The Relational Lens

Drawing on the authors' combined years of experience in both private and public sector organisations, this practical book highlights the importance of relationship building between individuals, groups and organisations in diverse contexts. It will make a valuable read for business professionals and graduate students in fields as varied as change management, leadership, organisational psychology and organisational behaviour. Employing the Relational Proximity® framework, it provides tools for:

- Informing assessment of the relational impact of policy and management decisions
- Enabling evaluation of organisational relationships
- Providing a language for constructive discussion of strained relationships
- Integrating a range of models and perspectives within one process

Using real-world case studies and models, the conditions within which people are more likely to form and conduct effective relationships are also examined. This combined approach provides the language and concepts to enable constructive discussion and actionable solutions in building trust and sustainable value.

John Ashcroft is Research Director at the Relationships Foundation and co-author of *Relationships in the NHS* and *The Case for Interprofessional Collaboration in Health and Social Care.*

Roy Childs has worked in organisations at senior levels for more than twenty years, focusing on developing capability and building. He is an Associate Fellow of the British Psychological Society and a Chartered Occupational Psychologist.

Alison Myers is an experienced consultant, facilitator and trainer. She has been a senior managing consultant with Accenture's Change Management and Human Performance practice and is now an ordained Anglican minister.

Michael Schluter is an economist and social entrepreneur who has launched ten not-for-profits and was awarded a CBE in the Queen's New Year's honours in 2009. He is also Chairman of Relational Analytics. He co-authored *The R Factor* and *The Relational Manager.*

THE RELATIONAL LENS

UNDERSTANDING, MEASURING AND MANAGING STAKEHOLDER RELATIONSHIPS

John Ashcroft,
Roy Childs,
Alison Myers and
Michael Schluter

CAMBRIDGE
UNIVERSITY PRESS

CAMBRIDGE
UNIVERSITY PRESS

University Printing House, Cambridge CB2 8BS, United Kingdom

Cambridge University Press is part of the University of Cambridge.

It furthers the University's mission by disseminating knowledge in the pursuit of education, learning, and research at the highest international levels of excellence.

www.cambridge.org
Information on this title: www.cambridge.org/9781107155763

10.1017/9781316659212

First published 2017

Printed in the United Kingdom by Clays, St Ives plc

A catalogue record for this publication is available from the British Library.

ISBN 978-1-107-15576-3 Hardback

CONTENTS

FIGURES

TABLES

FOREWORD BY VINCENT NEATE

I was introduced to the work of Michael Schluter, and subsequently to John, Roy and Alison, because of a relationship – in fact two. Two leaders who mentored me at KPMG introduced me to him within days of each other. I never found out if there had been collusion, but I remain grateful to both that they recognised that here was a new set of relationships that I would both enjoy and benefit from.

I have spent much of my career puzzling over what makes for a high performance relationship. Whether that is one of sales, in a supply chain or in a team, the person-to-person elements of business have always fascinated me. As an accountant by profession I would never underestimate the importance of keeping the score and measuring business success, but that doesn't mean I can't see how it is through relationship that creativity, innovation and invention are able to flourish and take hold. If we are to build better businesses, it will be through relationships that we do so.

The Relational Lens is, I think, the best articulation yet of what Relational Thinking is all about. We need a common language to take us beyond the simplicity of the satisfaction survey and to give us a foundation on which we can build future success. What the authors have given us is a robust description of the structure of relationships that can be applied one-to-one, one-to-many and many-to-many without losing any of its relevance. To this they have added real insight into the conditions for success within this structure.

I share their hope for a business paradigm where privileging relationship becomes the norm for leaders and managers. At the very least any leader or manager committed to responsible business should read *The Relational Lens*.

VINCENT NEATE,
PARTNER KPMG UK

FOREWORD BY PAUL DRUCKMAN

Market players around the world are starting to grapple with a fundamental economic truth: that the boundary of financial relevance has expanded. For example, when the *Financial Times* was bought by Nikkei in July 2015 for thirty-five times its operating profit, Nikkei was buying a stake in something more profound than a growing balance sheet: it was buying access to a global marketplace. In the past the stocks of value reported on by an organisation would have included principally the land, buildings, equipment and inventory owned by the business. For the world's largest corporations today – the likes of Google, Mitsubishi and Microsoft – the foundation of their value creation potential lies in their ability to attract talent, articulate ideas and build strong brands that sustain strong relationships with their employees, customers, suppliers and partners.

In order to manage and communicate their processes of value creation, businesses around the world are turning to the International Integrated Reporting (IR) Framework, which introduces the concept of multiple capitals. The framework is used to articulate the broad range of resources and relationships an organisation uses or impacts in its business model to create value over time. This concept enables organisations to articulate the multiple capitals they are using, including relational capital, giving full expression to the expanded boundary of financial relevance. By understanding and explaining the value-creating potential of these multiple capitals, organisations find themselves driven to change their corporate governance, abolish internal silos and manage risks and opportunities that may not have been triggered through an isolated focus on the financial statements alone.

When we started the process of developing the IR Framework it became apparent very quickly that the prominence of relational capital needed to be raised. It was important that it was recognised as part of the key capitals that an organisation uses and affects to create value over time. Subsequent research into relational capital is giving new depth to this previously undervalued capital. That is why the work done by the authors of this book is greatly appreciated. Readers will find here practical steps to help them understand, measure and manage stakeholder relationships inside and outside the boundaries of their organisations. This has not been done in a consistent way until now, but organisations that engage with IR will quickly discover the huge potential benefits of this new approach to measuring relational capital.

I hope that this book, that so effectively unpacks the concept of relational capital, will be widely read and applied, not just in the corporate world but also in public sector organisations, and in the international and national non-governmental organisation (NGO) sectors as well. For strong relationships are vital not just for the delivery of financial results, but for the broader sustainable development of the organisation.

PAUL DRUCKMAN,
CEO, IIRC

ACKNOWLEDGEMENTS

The development and honing of ideas over a long period creates many debts of gratitude to those who contributed new insights, corrected mistakes, encouraged progress, clarified communication, or tested application. With insights into relationships available from so many different academic and professional disciplines, and relevant to every aspect of a society, all that we have written has been shaped by the wisdom of others. There is, of course, much that we still have to learn from others and any weaknesses in the argument are entirely the authors' responsibility.

It is impossible to name and thank all those who have helped and encouraged at different stages of this project but the authors wish to acknowledge the particular contributions of a number of individuals and organisations.

Paul Sandham worked with us on the material for the book over many years, using the material with organisations, urging the deepening of the thinking, and financially supporting the research and writing. Without this constant encouragement we would not have come so far. Three experienced business consultants – Tim Young, Paul Shepanski and John Kay – have provided invaluable advice and guidance in strengthening our account of organisational relationships.

The ideas within this book have also been developed and refined in the context of partnership with KPMG. Tony Powell and Shonaid Jemmett-Page helped with the early application of this material in business. More recently KPMG's sustainability teams in South Africa, Australia and the UK have all tested new applications. We are also grateful for the support of four companies: Ogilvy, John Lewis Partnership, Land Securities, and TourAust. Each in different ways has recognised the vital importance of relationships to their business.

Using the framework in different contexts always offers new learning. The comments of Ncaba Hlophe of Stakeholder Relationship Assessments in South Africa and Peter Lacey of Whole Systems Partnership have been particularly insightful. Writing up the material has been greatly assisted by David Lee in particular, with help also from Guy Brandon, Josh Hemmings, David Wong and Jutta Nedden. We also wish to thank the colleagues, supporters and partners in our respective organisations who have patiently facilitated the work on which this book is based.

Introduction: The Dark Matter of Organisations

The Deepwater Horizon oil spill is a story about relationships between stakeholders.

It began on 20 April 2010, with the Macondo blowout – effectively an explosion separating the rig from the well. The rig sank and oil flowed from the seafloor gusher into the Mexican Gulf for eighty-seven days. It was the largest accidental marine spill known in the petroleum industry, with total discharge of crude oil estimated at 4.9 million barrels and eleven direct fatalities. The primary stakeholders in the well were BP, rig owners Transocean and rig operators Halliburton. There were millions more, but many didn't realise they were stakeholders until the oil slick began to spread: populations on the Gulf coast; owners and employees in the tourism and fishing industries; and, further out, savers across the world whose pension funds held BP stock.

Subsequent reports on the disaster – of which there were many – pinpointed specific failings in equipment, procedures, training and oversight. These came to some fairly predictable conclusions. For example, a US Government report released on 5 January 2011 stated that 'whether purposeful or not, many of the decisions that BP, Halliburton, and Transocean made that increased the risk of the Macondo blowout clearly saved those companies significant time (and money)'. At the same time, it was noted, government regulators did not have sufficient knowledge or authority to notice these cost-cutting decisions.[1]

In reality this is about more than whether people and companies are being greedy or irresponsible: it is about the ways in which stakeholder groups are connected together, and how those connections incentivise or disincentivise

[1] National Commission on the BP Deepwater Horizon Oil Spill and Offshore Drilling, 'Deep Water: The Gulf Oil Disaster and the Future of Offshore Drilling', January 2011.

certain types of behaviour. The pressure on all three companies involved in the spill to cut costs derived from the importance of good quarterly reports as a key ingredient in the way that public limited companies manage their relationship with investors. But that is not an issue any regulator is likely to act upon. The actual human relationships created between stakeholders by markets and systems of regulation are, for all practical purposes, invisible.

There is a strange parallel here with astrophysics. As far back as Galileo, astronomers have assumed that the universe is something you can see. Yet astrophysicists estimate that visible matter accounts for only 4 per cent of the mass of the universe, and doesn't come close to explaining how galaxies behave. What drives the motion of the universe is dark matter – material which exerts immense gravitational pull but which telescopes are unable to detect. At first this analogy might seem far-fetched. After all, relationships are all around us; no society exists without them; they enable life – personal life, business, communities – to function. And yet they are invisible in the sense of being so pervasive that their influence is often taken for granted. And, like dark matter, their impact is felt far more deeply and far more extensively than most people realise – and it doesn't need a major oil spill to show their effects.

The premise of the book, and of the tools and courses that complement it, is simple. It is that success – in business, in community building, in public service, in life – depends upon getting relationships right; that leadership (in whatever context and at whatever level it is exercised) depends upon the ability to build and sustain relationships; and that real change starts by realising that relationships are both measurable and a basis on which to improve performance. It is possible to create the conditions within which people are more likely to form and conduct effective relationships, and to approach relationships in organisations in ways that enable constructive discussion and actionable solutions.

Overall, that approach could be termed thinking relationally. This is sometimes easier to talk about than do, because effective management of relationships needs, first, a better understanding of the relational dynamic and, second, a better grasp of how to work with and through relationships to make realistic change possible. Most people do not read relationships accurately – partly because they inevitably view their own relationships from their perspective. They sometimes fail to anticipate the consequences of their choices and actions. Perhaps most important, the culture they live in determines their scale of values. People think individually, in terms of their own planning and interests. They think financially, by using currency as a means of comparison. It is not instinctive to think relationally – even though almost anyone will say that relationships are important. Thinking relationally requires effort.

In organisations, as everywhere else, relationships are key to getting things done, but can also be hard-to-shift obstacles; they create value, but destroy it when they go wrong. Cultivating healthy, effective relationships is no easy task. So this book, which reflects a single approach but a diversity of professional viewpoints, looks first at the vital importance of relationships themselves, exploring how they shape the way we think and act. It then moves on to examine a framework called Relational Proximity[2] – a scalable analytic tool which has been used successfully for twenty years to understand, measure and influence relationships in organisations, and which can be applied at almost any level in the private and public sectors worldwide.

---

[2] This builds on concepts first set out in M. Schluter and D. Lee, *The R Factor* (London: Hodder & Stoughton, 1993).

1   The Value and Importance of Relationships

Creating value, managing risk, achieving performance in a fast-moving business environment, improving wellbeing, building social capital, developing nations: all these challenges are affected by the health or otherwise of relationships.

Politics could be described as 'the art of relating',[1] and is concerned with the nature of the relationships between the individual and the state and between different interest groups, and in enabling those relationships that produce social goods, including health, welfare, education and security. Political leaders who stand at greater or lesser turning points in history – for example Oliver Cromwell, George Washington, William Beveridge, Margaret Thatcher or Nelson Mandela – have changed the pattern of relationships within and between nations in their reforms of constitutions, welfare, industrial relations, or relationships between ethnic groups. Reforms to public services are, fundamentally, about reshaping the relationships between the users and providers (professions and organisations) of services, and the relationships associated with the funding and accountability of those services.

Similarly, business decisions are essentially no more than choices about who to relate to (as customers, suppliers, employers, partners or investors), how to make entering these relationships more desirable, and how to make them more valuable. The processes of accessing resources (whether finance, people, ideas, or things), and producing and supplying goods and services include investing,

---

[1] Althusius published his Systematic Analysis of Politics in 1603 in support of the small city states and self-governing territories of the Holy Roman Empire. The 'art of relating' summarises his redefinition of politics as 'the art of associating men for the purpose of establishing, cultivating and conserving social life among them'. F. S. Carney (ed. and trans.), *The Politics of Johannes Althusius* (London: Eyre & Spottiswoode, 1995), p. 12.

borrowing, buying, selling, recruiting, or serving. These are all about the kinds of relationship between individuals and groups of people that define purpose, and create and distribute value and wealth.

The most important personal decisions are also fundamentally relational. Relationships are a key determinant of our wellbeing. Identity, security, purpose, belonging and happiness are all bound up in the relationships we forge and sustain. Choices about who we live with (or how we relate in the case of given relationships), work with and spend time with shape our lives.

When a relational risk is not seen, banks can go bust. When the relational dynamics of organisations are not understood, value is destroyed. When the relational impact of policy is not considered, social costs increase. Relationships are inherent in much of what we are about as human beings and as leaders of organisations and communities, but we don't always see things in these terms. Therefore, we begin by reviewing some diverse perspectives on the importance of relationships.

Relationships are a Fundamental Reality

Relationships, though, are not just about functional outcomes. They also describe the fundamental reality of existence. Margaret Wheatley, author of *Leadership and the New Science*,[2] argues that relationships exist at every scale in the way the universe works. At quantum level, what appear to be the most fundamental particles only exist, and are only visible, in relation to other particles: 'Everything in the Universe is composed of these "bundles of potentiality" that only manifest their potential in relationship.'[3]

There has been a long tradition of seeking a richer account of persons-in-relationship in politics, as a way between the polarities of capitalism and communism – hence the comment of J. H. Oldham: 'There is no such thing as the isolated individual. Reality is the lived relation.'[4] But this tradition has been masked to a great extent by the dominance of individualism in western culture. Descartes' aphorism 'I think therefore I am' is perhaps the best-known statement

---

[2] M. J. Wheatley, *Leadership and the New Science: Discovering Order in a Chaotic World*, 3rd edition (San Francisco, CA: Berrett-Koehler Publishers, 2006).

[3] M. J. Wheatley, 'Relationships: the basic building blocks of life', 2006, www.margaretwheatley.com/articles/relationships.html, accessed 15 October 2013.

[4] J. H. Oldham, *Real Life Is Meeting* (London: Sheldon Press, 1942), p. 31.

in western philosophy, drawing on a long tradition of understanding what it means to be a person.[5] Yet people are clearly more than just individuals. In his book *Herd*, Mark Earls argues that individualism is a cultural ideology that pervades and shapes our way of seeing the world[6] and that 'we are a we-species who do individually what we do largely because of each other'.[7]

Organisations, too, particularly in the West, are often based on the priority of the individual, ignoring the fact that we self-organise around relationships. Margaret Wheatley suggests that 'our neatly drawn organisations are as fictitious as building blocks are to physicists' and that 'the only form of organisation used on this planet is the network – webs of interconnected, interdependent relationships'. The lines and boxes of organograms are imaginary; 'the real organisation is always a dense network of relationships.'[8]

To those living and working in more relational or collectivist cultures this may be obvious. But to many of us it is still worth noting that organisations are, fundamentally, expressions of relationships, rather than relationships simply being the connections between the assumed fundamental reality of individuals and organisations.

Relationships Create Value

For an organisation, value is derived from assets and the future profits they may generate. In the 1990s there was a rapid growth in interest in new forms of capital, with new elements and models almost continually being proposed. Physical and financial assets are complemented, variously, by human capital (e.g. training and skills), emotional capital (e.g. brand affiliation),[9] intellectual capital (e.g. knowledge)[10] and spiritual capital (e.g. religious

[5] For example, the sixth-century philosopher Boethius (480–525), whose writing influenced much medieval thought, defined a person as 'an individual substance of a rational nature': originally 'Rationabilis naturae individua substantia'. Boethius, *De Persona et Duabas Naturis*, c. 2.

[6] Mark Earls, *Herd: How to Change Mass Behaviour by Harnessing Our True Nature* (Chichester: John Wiley, 2007), p. 92.

[7] Earls, *Herd*, p. 5.

[8] Wheatley, 'Relationships'.

[9] E.g. K. Thomson, *Emotional Capital: Maximising the Intangible Assets at the Heart of Brand and Business Success* (Oxford: Capstone Publishing, 1998).

[10] There is now an academic *Journal of Intellectual Capital*. Management books on this include, for example, T. A. Stewart, *Intellectual Capital: The New Wealth of Organizations* (New York: Doubleday, 1997).

values).[11] The wealth of a community is also derived from every one of these or their equivalents. The literature on each has grown rapidly alongside a range of metrics and consulting processes.

All these categories, however, focus on one thing: relationships. In an increasingly knowledge-oriented economy, for example, intellectual capital – the knowledge of products, processes and clients – may be a far more significant component of a company's valuation than its physical assets. In determining the value of intellectual capital to an organisation, however, two relational factors need to be considered which affect its robustness: stability and participation. The degree of stability within organisational relationships is important because intellectual capital can easily walk out of the door: whole teams with all their proprietary knowledge and client relationships can be poached. Buying in intellectual capital serves little purpose if the people are placed in an environment in which innovation and creativity cannot flourish – which is determined by the degree of participation embedded in the relationships. Relationships are therefore part of the content of intellectual capital. But not only this, the nature and quality of relationships are instrumental in an organisation's ability to retain and realise the value of intellectual capital.

The term 'social capital' has been coined to capture the vital contribution that relationships and social networks make to the value of an organisation, a community or a nation. Robert Putnam is one of its best-known advocates, defining social capital as 'the features of social organisations such as networks, norms and social trust that facilitate coordination and cooperation for mutual benefit'.[12] Putnam describes the core insight as 'extremely simple: like tools (physical capital) and training (human capital), social networks have value'.[13] The importance of these networks has been established in a wide range of contexts including income, health, crime, national development, democracy and economic performance.

Social networks are valuable because of the existence of relationships: networked people have access to resources held by others; people without the relationships don't. A classic study on 'the strength of weak ties'[14] demonstrated this

[11] E.g. D. Zohar, *Spiritual Capital: Wealth We Can Live By* (San Francisco, CA: Berrett-Koehler Publishers, 2004).

[12] R. Putnam, 'Bowling alone: America's declining social capital', *Journal of Democracy*, 6 (1995), pp. 65–78.

[13] R. Putnam, 'E pluribus unum: diversity and community in the twenty-first century', *Scandinavian Political Studies*, 30 (2007), p. 137.

[14] M. Granovetter, 'The strength of weak ties', *American Journal of Sociology*, 78 (1973), pp. 1360–1380. In the current social capital debate this may be linked to the benefits of bridging relationships as opposed to the narrower, stronger and more exclusive bonding relationships.

with respect to people's ability to find jobs. The wider the network, in this case, the quicker and easier it is to find employment. Specifically, Granovetter's study found that opportunities were *more* likely to be found among a person's 'weak ties' – friends of friends, acquaintances and less well-known connections – rather than within existing close relationships. Broad social networks are valuable, even if you don't know a lot of people well.

Value is also derived from the quality of relationships – visible in such norms as trust and reciprocity – that enables those relationships to be mutually beneficial. If our relationship is good you are more likely to help me out with my IT problem, and I am more likely to give you a lift to the station. Knowing someone who has no inclination to help and cannot be trusted is not seen as valuable. In this way, social networks create benefits in the wider community. In *Bowling Alone*,[15] Robert Putnam gives the example of the benefits he receives from neighbourhood relationships that reduce crime, even if he is often absent and not an active contributor to those relationships.

In organisations, trust and reciprocity and organisational stability have direct benefits: teams work more efficiently; resources are better shared to deal with issues; retention is improved; and the organisation becomes more resilient and adaptable. Yet, paradoxically, when an organisation's processes and structure are being re-engineered, the cost of breaking up the existing social networks is often not accounted for when assessing the anticipated efficiency gains.

Don Cohen and Laurence Prusak make the following case for investing in social capital in their book *In Good Company*. Social capital can benefit organisations through:

- Better knowledge sharing, due to established trust relationships, common frames of references and shared goals.
- Lower transaction costs due to a high level of trust and cooperative spirit (both within the organisation and between the organisation and its customers and partners).
- Lower turnover rates, reducing severance costs and hiring and training expenses, avoiding discontinuities associated with frequent personnel changes, and maintaining valuable organisational knowledge.
- Greater coherence of action due to organisational stability and shared understanding.[16]

[15] R. Putnam, *Bowling Alone: The Collapse and Revival of American Community* (New York: Simon & Schuster, 2000).
[16] D. Cohen and L. Prusak, *In Good Company: How Social Capital Makes Organizations Work* (Cambridge, MA: Harvard University Press, 2001), p. 10.

Relationships are a Source of Competitive Advantage

The central importance of relationships in achieving competitive advantage is well summarised by Waterman: 'the key to strategic success is mainly this: building relationships with customers, suppliers and employees that are exceptionally hard for competitors to duplicate.'[17] The benefits can be summarised as shown in Figure 1.1.

It takes time and effort to build relationships, in contrast to products that can be copied and potentially produced at lower cost. This is true whether we are talking about the social capital internal to an organisation and which

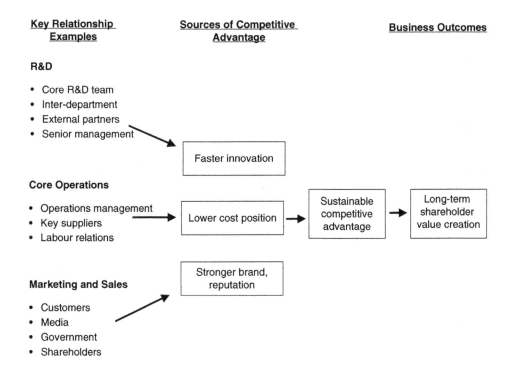

Figure 1.1:   The connection between key relationships, sources of competitive advantage and outcomes.
Source: J. Rushworth and M. Schluter, *Transforming Capitalism from Within* (Cambridge: Relational Research, 2011).

---

[17] R. Waterman, *The Frontiers of Excellence: Learning from Companies That Put People First* (Boston, MA: Nicholas Brealey Publishing, 1994).

underpins other types of capital, or the relationship between the organisation and its customers, suppliers and partners.

Relationships are also at the heart of those businesses that have risen to the top in the competitive dotcom field. Although the rise of dotcom companies was often primarily seen in terms of the adoption of new technology, the successes have been those that have changed the dynamics of relationships with customers, among social networks, or between providers and users of information. As they have matured, it is the relationships that have been developed or enabled, as much as the uniqueness of the technology, which keeps them at the top.

Moreover, this is not just a business issue. Voluntary sector organisations may need to compete for funding, contracts, public influence, or staff. In each of these areas it is often the quality of relationships that is a key ingredient in their ability to achieve their goals and thus make them attractive partners and fundable propositions.

Relationships are a Key to Better Risk Management

Relationships are assets and opportunities, but also a major risk factor. When relationships go wrong lives can be lost, environments damaged, reputations diminished, careers ended and value destroyed. As Chapter 11 shows, if you examine any business or public service failure you're likely to find weak, ineffective or dysfunctional relationships playing a dominant part.

Relational risk takes many forms. The relationship itself may be a source of risk as has been seen, for example, in scandals surrounding the care of children, elderly people or people with disabilities. Control systems may fail as relational weaknesses result in actions not being questioned or protocols neglected. Nick Leeson, the rogue trader who famously broke Barings Bank, described the ease with which he concealed his losses: 'they never dared ask me any basic questions since they were afraid of looking stupid.'[18] The relationship between London managers and Singapore traders was not up to managing the risks. Conflict within teams can impair performance and profitability. Staff may leave or strike. Customers may go elsewhere.

---

[18] N. Leeson, *Rogue Trader* (London: Little Brown, 1996), p. 161.

Models for analysing adverse events identify a number of types of poor conduct that increase risk: poor communication; poor leadership; conflict in interpersonal relations; poor preparation, planning and vigilance; lack of exposure to new ideas, systems and processes; and disempowerment.[19] While financial risk may be evident in the balance sheet and profit and loss accounts, data on the nature and extent of relational risk is typically far less evident until much too late.

Relationships are a Goal as well as a Means

For some organisations, relationships are more than a means to getting things done. They are also the thing that needs to *be* done – the end as well as the means. Public sector organisations, charities and social enterprises often have goals that are both defined by and dependent on relationships. A criminal justice system, for example, should be seeking to repair the relationships between victims and offenders, and between offenders and society.[20] The ability to do this depends on the relationships within prisons and between agencies such as police, courts and probation.

Some businesses define their purpose in relational terms. The John Lewis Partnership, for example, a large UK-based retailer, describes the partnership's 'ultimate purpose' as 'the happiness of all its members, through their worthwhile and satisfying employment in a successful business'.[21] Moreover, the resources (knowledge, finance, or connections) needed to achieve complex social outcomes are never (or rarely) located within any single profession or organisation. The capacity to make a difference therefore depends upon the contribution of others, not least the users of services. Relationships become the essential mechanism by which the necessary resources are both brought to bear and used effectively.

For example, reducing teenage pregnancy rates has been one of the key targets for UK health services in recent years. Many vulnerable young people

[19] R. Helmreich, 'On error management: lessons from aviation', *British Medical Journal*, 320 (2000), pp. 781–785; J. Higgins, 'Adverse events or patterns of failure', *British Journal of Health Care Management*, 7 (2001), pp. 145–147.

[20] See, for example, J. Burnside and N. Baker (eds.), *Relational Justice: Repairing the Breach* (Winchester: Waterside Press, 2004).

[21] John Lewis Partnership, 'Our Principles', last modified 16 September 2015, www.johnlewispartnership .co.uk/about/our-principles.html.

have limited contact with, and trust in, statutory services, particularly if they have been truanting from school and involved in criminal activity or anti-social behaviour. Statutory agencies may simply not have the relationships with the young people that are needed if they are to make a sufficient difference to pregnancy rates. A voluntary sector youth worker may, however, have known them for several years and gained their trust. The partnership between statutory agencies and voluntary or third-sector organisations may therefore become a key element in the ability of both to achieve their goals.

Relationships are a Skillset

While the language of capital has been used to describe the importance of relationships for organisations, 'intelligence' has been used to focus attention on the relational skills and capacities of individuals. Daniel Goleman[22] popularised the idea that emotional intelligence (EQ) is more important for leadership success than IQ: that self-awareness, self-regulation, empathy, motivation and social skills are more important than intellectual ability.

A significant (and earlier) description came from Salovey and Mayer, who defined emotional intelligence as 'the subset of social intelligence that involves the ability to monitor one's own and others' feelings and emotions, to discriminate among them and to use this information to guide one's thinking and actions'.[23] The thinking and language of emotional intelligence has pushed soft skills and the ability to relate to other people up the agenda. Education, recruitment, training and promotion are all now influenced by the recognition that the ability to understand both self and others is essential.

Claudio Fernández-Aráoz, a senior adviser to the leading executive search firm Egon Zehnder, summarises his conclusions about the importance of emotional intelligence in his book *Great People Decisions*:[24]

- EQ counts more than IQ for success, and the lack of EQ is very highly correlated with failure in senior managerial positions.

---

[22] D. Goleman, *Emotional Intelligence: Why It Can Matter More Than IQ for Character, Health and Lifelong Achievement* (New York: Bantam Books, 1995).

[23] P. Salovey and J. D. Mayer, 'Emotional intelligence', *Imagination, Cognition, and Personality*, 9 (1990), pp. 185–211.

[24] C. Fernández-Aráoz, *Great People Decisions: Why They Matter So Much, Why They Are So Hard and How You Can Master Them* (Hoboken, NJ: John Wiley, 2007), p. 140.

- If only two broad categories can be achieved in a search for a top manager, then experience plus EQ is in general the most powerful combination for achieving success.
- The traditional combination of relevant experience plus IQ (with limited EQ) is much more likely to produce a failure than a winner.

EQ does not, however, amount to the same thing as Relational Intelligence. EQ typically takes self-awareness as a starting point from which to build towards collaborative goals. In particular, it has focused on how individuals develop *themselves* in order to understand, motivate and lead others. Relational Intelligence, which incorporates these self-development ideas into a broader framework, focuses on developing an organisational culture within which relationships flourish.

Relationships are the Cornerstone of Wellbeing

> Well-being can't be measured by money or traded in markets. It can't be required by law or delivered by government. It's about the beauty of our surroundings, the quality of our culture, and above all the strength of our relationships ... What makes us happy, above all, is a sense of belonging – strong relationships with friends, family and the immediate world around us.[25]

Concepts of happiness and wellbeing are now at the fore of public debate, including the introduction of new national measures of wellbeing in the UK and elsewhere.[26] Wellbeing is a complex mix of subjective feelings ('happiness') and more objective indicators of, for example, physical and mental health, as well as the experience of meaning and purpose. While those on higher incomes tend to report higher levels of wellbeing than those on lower incomes, financial security does not compensate a loss of close, supportive relationships. Being separated (rather than married), for instance, decreases happiness by four times as much as losing a third of family income.[27]

---

[25] D. Cameron, 'David Cameron's speech to Google Zeitgeist Conference, Europe 2006', full text available at *Guardian*, 22 May 2006, www.theguardian.com/politics/2006/may/22/conservatives.davidcameron.

[26] Office of National Statistics, 'Measuring National Well-Being', last modified 22 October 2015, www.ons.gov.uk/ons/guide-method/user-guidance/well-being/index.html.

[27] R. Layard, *Happiness* (London: Allen Lane, 2005), p. 64. Data from the World Values Survey that covers 90,000 people in 46 countries.

There are many reasons why healthy personal relationships are so important for wellbeing. For a start, they bring the *practical benefits of support* as well as the feeling of security that comes from its availability. This can be manifested in a variety of different ways – it may be borrowing a tool from a neighbour, or money from a relative; it may be the performance of a 'favour' or provision of care when it is needed; it may be access to information or advice based on skills or personal experience. Practical support both provides a gateway to other sources of wellbeing and acts as a buffer against negative impacts on wellbeing. The nature and quality of a relationship influences its support-giving potential because some forms of support require physical presence or higher levels of trust and commitment.

Ed Diener and Martin Seligman put it like this:

The quality of people's social relationships is crucial to their well-being. People need supportive, positive relationships and social belonging to sustain well-being. Evidence [shows] that the need to belong, to have close and long-term social relationships, is a fundamental human need, and that well-being depends on this need being well met. People need social bonds in committed relationships, not simply interactions with strangers, to experience well-being.[28]

In our psychological development we come to understand who we are primarily through the way that other people relate to us. This is particularly the case for children,[29] although it may often be true in adult life as well. Beliefs about the value and ability of the self are shaped by what other people say – particularly as the concept of the self is being formed in a child's development, but also through significant experiences in later life, whether positive or negative. Two components of Ryff's model of psychological wellbeing, for example, are self-acceptance and autonomy.[30] While these may seem somewhat individualistic in their manifestation, they are thoroughly relational in their origin. In fact, if the basis for self-esteem or autonomy becomes too focused on the self it may result in greater levels of narcissism and anxiety, and thereby reduce levels of wellbeing.[31]

---

[28] E. Diener and M. E. P. Seligman, 'Beyond money: toward an economy of well-being', *Psychological Science in the Public Interest*, 5 (2004), pp. 1–31.

[29] Bowlby's work on attachment theory has been particularly influential here; see J. Bowlby, *Attachment*, Vol. 1 of *Attachment and Loss* (London: Hogarth, 1969).

[30] C. Ryff and C. L. M. Keyes, 'The structure of psychological well-being revisited', *Journal of Personality and Social Psychology*, 69 (1995), pp. 719–727.

[31] See, for example, J. M. Twenge, *Generation Me: Why Today's Young Americans Are More Confident, Assertive, Entitled – And More Miserable Than Ever Before* (New York: Free Press, 2006).

Relationships also influence health, which can be considered as an objective element of wellbeing as well as a factor that influences the experienced sense of wellbeing. Poor relationships can lead to health-threatening behaviour as well as eroding support. In contrast, positive relationships are linked to improved immune responses, improved buffering of stress and faster recovery from strokes and cancer. An early review of the link between relationships and 'allostatic load' (the long-term cumulative effect of physiological accommodations to stress), for example, concluded that 'nurturing social ties and maximising opportunities for valued, emotionally rewarding and meaningful interactions with significant others' may be as consequential for long-term health and wellbeing as widely promulgated messages regarding proper nutrition and adequate exercise.[32]

Relationships Impact Third Parties

At a wider community or societal level, wellbeing is also influenced by the health and effectiveness of relationships that we are not directly party to, and over which we have little influence. The ability of others to provide care for us is made more or less effective by their own inter-professional and inter-agency relationships. We can experience the negative consequences, such as increased antisocial behaviour, that result from broken relationships elsewhere. As new arrivals to a community we are affected by whether other people have, over time, created a community that we can join.

These third-party relationships can be close to us, or they may be at some distance and yet still exercise considerable impact on our wellbeing. Caring for an elderly relative or disabled child can place a strain on the wellbeing of a couple: a fairly clear and immediate impact. However, the relationship between investors and managers – typically much more distant – may influence investment decisions that have significant consequences for us as employees.

Conversely, the good relationships we enable will also have an impact on the wellbeing of others, directly or indirectly. On the positive side, good community relationships might result in better care for the local environment, or good business relationships might lead to increased productivity and more meaningful and engaging work. By the same token, relationship breakdown in

[32] C. Ryff, B. Singer, E. Wing and G. Love, 'Elective affinities and uninvited agonies', in C. Ryff and B. Singer (eds.), *Emotion, Social Relationships and Health* (Oxford University Press, 2001), p. 172.

a family context might lead to homelessness, antisocial behaviour, or crime. In cases like these, the immediate symptom of a lack of wellbeing might not appear to be a relational issue, but generally has its origins in the health or otherwise of one or more relationships.

Impact on third parties also provides a way to assess the quality of relationships. Trust, respect, empathy and commitment between peers will also have a third-party impact that may be negative rather than positive. A much-quoted example is the Mafia, but there are numerous other examples. In an organisation, internal stakeholders may enjoy more advantages than external stakeholders do – including customers, suppliers, the local community and society as a whole. IR provides a way of quantifying an organisation's impact on a wide range of third parties.

2 Why Organisations Should Think Relationally

In practice, organisations notice relationships mainly when they go wrong. A failure to perceive the relational dynamic of an issue, or the relational consequences of a decision, can surface in individual interactions, in dealing with organisational systems, or in public policy. Mike King, former Head of People at Ogilvy, recalls the time when Ogilvy moved to offices in London's Canary Wharf. At the time Canary Wharf was a new office development in the old docklands area, three miles from the City. 'Because we were one of the first wave of companies to move in, many of our clients were still in central London. Ogilvy staff spent more time at, or travelling to, client offices, and relationships within teams suffered.' A firm that prided itself on understanding relationships didn't fully anticipate the relational consequences of the decision to relocate.

The Problem of Filtering

In July 2003, around 500 of British Airways' check-in and ticket desk staff at Heathrow airport went on unofficial strike, affecting more than 500 flights and 100,000 passengers at one of the busiest times of year. The walkout was in protest at the introduction of a new automated 'clock in – clock out' system that was already being used successfully in other areas of the company. The management, it transpired, had not recognised the relational consequences of this aspect of its plan to 'improve the efficient use of staff and resources', on the largely female workforce. The desk staff were afraid that automation would reduce the flexibility that they valued and needed in order to juggle work and family responsibilities. This fear was exacerbated by the poor timing of the system's introduction, right at the beginning of the long summer school holiday in the UK, when such sensitivities would be heightened. Failure to notice and respond to the relational impact and resultant worries up front cost British Airways dearly.[1]

Thinking is about ordering data, ignoring that which is deemed irrelevant (we *notice* far less than we *see*), and seeking patterns, in order to find meaning and make predictions. In order to be able to make any decision we need to restrict, or 'filter', the amount of data that we are considering and apply some rules or shortcuts: otherwise we'd be no more effective than a churning computer. But this highly effective strategy has dangers: our perceptions and decision-making rules may mislead us. Recognising why our patterns of seeing and thinking are not always attuned to relational reality is an important first step in learning to manage and influence relationships more effectively. The second step is giving ourselves new tools to adjust our patterns of seeing and thinking so that we recognise that relational reality more clearly.

In a well-known experiment, researcher Daniel Simons videotaped students playing basketball. He then split viewers into three groups with different instructions. One group was instructed to watch a team, another to count the number of passes, while the third group was given no instructions. People in the third group were much more likely to notice that at one point a student in a gorilla suit walks onto the court, beats his chest and walks off. The people counting the passes, however, were often so focused on seeing what they needed to complete the task that they were oblivious to it. Viewers tended only to notice what they were looking for.[2]

Different patterns of seeing are not just shaped by the task, they are also a product of our culture and its rules and expectations. It may be that the inability to notice these 'gorillas' is a particularly western problem. Social psychologist Richard Nisbett has found that Asians are more likely to notice background events than westerners.[3] He describes experiments showing how 'Asians see the

---

[1] J. Arrowsmith, 'Strike grounds British Airways at Heathrow', European Industrial Relations Observatory Online, 17 August 2003, www.eurofound.europa.eu/eiro/2003/08/feature/uk0308103f.htm, accessed 4 October 2011.

[2] D. J. Simons and C. F. Chabris, 'Gorillas in our midst: sustained inattentional blindness for dynamic events', *Perception*, 28 (1999), pp. 1059–1074 (see also M. Earls, *Herd: How to Change Mass Behaviour by Harnessing Our True Nature* (Chichester: Wiley, 2007), p. 62).

[3] R. E. Nisbett, *Geography of Thought: How Asians and Westerners Think Differently ... and Why* (New York: Free Press, 2003), p. 109.

big picture and they see objects in relation to their environments – so much so
that it can be difficult for them to visually separate objects from their environments' while westerners focus on objects and 'literally see fewer objects and
relationships in the environment'.[4] This has important implications. Not only
do people differ in their capacity to notice what is going on, this capacity is
also bound up with cultural habits of how they view the world and, further,
how they interpret what they see. However, if the capacity to notice what is
going on is even partly a product of culture, then it is possible to learn new
habits of perceiving and interpreting information.

Arie de Geus looked at why many large companies fail to last more than a few
generations. He concluded that 'the signals of threat are always abundant and
recognised by many, yet somehow they fail to penetrate the corporate immune
system response to reject the unfamiliar'.[5] To start with, our own perception
of reality is filtered, and then collective decision-making processes create a
further set of filters. Significantly, the organisational processes involved in
decision-making are not usually designed to bring relational issues to the fore.
Financial information, for example, is readily available and can be factored in.
Relational information, all too often, is not.

A related problem is 'referred pain'. Sometimes, within an organisation or
community, the problem lies in failing to see the full picture – not looking at
the system in its entirety. In medicine it is often the case that a pain in one part
of the body signals a problem somewhere else. During a heart attack, pain can
often be felt in the back, neck and shoulders – not the chest. Runners often
experience pain in the knees and hips that can be addressed with corrective
orthotics in their shoes: misalignment in the way the feet strike the ground has
consequences elsewhere. The same is true in organisations. The poor relationship
between a company's procurement team and its suppliers might be the result of
a communication issue with the accounts department, meaning that suppliers –
who have no direct contact with accounts – aren't paid on time. Seeing the big
picture allows us to pinpoint the root cause, rather than the symptom.

Peter Senge gives an example of such a 'eureka moment'.[6] It came from a
study by Daniel Kim of the process of designing a new car. The problem was
that individual teams would apply quick fixes to design problems that in turn

---

[4] Nisbett, *Geography of Thought*, p. 109.

[5] A. de Geus, *The Living Company: Growth, Learning and Longevity in Business* (London: Nicholas
Brealey, 1999).

[6] The example, in the book *Presence*, is taken from G. Roth and A. Kleiner, *Car Launch* (New York:
Oxford University Press, 2000).

created problems for other teams. More fundamental and integrated solutions required collaboration with other teams, but they didn't have the time to do this – in part because of the additional time costs of solving problems created by other teams in the first place. He describes how 'seeing differently' was a pivotal moment in addressing the problem: 'It was as if they suddenly saw what they all knew but didn't know they knew.' The details of the situation were all familiar but now 'they were actually seeing the systemic pattern that caused this'. This larger system that their individual reactions created consistently produced poor technical solutions, stress for the workforce, and late cars.

But how do we change this? In his book *Presence*, Peter Senge worked with Otto Scharmer, Joseph Jaworski and Betty Sue Flowers to explore how change happens.[7] A key finding was that learning to 'see our seeing' was a fundamental starting point for change. By 'hanging our assumptions in front of us' we 'begin to notice our thoughts and mental models as the workings of our own mind. And as we become aware of our thoughts, they begin to have less influence on what we see.' This works for organisations, too. As we become more aware of how the processes for reporting, problem-solving and decision-making work we can begin to see and question the assumptions built into the system.

How Rational are You?

The way in which our perception of issues and consequent choices and actions may be distorted has been explored by Dan Ariely.[8] He and others have shown that, despite our assumption of rational decision-making, we are often 'predictably irrational'. Ariely emphasises the predictability of this irrationality – there are well-understood mechanisms that lead us to make decisions, often with relational consequences, that seem irrational when analysed. He compares these decisions to visual illusions:

Just as we can't help being fooled by visual illusions, we fall for the 'decision illusions' our minds show us. The point is that our visual and decision environments are filtered to us courtesy of our eyes, our ears, our sense of smell and touch, and the master of it all, our brain. By the time we comprehend and digest information, it is not necessarily a true reflection of reality, and this is the input we base our decisions on. In essence

---

[7] P. Senge, O. Scharmer, J. Jaworski and B. S. Flowers, *Presence* (London: Nicholas Brealey, 2005), p. 29.
[8] D. Ariely, *Predictably Irrational: The Hidden Forces that Shape Our Decisions* (London: HarperCollins, 2008).

we are limited to the tools nature has given us, and the natural way in which we make decisions is limited by the quality and accuracy of these tools.[9]

Factors that can lead to irrational decisions include comparisons that influence assessments of attractiveness or good financial value, expectations and social norms, risk aversion, overvaluing what we have, and sexual arousal. Ariely's experiments demonstrate that being asked to write down social security numbers influences the amount bid for items (the anchoring effect), that introducing unattractive options makes others more attractive (the decoy effect), and that people will spend fifteen minutes to save $7 on a $25 item, but not on a $455 item.

That we present a fully rational self in every relationship or subject every aspect of a relationship to rational analysis goes against the grain of our human nature. Herbert Simon, a Nobel Prize winner for his work on decision-making in organisations, suggests that most people are only partly rational – and are, in fact, emotional or even downright irrational in the remaining part of their actions and decisions.[10] Simon's concept of 'bounded rationality' accounts for the fact that perfectly rational decisions are often not feasible in practice due to the finite computational resources available for making them. Given that human relationships are complex, and that we do not have the capacity to understand or know everything within any given relationship, many of our decisions are not fully thought through, and we can therefore only be rational within such limits as time, resources and cognitive capability.

If this irrationality is predictable, then we must learn to be masters not slaves of it, by improving the quality of the 'natural tools' for perceiving and analysing data and making good decisions. That includes our predictable propensity to get relationships wrong.

Ways of Seeing

To summarise:

- *People filter data in different ways because they notice different things.*
- *People filter data based on their different task priorities and culture.*
- *People in organisations filter data through their processes.*
- *People often see only part of the picture rather than the whole.*

---

[9] Ariely, *Predictably Irrational*, p. 243.

[10] H. Simon, 'Bounded rationality and organizational learning', *Organization Science*, 2 (1991), pp. 125–134.

Consciously or unconsciously, people filter information so that they see what they believe to be important. Because relationships are largely taken for granted, most people don't filter to see what's happening to relationships, and this inevitably limits their ability to read relationships and to manage them effectively. Instead they use other filters.

The Filter of Individualism

Western culture is frequently described as individualistic and consumerist. The contemporary search to discover who we are and experience ourselves as autonomous individuals drives us to consume things in a way that distinguishes us from our neighbours. According to social scientist Zygmunt Bauman, consumerism, and the ability it gives us to choose or buy things, is the solution that society gives for our need to be individual.[11] Choice, change and ownership are ways to aid the construction and projection of self-image. Relationships are entered into, or left, in order to meet the needs of the self. Managers constrain or play upon the self-interest of the employee. Communication is more oriented to transmission than dialogue. Overall, the filter of individualism encourages us to see life as a series of experiences that enable our personal growth or promote our personal pleasure. On the same basis, policy treats people as isolated individuals: the choices, rights and freedoms of the individual are the governing concern.

Traditionally, psychology has been seen as the science of individual behaviour and sociology the science of group behaviour.[12] A deeper understanding of human relationships may naturally sit in the overlap between these two disciplines – social psychology. However, the traditional focus even of social psychology has been on how individuals behave in group settings rather than on how relationships shape their lives – a tendency not wholly corrected by the influence of systems thinking within psychology, which retains a heavily individualistic orientation.

The Filter of Finance

Not surprisingly, managers in organisations often see the world in budgetary terms. Profitability and gross domestic product (GDP) are considered to be primary measures of progress. Money is the principal measure of value. Financial health is audited, and cost is the key consideration in purchasing decisions.

---

[11] Z. Bauman, *Liquid Life* (Cambridge: Polity Press, 2005), pp. 19–24.
[12] There are notable exceptions, including Adlerian and Systemic therapy.

Higher-paying jobs are more sought-after, while cars, housing and clothing make statements about purchasing power. People invest in financial pensions, but not in the set of relationships – the 'relational pension' – that will bring support and happiness throughout old age. One reason for the influence of the financial filter is simply the availability of data: pay slips, bank statements, invoices, accounts, sales figures, investment returns and many others describe what is happening and inform decisions.

The Filter of Environment

When we see the world in terms of the environment, we scrutinise the use of resources and the production of waste for sustainability. We evaluate transport choices by levels of CO_2 emissions. We see energy efficiency or the ability to recycle as a priority in purchasing decisions. We seek the reduction of energy use in housing design and urban planning. We use inter-generational accounting so that we include natural capital as well as financial capital.

Thinking Relationally as Perspective

Scott Page, Professor of Complex Systems, Political Science and Economics at Michigan University, provides a helpful analysis of the four key components of what he calls our 'cognitive toolbox'.[13] These components enable us to notice and understand experience, and to analyse and solve issues. This is not about whether we think relationships are important in any particular setting, but whether we have the tools to enable us to see the relational dimension of issues and situations. Inside his toolbox, Page highlights three tools that are of particular relevance to thinking relationally: perspectives, interpretations and predictive models.[14]

Different ways of seeing things – new perspectives – can open up new solutions and make problems easier to solve. Examples from science include Dmitri Mendeleev constructing the Periodic Table, Copernicus describing a heliocentric universe, or Einstein linking space and time. But perspectives are not just

---

[13] S. Page, *The Difference: How the Power of Diversity Creates Better Groups, Forms, Schools and Societies* (Princeton University Press, 2007).

[14] His fourth component, heuristics (ways of generating solutions to problems), relates more to strategies in using information to reach solutions than in whether data is ordered in ways that help to make sense of relational issues.

about big breakthroughs in science: they can be about different ways of look-ing at the ordinary things. The same location can be described by the posi-tion of landmarks, or by the use of a postcode, depending on whether you are directing someone to the street or sending a letter. Neither is more true than the other: they are just complementary.

Similarly, different academic disciplines and professions tend to work with dif-ferent perspectives. History, geography, sociology, economics, biology, anthro-pology, politics and others all contribute to our understanding of relationships. Sometimes they combine – as economics and psychology have done in behav-ioural economics – to create a greater awareness of the relational dimension.

Taking a different perspective can also prompt different questions. When buying a microwave the options could be considered from an economic per-spective (Can we afford it? Which is best value?), from an environmental perspective (What's the energy consumption? Can it be recycled?), from an aesthetic perspective (Does it match the kitchen units?), or from a spatial per-spective (Is it small enough to fit on the counter?). A relational perspective, however, introduces these questions: Will it affect whether we cook and/or eat together? Will it give us free time to spend together?

Or consider the different perspectives that can be taken when looking at bank operations. A bank regulator might look at capital ratios, an analyst at earnings, a financial adviser at mortgage rates and an environmentalist at the carbon footprint. A relational perspective would pay more attention to the implications of ownership structure for the relationship between shareholders and directors, and the implications of this for lending and investment risks. Understood from this perspective it is not so surprising that many hedge funds – where managers have their own capital at risk and other owners of the business are more closely involved – have proved to be less risky than some large high street mortgage lenders, particularly those dependent on wholesale money markets.

To think relationally, then, we need a *relational interpretation* – deliberately asking questions about relationships and about how they define a situation, and about the relational impact of decisions.

Thinking Relationally as a Lens

Interpretations start to simplify the data within or across perspectives by finding patterns or types of objects. As Scott Page says, 'One financial ana-lyst might categorise companies by their equity value, while another might categorise them by industry'[15] – as FTSE 100 companies, say, as opposed to global oil companies. Other interpretive categories with which we are more or less familiar are those of the marketers, politicians and sociologists – for example, 'AB1s', 'Soccer Moms', 'Generation X'.

These interpretations against known categories are necessary because, as Page points out, political profiling works with as many as ten dimensions (for example gender, marital status, income, education), each with its own sub-dimensions (such as male or female for gender). This can easily create over 30 million different possible permutations – too many to be much use in simplifying analysis.[16] So political strategists and marketers identify larger groups based on selected categories, which then allow plausible inferences on their views and likely responses to policy proposals.

Managing relationships encounters the same problem. A model that describes the unique characteristics of every relationship wouldn't help to make useful, general inferences. If we are to have ways of assessing relationships and strategies for improving relationships that are generic, we need interpretations that group different relationships in meaningful ways without too many categories. Work conducted by the Relationships Foundation has shown that grouping relationships according to the factors that influence them can be helpful. Some relationships between prisoners and prison officers, between partners and senior solicitors in law firms, and between doctors and health authority managers, though in very different organisational sectors, could fit into the same group or category. This has helped in troubleshooting and in sharing the solutions most likely to work. So, for example, relationships characterised by limited opportunities to gain breadth of knowledge about the other party typically result in unnecessary friction due to misunderstanding.

So, by choosing a *relational interpretation*, we further increase the focus on the relational aspects of the decisions we make and the relational solutions to the issues we face. In order to do this we need a language of relational categories.

Thinking Relationally as a Predictive Model

In order to engage with the world, to make decisions, to meet challenges, it is necessary to forecast what might happen next. To do this we use predictive models – ways of inferring cause and effect and mapping interpretations onto outcomes.

[15] Page, *The Difference*, p. 8.
[16] Page, *The Difference*, p. 82.

These can be quite simple rules of thumb. For example, a person might say that one make of washing machine is likely to be more durable than another (based on personal or reported experience), or that people who smile are trustworthy. Predictive models can also be complex theories derived from different disciplines. Examples include the belief that global free trade will benefit low-income countries (or the reverse), or the belief that greater social capital leads to higher levels of innovation. In fact, economics often dominates predictive modelling, and therefore decision-making, because there is a simple language of comparison (price), a mechanism for allocation (markets and choices) and an ability to quantify inputs and outputs. Being able to quantify and compare inputs and outputs aids the development of predictive models as to what enables growth and profitability.

More recently, environmental sustainability has been quantified in terms of resources consumed and waste produced, with carbon (rather than dollars) being the unit of comparison. Other greenhouse gases (GHGs) can be compared to the global warming potential (GWP) of the same amount of CO_2.

It is widely recognised that social sustainability has been the weakest element of 'triple bottom line' reporting.[17] For example, the Global Reporting Initiative (GRI) concluded that 'in contrast to GRI environmental indicators ... reporting on social performance occurs infrequently and inconsistently across organisations'.[18] Modelling and quantifying social impact is more complex, not least because of fundamental differences of view over the desired nature of the social state to be sustained or worked towards.

For relationships, there are many predictive models. Some are proverbial (for example, men's jokes about mothers-in-law). Others are shaped by crude stereotyping about ethnic minorities and social classes. Those that arise from lived experience may be hotly debated. For example, does it matter how many hours you work when your children are young? Others are widely validated, like the assertion that supportive relationships improve your health and life expectancy.

In general, though, detailed prediction is difficult. A relatively simple model, with five different kinds of relationships (most people have many more), five influences on those relationships and five possible outcomes, will generate 125 different predictions (if only one influencing factor operates at a time). So it is

---

[17] The 'triple bottom line' promotes the assessment of companies or policies not just in terms of their economic success but also their environmental and social impact. See 'Triple bottom line', *Economist*, 17 November 2009, www.economist.com/node/14301663, accessed 12 February 2013.

[18] Global Reporting Initiative, 'GRI Sustainability Reporting Guidelines', June 2000, p. 33.

not altogether surprising that leaders may be cautious about seeking to influence relationships. The data supporting good decisions is limited. Experts offer competing and contradictory models. Some researchers have, for example, found that staff are more prepared to work harder for managers who treat them fairly and with respect, while others report that 'great intimidators' are the best motivators.[19] Moreover, predictions may be derived from correlations that do not explain how one thing leads to another. Knowing that trust in strangers is a good indicator of social capital does not, of itself, explain how to go about building trust. Or they may give us little indication of how to contextualise or apply known information. Psychological models may tell us something about ourselves – that we are 'introverts' or 'extroverts' – without telling us how this varies due to context, practice or preference, or how to extrapolate this to group and organisational levels.

Given these difficulties, and the fact that relational issues may seem personally sensitive and threatening, a financial perspective may seem a much simpler focus; giving people the freedom to make their own choices may appear to be a safer and more effective strategy. That means there is an urgent need for more robust *relational predictive models* – at both individual and organisational levels, whether in the workplace or in the community.

Thinking Relationally for Organisations

Thinking relationally is a perspective and an interpretation – a way to ask questions from a relational perspective and a language in which to speak about different types of relational problems and experiences. It can also be used as a *predictive model* that aggregates the insights from many other models and practices and that has the power to shed light on the specifics of very different situations.

In addition, it provides a basis on which to integrate other perspectives – individual, financial and environmental. It does this because, as noted earlier, relationships are a fundamental category. Individuals exist in relationship; economics shapes relationships and is influenced by them; environmental

---

[19] T. Qiu, W. Qualls, J. D. Bohlmann and D. E. Rupp, 'The effect of interactional fairness on the performance of cross-functional product development teams: a multilevel mediated model', *Journal of Product Innovation Management*, 26 (2009), pp. 173–87; and R. M. Kramer, 'The great intimidators', *Harvard Business Review*, 84 (2006), p. 88.

concerns are a function of relationships between communities and between generations, and our ability to live sustainably is influenced by the patterns of household and business relationships that we create.

The choice is not between relationships and something else, but about the kinds of relationship we choose and the intentionality with which we pursue them. We can leave relationships as the by-product of decisions taken from other perspectives and with other considerations in mind. We can work with a narrow and incomplete view of relationships, using one or more other evaluation criteria. But this will not enable us to do justice to the importance of relationships, nor to respond effectively to the relational reality of the situations we confront.[20]

Ambivalence and Pressure

Thinking and seeing relationally doesn't always translate into practice. Anyone can look back over the last week and come up with a list of relational failures: responses that were less than constructive, deficiencies in thoughtfulness, misunderstood emails, forgotten promises, neglected duties and difficult conversations. Accepting that relationships are important is one thing; getting the practice of relationships right is another. But there are good reasons why people – and particularly organisations – so often fare poorly in making relationships work.

The first reason is *ambivalence*: relationships are valued in theory but in practice we may shy away from their demands. What is best for building a relationship with another person or organisation may not be the most urgent priority. The desire to focus on building customer relationships may be insufficient to move from the comfort of existing ways of working. Partnerships goals in the public sector may be outweighed in practice by silo targets. Nationally we may question whether GDP addresses all our aspirations, but still make economic growth the main outcome to be pursued. At a personal level we may want both the security of belonging and the freedom to move away. Sometimes, other deeper needs compete with fulfilling relational obligations, however binding they appear to be. It is hard for teams to retain professional players who want to move, whatever the employment contract. Opportunities for greater self-fulfilment and realisation may be presented elsewhere.

---

[20] For more information on thinking relationally, see www.relationalresearch.org.

This ambivalence has been framed in various ways. Biologists might describe us as social animals with selfish genes. Psychologists have explored the deep roots of our desire for relationship as well as our fear, the needs for both attachment and independence. Theologians might describe a God-given desire to relate to others that is marred by destructive self-centredness. Game theorists explore the 'prisoner's dilemma' to see how cases can be made both for collaboration and for more self-oriented 'cheating'.

The ambivalence of our own motivations may be further distorted by organisational priorities and motivations: 'I'd like to but ... .' Organisations often say the right things about relationships but in practice set up conflicting demands. Relational commitments may be weakened by the demands of external stakeholders, such as investors or funding bodies. As the Director of Housing for a London borough said: 'I'd like to work more closely with the NHS but I can't help them meet their Accident and Emergency waiting time targets.' He had a strong personal vision of how long-term sustainable improvements in the lives and wellbeing of homeless families could be achieved. But the opportunity to pursue the vision that motivated his work was increasingly frustrated both by his own organisation's targets, which too often meant that the short-term provision of shelter was all that could be achieved, and by the needs of other organisations to focus on their own targets – to the detriment of any partnership working on other issues.

A second reason why people and organisations don't get relationships right is *pressure*. Time and structural constraints may prevent the building of strong relationships. A heavy workload may limit a manager's ability to invest in staff development and team relationships. Children may be geographically distant from elderly parents and so less able to deliver the care and support they would like to provide. The institutional structures that would enable certain kinds of relationship (for example, a trade union) might not exist or be allowed to operate.

Other pressures are inherent in the culture:

- *We are highly connected*: we have more relationships to maintain than we used to. Anthropologists have suggested a maximum capacity for an individual of about 150 relationships, but typically our number of connections far exceeds this, leading to real problems in managing competing demands. Although Facebook and other social networking sites can enable more contacts to be maintained, pressure arises when this moves from simply maintaining informational awareness to active acceptance of obligations, commitments and responsibilities, or even to demands for higher frequency of interaction.

- *We are mobile*: people migrate across the country or the world for work or lifestyle reasons; companies need their key staff to gain experience in different places; work functions are outsourced across entire continents, albeit for sound financial reasons. The physical distances between colleagues, organisations, or family members can be hard to bridge.
- *Life is fast*: computing time, communication time, even plot speed in films are all quicker than they used to be. We expect everything to be faster, so we don't anticipate the time it takes, or we are not allowed the time, to build deep relationships.
- *Time has to be productive*: specific outcomes are important, and less time is available for investment activities such as building relationships. The combination of more relationships and less time available creates pressure – both in the amount of time in contact and the opportunity for reflection.

A third problem for relationships is *complexity* arising from both the emotional and political dynamics of a situation, as well as the nature of systems with many influencing factors and feedback loops. Breakdown in personal relationships often results in what Douglas Stone terms 'difficult conversations', where issues are emotionally painful, hard to pin down, difficult to resolve and sometimes even to discuss. Similarly in organisations, data and metrics are frequently lacking. A Relational Audit of Scottish prisons conducted by the Relationships Foundation in the 1990s identified relationships within prisons as a key factor in reducing both unrest and recidivism. A regional director in the Scottish Prison Service commented that he could 'lick his finger and hold it in the wind' as a means of assessing relationships. Data on escapes, suicides and violent incidents were crude performance indicators.

The result of ambivalence, pressure and complexity is that people often treat relationships as a 'black box'. The inputs and influence can be seen, as can the outcomes – but what is inside the box is far from clear. One advantage of thinking relationally is that it allows us to get inside the black box in a way that makes relationships easier to handle, both individually and organisationally. Thinking relationally gives leaders and policy-makers a language to describe and troubleshoot difficulties in relationships; it connects the external environment (and its pressures) to relational outcomes, enabling a clearer identification of cause and effect; it generates metrics to assess relational health from inside the black box rather than by waiting for the outcome when it is too late; and it supports the development of relational intelligence.

3 How to Measure Relationships

Politicians cannot legislate better relationships into existence. Managers cannot make staff like their customers or colleagues. But it is possible to create an environment in which relationships that can sustain the desired outcomes are more (or less) likely to be established. We can think about how policies, organisational structures, working practices, technology, or culture influence the way in which contact is made, the time that is available and how it is used, the opportunities to gain greater breadth of knowledge about counterparts, the ways in which staff can exercise power or customers be empowered, or how shared purpose may be enabled or conflicting objectives increased. This opens up a far more constructive discussion and analysis of relationships, and one that is capable of drawing on a wealth of insight from different disciplines.

Michael Schluter's interest in relational policy was crystallised during his time in East Africa in the 1970s discussing questions of economic and social policy. If, from an ethical starting point, the goal is to create the right set of relationships, how might we best describe 'right relationships'? And how do land ownership, capital markets, finance, employment regulation and other policies influence a society's capacity to build such relationships?

These remain key questions. If we want to build social capital, increase well-being, or fix a 'broken society' (to quote UK Prime Minister, David Cameron) we need to understand the ways in which we are shaping the environment within which people relate. In considering this environment we are looking at relationships from the outside in. But if we stop at this, then we miss something that strikes at a deeper level. We also need to understand why relationships are psychologically important to human beings and how we influence them; we also need to work from the inside out.

Roy Childs, as a psychologist, approaches questions about relationships in just this way. Relationships are shaped by the actions and responses of individuals. These are the product of the 'relationship with self' – the pattern of needs, fears and desires that governs our choices and behaviour. Understanding the person is an important and valuable way of understanding the relationship. To give ourselves a fighting chance of building good, healthy, productive relationships we therefore need to come at them from three directions – from the outside in, from the inside out, and from in between. We need to understand how to create an environment in which relationships flourish. By combining the approaches of structural systems (from the outside in), psychology (from the inside out) and organisational development (from in between) we have identified a framework for deconstructing the way relationships between individuals or organisations and within groups work.

So What is a Relationship?

At this point, it is worth going back a few steps and asking the basic question: what exactly is a relationship – particularly in an organisational setting?

Any relationship between organisations will be expressed through interpersonal interactions – sometimes just between two individuals but more usually a complex weaving of relationships between many individuals. Moreover, an inter-organisational relationship is more than the sum of the interpersonal parts: the relationship between organisations has a history and culture of its own, which both governs and is governed by the constituent interpersonal relationships.

In the relationship between the President of the USA and the Prime Minister of Great Britain, personal chemistry is an important element. However, alongside the relationship of President to Prime Minister there are relationships between administrations: the Oval Office and No. 10 Downing Street, State Department and Foreign Office, government to government. These house a range of personal relationships: Secretary of State to Foreign Secretary, between defence secretaries, and so on. At any time, all of these combine to be just one instalment in a longer-term relationship, which is further influenced by each party's relationships with other nations. The dynamics of all these relationships are relevant to the understanding of the relationship between any two individuals involved.

By 'relationship' we also mean more than mere linkage or association. Individuals or organisations are both capable of thoughts, words and actions; and those thoughts, words and actions can be influenced by the responses of the other. Thus, while it is possible to talk of my relationship with an object, or a place, or a work of art, or a dog – none of these are relationships in the sense defined in this book.

In addition, an important distinction exists between relationships and connections. In a loose sense we are all connected to one another through global markets and political systems, but that is not the same as having a personal relationship. There has to be a degree of ongoing interaction. As Robert Hinde has argued, 'relationships involve a series of interactions between two individuals who know each other such that each interaction can be influenced by past interactions and by expectations of interactions in the future'.[1]

He gives an example of talking to a telephone operative every day for a week. 'If you did not know it was the same person, if each conversation was uninfluenced by what you had learned about the operator as an individual on previous occasions, you could not have a relationship with him or her. A relationship only exists when the probable course of future interactions between the participants differs from that between strangers.'[2]

In summary, we suggest that a relationship exists where there is:

- *a series of encounters* with another – a person or an organisation – or group of others
- ... which are *shaped by the experience* (memory) of past encounters *and the expectation* (imagination) of future encounters
- ... where *the other is known*, or at least knowable
- ... where *the actions of each can affect the other*
- ... within some *shared context or motivation*.

Another way to put this is to say that people who engage in a relationship – whether it is personal or role-based – usually look for a corresponding set of five characteristics that determine how willing they are to continue engaging with the other party. The relationship will have to:

- Involve a degree of mutual *presence* – physical, intellectual, emotional or spiritual.

---

[1] Robert Hinde, *Relationships: A Dialectical Perspective* (Hove: Psychology Press, 1997, p. 48.
[2] Hinde, *Relationships*, p. 38.

- Yield a *story* that provides retrospective meaning and sets expectations for the future.
- Produce some *breadth* of understanding as a basis for tolerance and reliability.
- Achieve *fairness* in the distribution of power, risk and rewards.
- Show a degree of *alignment* in purposes and values.

To some extent, in personal relationships these characteristics are self-selecting: we grow familiar with those we meet often and at close quarters, and we seek out those with whose interests we align and who we perceive as treating us fairly. From an organisational standpoint, however, it is important to note that these characteristics are often strongly influenced by the formal structures within which relationships have to operate. For example:

- *Presence* is influenced by the way in which contact is made, including choice of the medium of *communication*.
- *Story* is influenced by the *duration* over which these contacts take place and the ways gaps between them and transitions are managed.
- *Breadth* is influenced by the ability to interact within a variety of sources and *contexts*.
- *Fairness* is influenced both by the complex distributions of *power* and by the way that power is used and expressed.
- *Alignment* is influenced by *purpose* and the ways in which difference is both valued and managed.

These are sensitive mechanisms, and organisations often create connections between people and between stakeholder groups that either fail to utilise the momentum created by good relationships or actively interfere with good relating. It is quite possible, for example, that individuals may find themselves working closely with those they do not warm to personally; or that potentially vital relationships are constrained by silos and reporting structures; or that an organisation fails to encourage alignment of purpose, or creates resentment by widening power differentials with excessively unequal rates of pay. Where this is the case, relationships, morale and performance will suffer.

Such, in summary, is the rationale for the Relational Proximity Framework. This recognises the importance of the goals of presence, story, breadth, fairness and alignment. It also provides organisations with metrics to assess how far they fall short of these goals and therefore the degree to which they are exposed to relational risk. Relational Proximity is a measure of the 'distance' in the relationship between people or organisations that determines how well each is likely to engage with the thinking, emotions and behaviour of the other. It uses five scales:

- *Directness*: the use of contact to create an encounter, and enable clear and effective communication in the relationship.
- *Continuity*: the use of time over a period of time to create a storyline and sense of momentum and resilience in the relationship.
- *Multiplexity*: the way information is gained to build breadth of knowledge and an ability to anticipate and respond in the relationship.
- *Parity*: the use of power to promote fairness and participation in the relationship and build mutual respect.
- *Commonality*: the sharing of purpose and values to create alignment and a sense of synergy and unity in the relationship.

These are discussed in the following chapters, but we provide an overview of the model here.

Directness

When we say that relationships are a series of interactions we mean that there is some contact between the parties involved. The way we communicate, the media we use and the skills we employ are fundamental processes by which one party to a relationship engages with and perhaps influences another. Intentions, hopes, desires, fears, needs and information all need to be communicated in order to coordinate actions, generate desired responses, or fulfil the human need for connection. Without at least the potential for communication there is no relationship as the two parties become wholly disconnected. Wars can be won or lost, businesses thrive or go under, and marriages flourish or break up as a result of successful or poor communication.

Why does face-to-face communication matter? Why are emails sometimes great – but sometimes not? The extent to which either party to a relationship is physically, intellectually, or emotionally present affects what is communicated, how it is experienced and what is achieved. The nature and extent of presence is influenced by such factors as time, place and the medium of communication used, as well as the communication skills employed and the degree of openness. It is this that enables both the sense of connectedness and the effectiveness of the communication process.

Communication, and, by extension, the encounter, can be shaped by external factors (for example, the geography of the relationship, including the size and design of offices) as well as internal factors, including both openness and communication skills.

Continuity

Defining relationships as a series of interactions introduces the time dimension to a relationship. This includes both the overall duration of a relationship and the way in which some things continue from one interaction to another, so enabling us to say that these interactions are part of the same story.

It is time that allows relationships to grow, understanding to deepen and trust to be built. Most people prefer to see the same doctor, have the same person cut their hair, or repeat business with people who have served them well. It reduces risks and saves time, while the explicit or implied promise of continuity conveys security and belonging. It is certainly preferable to have confidence that your bank will continue to exist and that agreements made yesterday will still be valid tomorrow.

These interactions build up over time to create a storyline, or narrative, for the relationship that links the past both with the present and with an expectation of the future. A key element of successful relationships is that they can build on previous interactions to create a sense of momentum. Where encounters are positive, trust, understanding and information is carried through from one interaction to the next, enabling more to be achieved. Time is not wasted, or the scope of what can be achieved limited, by having to start over again. Conversely, building on negative experiences is likely only to deepen the bitterness of a feud: this is why peacemaking is often based around reframing the story of the relationship.

The sense of being part of a story is a major contribution to the feeling of rootedness or belonging – to an organisation or community, for instance – that gives us resilience in the face of challenge and the confidence to adapt and grow.

Building a shared storyline becomes more challenging when staff turnover is high – a team will risk breaking down. A lack of time and momentum through a series of interactions is also a major limiting factor. The time dynamic of relationships is shaped by external factors such as the demands of other relationships, as well as by such internal factors as the commitment and loyalty that influence time allocation.

Multiplexity

Part of what continues from one interaction to another is information. The conduct of a relationship is influenced by what we know, and the accuracy and completeness of that information. Misunderstandings and missed opportunities result when too little is known, or when information is false. The nature, extent and quality of information about each party to the relationship is shaped by external factors, such as whether there is the opportunity to meet in different contexts, as well as the openness of disclosure and discernment.

Over time, we see people in different contexts and situations. We deliberately or unconsciously gather information that we use to build up our knowledge of them. We use this knowledge to invite their contributions, assess their needs and interests, judge their character, or interpret their responses. The completeness and authenticity of this knowledge is influenced by varied sources of information, or contexts for gaining it, as well as the degrees of inquiry and disclosure that characterise the relationship.

There are times when privacy is valued and important, or when knowledge can be used against us. However, the sense of being known, which brings with it the possibility of being understood, is an important affirmation of our worth as human beings, as well as bringing practical benefits.

Parity

The way in which we engage with other parties in a relationship raises the issue of power and the consequences of the way in which power is used. This has a particular influence on the levels of participation and investment in a relationship – either because of the rational calculation of fairness of return, or the more emotive response to feelings of being used, imposed upon, or treated unfairly. There are many forms of power, each of which may be distributed and used differently by the various parties to a relationship.

The instinct for fairness is deeply hard-wired into our make-up and a powerful influence on relational behaviour. Broadly speaking, we can understand and willingly accept an apparently unequal distribution of power if we think and feel that it is fair – in a military unit, say, or in the management structure of a large corporation. The distribution of the various forms of power, the structures and processes that support it, and the way in which people use power and respond to it, combine in ways that seem to us either more or less fair, either more or less exploitative. How fair or exploitative we think it is influences our willingness to participate in and contribute to a relationship. Fear of being hurt or treated unfairly is a major disincentive. Confidence that there will be a positive return (whether in terms of finance, reputation, opportunity, pleasure or any other currency) encourages participation.

Our sense of self is shaped, in part, by how others treat us. Mutual respect within a relationship or group is important to its health. Social cohesion in part is based on respect between groups that might otherwise look down on each other. If we are treated fairly then we feel respected and are given dignity. This in turn encourages contribution, responsibility and loyalty.

Commonality

A common purpose is often what brings people or organisations together, and informs the desired outcomes of their relationship – perhaps a job of work or a campaign. Purpose may be influenced by the demands of and obligations to others, as well as being the more internally defined product of the things that motivate us. Sometimes people have different objectives and priorities in a relationship: the relationship between a customer who wants to buy something and a supplier who wants to sell for a profit. What matters is the degree of alignment of purpose and the extent to which different purposes can be accommodated.

Sometimes where a common purpose is less well defined it is common values that unite a community or provide the 'glue' in a relationship. Where both purpose and values are held in common there will be a strong bond.

Because people are different, different purposes, identities, preferences or accountabilities all need to be managed in a relationship. Difference has many benefits: the variety can be both interesting and creative. But difference that is poorly managed with little alignment of purpose – in the sense of person to task, between persons, or between organisations – leads to conflict and friction. In a complex system, this process of alignment can be both unstable and challenging, with actions in one relationship having knock-on consequences for others. Yet without successful management of difference any cooperative activity becomes fraught with risks and will lack any sense of synergy.

Without a sense of common identity that encompasses and respects difference, the scope of what we can achieve is severely reduced. Human civilisation has always been built upon the ability to coordinate actions with others. It still gives us problems today.

4 Directness: High Touch Organisation

Think about your communication today: calls, texts, emails, tweets and other social media, meetings and conversations, perhaps even a handwritten note. Some emails might be a brief couple of lines, others a more composed response. Some may be to people you know well, others to do business with people you will never meet. You might call to make sure an email had got through, having received no response for a few days, or text to confirm a date. A longer call might involve creative thinking with a colleague on a joint project. At a meeting over lunch you may take more time to catch up on family and work-related news.

Each of these *encounters* are different. In some you will be physically present; in others physically elsewhere but still mentally present in the exchange. In our encounters we exchange information, we act together, we connect with the other person or people and we build the relationship. In doing this, we experience to a greater or lesser degree the presence of the other person at a number of different levels – physically, emotionally, intellectually or spiritually, or in a combination of these – and they experience ours. The encounter can be constrained to a 'narrow bandwidth', operating on just one of these levels – an intellectual task focused via email, say. Or it can have 'high bandwidth', operating on several of these levels at once – a face-to-face meeting with a friend. The greater the bandwidth of the interaction the more of these levels can come into play, and the greater the experience of *connection*.

The quality and degree of connectedness is enabled by the way in which we make and sustain *contact*. In practice, the technology of phone or web facilitates contact. With email, for instance, there is usually a time delay before receiving a reply: in this case, both a time lapse and email technology define the contact,

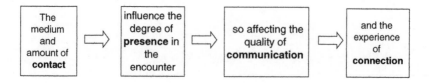

Figure 4.1:   How Directness influences the behaviour and outcomes of a relationship

and therefore influence the degree of connection, you make with the other person. In this way, we manage contact with the other person to create a level of connectedness appropriate to the relationship. In the workplace (and elsewhere), the nature of the connections we make is a key determinant of the *communication* process and its outcomes. The ability to reach the right person, to access them quickly and get a response, as well as the clarity and completeness of any communication, can all be influenced by the way in which contact is made.

At a psychological level we also impact the connection with the other person, or people, by how much of ourselves we consciously or unconsciously bring to the relationship. A highly Direct relationship is one in which the encounter is unmediated and integrates all four levels: the physical, emotional, intellectual and spiritual. Each person is truly and deeply present in the encounter and feels connected to the other (Figure 4.1).

A low level of Directness occurring inappropriately results in isolation, such as in the breakdown of a virtual team in the workplace, or the loneliness of young mothers on an estate with no communal meeting place. The sense of positive connectedness that is so important to a strong, healthy relationship is made possible by high levels of Directness – by closing the gaps of time and space, and by practising openness.

The degree of Directness in a relationship is not just a consequence of our choices about means of contact. Other people's choices and actions as well as the environment within which we relate influence the potential to achieve Directness in relationships. Working hours influence the time family members can be physically together. A high-quality transport infrastructure makes it easier for people to work further away from home, but also makes it easier to see those from whom they are geographically separated. The size and design of schools and offices shapes patterns of interaction. Local 'parliaments' can be created to give socially excluded users of public services an opportunity to meet and directly express their concerns to local policy-makers. This chapter is therefore not just about how we should conduct our own relationships. It is also concerned with how we influence the potential for other people to experience directness in their relationships, and the consequences of this.

Why Face to Face Matters

There is a reason why people cluster together. Companies often co-locate – as in the City of London or in Silicon Valley in the USA. Communities form settlements and gather together in public spaces. Humans attach significance to being together in the same place at the same time. With it, important things happen. Without it, opportunities are missed or communication impaired.

In terms of communication, being physically present enables a rich exchange of information that adds facial expression, tone of voice, dress and information from surroundings, even smell, to the actual words used. Used symbolically, it reinforces belonging in groups and communicates worth and importance; more practically, it supports joint activity and enables physical acts of care and support. That is why multinational companies spend heavily to get their staff together for the annual global conference and why there is such intense networking at such face-to-face events. It also explains why organisations cluster. As Michael Porter has shown: 'the social glue that binds clusters together also facilitates access to important resources and information. Tapping in to the competitively valuable assets within a cluster requires personal relationships, face-to-face contact, a sense of common interest, and "insider" status.'[1]

Places are the 'container' for an interaction or an opportunity to connect. Office buildings such as the British Airways corporate headquarters in the UK are designed with communal space and walkways that encourage people to bump into each other.[2] Some environments are more conducive to social and business conversations. And some configurations of office space, furniture, decoration, walkways, parks and playgrounds are more likely to create opportunities for contact and interaction. A criticism of post-war social housing developments in the UK is that they replaced community spaces with corridors and elevators that reduced interaction between neighbours, with a consequent impact on patterns of social contact and security. A particular place can

[1] M. Porter, 'Clusters and the new economics of competition', *Harvard Business Review*, 76 (November–December 1998), p. 88.
[2] F. Duffy, 'Working at Waterside – conduciveness as a workplace of the British Airways' Headquarters in Harmondsworth, England', *The Architectural Review*, 1218 (1998), pp. 44–45.

become intrinsic to a relationship or community, becoming part of its fabric, and giving identity and a sense of rootedness. Spaces shape communities, but communities also shape spaces and give them meaning, imbuing them with memories and associations shaped by past interactions.

Much dealing and trading has migrated to electronic platforms. In 2004, Leslie Willcocks and John Hindle looked at the future of the Lloyd's insurance market, exploring the tensions between the benefits and the inefficiencies of the face-to-face dealing that had developed from the market's origins in coffee houses.[3] In complex, hard-to-quantify deals, and in arranging cover quickly, some of the dealers noted the importance of being able to see whether someone sweated when they signed the contract. On the other hand, some feared losing business to more efficient, electronically driven markets. Much business at Lloyd's is still conducted face to face.

Face-to-face communication is unique in that it is the only form of communication that is linked to physical presence: the rise of speed dating is one illustration of how physical presence enables much information to be processed rapidly. Face to face is the only form of communication that does away with the filtering effect of technology, time and other people. It is only through face-to-face communication that all the elements of human interaction can be explored – it can engage the senses (sight, sound, touch, smell). This increases the bandwidth and magnifies the interaction. Emotional as well as factual information is rapidly exchanged. Creativity is facilitated; an experience is shared; opportunities for interaction multiply. There is a difference between seeing refugees on the news and physically being in the camp.

Interactions that require high levels of emotional engagement are usually most effective when face to face. In the business world, companies fly senior executives from, say, London to New York, to sign a contract. Agreements sealed with a handshake are more likely to be honoured than those made by videoconference. Conversely, it is easier to lie by phone than face to face. The same dynamic drives controversies over forms of dress. In October 2006, the then UK Foreign Secretary, Jack Straw MP, sparked controversy by revealing that he asked Muslim women wearing the niqab – the veil which covers the face – to remove it when they came to see him in his constituency office.[4] A few months later in the UK a classroom teaching assistant was dismissed for

---

[3] L. Willcocks, *The London Insurance Market: Modernisation or Muddle* (London: Knowledge Capital Partners, 2004).

[4] J. Straw, 'I felt uneasy talking to someone I couldn't see', *Guardian*, 6 October 2006.

refusing to remove the niqab. The ensuing national debate has continued over the years about the implications of face coverings for security, giving evidence in court, nursing care or teaching, focusing on the extent to which seeing the face was necessary for particular jobs and tasks.

The complex exchanges of ideas that enable creativity is far easier and faster when done face to face.[5] Spontaneity, particularly among a group, is almost impossible in a conference call. The subtleties of body language become part of the discussion – you and they can add something to the conversation by the way you use your hands, or sit forward, or get up and walk around. Instant feedback checks the understanding of what has been heard; the response immediately elicits a further exchange. A study for Corning found that 80 per cent of their ideas arose from face-to-face contact and that the engineers were only willing to walk 100 feet from their desk to talk to somebody else. Cohen and Prusak draw on this and other case studies to argue for the benefit of small offices.[6]

At the top end of the scale of Directness is physical contact. Margaret Atwood writes in *The Blind Assassin*[7]: 'Touch comes before sight, before speech. It is the first language and the last, and it always tells the truth.' Psychologists are becoming increasingly aware of the developing child's need for physical contact. Studies in orphanages and hospitals repeatedly tell us that infants deprived of skin contact lose weight, become ill and even die. Premature babies given periods of touch therapy gain weight faster, cry less, and show more signs of relaxed pulse, respiration rate and muscle tension. Avoidance of physical contact may indicate neurological damage or history of abuse.

Physical contact remains significant throughout life. In an experiment, librarians were instructed alternately to touch and not touch the hands of students as they handed back their library cards. When the students were interviewed, those who had been touched reported far greater positive feelings about themselves, the library and the librarians than those who had not been touched. This occurred even though the touch was fleeting and most of the students had not noticed it.[8] Attitudes and customs vary between cultures. Asian cultures generally regard physical contact between adults outside the

---

[5] L. Daft, R. H. Lengel and L. K. Trevino, 'Message equivocality, media selection and manager performance – implications for information systems', *MIS Quarterly*, 11 (1987), pp. 354–366.

[6] Cohen and Prusak, *In Good Company*, p. 88.

[7] M. Atwood, *The Blind Assassin* (London: Virago Press, 2001).

[8] J. D. Fisher, M. Rytting and R. Heslin, 'Hands touching hands: affective and evaluative effects of an interpersonal touch', *Sociometry*, 39 (1976), pp. 416–421.

family as inappropriate, but for children and elderly people in care it is not only acceptable but valued. In contrast, western countries are more likely to regard forms of physical contact between adults as acceptable, but to place restrictions around the forms of physical contact permissible between unrelated adults and children.[9]

Having ease of access to others is an important factor in care situations. There are certain kinds of support – both practical and emotional – that people cannot supply simply by making a phone call. This is particularly a problem for the growing numbers of elderly in western countries. Many elderly people have low levels of social contact, with over 1 million describing themselves as always or often lonely.[10]

Research and experience have discovered that the face itself is important to the way we encounter others. We base conscious and unconscious judgements about such traits as attractiveness, likeability, trustworthiness, competence and aggressiveness on people's faces. Furthermore, one study found that physicians spent more time looking at diagnostic scans when they were accompanied by a photograph of the patient. It is suggested that the picture of a face, the reminder that there is a real person behind the images, triggers greater ethical commitment.[11]

Charles Darwin was almost denied the chance to make his historic voyage on the *Beagle*. The captain did not believe that a person with such a nose would 'possess sufficient energy and determination'.[12] We also make very swift and more-or-less unconscious evaluations based on faces. Malcolm Gladwell brought to public prominence both the power and significance of our unconscious thinking and judgements such as these in his book *Blink*.[13] Some, though not all, research has shown that people make judgements about character traits on the basis of exposure to a face for a tenth of a second. These snap assessments correlate to assessments without time constraints, although

[9] See, for example, P. C. Earley and S. Ang, *Cultural Intelligence: Individual Interactions Across Cultures* (Stanford University Press, 2003), p. 176.

[10] TNS, TNS Loneliness Omnibus Survey for Age UK (April 2014).

[11] Y. Turner and I. Hadas-Halpern, 'The effects of including a patient's photograph to the radiographic examination', Radiological Society of North America 2008 Scientific Assembly and Annual Meeting, Chicago IL, February 18–20, 2008, abstract available at http://archive.rsna.org/2008/6008880.html, accessed 20 October 2015.

[12] F. Darwin (ed.), *Charles Darwin's Autobiography* (New York: Henry Schuman, 1950), p. 36, quoted in A. Todorov et al., 'Inferences of competence from faces predict election outcomes', *Science*, 308 (2005), pp. 1623–1626.

[13] M. Gladwell, *Blink: The Power of Thinking Without Thinking* (New York: Little, Brown, 2005).

longer exposure to a face increases confidence in the judgement and allows for more differentiated trait impressions.[14] The impact of face-based evaluations is revealed in the fact that one-second exposure to the photographs of unknown election candidates has a 70 per cent success rate in predicting election outcomes.[15]

The physical presence of others is not, of course, always a positive experience. Particularly where it is enduring and inescapable, it can intensify negative, rather than creative and positive, feelings. This point is well captured by Lawrence Stone in his historical study of the family:

In the 'face-to-face society' of the traditional village, whose virtues are often praised in this more impersonal and mobile world ... it was possible for expressions of hatred to reach levels of frequency, intensity and duration which are rarely seen today, except in similar close-knit groups like the Fellows of Oxford and Cambridge Colleges.[16]

The advantages of face-to-face communication are intuitively understood in organisations, but seldom analysed. They can be summed up as follows.

First, face-to-face communication *aids the quality of interaction*:

- It permits a wide range of clues and messages through touch, body language and tone of voice.
- Instant feedback allows miscommunication to be identified and corrected – you cannot tell so easily if your letter or email has caused offence.
- Eye contact aids attention management. This is much harder to do in, for example, videoconferences.
- Spontaneous communication doesn't happen to the same extent when people are not together. This often includes important information both in terms of building the relationship and sharing knowledge.
- It enables creative conversation: it is harder to be creative over the phone.
- Additional contextual information is communicated by physical presence – for example the additional information gleaned by visiting a business contact in his or her office.

---

[14] J. Willis and A. Todorov, 'First impressions: making up your mind after a 100-ms exposure to a face', *Psychological Science*, 17 (2006), pp. 592–598.

[15] C. Ballew and A. Todorov, 'Predicting political elections from rapid and unreflective face judgments', *PNAS*, 104:46 (2007), pp. 17948–17953.

[16] L. Stone, *The Family, Sex and Marriage in England, 1500–1800* (London: Weidenfeld & Nicolson, 1977), p. 95, quoted in L. Spencer and R. Pahl, *Rethinking Friendship: Hidden Solidarities Today* (Princeton University Press, 2006), p. 21.

Second, it impacts *obligation and accountability*:

- It is harder to lie face to face than by email, or fail to honour an agreement sealed with a handshake than one made by videoconference.
- It is harder to be concerned about the consequences of our actions on people we do not see.
- There is greater commitment to joint decisions made in face-to-face contact.
- It is easier to get people to do what you want, especially if you are a member of the more powerful group – distance reduces this influence.

Third, it *signals belonging and enables empathy*:

- Face-to-face Directness enables social bonding through, for example, greetings or eating and drinking together. Other forms of communication do not allow this so effectively.
- Shared experience is particularly effective in developing closer bonds if face to face.
- It is harder to forget or sideline group members if they are physically present; those present less often than the rest are more likely to be marginalised.
- It influences the extent to which 'badges' can be seen: e.g. clothes, accent, skin colour, age (however, the anonymity of more remote communication may sometimes be appropriate to inhibit discrimination).
- Physical presence may communicate comfort and support even if nothing is said. Sometimes the best hospital visitors are those who can be comfortable saying nothing.
- It reflects the fact that we are social, relational beings. Through work we address our relational needs – communication is more than task accomplishment.

The advantages are felt even when most interaction takes place by other means. Author and consultant Alison Myers was based in London, managing a virtual, dispersed team responsible for the global rollout of an assessment centre. Although one of her team members worked in the same office, one was in South Africa and two were in Milan. Managing the team relationships was difficult. Passing information around the team needed discipline from everyone involved, and she discovered that discussing strategic issues or problem-solving was almost impossible in a teleconference, let alone building a sense of collaboration.

Alison quickly found that a face-to-face day-long meeting once a month was both highly effective for relationship building and for the more challenging creative work, supplemented by regular teleconferences to go over ongoing tasks and by weekly email reporting. The relational benefit of the monthly day together extended over the following month but only lasted so long – gradually wearing off until the next away-day when the high level of Directness gave the team's relationships effectiveness another 'shot in the arm'.

Directness Without Face to Face

Quality communication – by which is meant communication that is clear, complete and open – is built upon well-managed encounters with other people or with organisations. Research has confirmed the importance of building social relationships in order to facilitate effective transfer of information – verbal and non-verbal – between the parties involved. Bonnie Nardi and Steve Whittaker, for example, argue that 'social linkages between people are a precondition of information exchange'. They argue that people create social 'fields' or 'communication zones': 'A zone is a potentiality for productive communication between two people. In everyday human activity, the management of communication zones involves long-term projects of creating appropriate social bonds of connection, which may stretch over years, or even decades, as well as much shorter-term projects of managing attention.'[17]

The reality, however, is that face-to-face communication isn't always possible. We are much more extensively connected, but with more people, and over far greater distances than we can effectively travel. Geographical clusters – jewellers in London's Hatton Garden, financiers on Wall Street – have been overshadowed by virtual clusters that are part of contemporary organisational life. Businesses are managed from the other side of the world. Relationships are stretched across geographical boundaries. Each of us can communicate with millions of others – via blogs and chatrooms. The trend that began with smoke signals and beacons, through carrier pigeons, semaphore and Morse code, has accelerated with current forms of electronic communication. Simultaneously, the range of interaction has widened. Videoconferencing allows a degree of emotional and quasi-physical communication that simply couldn't fit on a text message, still less on a semaphore flag.

So while it is important to many relationships – working or otherwise – meeting face to face is not always possible, practical or even desirable. It takes time, particularly if it requires travel (and therefore also has a carbon cost). It is not always most appropriate if emotional detachment is required, time for thought or a formal written record of communication is needed, or

---

[17] B. A. Nardi and S. Whittaker, 'The place of face-to-face communication in distributed work', in P. J. Hinds and S. Kiesler (eds.), *Distributed Work* (Cambridge, MA: MIT Press, 2002), pp. 83–113.

in addressing multiple audiences in different places. Similarly, a phone call may not be possible, across time zones for instance, or to catch up with a busy person. But an encounter by email will often facilitate communication that otherwise would not happen at all. Understanding this means that we can make choices about the type of encounter based upon the purpose of the communication; and we can manage the risks to communication derived from the limitations of particular types of encounter.

This has an impact on motivation, trust and accountability. Psychologist and author Roy Childs worked with a virtual team in the IT sector. Its sense of identity was based around its use of advanced technology: it was almost a matter of pride to say 'Hey, look, we can do all of this with technology – who needs the old-fashioned ways of running teams – and look at all the time we save with not flying all over the world and wasting all that time in meetings!' The team leader, however, was convinced of the need for everyone to get to know each other better, but found this hard to justify in the culture, especially as they delivered all that was expected of them. Judged by the yardstick of efficiency, actual meetings were a waste of time. Despite this, in spite of negative comments from his boss, the team leader authorised the budget for a facilitated two-day discussion. This was a brave decision, not least because, at the time, it was based on intuition and faith rather than on the much-favoured rational analysis.

Roy proposed that the two days would not address any work issues directly: the sole purpose would be to get to know each other. After the two days there was dramatic feedback. First, the amount of communication increased enormously – by phone rather than email. Second, several team members admitted that they had been demotivated and had started looking around for another job – but had now decided to stay. Third, they expressed a willingness to share ideas and solutions that they had been less inclined to do before. All of these benefits can be quantified, giving a useful reminder that you don't have to focus on performance to improve performance. In fact focusing on relationships can be one of the quickest ways to improve performance.

Directness, Presence and Absence

The ability to reach the right person, to access them quickly and get a response, as well as the clarity and completeness of any communication, can all be influenced by the channel through which contact is made. At a psychological level, it is also influenced by how much of ourselves we consciously or unconsciously bring to the relationship. A highly direct relationship could be described as one in which the encounter is unmediated and integrates more than one level: not only physical presence, but also emotional, intellectual and spiritual levels. All of these contribute to the experience of connectedness.

One way of describing presence in relating is 'being awake' to oneself, to others and to the wider context in which the relationship is set. In his book about leading in conflicted situations,[18] Mark Gerzon argues that we can only lead effectively if we are fully present – 'awake' – which means being:

- open to perceiving what is happening right now
- responsive to the needs of this moment
- flexible enough to shift gears
- able to notice if current behaviour or strategy is not working
- creative enough to invent a new approach in the moment
- honest enough to admit it if we don't have a new approach yet.[19]

Being present intellectually, or mentally, is probably at its most evident or necessary when there is a specific task to be achieved by those involved: problem-solving, decision-making, or processing information, in fact in any predominantly cognitive activity. We talk about a 'meeting of minds' when two people, or a group, encounter (and agree with) each other in this way. There is also an emotional dimension to an interaction in which we are fully present. To be fully attentive and committed to another person, or to a team or organisation, we must involve our emotions. Connecting intellectually can be hugely creative and intuitive, but risks being 'dry', without the accompanying emotional connection. As leaders, managing emotional presence is important to our impact on those around us and on our ability to motivate and be motivated. Organisationally, emotional connectedness brings with it a sense of engagement in the task at hand.

Technology plays an increasingly significant role in Directness, and its influence cuts both ways. On the one hand, it makes possible interactions that would have been impossible before. Businesses can run virtual teams and global companies existing in different time zones. Employees can have the option to work from home, juggling caring commitments with work. Companies can reach huge numbers of people worldwide with their brand and products. Technology

---

[18] M. Gerzon, *Leading Through Conflict: How Successful Leaders Transform Differences into Opportunities* (Cambridge, MA: Harvard Business School Press, 2006).

[19] Gerzon, *Leading Through Conflict*, p. 100.

can also increase Directness by cutting out the middle men, replacing them with more neutral forms of mediation. Blogging, for example, enables celebrities, politicians, journalists and others to be 'present' in a more unmediated form (at least in perception), thus bypassing the editing and interpreting mediation of the press.

On the other hand, technology places a filter on an interaction, by reducing the breadth of the communication channel. Technology is weighted towards connecting at an intellectual level, reducing the emotional connection of the exchange to little or nothing. A phone conversation is reduced to the words used and the tone of voice; in messaging, the focus is on the words alone and the way they are used. A videoconference allows us to see the person to whom we are talking and therefore to pick up some body language cues, but we may struggle to pick up a sense of physical presence.

Telephone or email interactions are well suited to connecting primarily on an intellectual task-focused level. Lack of physical proximity reduces the 'noise' of emotional data as well as wider contextual information, making it easier to focus in on the intellectual content of the conversation. For this reason, virtual working relationships tend to be at their best when highly tasked – that is, when the primary need is for 'dry' intellectual content. Of course, reduction to the intellectual can be a disadvantage when emotional or other contextual information would be helpful: for instance, when motivation is an issue or when brainstorming. It is also hard, though not impossible, to transfer emotional presence via a third person.

What we might term a 'spiritual' connection within a relationship is characterised by integrity, meaning and calling. At an individual level, the integrity of the encounter and its sense of spiritual connectedness means that it is true to one's beliefs and values. Organisationally, the spiritual level within a relationship is represented by the principles and integrity embedded within the ethos of the organisation.[20] In these cases, communication is characterised by openness, honesty and trust, and recognition of a connection to something beyond the everyday. An encounter that has a spiritual dimension derives its meaning and its values from something bigger than itself, from its contribution to other people and causes, and perhaps from a sense of responsibility to God.

Of course, it is possible to be in the same room but not engaged with others in any meaningful way: present physically but only partially present emotionally

---

[20] Stephen Covey includes spiritual intelligence as one of the four intelligences. See *The 8th Habit: From Effectiveness to Greatness* (New York: Simon & Schuster, 2006).

or intellectually. Thoughts can be elsewhere and feelings hidden, even when one appears to be engaged in conversation or discussion. Microsoft executive Linda Stone coined the phrase 'continuous partial attention' for this in 1998. Providing support – 'being there' – often requires not just physical proximity but also availability, attention and commitment. Continuous partial attention has become more of an issue in a technological environment where people are instantly reachable anywhere and from anywhere. Phones constantly bombard users with requests for action or interaction, with a well-documented impact on the conversations or meetings in which a person is currently taking part. The desire to connect, be accessible and value people by responding quickly to them is positive. The problem is that in trying to be more accessible to more people, we can become less accessible to those who are most important. Our world becomes, as Linda Stone puts it, like a never-ending cocktail party where you're always looking over your virtual shoulder for a better conversation partner.[21]

There is a sense, of course, in which people are always partially 'absent' when they deal with others. They present a *persona* – a version of the 'self' that is projected into the encounter. This is made up from a deep-seated sense of self (motivations, personality, values), beliefs about the situation (attitude to others) and current state (mood, fatigue, other events that are going on). Goffman captures this when he notes that we all live in a world of social encounters. These may be face-to-face or mediated contact with other people. In each of these contacts, he argues, a person tends 'to act out what is sometimes called a *line* – that is, a pattern of verbal and nonverbal acts by which he expresses his view of the situation and through this his evaluation of the participants, especially himself'.[22]

This means that people are often hard to 'read'. Personas may be variable, deceptive, robust or fragile and can create barriers to effective communication: the polished performance can convey emotion and sincerity while concealing contrary thoughts and feelings. Strong relationships are usually characterised by openness – but that is a state most people and organisations approach with caution. To reduce stress and build resilience in staff, change management practitioners urge organisations to be as open as they can be with their employees about changes that are taking place, even if not everything is yet

---

[21] L. Stone, 'Attention: the real aphrodisiac', Speech at the Emerging Technology Conference, San Diego, CA, December 2006.

[22] E. Goffman, *Interaction Ritual: Essays on Face-to-Face Behavior* (New York: Anchor Books, 1967), p. 5.

known. For some organisations mutual openness is a characteristic of their relationships with partners and suppliers through open book accounting and participation in briefings and strategy sessions.

Will Schutz, author of Fundamental Interpersonal Relations Orientation (FIRO) theory,[23] describes how a director he worked with found the yearly pay bargaining the worst part of his job. He claimed that the pay round discussion began as soon as the previous year's had been completed. It was characterised by covert conversations and criticism and was generally a negative and demotivating process. Will Schutz suggested that the whole team got together in one room to address the issue together and directly. After some persuasion the director accepted this proposal and Schutz began the meeting by outlining the issue. He asked whether anyone else found the process unsatisfactory. Everyone agreed. He then suggested that they all say what they earned in order to open up a discussion on how to manage the process more transparently. This – not unexpectedly – was fiercely resisted. So Schutz suggested that they guess what each other earned as a way of starting the discussion. This enabled them to transition to real issues: not just salaries, but personal value and eventually self-esteem, which they tended to attach to their salaries. The result was an open agreement about managing changes in pay levels that took thirty minutes instead of a whole year.[24]

Directness and Third Parties

A common way of managing Directness is to use intermediaries or third parties. Intermediaries play an important role in managing relationships, where officeholders or organisations may choose to conduct business using an advocate, ambassador, press secretary, or adviser, and in this way the intermediary acts both as a constraint on Directness and also as a point of contact and a specialist service. Brokers may be able to negotiate better deals, or advocates secure better care. An intermediary is beneficial to a relationship when the value of expertise or accessibility is added, and when the intermediary has personal access to the ultimate seller or decision-maker. Intermediaries' knowledge,

---

[23] W. Schutz, *FIRO: A Three Dimensional Theory of Interpersonal Behavior* (New York: Holt, Rinehart & Winston, 1958).

[24] W. Schutz, *The Human Element: Productivity, Self-Esteem and the Bottom Line* (San Francisco, CA: Jossey-Bass, 1994), p. 54.

skills, relationship with the other party, or ability to represent a group of people and aggregate their leverage can all mean that they enable us to have more influence in a relationship than we would have by acting on our own.

Mediation by people is distinct from mediation by technology in that it is not *our* words that reach the intended audience. Sometimes this is an advantage, but it is also prone to distortion and drift. PAs may edit a message or add interpretations. Hierarchy can limit access to senior people, meaning that suggestions or requests have to be presented by others further up the management line who are less motivated to press the point and more likely to misunderstand it. Where decision-making is distant from those who are affected, it can be difficult to preserve the sense of personal and emotional connection that trust and understanding rely on. Poor decisions and disaffection are risked as a consequence.

Mediation by other people may be built into the structure of the relationship. Capital providers in public limited liability companies, for example, are increasingly distant from directors. A financial adviser will place your money into a fund whose managers may or may not be active in voting or in getting to know people in the company. Some may even argue that 'objective' analysis of data provides better investment information than the 'subjectivity' of company meetings. The company in whose ownership you have a share thanks to your investments may operate on the other side of the world, and have a wide-ranging and largely invisible set of relationships with employees, customers, suppliers and other stakeholders. Lack of Directness means, in effect, disempowerment for the investor.

Organisations sometimes use branding to build a more direct connection with consumers. The producer's relationship with the customer, however, may be mediated by wholesalers and retailers, increasing the relational distance to a point where the producer feels the consumer's influence only in the form of a demand for a lower price. This lack of Directness is exactly what has driven the bullying behaviour of supermarket chains towards dairy farmers in the UK.

Building in Distance

Directness is a variable that individuals and organisations use to manage their relationships with others. Sometimes they need less of it, not more. Financial institutions may need 'Chinese walls', limiting communication to limit conflicts

Table 4.1: Appropriate and inappropriate experience of high and low degrees of Directness

High Directness	Intrusion	Connection
Low Directness	Isolation	Privacy
	Felt as inappropriate	Felt as appropriate

of interest. Managers sometimes need to make themselves 'absent' in order to give space for others to interact, to empower team members, to delegate tasks more fully, or to enable someone to occupy a role. In counselling, it is necessary to balance sufficient Directness to pick up verbal and non-verbal clues, with sufficient professional distance on an emotional level to remain objective.

The subjectivity of the effects is important, because Directness can be measured both by objective criteria (what kind of communication, how much distance) and by subjective criteria that are set by the parties involved (Table 4.1). Geoff Mulgan, former head of policy for Tony Blair, published his book *Connexity* during the first year of Tony Blair's administration. He noted the growing importance of connectedness for both nations and individuals:

In the past what made a city or island strong was to be part of a strong hierarchy (like an empire) or to provide raw materials. Today, strength and autonomy are more likely to flow from maximising the extent of connectedness to the rest of the world, through bandwidth and technologies, relationships and contacts. If in the past it was good to be left alone because being noticed meant being a likely target for invaders, today no fate is worse than to be cut off.[25]

But he goes on:

Remoteness and isolation were once the condition of the poor. Today it is only the extremely rich who can escape other people, and even they depend on armies of people and systems which need active maintenance.[26]

---

[25] G. Mulgan, *Connexity: How to Live in a Connected World* (London: Chatto & Windus, 1997), p. 32.
[26] Mulgan, *Connexity*, p. 19.

5   Continuity: Organisation across Time

At any point in time, a relationship looks simultaneously to the past and to the future. If it consists of more than a couple of chance encounters it begins to develop a storyline, and the content of that storyline, as told by each party, creates potential or 'baggage' for the relationship going forward. Relationships need Continuity – but Continuity itself is a complex thing. The interplay of past and future has an impact on all relationships. For example:

- In a nursing home an elderly resident may be distressed when a new carer helps her to get up in the morning but doesn't follow the same routines as the previous long-standing carer.
- In a negotiation it may be hard to interpret the responses of the other party because you have little or no experience of that person.
- In a long-standing project, a new manager may inadvertently offend project partners by being unaware of what had previously been agreed.
- In outsourcing, a client may decide to go with a known supplier, for the sake of track record and ease of communication, rather than accepting a lower bid from a competitor.
- In career building, a manager with an eye on the next rung up the ladder may prioritise tasks that will show measurable progress in the next few months – rather than tasks that are more crucial for the long-term growth of the company or without regard to longer-term risks that may be created.

In each of these examples, the present is affected either by the experience of the past, or the expectation of the future, or both. The present encounter is experienced as a moment in an ongoing narrative. The relationships people tend to rate as most significant, whether friends, family members or work colleagues, are the ones that carry a strong past history and the expectation of longevity. Many of these relationships will have a positive past and the prospect of more of the same. Others may be in the list for less positive reasons: their history is a difficult one and their future is viewed with resignation or worse.

Relationships 'involve a series of interactions between two individuals who know each other, such that each interaction can be influenced both by past interactions and by expectations of interactions in the future'.[1] The existence of a storyline in a relationship or group gives a sense of *momentum* or progression. It occupies time in two senses: the amount of time spent interacting and the frequency or regularity of contact. Continuity can be defined as 'time over time'. It also involves management of gaps between encounters, which can cause loss of information, failures in understanding, and a mismatch in expectations. Weekly or monthly team meetings frequently exhibit all three.

Being part of an ongoing storyline, in a single relationship or as part of a group or community, fulfils a human desire to *belong*. It gives a sense of rootedness and fosters those relational characteristics that take time to grow, such as trust, understanding, loyalty and best practice. These qualities can embed relationships to such an extent that it is sometimes possible to pick up 'as though you've never left off' even after a long separation. Conversely, the same qualities can be lost if storyline disintegrates and cannot be replicated instantly.

The Use of Time and Narrative in Relationships

Stories are basic to the way humans think. We understand the world through stories. The Nigerian novelist, Ben Okri, described people as *homo fabula* – storytelling beings.[2] This is echoed by Mark Turner, Professor of Cognitive

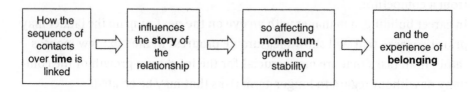

Figure 5.1:   How Continuity influences the behaviour and outcomes of a relationship

[1] R. Hinde, *Relationships: A Dialectical Perspective* (Hove: Psychology Press, 1997), p. 48.
[2] B. Okri, *A Way of Being Free* (London: Weidenfeld & Nicolson, 1997), p. 114.

Science at Case Western Reserve University, who argues that our most complex mental tasks are usually carried out not by the 'classical mechanics' of rational actor theory (where stories have no place), but rather by a set of analogy-making and metaphor-mapping abilities which together form the core of human cognition: 'Story is a basic principle of mind. Most of our experience, our knowledge, and our thinking is organised as stories.'[3]

Narrative therefore has a powerful grip on human cognition; it can restructure our mental spaces in ways that strongly influence our reasoning ability and, ultimately, what we make of the world.[4] The story of a relationship – as opposed to that told by an individual purely about him or herself – therefore shapes the relationship and its participants at a profound level; and the way in which interactions build a story of the relationship therefore has a deep impact on how that relationship, and often the world beyond, is experienced. When you receive an email from a colleague, you draw on the memory of previous interactions to 'read between the lines', to establish 'tone of voice', motivation, and so on. When an organisation renegotiates its contract with a supplier, it will be informed by the story of a previous late delivery.

In order to understand the ways in which interactions are linked to form relational continuity, and the consequences of success or failure in this, we need first to understand what we mean by the story of the relationship. For a story to sustain a relationship, a team or a community, it needs to have a pattern – a past and a future that frame the present, and make sense together. With this trajectory in time a story becomes an identifiable storyline. Without this, a story is unpredictable, disjointed, disconcerting; few deductions can be made from the past that will help us in the present; few clear expectations can be held of the future.

Each of these three points of focus – past, present and future – is linked to, and impacts, the others. The past may be construed in ways that make it harder (or easier) to deal with the present. Dwelling on betrayal may colour the future; glossing over your own part may mean that important lessons are not learned. Organisations or individuals who are too focused on the past

---

[3] G. Fauconnier and M. Turner, *The Way We Think: Conceptual Blending and the Mind's Hidden Complexities* (New York: Basic Books, 2002).

[4] Other classic works here include G. Lakoff and M. Johnson, *Metaphors We Live By* (University of Chicago Press, 1980); and D. Gentner, K. Holyoak and B. Kokinov, *The Analogical Mind: Perspectives from Cognitive Science* (Cambridge, MA: MIT Press, 2001). See also W. D. Casebeer and J. A. Russell, 'Storytelling and terrorism: towards a comprehensive "counter-narrative strategy"', *Strategic Insights*, 4 (2005), p. 1–16.

may fail to deal with the present or adapt to the future. However, an exclusive focus on the present may fail to prepare for the future as well as neglecting the culture and traditions that frame other people's expectations of the present. Living for the moment may capture an intensity of exhilaration, but with neither roots nor prospects to give meaning and context there may be little left when the moment passes. Furthermore, focusing primarily on the future may be visionary, but the prospect of jam tomorrow may not satisfy other people's needs for today. Always being restlessly future-focused precludes the enjoyment of the realised dream, the moment when an anticipated future becomes a present reality.

Sometimes, the lives of individuals or organisations may run more or less in parallel, sometimes closer, sometimes further apart and occasionally intersecting but without a much of a shared story. Some trigger is required to convert this coexistence into a relationship of Continuity – a task, an incident, a deliberate choice, perhaps. Once catalysed, the shared prehistory acquired through parallel lives may add meaning to the relationship, but without the catalytic trigger little or no meaning would have accrued. Life is a continuing unfolding of potential Continuity. Which lives we intersect with, and how often, is a product of both choice and chance. In whatever way the connections are made, they become key to the story of our lives.

The stories we live by also influence our perception of ourselves. A stable self-identity is based on an account of a person's life, actions and influences which makes sense to themselves, and which can be told to other people. It 'explains' the past and is oriented towards an anticipated future. Anthony Giddens describes this as a 'reflexive project' – an endeavour that we continuously work and reflect on. We create, maintain and revise a set of biographical narratives – 'the story of who we are, and how we came to be where we are now'.[5]

Continuity for the organisation as an entity is complex, and not quite the same as Continuity for the people who are a part of it. Organisations 'remember' by means of digital or paper records as well as the memories of individuals. In fact the latter constitute a relational risk because memories – including valuable intellectual property – can walk out of the door with the people who hold them. Start-ups typically endure a period of transition when founders step down, and all organisations struggle to maintain Continuity through

[5] A. Giddens, *Modernity and Self-Identity: Self and Society in the Late Modern Age* (Cambridge: Polity Press, 1991), p. 54. See also D. Gauntlett, *Media, Gender and Identity: An Introduction* (London and New York: Routledge, 2002).

replacements of key officers, particularly on the board of directors. Original visions can be lost beyond recall even when institutional frameworks remain.

Some organisations find novel ways to tackle the problem. In mid July, at the end of each school year, the head teacher of a primary school in the east of England invites all the current staff and governors to a tea party. They are each asked to bring an idea for one or more things they want to highlight from the past school year – school trips, plays, sports days, new people, projects and so on. Where possible they bring pictures or objects that relate to their memories. Then over tea and conversation, they write these memories onto a timeline of the year. Their collective timeline now covers four years, since the school's establishment. Each year, the new year and the old years are laid out again on the floor, on a series of rolls of paper, so that current members can walk along it as they tell the stories and remember together the stories of those now gone.

Continuity as the Key to Future Cooperation

An anticipated timeframe is a crucial part of investment. Longer-term franchises, for example, may be needed to make significant financial investment worthwhile. Similarly, when new people move into an area of high mobility, neighbours may ask whether it is worth investing time in getting to know them. When the Relationships Foundation looked at the relationship between a healthcare provider and the health authority that purchased the care it provided, they found that the average job tenure for commissioning managers could be as little as nine months. The main drivers were organisational change and restructuring, together with rapid career progression for people in these types of posts. The senior doctors in the trust, providing care to people who had long-term conditions, often remained in their post for over ten years, but were sometimes reluctant to invest in relationship building with managers who typically stayed in post for much shorter periods.

Anticipated Continuity opens up more possibilities for collaboration and reciprocity. Investing time at the outset in early-stage partnering in the construction industry, for example, can save time and costs, and may create competitive advantage in joint tendering. The chief executive of a social services department described, as he approached retirement, his frustration that one of the families he had first worked with as a junior social worker was still on their books thirty years later. He felt that if there had been a long-term view at the outset, and they had thought about where the family could be in twenty years' time, and how to support them in getting there, they could have made a real difference. In reality, numerous short-term interventions had not added up to an effective long-term strategy.

Expectations also influence conflict resolution and collaboration. If the relationship cannot or is not going to be severed, then the recognition of continued coexistence creates an incentive for negotiation and, ultimately, peaceful resolution. Game theorists have also demonstrated how Continuity incentivises collaboration. In a one-off interaction it may pay to cheat as no benefits of trust accrue, and no sanctions for trust breaking are possible. If further exchanges are anticipated then collaboration can become the optimum strategy.

Robert Axelrod's experiments with the prisoner's dilemma imagines that two bank robbers have been arrested and are held in separate cells with no contact with each other. Each is told that if they both confess they receive equal sentences of nine years. If only one confesses, and the other refuses to confess, the one who confesses is freed while the other gets ten years. If they both refuse to confess, they will be sentenced for one year on a lesser charge. Axelrod used computers to play the game repeatedly using a number of different strategies. The most successful strategy was called tit-for-tat, where each player mirrored the other's previous turn. In tit-for-tat, if one player 'cheated' by confessing, it was punished by the other in the next round. If it cooperated, it was rewarded because the other cooperated in the next round. Axelrod deduced from this that, once it is possible to monitor agreements and sanction behaviour over time, cooperative rather than individual or competitive strategies pay.[6]

There are limits. It is not unusual for two parties to bring to a relationship stories so different that even establishing dialogue is hard. Benjamin Barber in *Jihad vs. McWorld*[7] described a clash of cultures that has only become more entrenched in the two decades since the book's publication in 1995. Such incompatible cultural stories need not be theological or philosophical. Miners' unions in many countries were shaped by deeply rooted stories of fraternity and struggle. Industrial disputes are hard to understand or resolve if the stories through which relationships are tacitly or explicitly interpreted are not recognised on the other side. In business, there is a difference between the company's and the customer's view of the relationship. A sophisticated customer relationship management (CRM) system will keep not only static customer data –

[6] R. Axelrod, *The Evolution of Cooperation* (New York: Basic Books, 1984).
[7] B. R. Barber, *Jihad vs. McWorld* (New York: Crown, 1995).

name, address and so on – but also a record of previous interactions, orders taken and delivered, queries raised and so on – a factual, observational history of the relationship, which we could refer to as the 'plot' of the story. The customers, on the other hand, may have a factual record of orders and phone calls, but it is likely that they also have an interpretation of those facts. For them, what endures between interactions is an evolving web of judgements, deductions and inferences about the agenda of the organisation, how it deals with its customers, how well trained its staff are and so on.

Where parties converge, past and future are often divided with the use of a formal agreement – a treaty, a contract, a memorandum of agreement, a vow. Third parties are important here. Marriages are publicly witnessed events for precisely this reason. And the governance and regulatory arrangements surrounding businesses and their alliances provide a degree of confidence in future Continuity for the various stakeholders concerned. Sometimes Continuity is a product of shared rootedness in a place or shared membership of an organisation.

The power of a story to stimulate ongoing connection is well recognised in the organisational world. Brands want to create a shared story with the customer to encourage a relationship that involves repeated contact (as well as to influence the story the customer tells about himself). To bind the organisation together despite change, organisational change programmes have names such as Unilever's 'Path to Growth' – capturing the essence of an organisational storyline that moves from where we are now, through the overcoming of a problem, to a vision of the future. Careful analysis of the culture of an organisation includes identifying the myths and stories told about the organisation by its staff, as well as the key characters in those stories.

Continuity and Discontinuity

Like Directness, Continuity is a variable, and there are important points of discontinuity to be managed where a relationship is abusive or intervention is required to protect the wellbeing of vulnerable children. In a business context, contracts with suppliers may be terminated, employees may be dismissed or individuals may choose to search for new jobs.

There is a tension between individual stories and the stories attached to relationships. Phrases such as 'breaking the mould' and 'a breath of fresh air' point to the refreshing power of change. Long-standing, cosy, possibly collusive relationships sometimes need to be dropped, creating new opportunities. New

Table 5.1: Appropriate and inappropriate experience of high and low degrees of Continuity

High Continuity	Entrapment	Belonging
Low Continuity	Abandonment	Renewal
	Felt as inappropriate	Felt as appropriate

skills and fresh perspectives may reinvigorate an organisation or team, and this can be achieved either by switching over the team members or by exposing them to new and challenging relationships in other contexts, the experience of which they then draw upon in their future interactions in the group. Careers have to progress in a way that allows both personal development and the acquisition of new skills, contacts and experience.

As with Directness, it is possible to summarise the subjective impact of Continuity as a simple quadrant (Table 5.1).

In Relational Proximity, Continuity is a variable among other variables, which means that high levels of Continuity in a relationship can be destructive if there are not also adequate levels of Parity and Commonality to drive mutual respect and a sense of shared identity. Tribal feuds and bitter rivalries between business competitors have a strong storyline. So do relationships involving abuse, bullying and exploitation. Sometimes radical change is the only way to keep the narrative of an organisation going. A loss-making business may need repositioning before it can be profitable. A failed school may need to reopen under a new name and new management for a fresh start in student learning. Good delegators – and good parents – know there's a time to step back and give the team member or child more space.

Author and consultant Alison Myers took over as acting team leader on a community project when the manager left on a three-month sabbatical. During this time, the team had no contact with the manager over work-related matters. To cover his absence some tasks were delegated to different people, both inside and outside the core team. Alison used her own experience and that of other team members to respond to the needs of the community. Some practices they deliberately changed; some changes just happened naturally. On his return, the manager recognised that his absence had given space for the team to evolve and change. So rather than reverse the changes, he asked questions: How had team roles changed? How should the team define its roles going forward? Had the procedural changes worked? What innovations should be continued? Who had grown as a result of his absence?

Continuity and the Management of Time

The fixed division of time (days, hours, seconds), and the increasingly uniform ordering of societies in accordance with these constructs, is comparatively recent. France, for example, had fourteen time zones, and the USA eighty different railway times, until the Washington conference of 1884 that created World Standard Time.[8] Industrialisation and increasingly global communication changed our experience of time, with synchronisation and homogeneity changing the local seasonal rhythms of agricultural societies. Post-industrial time is less structured, with 24/7 processes and more flexible working.

Despite a significant reduction in working hours since Victorian industrialisation, many people experience acute time pressure while others, lonely and isolated, find that time hangs very heavily. This is partly a consequence of technology increasing the productivity of time and enabling us to engage in multiple relationships simultaneously. Technology increases productivity and busyness, but rarely saves time. The arrival of washing machines and vacuum cleaners meant that clothes and carpets were cleaned more often, thus nullifying their time-saving benefits. And time, unlike money, cannot be stored. The value of time has increased, as more can be produced within a unit of time. An hour's work is reckoned to be worth twenty-five times more than in 1830 as a result. Time is the currency of relationships and, as economies grow, becomes ever more valuable. The minute is rising against the dollar and the euro.

Time, like story, is rooted in change. If nothing happened, its passing would have no reference points. Time is, at least in part, an abstract construct to describe our experience of sequenced events but it is also within some worldviews the great story, the journey from the beginning of all things to their end. Our work lives have become ever more structured around our consciousness of time and the constant ticking of the clock. Time management is considered to be a key skill and 'poor time management' an indictment. Time is experienced as a finite resource and we become ever more fretful about making good use of it. We make choices about how and where – mainly meaning with whom – we spend our time. More specifically, we make choices about the amount of time spent together, or in conversation, and the frequency of meeting or contact. We need to maintain a 'presence' in the relationship or the group or the market,

---

[8] See M. Bartle, I. Briscoe, G. Mulgan, Z. Sar-Wiwo, J. Wade and H. Wilkinson, *The Time Squeeze* (London: Demos, 1995).

and are forced to rank priorities. Commuting time correspondingly decreases the time available to spend on relationships, impacting both family life and broader social cohesion.

While we can, if we choose, be more intentional about our own time use and allocation, we can also make decisions that have a positive or negative effect on other people's time and, as a consequence, their relationships. A change in personnel may require others to spend time investing in a new working relationship, potentially to the detriment of existing working relationships. Retail requirements to work unsocial hours, and the long hours culture of many professional services organisations, will inevitably have an impact on personal and family relationships. Increasing the formal reporting in police work will tend to erode time spent building local relationships and creating a positive story of police presence in the community. Income tax and other forms of self-assessment export time costs from the assessor to the assessed, which increases efficiency on one side but exerts time pressure on the other.

Choices about use of time are, inevitably, choices about relationships. You can divide a thousand pounds into ten lots of a hundred or a hundred lots of ten. But you can't turn it into a hundred lots of a hundred. Similarly with relationships: you only have 24 hours in a day. You can stretch the time thinly over many relationships, or you can give it out in larger amounts to fewer relationships. What you can't do is increase both the number of relationships and the time spent on each one of them.

When people talk about 'quality time' they generally mean time given wholly to another person, without interruptions – time when they are wholly present for the other person. Intensive scheduling, however, means that busy professionals tend to parcel out their quality time in fairly small units. This can work – within limits – in a business environment. At home it is often less successful, because children have a habit of demanding, expecting and needing time not only in quality but in quantity. Flexibility, and a degree of underoccupation, can be useful if you are really going to respond to the needs of dependants at the time required.

Ultimately, time management in Continuity is about using time to build relationships – working with time over a period of time – and answering the questions 'how often?' and 'how long?'

How often? In deciding the frequency of meeting or other kinds of contact, the lifecycle of the relationship, the pace of activity and the strength of common purpose will all be factors. Generally speaking, the greater the need for momentum and/or a sense of belonging, the greater the frequency of meetings required. Once momentum is gained and the relationship or community is healthy, frequency can be reduced. In fact in some relationships meetings can be infrequent and yet the relationship remains strong due to an initial burst of high-intensity encounters – for example, friends from university who easily resume their relationship when they meet every couple of years.

How long? The length of each meeting will be related to the frequency of encounter. Is it better to meet often for a short length of time or less frequently but for longer? Is brand awareness and the customer–brand relationship built best by daily but short-lived exposure, or longer exposure less frequently? It takes time to build relationships. The pressure is always on to achieve results quickly and at a low cost. Yet strong and sustained relationships between people, within communities, and between and within organisations, take time to grow. Trust may need to be built; real understanding of people's needs and prospects gained.

There may also be a 'right time' for a particular interaction or meeting, judged not only by the date (is it on the day we planned it?) but also by the context (is it at the right moment in the development of the project?) and by the stage the relationship has reached. There is a right and a wrong time to try to close a deal. Time invested at an early stage can save much more time (and money) if it helps to avoid problems later. The skills of chronological time are planning and coordinating. The skills of synchronous time are of working with the rhythm of the relationship and 'recognising the moment' for that encounter which moves the story on.

Continuity, Gaps and Handovers

No relationship anywhere is completely continuous, and for that reason managing time gaps can be crucial. Regular but infrequent meetings where notes or minutes are not taken can mean that all the business has to be done again next time around. Gaps can also weaken ties and dilute loyalty, purpose and commitment. Hence the importance for mail-order and online merchants of keeping up regular contact with customers by post or email, and of maintaining brand identity and brand awareness. The relationships involved in the gaps are, however, always under attrition. The supplier's account manager moves on, so the purchasing officer takes the opportunity to shop around when she next runs short of supplies. In a community, the older people in the village are unwilling to attend a church service in a new building, or feel uncomfortable with a new minister. Shift workers come and go.

In handovers, Continuity is at a premium, especially when complex or detailed information cannot easily be transferred through systems. Where the same people cannot be involved over time, the storyline becomes a joint endeavour, with different actors in effect taking over the same role. Handovers occur routinely in doctors' surgeries and customer service, and centralised records and CRM systems provide substantial assistance in supporting the relationship with patients or customers. They can prevent healthcare workers and customer service representatives literally losing the plot in the stories of those they are serving. In healthcare, reviews of continuity of care have highlighted its importance for patient satisfaction.[9] Three types of continuity have been identified, as follows:

- *Informational continuity*: the use of information on past events and personal circumstances to make current care appropriate for each individual.
- *Management continuity*: a consistent and coherent approach to the management of a health condition that is responsive to a patient's changing needs.
- *Relational continuity*: an ongoing therapeutic relationship between a patient and one or more providers.[10]

In the definition used in this book, of course, Continuity embraces all three. Two significant organisational developments in primary care have implications for Continuity in the relationship between patient and doctor. One is the move to larger practices or health centres. The other is the contracting out of out-of-hours care (evening and weekends), rather than family doctors doing this themselves. A review of the 'human effect' in medicine explores the significance for the relationship between family doctors and patients: 'It seems that patients who get to know their GPs ... are more likely to take their pills as advised ... [and] an improved knowledge of the patient's lifestyle correctly interpreted can help doctors to assess how an illness is developing and how serious it might be.' Conversely, a 'lack of continuity was associated with additional morbidity, an increase in the number of difficult consultations with the doctor and, finally, an increase in the number of appointments which these patients attended, or indeed made and failed to attend'.[11]

---

[9] For example N. Pandhi and J. Saultz, 'Patients' perceptions of interpersonal continuity of care', *Journal of the American Board of Family Medicine*, 19 (2006), pp. 390–396.

[10] J. L. Haggerty, R. J. Reid, G. K. Freeman, B. H. Starfield, C. E. Adair and R. McKendry, 'The continuity of care: a multidisciplinary review', *British Medical Journal*, 327 (2003), pp. 1219–1221.

[11] M. Dixon and K. Sweeney, *The Human Effect in Medicine: Theory, Research and Practice* (Oxford: Radcliffe Medical Press, 2000), p. 45.

Handover issues arise also with staff turnover and absenteeism. According to Sir Martin Narey's report in 2014, of 155 UK Local Authorities surveyed in 2012, half had a vacancy rate of over 10 per cent.[12] Camila Batmanghelidjh, founder of the charity Kids Company, described the impact and risks for vulnerable children: 'In deprived pockets of Britain, each social worker has to juggle as many as 20 cases of neglect and abuse. The load is worsened by having to pick up colleagues' cases: there are high rates of sickness and rapid staff turnover. Recently I dealt with a seven-year-old boy who had six new social workers within the year. How can a professional begin to understand that child's needs? And how can that vulnerable child build a relationship with a carer who will be moving on in weeks?'[13]

Sometimes it is necessary for an organisation or community to recognise and retell its story. An organisation or team can deal with a change more effectively if they sit down together to work out their common story leading up to this change and moving beyond it. The potential discontinuity then becomes part of an overarching continuous storyline and the team feels a greater sense of belonging and momentum. When orientating new staff it pays to give them time to listen to the story or stories of the organisation so that they can start to feel part of the organisation's narrative and develop a sense of belonging. A strong storyline enables people to envisage the future for the group, the relationship, or themselves.

The Benefits of Continuity

When a team is working well together, or when a community group is getting somewhere, it develops a sense of its own momentum. The synergy of a high-performing team comes in large part from the coherence and flow of a strong and positive shared story – a shared memory of the past achievements, a practical approach to the management of time and tasks in the present, and a clear-sighted view of the path towards future goals. The experience of fruitful

---

[12] M. Narey, *Making the Education of Social Workers Consistently Effective: Report of Sir Martin Narey's Independent Review of the Education of Children's Social Workers* (London: Department for Education, January 2014).

[13] C. Batmanghelidjh, 'The moral darkness that engulfed Baby P', Care Appointments, *The Times*, 2 December 2008, www.careappointments.co.uk/care-news/england/item/9268-The%20Moral%20 Darkness%20That%20Engulfed%20Baby%20P.

working together over time can, of course, also be true of one-to-one relationships between business partners or between a manufacturer and a retailer. This sense of momentum is a direct consequence of Continuity, and is of value to a relationship or team because it carries with it a number of allied and highly desirable outcomes for those involved.

Productivity

A class with a succession of supply teachers risks a breakdown in the learning relationship between staff and students. When gaps between interactions are poorly managed, something is lost: information, knowledge, understanding, direction. Not everything that was gained in one interaction is available to the next. Discussions may have to be repeated because no adequate record was kept. Actions that were meant to have been taken since the last meeting have not been followed up, so no further progress is possible. People have changed on the team so the ground has to be covered again for their benefit. The cost of time lost and action slowed may be imposed on others who have little or no control over the choices and actions that caused it. If Continuity is poor, less is achieved.

According to Sir Bobby Robson, the former England football manager, 'Successful football clubs are all about successful relationships and you don't get that overnight. It takes time and continuity; you can't do it in six months.'[14] He was commenting on the instability and frequent changes of manager at the UK football club Newcastle United. Research studying 678 managerial changes in the four football leagues from August 1992 to December 2005 found that the average length of a football manager's tenure was 2.19 years: only one manager had spent more than twenty years in a job and three had spent more than ten.[15] Newcastle had eight different managers in the seven seasons following Sir Bobby Robson's departure in 2004.

Looked at this way, the productive value of a unit of time – based on what can be achieved within it – is influenced by the legacy of previous interactions. You may be able to achieve more in one hour when working with someone you know well and when you are able to build on previous work, than in the same hour with a relative stranger. Thus not all time in a relationship is of

[14] *The Times*, 'Bobby Robson's sadness over Newcastle's implosion', 20 October 2008.
[15] S. Bridgewater, 'An analysis of football management trends 1992–2005 in all four divisions', *Warwick Business School Report for League Managers Association* (Coventry: University of Warwick, 2006).

equal value. So, later time in a relationship may be more productive, because it builds on the legacy of understanding derived from previous encounters. Time invested at an early stage in a relationship is less likely to be actively and immediately productive, but it can go on to save much more time (and money) in the longer term. The value of productive time – in which progress is made towards a goal – must be ascertained in a different way to 'investment time'. Thus, timeliness is also important to productivity. Not just the amount of time, but the right moment. A short input at the right moment can achieve much, while a lot of time can be spent unproductively if the moment is wrong.

Commitment, Investment and Loyalty

Knowing that a relationship is likely to endure affects the willingness to invest in it: this may be investment in getting to know the person or organisation, or investment to improve the relationship and its outcomes. Author and economist Michael Schluter lives in Cambridge, in the UK, a city with relatively high population mobility due in part to the numbers of people coming and going from the University. He has lived in his current house for the last thirty-three years. Over that time he has seen many neighbours come and go, and is conscious of considering how much effort it is worth making to get to know a new neighbour if they seem likely to move on in a few years.

The forward momentum of a continuing relationship can also change attitudes to the resolution of conflict. In the context of international peace building, where continuing physical proximity and shared issues (such as access to resources or a political settlement) are unavoidable, it becomes easier – though never easy – to establish incentives for engagement. The participants will be around to reap the continuing consequences of failure or the benefits of peace.

With investment, loyalty and commitment to the relationship or organisation increase over time. The momentum gained by ongoing contact with the coherence of a storyline tends to increase loyalty and commitment to each other as well as towards, or perhaps instead of, the cause or task. This may be experienced in the development of shared identity, the build-up of reciprocal obligations, greater trust, or greater ownership of the task or issue – all as a product of previous investment. Volunteers invest time in a community venture together. Serialised offers and free gifts encourage a customer's repeated purchase of a particular newspaper, say, in the hope that loyalty is built by repeated contact with the brand. Loyalty may also result not from proactive investment but from the cost of change and loss aversion (there may be more to be lost than gained in changing) – as among some bank or phone customers who live with 'the devil they know' because of the effort anticipated in changing supplier. This pseudo-loyalty lasts until its cost is greater than the cost of change. Here momentum may be a good thing for one party – the supplier or bank – but not for the other – the end customer.

Short-termism is increasingly becoming a problem in business. A survey found that the great majority of a sample of financial executives viewed short-term earnings as the most important performance measure they reported to outsiders.[16] Most executives today believe that meeting earnings expectations helps maintain or increase the stock price, while simultaneously boosting customers' and suppliers' confidence and enhancing the reputation of the management team. By contrast, failure to meet earnings targets is increasingly seen as evidence of managerial weakness and, if repeated over several quarters, may well lead to career-threatening dismissal.[17]

It is therefore hardly surprising when companies decide to delay or abandon potentially value-creating investments for the longer term in order to meet immediate earnings expectations. An astounding 80 per cent of executives surveyed would decrease discretionary spending on research and development (R&D), advertising, maintenance and hiring to meet earnings benchmarks, and more than 50 per cent would delay a new project even if it meant forgoing potential future value.[18] This mutually reinforcing obsession between the investment fraternity and corporate executives with short-term performance goals has been studied by Alfred Rappaport who observes: 'short-termism is the disease, while earnings and tracking error are the carriers.'[19]

Another facet of this problem is the relatively short typical holding period for shares that, according to the Bank of England, has reduced from five years in the 1960s to less than eight months in 2007. The Bank also notes a great increase in the level of high-frequency trading, which now accounts for 30–40 per cent of European trading in equities and futures.[20] The shorter the holding

---

[16] J. R. Graham, C. R. Harvey and S. Rajgopal, 'The economic implications of corporate financial reporting', *Journal of Accounting and Economics*, 40 (2005), pp. 3–73.

[17] F. Degeorge, J. Patel and R. Zeckhauser, 'Earnings management to exceed thresholds', *Journal of Business*, 72 (1999), pp. 1–33.

[18] Graham, Harvey and Rajgopal, 'The economic implications'.

[19] A. Rappaport, 'The economics of short-term performance obsession', *Financial Analysts Journal*, 61 (2005), pp. 65–79.

[20] A. Haldane, 'Patience and finance' (Beijing, Oxford China Business Forum, Beijing, 22 September 2010), available at www.bankofengland.co.uk/publications/news/2010/067.htm.

period, the more the sentiments of other players in the market, rather than long-term fundamentals, become central to investment decisions. Besides these relatively short holding periods, the patience needed for companies to grow organically is running very thin. As Andrew Haldane, Chief Economist and Executive Director, Monetary Analysis and Statistics at the Bank of England noted, market inefficiencies can 'support the myopic and irrational at the expense of the solvency of the far-sighted'.[21]

Reputation and Trust

The repeated honouring of promises, meeting of deadlines, or other types of successful encounter breed the confidence that future encounters will also be successful. Thus reputation is built, and trust can be placed in that reputation. In Chapter 4 we saw how face-to-face interaction can influence trust decisions. In the following chapters we will see how breadth of information, fair use of power and the alignment of purpose are also important in building trust.

Reputation is a kind of 'transferable Continuity'. We draw on the knowledge gained from other people's encounters over time. They recommend an architect, accountant, or training consultancy based on their experience of their past relationship with them. So when I start to build a relationship with the accountant recommended to me by someone whose judgement I trust, I am not starting from first base. I have a kind of 'second-hand' history with them: I know him or her by reputation.

Reputation and recommendation help us to place our trust in strangers. This reputation may attach to a particular individual or organisation – a professional coach for senior executives, or a business start-up asking for investment; or it could attach to a generic group – such as 'faith leaders', 'local politicians', or 'management consultants'. But this act of faith is a provisional assessment, ready to be modified in the light of the experience of the relationship.

Reputation reduces risk by reducing unknowns, and it saves time in, say, sourcing and evaluating partners from scratch. One of the benefits of the internet is in the increased accessibility of goods and more competitive prices available from a wide range of suppliers. However, ordering from an unknown company brings with it an unknown risk in the quality of both goods and services. A wise organisation will consider reputation as well as price when ordering goods from a supplier.

[21] Haldane, 'Patience and finance'.

There is pressure on reputation from high levels of mobility. Mobility around a large organisation, or geographic mobility, often means that relational histories are shorter, and in a particular community there are fewer people who know about the reputation in question. It becomes harder to find a recommendation of, say, a good local garage, or the person in the office to ask about a particular subject, or the best firm to manage an event. And the travelling con man can move from town to town before reputation and the law catch up. But there is an upside to mobility, too: the possibility of increased networking of reputation and recommendation beyond an established group. New business can be gained when a key client contact moves to another company and recommends your firm.

Although reputation is a valuable tool in business, where there is a choice between the potential trustworthiness of reputation and the proven trustworthiness of direct relationship, the latter is always likely to be a less risky option. Building trust takes time, and needs the context of an enduring relationship that brings with it the potential for sanctions and incentives, as well as the opportunity for the other dimensions of Relational Proximity to grow, all of which contribute to building trust. Indeed, there is a sense in which Continuity creates a context in which the other dimensions of Relational Proximity operate more effectively. There are more opportunities for real encounter (Directness). Breadth of knowledge can be gained (Multiplexity). The sense of common purpose can be both deepened and widened (Commonality). And if the relationship moves over time from formal roles to a different interpersonal dynamic, new forms of Parity can be possible.

Reduced Risk and Greater Accountability

Penny Campbell became suddenly and dangerously ill with blood poisoning. Although she was intelligent and articulate, and therefore able to describe symptoms, no fewer than eight doctors working in the UK National Health Service's out-of-hours service failed to identify the symptoms that would later kill her.[22] Four of the contacts had been phone calls to an out-of-hours service. As calls were taken by different doctors in different locations, and without electronic patient records, information from one was not available to the others. Doctors who took the calls failed to pick up the urgency of the situation

---

[22] A. Mackinnon, 'Death at the hands of the NHS: the tragedy of Penny Campbell', *Independent*, 10 October 2006.

as she sounded so calm. Without knowing the patient and so being able to interpret the calmness, without seeing the patient to gauge her health status, with poor informational Continuity (in some cases not even knowing there had been previous interactions), previous interactions did not build on each other to make progress, and the risk of service failure increased.

Momentum in a relationship ensures that single interactions build on one another to add to the narrative. Where momentum is broken or never gained – perhaps by staff changes or dealing with different people – it is hard for participants to see the pattern of the story. The pieces are not put together; knowledge and information are lost, or poorly coordinated; experience is not drawn upon. The risk that something will go wrong is much greater; problems may unfold without anyone noticing. Accountability mitigates this kind of risk by placing, or accepting, responsibility for understanding the story.

Without Continuity, however, accountability is a challenge, because the person or legal entity responsible in the present is not the same as that responsible for the past or that will be responsible for the future. And with little wider accountability, the risk will tend to be assessed more narrowly. The global banking crises of 2008 revealed considerable public anger that individuals who had personally profited from risky lending practices, but who were no longer employed, could not be held accountable for the costs to others of their actions. Taking narrowly defined financial risks had, in this case, been a 'rational' strategy for the individuals directly involved, because immediate benefits were there for the taking, and they did not need to have any long-term connection to, or liability for, the consequences.

Predictability

The past is used to make inferences about the present and the future. If every interaction was unrelated or completely novel, we could not make such assumptions. Continuity thus helps to interpret the moods and predict the responses of those with whom we deal. Knowing likely responses informs decisions on how best to reward, praise, encourage and motivate people, as previous interactions will have shown what works well.

6 Multiplexity: Context for Breadth

'You should have asked me ... I could have told you.' Opportunities are missed when we don't have the knowledge, skills or contacts that others could contribute.

'I'm shocked ... I had no idea he could do something like that.' Individuals and organisations are not always what they seem. Their activities in other areas may surprise us and cause us to question our original assessment of them.

'I thought it would help ... ' Good intentions can go wrong when the needs and circumstances of others, and the impact of actions on them, are poorly understood.

'I assumed that you ... ' Limited knowledge of the pressures people face, their capacity or priorities can lead to false assumptions and misunderstanding.

These are not just the problems of personal relationships. Management decisions can alienate employees when the impact on them is poorly understood. Joint ventures and mergers can fail when limited knowledge of the other party leads to unexpected problems. Customers can be poorly served when their needs are not well understood.

Information is useful. It aids the conduct of a relationship by enabling the interpretation of responses, avoiding misunderstanding and missed opportunities, and increasing awareness of how one party's actions might affect the other. Different sources, roles and contexts provide different streams of information, and that information adds up to knowledge – whether about people we have never met, casual acquaintances, or those we are emotionally closest to. A wider range of behaviours can be observed and a wider range of contextual information becomes accessible. This information and understanding is useful both in reading the person – interpreting responses and evaluating character – and in

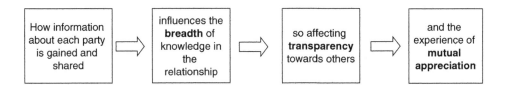

Figure 6.1:   How Multiplexity influences the behaviour and outcomes of a relationship

managing the relationship in ways that take due account of each party's needs, interests and potential contributions. As a result, *mutual understanding* develops and takes its place as a sustaining element of the relationship. Even groups and organisations can be known through membership, or known through dealings and interactions. *Transparency* towards other organisations, customers, voters – of culture, of working practices, of service provision – is the organisational equivalent, and goes hand in hand with the mutual integrity that results in long-term productive relationships.

Multiplexity describes a way of building up this information. Directness enables rich communication. Continuity helps build trust and understanding through cumulative exposure to the other party, and a sense of significance, narrative and meaning. Multiplexity – literally a many-stranded relationship – adds to this by increasing the opportunity for a wider range of sources and contexts to inform the relationship (Figure 6.1).

Multiplexity, Knowing and Knowing About

Managing and assessing stakeholder relationships requires considering the quality of knowledge, seen in terms of its breadth and authenticity, and the ways in which such knowledge can be gained. Breadth of knowledge enables us to interpret responses (moods, decisions, action), predict impact (understand how something will affect another party) and maximise involvement and contribution (know the range of skills, contacts, and so on that another party can offer). Its ultimate outcomes – mutual understanding and transparency – have clear benefits for both individuals and organisations. Breadth of knowledge means knowing more about 'what the other party does': it is context-driven and primarily functional. For an individual, this might include his or her wider brief, related responsibilities, or other roles in the same organisation; for a company, it might include who else they supply, other product lines, or other places in which they operate. It also means knowing more about 'who the other party is'. At an individual level this can be termed personal knowledge, which implies a degree of intimacy – values, character, interests and so on. In a relationship between organisations, this may involve mutual exploration of vision, culture and working practices. Somewhere between these two poles comes knowing about skills and pressures, responsibilities and potential contribution.

'Knowing about' nearly always precedes 'knowing'. Knowing about a person or an organisation takes us into the realm of factual information, and involves a degree of detachment from the other and the possible use of third-party sources. 'Knowing' a person or an organisation assumes direct experience and interaction, opens the possibility of empathy and the probability of mutuality, and is more likely to develop over time and through repeated encounters. The retail CEO who visits individual stores can see things and know the store in a way that he or she cannot from performance data alone. Such an event marks a step up in Multiplexity, where information becomes experience, and a list of facts morphs into a complex web of narrative, intuition, interpretation and understanding. As a result, relationships shift into a degree of mutual understanding which cognitive information-based knowledge can never wholly capture. This is the point at which prejudice and stereotypes are most challenged. If you think you *know about* the other person or community, getting to know them and developing mutual understanding may change your perspective entirely, and create a healthy relationship.

Multiplexity and Directness often coincide here. When the Relationships Foundation looked at the relationship between prison governors and headquarters staff in the Scottish Prison Service, governors with responsibility for life-sentence prisoners were frustrated by the perceived unresponsiveness of the relevant unit in prison service headquarters. One governor commented on the difference made by visiting the lifer management unit and seeing the number of staff employed, and the case volumes they were dealing with (physically piled on their desk). This didn't solve the problem of slow response, but took some misunderstanding out of the situation and enabled a more constructive approach to the issue.

Sometimes mutual understanding is a natural consequence of getting to know someone or a group of people better. Understanding is gained when knowledge is interpreted: it is a construct, a set of conclusions and inferences from the data available to us. This is the case whether we mean understanding of the way the relationship works in the present, its vagaries and its potential;

or the ability to predict, and make choices about, its ebb and flow in the future. Relational understanding depends upon this process of interpretation and its accuracy:

KNOWLEDGE + INTERPRETATION = UNDERSTANDING

The way we interpret the information we have gained is influenced by our frame of reference. Each participant brings certain skills and assumptions to the process of understanding the other in the relationship. Doctors take the information offered and use their existing expertise to understand the patient and the condition. An abused teenager may respond with aggressive suspicion to the youth worker who reaches out to help. Our frame of reference – values, assumptions, expectations, skills, role – will either help us reach a good level of understanding of the other person or hinder us from doing so by pushing us towards misinterpretation and misunderstanding. Lack of contextual information about the other party makes it more likely that assumptions will fill in the gaps. Being aware of your own and your organisation's frame of reference makes it easier to compensate for likely blind spots, bias and baggage.

Knowledge is rarely complete. Even an individual is impossible to encounter fully. As Walt Whitman's 'Song of Myself' says, 'I am large, I contain multitudes'.[1] In our most intimate relationships we may feel that we know someone deeply and well, yet also recognise that there will always be more that could be known; that other people can never be fathomed fully and will always be able to surprise us. Like organisations, people change. There is also a sense in which knowledge is a relational reality, and can only be built up from a wide variety of relational perspectives. Narnia author C. S. Lewis said of his friend J. R. R. Tolkien, who wrote *Lord of the Rings*, 'In each of my friends there is something that only some other friend can fully bring out. By myself I am not large enough to call the whole man into activity; I want other lights than my own to show all his facets.'[2]

Knowledge may also be limited because our sources of information are few or narrow – we only know a colleague from another department, say, via an occasional meeting – or because the relationship is new. Generally, therefore, we supplement our knowledge with best guesses and rules of thumb, weighing up the risks of our limited mutual understanding against the likely longevity of the relationship in question, and the relevance of the information to

---

[1] W. Whitman, 'Song of Myself', *Leaves of Grass* (New York: Penguin, 1986), section 51.
[2] C. S. Lewis, *The Four Loves* (New York: Harcourt, 1960), p. 61.

its purpose and activities. Arrive in a city you don't know, for example, and you might look up local restaurants on internet review sites. Failing that, you might pick the one that is full, on the assumption that popularity attests to the quality of the food.

The flipside of incomplete knowledge is that people deliberately edit their presentation of themselves to others. Jason Pontin has reflected on the authenticity of online identities, recognising that while the 'constructed persona' of his blog is always 'unchallengingly personable, humorous, and thoughtful' he is in reality 'none of those things very often'. While others may share everything about their lives online, or seem to, he wonders whether they are 'mere copies, cast from a few popular molds, endlessly reproduced among false friends?'[3] Politicians and celebrities may have staff to manage their Twitter accounts. In a different setting, Michelle Obama commented that the TV version of Barack Obama sounded really interesting and that she'd like to meet him sometime. It was, she said, hard at times to match the public persona with the domestic reality of the guy who 'still can't manage to put the butter up when he makes toast, secure the bread so that it doesn't get stale, and his 5-year-old is still better at making the bed than he is'.[4]

The Johari window, a tool created by Joseph Luft and Harry Ingham in 1955, provides a way to analyse interpersonal communication. It looks at the four possible combinations of what two parties in a relationship might know. The things known by both are public. Things you know about me, but I don't know, are my blind spots. The things I know about myself, but which you don't, may simply be private, but may also be part of a façade I create. Things that are unknown by both parties are considered as potential to be explored. There may, for example, be shared interests and possibilities for collaboration that have been missed.

'Façade' is perhaps a misleading term because, in itself, the slippage between what we know of ourselves and what we allow to be discussed in public is a kind of lubricant of social interaction. An experienced group leader may deliberately downplay his or her achievements in order not to overwhelm other members or make them feel their contributions are less valuable. There is also

[3] Jason Pontin is the Editor in Chief and Publisher of *Technology Review*. J. Pontin, 'Authenticity in the age of its technological reproducibility: do social technologies make us less sincere?', *Technology Review*, August 19, 2008, www.technologyreview.com/view/410686/authenticity-in-the-age-of-its-technological-reproducibility, last accessed 15 October 2012.

[4] M. Dowd, 'Michelle Obama's just a bit too quick to deflate hype', *San Jose Mercury News*, April 29, 2007, www.mercurynews.com/opinion/ci_5778824.

Table 6.1: Knowledge of others seen through the Johari window

	I know	I don't know
You know	Public	Blind spots
You don't know	Façade	Potential

the universal protocol – explicitly recognised in the East – of respecting the face of the other party: deliberately accepting another person's account of himself or herself in order to avoid causing embarrassment or humiliation – even if we know or suspect that the reality is rather different.

We should recognise, therefore, that our knowledge of another person or group will never be complete. While we may be able to act effectively within the limitations of current knowledge, and seek to be alert to the symptoms of crucial gaps such as misunderstandings and false assumptions, where there are 'known unknowns' or a recognised risk of 'unknown unknowns' we should consider ways of accessing and exposing ourselves to wider sources of information. Conversely, the more complete we are able to be within a relationship, the easier it is for aspects of a person or organisation to be an acknowledged presence or factor in the relationship, rather than simply intruding as contextual interference. This can enable better integration of different roles. Other commitments that are known about can be managed and, if appropriate, allowances made for them. Unknown commitments may appear only as unexplained distractions.

The Value of Multiplexity

Multiplexity is useful in organisations in understanding the other party in a relationship, managing the relationship in the light of this knowledge to make full use of the potential and to ensure that the needs of others are recognised and addressed. Breadth and depth of knowledge in a relationship expands possibilities, whereas breadth and depth of ignorance increases the potential misunderstandings, missed opportunity and uncontrolled risk. Multiplexity is also context specific: a one-off purchasing transaction may require little or no breadth, a long-term strategic partnership considerably more. A crisis meeting will focus quickly on immediate needs; there will be time and energy for cultivating relationships later.

Reading the Person

Multiplexity produces understanding, because knowing people well helps us to read them accurately and predict their responses. In different professional situations this may be, for example, the ability to interpret the moods and emotions that arise from bereavement in the family, or through being prone to migraines; or insight into the values and pressures behind the intensity of the other's response – why something matters so much to them. For a community worker, it might be recognising that a community's responses to a presented change are shaped by its history – and that coming at it a different way might provoke a different response.

Knowing We Can Trust

Multiplexity produces the assurance that trust is possible. It enables us to identify the range of risk factors and the likelihood of them occurring. When a City law firm was exploring a merger with a German law firm, some of the partners stayed in each other's homes rather than in hotels. The head of HR commented that arguments about who forgot to buy the milk for breakfast, as well as seeing the houses themselves, helped deliver a more rounded picture of potential partners and became an important aid to completing the merger. Partners knew the people, and not just the firm. Due diligence needs to be about trust and chemistry, not just the numbers, particularly in an organisation relying on high relational capital. You need to know the working styles, the range of contacts, the values and motivations of the people you will be working closely with. Here, Multiplexity is brought into play right at the start of a relationship by a deliberate and intensive investment of time.

Energy and Commitment

Aleksandra Kacperczyk and her colleagues when she was at the University of Michigan have shown that multiplex ties with co-workers – knowing them as friends as well as work colleagues – increase emotional energy at work. Emotional energy can be defined as the feeling that one is eager to act and capable of acting, or taking the initiative.[5] It is a continuum, ranging from

---

[5] A. Kacperczyk, J. Sanchez-Burks and W. E. Baker, 'Multiplexity and emotional energy in cross-cultural perspective', Unpublished paper, University of Michigan, 2008.

a high end of confidence and enthusiasm, to a low end of depression, lack of initiative and negative feelings. Some theories have suggested that the demands of managing relationships inside and outside the workplace deplete energy. The contrary theory, which this study supported, was that people tend to socialise with energising individuals and that socialising outside work, borrowing money from a co-worker and inviting a co-worker home all increase emotional energy. Connecting with others is an important and positive experience. Broadening the basis of that connection appears to increase not just energy in the relationship but, more broadly, the emotional energy at work.

Knowledge of What Can be Contributed

Multiplexity increases knowledge of another person's or organisation's skills and interests, helping maximise involvement and participation. Skills, knowledge and contacts that are unknown – either within a group or organisation, or in partner organisations – are less likely to be applied within a particular working relationship. In some situations an open question 'Does anyone know ... ?' or 'Can anyone ... ?' creates an opportunity to contribute – but such questions are often not asked. Accurate knowledge of people's capabilities also helps avoid the risks of unrealistic expectations, and that people will be placed in roles that exceed their capabilities. Tasks may be misperformed, or require expensive outsourcing, or simply not get done. Individuals' opportunity to grow their roles may be constrained, and poor decisions made, as relevant knowledge is not accessed. Research has shown that people who maintain multiplex relationships with a network of managers are also likely to have access to timely and accurate information or explanations about organisational issues.[6] Knowing that particular departments face staff shortages, are in the midst of a major bid, or are going through a disruptive change process helps inform a realistic basis for the working relationship.

Sharing Knowledge

Multiplexity facilitates the sharing of knowledge. It is often estimated that only 20 per cent of the knowledge in the average organisation is explicitly captured, generally as structured or unstructured data on some knowledge management

[6] R. S. Burt, *Structural Holes: The Social Structure of Competition* (Boston, MA: Harvard University Press, 1992).

systems. The other 80 per cent exists tacitly in the heads of employees. A study involving 1,000 employees found that up to 70 per cent of all workplace learning was informal. This refers to the type of learning that is unbudgeted, unplanned and not captured by the organisation, and that occurs in dozens of daily activities, including participating in meetings, interactions with customers, supervising or being supervised, mentoring others, communicating with peers and training others on the job.[7] Formal networks and structures become stale and somewhat inhibitive almost as soon as they are established, but informal networks that arise out of multi-stranded relationships, precisely because they are dynamic, never do. Although idle talk in the workplace has often been considered a waste of time, it is the way the organisation's knowledge network updates itself and tacit knowledge is shared around the organisation.[8]

Service and Care

Multiplexity allows more accurate knowledge of needs. Put the phrase 'a person not a number' into a search engine and you'll find a long list of companies who claim that this is how they will treat you. This experience of being a person rather than a number has much to do with being treated as a distinct individual. Customers, as well as patients, want to be treated as different from the previous customer and from the next one. A one-size-fits-all service that requires little knowledge of the customer can be cheap and effective: in-depth knowledge is not always needed, particularly when there is an extensive menu of options to choose from. But where advice, assistance and tailoring of service is required to meet individual needs and goals, then gaining adequate knowledge is essential. Good service requires understanding the needs and practices of the person or organisation to be served. Financial advisers should seek full client data to gain a good understanding of their financial circumstances, future needs and aims, as well as their attitude to risk. Supply chain partners need to understand both client requirements and the ways in which they work in order to innovate effectively. Health workers' diagnosis and care can be informed by better knowledge of patients' family and household circumstances.

[7] J. Pfeffer and R. I. Sutton, 'Knowing what to do is not enough: turning knowledge into action', *California Management Review*, 42:1 (1999), pp. 83–108; and J. Pfeffer and R. I. Sutton, *The Knowing–Doing Gap: How Smart Companies Turn Knowledge into Action* (Cambridge, MA: Harvard Business School Press, 1999).

[8] T. H. Davenport and L. Prusak, *Working Knowledge: How Organisations Manage What They Know* (Cambridge, MA: Harvard Business School Press, 1998).

Sally Thorne and her colleagues at the University of British Columbia considered the experience of cancer sufferers and the way in which they feel they are known by their doctors. They interviewed 200 cancer patients over a two-year period. They found that:

A powerful force often shaping their entire cancer care experience was the degree to which they had felt 'known' in profoundly fundamental ways by their health care providers. Implicit or explicit was the sense that one had made some form of human connection distinct from the diseased organ or mechanical body, that one was recognised for being a unique human being.[9]

However, the cancer patient study demonstrated that there is wide variation in desired knowledge. 'For many, personal information that the professional disclosed within the context of the clinical encounter was a precious bit of evidence that the professional was willing to extend the relationship beyond functional boundaries in an effort to know the patient.' For others, however, 'personal information was interpreted as slippage in relation to whose needs warranted priority within the therapeutic relationship, and could even detract from confidence in the professional's competence'. One useful model distinguishes knowledge of the 'case', the generalised knowledge that has to do with a theoretical patient, 'patient knowledge', which is knowledge of the particularity of an individual body, and 'person knowledge' – knowing the person as a subject who acts with her or his own desires and intentions.[10] The cancer study concludes:

The client on the receiving end of case, patient or person knowledge can discern the difference between that which is standardised and that which 'feels' individualised. Further, our findings seem to suggest that patients perceive that communication has been tailored toward their unique needs when it derives from a combination of all three types of knowledge rather than simply a close interpersonal relationship. Feeling that one 'is known' within the clinical cancer context can arise from exchanges ranging from the most profound to the most mundane.

The effort of gaining and 'remembering' knowledge conveys both respect and care. CRM systems facilitate this at a superficial level by, for example,

---

[9] S. E. Thorne, M. Kuo, E. A. Armstrong, G. McPherson, S. R. Harris and T. G. Hislop, 'Being known: patients' perspectives of the dynamics of human connection in cancer care', *Psycho-Oncology*, 14 (2005), pp. 887–898.

[10] J. Liaschenko, 'Knowing the patient?', in S. E. Thorne and V. E. Hayes (eds.), *Nursing Praxis: Knowledge and Action* (Thousand Oaks, CA: Sage, 1997), pp. 23–37.

allowing the bank call centre operative to bring up your account details on screen when you ring in. Companies like Amazon try to give us the experience of being known by their recommendations systems based on what we previously bought. Other examples include the doctor who asks after your family the next time you visit, the tailoring company that keeps your measurements on file, or the supplier who knows enough about your business to suggest a new product that might prove useful.

Conversely, being cut socially by a remark like 'Do I know you?' asserts Multiplexity in reverse and communicates social irrelevance. Unanswered emails made to a business partner, or calls by a customer to a service organisation, generate more than just frustration at the lack of communication. Being – or feeling – ignored, or having a certain part of one's abilities ignored, deprives us of meaning and value. Our sense of our own significance is bound up in the extent to which we are known and understood by others. Children want their presence to be acknowledged, their thoughts and opinions listened to, their achievements witnessed and noted. Adults are often little different. Eli Siegel, founder of the Aesthetic Realism movement, wrote in the 1960s: 'We live not only in our minds, but in other minds; our minds depend, for their full existence, on being apprehended by other minds ... The self is a to-be-known reality ... '[11] The significance of who we are and what we have achieved is usually linked to being known by others. Being known truly and deeply is a sign that not only have you connected and become part of a story, but that there is also some authenticity and completeness to that connection.

One analysis of the experience of being known in a group or community notes:

> We explored the concepts of authenticity and belonging, as a response to being confronted in our work by people who feel neither and, as a result, feel disconnected, hopeless and despairing ... In a containing environment we believe that it is possible to develop a sense of being real through being known, leading to a greater ability to connect with others.[12]

The pastoral carer and the executive coach, among others, recognise that by listening to someone's story, by taking a moment to know them a little better,

---

[11] E. Siegel, 'The ordinary doom' first appeared in the journal *Definition* (1961), and was reprinted in the Reverend J. T. Browne (ed.), *A Book of Non-Fiction* (New York: Macmillan, 1965). The Preface was written to accompany the essay's publication in E. Siegel, *The Frances Sanders Lesson and Two Related Works* (New York: Definition Press, 1974).

[12] D. Menzies and B. Davidson, 'Authenticity and belonging: the experience of being known in the group', *Group Analysis*, 35 (2002), p. 43.

we give solidity to their existence, making them more present in the world. And this can be the beginning of them finding their own resources to deal with whatever is in front of them.

One further point: beyond individuals and groups, brands also exist to be known and experienced – indeed they exist only in their apprehension by customers or other players in the market. A brand that is not known by anyone is only a project or an aspiration – it has not yet come fully into existence. The sustainability and credibility of a brand must also survive exposure to multiplex knowledge across its relationship with its customer base: it must be experienced consistently across all the critical points of connection – the touch points – with customers.

Privacy and Detachment

While good mutual understanding aids the conduct and management of relationships, there is often ambivalence about the extent to which people want to be known. On the one hand, being known brings a sense of acceptance and affirmation – connectedness with the 'real' person or organisation – and breeds trust and confidence – we know that our assessments are well founded. But, on the other hand, personally or organisationally, privacy and anonymity can be necessary or desirable; knowledge conveys power or can be a burden; and transparency can reveal uncomfortable truths as well as the things we are happy to disclose. Sometimes it is better not to know everything about the other in the relationship. Knowledge is a burden that cannot easily be put down: wilful forgetfulness is not easy.

People will vary in the extent and manner in which they wish to be known in particular contexts. Anonymity can provide the freedom to experiment and explore, without every mistake colouring people's attitude towards us ever after. This has long been the lure of the city, escaping the constricting knowledge of tight communities and their limiting expectations, to find the freedom to be whoever we want to be. But that freedom also comes with a risk – that of being lost and unknown.

The knowledge held by third parties to the relationship may be better kept out of the way. Clergy, lawyers, doctors and others may hold confidential information about people which, ethical issues notwithstanding, it may not be helpful for others in the community to know. Gossip about one in the relationship when relayed to the other may damage the dynamic between them. Relationships may be complicated and perceptions of others changed for ever by information that is not directly material to the role or task.

Within the relationship itself, generally, relational ties are strengthened by the multiplex knowledge that comes from knowing the other in more than one role. However, sometimes knowledge gained from working with the other in *one* role may not be helpful when you need to relate to them in *other* roles. For some people, this is an occupational hazard. Rob works as a counsellor in a town with comparatively low mobility. Over the years, as the number of his clients has grown, he has encountered more awkward situations when unexpectedly meeting clients in social contexts. More broadly, studies have noted that professional integrity or objectivity can be compromised by another strand of a multiplex relationship.[13] Roles that require professional detachment, or which involve actions that would be unsustainable in other roles, may not be the most appropriate content of multiplex ties – you might not want your boss to encourage you in the same way as your fitness coach.

Not knowing can sometimes change behaviour positively. In the workplace, sometimes not knowing a person's relatively senior position in the organisation enables you to relate to them more naturally than you are able to later, when you do know. Not revealing something key about yourself is a risky ploy but may in the short term be constructive: Shakespeare's Henry V, roaming the camp anonymously before the battle of Agincourt, is able to gain a better sense of what his soldiers think of him and of the battle than he would if he had revealed himself as the king.

Similarly, the range of possible roles of a multiplex relationship may confuse those involved. Are you relating as line manager or friend? Alison has been involved in a team in which, taking a strictly hierarchical interpretation, in one role a particular colleague is a peer relating to the team's leader while in a separate role they could be considered to be senior to that team leader. In this case a strongly collaborative approach is called for with careful role boundary management. In cases such as these, the opportunity brought by high Multiplexity to relate via a range of roles may confuse those involved as to which role or identity prevails in a given context.[14]

---

[13] S. M. Plaut, 'Boundary violations in professional–client relationships: overview and guidelines for prevention,' *Sexual and Marital Therapy*, 12 (1997), pp. 77–94; and G. N. Powell and S. Foley, 'Romantic relationships in organisational settings: something to talk about', in G. N. Powell (ed.), *Handbook of Gender and Work* (Thousand Oaks, CA: Sage, 1999).

[14] Plaut, 'Boundary violations'.

Table 6.2: Appropriate and inappropriate experience of high and low degrees of Multiplexity

High Multiplexity	Intrusion	Transparency, mutual understanding
Low Multiplexity	Secrecy, misunderstanding	Privacy, detachment
	Felt as inappropriate	Felt as appropriate

Tough decisions can require emotional distance. It is not easy to sack friends, or to drive hard bargains with those with whom you have built close relationships. The independence of judges who play golf with prosecutors or defendants may be questioned. As noted in Chapter 5, this is one reason why Continuity may be discouraged – for example, when retailers move their buyers around to avoid the development of too close a relationship with suppliers (Table 6.2).

So, in some circumstances, not knowing the other person, or limiting the ways in which one knows them, may well produce the most desirable outcomes in the relationship. On the other side of the coin, however, knowing too much may be intrusive and controlling. Teenage reticence is one response to the instincts of 'helicopter parents' who hover anxiously over every activity and element of their children's lives in their quest to ensure safety, development and success. A corporate customer's requirement for open book accounting may be more about gaining power and control over a key supplier than about looking for efficiency gains. Where independence is not firmly established, the space of more limited knowledge may be valued.

In multiplex relationships that also involve substantial power differentials, the more powerful party may be tempted to exploit information provided by the less powerful party for personal gain,[15] blackmail, or bullying. Asymmetry of information, entirely correct in some professional relationships – therapist, social worker, doctor, and so on – can elsewhere be a warning signal that something is wrong with the way power differentials are being handled. There are some fairly easy ways to reduce Multiplexity in one-on-one relationships. You can reduce the number of roles or contexts in which you meet the other party. You can clarify the role in which you are interacting with them ('speaking with my ... hat on' is a familiar phrase used to segment through processes

---

[15] Plaut, 'Boundary violations'; and Powell and Foley, 'Romantic relationships'.

in meetings). Or you can simply reduce the information available about you on social media, or be less open with information about other parts of your life.

The latter is an issue in job applications. In the West, as a protection against prejudice, there is trend for recruitment decisions to rely on a more narrow information base, with references to age, gender, sexuality, race, marital status, or religion being removed from both curricula vitae and interview questions where such information may be deemed irrelevant to the job and a potential basis for discrimination. Instead, attention focuses on experience, skills, past performance and personality. Nevertheless, breadth of knowledge of the applicant is still viewed positively. One UK newspaper advised job-hunters to 'make what you do in your private life as public as possible' on the grounds that that 'your CV will probably be read by people who will have no other insight into your personality, skills or potential than what is laid out before them'.[16]

Not all aspects of private lives will be attractive to potential employers, and some have come to regret their own and their friends' postings on Facebook and other social networking sites. Information cannot be controlled, and the web makes background information on people readily accessible. In the run-up to the 2010 general election in the UK, when a constituency party discovered that the candidate they had recently selected had had an extramarital affair, they were seen in the press as naïve for not having googled the individual before putting him forward.

Ways to Build Multiplexity in Organisations

To increase Multiplexity, and gain better knowledge and understanding, we can seek to increase the information. First, by making better use of encounters that already take place in the context we know, we can broaden the range of information exchanged and experienced between those involved. Second, we can further broaden the range of information exchanged and experienced by creating opportunities for different types and contexts of encounter between participants. Third, and sometimes where opportunities for actual encounter are limited, we can make use of other information sources – databases, third parties and so on – outside the relationship or organisation.

---

[16] 'Interests and hobbies', *Guardian*, 15 April 2009, www.theguardian.com/careers/cv-interests-hobbies.

Continuity and Multiplexity often go together. The more often you see people, the greater your chances of observing them under different circumstances, and thus displaying a wider repertoire of skills and behaviours. A broader picture emerges from seeing someone in success and failure, when things are easy and when the going is tough, in difficult arguments and easy conversations, managing and being managed. But there are other ways to build up Multiplexity.

Take Advantage of Opportunities

The simplest way is *taking the opportunities already presented*: checking in at the start of meetings, not just getting straight down to business; taking time now and again to ask team members what they like about the job and what they'd like to change; initiating a conversation about what's in the news as you walk down the stairs together; creating an environment where it is OK to acknowledge the challenges of the job.

The neighbour of a New York 9/11 victim wrote about his failure to take opportunities when he had them:

I stood with you nearly every morning and we greeted each other simply with a head-nod and a pleasant hello. I stood next to you for more than two years, and we never even exchanged names. Always that simple head-nod and a pleasant hello. I learned your name after you died – I read it below your photo in the newspaper. I knew of your death earlier though. As the search for you went on, and your fate became more obvious I would watch your mother walk up and down the street crying. I didn't go out there and introduce myself to her either. I guess I haven't learned my lesson. So now I am reminded of you every day by simply looking out my window and seeing your car, still unmoved since the day you left for work. I can't say I miss you, as I never really knew you. But that is the part I find myself thinking about all the time ... why didn't I get to know you?[17]

Create 'Talk Spaces'

Going one step further, *creating 'talk spaces'* encourages exchange of information. These can be as simple as the areas around the water cooler or coffee bar, or as full-fledged and sophisticated as specially built 'chill-out' rooms. It is because there is so much interchange of intellectual capital within seemingly idle talk that the value of downtime 'talk spaces' has become increasingly

---

[17] www.september11victims.com/september11victims/VictimInfo.asp?ID=2351, last accessed 20 September 2008.

understood. Proponents have argued that dedicated 'talk places' have shown that the conversations employees have with one another are the way knowledge workers discover what they know, share it with their colleagues and, in the process, create new knowledge for the organisation.[18] It has to be added, though, that talk spaces must fit in with the broader existing organisational culture. For example, Clear Communications, a New Zealand telecommunications company that merged with Telstra in 2001, had 'chill zones' complete with comfortable sofas, televisions and DVD players, and furnishings chosen by the employees themselves.[19] And there are extensions of the same idea: knowledge can deepen and broaden when meeting colleagues at the local football ground, or seeing them perform at the conference revue.

Co-Locate

Being *located in the same place* increases the opportunities for encountering one another in different contexts. If, for example, work and home are geographically distant, you may be less likely to meet work contacts while shopping at the weekend. The more roles that are linked to the same place, the greater the chances of meeting the same people at the school gate, in the street, at the sports club, or on the commuter train. When building a community, enabling these different types of meeting-contexts is important. Bumping into and chatting to the same people – at the supermarket, in the exercise class, the faith meeting place, the café, the bus stop – helps to develop multiplex, cross-community relational ties.

Note that there are limits to this. 'Living above the shop' may not always be the best option. Teachers may deliberately choose not to live in the catchment for their school so as not to blur their role in the eyes of students. Clergy, accustomed to living in the community in which they minister, recognise both the strength of this approach in developing authentic relationships, but also the vulnerability they then carry. An intelligent choice needs to be made on balancing the advantages of privacy and transparency.

Network

Today we meet in multiple *virtual contexts*, with the growth of Twitter, Facebook, YouTube, blogs and other online forms of communication. Organisations and individuals actively seek to make contact with others via a range of different

---

[18] Davenport and Prusak, *Working Knowledge*, p. 46.
[19] *New Zealand Herald*, 'Clearly, sofas are a winner', 8 August 2001.

media. Organisations may take this further as the range of contexts in which they 'meet' their customers and communicate something about themselves can range from different types of advertising, through news media to product placement.

Use Lunch

Eating together works on two fronts. Firstly, it encourages a broader field of conversation. At Google's Googleplex headquarters almost everyone eats in the Google café, sitting at whichever table has an opening and enjoying conversations with Googlers from different departments.[20] This allows Googlers from across units, departments and functions to interact informally, thus enhancing the possibility of enriching their networks within this giant organisation. There are creative variations on this. One oil company senior executive described his preference for picnics rather than restaurants in corporate hospitality: seeing how people opened the wine and distributed the food was more revealing than simply sitting and being served, as well as encouraging some less work-focused conversation.

Refer to Third-Party Sources

Multiplexity need not only be built from first-hand knowledge. When building mutual knowledge between organisations, individuals will often not gain all the knowledge they need first-hand. Colleagues may gain insights from each other about customers, suppliers or other colleagues. In pitching for new business, many people may be sounded out to get a feel for the needs and interests of a prospective client. Parents may ask friends and neighbours about their experiences of local schools or other service providers. This knowledge building process may be deliberate or accidental, formal or informal, clearly targeted to fill specific gaps or a less focused 'fishing expedition'.

One way of gaining knowledge from other people is through *references and testimonials,* or less directly through endorsements. 360-degree reviews are also used to build a more rounded view of an employee's performance. All these processes can raise questions about the accuracy and honesty of the information. Knowledge about other people and organisations is also gained through *reputation and gossip.* The grapevine can circulate information

---

[20] Google' 'The Google culture', https://www.google.co.uk/intl/en_uk/about/company/facts/culture, accessed 16 October 2015.

quickly. People may know about organisational decisions before the official announcement; such information is not always right, though at its best it can be a useful complement.

Reputation needs a basis. There is a difference between being skilled (perceived quality) and being known (prominence in mind). If things are repeated often enough they are more likely to be believed. We also need to ask whether the reputation is deserved – it may have been true in the past but is not true now, or it may not have been true at all. On whose judgement does the reputation depend? The speed and reach of new communication technologies have significantly increased the risk to high-profile reputations.

Finally, many organisations use structured *knowledge management* processes:

- *Relationship managers*: key contacts sift and share information: these gatekeepers of Multiplexity can be effective channels or limiting filters.
- *Knowledge management* systems: IT databases that capture information about customers and other contacts and pool it from diverse sources.
- *Data mining*: companies try to build a broad profile about customers from a range of data sources and types, e.g. data about purchases. This automated form of Multiplexity is behind the specific-to-you product recommendations made to individual customers by companies such as Amazon.
- *Network management*: facilitating the right contacts and ensuring that people have the information to make the right connections. The business social networking site LinkedIn provides a network management service that explicitly links people either directly or via third-party contacts.

A large consumer products company held a global meeting of its researcher community. Each participant's name badge contained a radio frequency identification (RFID) chip, coded with data about that person and his or her work: some personal background, some areas of expertise and current research interests. As the attendees mingled during the cocktail hour, their name tags glowed whenever two people with common or complementary interests passed. As people responded to the lights and made introductions, a computer tracked the connections and continuously updated a sociogram of the participants on a large projection screen. By the end of the evening, a poorly connected network had evolved into a richly linked community of practice.[21]

---

[21] T. Laseter and R. Cross, 'The craft of connection', *Strategy + Business*, 44 (2006), www.strategy-business.com/article/06302?gko=ee374.

7 Parity: Power, Balance, Fairness

When people or organisations feel used, bullied, unfairly treated, not listened to and not respected they are more likely to withdraw from a relationship or to engage negatively. Conversely, those who are confident in the fairness of a relationship are more likely to invest in it, and those who feel listened to and respected are more willing and able to participate.

These feelings, both positive and negative, are often experienced strongly and with significant implications for the relationship. At the root of this is the *power* dynamic present in every relationship. A boss uses her power in her relationship with employees to direct their activities. A brand uses its power to influence what its customers buy. A community leader galvanises neighbourhood action. Staff withdraw their labour from their employer. A manager decides who gets a bonus, and how much. A sports coach motivates his team. Your fellow board members listen to your ideas or, perhaps, ignore them. Voters change the way they are governed. Local politicians fund some projects and not others for local residents.

However, across these various relationships power is focused on different things – sometimes power is used to affect another person or organisation; sometimes to direct or initiate common tasks; sometimes to change the nature of the relationship. And power is derived from different sources: the power of reward or coercion; the power of expertise; the power that celebrities have to generate imitators; the power of cultural norms; or the power of controlling resources; and a whole subtle network of advantages based on age, education, opportunity, precedent, psychology and personality.

Power is never evenly distributed, and authority systems and reporting structures depend on power asymmetries. Decisions made in one relationship can affect the power dynamics in others. Reactions to power asymmetries are also important. Negative and defensive reactions rarely make for constructive solutions and effective collaboration. Indeed, recognising that there is always a choice about how to respond is perhaps the most fundamental and inalienable power of all. Parity therefore involves paying attention both to the distribution of power and to the way in which it used.

The instinct for justice is deeply ingrained. The child's cry of 'That's not fair!' indicates that human beings are highly attuned to it from an early age. A sense of fairness may deal in rational calculation – for instance, in comparing the relative value or rewards or opportunities – but it is rooted in the emotions. A sense of unfair treatment touches on important elements of our self-perception and self-respect: often what hurts is not so much the outcome itself, but the implications of the disregard of the other for us. That is why restitution without apology still disappoints – the relational nature of the problem has not been addressed. It also illustrates why Parity is such a potent factor in relationships: it is because it can be experienced so strongly that it can have such a significant effect on how people, groups and organisations participate in relationships, and the outcomes that result.

Parity is not equality; rather, it is a configuration of power asymmetries that acknowledges our common humanity and which tends to produce respect, self-respect and fairness. It is partly structural and partly attitudinal. Power exercised in a stance of *respect* towards the other is far more likely to be experienced as fair. Individually, this may be demonstrated by acknowledging positively physical presence, social importance, ideas and values, needs and interests, achievements and efforts, qualities and virtues or rights.[1] In organisational terms, it may involve recognising the other company's working practices, history and market challenges, for example, as well as its values, interests, or achievements and qualities. In our actions and decisions we either take account of these things or ignore them.

Relationships involve *participation* on both sides. Power, on the other hand, is often defined as 'that which enables one person to make another act in a certain way'.[2] In reality, there are many forms of power, and in many situations different forms and levels of power and advantage run in different directions and confine one party's practical advantage to a narrow sphere. In organisations,

---

[1] See, for example, R. Wolf, 'Respect and international relations: state motives, social mechanisms and hypotheses', Paper presented at 49th Annual Convention of the International Studies Association, San Francisco, CA, March 26–29, 2008, or R. Dillon, 'Respect: a philosophical perspective', *Gruppendynamik und Organisationsberatung*, 38 (2007), pp. 201–212.

[2] R. A. Dahl, 'The concept of power', *Behavioural Science*, 2 (1957), pp. 201–215.

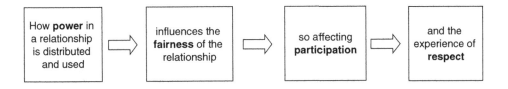

Figure 7.1:   How Parity influences the behaviour and outcomes of a relationship

Parity is about distributing and using power in a way that encourages effective participation, increasing the scope of what can be achieved by combining the contributions of others – their time, contacts, knowledge, skills, finance, or other resources. The ability to influence the extent and nature of others' participation is dependent on perceptions of the fairness of the exchange and of the use of power within it (Figure 7.1)

Parity in relationships helps to reduce risk. Accidents happen when warning voices aren't heard. In aviation, this is described as the cockpit gradient, with some analysts attributing 20 per cent of crashes to the powerlessness of co-pilots to question the actions of more senior pilots.[3] Similarly, when a cluster of young children died during heart operations at a Bristol hospital it was found that the nurses and anaesthetists had been unable to make their concerns heard.[4] Get Parity wrong, and less is achieved, with the risk of the relationship becoming destructive. Get it right, and people engage fully and constructively in the relationship.

Power Sources

Building and maintaining Parity within a relationship or group has to address the use and distribution of power between those involved. This is not simple. Power comes in multiple forms, and it is not always clear where they are located. All parties to a relationship are likely to have more than one form of power, but not all those forms are equally easy to use. Actual power is also a function of the skill with which it is deployed. Weak hands can be played well, or strong positions squandered. So how do we understand the power dynamic in a relationship or group, particularly as it affects fairness, participation and mutual respect?

---

[3] E. Tarnow, 'Towards the zero accident goal: assisting the First Officer monitor and challenge Captain errors', *Journal of Aviation/Aerospace Education and Research*, 10 (2000), pp. 29–38.

[4] I. Kennedy, *Final Report, Bristol Royal Infirmary Inquiry* (London: HMSO, 2001).

Coercive Power

This is the type of power most likely to be encountered within the structures of organisations and communities. It is strongly, though not exclusively, linked to position and role, and resides in the perception that one person is able to make another act in a certain way.[5] It often includes the ability to punish or to incite fear of punishment should another fail to comply. In some cases this may take the form of violence – the power of the mugger with a knife to persuade you to hand over your wallet or phone. More often, as in the workplace, it involves the crude use of threats. For example, a manager might use the threat of a poor appraisal or block on promotion to ensure compliance.

Coercive power may be legitimate if exercised within bounds. Many authority structures confer on certain office-holders a degree of coercive power over those further down in the system.[6] For example, the legitimate power of the police to enforce the law by physically restraining a suspect depends both on the authorisation of the officer and on observance of limits set to prevent abuse. For this reason the conduct of police officers in a case where the suspect has died in custody is brought under intense scrutiny. Similarly, the rights of a prisoner – to remain silent or to see a lawyer – operate as a check on what might in other circumstances become the unfettered coercive power of law enforcement. To be considered fair, this type of power – between manager and staff, state and citizen, teacher and student – has to be accepted as appropriate by all parties, along with the checks and balances that prevent power being abused.

A wide variety of situations involve the use or threat of coercive power: in effect, the ability to induce compliance in others through the fear of loss:

- *Exit rights, veto and sabotage*: this is the 'nuclear option' of the weaker party: no one gets anything if I don't get more.
- *Choice* rights: the ability to choose different suppliers of services (for example, in health, education and utilities) is designed to empower consumers and works because the loss of custom or contract inflicts damage on suppliers.
- *Voice rights*: within power structures, appealing to a higher jurisdiction confers the ability to hold accountable, to gain redress, and to influence policy and strategy.

---

[5] Dahl, 'The concept of power'.

[6] See for example, M. Weber, *The Theory of Social and Economic Organization* (Glencoe, IL: Free Press, 1924); H. Fayol, *General and Industrial Management* (London: Pitman, 1949); and P. M. Blau, *Exchange and Power in Social Life* (New York: Wiley, 1965).

- *Political power*: political authorities have the sanctioned ability to compel and prohibit behaviour and to allocate resources. Highly centralised 'winner-takes-all' political systems allow significant patronage and have been a major factor in ethnic conflict in post-independence Africa.
- *Financial power*: as Marx pointed out, significant power belongs to those who own the means of production. More widely, control of the budget brings influence in a relationship. Access to financial resources can also distort other forms of power. If the costs of a justice system are too high, or one party cannot risk the financial costs of losing, this confers power on those with greater financial resources.
- *Market power*: for companies, size and position in the market influences the pricing power and access of others to the market. This is linked to the producer power that comes with control over access to goods and resources, such as scarce commodities, or through proprietary technology.
- *Administrative* power: administrations have the capacity to delay, enable or distort implementation through control of key mechanisms. This brings potential for corruption and for the protection of vested interests through inertia and sabotage of reform initiatives.

Reward Power

The converse of coercive power is reward power – the ability to distribute rewards that are perceived to be valuable: the carrot rather than the stick. Reward power relies on inner motivation, and has particular potency when there are no – or few – other routes to those rewards other than by the patronage of the one making the offer. Reward power may be exercised fairly – fair pay for work done, for instance – or, beyond what is strictly fair, with generosity. Often coercive power has the appearance of reward power, insofar as coerced parties comply by choosing the best of available options – though the more powerful party is defining the options available.

Persuasive Power

In a weaker form, power asymmetries exist in the form of one individual's ability to exert influence over others, without explicitly offering either threats or rewards.

Some theorists go beyond individual charisma and focus on the more complex impact of ideas, preferences, self-image and self-reflection on the power structure of the relationship. They argue that the greatest conceivable power lies in 'pre-forming' people or organisations in such a way that they do what one wants them to do without any need for explicit domination or displays of power.[7] In this per-spective, the most important forms of power are those where someone does not need to make another do something because the latter will do it anyway.[8]

It can be argued that many covert forms of power are exercised through organisational or societal culture.[9] Cultural power influences, or even con-trols, subjects by inducing them to accept and internalise a set of more widely espoused norms, values and practices. Where coercive power may influence behaviour directly, cultural power works at a deeper level through mind and emotions.[10] There may be a deliberate attempt to influence people via the shap-ing of cultural norms and expectations – such as a government health pro-gramme, or a marketing campaign; this influence may be a side-effect of other identifiable activities – such as the broadcast of particular storylines in popular TV soaps, or the media commentary and reporting of a current event. In prac-tice, because any kind of group develops its own culture, the power of cultural norms is always present – to a greater or lesser degree. For example, in the UK, northerners visiting the south often remark upon how unfriendly southerners appear to them. In the north of England it is more usual to acknowledge pass-ers-by than it is in the south. Northerners relocating to the south of England may appear overfriendly. This is the power of cultural norms in action.

When used deliberately, this form of power, also known as normative con-trol, seeks to manage the inner psyche of people so that they act in the best interests of the organisation or community, not because they are externally coerced, nor purely from concern with rewards and sanctions, but driven by internal commitment, strong identification with organisational norms and goals, and intrinsic motivators such as satisfaction from work.[11]

An example is when subordinates voluntarily choose to work on week-ends in order to meet a deadline. Their decisions do not arise out of the overt

[7] C. Castoriadis, 'Power, politics, autonomy', in A. Honneth, T. McCarthy, C. Offe and A. Wellmer (eds.), *Cultural–Political Interventions in the Unfinished Project of Enlightenment* (Cambridge, MA: MIT Press, 1992).

[8] S. Clegg, 'The power of language, the language of power', *Organisation Studies*, 8 (1987), pp. 60–70.

[9] C. A. Ray, 'Corporate culture: the last frontier of control?', *Journal of Management Studies*, 23 (1986), pp. 287–297.

[10] T. Mitchell, 'Everyday metaphors of power', *Theory and Society*, 19 (1990), p. 545–578.

[11] G. Kunda, *Engineering Culture: Control and Commitment in a High-Tech Corporation* (Philadelphia, PA: Temple University Press, 1992).

wielding of a stick or the dangling of a carrot by their managers. Instead, it is the structural and systemic character of power embedded in the wider culture. The subordinates have internalised the belief that working on weekends is a norm if the situation warrants it.

Another variant is referent power. Its source is a collection of desirable resources or personal traits in an admired person. This form of power is often the result of another's admiration and the desire to follow or to be like the admired person. This is demonstrated in the ability of celebrities to attract cult followings and is recognised by advertisers in the huge paycheques such celebrities command for endorsing products.

Networks, Power and Dependence

Gillian Shephard, a member of a 1990s UK government that was famously described by a former member as being 'in office but not in power',[12] describes the elusiveness of power:

Like others, I observed power receding as you think you are approaching its source. You become a minister and find that somehow it isn't you that has the power, it's maybe the civil servants, or it could be your secretary of state. Then when you get into cabinet it isn't there either, so you think it has to reside with the prime minister. Then you see prime ministers constrained by their circumstances.[13]

Power and dependence are inter-related. One party is dependent upon the other if the other controls a resource that is important, scarce and non-substitutable. The power resides with the resource-holder, whether we are talking about goods, labour, finance or something else. Dependency is not limited to material resources: any need that is perceived as a reward or lack of it as a punishment is a potential dependency – perhaps for affection, approval, information, opportunities, or permission. Dependence also occurs when the resource concerned is expertise. In every case, if one party needs the resource, then the other party holds a degree of power that he may or may not recognise and may or may not choose to exercise. Only by the first party not desiring the rewards, or not fearing the sanction, can the other party's power be

---

[12] The former Chancellor of the Exchequer, Norman Lamont, on John Major.
[13] G. Shephard, *Shephard's Watch: Illusions of Power in British Politics* (London: Politico's Publishing, 2000).

diminished. If you do not care about your future prospects within the firm, the CEO has little power to coerce or motivate you.

Dependence is inversely proportional to the number of accessible alternative sources of supply. High dependence occurs where there are few alternatives. People in occupations where there is scarcity in the labour market can often negotiate remuneration packages that are far more attractive than those in occupations where there is excess supply in the labour market. If a product is only manufactured by a single company, the company will tend to charge a high price. This is a major reason for governments to seek to promote competition and restrict monopolies.

Dependency is also inversely proportional to the degree of substitutability of a resource or outcome. The fewer similarly viable and attractive substitutes for a resource there are, the more one depends on those who control that resource. Dependency on Middle Eastern oil or Russian gas, for example, is only a problem as long as countries lack alternative means of generating energy. Similarly, agencies encourage young people at risk of influence by gang culture to think and act more independently by increasing their range of cultural reference points, role models and sources of affirmation.

In the economic and political spheres, dependence is often mutual. China depends on US consumers purchasing Chinese goods, while the US depends on China to fund its borrowing. The degree of *mutual dependence* is raised by empowering the more dependent party. In a conflict situation, this might involve active listening – to listen properly to someone else's point of view is to empower them without disempowering yourself. In a management situation, staff may be dependent on a manager because he has the power of reward and coercion vested in him by virtue of his position in the company reporting structure, but the manager will also be dependent on his staff for expertise and labour supply. The combination of powers is difficult to quantify, but both parties will be aware of it, and that awareness is an important foundation of Parity.

Why Fairness Matters

In any group or one-to-one relationship, fairness carries a value. It signals respect for, and recognition of, the dignity of the individual and confirms his or her 'right to belong' in a given relationship or group.[14] More pragmatically, the

[14] E. A. Lind and T. R. Tyler, *The Social Psychology of Procedural Justice* (New York: Plenum, 1988).

perception of unfairness in a relationship can trigger an emotional response and a rational appraisal as to whether to continue on the same terms. Many business deals have foundered for lack of agreement on a fair return for both parties.

It seems that an instinct for fairness is hard-wired. Sarah Brosnan[15] has demonstrated evidence of quite nuanced concepts of fairness in the behaviour of primates. One chimpanzee will not tolerate being rewarded with a cucumber when another has been given grapes for the same task. Kenneth Binmore[16] has demonstrated, using game theory, how fairness has a evolutionary adaptive advantage. A simplified explanation is that sharing food helps protect against hunger where some people have been successful in finding food, but others have not. Game theory suggests that people who don't share are less likely to be shared with, and thus less likely to access the protective benefits of sharing. In repeated encounters the development of norms for sharing, together with graduated measures for enforcing them, offers consistently better outcomes than if both parties presume the worst and act accordingly.

Another example of an instinct for fairness comes from 'dictator games'. If one person is given a sum of money and instructed to share it and, at the same time, told that both parties will keep their allocation if the offer is accepted, but both parties will lose it if it is refused, then it would make sense to accept any offer if the game is played once – even if you are offered only 10 per cent – because something is better than nothing. But economics experiments like this one consistently show that people will *turn down* an offer that they feel is unfair, thereby punishing the donor for their inequitable suggestion. The theorists argue that it makes sense to 'punish' unfair people, because that preserves the rules of fairness and makes it more likely that you will be treated fairly in the future. This is known as 'inequity aversion'. Similarly, in other experimental situations, participants will tend to reduce the wealth of the richest participants and increase the wealth of the poorest, even when they themselves do not gain.[17]

While an aversion to inequity and an instinct to maintain the social rules of fairness may be deeply ingrained, fairness can also be a matter of rational calculation, particularly when both parties are free agents with other options. Each can make their own calculation of what something is worth. This freely made calculation is what is held to be the basis of a just price: a balancing of

[15] S. F. Brosnan, 'Justice- and fairness-related behaviors in non-human primates', *Proceedings of the National Academy of Sciences*, 110, Supplement 2 (2013), pp. 10416–10423.

[16] K. Binmore, *Natural Justice* (Oxford University Press, 2005).

[17] C. T. Dawes, J. H. Fowler, T. Johnson, R. McElreath and O. Smirnov, 'Egalitarian motives in humans', *Nature*, 446 (2007), pp. 794–796.

one's own self-interest with that of another. Equality of power is not always available or appropriate (though one could argue about the balance of different types of power), but it is nearly always possible to achieve a mutual sense of fairness in a relationship. In practice, research has shown that the experience of fairness within an active relationship or group has three interconnected components: fair outcome, fair process and fair conduct.

Fair Outcome

Participants perceive Parity in a relationship if the outcome of joint action is judged to have been fairly *distributed* and fairly *deserved*. These two aspects together are termed 'distributive justice' in the literature.[18] At its simplest, where the 'inputs' to the activities of the relationship are equal, a fair *distribution* requires that rewards are shared equally among the participants in the relationship. Again, at a simple level, a fairly *deserved* outcome in a one-to-one relationship means that the input matches the outcome. As an employee, I feel that I am dealt with fairly by the organisation if my salary has some correlation with the amount of work done, the skill required, or the profitability of the transaction. The client perceives fairness (or not) in the work that is delivered by the contractor for the fees paid. For a punishment to be deemed fair, it must be commensurate with the transgression: if every employee who turns up late for work is invariably fired, regardless of how late or the reasons why, such a penalty is unlikely to be considered fair.

The question of fair outcomes – fairly deserved and fairly distributed – quickly becomes more complicated as soon as the outcome is a consequence of differing inputs across a group or organisation. Within an organisation, fair pay is judged both on input criteria such as hours, skills and responsibility, and also by how it is distributed, based on those same criteria, among others in the organisation. Of course, the outcomes received by third parties outside the immediate relationship will also affect our perception of a fair relational outcome – the money earned by others in the organisation or in society as a whole, the quality of work delivered elsewhere for the same contractual fee. Ultimately, this indicates that questions about, say, whether bonuses in the financial services industry are fairly deserved, or whether relative pay rates between men and women in the same organisation are just, are questions of Parity.

---

[18] See, for example, D. P. Skarlicki and R. Folger, 'Retaliation in the workplace: the roles of distributive, procedural and interactional justice', *Journal of Applied Psychology*, 82 (1997), pp. 434–443.

This is why fairness differs from equality. If treating people equally means giving them the same reward for very different contributions, in most circumstances that would not be perceived as fair. Aristotle argued that equality should mean treating people according to their differences. Parity, therefore, recognises difference, whether this is in terms of role, skill, authority, experience, effort, or other relevant factors. Any difference in outcome should be a fair outworking of these differences. But if the starting point is perceived as being in some way unjust or unfair then it cannot be used to legitimise differences in outcome.

Fair Process

Outcome alone is not a sufficient gauge of fairness in a relationship or group activity. The fairness of the *process* used to determine outcomes, or allocate reward, is also important to the Parity of the relationship. A fair process is, first of all, one that is seen to be *applied consistently, without bias, based on accurate information*. If one employee is given twenty days' annual leave, and another doing an identical job for identical pay is given twenty-five days', this will normally be perceived as unfair.

A sense of fair process – or 'procedural justice'[19] – is also more likely when those affected are given some *involvement* through giving input, providing explanation or exercising right of appeal. In one study, people were asked to come up with innovative names for household products, with a supervisor evaluating the suggestions and handing out rewards. Participants who were allowed to give explanations along with their suggestions rated the process as fairer and gave higher ratings to the supervisor.[20] The opportunity for a participant to be heard within the process affords them respect by giving them use of the power of voice. However, giving people a chance to provide input does not, in itself, ensure perceptions of fair process. When decision-makers fail to respond to the input given, either in terms of action or giving reasons for not doing so, perceptions of unfairness may be higher than if input had not been solicited at all.[21]

---

[19] Skarlicki and Folger, 'Retaliation in the workplace'.

[20] R. Kanfer, J. Sawyer, C. P. Early and E. A. Lind, 'Participation in task evaluation procedures: the effects of evaluative criteria on attitudes and performance', *Social Justice Research*, 1 (1987), pp. 235–249.

[21] J. Greenberg and R. Folger, 'Procedural justice, participation, and the fair process effect in groups and organisations', in P. B. Paulus (ed.), *Basic Group Processes* (New York: Springer-Verlag, 1983), pp. 235–256.

A third source of a sense of fair process is an adequate *explanation* of how the outcome was reached, which is particularly true for formal decision-making procedures. A study to gauge employee reactions to a company's decision to relocate its facilities revealed that individuals reacted more positively when the move was adequately explained than when it was not.[22] Here, fair process plays an even more pivotal role when the outcome may be perceived as unfair. When someone does not get what they think they deserve, it is important that the reasons why are explained. Unfavourable outcomes, such as a planning decision that goes against your preferences, can be considered, at least, acceptable provided they are based on a process that is perceived as fair.[23] In addition, procedural fairness has a strong impact on self-esteem. One relational model suggests that people's socio-psychological needs – including not just self-esteem but also self-identity and affiliation – are likely to be met when they interact with others who are procedurally fair.[24]

Fair Conduct

A sense of fairness is also derived from the degree to which one is treated with dignity, concern and respect, independent of the fairness of any process inherent in the relationship. This is referred to as 'interactional justice'.[25] Studies show that people pay considerable attention to the interpersonal treatment they receive from the decision-maker in a working relationship.[26] Parity can be achieved even where one party holds the decision-making power, if other parties perceive that they are being treated fairly and with respect. In contrast, people who are treated in what they perceive as an unfair, disrespectful, or undignified manner are likely to retaliate – often leading to a vicious circle of disharmony and conflict in the organisation.[27]

---

[22] J. P. Daly and P. D. Geyer, 'The role of fairness in implementing large-scale change: employee evaluations of process and outcome in seven facility relocations', *Journal of Organisational Behavior*, 15 (1994), pp. 623–638.

[23] J. Greenberg, 'A taxonomy of organisational justice theories', *Academy of Management Review*, 12 (1987), pp. 9–22.

[24] Lind and Tyler, *The Social Psychology*, and R. Folger and R. Cropanzano, *Organisational Justice and Human Resource Management* (Thousand Oaks, CA: Sage, 1998).

[25] Skarlicki and Folger, 'Retaliation in the workplace'.

[26] R. J. Bies, D. L. Shapiro and L. L. Cummings, 'Causal accounts and managing organisational conflict: is it enough to say it's not my fault?', *Communication Research*, 15 (1988), pp. 381–399.

[27] Skarlicki and Folger, 'Retaliation in the workplace'.

Fair treatment can be exemplified by procedural fairness – explaining decisions, for instance – or by application of fair reward, a form of outcome fairness. But it could also be demonstrated in fair conduct in day-to-day inter-actions. Bullying and sexual harassment in the workplace are both examples of unfair conduct. Organisationally, unfair conduct may be seen in a relationship between a global company and its small local supplier if the larger and more powerful organisation uses its advantage to delay payment unacceptably or drive margins down to unsustainable levels.

All forms of fairness reflect an implicit psychological contract between organisations and their members. A psychological contract is not a formal, written document, but an implicit set of unwritten obligations between two parties engaging in a relationship that are governed by the prevailing culture. It comprises two key aspects, namely 'transactional' factors and 'relational' obligations.[28] The former includes many of the outcomes discussed under the concept of distributive justice. Financial rewards and career advancement are among the rewards that employees can reasonably expect in exchange for excellent performance. The latter aspect refers mainly to relational expecta-tions that include fair processes and dignified treatment – themes associ-ated with procedural justice and interactional justice. The emotions that are evoked when a psychological contract is violated are not merely dissatisfac-tion or disappointment, but usually the more intense feelings of betrayal and deeper psychological distress, leading possibly to disengagement and withdrawal, particularly when both transactional and relational elements are violated.

Respect and Disrespect

Human beings are highly sensitive to respect:

- The chief executive and her entourage sweep through the corridor with ev-eryone else having to make way, entering offices and interrupting conversa-tions without acknowledging the people who have been edged out. (Using physical presence to disrespect)

---

[28] See, for example, C. Argyris, *Understanding Organisational Behavior* (Homewood, IL: Dorsey Press, 1960); E.H. Schein, *Organizational Psychology* (Englewood Cliffs, NJ: Prentice Hall, 1980); and D. Rousseau, 'Psychological and implied contracts in organisations', *Employee Responsibilities and Rights Journal*, 2 (1989), pp. 121–139.

- The youth worker acknowledges the status of the gang leader in drawing teenagers into a football game. (Giving social respect)
- Contributions to discussion by particular team members are disregarded in a team meeting. (Disrespecting ideas and values)
- Care responsibilities are given consideration by employers; an organisation's needs are accommodated in negotiation. (Respecting needs and interests)
- Extra effort to meet a deadline is unacknowledged and taken for granted. (Disrespecting achievements and efforts)
- Crowds turn out to honour a national public figure. (Respecting qualities and virtues)
- A court requires a government to recognise a citizen's rights. (Respecting the individual)

Respect is fairness brought into human interaction. It asks for recognition of what one party brings to a relationship. We may want to experience respect for our participation, for our particular contribution, for the existence of our organisation, or for ourselves as human beings. Respect recognises individual identity; mutual respect reinforces relational identity. It does so in a way that balances the individual with the group, so that the former is not entirely subsumed into the latter. Mutual respect provides a foundation for diversity. In business life, mutual respect between members of a team makes it possible to explore different approaches constructively, or to disagree when problem-solving. In community life, mutual respect encourages those of differing opinions or backgrounds to acknowledge and perhaps meet each other's needs and concerns. Dialogue starts from a position of mutual respect, perhaps initially based only on acknowledgement of fellow humanity.

While mutual respect between organisations helps to sustain healthy relationships, a lack of respect between organisations can make collaboration almost impossible. The CEO of a charity working with vulnerable people was frustrated in negotiating funding with a local authority. He had been publicly critical of their lack of imagination and quality of service. He felt strongly that the needs of service users should shape policy, not the organisational and financial needs of statutory authorities. He also felt that scant regard was paid to the significant additional resources the charity was bringing into the sector through trusts and corporate donors. For their part, service managers in the local authority saw the charity CEO as a self-promoting egotist with little commitment to partnership and rather arrogant and unfounded views of his own organisation's excellence. Limited personal respect between individuals,

overlaid on a lack of respect for the roles and contributions of the two organisations, made effective partnership working very difficult.

   At a global level, the desire of nations (and their leaders) to be shown respect
by others may be linked to the need to bolster national identity, or to recent
experiences of disrespect or humiliation, or perhaps to a need to strengthen
internal political relationships through the conduct of international relations.
A perceived lack of respect may then contribute to more aggressive respect-
seeking stances. Examples include Russia, which has endured the break-up of
the Soviet Union and the loss of superpower status, and Iran, with its proud
history and struggle to be recognised as a regional power. For both countries,
the need for respect, particularly from militarily more powerful countries like
the USA, has shaped their approach to many issues. Vladimir Putin has said
his determination to make Russia strong had nothing to do with aggression,
but with providing security and comfort – both economic and psychological –
for Russian citizens. What he made clear, however, was that Russia wanted to
be treated with respect, and that he personally was determined that its view
should carry weight in international relations.[29]

   Low Parity tends to produce either resentful compliance or resistance. A
dictatorial boss, an ill-tempered and abusing partner, members of a notorious
inner-city gang, or a bullying and uncompromising football manager will create a matching counterpart: acquiescent employees, a submissive spouse, cautious neighbours and players who toe the line. The low Parity, of course, may
be legitimated by social norms. In football, Alex Ferguson, former manager
of Manchester United, was a notoriously tough boss – but nobody suggested
that this was inappropriate, in spite of the fact that the 'respect' he enjoyed
probably involved 'an uneasy watchful attitude that has the element of fear'.[30]

   Overbearing leadership and consequent attrition in the quality of relationships easily breeds resentment, covert resistance, or open conflict and may
even lead to litigation. While disputes over the fairness of outcomes or decisions, such as annual bonuses or redundancy compensation, and the fairness of
the process of arriving at those outcomes, have at times ended in acrimonious
lawsuits, the lack of 'interactional fairness', or in simple terms the ill treatment

---

[29] From Vladimir Putin's first television interview with a foreign journalist after becoming President
elect: S. Mulvey, 'Analysis: Putin wants respect', BBC, last modified 5 March 2000, http://news.bbc
.co.uk/2/hi/europe/666768.stm, accessed 15 October 2008.

[30] J. Feinberg, 'Some conjectures on the concept of respect', *Journal of Social Philosophy*, 4 (1973),
pp. 1–3.

of people, has been the main factor behind many legal actions. The abuse of power in the form of sexual harassment often results in lengthy and expensive litigation. One study on layoffs discovered that the perceived fairness of the social treatment people received as their redundancies were announced was the strongest predictor of their interest in seeking legal damages: 66 per cent of those who perceived themselves as having been treated disrespectfully considered suing their former employer, while only 16 per cent of those treated well were considering the same.[31]

To a degree, respect is internalised and formalised by social rules and norms. People show respect to others – to others in general or to particular groups – because it is socially reinforced, understood as the proper way to act, or simply conducive to an easier life. This form of respect includes elements of courtesy and civility, treating and being treated politely and with dignity,[32] honour or appreciation for the characteristics of others,[33] inclusion[34] and a relationship or exchange based on consideration and friendliness.[35]

Some individuals may inspire greater respect on the basis of their uniquely valuable characteristics. They may be trustworthy or hardworking. They may have done a favour in the past. The stimuli for respect will differ with the individuals on either side of the relationship. Some prominent individuals – sportspeople who excel, political leaders who inspire by their example – win the respect of populations. In other cases the respect may simply be a quality of the relationship between two particular parties. In contrast to respect through common humanity, respect based on attributes is founded on differences rather than similarities.

---

[31] E. A. Lind, J. Greenberg, K. Scott and T. Welchans, 'The winding road from employee to complainant: situational and psychological determinants of wrongful termination claims', *Administrative Science Quarterly*, 45 (2000), pp. 557–590.

[32] L. Heuer, E. Blumenthal, A. Douglas and T. Weinblatt, 'A deservingness approach to respect as a relationally based fairness judgment', *Personality and Social Psychology Bulletin*, 5 (1999), pp. 1279–1292; and T. R. Tyler and E. A. Lind, 'A relational model of authority in groups', *Advances in Experimental Social Psychology*, 25 (1992), pp. 115–191.

[33] T. Hedinger, 'Assessing interpersonal respect: its psychological and philosophical implications', Master's Thesis at Southern Illinois University, Carbondale, IL, *Master's Abstracts International*, 30 (1992), p. 908.

[34] T. Hedinger, 'To learn respect: four adults share their stories of respectfulness', Doctoral Dissertation at Southern Illinois University, Carbondale, IL, *Dissertation Abstracts International Section A: Humanities and Social Sciences*, 61 (2000), p. 3068.

[35] D. DeCremer, 'Respect and cooperation in social dilemmas: the importance of feeling included', *Personality and Social Psychology Bulletin*, 28 (2002), pp. 1335–1341; and B. Simon and S. Sturmer, 'Respect for group members: intragroup determinants of collective identification and group-serving behavior', *Personality and Social Psychology Bulletin*, 29 (2003), pp. 183–193.

The fundamental basis of Parity is a recognition of shared humanity: that respect is due to others simply because they are people, and it would be unfair to discriminate on this basis between one person and another. This has a variety of philosophical and ethical roots, or can be expressed politically through constitutional commitments to equality and human dignity. Immanuel Kant's moral imperative to treat people only as ends and never as means is a classic example of this view. A variant on this is the expression of respect through intentional acts of care or compassion, which goes beyond the minimum requirements of human dignity and recognises that fairness makes legitimate demands on time and resources.

Respect and Self-Respect

Psychologically, respect and self-respect are closely connected. If we feel disrespected by those around us, our sense of self-worth is likely to suffer. American psychologist Carl Rogers considered 'unconditional positive regard' for self and for others to be the foundation for meaningful human relationships.[36]

Self-respect has a number of elements. Nathaniel Branden suggests six key pillars: living consciously; self-acceptance; self-responsibility; self-assertiveness; living purposefully; and personal integrity.[37] These bear close resemblance to models of wellbeing such as that proposed by Carol Ryff which covers the six dimensions of autonomy, personal growth, self-acceptance, life purpose, mastery and positive relatedness.[38] Issues of self-respect can have significant impacts on both organisations and on workers. A perception of organisational fairness is particularly important to members because the experience of fairness is often taken as an indicator of an individual's status in, and value to, an organisation. If we believe we are consistently treated worse than we deserve, we are likely to translate this into a decreasing personal assessment of our worth at work.[39] Indeed, empirical findings from both cross-sectional field studies[40]

[36] C. Rogers, *On Becoming a Person* (Boston, MA: Houghton Mifflin, 1961).

[37] N. Branden, *The Six Pillars of Self-Esteem* (New York: Bantam Trade Paperback Edition, 1995).

[38] C. D. Ryff and C. L. M. Keyes, 'The structure of psychological well-being revisited', *Journal of Personality and Social Psychology*, 69 (1995), pp. 719–727.

[39] J. Brockner, *Self-Esteem at Work* (Lexington Books, 1988).

[40] B. M. Wiesenfeld, J. Brockner and V. Thibauh, 'Procedural fairness, managers' self-esteem, and managerial behaviors following a layoff', *Organisational Behavior and Human Decision Processes*, 83 (2000), pp. 1–32.

and controlled experiments[41] indicate that fairness perceptions are associated with context specific self-esteem.

The self-worth of employees has value for organisations. In 1890 William James, one of the leading figures in the development of psychology as a discipline, argued that people seek to achieve success or avoid failure in those areas in which they have staked their self-worth.[42] People want to feel good about themselves, and want this to be expressed in, and validated by, the behaviour of others towards them. In turn, a sense of self-worth makes the praise and affirmation of others credible and reinforcing. People make choices about their degrees of engagement based on the respect that they feel they receive from the other party, which means that the ability of managers to show and convey respect to others is an important influence on their behaviour and reactions.

The desire to be respected, and the attributes on which that desired respect is based, is not always healthy. Alain de Botton, in his study of status anxiety,[43] acknowledges the relationship between the respect and recognition we desire from others, and the needs of our own sense of self. The desire for respect and admiration from our peers is an aspect of the 'two great quests' – 'the search for sexual and romantic fulfilment, and the search for recognition in the world'. The fight for status is seen as a fight for identity with the answer to the question 'Who am I?' 'often contingent on the very things that make us doubt ourselves in the first place'.

At the same time, the obsession with one's own self-esteem, often a product of low-Parity situations, has been shown to inhibit interaction. Jennifer Crocker has shown how, among students, the prioritisation of self-esteem has a negative impact on connections with others:

People engaged in the pursuit of self-esteem respond to self-threats with avoidance, distancing, and withdrawal, or with blame, excuses, anger, antagonism and aggression. All of these responses take a tremendous toll on meaningful, authentic and supportive connections with others. When our super-ordinate goal is demonstrating our worth or value as a person, we become isolated and disconnected from others.[44]

---

[41] C. Koper, D. van Knipperberg, F. Bouhuijs, R. Vermunt and H. Wilke 'Procedural fairness and self-esteem', *European Journal of Social Psychology*, 23 (1993), pp. 313–325.

[42] W. James, *Principles of Psychology* (Cambridge, MA: Harvard University Press, 1890) cited in L. E. Park, J. Crocker and K. D. Mickelson, 'Attachment styles and contingencies of self-worth', *PSPB*, 30 (2004), pp. 1243–1254.

[43] A. de Botton, *Status Anxiety* (London: Penguin, 2005).

[44] J. Crocker and N. Nuer, 'The insatiable quest for self-worth', *Psychological Inquiry*, 14 (2003), pp. 31–34. See also J. Twenge's study, *Generation Me: Why Today's Young Americans Are More Confident, Assertive, Entitled – And More Miserable Than Ever Before* (New York: Free Press, 2006).

This has important implications for the workplace. In organisational psychology, a narcissist is a person with a grandiose sense of self-importance, who demands excessive admiration, has a sense of entitlement and who is often arrogant in relating to colleagues.[45] Narcissistic behaviour often has detrimental impact on employee morale and leads to breakdown in otherwise healthy and effective working relationships. In order to obtain the admiration of others and to affirm their superiority, narcissists tend to be selfish and exploitative and invariably treat others as inferior and view others as existing for their benefit.[46] While narcissists may think they are better leaders than others as a result of their ostensibly overt self-confidence, studies have found that their superiors considered them to be worse leaders and less effective at their jobs, particularly when it comes to helping and leading people (Table 7.1).[47]

Low-Parity relationships may cause one or more parties to seek to leave the relationship. Or they may remain in the relationship but be more disengaged, contribute less, or deliberately seek to damage the other through sabotage or conflict. In effective relationships all parties feel respected – for themselves, for their contribution, for their position. People who feel their contribution will be heard are more likely to speak. An organisation that feels it will not be dismissed out of hand is more likely to come to the negotiating table. A leader who is respected by his team is more likely to work without throwing his weight about. This respect is powerfully communicated through fairness: fair process, fair treatment, a fair hearing. And it has a future aspect: confidence

Table 7.1: Appropriate and inappropriate experience of high and low degrees of Parity

High Parity	Overfamiliarity, presumption	Fairness, respect
Low Parity	Unfairness, bullying	Legitimate authority
	Felt as inappropriate	Felt as appropriate

[45] R. P. Brown and V. Zeigler-Hall, 'Narcissism and the non-equivalence of self-esteem measures: a matter of dominance?', *Journal of Research in Personality*, 38 (2004), pp. 585–592.

[46] W. K. Campbell and C.A. Foster, 'Narcissism and commitment in romantic relationships: an investment model analysis', *Personality and Social Psychology Bulletin*, 28 (2002), 484–495.

[47] M. Maccoby, 'Narcissistic leaders: the incredible pros, the inevitable cons', *Harvard Business Review* (2000), pp. 69–77; and T. A. Judge, J. A. LePine and B. L. Rich, 'Loving yourself abundantly: relationship of the narcissistic personality to self and other perceptions of workplace deviance, leadership, and task and contextual performance', *Journal of Applied Psychology*, 91 (2006), 762–776.

in a fair share of the rewards encourages the risk of investment in terms of time, energy, reputation, or money. High-Parity relationships are high-capacity relationships. They enhance participation and involvement, because each party is enabled to contribute more and each party is enabled to gain more. In particular, there are four advantages to Parity.

Openness to Risk

Where we have a choice, the decision to participate in a particular relationship – to join a network, to form a partnership, to negotiate a contract – is informed, consciously or unconsciously, by the potential *reward*. The term 'reward' is used in the broadest sense: from, for example, the goods or money gained from a business relationship; through recognition, a sense of identity, or the potential to make a difference, perhaps; to the fun or the emotional support of a friendship.

In practice we are usually aware whether the distribution of rewards is likely, over time, to be (a) fairly shared, (b) in our favour, or (c) in the other's favour. If this is a strategic business partnership we will make this analysis carefully and explicitly. At other times it will be based on gut feel and intuition. If we detect that the reward is unfairly biased away from us, other relationships may be more attractive, or the investment simply deemed to be not worthwhile. If, conversely, the reward is unfairly skewed in our favour, we might gain in the short term but the relationship is likely to be difficult once the other party notices the inherent unfairness.

Of course, the assessment of fair shares depends upon the value of the rewards in question. And different participants in the relationship may place different values on particular types of rewards. We might want the business contacts that membership of a network gives us; the network organiser may want our cash. The more this is perceived as a fair exchange, the more stable the relationship will be. We also weigh up the potential costs and risks of a new relationship – the costs of time and money that will be sunk into a new business venture, say, or the risk to reputation and bank balance if it fails. As with reward, we assess whether the costs and risks are likely to be fairly distributed both across the parties to the relationship but also when offset against the possible rewards. If it looks as though I will have to do most of the work for a particular project, then I may be reluctant to get involved at all without the promise of greater recognition or recompense. Sometimes, people either do not enter or they withdraw from the relationship because they fear getting hurt – an emotional risk – or because they lack the capacity to manage and contain risks such as these.

When a relationship becomes unfair to one or other participant, sometimes those involved feel that the withdrawal of their active participation in the relationship is the only way to alter its balance back in their favour. The unfairness is experienced as an imbalance of power and, in effect, this exercise of the power of withdrawal is an attempt to change the distribution of power in the relationship in favour of the withdrawers. Examples range from strike action to a simple refusal to continue a correspondence. When Dave Carroll's guitar was broken by baggage handlers, and United Airlines refused compensation, he wrote three songs and posted videos on the net. The first song, *United Breaks Guitars*, was played over 3 million times on YouTube. Press reports suggest that within four days of the song going online, 'the gathering thunderclouds of bad PR caused United Airlines' stock price to suffer a mid-flight stall, and it plunged by 10 per cent, costing shareholders $180 million'.[48]

If one party has more to gain, or risks less, in a particular relationship than the other or others, it affects the distribution of power within that relationship. The net gainer is more powerful than the net losers. Those who lose out, with a lesser reward or a greater risk, feel used. The expected fair distribution of reward, cost and risk is an indicator of a fair distribution of a particular type of power – 'reward-power' – and is an important incentive for participating in a relationship.

Productivity and Performance

Once a working relationship or team membership is embarked upon, studies show that its foundations of mutual respect and fairness are associated with improved job performance and job satisfaction.[49] One study sought to establish the direct impact of fair process (termed procedural justice) on performance outcomes by looking at forty product development teams in large companies. Team members were asked to rate, firstly, their satisfaction with the decisions made by the team and the top management and, secondly, the perceived fairness of that

[48] www.timesonline.co.uk/tol/comment/columnists/chris_ayres/article6722407.ece.

[49] J. L. Pierce, D. G. Gardner, L. L. Cummings and R. B. Dunham, 'Organisation-based self-esteem: construct definition, measurement, and validation', *Academy of Management Journal*, 32 (1989), pp. 622–648; D. G. Gardner and J. L. Pierce, 'Self-esteem and self-efficacy within the organisational context', *Group and Organisation Management*, 23 (1998), pp. 48–70, 177–198; J. R. Frei and P. R. Shaver, 'Respect in close relationships: prototype definition, self-report assessment and initial correlates', *Personal Relationships*, 9 (2002), pp. 121–139.

decision-making process. The study then compared team performance with the data on satisfaction and perceived fair process. The correlation between satisfaction and team performance was found to be statistically insignificant – some 'satisfied' teams performed badly and some 'unsatisfied' teams performed well. However, there was a strong positive correlation between perceived fairness of the decision-making process and team performance, implying that people who felt that they were treated fairly also performed better.[50]

There is evidence, too, that fairly treated and respected employees will in turn treat customers well. The link between satisfied employees and satisfied customers, particularly in the services industries, is well known.[51] But there is also direct evidence that *fair treatment* of employees has a clear impact on customer satisfaction.[52] Further studies show links between perceptions of fairness and a whole host of other desirable outcomes, including a willingness to participate beyond the call of duty.[53] A perception of fair treatment – 'interactional fairness' – is credited with a wide range of organisational citizenship behaviours, including those helpful and supportive actions by employees that are not part of their formal job description.[54]

Good Decision-Making

Fair treatment respects the views of others; and fair process requires openness about agendas and procedures – or at least honesty that some things have to be confidential. In a relationship characterised by fairness people

[50] H. Korine, 'Strategic decision-making processes and performance: multiple levels, reciprocal influences', Working Paper, 40, London Business School Strategic Leadership Research Programme (1998).

[51] See, for example, J. Heskett, C. Hart and W. E. Sasser, Jr, *Service Breakthroughs: Changing the Rules of the Game* (New York: Free Press, 1990); J. Heskett, W. E. Sasser, Jr and L. A. Schlesinger, *The Service Profit Chain* (New York: Free Press, 1997); and J. Heskett, W. E. Sasser, Jr and L. A. Schlesinger, *The Value Profit Chain: Treat Employees Like Customers and Customers Like Employees* (New York: Free Press, 2003).

[52] S. Masterson, 'A trickle-down model of organisational justice: relating employees' and customers' perceptions of and reactions to fairness', *Journal of Applied Psychology*, 86 (2001), pp. 594–604.

[53] W. C. Kim and R. A. Mauborgne, 'Implementing global strategies: the role of procedural justice', *Strategic Management Journal*, 12 (1991), pp. 125–143.

[54] See, for example, R. H. Moorman, 'Relationship between organisational justice and organisational citizenship behaviors: do fairness perceptions influence employee citizenship?', *Journal of Applied Psychology*, 76 (1991), pp. 845–855; and C. Lee, 'Prosocial organisational behaviors: the roles of workplace justice, achievement striving and pay satisfaction', *Journal of Business and Psychology*, 10 (1995), pp. 197–206.

are more likely to be given a voice in the decision-making process. As a result they are often more satisfied with, and accepting of, the outcomes, even when the outcomes are not the expected or favoured ones. Studies have shown that managers may gain greater support for their decisions and for themselves by being procedurally fair, especially when the outcomes of the decision are unfavourable.[55] Employees have been shown to react less negatively to a pay freeze when it is implemented in a procedurally fair manner than when the procedure was deemed unfair.[56] The stakes are high because decisions that are not accepted can lead to resistance and sabotage; and this is particularly evident in cases where procedural fairness is perceived to be lacking.

One way of detecting the distribution of power in a group of people is to discover who is involved in making decisions for the group – both officially and behind the scenes – and how decisions are made. Is there a clear process, or are decisions driven by whispering campaigns and conversations on the golf course? To be asked for one's views both demonstrates respect and empowers participation in the decision-making process. It is likely to have a positive knock-on effect on ownership of the shared task and its completion. The converse of this is the deliberate exclusion of views. Symptoms of power being exercised unfairly include hidden or controlled agendas, controlled participation in the process, limiting the information made available or limited time to consider it. Even when all participants seem to be involved in the decision-making process, clear signals can be given as to whose views are considered important and influential, and whose are to be ignored as unhelpful or irrelevant.

The Growth of Trust

Trust is encouraged by respect and fair treatment. Although much is made of a 'crisis of trust', many people every day continue to place active trust in a wide range of individuals, professions and organisations, such as doctors,

---

[55] See, for example, Lind and Tyler, *The Social Psychology*; J. Brockner and B. M. Wiesenfeld, 'An integrative framework for explaining reactions to decisions: the interactive effects of outcomes and procedures', *Psychological Bulletin*, 120 (1996), pp. 189–208; W. C. Kim and R. A. Mauborgne, 'Fair process: managing in the knowledge economy', *Harvard Business Review*, 75 (1997), pp. 65–75.

[56] J. Schaubroeck, D. R. May and F. W. Brown, 'Procedural justice explanations and employee reactions to economic hardship: a field experiment', *Journal of Applied Psychology*, 79 (1994), pp. 455–460.

plumbers, suppliers, investment managers, or business partners.[57] Placing trust is, in part, an assessment of the likely Parity of a relationship: whether there is a risk of creating a form of dependency, whether the other party will use the power – of expertise, monopoly supply, access to your property, and so on – appropriately, whether they will treat you fairly or use you. Trusting people or organisations that have the potential to harm us or let us down is difficult, particularly when trust has not been built up over time. People use perceptions of fairness – especially fair process – to make decisions about how much to trust another.[58]

Key Ways to Build Parity

Every decision and every action is an opportunity to build or undermine Parity. In turn, Parity influences the mechanics of almost every area of practice, including negotiation, leadership style, remuneration, teamwork, recruitment, partnership and collaboration. The distribution of outcomes is always an important element of fairness. Confidence in this area encourages both entry into a relationship and contribution to the relationship and its associated tasks. People calculate fairness in advance when they consider embarking on a new relationship or taking an existing relationship into a new phase. The cost–benefit calculation is often done intuitively, and using different currencies: time, reputation, contacts, energy and knowledge are all key components of the relationship investment. Ultimately fairness is a subjective judgement – it matters that I *feel* the terms are fair, whatever the rational assessment. Loss of the sense of fairness in a relationship may have several causes. For example, a request for more remuneration from an employee may mask frustration at a lack of acknowledgement or feedback. In some cases parties in a relationship who appear to be demanding a sense of fair return from a specific exchange will be satisfied by responses that address the issue more widely.

[57] O. O'Neill, *A Question of Trust: The BBC Reith Lectures 2002* (Cambridge University Press, 2002).
[58] Lind and Tyler, *The Social Psychology*, and M. A. Konovsky and S. D. Pugh, 'Citizenship behavior and social exchange', *Academy of Management Journal*, 37 (1994), pp. 656–669.

Parity through Participation

Parity is built by giving people the capacity both to influence a relationship and its outcomes, and to participate directly in its activities and purpose. Ways of improving the capacity for involvement include:

- *Giving a 'voice'*: Those who are in vulnerable and weak positions can be helped to achieve greater Parity in their relationships when they are given the opportunity and the means for their voice to be heard. Voluntary sector work with disabled people and their relationships with family members, carers, service providers and employers illustrates this. 'Voicelessness' occurs for many reasons: individuals may not be able to articulate their desires, hopes and concerns; they may be daunted by professional knowledge or the complexity of the process; or they may lack the confidence to contradict the views of those on whom they are in some way dependent. The concerns of sections of the community may not be heard through normal democratic or decision-making processes.

In some cases merely stopping, listening and attending to what is said will be enough for those involved to feel they have a voice and a new stake in the relationship. In other cases, the use of advocates or the creation of specialist consultation processes will be the most appropriate way forward. This is a gift that the powerful can give to the 'voiceless'. Listening to the other point of view is the first step in conflict resolution – it empowers the speaker without the listener losing power. For those who have had little control over their own lives this can be a transforming experience. However, empowerment through 'giving a voice' is not just an issue for vulnerable and marginalised people. Most people use someone to speak for them at some point. Financial advisers act as advocates, seeking better deals or resolving complaints about service. Lawyers represent clients in situations where they may lack the knowledge and skills themselves.

- *Enabling collective action*: When individuals come together and act as a group they empower each other. Collective action in the face of the relational participant who up until that point holds all the cards can transform the distribution of power and have a major impact on the Parity of the relationship. Trade unions were formed in the early years of the industrial revolution to re-balance the power between individual workers and owners of capital. In Iceland at the end of 2009, a quarter of the voting population signed a petition to prevent their government from repaying money owed to Britain and the Netherlands after the failure of Icelandic banks.[59] The recent emergence of viral communication – for example, the rapid circulation of video clips on sites such as YouTube – means that collective action need not be formalised. Similarly, collective political concern can be rapidly gathered and expressed, exposing gaffes or forcing retractions.

- *Informing choice*: Information and guidance is an essential element in making choice a reality. The internet has enhanced consumer power by making price comparison easier and opening up access to non-geographically proximate suppliers. The recent UK experience of publishing MPs' expenses and receipts online has, in many people's view, strengthened accountability, as MPs have been forced to address their local communities and associations to ascertain future support.

- *Financing involvement*: Just as information enables choice, so also reallocation of finance within a relationship can unlock a greater range of choices and the power to make them for oneself. A strategy for empowering vulnerable service users, including people with disabilities, is the use of 'personalised budgets' that give them more control over choices in care. Rather than simply being the recipients of pre-allocated public services, control over their personal budget allocation allows them to seek other services and solutions. And because service users have greater opportunity to seek alternative provision, service providers become more responsive to their needs and preferences.

- *Providing resources and training*: Successful engagement in shaping policy and strategy, or in political or commercial negotiations, requires time, skills and knowledge. Smaller and weaker groups or individuals may lack the resources to influence the process and outcomes as effectively as other participants. It is hard for small businesses to bid against large corporations to win government contracts, for instance. Where their contribution is considered valuable, or their acceptance of the outcome important, participants in the relationship, or even third parties, may invest in capacity building: providing resources, training, or advice to enable them to contribute more effectively.

- *Providing fair process*: Process, whether formal or informal, is the mechanism by which partners, team members and others involved in a relationship achieve their shared purpose. In some cases, the process is tacit and minimal – mutual support between family members, say; in others, it is explicit and

[59] NRC Handelsblad Staff, 'Setback in Reykjavik: Iceland blocks 3.8 billion euro repayment to Dutch, British', *Der Spiegel*, 5 January 2010, www.spiegel.de/international/europe/setback-in-reykjavik-iceland-blocks-3-8-billion-euro-repayment-to-dutch-british-a-670294.html.

detailed – the provision of quality service to customers by an IT company. A process that is perceived as fair engages participation.

- Research has discovered six critical *attributes of a fair process*.[60] In order to foster Parity, a fair process must be:
  - *consistent* in applying standards across people and over time
  - *unbiased* by self-interest
  - *accurate*, in that decisions ought to be based on reliable information
  - *correctable*, in that decisions must allow for challenge or appeal
  - *representative* of the concerns of all involved
  - *ethical* in its foundations.

To raise the level of Parity in a relationship it is imperative that those with power – leaders, managers and supervisors – are responsive, consistent and unbiased, that they make decisions based on objective and accurate information, and thereafter adopt an open mind to appeals.[61] While it is paramount to institutionalise fair procedures, it is equally crucial to ensure that they are perceived as adequate and sincerely delivered. Merely putting in place systems that ensure fair processes but neglecting the implementation aspects that include carrying out those processes adequately and with empathy is likely to render them less effective.[62]

- *Doing equitable evaluation*: The 360-degree method of appraising performance is a useful tool to foster Parity throughout the organisation right from top management through to rank and file employees.[63] When carefully and correctly implemented, it is more equitable than traditional superior–subordinate appraisal methods – performance feedback is obtained from the full circle of substantial daily contacts that an employee has. Because it relies on feedback that ranges from superiors, peers and subordinates to customers and suppliers, the 360-degree process, besides merely providing a more accurate reading of employee performance, also helps develop a sense of participation and responsibility among all employees regardless of position.

---

[60] G. S. Leventhal, J. Karuza and W. R. Fry, 'Beyond fairness: a theory of allocation preferences', in G. Mikula (ed.), *Justice and Social Interaction* (New York: Springer-Verlag, 1980), pp. 167–217.

[61] G. S. Leventhal, 'What should be done with equity theory? New approaches to the study of fairness in social relationships', in K. Gergen, M. Greenberg and R. Willis (eds.), *Social Exchange: Advances in Theory and Research* (New York: Plenum, 1980), pp. 27–55.

[62] D. E. Conlon and N. M. Murray, 'Customer perceptions of corporate responses to product complaints: the role of explanations', *Academy of Management Journal*, 39 (1996), pp. 1040–1056.

[63] See, for example, W. W. Tornow and M. London (eds.), *Maximizing the Value of 360-Degree Feedback* (San Francisco, CA: Jossey-Bass, 1998); and J. F. Brett and L. E. Atwater, '360-degree feedback: accuracy, reactions and perceptions of usefulness', *Journal of Applied Psychology*, 86 (2001), pp. 930–942.

Parity through Rules

Well-crafted rules and regulations can increase Parity by constraining the accumulation or inappropriate exercise of power in a relationship. Confidence that rules operate and will be followed, and that breaches will be dealt with, acts as a safeguard in relationships where power might be unfairly used. This confidence might be based on a contract – hours of work, duties and responsibilities, remuneration, grievance and disciplinary procedures. It might also introduce a third party to the relationship who can enforce rules and perhaps develop them, too – a regulator, watchdog, professional body, tribunal, or mediator. In each case, they are vested with the authority to enforce rules and to safeguard the Parity in the relationship or group.

In the UK, the role of these third parties has been pivotal in helping to foster greater Parity in relationships between businesses and consumers. Examples include regulatory action against monopolies to prevent or limit abuse of market power, professional bodies protecting the interests of the public against misconduct (although there can be a risk of protecting the professions' vested interests against the public), planning regulations that seek to ensure that the concerns of all interested parties are considered, or employment rules to protect people against harassment and discrimination.

Parity through Conduct

Robert Sutton has coined the term 'asshole factor' to describe the risk that power creates 'jerks at work':[64]

A huge body of research – hundreds of studies – shows that when people are put in positions of power, they start talking more, taking what they want for themselves, ignoring what other people say or want, ignoring how less powerful people react to their behaviour, acting more rudely, and generally treating any situation or person as a means for satisfying their own needs. What is more, being put in positions of power often blinds them to the fact that they are acting like jerks.[65]

Conveying respect involves giving adequate consideration to another person's physical presence, social importance, ideas and values, needs and

[64] R. I. Sutton, *The No Asshole Rule: Building a Civilized Workplace and Surviving One That Isn't* (London: Sphere, 2007).
[65] R. I. Sutton, 'Are you a jerk at work?', *Greater Good: The Science of a Meaningful Life*, 1 December 2007, http://greatergood.berkeley.edu/article/item/are_you_jerk_work.

interests, achievements and efforts, qualities and virtues, or rights. The con-duct of interpersonal relationships has significant implications for the extent to which respect is experienced and whether power is used to build Parity.

Awareness of your impact on others is one essential element in building Parity. Low levels of Directness make it more likely that the impact of deci-sions on others goes unnoticed. Low 'emotional intelligence' also tends to increase problems in Parity through the individual's lack of awareness of their impact on others. A range of psychology-based models, including Schutz's account of the need for inclusion and control, together with approaches to defining and building emotional intelligence (see Chapter 1), offer ways of understanding both self and other and so managing relational conduct in ways that sustain Parity.

One unusual study asked people to paint a letter 'E' on their foreheads. They found that people asked to recall and write about incidents when they had power over other people were three times more likely to paint an E that was the right way round when they looked at themselves in a mirror, but the wrong way round for anyone looking at them. The comparison group were asked to recall times when someone had power over them, and they wrote the E the right way around for others to see, but they saw a reflected E in the mirror.[66] The conclusion made by the researchers was that feeling powerful tends to reduce awareness of other people's perspectives, the ability to 'see the world through other people's eyes'.

Parity will not always be promoted by other participants in a relationship. Some people are more assertive than others; some bully their employees. This means that those on the receiving end of difficult behaviours need a degree of resilience. For example:

- *Check your sensitivity*: actions that annoy you might not affect others the same way. Previous negative experience may increase sensitivity.
- *Don't take it personally*: the ability to dissociate personal anxieties or slights from organisational needs and processes may reduce sensitivity to some Par-ity issues.
- *Take responsibility for your response*: recognising that you have choices in how you react may be empowering and so reduce the perception of unfair-ness.
- *Recognise respect from elsewhere*: respect from a broader range of others can be internalised and acts as a buffer.

[66] Sutton, 'Are you a jerk at work?'

Parity through Structure

When the Relationships Foundation worked with healthcare organisations during a period of constant organisational and policy change, everyone seemed
to think someone else held the power in their relationships. So, for example,
providers of services felt that those controlling the budgets that purchased
their services held the power in the relationship. But because the holder of
the budget was accountable to politicians for improvements in healthcare
outcomes and patient waiting times, they perceived those who delivered the
services for which they were accountable as holding the power in the relationship. Recognising that both parties had concerns about power and its distribution was an important step in moving towards more effective collaboration.
Developing a better understanding of shared strategic goals, more face-to-face
contact during contract negotiations, and better management of the impact of
staff turnover on Continuity in the relationship were all important. But dealing with perceptions of Parity was essential in creating the space for progress
in other areas.

Concentrations of power are inherently risky and therefore carry great responsibility. However, when the many different forms of power are considered –
power of expertise, power of withdrawal, power of choice and so on – the
concentration may be less, and the distribution greater, than it first appears.

The way power is distributed among the connected individuals or bodies
may be a product of the design of systems and institutions, but can also be a
matter of choice about the extent to which power is centralised or, conversely,
distributed. Multipolarity in the distribution of power – the situation where
different institutions such as judiciary, press, professions, central bank governors, parliament, or civil service all have independent powers and can act
against abuse of powers by the others – offers one mechanism for increasing
Parity through the wider distribution of power.

Parity problems sometimes arise through the sheer size of organisations
and the resources and market share they command. Deliberate action to limit
the size of organisations is thus one strategy for promoting Parity – notable
examples being the use of antitrust law in the USA in the twentieth century to
break up Standard Oil and AT&T. While the break-up of organisations is less
common, companies may be required to divest divisions or operating units as
a condition for approval of mergers or takeovers.

8 Commonality: Overlap of Purpose

Nikos Mourkogiannis says in his analysis of the nature and role of purpose in companies: 'Purpose increases morale, strengthens the ability of the firm to innovate, solidifies position and guides leadership. In all of these ways explicit attention to Purpose can lead companies closer to their potential for greatness.'[1]

From the point of view of relationships – whether between two individuals, or two organisations, a team or a community – purpose is the raw ingredient but what yields relational health and strength is its *alignment*, the degree to which purpose is shared. If their purposes are too divergent then the parties to a relationship will experience friction and conflict, will achieve less, and may come to see no reason for remaining in the relationship. Conversely, a greater alignment of purpose – in a way that accommodates and values difference – increases the *synergy* in the working relationship. Tasks are more easily shared; motivation, satisfaction and commitment are higher; better outcomes can be achieved working together than separately (Figure 8.1).

The alignment of purpose can both encourage and reflect a sense of shared identity and unity. Where there is a strong 'them' and 'us' culture, the interests of each group may inhibit the identification and pursuit of a shared purpose (which may include serving a third party). But where people are working together, a strong team identity may be forged: 'I' becomes 'we' and other aspects of a shared identity may develop within the context of shared purpose.

Sharing purpose is not, however, a straightforward matter of agreement or disagreement. Purpose can be fuzzy and inarticulate. Purpose itself often

---

[1] N. Mourkogiannis, *Purpose: The Starting Point of Great Companies* (London: Palgrave Macmillan, 2006), p. 112.

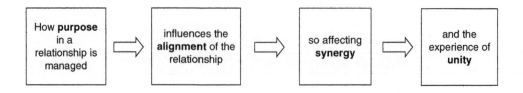

Figure 8.1:   How Commonality influences the behaviour and outcomes of a relationship

changes over time. Any individual or organisation may have multiple purposes, reflecting different roles and relationships. Each of these purposes is
influenced by many factors, making alignment with another individual or
organisation difficult. Shared purpose is thus best understood as a dynamic
construct, the unstable product of forces in balance, always liable to being
pulled apart by conflicting demands. This makes realising the dividends of
shared purpose a constant challenge. These forces can, however, be changed
and managed. The decisions you make as a leader can therefore make it more
or less likely that a satisfactory alignment of purpose is achieved.

What Shared Purpose Is and Does

People use a wide range of words to describe *what* they want to achieve or do
together, *why* it is important, *how* to get there, or how it works out in practice.
Here, we are taking a broad definition of the term 'purpose' to include both
the 'what?' of the relationship and behind it the 'why?' In practice, however,
there is considerable blurring between these categories and many of the related
words are used in more than one way.

At an emotional level, individual purpose draws on motivators and interests, values and beliefs. Corporately, this might find expression in a set of
founding principles, a clear raison d'être, a core ideology, or the beliefs and
values embedded in the organisation's culture. These answer the question
'why?' They may be clearly articulated, communicated and reinforced via
a corporate brand or they may be implicit within the life of the individuals
or the organisation. More pragmatically, the 'what?' dimension of purpose
can be defined by strategies or visions, goals and even tasks that express the
core ideology or the interests of those concerned. Whether strategies, goals
and tasks are answers to the 'how?' question depends on your field of view.
If all you can see is the task you have been assigned rather than a broader

field in which it is part of how to reach a further horizon, then it functions as the answer to 'what is this relationship for?' or even 'why does this relationship exist?'

Nikos Mourkogiannis offers his definition of purpose in reflecting on the failure of the energy company, Enron:

Purpose is bigger than tactics. Tactics represent the 'how', the means by which leaders pursue their goals. Purpose is bigger than strategy. At best, strategy is short-term Purpose, a step-by-step path towards optimal results. Enron had strategy – indeed, it had many strategies. But strategies are about means; they cannot be an end in themselves. An end is a reason. Enron lacked a reason – it lacked Purpose.[2]

A study of more than 200 organisations across industries from regions including Europe, North America, Asia, the Middle East and Africa underscores the importance of shared purpose, direction and vision. Organisational cultures with a clear strategic direction and intent, coupled with a strong and recognisable vision, were found to be critical to the success of the firms studied.[3]

Employment in or membership of an organisation almost by definition involves overlaps in purpose: people are working to the same overall goal. But in detail the picture is more complex. For one thing, there are degrees of alignment, ranging from substantial common ground and shared purpose at one end of the scale, through compatibility of purpose, to incompatibility, and to actively conflicting purposes at the other end. Purposes do not need to be identical. It may be enough that they don't conflict and are perceived to be fair. Transactional agreements are like this: 'I will enter into employment with your organisation because I need the money, and you need my skills.' However, compatible purposes of this kind seldom create high engagement. Conversely, successful teams rely on much higher degrees of Commonality, which often develops over time. Once the tentative initial discussion of the task is over, a process, direction or goal emerges, and shared purpose unlocks the latent energy of the group and allows it to be focused on achievement. The sense of working together, of pulling in the same direction, does not preclude disagreement, and difference is often beneficial – but shared purpose allows differing contributions to be aligned.

Shared purpose has a number of benefits.

---

[2] Mourkogiannis, *Purpose*, p. 6.

[3] D. R. Denison, S. Haaland and P. Goelzer, 'Corporate culture and organisational effectiveness: is Asia different from the rest of the world?', *Organisational Dynamics*, 33 (2004), pp. 98–109.

Shared Purpose Provides *a Reason for Entering into a Relationship*

Shared purpose can act as the rallying call for potential team members. It answers the question: is there something we really want to do together? It provides the context for the story of the relationship to develop and for its participants to have expectations of its future. The prospect of its fulfilment provides the incentive for the relationship to continue, despite difficulties and differences, perhaps. A lack of shared purpose can lead to higher levels of conflict within a relationship, as other forms of diversity become harder to harness and differences about fundamental preferences become a major source of contention.

Shared Purpose *Motivates*

Shared purpose unlocks energy, passion and commitment. It strengthens and directs contribution. Thus, not only can a wider range of resources be brought to bear, they can also be applied more effectively. Team members are likely to participate more fully, perhaps even going 'above and beyond the call of duty'. High levels of Commonality coupled with a lack of Parity in the relationship can therefore lead to the exploitation of some of those involved. On the other hand, a lack of Commonality, even where there is Parity, reduces both ownership of the issues and investment in the common good.

Shared Purpose *Improves the Quality of Outcomes*

Shared purpose increases focus on the activities of the relationship, and acts against forces that push towards compromise, narrowing and distortion:

- Poor service or product design may be the result of seeking to achieve a range of different goals, but meeting none of them well.
- When a lack of shared purpose reduces the ability to harness a wider range of resources, ambitious objectives that require the contribution of others cannot be realised.
- Perverse incentives, which neglect the real purpose of an organisation, arise when targets distort or replace the agreed outcomes. The overall quality of the outcomes is reduced – as is the case, for example, in education systems when teachers 'teach to the test' rather than seeking the development of cognitive and relational skills and the ability to apply a robust grounding of knowledge and understanding.

Shared Purpose *Enables Efficient Use of Resources*

Resources like time, finance, ideas or contacts can be brought together to achieve an objective. More can be achieved if the contributions of others are oriented towards a shared goal – more than any one individual or organisation could achieve alone. This has the side-effect of influencing the nature of the relationship and the satisfaction of the participants. Synergy is satisfying, productive and strengthens relationships. It also generates processes that work like chain reactions: one contribution sparks another, each being catalysed by, and taking up, some elements of what has gone before to create something new.

Shared Purpose *Provides a Basis for Collective Identity*

An organisation with a shared sense of purpose knows what it does, and why it does it. It will communicate organisational values and purpose to potential recruits through a carefully articulated brand identity. Likewise, a shared cause – such as the 'Make Poverty History' campaign of the early 2000s – brings together previously disparate individuals and organisations, giving them a collective sense of identity recognised both by participants and by those on the outside.

As with synergy, the degree to which shared identity or unity develops depends upon the degree of alignment of purpose. Also, the sense of collective identity and the feeling of belonging that derives from Continuity are closely allied, as are alignment and the development of a storyline to the relationship. Each can be the primary source of the sense of 'us' for the participants, and that sense of 'us', of belonging, may in some cases be more important than the purpose the group represents. Volunteers may assist a charity because they feel aligned with the cause or they may simply want a worthwhile activity and a feeling of companionship.

One model suggests that there are four main components to shared identity:[4]

1. *social goals*: shared by members of the group
2. *cognitive models*: shared worldviews or understandings of political and material conditions and interests
3. *'out-group' comparisons*: where there is a strong, threatening 'out-group' – those with whom raison d'être is not shared – 'in-group' identity and cohesion can be strengthened
4. *constitutive norms*: formal and informal rules that govern group membership.

---

[4] R. Abdelal, Y. Herrera, A. Johnston and R. McDermott, 'Identity as a variable', *Perspectives on Politics*, 4 (2006), pp. 695–711.

A strong sense of collective identity can, however, make it harder for those outside to join in. Sharing a sense of purpose is particularly important, but even beyond that, the separation between the 'us' of the insider and the 'them' of the outsider can be strong. The potential for a 'them and us' mentality to create a strong sense of unity within one group but at the expense of the relationship with other groups can be seen in ethnic conflict, industrial relations between unions and management, between different professions in public services, or in the competition between operational divisions or offices in companies, perhaps particularly when post-merger integration has been ineffective.

A membership ritual or induction is sometimes consciously or unconsciously employed to solve the problem of transforming the outsider into an insider – the boot camp, the graduate induction scheme, the payment of membership fees or other financial investment, shaking hands on a contract and so on. In other cases, such as moving into a new community or starting a new job, it just takes time and the development of a shared storyline.

A noteworthy study of the way purpose shapes identity was conducted on an American summer camp for boys in the early 1960s.[5] The experimenters found it easy to introduce 'them and us' feelings among the boys by splitting them into different cabins, giving the groups different names and encouraging competitive games between groups. Name-calling, food fights and cabin raids soon resulted, even in the context of joint activities. The purpose of each group was, sometimes implicitly, sometimes explicitly, wrapped up in competing against the other groups, in coming out 'on top'. Robert Cialdini summarises how the experimenters successfully reversed this through introducing situations where competition would have harmed everyone's interests and where cooperation between groups was necessary to achieve an overarching common purpose, for example by arranging an interruption to the camp's water supply:

We can trace the roots of this surprising turnaround to those times when the boys had to view one another as allies instead of opponents. The crucial procedure was the experimenters' imposition of common goals on the groups. It was the cooperation required to achieve these goals that finally allowed the rival group members to experience one another as reasonable fellows, valued helpers, and friends. And when success resulted from mutual efforts, it became especially difficult to maintain feelings of hostility towards those who had been teammates in the triumph.[6]

---

[5] M. Sherif, J. White, C. W. Sherif, W. R. Hood and O. J. Harvey, *Intergroup Conflict and Cooperation: The Robbers' Cave Experiment* (Norman, OH: University of Oklahoma Institute of Intergroup Relations, 1961).

[6] R. B. Cialdini, *Influence: The Psychology of Persuasion* (New York: William Morrow & Co., 1984), p. 181.

Problems with Purpose

Although shared purpose is an emotive aspiration, in practice what organisations seek to achieve is more modest: a greater degree of alignment. Two problems in particular, fuzzy purposes and evolving purposes, stand out:

Fuzzy Purposes

Purpose can be fuzzy because different views have not been articulated or reconciled. Organisations lack a clear purpose when multiple individual views have not been resolved. Bringing clarity and agreement is therefore a key leadership task. The CEO of VeriSign, a provider of internet infrastructure services, put it like this: 'It comes down to charting a course – having the ability to articulate for your employees where you're headed and how you're going to get there.'[7]

Individual participants in the relationship can also lack a clearly defined purpose. For some people, purpose is tied to clearly defined goals which they may pursue with adamantine willpower – hard to deflect, unwilling to give up – making others bend to the force of their sense of purpose. But others have little sense of purpose at all. Still others are more process-oriented, happy to serve a wide range of purposes and finding their satisfaction in the use of skills that enable the goals of others to be achieved. Some people are happiest working for an organisation in whose goals they passionately believe. But others feel great satisfaction in knowing that their skills and experience are well used and valued by their employer, more or less regardless of what the company does. Still others fail to engage at all. William Damon, a Stanford University psychologist, surveyed 1,200 young people between the ages of twelve and twenty-six over a period of five years. He found that a quarter of the young people were 'disengaged', meaning that they expressed no particular wider purpose for their lives and were not involved in activities that might help them find one.[8]

Fuzzy purpose can also be the result of poor delegation. The team is not quite sure of the extent of its responsibilities because they have not been spelled out, because there are tacit assumptions on one or more sides, or because activities

---

[7] S. Shinn, '21st century engineer', *BizEd* (January–February 2005), pp. 18–23.

[8] W. Damon, *The Path to Purpose: Helping Our Children Find Their Calling in Life* (New York: Free Press, 2008). See also W. Damon, 'Majority of youths found to lack a direction in life', interview in *Education Week*, June 11, 2008.

which appeared to have been clearly delegated have been retrieved, perhaps unconsciously, by the delegator or are being carried out by someone else. The reality for many people is that purpose is a poorly articulated approximate direction that often has more to do with instinct than reason. When allying purpose with values, Goleman states: 'Personal values are not lofty abstractions, but intimate credos that we may never quite articulate in words so much as feel. Our values translate into what has emotional power or resonance for us, whether negative or positive.'[9] A fuzzy purpose is, therefore, not necessarily a clear-cut disagreement, but may be experienced more as a sense of unease – feeling uncomfortable about the direction of travel without being able to explain precisely why.

Evolving Purposes

Purpose is often not fixed. Circumstances, beliefs and values can all change. Organisational or community purpose can change as leaders or other participants change. Policy change following elections may lead to different objectives for public services and other agencies. New CEOs may seek new strategic directions, reflecting fundamental changes in value and purpose. The raison d'être may change with company ownership, when private firms go public or following hostile takeovers.

In partnership contexts, change in purpose can be more difficult to manage. It may lead to a parting of the ways, amicable or otherwise. Business partners, pop groups, faith communities and campaign groups have all split to pursue different interests and objectives. Alternatively purpose can change in tandem, with participants continuing to hold their alignment and sense of corporate identity. Long-lasting marriages negotiate changes in child-rearing, work and leisure over decades. Adaptive organisations reinvent themselves to take into account changing market conditions or cultural context. Interface, for example, is a global floor coverings company whose founder and chairman has led a journey towards a commitment to sustainability – a shift in purpose that had many implications for employees and suppliers.[10] Following what he describes as an 'epiphany', Ray Anderson provided his global team with a mission to convert Interface to a restorative enterprise; first by reaching sustainability in business practices, and then becoming truly restorative – a company returning more than it takes – by helping others reach sustainability.

---

[9] D. Goleman, *Working with Emotional Intelligence* (New York: Bantam Books, 1998).

[10] Interface Global, 'Our sustainability journey – mission zero', www.interfaceglobal.com/Sustainability/Interface-Story.aspx.

Multiple Purposes

Developing shared or aligned purpose is also complex because the individuals in a relationship or team may be working to fulfil multiple purposes linked to different roles and relationships with others. If I am a member of a team with a shared purpose defined by its responsibility for a set of activities, say, then I will meet with them regularly to make sure that we are making effective progress. But at the same time I also want to:

- ensure access to resources for another project in which I am involved with another team
- ensure that longer-term organisational objectives are not minimised
- develop the relationship with particular participants
- maintain my status in a wider community of interest, and
- ensure the work is finished by a certain time to meet family commitments.

Each of these may impinge upon the way in which the purpose of any given relationship, and my personal purposes in participating in it, are articulated, and on the way in which purposes are aligned or shared. At worst, the presence of multiple purposes may encourage only a shallow and temporary sense of common purpose, or none at all.

Role conflict is sometimes cited as a cause of tension and stress in working life. But lying behind the conflict between different roles is often the conflict between different relational purposes. Different relationships are required by the different roles, and trouble arises when the purposes of each of the relationships is not compatible. When UK health policy assigned greater priority to public health, and gave family doctors a greater role in the commissioning of healthcare, they reported purpose conflict across different relationships. In their relationship with an individual patient a doctor prioritises advocacy of their needs in order to make the best medicines available to them. But in their relationship with the public authority managing the budget (for a taxpayer-funded national service) family doctors also have a responsibility to manage health resources for the community appropriately, keeping prescribing budgets under control, and meeting targets in doing so. These two purposes will at some point conflict.

Sometimes 'purpose conflict' arises because a single relationship has to bear more than one purpose. In the Relationships Foundation's work in prisons, a single relationship – between officers and offenders – had to fulfil two purposes: maintaining security and control, and seeking the effective rehabilitation of offenders. These different tasks involve different relationship styles. A similar tension can exist where a relationship is built around the activities of both managerial supervision and pastoral care. Systems may be in place to identify and remove such conflicts of purpose – for example, if you are involved in the purchase or commissioning of a service from companies in which you or your relatives have a financial interest. But with multiple purposes in a single relationship, or overlapping between relationships, you cannot always simply abstain from decisions. Scott Page, Professor of Complex Systems, Political Science and Economics at the University of Michigan, recognises the dilemmas and tensions to which this might lead, but also the creative richness of those who work with multiple roles and purposes:

The fullness of their lives produces these inconsistencies. Most of us would accept this trade-off. We would willingly accept contradictions in exchange for a fullness and richness of roles and ideas. Teams, groups and entire societies might well accept this same compromise, for to be large enough to contain contradictions also makes them large enough to solve problems.[11]

Time-Bound Purposes

Different stakeholders in a relationship may have different time horizons for their purposes. Financial markets are often accused of pursuing short-term financial returns at the expense of the long-term interest of companies and society. Hedge funds, for example, were notoriously described by the German politician Franz Müntefering as locusts – profiting without any interest in, or responsibility for, longer-term consequences: 'Some financial investors don't waste any thoughts on the people whose jobs they destroy. They remain anonymous, have no face, fall like a plague of locusts over our companies, devour everything, then fly on to the next one.'[12]

The Relationships Foundation's examination of the relationship between a health authority and a provider trust revealed that the average time in post for a commissioning manager was around nine months. However, the doctors providing care often held the same job for many years and were working with patients with long-term conditions. They had a view of the change that could be made which extended over years. Alignment can be achieved through a

[11] S. Page, *The Difference: How the Power of Diversity Creates Better Groups, Forms, Schools and Societies* (Princeton University Press, 2007), p. 284.
[12] A. Evans-Pritchard, '"Swarms of locusts" man in German coalition', *Telegraph*, 14 October 2005, www.telegraph.co.uk/finance/2923841/Swarms-of-locusts-man-in-German-coalition.html.

shared strategy that reconciles the different time horizons if it takes a clear view of how shorter-term targets contribute to longer-term goals. But in this case the nominally agreed shared strategy was rarely in the frame when critical contract discussions were being held.

There may also be time-related differences in purpose in a single relationship or within the same organisation. Acute immediate financial needs, or pressure to achieve targets, can undermine longer-term goals. Companies may cut the investment that is key to their future to meet short-term targets. A commissioner of a service facing a budget shortfall may squeeze the provider who is the weakest negotiator in order to meet short-term savings targets, but at the risk of losing a better-value supplier in the long term. Opposition parties such as the Conservatives in the UK following their defeat in 1997, Labour in Australia during the Howard premiership between 1996 and 2007, and perhaps Republicans in the USA following their 2008 defeat, needed to resist the temptation to demonstrate short-term progress at the expense of the longer-term project of building a winning philosophy and support base.

Prioritised Purposes

Purpose can be shared in many contexts: individuals share purpose in groups, organisations share purpose in partnerships, individuals and organisations share purpose in aligning motivation, while organisations and society may share a purpose where legitimacy and licence to operate requires corporate social responsibility. There is, for example, increasing expectation that social and environmental concerns will be part of corporate purpose. The multiple purposes of an individual applied across the many relationships to which they are party then raises the question of the extent to which purpose can be aligned in each of these relationships.

This is partly a question of priority. Professional ethics for doctors and lawyers require that client or patient interests come first. It may be a consequence of power: some individuals or organisations will have greater 'gravitational pull' to ensure that the purposes of others are aligned around their interests. It may be a consequence of presence: those who are visible and 'at the table' shape purpose while others are out of sight and out of mind. It may also be a consequence of Continuity: long-term valued customers are prioritised over those who are perceived to offer one-time-only contracts.

Purpose may be misaligned, and the prioritisation of interests contested. One of the lessons from the 2008 credit crunch has been the need to revisit the problem of agency in organisations. Directors are, formally, agents of share-holders, but may in practice act as principals. Pay is increased by taking risks, but with the costs of those risks being borne by the providers of capital – shareholders and lenders. Thus the goals of directors (the ego and financial rewards of big deals) may be served by riskier and more extensive borrowing, acquisition, or lending than is in shareholders' interests. Shareholders may be complicit in this in chasing short-term returns with the option (not always exercised in time) to sell out before long-term realities put the company out of business.

Diversified Purposes

Aligning purpose quickly confronts the challenges – and opportunities – presented by difference and diversity. People differ in many respects, as do organisations: different preferences, different ways of doing things, different skills and different ways of thinking. Even when our goals are the same, our ways of achieving them or living them may be various. Moreover, creativity and innovation are sparked by the interplay of different insights. High-performing teams harness a diversity of skills. At a basic level, difference is an inevitable property of human life; at its best difference is the driver of creativity and produces the complex beauty of harmony.

Commonality can be described as all the participants in a relationship or team pulling in the same direction. But it is important to understand how complementarity and homogeneity connect. In musical terms it is the difference between singing in harmony and singing in unison. When a choir sings in unison, its members all sing the same notes: it is not discordant, but it also lacks colour and depth. Harmony, on the other hand, is the product of many voices singing different notes: its effect depends on the various patterns of notes complementing and reinforcing each other. Similarly, in teams and organisations, homogeneity is not the same as complementarity, though both exhibit an absence of discord. It generally takes more work to maintain harmony among a diverse group than unison among one that is uniform. However, although homogeneous teams tend to experience less conflict, they are also less good at reaching effective solutions. High levels of Commonality, and specifically high levels of alignment, can be achieved through either complementarity or homogeneity but the loss of diversity carries with it the risks of 'groupthink', lack of innovation and insularity.

Scott Page, Professor of Complex Systems, Political Science and Economics at the University of Michigan, has analysed how difference can create better groups, firms, schools and societies.[13] He provides the detailed mathematical modelling and theories to explain why crowds can be wise, and better at prediction, than experts, and the importance of diversity in this. Behind the modelling is the insight that a diverse group will use a wider range of predictive models and be able to see solutions that more homogeneous groups miss.

The availability of multiple resources and skills enables diverse groups to be more innovative and creative in problem-solving than homogeneous groups.[14] Diversity enables groups to avoid becoming stuck at sub-optimal solutions, in contrast to groupthink, where shared assumptions and patterns of thought have become so entrenched that existing solutions are not challenged and problems may not be recognised.

The benefits of difference in groups also apply at a national policy level. This is the basis of the argument for greater plurality of provision in public services. By 'letting a thousand flowers bloom', a choice-based approach can weed out the worst and encourage the best. Allowing different providers to try different ways of working makes it more likely that service improvements will be identified. Plurality not only gives space for different thinking, it also allows experimentation and testing that would be less likely in a monopolistic monoculture.

Low levels of Commonality, whether there is diversity or not, mean that teams don't work well together, staff retention rates decrease and sub-groups become isolated within their communities. Diversity in the context of low levels of Commonality can lead to either conflict or withdrawal. Drawing on current US data, for example, Robert Putnam concludes that ethnic diversity does not necessarily trigger in-group/out-group division and conflict, but more often can be a source of anomie and isolation:

Diversity does not produce bad race relations or ethnically defined group hostility, our findings suggest. Rather, inhabitants of diverse communities tend to withdraw from collective life. To distrust their neighbours, regardless of the colour of their skin, to withdraw even from close friends, to expect the worst from their community and its leaders, to volunteer less, give less to charity and work on community projects less often, to register to vote less, to agitate for social reform more, but have less faith that

[13] Page, *The Difference.*
[14] F. Rink and N. Ellemers, 'Diversity as a basis for shared organisational identity: the norm congruity principle', *British Journal of Management*, 18 (2007), pp. S17–S27.

they can actually make a difference, and to huddle unhappily in front of the television. Note that this pattern encompasses attitude and behaviour, bridging and bonding social capital, public and private connections. Diversity at least in the short run, seems to bring out the turtle in all of us.[15]

Putnam comes to some pointed conclusions about the effect of diversity without shared purpose:[16]

- Across workgroups in the USA and Europe internal heterogeneity (in terms of age, professional background, ethnicity, tenure and other factors) is generally associated with lower group cohesion, lower satisfaction and higher turnover.
- Across countries greater ethnic heterogeneity is associated with lower social trust.
- In local areas ethnic diversity is sometimes associated with lower investment in public goods, default in micro-credit cooperatives, less voluntary fundraising, or collective infrastructure maintenance.
- In experimental game settings such as the prisoner's dilemma, players who are more different from one another (regardless of whether or not they actually know one another) are more likely to cheat or defect.
- Within companies of the Union Army in the American Civil War the greater the heterogeneity in terms of age, hometown and occupation, the greater the desertion rate.

Putnam is ultimately hopeful for the long-term benefits of diversity, not least because of the increased creativity and growth it can generate. He sees the solution in recognising that identities can be reformed and reconstructed. Writing again about ethnic diversity and social cohesion he states: '[I]n particular it seems important to encourage permeable, syncretic, hyphenated identities; identities that enable previously separated ethic groups to see themselves, in part, as members of a shared group with a shared identity.'[17]

Another possible outcome of diverse preferences results from the underprovision of common resources, where the available resources for things of shared interest or value are spread thinly. Page offers the illustration of the allocation of space in a house. A family that likes doing the same things would be expected to choose a house with more shared space. A family with very

---

[15] R. Putnam, 'E pluribus unum: diversity and community in the twenty-first century', *Scandinavian Political Studies*, 30 (2007), pp. 137–174.
[16] *Ibid.*
[17] *Ibid.*

different interests may end up with a tiny kitchen and living room combination to create more individual space for their diverse preferences.[18] Similarly, there is a tendency for there to be less willingness to invest in common goods in diverse communities. Ethnically diverse villages, for example, have been shown to be less likely to build or maintain wells and bridges. Shared communal responsibility for common goods is dissipated, and there is less willingness to invest in things that benefit 'others'.[19]

Thoughtless Purposes

'Groupthink' refers to a phenomenon where members of a group tend to seek concurrence to the extent that any attempt to critically consider, analyse and appraise alternative ideas or options is non-existent, discouraged or actively undermined. Members refrain from expressing deviant, minority, or unpopular views because they don't want to rock the boat or anger others, they are afraid that others will think their ideas are foolish or embarrassing, or they simply hope to avoid conflict.[20] An illusion of unanimity is created by the lack of views and alternative voices. Abstention is taken as a 'yes' vote.[21] This is, in part, a failure of Parity, but gives rise to a false sense of Commonality, where surface-level agreement can mask deeper disagreement and disillusionment. The group risks making decisions that are hasty, irrational and poorly thought through.

Studies have noted symptoms of groupthink in the US Navy's lack of preparation at Pearl Harbor, the American invasion of North Korea, the Bay of Pigs fiasco, the escalation of the Vietnam War, the Challenger and Columbia space shuttle disasters and the NASA decision processes in relation to the failure of the main mirror on the Hubble telescope.[22] Following the Bay of Pigs invasion,

---

[18] Page, *The Difference*, p. 282.

[19] Putnam, 'E pluribus unum'.

[20] See, for example, I. L. Janis, *Groupthink* (Boston, MA: Houghton Mifflin, 1982); J. N. Choi and M. U. Kim, 'The organisational application of groupthink and its limits in organisations', *Journal of Applied Psychology*, 84 (1999), pp. 297–306; and W. W. Park, 'A comprehensive empirical investigation of the relationships among variables of the groupthink model', *Journal of Organisational Behavior*, 21 (2000), pp. 873–887.

[21] Janis, *Groupthink*.

[22] Janis, *Groupthink*; G. Moorhead, R. Ference and C. P. Neck, 'Group decision fiascos continue: space shuttle Challenger and a revised groupthink framework', *Human Relations*, 44 (1991), pp. 539–550; E. J. Chisson, *The Hubble Wars* (New York: Harper Perennial, 1994); and C. Covault, 'Columbia revelations: alarming e-mails speak for themselves. But Administrator O'Keefe is more concerned about Board findings on NASA decision-making', *Aviation Week & Space Technology*, March 3, 2003, p. 26.

and purportedly having learned the lessons, President John F. Kennedy sought to avoid groupthink during the Cuban missile crisis by inviting external experts to share their opinions and allowing for critical questioning during meetings. President Kennedy also actively encouraged group members to discuss possible solutions with trusted members of their separate departments, and was deliberately absent from some meetings in order to avoid members acquiescing in his opinion.[23]

Not unexpectedly, research into groupthink has found that it is more likely to occur where there is a clear – and by implication, strong – group identity, when members hold a positive image of their group that they want to protect, and when the group perceives a collective threat to this positive image.[24] These are also symptoms of healthy Commonality. The key to recognising the difference is to explore how diversity is handled.

How to Manage Commonality

As with other types of Relational Proximity, Commonality can be represented on a grid (Table 8.1).

For the individual, purpose can be set internally or externally, with both factors usually operating together: I am accountable to other people and also have my own purposes. When participants come together, relational purpose is formed from the alignment of individual purposes, which in turn come from internal or external sources. People differ in their strength of purpose and the extent to which it is internally or externally determined. For organisations,

Table 8.1: Appropriate and inappropriate experience of high and low degrees of Commonality

High Commonality	Groupthink	Synergy
Low Commonality	Internal conflict	Autonomy
	Felt as inappropriate	Felt as appropriate

---

[23] I. L. Janis, *Victims of Groupthink* (Boston: Houghton Mifflin, 1972).

[24] M. E. Turner and A. R. Pratkanis, 'Mitigating groupthink by stimulating constructive conflict', in C. De Dreu and E. Van de Vliert (eds.), *Using Conflict in Organisations* (London: Sage, 1997), pp. 53–71.

purpose can be set within the organisation, or imposed from outside – by a parent organisation, the market, regulators or government policy.

The internal and external sources of purpose can be categorised in terms of ethics, needs, identity and targets.

'Because I Believe it's Right'

Purpose that derives from internal beliefs and values has considerable strength. Nikos Mourkogiannis argues that: 'Purpose is your moral DNA. It's what you believe without having to think.' It is inextricably linked to the values of an individual or an organisation, those things which a person, company or community believe to be of most importance in their life or existence – profit, learning, friends, caring, faith, success and so on. He goes on to argue that it is 'the primary source of achievement' and 'reveals the underlying dynamics of any human activity, the most fundamental issues involving motivation and behaviour, in either a community or an organisation. It's the core energy, the element that fuels everything else, big and small.'[25]

For companies, Mourkogiannis suggests four basic orientations of value-based purpose:

- discovery – which celebrates the new and is oriented towards choice
- excellence – which celebrates the good and is oriented towards fulfilment
- altruism – which celebrates the helpful and is oriented towards happiness, and
- heroism – which celebrates the effective and is oriented towards achievement.

Mourkogiannis argues that there is increasing evidence that these purposes are more motivating and transformational, and are more attuned to relational complexity and behaviour, than task/financial purpose.[26]

Ownership structure and leadership style affect the extent to which, and the manner in which, moral purpose shapes organisations. We have already mentioned how Ray Anderson's belief in sustainability changed the purpose of Interface. Business owners have greater freedom to shift collective purpose in this way. So the implications for organisational purpose are an essential factor to consider in floating companies or in demutualising. When John

---

[25] Mourkogiannis, *Purpose*, p. 6.
[26] *Ibid.*, p. 112.

Lewis turned his retail business into an employee-owned enterprise in 1929 he enshrined his concern for employees in this statement to safeguard the link between the organisation's purpose and his values: 'The Partnership's ultimate purpose is the happiness of all its members, through their worthwhile and satisfying employment in a successful business.'

Conviction politicians pursue their purpose despite opposition and difficult circumstances. Margaret Thatcher's commitment to policies to counter inflation and restructure the British economy was not solely rooted in the belief that a particular policy was the best way to achieve a goal, but also in her belief in the importance of that goal. The close relationship between her political purpose and her beliefs is illustrated in her famous statement: 'to those waiting with bated breath for that favourite media catchphrase, the U-turn, I have only one thing to say: You turn if you want to. The lady's not for turning!'[27] In the 2000s, New Labour sought to pursue what was termed 'tight–loose' policy: a tight definition of key goals with a loose and pragmatic approach to what works. This was in contrast to the 'tight–tight' policy of 'old' Labour with its ideological commitment to such policies as nationalisation as the means by which social justice goals should be pursued.[28]

Beliefs may, of course, be wrong. Ideological purity can be pursued with destructive fanaticism. But a resonant and coherent political narrative – a sense that political purpose is anchored in personal and collective party values – is recognised as important in defining the relationship between the electorate and those who seek power. David Boyle, co-founder of Time Banks UK, explains:

A narrative is not a slogan and not a USP. It is – for a political party at least – an idea or set of linked ideas that lies behind what we say and believe. It provides an explanation for the policies we have, a way of remembering and believing them. Supermarkets can sell anything, after all. Political parties are there for a purpose – get that purpose across to people and they might begin to hear what we say.[29]

Developing a shared sense of purpose between two individuals or organisations, or within a group, may well involve a conversation in which values

---

[27] Margaret Thatcher, 'The lady's not for turning', Speech to Conservative Party conference, 10 October 1980.

[28] The two-by-two matrix describing end and means as tight or loose is used by a number of management writers including, for example, J. Birkinshaw, *Reinventing Management: Smarter Choices for Getting Work Done* (San Francisco, CA: Jossey-Bass, 2010).

[29] D. Boyle, 'In search of a political narrative', D. Boyle: Politics of the future (blog), August 2005, www.david-boyle.co.uk/politics/narrative.html.

are explored. Common values or a shared ethical framework create their own sense of alignment upon which shared or aligned purpose can be built. When communities of different faiths recognise the shared values – of care, of the importance of family relationships, of a critique of consumerism, say – then collaboration in dealing with local social problems or lobbying government is realisable.

Purpose may have a range of ethical roots. In some cases profoundly different philosophical views may give rise to different organisational purposes. In criminal justice, for example, the purpose of prisons will differ if they are shaped by a commitment to retribution, rehabilitation, or an understanding of justice as resolving the relationship between victims, offenders and society.[30] The nursing profession has had to reflect whether care is rooted in compassion and love, and focused on the needs of the patient, or more narrowly defined technical competence constrained by organisational targets.[31] When trust in business has been compromised – for example, following the 2008 banking crisis – the businesses involved are often accused of losing sight of their purpose. So, for example, the Salz Review on Barclays' business practices suggested that: 'Bank leaders became identified with driving profit and shareholder return rather than promoting a clear sense of purpose, instilling good values, and doing the right thing for the customer and the long-term good of the organisation.'[32] Purpose, values and organisational culture are all interrelated. Organisations need to be alert both to fundamental disagreements about the values and beliefs that inform purpose, and to the ease with which such drivers of purpose can be squeezed out by other demands.

'Because I Need It'

Need can range from hard-wired biological responses to stimuli such as hunger, to choices that support emotional and psychological wellbeing. A drug addict may steal to fund their habit, a woman enter prostitution as the only

---

[30] See, for example, J. Burnside and N. Baker, *Relational Justice: Repairing the Breach* (Winchester: Waterside Press, 2004).

[31] Such issues are often raised in the context of public concerns about the quality of care, but have deeper philosophical roots, as discussed, for example, in A. Bradshaw, *Lighting the Lamp: Spiritual Dimension of Nursing Care (RCN Research)* (London: Scutari Press, 1994).

[32] A. Salz, 'The Salz Review: an independent review of Barclays' business practices', April 2013, para 8.6, http://online.wsj.com/public/resources/documents/Review04032013.pdf, accessed 15 October 2015.

way to provide for her children, a worker choose a less fulfilling career for higher pay, or an organisation make tactical choices to ensure survival rather than any deeper-rooted purpose. Organisations also have needs – for example, to maintain cash-flow in order to secure short-term survival.

Our needs, though, are not only at the level of survival. 'I wanted something more' is often the explanation for leaving one work or personal relationship and entering another. The desires for meaning, fulfilment and recognition, for instance, are powerful forces. Rosenberg avoids the idea of a hierarchy of needs (unlike Maslow) and identifies a range of needs that may be important to people. These are grouped as the need for connection, physical wellbeing, honesty, joy, peace, meaning and autonomy.[33] Doyal and Gough suggest this can be reduced to three basic needs of relatedness, autonomy and competence.[34]

Needs such as these are firstly a driver for the purpose of individuals, but they will also be a strong influence on shared purpose. Companies that seek to align staff to an organisational purpose will be more successful if the need-driven purposes of its staff are, at least partially, met in the course of organisational life. The principles of these individually located needs can be extrapolated to a larger organisational scale. They include the drive to survive – maintaining share price or profit, keeping investors happy, sourcing funding – or organisational versions of self-actualisation such as a decent market share, recognition as a market leader, or making an impact. So the development of shared or aligned purpose must take into account, implicitly or explicitly, the needs and expectations of those involved. And choices must be made as to whether those needs can reasonably be met by this relationship, and the risks to a sense of common purpose if they are not.

The organisational psychologists Robert Kegan and Lisa Laskow Lahey have explored why some employees won't change.[35] They suggest that 'Resistance to change does not reflect opposition, nor is it merely a result of inertia. Instead, even as they hold a sincere commitment to change, many people are unwittingly applying productive energy toward a hidden *competing commitment*.' These commitments may be rooted in quite complex personal needs. The authors cite a range of examples such as a manager unable to change

---

[33] M. Rosenberg, *Nonviolent Communication: A Language of Life* (Encinitas, CA: PuddleDancer Press, 2003).

[34] L. Doyal and I. Gough, *A Theory of Human Need* (London: Palgrave Macmillan, 1991).

[35] R. Kegan and L. Laskow Lahey, 'The real reason people won't change', *Harvard Business Review*, November 2001, pp. 85–92, emphasis in the original.

his behaviour to enable better integration with the team because it felt like disloyalty to his racial group. 'In short, while John was genuinely committed to working well with his colleagues, he had an equally powerful competing commitment to keeping his distance.' Kegan and Laskow Lahey conclude that success in addressing this is about 'understanding the complexities of people's behaviour, guiding them through a productive process to bring their competing commitments to the surface, and helping them cope with the inner conflict that is preventing them from achieving their goals.'

The nature and strength of people's needs, and therefore the nature of their purpose, can be shaped by external factors. Advertising and peer pressure influence the sense of material need or focus it in particular directions. Satisfaction of need in one relationship may reduce that need in another. Thus, addressing the influence of needs on shared purpose is not solely about individually located interventions, but also about shaping the environment in which the needs are formed or exist. It is this that gives organisations, governments and the media the opportunity to change the perception of needs and collective purpose. We should note, however, that any external influence on purpose will also be shaped by people's experience and thus the same external factors may influence the purpose of different relationships in different ways.

'Because This is Who I Am'

Anthony Giddens has highlighted how the shift to a post-modern culture has brought questions of personal identity to the fore: 'What to do? How to act? Who to be? These are focal questions for everyone living in circumstances of late modernity.'[36]

In this context the questions of meaning, purpose, identity and significance are all closely inter-related as individuals work to make sense of their lives. The relationships of work, family, politics and leisure can become increasingly suborned to this personal project, which struggles with a fundamental tension between the identity of individual uniqueness and the identity bestowed by social belonging. Purpose becomes part of this creative project. As we have already explored in this chapter, purpose generates a sense of corporate and individual identity – a team finds its sense of 'we're all in this together' as it coalesces around its purpose of managing a crisis. But purpose, whether group

---

[36] A. Giddens, *Modernity and Self-Identity: Self and Society in the Late Modern Age* (Cambridge: Polity Press, 1991), p. 70.

or individual, can also be an expression – sometimes experimental – of existing or emerging identity. Thus identity can also be a *source* of purpose.

Organisational purpose can also be internally driven, not just as a product of the internal purpose of the leaders, but as an expression of corporate culture and identity. While some organisations' statements of purpose are transient, communicating the latest strategy, others have deep historic and cultural roots that influence the way the organisation operates.

'Because I'm Required To'

Sometimes it is necessary to serve a purpose set by someone else – your boss, head office, a regulator, a politician or 'the market'. Whether we agree with it or not we are required to pursue this purpose, face sanctions, or leave. The purpose of public services is defined, at least in part, by legislation, although professional ethics and user priorities are also powerful influences – both directly and through their impact on legislation. Different political and ideological views of the purpose of an institution may be enshrined in legislation and expressed in legal duties, contracts and targets. Central banks in different countries or currency unions differ with regard to how goals of price stability, growth and employment are to be balanced. These external purposes and expectations are not always consistent.

An example of how legislation can change the purpose and culture of an organisation can be seen in reforms to the Probation Service in the UK and its subsequent integration into a new National Offender Management Service (NOMS). A key change was explained in Parliament:

The statutory requirement to 'advise, assist and befriend' was deleted from the relevant legislation when the Probation Order became the Community Rehabilitation Order under the 1991 Criminal Justice Act. The Criminal Justice Act 2003 (s. 142) sets down five purposes of sentencing. Within this approach, Offender Managers will select one of the four broad options for which the one-word labels – PUNISH, HELP, CHANGE and CONTROL – are a 'shorthand'.[37]

However, externally set targets can distort organisational purpose when they become ends in themselves and orient activity to achieve targets – often in ways that 'fix' the figures – rather than in achieving less clearly articulated,

---

[37] Written answer, *Hansard*, 10 September 2007 Column 1996w, www.parliament.the-stationery-office.co.uk/pa/cm200607/cmhansrd/cm070910/text/70910w0024.htm.

and perhaps unmeasured, outcomes that matter to stakeholders. This is a particular problem when accountability to the target-setter is much stronger than to other stakeholders and therefore has the power to distort purpose.

Businesses can also undermine common purpose and create perverse incentives through targets. Professor Michael Mainelli describes the impact of targets on call-centre agents in a bank.[38] Given a target to complete calls within a specified time limit they often prematurely ended many of the profitable, but complex and time-consuming, transactions. The situation was made worse when a second help-line, set up to catch dissatisfied customers threatening to leave, reduced the resources available to the main help-line. The time available per customer was thus further reduced, increasing the temptation to end calls to meet targets. While the second help-line was successful at retaining customers, the rate of customers threatening to leave increased. A series of misselling scandals by banks and other financial institutions has also illustrated the way in which performance targets and bonus systems can undermine the relationship with customers. As the Salz Review into Barclays Bank reported:

There has been much debate on the moral hazards of basing the incentives of a retail bank sales force on achieving sales volumes thereby underemphasising customer needs and suitability. We have concluded that the sales focus of the incentive schemes in place [in two divisions] were likely to have contributed to alleged mis-selling of certain products.[39]

When the UK government introduced a target for waiting time for Accident and Emergency care, with the clock starting to tick when a patient is officially handed over to hospital staff, the John Radcliffe Hospital in Oxford started to delay taking on patients from ambulances and created an ambulance waiting area. Although Department of Health guidelines indicated that patients should wait no more than fifteen minutes before being transferred into the care of hospital staff, neither the hospital nor ambulance trust was held accountable for this. Many ambulances ended up waiting at the hospital and so they struggled to meet their target eight-minute response time. One paramedic commented to a BBC reporter: 'The longest I actually waited was five hours, sometimes half the crews were waiting so the other half of the crews were running from one end of the county to the other, taking longer and longer to get to the calls. When it

---

[38] M. Mainelli, 'The perverse and the reverse: how bad measures skew markets', Lecture, Gresham College, London, 17 October 2005, www.gresham.ac.uk/lectures-and-events/the-perverse-and-the-reverse-how-bad-measures-skew-markets, accessed 20 October 2015.

[39] Salz, 'Salz Review', section 11:34.

was really bad, there could be as many as seven ambulances just waiting.' The trust chief executives were able to resolve the issue, but it is a stark example of how targets can displace proper purpose – in this case, patient care.[40]

A weaker form of compulsion in purpose, of course, is simply following the herd. Philip Zimbardo has described this as 'the Lucifer effect',[41] arguing that rotten barrels can make rotten apples. He also sees this as at least part of the explanation for the abusive conduct of US military prison guards at Abu Ghraib in Iraq.

Ways to Create Commonality

- What is the task that the team has been asked to undertake?
- How does the organisation define its purpose?
- What is it that the group has gathered together to do?
- What difference are we going to make to the community?
- Why are we here?

These are in a broad sense all questions about purpose in group relationships. It is possible for a relationship to have a strong sense of belonging based on the story of being together in the past, but without a sense of purpose the relationship risks aimlessness. The purpose may be something with a strong forward movement like a task to undertake, a problem to solve, or a mission to support or nurture. It may need to include a definition of long-term raison d'être or some clear time-limited goals. It may need to be explicitly aligned with closely held values, or imagined as a future vision. It will normally involve more than one of these.

Sometimes the purpose pre-dates the relationship: it is already apparent, perhaps in the form of something that needs to be done, and a team is assigned to undertake it; or, in the case of a campaign, say, a team or group coalesces around it. Sometimes the relationship exists first without there being much sense of purpose or vision: then, there are two paths to follow. Either it is the work of the group together to define or discover a purpose, in which case, the leader's role may be to facilitate the process of discovering common ground. Or a leader or group of leaders defines the purpose for the organisation and then works to enable others to catch the vision. There are five strategies that help with this.

[40] BBC Panorama, 'Fiddling the figures', BBC, Transcript, 26 June 2003, http://news.bbc.co.uk/nol/shared/spl/hi/programmes/panorama/transcripts/fiddlingthefigures.txt.
[41] P. Zimbardo, The Lucifer Effect: How Good People Turn Evil (London: Rider & Co., 2007).

Articulate Purpose

One of the primary tasks of an organisational or team leader is to articulate purpose and vision. It is hard to share purpose among a group or within a relationship unless it is expressed to those involved in terms they can understand – whether this is in writing, in an image, verbally or, in some circumstances, enacted. The most powerful purpose is usually presented and shared in more than one of these ways. Churchill's reference in 1940 to 'the broad, sunlit lands' of freedom[42] in his speech in Parliament, though delivered verbally, created emotive images in listeners' minds that significantly added to its ability to inspire a nation.

In a similar way to the use of images, symbols and symbolic actions can help to articulate an organisation's or team's purpose at an emotional level, connecting those sharing it more deeply. These could range from the choice of workplace furnishing (expensive, functional, minimal, or fun) to choice of layout (private offices, open plan, café space, hot desks), or to the way in which people are celebrated (team parties, individual thanks, birthdays). The emotional connection that images and symbols enable is described in Chapter 4 on Directness, together with practical approaches to supporting the emotional component of communication.

In the same speech, Churchill also uses a technique that could be termed the 'anti-purpose', in his reference to 'the abyss of a new Dark Age, made more sinister, and perhaps more protracted, by the lights of perverted science'. If purpose is described in terms of where a relationship or organisation is heading, then the 'anti-purpose' describes what it is avoiding. Darryl Conner, in his book *Managing at the Speed of Change*, terms this the 'burning platform' – the need to escape is what propels you forward.[43]

Some of the most engaging leaders are those who model purpose and in doing so articulate, or perhaps reveal, it to those around them, enabling it to be adopted by others. Where purpose is structured around achieving a task, this is a leader who is prepared to muck in. But where purpose is congruent with a leader's identity the effect is even more charismatic. Writing about leadership and followership, Alexander Haslam suggests that it is useful to think of leaders as 'entrepreneurs of identity' who help 'create, coordinate and control the sense

---

[42] W. Churchill, 'Their finest hour', Speech to the House of Commons, 18 June 1940, HC Deb., 18 June 1940, vol. 362 cc51–64.

[43] D. Conner, *Managing at the Speed of Change: How Resilient Managers Succeed and Prosper Where Others Fail* (New York: Random House, 1993).

of shared identity that is the source of both a leader's charisma and followers' enchantment and which motivates all parties to extra effort in pursuit of group goals'.[44] The opposite exemplar is those who say their purpose is one thing, but then do another – think of the outcry when politicians, say, extol the virtues of state-funded education while opting to send their children to private schools.

Create Breadth of Alignment

How much of our individual sense of purpose do we share? How many of my interests are involved in the shared purpose? If the shared purpose is narrow, it may not capture much of that which motivates and interests me, and little may be left to sustain the relationship if this limited shared purpose is eroded. Increasing the shared territory of relational purpose and its accompanying interests and values will create a more stable relationship. The more of my own sense of purpose that is inside the shared purpose of the relationship, the lower the risk that developing greater shared purpose in other relationships will erode the base here.

This may be as simple as finding out more about the other person's or organisation's raison d'être, enthusiasm and needs, and discovering what is already held in common. When a team leader allocates and adapts team roles, taking into account the interests and motivations of team members, he is enabling members' sense of purpose to come within, and strengthen, the shared sense of the purpose of the team.

Or it may mean deliberately altering or expanding the shared purpose of the relationship to cover or achieve a slightly different set of things. In deciding what kind of book this would be, we took into account the varying purposes – both individual and organisational – within the group. Then we defined the thinking and writing task in a way that created enough shared ground to give the project energy.

However, perhaps the common ground between you is already so broad that the purpose is unclear, its ambiguity preventing a clearly understood reason for the relationship. This, too, presents a risk to the long-term stability of the relationship. If this is a problem, then the lack of clarity and possibly conflicting demands can be handled as questions of priority within the relationship. In the Relationships Foundation's work with police forces, for example,

---

[44] S. Reicher, A. Haslam and N. Hopkins, 'Social identity and the dynamics of leadership: leaders and followers as collaborative agents in the transformation of social reality', *Leadership Quarterly*, 16 (2005), pp. 547–568.

senior officers described the frustration of the pendulum swinging between visible neighbourhood policing to tackle, for example, antisocial behaviour, and intelligence-led policing to tackle serious crimes. Prioritising the conflicting demands within a broad purpose involves tough choices.

Beyond what is shared or closely aligned, a sense of purpose can be strengthened further by compatibility – the existence of other motivations, interests and goals that, although not directly shared, do not conflict. The degree of compatibility of these 'outside interests' will have an impact on the relationship's stability. Two organisations working in unison do not overlap at every point: there are many things each organisation does that are outside the scope of the purpose named in the joint venture. Nevertheless, those areas may represent a source of creativity that can enrich and reinforce the relationship.

Organisations often struggle to clarify their purpose and get others to share it. For national governments the task is perhaps even harder, except when a common enemy can be identified. The challenge of articulating a shared purpose when dealing with a large and diverse constituency is captured by the pollster Mark Penn in his book *Microtrends*. He identifies seventy-five distinct, new demographic groups who need to be appealed to. 'America and the world are being pulled apart by an intricate maze of choices, accumulating in small, under-the-radar forces that can involve as little as 1 per cent of the population, but which are powerfully shaping our society.' Coherence of collective national vision is hard to sustain in the need to appeal to increasingly fragmented interests and identities. As Penn says:

Today, changing lifestyles, the Internet, the balkanization of communications, and the global economy are all coming together to create a new sense of individualism that is powerfully transforming our society. The world may be getting flatter, in terms of globalization, but it is occupied by 6 billion little bumps who do not have to follow the herd to be heard.[45]

In both politics and organisations, shared purpose may be most easily achieved by focusing on the 'big picture' that can accommodate differences. In the UK, local authorities and public services have been required to form local strategic partnerships. Partnership working does not come easily, and many members do not see the partnerships as particularly useful in furthering their own purposes. Any vision for the future has to be of a community within which individual organisational purposes can fit.

[45] M. Penn, *Microtrends: Surprising Tales of the Way We Live Today* (London: Penguin, 2007).

Deepen Alignment

It is possible that a shared purpose is little more than a temporary tactical alignment of interests. It can be an 'unholy alliance' where people with otherwise conflicting or divergent interests come together to achieve a specific shared goal. Such shared purpose is unlikely to be long-lasting, as fundamental differences in values tend to lead to divergence of purpose. Alternatively, shared purpose can be built on the basis of deeply rooted, shared convictions. This need not be evident at the start of the relationship, but can be a product of the growth of the relationship and the influence the different parties to it have on each other. A deep root can give rise to varied expression and may enable the relationship to survive a 'drought' when short-term shared purpose is hard to identify.

Between organisations and groups, the depth of alignment, beyond the tactical alignment of short-term goals, is demonstrated by the alignment of organisational structures, processes, power and so on between departments and organisations. Within organisations, corporate culture can reinforce organisational purpose by seeking to strengthen and embed organisational values or by recruiting for motivation towards the organisation's purpose as well as technical competence.

We can see how these various aspects of shared purpose come together in the concept of collaboration. The type of goal may be to achieve functional outcomes or to build the relationship itself. They may be focused on different levels of the organisation: technical teams can share a purpose even if there is little strategic shared purpose between their organisations. Sharing may be expressed in different processes, through different organisational structures, and with different ways of using power. Shared purpose may be expressed in physical proximity, or may be a synchronous or asynchronous virtual collaboration. The time horizon and the number of partners, and consequent complexity, can also vary.

Think with Diversity

What can be done to prevent, or at least minimise, groupthink while preserving the all-important elements of Commonality in a group? Holding the formed identities and shared purposes of the group constant, leaders ought to play an impartial role where they should proactively seek input and ideas from all group members without laying down their own opinion as a marker in the early stages of any discussion. By the same token, senior leaders, when assigning tasks to a group, should also consider refraining from expressing an opinion. This minimises the potential for group members acquiescing with or deferring to the senior leader's opinion. Different ideas should be actively sought and not discarded until properly analysed: even if the idea itself is a non-starter, the discipline of considering it might shed new light on a team's tasks. It is also valuable for a team or group to work to understand its diversity – roles, personality, experience – and to value what others bring to the whole.

Neutralise Division

Where forces that may undermine Commonality can be identified there are several ways in which they, or their impact, can be neutralised. One is for leaders to provide 'air-cover' to protect those working for them from distorted targets. This means taking responsibility for targets being met, and giving people the space to get on with what really matters. Those who are least competent and confident may stick most slavishly to targets, which become a 'painting-by-numbers' approach to leadership, while trusted success generates more room for manoeuvre.

Governments concerned with the perverse incentives of targets may focus on a smaller number of higher-order outcomes (for example, do patients recover and are they satisfied with the quality of care?). Giving service users control of budgets means they can potentially 'purchase' common purpose, ensuring that all providers are focused around their needs. Those who don't share the purpose don't get the business. However, as Chapter 7 on Parity has discussed, consumers are not always in positions of power when they purchase.

One way of picturing this role is to think in terms of creating a centre of gravity that is sufficiently strong to counter the competing forces that might pull the parties to a relationship apart. Where consumers or users of services lack sufficient gravitational pull, however empowered they may be, the extent to which organisational culture is infused by common values and purpose may be key. Where this is weak, an individual's purpose may be shaped by the perceived priorities of their manager, and with different divisions developing their own cultures.

Commenting on the implications of the rapid growth from a primarily domestic retail bank to a global universal bank, the Salz Review into Barclays' business practices suggested that it resulted in an organisation that was complex to manage, tending to develop silos with different values and cultures.

It found that there was 'no sense of common purpose in a group that had grown and diversified significantly in less than two decades' and that 'there were no clearly articulated and understood shared values – so there could hardly be much consensus among employees as to what the values were and what should guide everyday behaviours'. But while 'there was no consistency to the development of a desired culture', culture exists regardless as if 'left to its own devices, it shapes itself, with the inherent risk that behaviours will not be those desired'. This was seen in the tendency for employees to 'work out for themselves what is valued by the leaders to whom they report'. The Salz Review concluded that 'the developing cultures across Barclays were still less consistent as a result of a highly decentralised business model, that tended to give rise to silos' leaving 'a cultural ambiguity at the heart of the bank'.[46]

[46] Salz, 'Salz Review', sections 2:14–2:16.

9 What Relational Proximity Builds

The previous chapters have explored five different domains of relationship: communication, time, information, power and purpose. The Relational Proximity model provides a way of looking at how, in each of these domains, skills, values, working practices, organisational structures, policy and other factors influence the ways in which relationships are formed and conducted, and the outcomes that result:

- *Directness* deals with the ways in which presence in a relationship may be mediated by time, technology, or other people, so influencing the quality of communication and the experience of connection.
- *Continuity* is concerned with how interactions are sequenced over time, enabling growth and momentum, and building the story of the relationship that can convey belonging and loyalty.
- *Multiplexity* looks at the way in which information is gained, enabling the appropriate breadth of knowledge that allows effective interpretation and management of the relationship, as well as the sense of being authentically known and appreciated.
- *Parity* addresses how the distribution and use of power can influence participation, fairness and the experience of mutual respect.
- *Commonality* considers how the depth, breadth and clarity of alignment of purpose influences unity and synergy in a relationship.

These experiences are distinct, but not unrelated. Each influences the others, with the potential for reinforcing benefits and toxic combinations. The way in which they combine influences the overall outcomes of the relationship. In this chapter we explore how they fit together, and the implications of this for approaches to developing and assessing relationships, and considering the impact of personal, organisational and policy choices.

The Mixing Desk

It can be helpful to think of building relationships as like working with a sound mixing desk, dialling different channels up or down to create the desired sound. Where weaknesses in one particular aspect of Relational Proximity cannot be addressed directly, others may be increased either to compensate for the effects or to create the space for other interventions. Different patterns of Relational Proximity create, and are suited to, different types of relationship. Limits or imbalances in Relational Proximity may be deliberately set and may be appropriate – for example in the armed forces, the criminal justice system or, less formally, between doctors and patients or between job candidates and selectors. It is important to note, however, that just as a mixing desk can create very different sounds, so too different combinations of Relational Proximity will create different types of relationship. These may be appropriate, but may be unhealthy. Consider, for example, the following pairings.

Directness and Multiplexity

Multiplexity broadens the experience of connection and enables more of a person to be present in the relationship (Figure 9.1). Where the Multiplexity involves different roles, it may bring opportunity for different types of presence, or make differing degrees of connection more appropriate. Doctor and patient may relate in different ways, for example, when watching their children

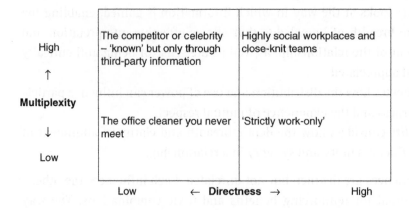

Figure 9.1: Illustrations of interaction between high and low levels of Directness and Multiplexity

play sport together. A high degree of Multiplexity can, however, mean that there is less escape from unwelcome Directness: you may not be thrilled to have your boss move in next door.

Directness and Parity

Parity increases perceived safety and willingness to be present, and invites the presence of other parties to the relationship (Figure 9.2). Some bosses make all the staff feel comfortable, whatever their rank or status, while others set out to intimidate. The interaction between Parity and Directness can be illustrated in different lending relationships. Regulation can increase the Parity in some consumer lending while paring down Directness to the functional use of phone or internet. This contrasts with the Directness involved in dealings with a loan shark, where the lack of Parity makes Directness itself uncomfortable and unwelcome. The low-Parity low-Directness environment of much commercial bank lending is routine but can create severe problems for the indebted business if the unreachable decision-makers at the bank decide to rein in their lending or if the business breaches its loan covenants.

The reason why Relational Proximity is not the same as simple 'closeness' is partly that social situations where people are sometimes stiflingly 'close' in fact also lack meaningful Commonality and Parity. In business, time pressure can mean that people feel too busy to delegate effectively, so minimising the participation of others, just as insufficient time to build trust can make power differentials between organisations more difficult to handle. In Multiplexity, lives become compartmentalised, with interactions taking place within just one sphere of activity and producing a one-dimensional view of other parties. As a result, limited understanding can mean that sensitivity to Parity issues

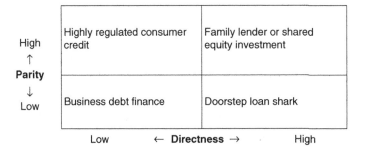

Figure 9.2: Illustrations of interaction between high and low levels of Directness and Parity

is underestimated (for example, the contract for a small supplier, which is a large part of their turnover but only a small cost to the customer), and lack of knowledge about a colleague's potential to contribute may be misconstrued as a desire not to involve them fully. Similarly, with Commonality, if the goals are shared and being achieved, team members will often be less concerned about a fair return than they would be if goals diverge.

Conversely, it is possible to compensate for deficiencies and encourage improvement by addressing imbalances in Relational Proximity. Directness increases the opportunity for contextual information. If I visit your office I may see family photos on your desk and meet your colleagues. Using only mediated communication (phone, email, text) reduces this contextual information. Continuity provides more time to gain knowledge, particularly as people often take a little while to build trust. Higher Parity gives people greater permission to do this. As a junior member of staff I might be reluctant to talk about life outside of work unless my superiors intentionally take an interest. And if there is Commonality in one area, then shared interests are more likely to be explored in another – perhaps in a sporting or social setting.

Relational Outcomes

In managing stakeholder, professional, or personal relationships we may seek relationships that display a variety of characteristics: trust, empathy and understanding, commitment or accountability, for example. While these can be measured directly, looking in more detail at the extent to which Relational Proximity creates the conditions that support these outcomes is more likely to point to actions that can be taken to improve the relationship, or identify risks.

Trust

The initial decision to trust may be taken in a split second, but sustained trust that enables significant risk or investment doesn't generally happen overnight. It is typically a long-term process that involves each party taking small steps towards each other. It is in the nature of building trust that a degree of vulnerability is required. As Chapter 4 discussed, Directness is an important factor in establishing trust. This is partly because we rely on so many different cues to gain a sense of a person, including their reliability, body language, tone of voice, facial expression, as well as physical setting. Mediating a conversation unnecessarily through technology distances us and denies us opportunities to gain information about the other person. This is acutely relevant in the earliest stages of a relationship when you may have literally nothing else to go on. If you start a relationship over the internet – whether a freelance job or a prospective romance – it can be impossible to know whether you are actually dealing with the person you think you are dealing with. Given the high-profile cases of fraud and exploitation regularly in the media, it is understandable that such an easily addressed lack of information might breed suspicion.

Continuity allows an individual's or organisation's reliability to be demonstrated over time and incentivises trustworthiness, as there is greater likelihood of being around to reap the dividends. If you can always shed your reputation by moving to the next town, or closing the business and reopening under a different name, the consequences of untrustworthiness are less likely to catch up with you.

Multiplexity gives us a more rounded picture of a person than is evident from a single context. Seeing how someone behaves and responds in a variety of contexts and situations can build trust in their ability to deal with new situations. A campaigning politician may be convincing in his appeal to trust him in office, and may even have delivered on his promises in the past. But public confidence can be badly shaken by the revelation that he is not trustworthy in his personal life or business dealings, as numerous high-profile figures caught in extramarital affairs or fraud have found out to their cost. Another form of Multiplexity is a recommendation of a third party by someone we already trust. We might have little reason for confidence in a builder found in the classified advertisements of the local paper, but would readily hire the same builder on the information that a friend had done so and found him competent, considerate and reliable. Online star ratings and reviews are forms of Multiplexity.

Greater Parity has the effect of reducing the scope for, and therefore concern around, untrustworthy behaviour. If advantage is concentrated on one side of the relationship, the other party may feel that he or she has little recourse if things go wrong. The phrase 'abuse of trust' is often used of a situation in which a power differential that gives rise to an implicit situation of trust, such as between a GP and patient, or a teacher and pupil, has ostensibly been exploited for personal gain.

Finally, Commonality can contribute to trust because it is recognised that both parties are acting out of the same interests, and therefore breaking trust would be detrimental to both their goals. If a joint project has a significant upside to my business partner, I can be confident that she will work hard to meet her obligations; if, on the other hand, she has no real interest in completing the project – or, worse, feels its completion could harm her in some way – then trust will likely be deferred until I know she has delivered her part of the bargain.

Empathy and Understanding

Mutual understanding is fundamental to the effective conduct of a relationship. The ability to interpret actions, predict responses and understand needs is essential if better outcomes are to be pursued intentionally and effectively. Serving, supporting, motivating and influencing other people and organisations all require understanding of their circumstances, hopes, fears, needs and expectations. Policy and management cannot make people like one another, but creating the conditions for improved mutual understanding enables the development of better relationships. Empathy is the capacity to understand others by putting yourself 'in their shoes'. A high degree of empathy facilitates relationships, because it enables us to understand *why* a person acts the way he or she does. It gives me a connection to the other person and allows me to identify with their needs and motivations – without which insight they may appear unreasonable or unpredictable.

Directness improves the quality of communication, and thus understanding, through greater openness, higher bandwidth to aid interpretation of messages and the opportunity for synchronous moderation of responses to aid dialogue. Directness enables empathy for another person through the wide range of verbal and non-verbal cues, which is one reason why counsellors tend to work face to face wherever possible; it allows them a better chance of gaining a realistic picture of a client and establish a 'connection'.

Understanding is built up over time; there are few shortcuts. The importance of Continuity is evident in the understanding that is built up between players in a sports team where moves and reactions can be anticipated, or in the investment of time in early-stage partnering. Continuity also brings a narrative to the relationship. A one-off event can be given context within a longer-term knowledge of someone, allowing you to position their impatience or irritation on first meeting within a wider understanding of their situation that might include tiredness, stress, or bereavement.

Understanding is aided by the full, rounded and accurate knowledge that comes with Multiplexity, which also helps in reading the person and increases awareness of circumstances that may impact on the relationship. A certain action may have implications within one setting that are better explained with reference to another. If my employee regularly finishes work early every Friday afternoon, I may jump to the conclusion that he is simply getting a head start on the weekend commute at my expense. If I later learn that he has childcare arrangements to fulfil or a sick relative who requires his time, and take into account that he comes into work before me most days to make up the difference, then I will take a different view of his actions.

If there is Parity in a relationship, empathy is easier. It lends motivation to understand, where a lack of Parity tends to breed resentment and defensiveness. Similarly, shared vision and purpose (Commonality) make it easier to empathise simply because it requires less imagination. If I have the same values, I am immediately more likely to understand another person's worldview. Seeking shared purpose also requires understanding of the real goals and motivations so that they can be better aligned.

Commitment

Commitment to a particular relationship is a key factor for success, on both corporate and individual levels. Companies depend on brand loyalty for a secure customer base, without which they risk losing market share. Employee commitment reveals itself in low staff turnover, enabling productive relationships to develop over the long term as well as reducing hiring costs. In personal terms, commitment is even more highly valued. We want to know that our friends will still be friends in the future, and that we will be still married to our spouse next year.

Often we will only feel committed to a relationship when we believe the other party shares our commitment – making commitment dependent on trust. Directness can be a significant factor here, since without it people can be left feeling isolated, and lacking the assurance that their own commitment and contribution matters. Despite the advantages of working from home, teleworkers often report feeling disconnected from the wider company and aware that they may be missing opportunities for advancement that are more readily available for those who can interact in the office. As Chapter 4 discussed, there is also some evidence that commitments made face to face are more likely to be adhered to.

Continuity and commitment are closely related, since commitment is an expectation and intention of future Continuity. Commitment can also be a function of the stake we feel we already have built up in an organisation or relationship; a valued, long-term shared history will often sustain a relationship through difficult times. In a shorter relationship, the participants may feel that they have less to lose by cutting and running.

Greater Multiplexity gives broader information about a person or organisation, allowing you to know better what they are really like. If I am offered a job with a retail company, my decision to accept or refuse it may well be influenced by my experience as one of their customers. If I suspect they don't 'walk the talk', and their supposed focus on customer satisfaction or employees' wellbeing is just PR, I may question whether I really want to be a part of that culture.

Parity affects commitment because people want to feel safe to commit. As with trust, if all of the power is held by one side, it can be difficult to feel that there is a good reason to commit; I might believe in the work an organisation is doing and want to commit to it, but if there is no reciprocal commitment to me then I am unlikely to feel at ease with the decision. Few employees would be willing to remain on temporary contracts indefinitely, because they have little assurance of job stability. In the same way, Commonality increases morale and reduces reasons for tension, raising the chances of success and synergy occurring. Where values as well as tasks are shared, commitment is likely to be correspondingly greater: there are more reasons to remain in the relationship and make it work.

10 Relationships between Stakeholders

Any organisation – whether a company, school, hospital or NGO – can be viewed as a matrix of relationships. For a school, for example, these might connect pupils, their peers, parents, teachers, departmental heads, head teachers, governors, central and local government, the local community, other schools, universities, teacher training departments, companies providing work experience, as well as all the suppliers of equipment and services. For any organisation – whether private or public sector, or a voluntary or community organisation – relationships with stakeholders are important in different ways, and all need to be carefully monitored and managed.

Mervyn King, chairman of the International Integrated Reporting Council (IIRC), summarises the business case for doing this:

Every company is dependent on good relationships with its key stakeholders and on the essential resources which it relies on. They are an integral part of how the company makes its money, its risks and opportunities, and its future outlook. And yet, the interrelated, interconnected and interdependent nature of many of these resources and relationships is not usually explicitly recognised by the company's board. Bringing the reality of these resources and relationships into the active awareness of the board and management leads to a better directed and better managed company. The resources and relationships should be built into the company's business model, strategy, risks and opportunities. They should be measured and monitored and their performance reported internally and externally.[1]

---

[1] M. E. King and L. Roberts, *Integrate: Doing Business in the 21st Century* (Johannesburg: Juta & Co., 2013), p. 55.

King suggests that there are five forces that will require organisations to adopt new tools in responding to social, economic and environmental challenges:

- The power of investors to drive change
- Large corporate customers demanding compliance with ethical standards as part of their reputation and brand management
- Increasing regulation
- Government expectations on business support in addressing social issues such as inequality
- Pressure on natural resources, including water, forests, soil and minerals.[2]

As shown in Figure 10.1, there are alternative models for understanding both the contributions made by stakeholder groups and the means by which they can be rewarded. Nevertheless, there are countervailing forces that can lead to the role of stakeholders being ignored. The integrated thinking that King describes as 'seeing the connections of the resources and relationships', and the way they work together in achieving strategic objectives, contrasts with the tunnel vision that Paul Seabright sees as a necessary corollary of dealing with strangers. His book, *The Company of Strangers: A Natural History of Economic Life*,[3] describes how much of our life depends on

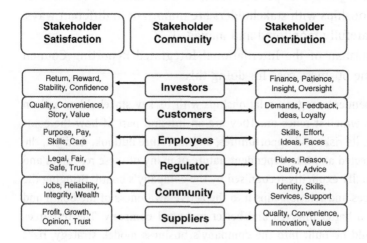

Figure 10.1:   How the main stakeholder communities in a company can contribute and be rewarded

[2] King and Roberts, *Integrate*.
[3] P. Seabright, *The Company of Strangers: A Natural History of Economic Life* (Princeton University Press, 2004).

relationships between strangers. He gives the simple example of how buying a shirt is the outcome of a complex series of interactions over many years, including the development of new varieties of cotton seed and all the supporting agricultural technology; the growth, harvesting and processing of the cotton; and the design, manufacture and merchandising, all with supporting financial, IT, transport and administrative processes. This 'cooperation with no-one in charge' relies on what he calls 'tunnel vision' – 'the capacity to play one's part in the great complex enterprise of creating the prosperity of a modern society without knowing or necessarily caring very much about the overall outcome'.[4]

While such tunnel vision may be necessary in many of our daily interactions it brings risks, not least that the cumulative consequences of these interactions can be profoundly economically, socially and environmentally damaging. Seabright explores how institutions have developed over the centuries to help the 'shy, murderous ape emerge from his family bands in the savannah woodland in order to live and work in a world largely populated by strangers'.[5] Our interest in stakeholder relationships is to consider how well these institutions, processes and ways of working shape relationships. This means not only working well with strangers but also enabling encounters with strangers to become relationships that create real value.

Ownership, Purpose and Responsibility

One key area is the ownership, financing and purpose of companies. The credit crisis of 2009 placed both business and capitalism under greater scrutiny. Public confidence in the social benefit of business has been dented. In the UK, an opinion poll by Populus for the BBC reported that 49 per cent of people agreed with the statement 'the public has more to fear from the conduct of Big Business than the actions of trade unions these days', with only 13 per cent disagreeing.[6] Key issues have been high-profile examples of corporate malpractice (such as banks fixing the LIBOR rate or misselling products), low tax payments by some multinationals, or levels of executive remuneration. The Governor of the Bank of England, Mark Carney, is one of many who

---

[4] Seabright, *The Company of Strangers*, p. 15.
[5] *Ibid.*, p. 257.
[6] Poll for BBC *Daily Politics*, May 2014.

have highlighted the need for reform. In a speech on 'inclusive capitalism' he noted that:

just as any revolution eats its children, unchecked market fundamentalism can devour the social capital essential for the long-term dynamism of capitalism itself. To counteract this tendency, individuals and their firms must have a sense of their responsibilities for the broader system.[7]

Such responsibility can only flourish if it is more than incidental to the goals of an organisation, and this leads to a number of important questions.

Are Companies Aiming for the Right Goals?

Commonality can be assessed both in terms of depth (the significance of the shared values that the alignment reflects) and breadth (whether the alignment represents a limited or extensive element of each party's overall purposes). The nature and extent of this alignment has implications for other aspects of Relational Proximity and for other relationships. High Commonality, for example, creates a reason for Continuity and investment in Directness, but the shared purpose of suppliers in maintaining a cartel affects customers.

Company structure, law, ownership, reporting and culture can all influence the ways in which organisations are able to align purpose in their stakeholder relationships. In a Michael Shanks Memorial Lecture entitled 'What is a company for?'[8] Professor Charles Handy relates the answer (inscribed above the blackboard in every class) he and his classmates were taught in business school in the 1960s: 'to maximise the medium-term earnings per share.' From this, Handy remarked, 'all else flowed, given, of course, a perfect market and an intelligent one and managers who were clever, energetic and wise'. Over the last fifty years such an assumption has proved unwarranted.

Yet management theory, and the thinking and behaviour of those who have been schooled in different perspectives, changes, with significant implications for relationships. 'Conscious Capitalism' provides one example. The ideas behind this are articulated in the book of the same name by John Mackey, Co-CEO of Whole Foods Market, and Raj Sisodia.[9] Conscious Capitalism seeks

---

[7] M. Carney, 'Inclusive capitalism: creating a sense of the systematic', Speech given at the Conference on Inclusive Capitalism, Bank of England, London, 27 May 2014, www.bankofengland.co.uk/publications/Documents/speeches/2014/speech731.pdf.

[8] C. Handy, 'What is a company for?', Michael Shanks Memorial Lecture, 5 December 1990.

[9] J. Mackey and R. Sisodia, *Conscious Capitalism* (Boston, MA: Harvard Business School Publishing, 2013).

to return financial and social wealth to stakeholders and is governed by four guiding principles: Higher Purpose, Stakeholder Integration, Conscious Leadership and Conscious Culture.

The idea is that 'Well run, values-centred businesses can contribute to humankind in more tangible ways than any other organisation in society'. The book also makes the business case for Conscious Capitalism, demonstrating that it need not compromise shareholder return, as the companies that were identified as most conscious outperformed the S&P 500 index by a factor of 10.5 over the years 1996–2011. People working in a company that is governed by principles such as these are more likely to be supported in considering and managing the relational distance in all their relationships than those in a company with a more narrowly conceived sense of purpose.

Have We Got Ownership Patterns Right?

The nature of company ownership is influenced by both law and technology, that impacts on the relationship between owners and other stakeholders, and the capacity to manage relational distance in these relationships. These are not new issues, as the prescient concerns of John Maynard Keynes in the 1930s illustrate:

The divorce between ownership and the real responsibility of management is serious within a country when, as a result of joint stock enterprise, ownership is broken up among innumerable individuals who buy their interest today and sell it tomorrow and lack both knowledge of and responsibility towards what they momentarily own.[10]

The relational problem cuts both ways. If I am irresponsible towards what I own, then by the same token those who operate what I own are irresponsible towards me. There may be some financial calculation that shows it to be advantageous that my savings should be invested where there is the greatest marginal efficiency of capital or the highest rate of interest. But evidence tends to show that remoteness between ownership and operation is a weakness tending in the long run to set up strains and enmities that will nullify the financial benefits.

This 'divorce between ownership and the real responsibility of management' is facilitated by three things.

First, a high proportion of shares are owned by large pension and insurance companies, and other institutional investors, who represent their customers'

---

[10] J. M. Keynes, 'National self-sufficiency', *The Yale Review*, 22 (1933), pp. 755–769.

interests but do not consult them on their investment strategies. This relationship is also only one link in the chain – the relationship between the investor and other stakeholders (for example, employees, suppliers, customers and local communities) is mediated through the company. Looking at these issues through the lens of Relational Proximity can identify the risks at a general level but also, by considering the conditions that might enable stronger and more effective relationships to develop and thrive, enables more informed reflection on possible responses:

- *Directness*: Layers of mediation mean that there is no direct contact between the provider of capital and its user. If you pay into a pension fund, you hand over responsibility for how your money is invested to a fund manager who is legally required to maximise financial returns. You probably will not even know in which company the money ends up, or how that company uses it to further their work. With no other information, the choice of where to put the money will take no account of its impact on community or employee welfare.
- *Continuity*: The trend towards short-term financial returns places pressure on companies to make gains today at the expense of tomorrow. Companies know that if they don't perform well enough then investors will take their money elsewhere. Immediate returns are sometimes engineered through cuts to staff and research. Borrowing to fund a takeover can result in a temporary boost in the share price, again at the expense of the company's future profitability. The global thinktank Tomorrow's Company, in their work on long-term value,[11] highlight research from Deutsche Bank on how long-term investing can outperform the market. But they also highlight how the intentions to pursue long-term value can be eroded and distorted through 'the magnitude and power of behavioural pressures in the system' so that 'intentions are barely formed, and if they are they get lost in the complexity of the investment chain'. A strong and focused investment mandate is seen as essential if pension fund trustees are to ensure that advisers and investment managers support long-term investment decisions and relationships.
- *Multiplexity*: Investors may relate to a company in one narrow domain – their share ownership and disposal. They may have no other interaction with a company or its personnel, even as a customer. Small investors will probably not attend shareholder meetings, either because of geographical distance, or because they feel they have limited influence. The knowledge and under-

[11] Centre for Tomorrow's Company, *Tomorrow's Value: Achieving Long Term Financial Returns. A Guide for Pension Fund Trustees* (London: CTC, 2014).

standing of other stakeholders is even more constrained, not least because the lack of Directness and Continuity provide few opportunities to gain such knowledge.

- *Parity*: Executives may feel shackled by the demands of quarterly reporting targets, while shareholders may feel that executives secure high pay that is only loosely connected to shareholder returns. In highly mediated relationships, Parity becomes far less a product of individual choices and conduct and becomes more a consequence of the extent to which institutions and processes foster Parity.
- *Commonality*: New company structures, such as Benefit Corporations (see below) are intended to create a more supportive context or pro-social common purpose between investors and other stakeholders. Regulation can, to a certain extent, require Commonality, though if only the letter rather than the spirit of the law is applied Commonality is easily eroded.

Second, owners and managers are separated by the construct of limited liability (realised in the UK in the Limited Liability Act 1855). Limited liability almost invariably creates relational distance between shareholders and the company. There are some economic advantages of this arrangement: without protection from the full impact of potential losses, many investors would not invest in a company and much technological, financial and medical progress would be curtailed. However, limited liability means that shareholders don't need to worry *too much* about what a company is doing. If the company goes bankrupt, they will lose their money, but they will not be held responsible for all the losses incurred. Although shareholders are thought of as owners of the company, they have in reality no responsibility for the way it is run, and so have less incentive to track its activities.

Third, ownership itself has become increasingly transitory. In 1940, the mean duration of US equity holdings by investors was around seven years. For the next thirty-five years up until the mid 1970s, this average holding period was little changed. But in the subsequent thirty-five years average holding periods have fallen spectacularly. By the time of the stock market crash in 1987, the average duration of US equity holdings had fallen to under two years. By the turn of the century, it had fallen below one year. By 2007, it was around seven months. At that stage, 'high-frequency' meant seconds; today, shares might be held for just milliseconds or microseconds. Estimates suggest that High Frequency Trades (HFTs) account for roughly 70 per cent of all trading volumes in US equities. When traders speculate on the value of a stock for such incomprehensibly brief periods (the fastest algorithms can make thousands of trades in the time it takes to blink an eye), their transient owner-ship of the stock is completely disconnected from the operation and success of the company.

HFTs are a relatively new entrant to the markets and their full impact is yet to become clear. They provide liquidity. On the other hand, the 6 May 2010 'Flash Crash' – in which the Dow Jones lost and regained around 600 points in the space of twenty minutes – was partly blamed on HFTs, which vastly exaggerated falls on an already fragile and volatile market. In August 2012, a 'trading error' caused by disused software becoming reactivated lost US Knight Capital Group $440 million in forty-five minutes, causing wild fluctuations in the share prices of dozens of other companies along the way.

The problems of incentivising shareholders financially were illustrated in *Dodge* v. *Ford Motor Company* in 1919 (though contrary to popular opinion this case did not legally establish the principle of shareholder value). Henry Ford, the president and majority stockholder, wanted to end special dividends in order to increase investment in new factories, thereby employing more peo-ple and decreasing prices for customers. Two minority shareholders, the Dodge brothers (co-founders of the rival Dodge Brothers automobile company), took Ford to court. The judge ruled that the company was in business for profit, and could not be turned into a charity – as was, effectively, Ford's intention. The directors were forced to declare an additional dividend.

Despite all this, share ownership may be the funding option with most rela-tional potential. For example, many problems of short-term share ownership are fuelled by speculators' needs for an immediate return. Having a greater proportion of long-term owners would reduce volatility and help to give a better impression of the true value of a company, though a certain amount of continuous trading is necessary for liquidity.[12] Additional shares could be issued to shareholders who have held their shares for a minimum amount of time, perhaps three years, with additional incentives at multiples of that period. Long-term shareholders could be recognised and rewarded in other ways, perhaps by allowing them to buy the company's products or services at a discounted price, or inviting them to hospi-tality events from time to time – also fostering Multiplexity.

In general, funding through profits generated by the company, or by issuing further stock, ensures that risk and reward are shared. For smaller companies,

---

[12] See J. Rushworth and M. Schluter, *Transforming Capitalism from Within* (Cambridge: Relational Research, 2011), pp. 37f.

other options for more direct borrowing may be open. For example, crowd-funding or social lending – in which individuals access finance from a group of providers on a P2P lending site – has high Parity, though relatively low Directness. They will never meet the lenders and the relationship is mediated through technology. The providers of capital may lend, donate, or receive an equity stake in the company. Since crowdfunding is increasingly used for start-up companies, the money could start as a loan and evolve into equity if and when the company becomes profitable. Alternatively, a shared equity investment from a friend, associate or family member is likely to be characterised by high Parity and Directness.

One response to this form of relational distance is to develop new forms of ownership. In the US, a new form of business known as a Benefit Corporation is starting to gain traction. Like other corporations, these are for-profit organisations. However, their business purpose has been redefined to address the legal difficulties that surround businesses obligated to place their financial duties to shareholders ahead of the interests of other stakeholders, including the wider society. 'Benefit Corporation' is a legal status. It is distinct from 'B Corporation', which is a third-party certification – a kind of 'Fair Trade label for a whole company', though one which is far more comprehensive than single-issue certifications (such as 'Organic' or 'Forestry Stewardship Council'). It is also more rigorous and credible than companies' own claims of ethical practice, which are often dismissed as 'greenwashing'.

'The distinctive features of a Benefit Corporation are: (1) it has a corporate purpose to create a material positive impact on society and the environment; (2) the duties of its directors are expanded to require consideration of interests in addition to the financial interest of its shareholders; and (3) it is required to report each year on its overall social and environmental performance using a comprehensive, credible, independent, and transparent third-party standard.'[13]

Have We Got the Financing Model Right?

Organisations of all sizes borrow money, from the entrepreneur who starts a small business with a credit-card advance to the multinational that borrows billions to fund a takeover. Whatever the scale, the relationship

---

[13] W. H. Clark, Jr and E. K. Babson, 'How benefit corporations are redefining the purpose of business corporations', *William Mitchell Law Review*, 38 (2012), p. 818.

between borrower and lender is likely to have a significant impact on the company's future.

- *Directness*: As with share capital, there may be several intermediaries between the ultimate providers and users of capital – and the provider will likely have no knowledge of how their money is being deployed. There is an important difference between lending directly to a business (perhaps as an 'angel' investor or to a friend) and lending money to a bank, which lends it on to a company, perhaps via another intermediary.
- *Continuity*: Short-term ownership is less of a problem with debt than it is with share capital. However, like shares, loans can still be traded. The most infamous example of this was the mortgage-backed securities that played a key role in the global financial crisis in 2008. Loans are also likely to be for a set term, to be paid off in monthly instalments. Once the loan is paid off, there is no guarantee that another will be granted – or of the rate and terms at which it will be available. Loans may be called in at the first sign of default, and because the purchaser has no expectation of making another loan to that company in the future and no interest in their business, there is no incentive for a long-term relationship.
- *Multiplexity*: Again, lenders may have little contact with the end-user of capital, particularly if the loan is provided through intermediaries. They may not even know that they are funding the particular company that is closing down a production facility in their locality.
- *Parity*: There is a reason that being 'in debt' to someone can mean more than owing them money. Debtors are almost always at a disadvantage to their creditors. Depending on the fine print, lenders can call in certain loans at any time (overdrafts being one example), or for a minor breach of contract. Even if this is not the case, loans are structured in favour of the lender – they receive instalments every month, regardless of the profitability of the business, and a single missed payment can represent 'default' in the contract. For the lender, any risk is offset by the borrower's collateral, with unsecured loans bearing higher rates to compensate the lender.
- *Commonality*: As with share capital, the priority for the intermediate lender (particularly an institutional lender) is likely to be making a steady financial return. The ultimate provider of capital – the individual who has money in a current or savings account – might have different priorities. If they are lending directly to a local business, there will be common benefits in

terms of a relationship between provider and user of the capital, which can potentially produce benefits for the health of the local economy, jobs and services.

These are not theoretical issues. They have an immediate impact on the funds that an organisation can secure and the terms under which they can access them. Having distant and short-term owners with no meaningful relationship, as is often the case with share capital, means that a company may not be able to formulate a long-term strategy, since the capital may be withdrawn because the funder has little interest in the organisation's future. Loans may address some of these problems, but bring other pitfalls – such as being unable to guarantee new funding when a loan is repaid, or the borrower being required to assume most of the risk associated with a loan rather than sharing it with the provider of capital.

The different ways in which capital is accessed also causes problems for companies' owners – meaning shareholders in this context. A new CEO can load a company up with debt, perhaps to fund a takeover, bringing short-term financial rewards under good economic conditions but storing up problems for the future when circumstances are tougher. If the company begins to struggle, the CEO can walk away, often with a huge bonus and pension, leaving shareholders out of pocket and employees vulnerable to the 'restructuring' to cut costs that is likely to follow.

The way that loans are typically structured creates an inherent relational problem with other stakeholders. In the event of bankruptcy, the creditor has priority over anyone else except for the lawyers who untangle the contracts. However, loan providers are not the only ones who lend to companies. Employees do work, which has a monetary value. They are usually paid at the end of the month but they are last in the queue of payment priorities if there is a problem. Employees are, therefore, in effect lending without security. Loans are usually arranged bilaterally, between the company and the bank, without involving the other interested parties such as trade creditors and employees. Multilateral agreements would avoid some of the relational imbalances that lending creates.

This Parity issue can be seen in other areas of business. Suppliers also lend to businesses, since they are paid in arrears unless the terms are cash on delivery. How long in arrears may or may not be agreed; suppliers will often state thirty days but find the business takes much longer to pay. They are rarely in a position to chase up the money because the legal costs are too high and they will lose the client if they 'rock the boat'. If the company goes out of business in the meantime, the supplier may well never be paid.

This form of injustice is also often the experience of the customer. Goods may be paid for up front but not arrive – or even be shipped – for days or weeks. The furniture industry is notable in that customers will often be paying for items that don't even exist: the company only makes the furniture after they have accepted the customer's money. This is not necessarily a bad thing, so long as there is adequate transparency. Often there is not: customers aren't told why there is such a long delay. Again, if the company goes out of business, they may never receive the goods or get their money back.

During the 2008 global financial crisis, the main problem for many banks was the lack of relationship between lenders and borrowers. Irresponsible mortgage lending was compounded as individual homeowners' loans were packaged up and sold on in increasingly large bundles of up to several thousand mortgages. There was then no Directness, no Continuity and no Commonality between lender and borrower: the selling of debts on to a third party without detailed checking of each mortgage in the bundle meant that no one involved felt responsibility to worry about their true contents. The mortgage-backed securities were AAA-rated, but no one took the trouble to dig into them and find out how good the individual mortgages were. There was just an assumption that prices would continue to rise across the USA taken as a whole, as they always had. This incentivised bad practice and eventually cost hundreds of billions of dollars in write-downs.

RBS bought a large part of the Dutch bank ABN AMRO right at the top of the market. It financed the purchase primarily through debt, just before the credit crunch. The next year RBS reported the largest loss in UK corporate history, £24 billion, in large part due to the bad debts it had taken on from ABN AMRO. Because RBS was seen as 'too big to fail' – the consequences for the economy would have been catastrophic – it had to be bailed out with £45 billion of taxpayers' money. The CEO who had arranged the purchase of ABN AMRO, Fred Goodwin, was able to retire with a pension fund of £16 million. There was a lack of Commonality between the bank's managers and its stakeholders, including both shareholders and the wider public: the health of the bank didn't matter much to its management, because they could make risky 'bets' in financial markets without being exposed to the downside. Parity was minimal between bank and public: the public couldn't refuse the bailout, partly because the fallout would have been too serious and partly because the decision was taken by politicians on their behalf.

Public Services

Relationships in public services are influenced by the understanding of the goals of the services, patterns of funding and accountability and the nature of professions. In recent years there has been growing interest in how a better understanding of relationships can inform both the goals of services and how they can be more effectively delivered. In the UK, the 2012 IPPR Report, *The Relational State*,[14] provides an example from the political left wing. This is complemented by interest in how family and community relationships are both a cause of social problems and a solution. So, for example, UK Prime Minister David Cameron argued that:

for those of us who want to strengthen and improve society, there is no better way than strengthening families and strengthening the relationships on which families are built. Whether it's tackling crime and anti-social behaviour or debt and drug addiction; whether it's dealing with welfare dependency or improving education outcomes – whatever the social issue we want to grasp – the answer should always begin with family.[15]

Similarly the Labour MP John Cruddas argues that:

We will not be able to increase public spending to solve all our social problems. Life in many of our communities is going to be tough for a long time – it will take a long time for the economic recovery to reach them. But many of the major social problems we face do not need more money. They need radical new ways to use existing resources. Putting relationships centre stage in service design. Helping people to help themselves and each other. Drawing on the assets of local communities to build resilience and break cycles of deprivation.[16]

Public Sector Goals

In contrast to private companies, the purpose of public sector organisations can be more politically determined. How their purpose is understood can have

[14] R. Muir and G. Cooke (eds.), *The Relational State: How Recognising the Importance of Human Relationships could Revolutionise the Role of the State* (London: IPPR, 2012), www.ippr.org/publications/the-relational-state-how-recognising-the-importance-of-human-relationships-could-revolutionise-the-role-of-the-state, last accessed 19 October 2015.

[15] D. Cameron, 'David Cameron on families', Speech, Relationships Alliance Summit, Royal College of GPs, London, 18 August 2014.

[16] J. Cruddas, 'John Cruddas's speech on love and work: full text', *New Statesman*, 29 January 2015, www.newstatesman.com/politics/2015/01/jon-cruddas-s-speech-love-and-work-full-text, last accessed 19 October 2015.

a profound impact on their relationships with their stakeholders. A health service, for example, that focuses on the promotion of public health will need to prioritise a different set of relationships than one which is focused on the medical treatment of disease:

- *Criminal justice*: Justice can be defined as the process of restoring the relationships between victims and offenders, and between offenders and society – not just housing offenders as efficiently (cheaply) as possible. Punishment is not intended to be an end in itself; its purpose is more than retributive and imprisonment seeks to do more than contain offenders. Crime is not simply considered an act against the state, but against victims – whose needs are a proper concern of the system. Sentencing seeks to redress harm to victims as well as to protect society. The relational causes of crime will be given real priority. This includes investment to address antisocial behaviour – not just to manage the symptoms. Punishments and prison regimes aim to tackle the causes of offending behaviour, and seek to strengthen (or at least not further weaken) the relationships that are key to rehabilitation. This context creates new opportunities for resolving the relationship between victims and offenders, requires different relationships between prisoners and prison officers, as well as creating a more supportive environment for more effective relationships between offenders and those who can help them address issues relating to drugs, mental health, education, or the family relationships which have a significant role to play in reducing recidivism.
- *Welfare*: Relational poverty and material poverty are recognised as being mutually reinforcing – and relational poverty is acknowledged as a serious problem. It is those on the margins of society, and those with the weakest networks of relationships, who are also most likely to be in financial poverty. Welfare seeks to strengthen family and community relationships rather than just relieve material need by lifting people over a certain income threshold. Where appropriate, employment is a key focus, maintaining the recipient's dignity and independence: welfare empowers and engages people, rather than trapping them in dependency and further exclusion.
- *Education*: PISA (the OECD's Programme for International Student Assessment) aims to evaluate and compare education systems worldwide by assessing fifteen-year-olds' competencies. However, these are restricted to just three core subjects: reading, maths and science. The Whole Education movement recognises the relational inadequacy of the PISA framework and seeks to articulate something more complete: 'a fully rounded education, developing the knowledge, skills and qualities needed to help [young people] thrive

in life and work'. This goes far beyond performance in national tests and exam results. Character and relational skills become a core part of the curriculum. Education policy recognises the contribution to learning of many different relationships and types of relationship. These are given appropriate weight in the location and design of a school and in the syllabus and ethos of the institution. Schools, colleges and universities are integrated into their communities, with strong links to local businesses and other organisations.

- *Health*: Healthcare is seen as more than fixing the mechanics of a damaged or failing body. There is a much greater emphasis on long-term health, and on prevention as well as cure. The links between mental and physical health are fully recognised, and the contribution of the health and strength of our relationships to each of these are also now more widely acknowledged.[17] The role played by informal carers – often family members – is recognised, as well as the mental and physical health impacts on them in turn. Consequently, relationships are seen as a public health issue, rather than dismissed as a solely private matter.

- *Housing*: Building programmes reflect the idea that they are creating communities, not just providing shelter. House design takes account of the needs of families, including extended families, and overall layout includes shared space for neighbours to meet together. Housing policy may allow and encourage families to live close to each other, in order to mobilise relational support. Hong Kong, for example, offers tax allowances if elderly parents live with their children.

It should be recognised that these areas of public policy cannot be dealt with in isolation, since they are interconnected. For example, housing has an impact on levels of relational support, which affect mental and physical health. Similarly, if the purpose of welfare is to reintegrate people into their community and strengthen their networks of relationship, where they live is a critical strand of this. These domains cannot be addressed without reference to each other.

Does Accountability Work in the Public Sector?

Public sector organisations do not, in most cases, have shareholders, though private companies and social enterprises may be significant providers of services. But, whether publicly or privately owned, they are subject to political

---

[17] See, for example, the chapter 'The relational shift in health and healthcare', in C. Spretnak, *Relational Reality* (Topsham, ME: Green Horizon Books, 2011), pp. 61–111.

accountability in a way that other businesses are not. This accountability can operate through a number of processes: contracts to providers, targets, inspection, or the empowered choice of service users. In the latter case, the data that is collected – for example, the measure of educational attainment and progress that is selected, and the way that it is made public – can influence the nature of the choices and the relationships between service users and providers.

The pattern of accountability shapes the context for relationships in the way it incentivises or discourages particular activities, and also through the impact of the time involved on other relationships. While leaders of organisations who are in a strong position may provide 'air-cover' for their staff, encouraging them to focus on what they believe is most important, too often the accountability process distorts purpose and relationships. In the case of schools, for example, there is the relational opportunity cost for teachers of reading and supplying the information required by government. Under the last Labour government in the UK, the burden on schools increased to 'a total of 207 different targets, measures and "compliance requirements" ... And these are just the targets relating to central government and national bodies such as Ofsted. In addition, one local education authority plan was found to have 307 targets. And this was said to be typical.'[18] Government emails of guidance and legislation totalled some 6,000 pages. In relational terms, the extra reading and form-filling involved detracts from a number of other areas: teachers' sleep, lesson-planning, family time, overall energy and, crucially, their relationships with pupils and other teachers in the school.

Targets are often poor proxies for the rich complexities of desired outcomes, and can be pursued without regard for the impact on other organisations' ability to fulfil their purpose. Targets have been an important part of the process for pursuing improved performance in healthcare in the UK, sometimes with disastrous consequences. In one case, a hospital's attempts to meet a target for the time taken to treat patients arriving at Accident and Emergency conflicted with the ambulance service's (a separate organisation) ability to meet a response time target. The hospital wanted to delay the moment when the clock started ticking for them, so delayed admitting patients, leaving them in ambulances or the care of paramedics, so delaying the ambulances. In another case, managers at the Mid Staffordshire NHS Foundation Trust Hospital were accused of pressuring surgeons into performing less urgent cases in order to

---

[18] M. Baker, 'A bonfire of school targets?', BBC, 20 March 2004, http://news.bbc.co.uk/1/hi/education/3551627.stm.

meet the eighteen-week target time from GP referral to treatment. The president of the Royal College of Surgeons, Professor Norman Williams, said that they were so focused on financial and waiting time targets that they 'forgot why they were there'.[19]

Public Sector Funding

Public services in many countries have increasingly operated as markets or quasi-markets: rather than government itself being the provider of services, they are commissioned from providers. These may be other independent public bodies (foundation hospital trusts or academy schools in the UK), charities or private sector contractors. Commissioning services involves purchasing on behalf of others (service users) with trade-offs between maximising quality, minimising costs, as well as nurturing the economy of providers so that the risks of future reliance on monopolies is diminished.

When budgets are cut, the weighting given to costs in any tendering process is likely to be higher. Funding decisions will also involve issues of Parity, but where these impinge on the nature and quality of services they will affect other aspects of Relational Proximity. This may include erosion of the richer aspects of Commonality (more limited goals are pursued) and lower levels of Directness and Continuity with service users, as staff manage higher workloads. Because many government departments operate as silos, the consequences of reductions in the quality or accessibility of services may fall on other departments or agencies, leaving commissioners little incentive to secure the best overall integrated service. A common example of this is the care of older people, where lack of funding for residential care can mean that hospital services are less able to discharge frail older patients to appropriate residential care (funded by local government), increasing costs and restricting bed availability for others.

Commissioners of services may also seek to pass risks and costs on to providers via super-contracts, where a lead provider takes over responsibility for managing smaller providers. Small voluntary sector providers may be less experienced in contracting and financially vulnerable to changes in contracts. This lack of Parity may mean that it is easier for those commissioning services to squeeze smaller, weaker providers whether or not they provide the

---

[19] R. Smith, '"Target culture" that led to Mid Staffs still exists in NHS, claims top surgeon', *Telegraph*, 25 January 2013, www.telegraph.co.uk/health/healthnews/9824256/Target-culture-that-led-to-Mid-Staffs-still-exists-in-NHS-claims-top-surgeon.html, accessed 19 October 2015.

best quality or value in services. Where local government is also a provider of services there will also be the temptation to maintain their own services rather than those of independent providers.

Overprescription of outcomes may distort activity and inhibit the effective development of relationships. When dealing with, for example, troubled families or young people, the development of trust should be an outcome itself as it is often the essential foundation for successful intervention thereafter. Funding decisions may have unrealistic expectations of case load, or the time that relationships require, resulting in unplanned relational costs of difficult financial decisions. Better analysis of the relationships may enable some of the costs to be avoided or mitigated, or even demonstrate that funding cuts will actually increase costs once the relational consequences are recognised.

Can Independent Agencies Coordinate Properly?

When the Relationships Foundation reviewed the inquiries into major service failures in the UK health sector,[20] relational failures were constantly highlighted. The tragic case of Victoria Climbié is a case in point.

Victoria Climbié, a young girl in the care of her aunt, was referred to UK social services in April 1999. She died in February 2000 having spent much of the last weeks of her life wrapped in a bin liner, lying in a bath with her faeces and urine, with her hands and legs tied. The post-mortem, recording 128 separate physical injuries, indicated that she was regularly beaten. Counsel for the Inquiry identified twelve missed opportunities by public services to save Victoria. In each case weak inter-professional and inter-agency relationships resulted in misunderstanding and failure to act. In Figure 10.2, the map of organisations surrounding Victoria Climbié's case shows no lack of resources. Nevertheless, the conclusion of the inquiry into her death was blunt:

The future lies with those managers who can demonstrate the capacity to work effectively across organisational boundaries. Such boundaries will always exist. Those who are able to operate flexibly need encouragement, in contrast to those who persist in working in isolation and making decisions alone. Such people must either change or be replaced.[21]

---

[20] G. Meads and J. Ashcroft, *The Case for Interprofessional Collaboration in Health and Social Care* (Oxford: Blackwell, 2005).

[21] Lord H. Laming, *The Victoria Climbié Inquiry* (London: HMSO, 2003), p. 8.

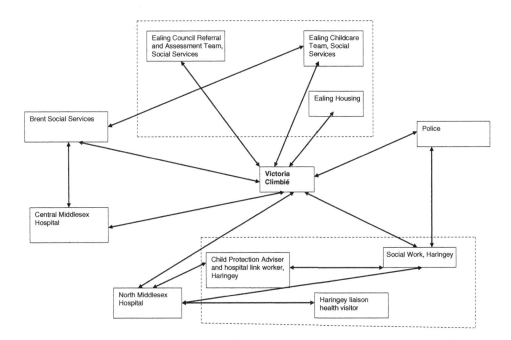

Figure 10.2:   Simplified map of the Relational Network of Care for Victoria Climbié
Source: Derived from evidence submitted to the Public Inquiry into the death of Victoria Climbié 2002.

Relational distance between the various individuals and organisations involved is not simply a consequence of their decisions, or of those immediately around them. Technology, culture and legislation, among other factors, have all influenced the way in which purpose is construed, accountability practised, business processes designed, or the size of the organisation deemed optimal.

Failures in collaboration are not always fatal. They can impede innovation, reduce satisfaction and increase costs. In the Relationships Foundation's work on healthcare it became clear that professionalism cannot be solely about technical knowledge and skills but must include the ability of professionals to conduct six key types of relationship, each of which brings its own challenges and issues:[22]

- *With one's own profession*: e.g. peer review mechanisms on treatment and prescribing, professional ethics regulation, contracts with the healthcare organisation rather than individual practitioner contracts.

---

[22] Meads and Ashcroft, *The Case for Interprofessional Collaboration*, pp. 10–11.

- *With other professions*: e.g. shared referrals and procedures; larger multi-specialist teams; integrated training and professional development; joint service management.
- *With new partners*: e.g. sponsorship and shared data systems; joint investment and risk-taking; mixed income streams and multiple accountabilities including voluntary, private and commercial agencies.
- *With policy actors*: e.g. innovation and increasing pilot/pioneer programmes; links to devolved political units and pressure groups; decision-making on healthcare options and priorities.
- *With the public*: e.g. publicly available performance comparators; NGOs and locally elected representatives with health-related roles; public scrutiny through media and participatory democracy.
- *With patients*: e.g. informed consumers; litigation; direct access to services; incorporation of social care into a more holistic concept of health.

Inter-Professional Relationships

Different silos, departments, office sites, or professions can all create barriers to effective relationships within organisations. Major service failures in healthcare provide an example of how the different elements of Relational Proximity can be impaired. The Kennedy Report into the high mortality of children undergoing paediatric cardiac surgery (PCS) at the Bristol Royal Infirmary highlighted the importance of those in leadership roles ensuring that these barriers are not created or are overcome:

relations between the various professional groups were on occasions poor. All the professionals involved in the PCS service were responsible for this shortcoming. But, in particular, this poor teamwork demonstrates a clear lack of effective clinical leadership. Those in positions of clinical leadership must bear responsibility for this failure and the undoubtedly adverse effect it had on the adequacy of the PCS service.[23]

The report's synopsis describes the combination of factors that contributed to these failings:

The story of the paediatric cardiac surgery (PCS) service in Bristol is not an account of bad people. Nor is it an account of people who did not care, nor of people who wilfully harmed patients. It is an account of people who cared greatly about human suffering,

---

[23] Department of Health, *Learning from Bristol: The Report of the Public Inquiry into Children's Heart Surgery at the Bristol Royal Infirmary 1982–1995* (London: HMSO, 2001), Summary point 24, p. 4.

and were dedicated and well-motivated. Sadly, some lacked insight and their behaviour was flawed. Many failed to communicate with each other, and to work together effectively for the interests of their patients. There was a lack of leadership, and of teamwork.

This was not, however, simply a consequence of individuals' inability to forge effective collaborative relationships. The systems and structures hindered effective relationships so the inquiry concluded that the medical staff 'were victims of a combination of circumstances which owed as much to general failings in the NHS at the time than any individual failing'.

The work environment was influenced by the split site and limited resources. Organisational and management factors were reflected in the 'silo' structure and club culture which hindered a multi-professional approach to reviewing quality of care. The wider institutional context included the lack of an effective system for external monitoring of quality, as well as an ethos of 'getting by'. This was seen in the dedication of health professionals to do their best, even with inadequate buildings, staffing and equipment, becoming the enemy of excellence:[24]

- *Directness*: In emergencies, access to people can become critical. In the context of heart surgery on babies it was found that junior doctors who were physically present in the Intensive Care Unit [ICU] for most of the time did not have ready access to experienced colleagues to address the more rapidly changing condition of babies.[25] Effective collaboration requires time and good communication. Although the children at Bristol were admitted under the joint care of cardiologists and surgeons the 'meetings between cardiologist and surgeon were a casualty of the cardiologists being overstretched'. The consultant paediatric cardiologist reported that being based on different sites limited 'the ordinary communication that exists in a unit where consultants and various doctors can meet with each other and bump into each other in a corridor, and so on, which facilitates the overall management'.[26] Advice from cardiologists at critical moments during surgery was thus not readily accessible.
- *Continuity*: In the Bristol inquiry it was found that 'exhaustion and low morale lead to stagnation and an inability to move forward in response to new developments [in other Paediatric Cardiac Services], despite the

[24] R. Kelin, 'No quick fix', *Health Service Journal*, 30 August 2001, p. 29.
[25] Department of Health, *Learning from Bristol*, p. 215.
[26] Department of Health, *Learning from Bristol*, p. 212.

stimulus provided by the new generation of consultants'.[27] Maintaining and building Continuity requires a positive decision: maintaining the status quo in a relationship or neglecting it can all too easily become the path of least resistance for those without the time or energy to invest in relationships. Yet this can mean that problems are unresolved and pressures increase. In another health sector context, different lengths of job tenure between senior doctors (many years) and non-clinical managers (averaging nine months) hindered the effective commissioning and development of services as well as undermining doctors' willingness to repeatedly invest in the relationship.

- *Multiplexity*: Silos and split sites reduce the likelihood of the informal sharing or gleaning of knowledge through chance encounters in the corridor, while 'club cultures' and strong professional divides limit the opportunities to build better understanding of roles, skills, pressures, or indeed weaknesses. Myths and stereotypes about other professions' cultures, values and practices can easily develop, and without adequate Multiplexity these can go unchallenged and uncorrected.

- *Parity*: There were also cultural problems in the relationships at Bristol with the inquiry finding that there was a mindset among younger clinicians that 'older established consultants had been left behind by recent developments', with a 'degree of resentment and defensiveness among the older consultants if practices were challenged' and that the 'club culture' created an 'environment that was not such as to make speaking out or openness safe or acceptable'.[28] Collaboration between professions is one of the key control factors against risk. At Bristol, however, nursing staff 'were let down by a culture that excluded them'. The Kennedy Report concluded that 'the hierarchical system common at the time (and regrettably still too prevalent now) made it difficult for the nursing staff to voice concerns and to be heard'.[29] Strict vertical hierarchies within clinical directorates can also mean that junior colleagues are unable to question or even validate consultant assessments, and prevent open discussion of clinical standards, hindering the development of corporate strategies to improve clinical outcomes.

---

[27] Department of Health, *Learning from Bristol*, p. 231.
[28] Department of Health, *Learning from Bristol*, p. 165.
[29] Department of Health, *Learning from Bristol*, p. 175.

- *Commonality*: The Kennedy Report also found that 'there was poor under-standing of the importance of teamwork, most particularly in the case of collaboration between cardiologists, anaesthetists and surgeons in the management of ICU; that teams are necessarily multidisciplinary'.[30] Shortfalls in teamwork were compounded by 'the uneasy relationship between anaesthetists and surgeons'. The difficulties the anaesthetist encountered in raising his concerns were described by the inquiry as revealing 'both the territorial loyalties and boundaries within the culture of medicine and of the NHS, and also the realities of power and influence'.[31] This illustrates some of the interplay between Parity and Commonality whereby the development of distinct professional identities and loyalties exacerbates the Parity problems discussed above.

In the case of Bristol there was a sharp distinction between clinical and managerial responsibilities as well as a 'silo structure' that impeded horizontal communication. The Chief Executive who instituted this structure was a strong believer in clinical freedom and autonomy. 'Leadership in Bristol was fragmented; clinical leaders were expected to take responsibility for discrete areas of clinical care; managers were expected to focus on non-clinical matters. A separation was created which was hard to sustain. Delegation of authority from the Chief Executive to clinical directorates created "silos" (discrete organisational units with very little communication between them) within the Trust. These were almost separate organisations. Strategic leadership from the centre was weak. Communication was up and down the system but not across it.'[32] The risk of this is that the sense of common purpose is eroded.

At Bristol the patient was not the focus. Although 'the consultants, particularly the surgeons, saw themselves as having very effective teams' the inquiry found that they saw them as their teams, which they *led* but were not *part of*, other than as leaders. The inquiry also found that the teams were 'teams of like professionals: consultant surgeon leading surgeons, consultant anaesthetist leading anaesthetists. The teams were not organised primarily around the care of the patient, they were not cross-speciality nor multidisciplinary, and they were profoundly hierarchical.'[33]

---

[30] Department of Health, *Learning from Bristol*, p. 231.
[31] Department of Health, *Learning from Bristol*, p. 161.
[32] Department of Health, *Learning from Bristol*, p. 302.
[33] Department of Health, *Learning from Bristol*, p. 198.

Stakeholder Organisations

Stakeholder relationships cannot be just a bolt-on to an organisation: getting relationships right means changes to the way an organisation sees issues and how it acts. It fundamentally changes the nature of the organisation, with implications for culture, size and processes, among other issues.

Within any organisation, there is a constant tension between simplicity of structure and process (work breakdown, performance appraisal, individual targets) and the relational and behavioural consequences. These may include completing tasks that turn out to be irrelevant, people not able to give their best, or people or groups competing with others. While the structure and process may look efficient, relational distance can cause long-term inefficiency. For example:

- *Reliance on contracts and formal procurement processes* can reduce prices, but it can also (by reducing Parity and Commonality) prevent a strong relationship forming with suppliers that could have reduced costs even more in the long term.
- A *hierarchical structure* breaks the organisation down into manageable units, but can create silos (disrupting Commonality and Multiplexity) that at best act independently and at worst compete or play politics, destroying value.
- *Performance appraisal systems* can ensure that people are aware of what they need to do, and receive the opportunity to talk about it with their managers. However, there is an inherent lack of Parity in the review process. Different types of target operate at different levels (reducing Commonality – see further below) and regular role changes within the organisation (affecting Continuity) can make it difficult for the process to add true value.
- *Business process re-engineering and workflow systems* can speed things up, but the focus on the internal process leaves customers at a Parity disadvantage, and makes it hard for people to understand each other fully (a reduction in Continuity).
- *Uncritical reliance on IT* can reduce Directness inside and outside the organisation.

All of these can increase costs through rework or lost custom. Many of the structures and processes that lead to unintended consequences are built into organisations at the point of initial design. Organisational structure tends to be functional, rather than relational – putting unnecessary boundaries between people that means they can sleepwalk into relational problems further down the line. Restoring the balance between relationships and 'the organisation as a machine' can significantly reduce the friction that all of these issues cause, reclaiming productivity that has been needlessly lost. Patrick Lencioni's book *The Advantage*[34] makes the point that real competitive advantage derives from organisational health – defined as when an organisation's management, operations, strategy and culture are unified. The Relational Proximity Framework is designed to bring this about.

Management and Scale

The way that staff and departments relate – or fail to relate – to each other is critical for the success of an organisation. Dysfunctional relationships or a 'silo' mentality can mean that different parts of an organisation pull in opposite directions.

Although management has a long and complex history, in its present form it dates back to the late nineteenth century and the work of Frederick Taylor, who pioneered 'scientific management'. He advocated low-Parity relationships with rigid training of employees in their given tasks, and managers assigned to ensure they carried them out properly – believing manual workers themselves too stupid to understand the true nature of the task they were doing. 'It is only through *enforced* standardisation of methods, *enforced* adoption of the best implements and working conditions, and *enforced* cooperation that this faster work can be assured. And the duty of enforcing the adoption of standards and enforcing this cooperation rests with *management* alone.'[35]

Fortunately, this is a caricature of most management today, but the idea of management itself remains a modern obsession. By one estimate there are some 5 million managers in the UK – ten times more than 100 years ago.[36] The profusion of managers is partly attributable to the increase in organisations' size and complexity: when there are so many managers, the managers themselves need managing. This creates stratified, bureaucratic organisations, which has a series of negative effects. These are compounded by poor training

[34] P. Lencioni, *The Advantage: Why Organizational Health Trumps Everything Else in Business* (San Francisco, CA: Jossey-Bass, 2012).

[35] F. W. Taylor, *Principles of Scientific Management* (New York: Harper & Brothers, 1911), p. 64, emphasis in the original.

[36] L. Kellaway, 'Are there too many managers?', BBC, 29 July 2013, www.bbc.co.uk/news/magazine-23462290. As a caveat, many of these are just managers in name, and do not manage people.

(only one in five managers holds a professional qualification) and low investment (the UK spends less on management development than almost anywhere else in Europe).[37]

One impact is simply that Directness suffers, leaving more room for misunderstandings and miscommunication. In a rigidly hierarchical organisation, top management may never speak to the most junior employees, meaning that they can feel isolated and unimportant – small cogs in a very large machine. It also means that executives are distant from the concerns of their staff, and may be unaware of developing problems. Where there is direct contact, there may be little Continuity.

Although managers are apparently in a position of power over their employees, their approach to those they manage can reveal one of the flipsides of Parity. Particularly where there are many and redundant rungs of management, managers may be unwilling to develop their staff too quickly for fear that they may end up in direct competition with them. Promising employees may find their advancement blocked. The managers' lack of security in their position – which is perhaps well founded if their job is unnecessary in the first place – means that their own careers become more important to them than the objectives of the organisation as a whole (undermining Commonality).

Many organisations have to be large and relatively hierarchical, but they are often unnecessarily so, risking a range of relational issues. This is a compelling argument for smaller, flatter organisations where possible. Where it is not possible, measures can still be taken to increase Relational Proximity. A Relational Health Audit can highlight where vulnerabilities lie and the problems that are arising or may in future arise from them.

Regardless of organisational size and structure, there are clear advantages to devolving decision-making closer to the client or customer. But this comes at the expense of lower consistency between divisions. It is easier to adapt and innovate, but there is less overall control.

Where decision-making responsibilities are devolved through a flat organisation, silos naturally – almost inevitably – arise as the groups involved look to their own interests as well as, and perhaps ahead of, those of the organisation. The obvious solution to this is to centralise decision-making, bringing the silos back in line with the organisation's overall vision and purpose – re-establishing Commonality, though generally reducing Directness. There is a trade-off between vertical and horizontal Relational Proximity.

---

[37] R. Spellman, 'Acknowledge managers as professionals', *Financial Times*, 10 October 2010.

Of course, greater centralisation leads to the bureaucracy and slow decision-making that the organisation was trying to overcome in the first place. Neither is necessarily 'better', as shown in the former USSR, where planners alternated between policies of economic centralisation and decentralisation without success.

This discussion is often seen primarily in terms of physical proximity to an organisation's HQ. In cases of both wide/flat and narrow/deep organisations, the Relational Proximity Framework gives more options in adjusting proximity beyond a monochrome near–far analysis. Organisations can build Continuity, Multiplexity and Commonality by training their senior management together, and only then decrease Directness by sending them out to the periphery. Working with all five dimensions allows organisations to build story and increase Parity at the beginning, improving overall cohesion.

Is Big Beautiful?

Size can make sense. Larger organisations can often do more than smaller ones. Larger schools can offer a greater breadth of subjects. Surgeons and their patients benefit from the greater volume of experience and support that larger specialist hospitals can provide. Many new technologies and products, such as drugs or new models of cars, are expensive to develop, something that is easier for larger firms. Nevertheless, size is a relational issue. While larger organisations can sometimes do more, this can easily come at the price of greater relational distance. Large organisations may have small teams, which have greater Relational Proximity within them, but across the organisation as a whole there may be disconnection. It is impossible for a head teacher to know everyone in a school of 1,000 or more pupils, however small individual classes are. The human mind is capable of maintaining a limited number of current social relationships in which we keep track of how each person relates to the others – and therefore of the dynamics within an organisation. Based on the relative sizes of the neocortex and social group sizes among human and non-human primates, the anthropologist Robin Dunbar estimated a mean group size of around 150. Much more than this, and group cohesion becomes increasingly difficult to sustain.

Alexander Hoare, partner of C. Hoare & Co, the oldest private bank in the UK, discusses this in the context of Continuity and Directness of relationship. The size of Hoare & Co., which is relatively small for a private bank, with assets of around £2 billion and 350 employees, means they can provide excellent service. Economy of scale is a well-established principle, but Hoare argues that it is easy to overlook the diseconomies of scale: 'While you can measure and demonstrate the economies of a larger dealing room, or the savings from merging two small banks, it is harder to identify the impact of colleagues who are competing for their jobs, the incompatible computer systems, the failure of offices to co-operate with each other.' He also argues that small size creates competitive advantage in relationships: 'We compete on dimensions where we have a clear advantage over a larger clearing bank: relationship, flexibility, care, independence, and speed of service (to name just a few).' The small size of the bank means, for example, that 'we are able to turn around all decisions in 24 hours, only because we know each customer personally'.[38]

In reflecting on specific relationships it is therefore important to consider how much organisational size or other factors that define the context of the relationship play a significant role in determining the ease with which Relational Proximity can be built. Size is perhaps most likely to affect the face-to-face interaction, the ability to develop Multiplexity with key contacts, Parity (given the power that size can bring and the more layers of hierarchy that may be required) and Commonality, as more departments or groups with their own identity and purpose are created.

A Relational Business Charter

The Relational Business Charter developed by Relational Research offers a specific set of principles designed to increase Relational Proximity in an organisation's relationships.[39] Directness is promoted, for example, through stakeholder dialogue, and continuity of ownership encouraged, alongside fairness and shared purpose across stakeholder relationships. A company will be recognised for the purposes of the Charter as having a relational ethos and operating in a relational manner if it can be seen to do the following:

1. *Set relational goals*: The company includes a Relational business objective in its constitution, and demonstrates a commitment to implement it, providing appropriate training to investors, directors and employees.

---

[38] A. Hoare, 'Why small is beautiful', *Spear's*, 20 March 2012, www.spearswms.com/news/alexander-hoare-on-why-small-is-beautiful-for-c-hoare-amp-co-private-bank/#.Vin_8H6rTIU, accessed 20 May 2015.

[39] Rushworth and Schluter, *Transforming Capitalism*.

2. *Create stakeholder dialogue*: Dialogue is promoted among all significant stakeholder groups, through regular face-to-face meetings and, where that is not possible, through regular online communication.

3. *Demand shareholder transparency*: There is direct and transparent (named) ownership of a significant proportion (perhaps 25 per cent) of the shares by individuals or family trusts.

4. *Encourage long-term ownership*: A high proportion of the shares are owned on a long-term basis that may be incentivised by issuing additional shares to long-term shareholders.

5. *Safeguard work–life balance*: There is evidence of management having respect for the interests of employees, e.g. with regard to length of working hours, atypical hours and other employment conditions.

6. *Lower pay differentials*: The dignity of all employees is respected by minimising remuneration differentials within the business – taking, for example, a 20:1 ratio between top and bottom as a benchmark.

7. *Build supplier partnerships*: Suppliers are treated fairly and with respect, paid promptly, and given support to develop their businesses.

8. *Respect customers and communities*: Customers and the local community are treated fairly and their concerns are respected, e.g. with regard to service provided and payment terms.

9. *Promote financial stability*: The risk of company financial instability is minimised to protect the company and its stakeholders, assessed with reference to debt-to-equity ratios and/or levels of interest cover.

10. *Fulfil social obligations*: Obligations to the wider society are fulfilled, assessed with reference to the percentage of profits paid in tax in the country where those profits are earned and also the percentage of profits spent on corporate social responsibility.

11 Managing, Measuring, Reporting, Regulating

The purpose of any organisation, the means of fulfilling that purpose, and the impact of this on other people and organisations all require organisations to consider their stakeholder relationships. Organisations are not ends in themselves, although they can sometimes act as if they were, serving neither customers, investors nor the wider society particularly well, while generating large returns for those who lead them. This is not sustainable: if customers are not served, the reliance on others for the resources that are needed to enable this not recognised, and the impact on third parties ignored, then administration, dissolution, or takeover will generally follow.

As shown in Figure 11.1, Relational Proximity provides a framework for analysing existing relationships and the likely impact of policies and actions on those relationships. Regulatory, supply chain, customer, investor, employee and community relationships are all well covered in management theory and literature. Within different sectors of business there are specialist tools, expertise and advisory services that can help organisations address the many presenting problems in their relationships. These include maintaining appropriate distance but building understanding in regulatory relationships; reducing costs, increasing innovation and managing risks in supply chains; improving teams; increasing customer loyalty and satisfaction; accessing funding and aligning time horizons with investors; or managing the impact on and relationship with local communities. A better understanding of the relational roots and nature of these problems opens up different responses that can save time, increase productivity and reduce risk.

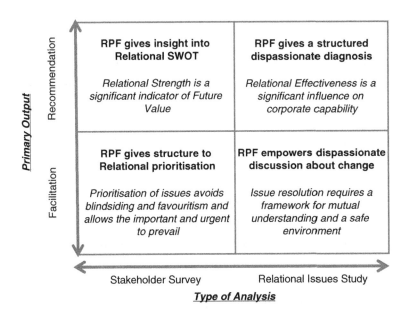

Figure 11.1: Ways of using the Relational Proximity Framework

Managing

Managing stakeholder relationships – i.e. all the relationships that are part of your work – is not just a task for leaders or a product of formal processes and interventions. Everyone can reflect on and improve their relationships. Sometimes, of course, the involvement of other parties is needed to make changes. And joint reflection can highlight the differences in perception, bringing into focus the blind spots in our own analysis. Yet there will always be steps that one party can take to improve, or at least ameliorate the negative impact, of a relationship.

Relational Analytics have a self-assessment tool that draws on the Relational Proximity model.[1] Taking just one driver as an example, this can help structure reflection on aspects of Directness:

- Who do you need to see *face to face*? Given the limits on the numbers of people you can meet in this way, are you present in person when and where it is most needed? Or are you trapped in a bubble, insulated from those with whom you need face-to-face contact?

[1] www.relational-analytics.com.

- Who needs a more *direct relationship* with you? You may be clear about who you want greater access to, but are you aware of those who are struggling to establish greater Directness in their relationship with you – this might be family members, neighbours or stakeholders in your work? Or it might be someone who you do not initially think of, but on deeper reflection ... ?
- Are you creating the right 'media ecology' in your communication? Reflecting on key relationships, do you have the right *balance between forms of communication*? What pushes this out of balance, and how could you address this?
- How can you *maximise 'presence'*? Reflecting on a particular medium of communication, or a particular instance, how could you make yourself more present? Could you change the way in which you write emails or use the phone? Are you fully emotionally and intellectually present in each exchange?
- What are the relational consequences of *where you live or work*? For instance, how does it affect who you meet face to face?
- What could you do to *increase Directness* with your local community?
- How well do you use *mealtimes* for building relationships, at work or at home?
- How good are your *listening and dialogue skills*? How can you develop them further?

Managing through Regular Review

Review of key partnerships should be an element of the regular management cycle – not just a response to problems. This allows risks to be identified early and the benefits of the relationships to be maximised.

For example, KPMG used relational metrics to examine and improve the relationship between a major UK food and clothes retailer and a major global NGO. The NGO had been working in partnership to ensure that the retailer's decisions about sourcing of commodities such as cotton and fish were as sustainable as they could be. This relationship was up for renegotiation and the two individuals in the respective organisations with responsibility for making the partnership work wanted to do everything they could to set the next seven-year agreement off on the soundest possible footing.

Both organisations stated their desire to build on their history together and 'make the relationship great'. However, the two organisations had very different cultures, oriented respectively towards financial return and the environment. Although both parties were immensely committed to a shared vision, they nevertheless clashed when historic prejudices got in the way. In particular, the NGO believed it could do much more to support the retailer on its sustainability journey if this artificial barrier could be broken down.

It became apparent that the most senior individuals from each party were judging the organisation-to-organisation relationship on the quality of their personal relationship. This personal relationship was particularly strong. Problems in the relationship between their respective teams would then be escalated for these leaders to resolve. The two leaders would resolve the problem, but neither could implement the changes needed to prevent the problem arising again.

Strong one-to-one relationships, particularly at senior levels, do not inevitably produce strong organisational relationships – though this may not be immediately obvious. The methodology was easily able to highlight where change was needed – in the degree of access each party felt they had, in how responsive they felt the other party were, and in the breadth and depth of their understanding of each other. All these were highlighted as areas for improvement. As a result, a new basis for the relationship was established to which both parties were able to commit.

Similarly, the CEO of a Professional Membership and Qualification body in Accountancy was concerned about the relationship with two partner organisations, who recruited and trained the students who would become the membership of the future by qualifying in the professional standards set. The relationship was not financial but was entirely symbiotic. There was no particular issue with either of the relationships; however, they were going through a process of setting mutually beneficial strategies on the basis of collaboration and the CEO wanted to set their path on the basis of the best possible relationship that he could create. Led by the CEO, the parties adopted an appreciative approach to the discussion, offering improvement actions to help the other party achieve their relational ideals. This was extremely effective.

When two organisations' leadership teams have an evidence-based discussion about their respective organisations' perceptions, commitment to cascade the findings throughout the organisations is easily forthcoming. The CEO of one organisation had a moment of important realisation when he said to his counterpart: 'I want our organisations to have a good relationship. If your team are telling us they only get 90% of what they expect for any of these drivers, I want my team to be moving that to 100%.' Every incremental gain must be worth having. The parties agreed to a relational action plan that they would cascade through their organisations. As a result of the intervention the parties' strategic discussion was recognised by all to have been more productive and efficient than it otherwise would have been.

Managing through Support

Managing stakeholder relationships is also about consciously creating the most supportive environment possible. In the case of supply chain relationships, for example, this will often be in the context of the greater relational distance and complexity that occur as goods are sourced from all over the world. The complexity of modern consumer products means that many components may be needed, each with their own supply chains. Manufacturers may buy the finished component without having any knowledge of its provenance. And, of course, competition from overseas means that manufacturers may compete on price alone, and there is little incentive to ask where materials or components have come from. Managing relational distance in supply chains therefore involves a number of relational dilemmas. The decision to be local or global may be influenced by production costs, speed and reliability of delivery, capacity to integrate effectively with other business processes, carbon footprint and commitments to employees and local communities. Technology may help to reduce the relational distance in global relationships, but also makes more relationally distant options viable. There are other drivers of relational distance and a relationally attentive but geographically distant supplier may be relationally closer than a local supplier.

For manufacturers, there are questions surrounding how supply chains are managed. It may be difficult, or even impossible, to have full oversight of the entire supply chain, from raw materials through to finished product. The way products are sold means that the market often doesn't offer any real transparency; coffee, for example, is produced by different sizes of farm (large estates, small family-owned farms, or cooperatives) but the beans are pooled and sold on the wholesale markets so that buyers have no way of telling how workers on individual farms are treated, how much they are paid, or the businesses' environmental policies. Some initiatives such as Fair Trade have sought to address this, but the certification criteria are geared towards certain types of producer (cooperatives) and so don't apply as well to others, such as those farmers that are too small to join a cooperative. Additionally, it does not tackle the ultimate problem of oversupply, which has the effect of decreasing Continuity and Parity between buyers and sellers: demand for coffee is inelastic, so greater supply than demand incentivises buyers to shop around constantly for the cheapest source, dropping one supplier when a cheaper one becomes available.

Many companies overcome relational distance in their supply chains through close integration into the business process, through just-in-time (JIT) supply models, and sometimes simply by excellent attention to customers. Hallmarks of success, seen through the lens of Relational Proximity, might be:

- *Directness*: Supplier staff are easy to get hold of when there are issues or problems and they can be addressed openly and honestly; the contact management processes are experienced as means of getting quickly to the right person rather than as a set of filters or barriers to be overcome; creative, engaged and value-creating discussions about needs and solutions take place; while the geography, technology and skills of the relationship are all carefully managed to support improved service.
- *Continuity*: Account managers stay long enough to build a good understanding of customers' needs; knowledge is not lost during handovers; issues in previous transactions are remembered so that the same information does not have to be given many times; while trust, confidence and the willingness to invest in better service are all enabled by the developing experience of the relationship.
- *Multiplexity*: Customers' needs and preferences are sufficiently well understood to inform the design of better services, while the impact of any changes to systems and processes on customers is accurately understood; customers have realistic expectations of their suppliers through knowing their capacity, skills and experience; individual relationships do not cause friction in the relationship due to insufficient mutual understanding; while careful attention is given to how such knowledge is gained and shared.
- *Parity*: Pricing and problem resolution are felt to be fair by both parties, with markets structured and regulated so that no one has undue pricing power; where one party has much greater power to set prices, this is used to drive up quality in ways that offer benefit to both parties; decisions are made fairly and can be influenced, while opportunities to participate and add value are opened up; fear of the abuse of power does not preclude investment or participation; while the respect for both individuals and organisations involved fosters participation and investment in the relationship.
- *Commonality*: There is a shared understanding of the basis of the relationship and its goals; purpose is sufficiently aligned so that both parties are fully motivated, particularly if more creative and supportive investment is required than a transactional relationship in order to achieve the required outcomes; suppliers are an important contribution to achieving goals that require action across the supply chain (for example, in reducing the carbon footprint); differences in the relationship prove to be an enriching source

of creativity rather than an impediment to effective operation; while when things go wrong, or pressure is experienced, the relationship does not break down into a them-and-us confrontation but joint ownership of the issues is retained.

Managing People

Team Focus assessed a highly successful consultancy business offering engineering solutions to its clients. Started thirty years ago by an entrepreneurial engineer, it had grown to a turnover of £15 million when the owner appointed a new MD. It now turns over £25 million. The top team was concerned about 'the next step'. It was no secret that the MD would retire in less than five years. Under his guidance they had agreed direction and strategy, and yet there was a level of disharmony in the team. The CEO invited Team Focus to run a 'Team Build' event to sort things out.

Team Focus agreed to run a two-day event but requested confidential one-to-one sessions with each member of the Executive Board prior to the event. This was for the consultants to get to know the participants, begin to build a relationship, and to uncover some of the underlying attitudes and issues. The one-to-one sessions revealed great concern about climate, direction and particularly the question of succession. Some believed that decisions were being made behind closed doors. Many were unclear how decisions were being taken and who was being consulted. It was agreed that the proposed two-day event would go ahead with an agenda for 'getting to know each other better and creating a more open climate'. The first day was designed around activities to get people talking and sharing. The second day moved the agenda back to work issues and concerns.

The event revealed that the team was unclear about what was happening and how decisions were to be taken. It was also clear that the issue of succession was surprisingly urgent. However, it was also clear that there were rivalries concerning internal applicants. As a result Team Focus proposed and then implemented the following process:

- Building a competency framework to describe the key attributes required by the new CEO, followed by a process for clarifying their emphasis and importance. Since this was a consultative process, an open debate arose around some fundamental differences concerning issues of technical knowledge and orientation (i.e. should the CEO focus outwards to build the company's image and presence in the market, or should he or she focus inwards to build the team, facilitate the relationships and grow the talent?).

- To inform this debate, the Relational Health Audit was administered online to a wide sample within the company. This demonstrated that relational issues were of greater importance than the top team realised, which resulted in a changed emphasis away from an analytical and networking style to a more developmental and facilitatory style.
- Internal aspirants were invited to discuss issues with the current CEO and to sign up for a process called Reality Coaching. This enabled them to consider their own strengths and weaknesses prior to formal application for the CEO role. Part of Reality Coaching is to go through a rigorous assessment procedure benchmarked against other top jobs and for the person to consider the results and implications with a coach.

The result was that several aspirants to the CEO role self-selected out, recognising that they did not have what is needed going forward. The climate in the top team became more open and positive as a result of having a clear and open process. The potential fallout which often comes from succession battles appears to have been averted or at least reduced.

The company has since acknowledged that without the Relational Health Audit they would not have identified the significance of the relational issues. Having a tangible metric for relationships transformed a debate concerning basic differences in opinions into a discussion based on meaningful evidence. The significance of the Relational Agenda would have remained where it is in most companies – recognised as important but having little impact on thinking and process. The appointment of this CEO has clearly shifted towards a more relational style with clear buy-in from the team.

Any job entails a mixture of technical/practical and relational skills. The maxim goes that employees are most likely to be hired for their hard skills but fired for their lack of soft skills. We are used to focusing on technical proficiency, but it is the lack of relational skills that tends to cause the most difficulties – tensions in the workforce, lack of commitment, problem behaviour and, in the end, increased turnover, instability and recruitment costs. Getting relationships right has effects that go far beyond the happiness of your employees.

Employers have historically focused on technical skills alone in recruitment. These can be taught and measured more easily than social skills, ostensibly making the process far simpler: the employer only needs to see evidence of a qualification or relevant experience. However, soft skills are generally necessary for successful long-term employment, as well as being more readily transferable to other sectors. Even if the job itself is highly technical, such as software design or engineering, employees don't work in a vacuum. They interact with a combination of other employees, management, clients, customers and wider stakeholders.

The lack of hard skills – particularly in engineering and science – may receive more media attention, but it is the difficulty in finding people with the right soft skills that tends to hold organisations back. According to the Chartered Institute of Personnel and Development (CIPD): 'The skills which employers say they need to focus on in order to meet their business objectives in two years' time are mainly leadership skills (sixty-five per cent), front-line people management skills (fifty-five per cent) and business acumen/awareness (fifty-one per cent). Looking more closely at leadership skills, the main gaps identified by employers are performance management (setting standards for performance and dealing with under-performance), and leading and managing change.'[2] These gaps both point to the importance of relational skills.

Getting relationships right draws on a wide range of skills. As we have noted, technical skills are important up to a point, especially in an organisational context: relating to someone who cannot fulfil their role in the relationship is deeply frustrating and usually short-lived. Hiring someone who turns out not to have the training or experience they need for the job presents an immediate problem. But beyond the 'hard' skills that employers tend to focus on – such as numeracy, proficiency in a software package or knowledge of a foreign language – there is also a wide range of relational skills that can be taught and developed: parenting, negotiating, active listening – even the ability to start and build a trusting relationship in the first place. Some of these are specific to certain circumstances. Others are valuable, whatever the nature of the relationship.

It is not just employees who may need to learn these skills. It is likely that leaders will be highly knowledgeable in one or more areas. In many cases, such technical knowledge is assumed to be enough. It does help to be an expert in your field but it doesn't matter how much you know if you can't communicate effectively with other people. Unsurprisingly, people with the highest qualifications don't necessarily make the best teachers. Speaking for Teach First, a

[2] CIPD, *Learning and Talent Development, 2010 CIPD Annual Survey Report*, www.cipd.co.uk/binaries/5215_Learning_talent_development_survey_report.pdf.

national charity that takes the best graduates, trains them and places them in under-achieving schools,[3] Ofsted's chief inspector Sir Michael Wilshaw suggested that the best teachers were 'incredibly reflective ... resilient, perceptive and interventionist'. These are emotional and relational skills, rather than technical ones. They allow teachers to understand their own motivations and show patience, insight and creativity in planning lessons, adapting and dealing with issues of classroom management.

Neither do the most knowledgeable people necessarily make the best managers. Some of the most technically proficient people have the worst relationship skills. But the relational shortcomings of organisational leaders are just as likely to cause problems as those of employees – arguably more so, because an employee is less able to manage their boss's problem behaviour and attitude, and is more vulnerable to dismissal. The result can be both disruptive and expensive for an organisation.

Managing through Appraisal

Overly complex organisational structure leads to a lack of Relational Proximity – not least Directness, which suffers due to the layers of management that are inherent in hierarchical organisations. Some of these layers will be redundant, and their ineffectiveness can result in a lack of Parity and Commonality between junior staff, managers and the organisation as a whole. Worse, the *explicit* objectives of various levels of staff and management can point in different directions, and are sometimes even directly contradictory.

A Relational Audit of a major accountancy firm showed a serious tension between junior staff, who were encouraged to maximise their billing hours, and managers who were appraised on whether they brought a project in on budget. Managers would discourage their staff from stating their work was chargeable, because it meant they were less likely to meet their profit targets. The conflict meant that the appraisal system could only ever be misleading, at best – it could not reflect both the realities and the organisational values at the same time. The same problem is true in almost any management consultancy firm.

The solution is to increase Commonality – or, where that is not possible, Parity. Ideally, all levels of an organisation should have the same objectives. Alternatively, both parties should manage competing objectives together. Continuity can also be an issue in these situations, since staff can work on

[3] Teach First homepage, www.teachfirst.org.uk/TFHome/.

several different projects with different managers for each, so it is hard for any one person to have full oversight of the employees' targets and time utilisation.

A similar tension in Commonality can be found in the example of a financial services organisation where, in order to improve 'efficiency', call centre agents were set a target of only spending a set number of minutes on each customer query – regardless of how profitable its outcome might be. As their bonuses were linked to achieving this target, the effect was to incentivise staff to wrap up calls within the allotted time, regardless of whether the customer had concluded his or her business satisfactorily – which led to many customers leaving the company. A drive for efficiency in one department undermined the profitability of the company as a whole.

Measuring

Although HR strategy is inherently concerned with managing people, it often overlooks relational criteria in favour of technical or practical ones. One of the chief problems is that relationships have traditionally been seen as resistant to quantification. Consequently, HR may tend to focus on processes rather than relationships. The Relational Proximity Framework helps HR departments report convincingly and accurately on the quality of relationships. A Relational Health Audit, for example, goes beyond the measures typically in use, such as employee attitudes surveys, and offers more ways to identify and resolve problems. A further advantage is that by allowing both parties to a relationship to assess it in terms of Relational Proximity it is possible to identify differences in perception. Relational Proximity helps identify ways to influence and change the relationship, not just a general assessment of its quality.

A professional services firm was losing senior professionals before they became partners. This mattered because the firm highlighted its workplace relationships in recruitment, and because it represented a significant loss of skilled staff with both technical knowledge and understanding of client needs. The HR director recognised that some partners were less good in managing relationships with their teams but needed to build a stronger case to inform and support changes to partner selection and development.

The firm's senior partners asked the Relationships Foundation to undertake a Relational Audit to identify key strengths and weaknesses in the relationship between partners and senior staff. The Relationships Foundation and the firm's personnel director jointly organised group discussions and interviews, and a confidential questionnaire using the Relational Proximity methodology was circulated to all partners and senior staff. It was found that underneath the superficially positive responses there were some deeply held concerns about flaws in the structure and operation of the partnership.

The output of the Relational Audit was fed back to all the partners and senior staff in the firm. Each department formed a group of partners and consultants to discuss concerns and put together action plans. The work of these groups was sponsored by the senior partners and coordinated by the personnel director who, with his team of personnel managers, undertook the cross-selling of ideas to improve relationships between groups and the development of initiatives across the firm.

The Relational Audit looked at the relationship from both sides, providing an assessment of areas of strength and weakness in the partner/senior professional relationship and highlighting concerns over specific aspects of Relational Proximity:

- *Directness*: Despite high levels of face-to-face communication there were concerns about the accessibility of partners and the degree of openness and honesty in the relationship. Nearly half of the partners and senior staff believed that they could not normally be open with each other. Two-thirds of senior staff and half the partners considered there was no regular feedback on performance given by partners. Almost all partners and senior staff believed that the ability to manage their relationship varied widely across the firm.
- *Continuity*: Two-thirds of senior staff and partners considered that there was not enough time to invest in building better relationships. Pressure of work often led to staff leaving the firm early on in their career, breaking the Continuity of relationships. The low retention rate was a destabilising factor, affecting morale and leading to the loss of important clients.
- *Multiplexity*: While partners and staff both agreed that getting to know one another well was an important factor in a good working relationship, perceptions differed as to whether or not this actually happened. Half the senior staff thought that opportunities for social contact were very limited, but few of the partners agreed. Nearly half of the staff believed that they had skills and experience that partners were not aware of, and little confidence in partners' knowledge of them as individuals.
- *Parity*: There was concern about the fairness of benefits in the relationship, particularly by senior staff, half of them being concerned about the fair

distribution of risk and reward. Some of the partners were far more concerned about this than others. Half of the female staff believed they were not treated equally by partners, and this view was supported by a quarter of the male staff. There was a culture of senior staff being unable to say 'no' to a partner giving them work even when overloaded.

- *Commonality*: While there was a strong shared view of commitment to clients and quality of work, views differed on internal issues. The majority of partners and half of all senior staff believed that there was little understanding of joint objectives or their needs for guidance in the ways to achieve them. Synergy between senior professionals' personal goals and the firm's corporate goals appeared to be weak – and was aggravated through there being different operating styles in different departments (and between different partners).

The use of the Relational Audit tools provided the partners and consultants with a common language that they could use to begin discussing the issues more openly and hence make progress towards a shared solution. A number of suggested changes emerged from the initial discussion groups and were evaluated in the interviews and questionnaire results. For example, it was felt that:

- Upward reviews would provide a formal process by which consultants could voice their concerns about the partner–consultant relationship.
- Consultants could be encouraged to work with different partners to gain a variety of experience and to develop partners' knowledge of them as individuals.
- Greater effort should be put into internal public relations by making information about the business available to all consultants.

Following meetings of the departmental groups, the personnel director led a development programme for partners, helping them to develop their role as managers and to change the approach of some of the partners to consultants – for instance, through training in such areas as mentoring and listening skills. Senior partners in the firm supported a 'new deal' for consultants, including the restructuring of pay scales and chargeable work procedures, and the introduction of a flexible working policy and planned secondments to client companies. The groups are continuing to work on a range of internal initiatives to improve the structure and operation of the partner–consultant relationship. The personnel director said of the audit process: 'Effective relationships are key to our business performance. The Relational Audit enabled us to target specific areas for improvement. We intend that these improvements will ultimately be reflected in the quality of our service to clients.'

Measuring Provides Accurate Diagnosis

Sometimes the issue is not establishing that action is needed, but identifying what needs to be done. Relational problems can be avoided because they are perceived as emotionally difficult, hard to pin down and likely to be time-consuming to resolve with limited prospect of success. In these situations, Relational Proximity can reveal the extent to which the conditions for effective relationships are in place, and can allow a potentially difficult conversation to take place in a safer and more constructive way. Assumptions about the nature of the problem will often be challenged, while identifying opportunities to strengthen the relationship in other areas can make it easier to address issues that have previously seemed intractable. This applies to individuals, teams, as well as organisations and communities.

A good example is a Relational Audit conducted by KPMG. The client organisation was a business going through a significant process of change. In one division a new leadership group had been formed, bringing together disparate sales leadership to increase collaboration and learning from best practice. The group had not gelled well for more than a year and performance was suffering.

On the face of it everyone in the team stood to gain if they worked together but the necessary collaboration wasn't happening. The individuals had been extremely autonomous in the past and resented what they perceived as an attempt to impose central control. The individual appointed to lead them assumed he had more respect from them than was actually the case. The behaviours in the team were challenging and unsupportive and could occasionally descend into hostility. The leader of the team felt he was running out of options.

A major relational problem was that the team members all disputed the right of the leader to instruct them. While instructing them was not his intent, this damaged all the relationships. The team met regularly but had no face-to-face communication between meetings. A lot of assumptions were made about what they knew about each other as people, and also about whether they shared a common purpose. There was such a degree of dispute between the individuals that the leader of the team was unable to see how he was contributing to the problems.

KPMG conducted a stand-alone team intervention involving the use of a Relational Health Audit followed by a facilitated workshop to discuss the results. Deficient scores were observed across all of the audit driver categories, confirming the initial feelings that a poor relationship existed within the group. Particularly low scores were found in aspects of Directness, Multiplexity and Parity. These low scores, with the exception of Parity, had a high consensus, indicating that there was a common recognition of the problem.

Before the intervention it was clear to an outside observer how dysfunctional the group was. However, the members of the group were telling themselves a number of narratives that placed all responsibility on the leader or one or more other members of the group. After the intervention, it was possible for the group to discuss their dysfunctionality dispassionately. In the end, this allowed for a realignment of purpose and this in turn led to a reorganisation and disbanding of the group. It was only through the objective analysis of the relationships that the problem could be moved away from mutual recrimination, providing both a clearer view of the situation and a way forward.

Similarly, the consulting firm Sandhams, working with the Relationships Foundation, conducted a Relational Audit for a client supplying services to a European manufacturer. The relationship was a long-standing one and both parties had been broadly happy with the transactional service arrangements in the past. Immediately prior to the involvement of Sandhams, however, there had been signs of increasing frustration from both sides. A number of staff on the supplier's team said they didn't want to work on the account and the customer was experiencing some concerns about the overall direction of the relationship. The customer was a large values-driven business and didn't want to use its advantage to demand change from the supplier. The supplier didn't know how best to approach the sensitive topic of why his team didn't want to work on the customer's business.

Sandhams met with both sides and conducted confidential interviews with the key people involved with the day-to-day relationship. They also met with the senior managers in the customer and the supplier so as to gauge their commitment to a mutually beneficial outcome. Having gained some sense of where the issues lay, Sandhams created a forum where both sides could voice the issues directly. To do this they designed a Relationship Review Process that included a Relational Audit. This comprised a one-day workshop and audit followed six weeks later by a follow-up workshop and review.

At the first workshop each side used the language of Relational Proximity to voice their concerns. For the supplier the main issue was around 'fair conduct'. They were able to describe how some of the ways a particular customer behaved were experienced by them as abrasive and intimidating. They said some hard things that the customer was unaware of. Those on the customer's side shared how they felt they were continually being 'sold' a strategic partnership style of relationship when in fact they wanted only a 'commodity service'. The issue was around shared objectives. This mismatch in expectation had led to much misunderstanding.

The outcomes of this intervention included:

- The 'intimidating' behaviour of the person concerned was addressed by the line manager.
- New working practices were agreed, including working in each other's offices for one day a week.
- A new vision for the longer-term relationship was articulated that embraced the 'strategic partner' and 'commodity supplier' needs of each side.
- A new climate of openness was created in which both sides could voice their concerns more directly.
- New contract discussions included relationship issues as a topic.
- The tone of the working relationship improved considerably such that people were happy to work on the team/account.

Although both organisations wanted to use their power in the relationship responsibly, differing views about the nature of Commonality had meant that actions were perceived in different ways. At the individual level, the corporate commitment to address the stakeholder relationship created the context within which concerns about an individual's conduct of a relationship can be identified and addressed. Without a commitment to address and improve the relationship, it is more difficult for suppliers to highlight ways in which their customers can improve the relationships to the benefit of both parties.

Sometimes Relational Audits throw up unexpected information. An audit of a South African mining company and its workforce showed that it had a significant impact on the communities where it was located. This is as expected: the provision of labour and the need for employment often create the potential for a strong foundation of Commonality, though concerns about local environmental impact can be a source of difference. The most likely relational issue is Parity, particularly when changes in commodity prices create significant financial pressures in the industry. In some cases, there is also a legacy of rather paternalistic provision of services to the community, and low workforce participation in decision-making. In the case of this particular company, however, it was found that one of the main concerns was lack of Continuity in the relationship between the community and the representatives of the mining company. The community had a much better understanding of the constraints facing the company than the company realised, but the high turnover of management tasked to interface with the community meant it was hard for the community to know who to deal with, or to build trust and understanding. This was relatively easy for the company to address, creating a context in which other issues could be addressed more effectively.

Measuring Allows Realistic Risk Assessment

Given the extent to which relationships represent a major risk factor for all organisations, there is a strong case for regular review of relationships to identify risks. As indicated in the next section this can, and probably should, be a requirement in company reporting.

With many relationships at stake, and each expressed in interpersonal and organisational terms, as well as through products and processes, it is a challenge for any organisation to consciously monitor and review performance in all these areas. This is not helped by the lack of lead responsibility for relationships within organisations: marketing, public relations (from a reputation perspective), HR, business development, procurement and other functional roles all have responsibilities.

While individuals and groups can continuously review and develop their own relationships, organisations need to prioritise the relationships they seek to develop. Rather than undertake a time-consuming, comprehensive mapping of all stakeholder relationships as a starting point for prioritisation, one option is to identify relationships based on an understanding of the organisation's specific sources of competitive advantage and key risks to cash-flow. Specifically, the relative importance of the various key stakeholder relationships in any organisation can be assessed according to two broad criteria: the importance of each relationship in supporting the business's strategic priorities and its potential to reduce short-term financial risk.

Long-term success results from the development and maintenance of competitive advantage that, in turn, is often largely dependent on key stakeholder relationships. For example, a strong relationship with customers can enable brand leadership, the ability to achieve a price premium and lower rates of customer churn. Strong relationships with key suppliers can enable industry-leading Continuity of supply, responsiveness and flexibility, and the achievement of the lowest-cost position. Strong relationships with employees/unions may be seen as vital in achieving industry-leading employee productivity and levels of process innovation. Examples of the contribution different stakeholders might make, and what might constitute their satisfaction, are given below.

To keep an organisation viable, management must ensure that adequate cash-flow is maintained to fund operations and to repay debt. This can inform relationship prioritisation by identifying the various scenarios that could threaten cash-flow and then identifying and strengthening the key stakeholder relationships that will help prevent these negative scenarios from occurring, or which will be critical in avoiding negative outcomes should they occur.

Within different types of external relationship it is then possible to identify which relationships are of most concern. Not only may, for example, relationships with different suppliers have very different characteristics but there may also be considerable variety within any one of them. Chief executives in the two organisations may have strong personal relationships, with relationships at the coalface being very different. The strategic collaboration that is frequently discussed by senior management may not be seen in the friction and conflict between those implementing it on the ground. Purchasers and suppliers may work well together, while their respective finance departments have a poor working relationship.

A South African utility company reviewed five of its key stakeholder relationships. An example of the insights this generated can be seen in the relationship with the government department. A Relational Audit revealed that the company's relationship with the department scored significantly lower than its relationship with other external stakeholders such as suppliers and customers. Also, the company's view of the relationship was significantly worse than the government department's view of the same relationship, with particular concerns about Continuity and Multiplexity.

Discussions with the utility company quickly showed why there were problems in the relationship and what could be done about it. It turned out that the utility company sent representatives into the office of the government department many times each week. However, it did not keep a record either of who was attending such meetings or of the messages that were communicated to the department's office. Nor did the company have a point person who was keeping a record of the issues raised by the department's office and the concerns expressed.

The company's board and executive committee, therefore, had little idea of how the company's relationship was developing, and what attitude the department's office might take to various questions. In practice, the company relied simply on its chief executive meeting with the relevant government minister once or twice a year for a half-hour discussion on the major issues affecting the industry, including the price appropriate to charge to consumers. The department, with fewer participants in the relationship, was better able to join the dots of the many different interactions and was therefore more confident in the relationship.

Without a measurement process to demonstrate how bad the relationship was with the department, especially relative to other stakeholder groups, this problem would have been difficult to identify and prioritise, and even more difficult to fix. Concerns about a relationship can too easily be attributed to some of the inherent tensions in that relationship: in dealings with a government department there is always potential for concern about Parity and Commonality. Yet in this case, closer analysis of the relationship showed that the problems lay elsewhere: in the management of the various interactions and the knowledge these could generate – issues that were far easier to address. Without such a review process, these issues may have gone unrecognised, symptoms of problems may have been misdiagnosed, and action to develop and improve the relationship been misinformed.

Measuring Informs the Evaluation of Structures and Processes

Measurement is also important for research and evaluation purposes. A good example is how different aspects of school structure and practice influence relationships.

Relational Schools works to put relationships at the core of school life. The starting point is a belief that supportive relationships between all members of a school are fundamental. Strong, secure relationships can surmount social inequality, whereas weak or fragile relationships reinforce educational disadvantage.

Many studies support the assertion that the quality of relationships in schools matters. This has enormous implications for structuring classroom environments. Children cannot learn if they are frightened, unhappy or feel that they don't belong. In addition, problems that remain into adolescence often last into adulthood. Students with insecure attachments in the home tend to experience dysfunctional and insecure relationships with staff. So if teachers can 'disconfirm' historical insecurities then those students will fare better socially, emotionally and academically.

Until now, the inability to measure relationships has been a major barrier in persuading schools and government to engage with relationships as a policy imperative. Relational Schools, however, has been working with a number of secondary schools across England to exploit Relational Audit methodology to achieve a formal, structured analysis that is unique in the field.

In a pilot study, most of the schools were either situated in areas of high material deprivation or drew much of their intake from materially deprived communities. It also focused on schools whose leadership team emphasised a Relational approach to issues such as class size, curriculum design and enrichment entitlement, with relationships acting as a driving imperative. Over 2,000 student-to-student relationships were assessed, as well as a large number of student-to-teacher relationships.

Early findings suggested that traditional pastoral structures in the UK tend to lead to fragmented relationships that become more fragmented as children progress through school. By the time they reach Year 11, the key domain of concern is Commonality: their shared goals and shared values were so weak that there was no sense of community or fraternity.

By contrast, the more Relational schools were remarkable in revealing the benefits of a Relational focus, as well as the potential to improve more dysfunctional relationships through a range of targeted interventions. For example, students in the schools that were intentional about relationship building:

- had a perception of being known and valued
- made more progress than predicted based on their socio-economic context
- reported feeling respected and feeling equal
- were happier and healthier than their counterparts in the other schools and had less time off school
- experienced declining levels of bullying as they progressed through the year groups.

Bullying is a significant indicator of wellbeing. An estimated half a million ten- and twelve-year-olds are physically bullied at school, according to a recent study by the Children's Society, which found that children in England were unhappier with their school experience than their peers in eleven other countries, including Ethiopia and Algeria.

In one case a school, described as a 'family' by students, was considered by social services as the best environment in the region for looked-after children. This last point is tangible evidence that demonstrates the impact of Relational systems and processes at school level.

Reporting

In South Africa, compliance with the King III code of corporate governance is now a requirement for any company that wants to be listed on the Johannesburg Stock Exchange. A draft King IV code aimed at broadening the acceptance of this approach by making it accessible to a wide range of organisations was released for public consultation on 15 March 2016. King III emphasises the need for sustainability in business – financially, environmentally and for society. It seems likely that as this becomes better known and established – and as the importance of factors beyond the financial and environmental becomes better accepted – that other countries will start to require some form of integrated reporting for their corporate governance.

The growth of relational reporting illustrates this, adding another dimension to the financial (and perhaps environmental) bottom lines employed by most companies. 'Integrated reporting', 'triple bottom line reporting', 'social accounting/auditing', 'sustainability reporting' and other similar terms all reflect a desire to capture the social and relational costs and benefits of a business, as well as the financial and environmental outcomes.

The International Integrated Reporting Council (IIRC) is one such major initiative, comprising 'a global coalition of regulators, investors, companies, standard setters, the accounting profession and NGOs'. Integrated Reporting (IR) aims 'to inform resource allocation by providers of financial capital that supports long term, as well as short and medium term, value creation. It promotes integrated thinking, decision-making and actions that focus on the creation of value in the long term, as well as short and medium term. IR enhances accountability and stewardship with respect to the broad base of capitals (financial, manufactured, human, intellectual, natural, and social and relational) and promotes understanding of the interdependencies between them.'[4] Even from a purely financial perspective, this may be desirable since IR seeks to understand the long-term sustainability of a business. Attracting long-term investors is often challenging for companies, since so many shareholders are interested only in short- or medium-term gain at the expense of long-term strategy. IR gives them a set of tools to communicate the viability of a business over more than the next few months or years.

[4] International Integrated Reporting Council, 'The International <IR> Framework', December 2013, http://integratedreporting.org/wp-content/uploads/2015/03/13-12-08-THE-INTERNATIONAL-IR-FRAMEWORK-2-1.pdf.

The Global Reporting Initiative (GRI) is another 'non-profit organisation that promotes economic, environmental and social sustainability. GRI provides all companies and organisations with a comprehensive sustainability reporting framework that is widely used around the world.' Again, this seeks to measure long-term financial profitability in the context of social justice and concern for the environment.

Currently, these corporate governance codes are designed for businesses. However, we believe that similar frameworks could and should be applied to the public sector as well. In particular, schools would benefit from relational reporting. At present, Ofsted places little weight on the quality of relationships within the school, or between the school and other stakeholders, or relational skills that pupils display – although there is a requirement for inspectors to consider 'the spiritual, moral, social and cultural development of pupils at the school'. The OECD's Programme for International Student Assessment (PISA), too, focuses solely on the three key competencies: reading, maths and science. However, there is growing evidence that employers value more than technical knowledge alone, with 'soft skills' increasingly sought during recruitment. Even on the highly reductionist criterion of accessing jobs, the frameworks used by Ofsted and PISA are deficient.

For companies, Relational Proximity provides a way of structuring stakeholder relationship assessments. The advantage of this approach is that it looks beyond the symptoms in a way that enables constructive reflection by both parties to the relationship and identifies ways in which relationships can be changed to support improved outcomes. So, for example, rather than simply reporting on employee or customer satisfaction, brand reputation, or specific indicators such as customer retention, it can identify the particular aspects of the relationships that give rise to these outcomes. This can be done by surveying a broad range of stakeholders, or more detailed investigation of specific relationships.

One level of analysis is provided by a Relational Balance Sheet. The Relational Proximity Framework provides the architecture for a variety of assessment tools. These can focus reflection and dialogue in three main ways. The first is to identify overall areas of strength and weakness in a relationship. This can be linked to specific stakeholders, individual drivers of Relational Proximity (Directness, Continuity, Multiplexity, Parity, Commonality) or sub-drivers. Such an approach might show that Continuity is consistently weak across all relationships (perhaps because of high levels of staff turnover and poor institutional memory), that particular suppliers are concerned about Parity and may thus be reluctant to be drawn into deeper collaboration, and whether this is due to the fairness of return or concerns about the way in which their staff are treated.

A second level looks at the perception gaps between the parties in a relationship. It is possible to create a Relational Balance Sheet (see Table 11.1) based on the differing perspectives from two sides of a relationship. If one party thinks Commonality is fine but the other party reports major concerns, then this helps set the agenda for discussion in a more concrete way.

A third level explores the degree of consensus among respondents about the quality of each domain in the relationship. An overall middling rating can mean that everyone is lukewarm about the relationship, or that half are highly positive and half are highly negative. Identifying pockets of dissatisfaction or divergent experience within a specific relationship can be vital means of identifying leading indicators of more critical problems. The sample balance sheet in Table 11.1 shows how a snapshot of stakeholder relationships can be provided.

Reporting on Progress

Accountability can require reporting on progress. One example of this comes from the United Nations Environment Programme (UNEP) on the link between peace building and the management of natural resources in Sudan.[5] The programme ran between 2007 and 2014 based on the recognition that building and restoring cooperation over natural resources and the environment is important for both peace building and governance. Three types of relationship were highlighted as essential for progress:

- *Institution–Institution*: including increased collaboration and coordination within and between government organisations and other institutions, such as civil society, international organisations or the private sector.
- *Institution–Community*: effective relationships between government and communities, characterised by consultations, participation in decision-making, accountable and effective service delivery, cost recovery and timely maintenance.

[5] Brendan Bromwich, *Relationships and Resources: Environmental Governance for Peacebuilding and Resilient Livelihoods in Sudan* (Nairobi: United Nations Environment Programme, June 2014).

Table 11.1: A sample Relational Balance Sheet

Relational Balance Sheet	Overall Score	Relational Proximity Drivers					Corporate Score	Institutional Gap	Counterparty Score
		Directness	Continuity	Multiplexity	Parity	Commonality			
External Stakeholders									
Trading Parties									
Suppliers	74	74	76	72	75	74	71	7	77
Customers	74	77	76	69	75	73	76	−4	72
Partnerships	74	74	78	73	71	74	76	−4	72
Trading Parties Score	74	75	76	71	74	73	74	−1	74
Authorities									
Regulatory Authorities	54	55	58	53	54	52	48	13	61
Stock Markets	76	81	80	76	74	68	73	5	79
Authorities Score	65	68	69	65	64	60	60	9	70
Indirect Stakeholders									
Communities	70	73	74	65	68	69	71	−2	69
Media Organisations	67	72	66	65	67	64	64	6	70
Trade Unions	62	65	70	60	59	58	64	−3	61
Industry Bodies	62	63	64	55	65	61	67	−11	56
Indirect Stakeholders Score	65	68	69	61	65	63	66	−3	64

Note: Scores of 65 or below were highlighted (here, in *italic*) for stakeholder attention.
Source: A pilot study conducted by Stakeholder Relationship Assessments (Pty Ltd) in South Africa in 2011 with five major corporates covering insurance, energy, utilities, telecoms and private healthcare provision. All figures in the table are aggregates across the results of the five companies which each chose a different selection of stakeholders to analyse.

- *Community–Community*: seen, for example, in collaboration at the community level, including agreements over access to resources and trade between livelihood groups.

The programme required a new approach to describing softer project outcomes and demonstrating progress – showing that the relationships essential to the improved governance of natural resources and building peace were being successfully supported and developed, alongside more tangible results such as construction of water-management structures. Where the development of relationships is both essential to programme outcomes, and likely to take significant time, then the ability to demonstrate progress to secure continuing programme funding becomes particularly important. Similar issues might apply, for example, in funding work with troubled young people, where the development of a relationship of trust is the essential foundation for being able to tackle other issues such as substance abuse, antisocial behaviour, or non-participation in education. Drawing on the Relational Proximity Framework, a new approach on measuring project outcomes in terms of relationships was developed. For each of the three key types of relationship, six typical stages of development were identified, each of which could be characterised by different degrees of Relational Proximity. This represented a measured pathway for monitoring progress.

The programme reached a number of conclusions about this relationships-based approach. The first is around the improved analysis of governance and peace building contexts. The use of relational metrics and the measured pathway to describe improving relationships was seen as extending the availability of practical tools. Measuring the impact of interventions was thought to be enhanced 'through the formulation of the measured pathway against which developing relationships can be compared'. The steps in the pathway enabled analysis of relationship progress. The approach was also seen as providing a new way to design interventions. If problems can be identified in relationships terms then the solution may be tailored accordingly. At a larger scale, 'the relationships-based theory of change provides a narrative of how effort in aid leads to impact for communities that can be applied in many contexts in which governance and peacebuilding are relevant'.[6]

---

[6] Bromwich, *Relationships and Resources*, pp. 48–51.

Regulating

Reporting underpins effective regulation, with reports forming some of the key data that regulators work with. But regulation also requires effective relationships:

Successfully managing various stakeholders and balancing their priorities is critical for all organisations. For banks, regulators are a vitally important stakeholder: they set the rules, supervise prudential financial strength and business conduct, challenge, and ultimately approve a bank's licence to operate. A poor regulatory relationship can result in onerous challenges for management including withdrawal of a banking licence, increased capital and liquidity requirements, financial penalties, mandatory remediation exercises, restrictions on activities and, as was the case for Barclays, the departure of senior executives and Board members.[7]

For organisations, both corporately and for individuals responsible for key relationships, Relational Proximity helps identify the risks, weaknesses and development opportunities in those relationships. From a public policy perspective, Relational Proximity helps model how regulatory effectiveness will be influenced by a range of relationships, including those with other companies, with regulators, with government and with consumers. The process works in both directions: regulation shapes relationships and is influenced by relationships. Greater clarity in understanding how relationships are shaped and influenced is a vital ingredient for better policy-making where relational literacy should be recognised as being as important as economic literacy.

Regulatory relationships take many forms, with the dynamics of the relationship varying according to the purpose and impact on business or service: protecting consumers in dealing with powerful organisations due to size, monopoly position, or technical complexity; reducing risk or improving standards; all have slightly different relational requirements. A simplified analysis of different regulatory relationships might highlight:

- *Utilities*: Protecting consumers and the environment, and maintaining the quality of national infrastructure, particularly in the context of local monopolies post-privatisation. The degree of independence from government may

---

[7] A. Salz, 'The Salz Review: An Independent Review of Barclays' Business Practices', April 2013, http://online.wsj.com/public/resources/documents/SalzReview04032013.pdf, para. 7.4, p. 68.

be compromised by continuing need for government subsidy and the political sensitivity of price increases.

- *Banking/finance*: Consumer protection, where Parity may be compromised by complexity of products, lack of consumer knowledge, or difficulty in switching. Regulators may also be concerned with risk, particularly the impact on the wider economy and government liabilities as 'lender of last resort'.
- *Retail*: General consumer protection may be advanced through advertising standards, food standards, competition or fair trading. As well as protecting consumers, businesses also benefit from a level playing field, where they will not be undercut by competitors who ignore these standards.
- *Professions*: Doctors, solicitors and other professions tend to seek self-regulation to maintain professional status, standards and independence. An important aspect of self-regulation has been the codification of the values that should govern relationships, with professionalism increasingly seen in terms not just of the knowledge required for entry, but of the way in which relationships with the public, other professions and other services are conducted.
- *Public services*: Regulation focuses on quality and safety, and may be at least semi-independent of government where there is plurality of provision. Ultimate government accountability for standards can mean that there is rather complex mediation of the relationship between public and services via both government and regulators, with professions also staking a claim to be guardians of both quality and ethics.

In theory, the relationship between organisations and regulators should be perfectly straightforward: the regulators are there to ensure that companies act within certain parameters to maintain safety and fairness. In practice, things are more complicated, and the relationship can be abused in a number of ways. The Relational Proximity Framework can begin to unpack what might be going on in cases of regulatory failure. Modern western regulatory frameworks place a lot of emphasis on 'independence'. The intention is that there is some degree of relational distance between the regulator and market participants. Where, however, expert knowledge of an industry is in limited supply, and so staff move between regulator and industry, it is easy for regulators to become much closer to people in the industry, whom they see frequently and who may often be former colleagues or personal friends, than to the public they represent.

Regulators, particularly where they are less independent of government, may be reluctant to be seen to be damaging a market that has strong political support. Companies can take advantage of this by artificially making losses, or organising their accounts to give that impression. Then the regulator will come under pressure from the government for being too tough. An overly powerful regulator can also create Commonality between competitors, to the detriment of Commonality with customers. The interplay of Commonality and Continuity allows competitors to build collusion. In the LIBOR scandal, there were many banks involved: competition was theoretically strong and so any effective collusion had to be direct and overt. In other cases, there are more subtle (less Direct) ways that different players in the market communicate with each other to collude in price-fixing in a way that may not seem to be unscrupulous to the players. One player might drop their prices for a week and thus send a signal to their competitors – like an opening bid in an auction – then raise them the next week. Competitors shuffle prices up and down to indicate their preferred levels.

Involving and empowering customers as a third party would enable them to look out for their own interests better, reducing the need for regulators to protect them. Customers typically act – and are treated – as individuals. When they speak with a consistent voice or are jointly represented then there is greater Parity with the companies whose goods and services they use. Neighbourhood and community purchasing is one example of this. Instead of customers buying power individually, they could club together to buy it as a whole village or town. They would invite power companies to tender for the large joint contract – benefiting both parties. Community broadband, in which groups of people get together to buy fast internet access in remote areas, is another example. This kind of initiative is normal in the business-to-business (B2B) world, but not in the retail sector. Unions serve the same function of collective influence for employees; action groups do the same for shareholders. There are some exceptions. The IBM user group SHARE, Inc. is a voluntary and independent partnership,[8] but retains strong links with the company and its subsidiaries. It is large enough to represent a significant proportion of IBM users and to influence company direction. Workplace insurance and pension schemes, in which employers secure favourable rates for their staff through a group discount, go some way to addressing imbalances in Parity, but these are mediated through third parties, meaning that rates could often be better with greater Directness.

From the perspective of Relational Proximity, then, power and purpose are key elements in regulatory relationships that seek to use the power of the state to protect the interests of others, as well as to ensure that the purposes of organisations reflect public interests. The other drivers of Relational Proximity are

---

[8] SHARE, Share homepage, www.share.org/.

important in understanding how regulatory relationships are best conducted, as well as in describing aspects of the relationships they seek to protect. For Commonality, one lesson is that the content and not just the degree matters. It must be compatible across all stakeholders and cannot be represented in the collusion of some against the interests of others. The Commonality of individual traders or participants in the market must also be aligned with the requirements of the nature and quality of relationships that their organisations are trying to build with stakeholders.

With respect to Parity, third parties such as regulators can act to alter Parity in other relationships, such as those between banks and customers. Governments should consider all options for influencing Parity (for example, community group purchasing) and not simply rely on regulation, while regulators may discover that closer analysis of how relationships operate offers alternative mechanisms of influence beyond the traditional levers of regulating pricing and mandating investment.

Regulators need a broad-based understanding of the organisations they regulate, and that requires Multiplexity. The relational distance that ensures impartiality may be important in regulating prices, but regulators may need to be more closely engaged to monitor risk and malpractice in, for example, banks. Discontinuity can bring a fresh perspective on relationships, disrupting collusion, but a lack of Continuity can mean that the individuals with the knowledge and experience to make the best decisions move on too often. The stability and predictability of the regulatory regime is also important for companies: without this Continuity the confidence to invest is diminished, particularly where the return on investment takes place over long timescales, such as in new power generation capacity.

The Salz Review[9] was commissioned as an independent assessment of Barclays' values, principles and standards of operation. Published in April 2013, it touches on many relational issues, illustrating how relationships with one stakeholder can impact on others. Internal relationships within the bank impacted on relationships with the regulator, which limited their ability to moderate the bank's relationships with customers or the wider social and economic impact of the bank's actions. Aspects of Relational Proximity that were highlighted included:

- *Commonality*: The fundamental importance of Commonality is seen in 'the absence of a common purpose or set of values'. A lack of Commonality within

[9] Salz, 'The Salz Review'.

the bank was seen in 'silos with different values and cultures'. A specific example was the relationship between the business and the Compliance function that was 'adversarial rather than collegiate, with Compliance seen as an obstacle to overcome in doing business'. A lack of Commonality within the bank impacted on Commonality in other relationships. For customers, 'despite some attempts to establish Group-wide values, the culture that emerged tended to favour transactions over relationships, the short term over sustainability, and financial over other business purposes.' This is linked to 'the moral hazards of basing the incentives of a retail bank sales force on achieving sales volumes thereby underemphasising customer needs and suitability'.

- *Parity*: The relationship with regulators was compromised by a perceived lack of Parity. The review noted the 'risk that at times the resources available to large universal banks on matters that have a bearing on these complex regulatory determinations significantly outweigh the resources available to the FSA [the regulator]'. The 'technically expert and well-supported' bank team 'came across to some as being "clever" or what some people have termed "too clever by half", even arrogant and aggressive'. There was also a lack of Parity in some internal relationships: 'Employees felt unable to question the new growth targets' and attributed this to a 'culture of fear' (particularly, it seemed a fear of not achieving targets) as well as to weak central oversight. Bonus decisions that were 'highly dependent on the judgment of individual line managers' were also an issue, creating 'a culture which encouraged individuals to follow their manager – resulting in complex dynamics around loyalty and willingness to offer challenge'. When the financial crisis broke, other weaknesses in Parity emerged, not least the 'disproportionate sharing of risk between employees and shareholders [that] became apparent'.

- *Multiplexity and Continuity*: Aspects of Relational Proximity were seen as likely to improve the regulatory relationship: 'One example would be for banks to recognise the value to bankers, as part of their careers, of spending time (probably for around two years to be valuable) working in a regulator, and vice versa.' Another recommendation was 'regular engagement by the Chairmen and Chief Executives of the banks with the leadership of the PRA [Prudential Regulation Authority] and the FCA, as well as with other public authorities with an interest in regulation'. Such ideas were seen as important in helping 'both regulators and the banks improve mutual understanding'.

- *Directness*: More open communication was a key recommendation: 'Openness is a value which goes directly to the heart of relationships with all stakeholders, for example: providing clarity about product suitability and pricing for customers; resisting ambiguity and applying high standards of disclosure to shareholder communication; promoting cooperative and straightforward discourse with regulators; and encouraging staff to raise concerns with no need to fear the consequences.' Misunderstanding is a risk: 'At times there has been confusion between some bankers and regulators as to the precise message that the regulators are sending. Clarity of message is more complicated in times of financial stress when there are interactions at many levels and the matters being discussed are sensitive.' Clarity of communication and listening are therefore essential: 'regulators should seek to be as clear as possible in their messaging and banks should listen carefully and seek clarification where any message is unclear.' Facilitating trust through greater openness and transparency is described as requiring 'two-way communications, both internally with all staff, management and the Board, and externally with all stakeholders – including, importantly, regulators. It involves better listening.'

Epilogue

Relational Proximity is an effective tool for measuring relationships – the 'dark matter' in organisations. It has been developed across twenty years of research, consultancy and social reform. Working with relationships over many years in business, public services, public policy and peace building, combined with the insights into relationships that many different academic disciplines afford, has built a rich picture of how organisational and personal relationships are influenced by a multitude of factors. Across multiple sectors, the same five drivers of Relational Proximity apply, and for people struggling with the nebulous complexity of relationships, this can be empowering: a few key insights can point to ways in which relationships can be more effectively influenced.

Organisations can work instrumentally with relationships as a means to an end. Reducing risk, increasing staff retention or productivity, improving the efficiency of supply chains and production, or enhancing customer loyalty and satisfaction are all important and valuable in their own right, and have an impact on the bottom line. But the challenges of recognising the relational nature of the world we live in, and of getting relationships right despite their complexity and the many pressures we may be under, raises a much more significant agenda than better management of the organisational relational environment.

Thinking relationally involves reappraising issues, seeing both self and other in a different way, changing goals, reforming institutions and implementing better practice. Seeing the relational dimension of issues, and the importance of relationships, leads to doing things differently. But ultimately it leads to *being* different. Becoming a relational organisation can involve rethinking purpose, changing culture and reforming structures. Though such transformations may be rewarding, they are also challenging. The challenge is not just for organisations, but for individuals and for societies as well.

We also began by acknowledging that relationships are often conducted under pressure. Lack of time, challenging targets or financial worries can all lead to relationships being neglected, or inadequate consideration given to the impact of actions and decisions on others. New technologies, globalisation of finance, as well as cultural changes, can all open up new relational possibilities but also create a more difficult environment. Some are pessimistic about the future – seeing the decline of social capital and the growing dangers of divorcing the ownership and use of capital from relational responsibilities. How will we build connectedness, when we connect globally to strangers? Will our stories become increasingly fragmented in a world of choice and rootless mobility? Will we only be known within the small and ephemeral enclaves we create? Will only power be respected as inequalities grow? Will the clash of civilisations be internalised within nations, fragmenting common purpose?

Relational distance is in some ways the defining characteristic of the age in which we live. And there are many ways in which it can be overcome. There are also new relational opportunities, with many organisations and individuals recognising the vital role of relationships in their effectiveness and wellbeing. New technology brings unprecedented opportunities for Directness, reducing the mediating power of media or political parties and opening up new business opportunities. The Continuity of personal contacts can be sustained through Twitter, Facebook, mobile phones and other media. Multiplex knowledge can be broadened by search engines. Parity is enhanced when a single customer can humble a mighty corporation through a viral complaint. The opportunity and the means to build common purpose with others is increased as it becomes easier to connect to people with shared concerns.

Public policy and organisational change can increase relational distance, or overcome it. This means that Relational Proximity is an important tool of political leadership. Relationships can be assessed, and impacts modelled. Good relational practice can be incentivised. More supportive environments for relationships can be created. But perhaps, above all, that hard-wired human desire for relationship means that we (and those to whom we relate) cannot remain endlessly content with the consequences of our personal and organisational flaws and weaknesses. Improvement is always a journey. For those seeking to improve relationships it is a rich and rewarding journey, with many fellow travellers.

BIBLIOGRAPHY

Abdelal, R., Y. Herrera, A. Johnston and R. McDermott, 'Identity as a variable', *Perspectives on Politics*, 4 (2006), pp. 695–711

Alexander, S. and M. Ruderman, 'The role of procedural and distributive justice in organisational behavior', *Social Justice Research*, 1 (1987), pp. 177–198

Argyris, C., *Understanding Organisational Behavior*, Homewood, IL: Dorsey Press, 1960

Ariely, D., *Predictably Irrational: The Hidden Forces that Shape Our Decisions*, London: HarperCollins, 2008

Arrowsmith, J., 'Strike grounds British Airways at Heathrow', European Industrial Relations Observatory Online, 17 August 2003, www.eurofound.europa.eu/eiro/2003/08/feature/uk0308103f.htm

Atwood, M., *The Blind Assassin*, London: Virago Press, 2001

Axelrod, R., *The Evolution of Cooperation*, New York: Basic Books, 1984

Ballew, C. and A. Todorov, 'Predicting political elections from rapid and unreflective face judgments', *PNAS*, 104:46 (2007), pp. 17948–17953

Barber, B. R., *Jihad vs. McWorld*, New York: Crown, 1995

Bartle, M., I. Briscoe, G. Mulgan, Z. Sar-Wiwo, J. Wade and H. Wilkinson, *The Time Squeeze*, London: Demos, 1995

Bauman, Z., *Liquid Life*, Cambridge: Polity Press, 2005

BBC, 'A bonfire of school targets?', 20 March 2004, http://news.bbc.co.uk/1/hi/education/3551627.stm

  'Analysis: Putin wants respect', http://news.bbc.co.uk/2/hi/europe/666768.stm, accessed 15 October 2008

  'Are there too many managers?', 29 July 2013, www.bbc.co.uk/news/magazine-23462290

BBC Panorama, 'Fiddling the figures', BBC, Transcript, 26 June 2003, http://news.bbc.co.uk/nol/shared/spl/hi/programmes/panorama/transcripts/fiddlingthefigures.txt

Bies, R. J., D. L. Shapiro and L. L. Cummings, 'Causal accounts and managing organisational conflict: is it enough to say it's not my fault?', *Communication Research*, 15 (1988), pp. 381–399

Binmore, K., *Natural Justice*, Oxford University Press, 2005

Birkinshaw, J., *Reinventing Management: Smarter Choices for Getting Work Done*, San Francisco, CA, Jossey-Bass, 2010

Blau, P. M., *Exchange and Power in Social Life*, New York: Wiley, 1965

Bowlby, J., *Attachment*, Vol. 1 of *Attachment and Loss*, London: Hogarth, 1969

Boyle, D., 'In search of a political narrative', D. Boyle: Politics of the future (blog), August 2005, www.david-boyle.co.uk/politics/narrative.html

Bradshaw, A., *Lighting the Lamp: Spiritual Dimension of Nursing Care (RCN Research)*, London: Scutari Press, 1994

Branden, N., *The Six Pillars of Self-Esteem*, New York: Bantam Trade Paperback Edition, 1995

Brett, J. F. and L. E. Atwater, '360-degree feedback: accuracy, reactions and perceptions of usefulness', *Journal of Applied Psychology*, 86 (2001), pp. 930–942

Bridgewater, S., 'An analysis of football management trends 1992–2005 in all four divisions', *Warwick Business School Report for League Managers Association*, Coventry: University of Warwick, 2006

Brockner, J., *Self-Esteem at Work*, Lexington Books, 1988

Brockner, J. and B. M. Wiesenfeld, 'An integrative framework for explaining reactions to decisions: the interactive effects of outcomes and procedures', *Psychological Bulletin*, 120 (1996), pp. 189–208

Bromwich, B., *Relationships and Resources: Environmental Governance for Peacebuilding and Resilient Livelihoods in Sudan*, United Nations Environment Programme, Nairobi: UNEP, June 2014

Brosnan, S. F., 'Justice- and fairness-related behaviors in non-human primates', *Proceedings of the National Academy of Sciences*, 110, Supplement 2 (2013), pp. 10416–10423

Brown, R. P. and V. Zeigler-Hall, 'Narcissism and the non-equivalence of self-esteem measures: a matter of dominance?', *Journal of Research in Personality*, 38 (2004), pp. 585–592

Browne, J. T. (ed.), *A Book of Non-Fiction*, New York: Macmillan, 1965

Burnside, J. and N. Baker (eds.), *Relational Justice: Repairing the Breach*, Winchester: Waterside Press, 2004

Burt, R. S., *Structural Holes: The Social Structure of Competition*, Boston, MA: Harvard University Press, 1992

Cameron, D., 'David Cameron's speech to Google Zeitgeist Conference, Europe 2006', full text available at *Guardian*, 22 May 2006, www.theguardian.com/politics/2006/may/22/conservatives.davidcameron

'David Cameron on families', Speech, Relationships Alliance Summit, Royal College of GPs, London, 18 August 2014

Campbell, W. K. and C.A. Foster, 'Narcissism and commitment in romantic relationships: an investment model analysis,' *Personality and Social Psychology Bulletin*, 28 (2002), pp. 484–495

Carney, F. S. (ed. and trans.), *The Politics of Johannes Althusius*, London: Eyre & Spottiswoode, 1995

Carney, M., 'Inclusive capitalism: creating a sense of the systematic', Speech given at the Conference on Inclusive Capitalism, Bank of England, London, 27 May 2014, www.bankofengland.co.uk/publications/Documents/speeches/2014/speech731.pdf

Casebeer, D. W. and J. A. Russell, 'Storytelling and terrorism: towards a comprehensive "counter-narrative strategy"', *Strategic Insights*, 4 (2005), pp. 1–16

Castoriadis, C., 'Power, politics, autonomy', in A. Honneth, T. McCarthy, C. Offe and A. Wellmer (eds.), *Cultural–Political Interventions in the Unfinished Project of Enlightenment*, Cambridge, MA: MIT Press, 1992

Centre for Tomorrow's Company, *Tomorrow's Value: Achieving Long Term Financial Returns. A Guide for Pension Fund Trustees*, London: CTC, 2014

Chisson, E. J., *The Hubble Wars*, New York: Harper Perennial, 1994

Choi, J. N. and M. U. Kim, 'The organisational application of groupthink and its limits in organisations', *Journal of Applied Psychology*, 84 (1999), pp. 297–306

Churchill, W., 'Their finest hour', Speech to the House of Commons, 18 June 1940, HC Deb., 18 June 1940, vol. 362 cc51–64

Cialdini, R. B., *Influence: The Psychology of Persuasion*, New York: William Morrow & Co., 1984

CIPD, *Learning and Talent Development, 2010 CIPD Annual Survey Report*, www.cipd.co.uk/binaries/5215_Learning_talent_development_survey_report.pdf

Clark, W. H., Jr and E. K. Babson, 'How benefit corporations are redefining the purpose of business corporations', *William Mitchell Law Review*, 38 (2012), pp. 817–851

Clegg, S., 'The power of language, the language of power', *Organisation Studies*, 8 (1987), pp. 60–70

Cohen, D. and L. Prusak, *In Good Company: How Social Capital Makes Organizations Work*, Harvard, MA: Harvard University Press, 2001

Conlon, D. E. and N. M. Murray, 'Customer perceptions of corporate responses to product complaints: the role of explanations', *Academy of Management Journal*, 39 (1996), pp. 1040–1056

Conner, D., *Managing at the Speed of Change: How Resilient Managers Succeed and Prosper Where Others Fail*, New York: Random House, 1993

Covault, C., 'Columbia revelations: alarming e-mails speak for themselves. But Administrator O'Keefe is more concerned about Board findings on NASA decision-making', *Aviation Week & Space Technology*, 3 March 2003

Covey, S., *The 8th Habit: From Effectiveness to Greatness*, New York: Simon & Schuster, 2006

Crocker, J. and N. Nuer, 'The insatiable quest for self-worth', *Psychological Inquiry*, 14 (2003), pp. 31–34

Cruddas, J., 'John Cruddas's speech on love and work: full text', *New Statesman*, 29 January 2015, available at www.newstatesman.com/politics/2015/01/jon-cruddas-s-speech-love-and-work-full-text

Daft, L., R. H. Lengel and L. K. Trevino, 'Message equivocality, media selection and manager performance – implications for information systems', *MIS Quarterly*, 11 (1987), pp. 354–366

Dahl, R. A., 'The concept of power', *Behavioural Science*, 2 (1957) pp. 201–215

Daly, J. P. and P. D. Geyer, 'The role of fairness in implementing large-scale change: employee evaluations of process and outcome in seven facility relocations', *Journal of Organisational Behavior*, 15 (1994), pp. 623–638

Damon, W., *The Path to Purpose: Helping Our Children Find Their Calling in Life*, New York: Free Press, 2008

   'Majority of youths found to lack a direction in life', interview in *Education Week*, June 11, 2008

Darwin, F. (ed.), *Charles Darwin's Autobiography*, New York: Henry Schuman, 1950

Davenport, T. H. and L. Prusak, *Working Knowledge: How Organisations Manage What They Know*, Cambridge, MA: Harvard Business School Press, 1998

Dawes, C. T., J. H. Fowler, T. Johnson, R. McElreath and O. Smirnov, 'Egalitarian motives in humans', *Nature*, 446 (2007), pp. 794–796

de Botton, A., *Status Anxiety*, London: Penguin, 2005

de Geus, A., *The Living Company: Growth, Learning and Longevity in Business*, London: Nicholas Brealey, 1999

DeCremer, D., 'Respect and cooperation in social dilemmas: the importance of feeling included,' *Personality and Social Psychology Bulletin*, 28 (2002), pp. 1335–1341

Degeorge, F., J. Patel and R. Zeckhauser, 'Earnings management to exceed thresholds', *Journal of Business*, 72 (1999), pp. 1–33

Denison, D. R., S. Haaland and P. Goelzer, 'Corporate culture and organisational effectiveness: is Asia different from the rest of the world?', *Organisational Dynamics*, 33 (2004), pp. 98–109

Department of Health, *Learning from Bristol: The Report of the Public Inquiry into Children's Heart Surgery at the Bristol Royal Infirmary 1982–1995*, London: HMSO, 2001

Diener, E. and M. E. P. Seligman, 'Beyond money: toward an economy of well-being', *Psychological Science in the Public Interest*, 5 (2004), pp. 1–31

Dillon, R., 'Respect: a philosophical perspective', *Gruppendynamik und Organisationsberatung*, 38 (2007), pp. 201–212

Dixon, M. and K. Sweeney, *The Human Effect in Medicine: Theory, Research and Practice*, Oxford: Radcliffe Medical Press, 2000

Doyal, L. and I. Gough, *A Theory of Human Need*, London: Palgrave Macmillan, 1991

Duffy, F., 'Working at Waterside – conduciveness as a workplace of the British Airways' Headquarters in Harmondsworth, England', *The Architectural Review*, 1218 (1998).

Earley, P. C. and S. Ang, *Cultural Intelligence: Individual Interactions Across Cultures*, Stanford University Press, 2003

Earls, M., *Herd: How to Change Mass Behaviour by Harnessing Our True Nature*, Chichester: John Wiley, 2007

Economist, 'Triple bottom line', 17 November 2009, www.economist.com/node/14301663, accessed 12 February 2013

Fauconnier, G. and M. Turner, *The Way We Think: Conceptual Blending and the Mind's Hidden Complexities*, New York: Basic Books, 2002

Fayol, H., *General and Industrial Management*, London: Pitman, 1949

Feinberg, J., 'Some conjectures on the concept of respect', *Journal of Social Philosophy*, 4 (1973), pp. 1–3

Fernández-Aráoz, C., *Great People Decisions: Why They Matter So Much, Why They Are So Hard and How You Can Master Them*, Hoboken, NJ: John Wiley, 2007

Financial Times, 'Acknowledge managers as professionals', 10 October 2010

Fisher, J. D., M. Rytting and R. Heslin, 'Hands touching hands: affective and evaluative effects of an interpersonal touch', *Sociometry*, 39 (1976), pp. 416–421

Folger, R. and R. Cropanzano, *Organisational Justice and Human Resource Management*, Thousand Oaks, CA: Sage, 1998

Frei, J. R. and P. R. Shaver, 'Respect in close relationships: prototype definition, self-report assessment and initial correlates', *Personal Relationships*, 9 (2002), pp. 121–139

Gardner, D. G. and J. L. Pierce, 'Self-esteem and self-efficacy within the organisational context', *Group and Organisation Management*, 23 (1998), pp. 48–70, 177–198

Gauntlett, D., *Media, Gender and Identity: An Introduction*, London and New York: Routledge, 2002

Gentner, D., K. Holyoak and B. Kokinov, *The Analogical Mind: Perspectives from Cognitive Science*, Cambridge, MA: MIT Press, 2001

Gerzon, M., *Leading Through Conflict: How Successful Leaders Transform Differences into Opportunities*, Cambridge MA: Harvard Business School Press, 2006

Giddens, A., *Modernity and Self-Identity: Self and Society in the Late Modern Age*, Cambridge: Polity Press, 1991

Gladwell, M., *Blink: The Power of Thinking Without Thinking*, New York: Little, Brown, 2005

Global Reporting Initiative, 'GRI Sustainability Reporting Guidelines', June 2000

Goffman, E., *Interaction Ritual: Essays on Face-to-Face Behaviour*, New York: Anchor Books, 1967

Goleman, D., *Emotional Intelligence: Why It Can Matter More Than IQ for Character, Health and Lifelong Achievement*, New York: Bantam Books, 1995
Working with Emotional Intelligence, New York: Bantam Books, 1998

Graham, J. R., C. R. Harvey and S. Rajgopal, 'The economic implications of corporate financial reporting', *Journal of Accounting and Economics*, 40 (2005), pp. 3–73

Granovetter, M., 'The strength of weak ties', *American Journal of Sociology*, 78 (1973), pp. 1360–1380

Greenberg, J., 'A taxonomy of organisational justice theories', *Academy of Management Review*, 12 (1987), pp. 9–22

Greenberg, J. and R. Folger, 'Procedural justice, participation, and the fair process effect in groups and organisations', in P. B. Paulus (ed.), *Basic Group Processes*, New York: Springer-Verlag, 1983

Guardian, 'Interests and hobbies', 15 April 2009, www.theguardian.com/careers/cv-interests-hobbies

Haggerty, J., R. J. Reid, G. K. Freeman, B. H. Starfield, C. E. Adair and R. McKendry, 'Continuity of care: a multidisciplinary review', *British Medical Journal*, 327 (2003), pp. 1219–1221

Haldane, A., 'Patience and finance', Beijing, Oxford China Business Forum, Beijing, 22 September 2010, available at www.bankofengland.co.uk/publications/news/2010/067.htm

Handy, C., 'What is a company for?', Michael Shanks Memorial Lecture, 5 December 1990

Hedinger, T., 'Assessing interpersonal respect: its psychological and philosophical implications', Master's Thesis at Southern Illinois University, Carbondale, IL, *Master's Abstracts International*, 30 (1992)

'To learn respect: four adults share their stories of respectfulness', Doctoral Dissertation at Southern Illinois University, Carbondale, IL, *Dissertation Abstracts International Section A: Humanities and Social Sciences*, 61 (2000)

Helmreich, R., 'On error management: lessons from aviation', *British Medical Journal*, 320 (2000), pp. 781–785

Heskett, J., C. Hart and W. E. Sasser, Jr, *Service Breakthroughs: Changing the Rules of the Game*, New York: Free Press, 1990

Heskett, J., W. E. Sasser, Jr and L. A. Schlesinger, *The Service Profit Chain*, New York: Free Press, 1997

The Value Profit Chain: Treat Employees Like Customers and Customers Like Employees, New York: Free Press, 2003

Heuer, L., E. Blumenthal, A. Douglas and T. Weinblatt, 'A deservingness approach to respect as a relationally based fairness judgment', *Personality and Social Psychology Bulletin*, 25 (1999), pp. 1279–1292

Higgins, J., 'Adverse events or patterns of failure', *British Journal of Health Care Management*, 7 (2001), pp. 145–147

Hinde, R., *Relationships: A Dialectical Perspective*, Hove: Psychology Press, 1997

Interface Global, 'Our sustainability journey – mission zero', www.interfaceglobal.com/Sustainability/Interface-Story.aspx

International Integrated Reporting Council, 'The International <IR> Framework', December 2013, http://integratedreporting.org/wp-content/uploads/2013/03/13-12-08-THE-INTERNATIONAL-IR-FRAMEWORK-2-1.pdf

James, W., *Principles of Psychology*, Cambridge, MA: Harvard University Press, 1890

Janis, I. L., *Victims of Groupthink*, Boston, MA: Houghton Mifflin, 1972

Groupthink, Boston, MA: Houghton Mifflin, 1982

John Lewis Partnership, 'Our Principles', last modified 16 September 2015, www.johnlewispartnership.co.uk/about/our-principles.html

Judge, T. A., J. A. LePine and B. L. Rich, 'Loving yourself abundantly: relationship of the narcissistic personality to self and other perceptions of workplace deviance, leadership, and task and contextual performance', *Journal of Applied Psychology*, 91 (2006), pp. 762–776

Kacperczyk, A., J. Sanchez-Burks and W. E. Baker, 'Multiplexity and emotional energy in cross-cultural perspective', Unpublished paper, University of Michigan, 2008

Kanfer, R., J. Sawyer, C. P. Early and E. A. Lind, 'Participation in task evaluation procedures: the effects of evaluative criteria on attitudes and performance', *Social Justice Research*, 1 (1987), pp. 235–249

Kegan, R. and L. Laskow Lahey, 'The real reason people won't change', *Harvard Business Review*, November 2001, pp. 85–92

Kennedy, I., *Final Report, Bristol Royal Infirmary Inquiry*, London: HMSO, 2001

Keynes, J. M., 'National self-sufficiency', *The Yale Review*, 22 (1933), pp. 755–769

Kim, W. C. and R. A. Mauborgne, 'Implementing global strategies: the role of procedural justice', *Strategic Management Journal*, 12 (1991), pp. 125–143

  'Fair process: managing in the knowledge economy', *Harvard Business Review*, 75 (1997), pp. 65–75

King, Mervyn E. and L. Roberts, *Integrate: Doing Business in the 21st Century*, Johannesburg: Juta & Co., 2013

Klein, R., 'No quick fix', *Health Service Journal*, 30 August 2001

Konovsky, M. A. and S. D. Pugh, 'Citizenship behavior and social exchange', *Academy of Management Journal*, 37 (1994), pp. 656–669

Koper, C., D. van Knippenberg, F. Bouhuijs, R. Vermunt and H. Wilke, 'Procedural fairness and self-esteem', *European Journal of Social Psychology*, 23 (1993), pp. 313–325

Korine, H., 'Strategic decision-making processes and performance: multiple levels, reciprocal influences', Working Paper, 40, London Business School Strategic Leadership Research Programme (1998)

Kramer, R. M., 'The great intimidators', *Harvard Business Review*, 84 (2006)

Kunda, G., *Engineering Culture: Control and Commitment in a High-Tech Corporation*, Philadelphia, PA: Temple University Press, 1992

Lakoff, G. and M. Johnson, *Metaphors We Live By*, University of Chicago Press, 1980

Laming, Lord H., *The Victoria Climbié Inquiry*, London: HMSO, 2003

Laseter, T. and R. Cross, 'The craft of connection', *Strategy + Business*, 44 (2006), www.strategy-business.com/article/06302?gko-ee374

Layard, R., *Happiness*, London: Allen Lane, 2005

Lee, C., 'Prosocial organisational behaviors: the roles of workplace justice, achievement striving and pay satisfaction', *Journal of Business and Psychology*, 10 (1995), pp. 197–206

Leeson, N. *Rogue Trader*, London: Little Brown, 1996

Lencioni, P., *The Advantage: Why Organizational Health Trumps Everything Else in Business*, San Francisco, CA: Jossey-Bass, 2012

Leventhal, G. S., 'What should be done with equity theory? New approaches to the study of fairness in social relationships', in K. Gergen, M. Greenberg and R. Willis (eds.), *Social Exchange: Advances in Theory and Research*, New York: Plenum, 1980, pp. 27–55

Leventhal, G. S., J. Karuza and W. R. Fry, 'Beyond fairness: a theory of allocation preferences', in G. Mikula (ed.), *Justice and Social Interaction*, New York: Springer-Verlag, 1980, pp. 167–218

Lewis, C. S., *The Four Loves*, New York: Harcourt, 1960

Liaschenko, J., 'Knowing the patient?', in S. E. Thorne and V. E. Hayes (eds.), *Nursing Praxis: Knowledge and Action*, Thousand Oaks, CA: Sage, 1997, pp. 23–37

Lind, E. A., J. Greenberg, K. Scott and T. Welchans, 'The winding road from employee to complainant: situational and psychological determinants of wrongful termination claims', *Administrative Science Quarterly*, 45 (2000), pp. 557–590.

Lind, E. A. and T. R. Tyler, *The Social Psychology of Procedural Justice*, New York: Plenum, 1988

Maccoby, M., 'Narcissistic leaders: the incredible pros, the inevitable cons', *Harvard Business Review*, 2000, pp. 69–77

Mackey, J. and R. Sisodia, *Conscious Capitalism*, Boston, MA: Harvard Business School Publishing, 2013

Mackinnon, A. 'Death at the hands of the NHS: the tragedy of Penny Campbell', *Independent*, 10 October 2006

Mainelli, M., 'The perverse and the reverse: how bad measures skew markets', Lecture, Gresham College, London, 17 October 2005, www.gresham.ac.uk/lectures-and-events/the-perverse-and-the-reverse-how-bad-measures-skew-markets

Masterson, S., 'A trickle-down model of organisational justice: relating employees' and customers' perceptions of and reactions to fairness', *Journal of Applied Psychology*, 86 (2001), pp. 594–604

Meads, G. and J. Ashcroft, *The Case for Interprofessional Collaboration in Health and Social Care*, Oxford: Blackwell, 2005

Menzies, D. and B. Davidson, 'Authenticity and belonging: the experience of being known in the group', *Group Analysis*, 35 (2002), pp. 43–55

Mitchell, T., 'Everyday metaphors of power', *Theory and Society*, 19 (1990), 545–578

Moorhead, G., R. Ference and C. P. Neck, 'Group decision fiascos continue: space shuttle Challenger and a revised groupthink framework', *Human Relations*, 44 (1991), pp. 539–550

Moorman, R. H., 'Relationship between organisational justice and organisational citizenship behaviors: do fairness perceptions influence employee citizenship?', *Journal of Applied Psychology*, 76 (1991), pp. 845–855

Mourkogiannis, N., *Purpose: The Starting Point of Great Companies*, London: Palgrave Macmillan, 2006

Muir, R. and G. Cooke (eds.), *The Relational State: How Recognising the Importance of Human Relationships could Revolutionise the Role of the State*, London: IPPR, 2012, available at www.ippr.org/publications/the-relational-state-how-recognising-the-importance-of-human-relationships-could-revolutionise-the-role-of-the-state

Mulgan, G., *Connexity: How to Live in a Connected World*, London: Chatto & Windus, 1997

Mulgan, G. and H. Wilkinson, 'Well-being and time', *Demos Quarterly*, 5 (1995), pp. 2–77

Nardi, B. A. and S. Whittaker, 'The place of face-to-face communication in distributed work', in P. J. Hinds and S. Kiesler (eds.), *Distributed Work*, Cambridge, MA: MIT Press, 2002, pp. 83–113

Narey, M., *Making the Education of Social Workers Consistently Effective: Report of Sir Martin Narey's Independent Review of The Education of Children's Social Workers*, London: Department for Education, January 2014

National Commission on the BP Deepwater Horizon Oil Spill and Offshore Drilling, 'Deep Water: The Gulf Oil Disaster and the Future of Offshore Drilling', January 2011

New Zealand Herald, 'Clearly, sofas are a winner', 8 August 2001

Nisbett, R. E., *Geography of Thought: How Asians and Westerners Think Differently ... and Why*, New York: Free Press, 2003

NRC Handelsblad Staff, 'Setback in Reykjavik: Iceland blocks 3.8 billion euro repayment to Dutch, British,' *Der Spiegel*, 5 January 2010, www.spiegel.de/international/europe/setback-in-reykjavik-iceland-blocks-3-8-billion-euro-repayment-to-dutch-british-a-670294.html

Office of National Statistics, 'Measuring National Well-Being', www.ons.gov.uk/ons/guide-method/user-guidance/well-being/index.html

Okri, B., *A Way of Being Free*, London: Weidenfeld & Nicolson, 1997

Oldham, J. H., *Real Life Is Meeting*, London: Sheldon Press, 1942

O'Neill, O., *A Question of Trust: The BBC Reith Lectures 2002*, Cambridge University Press, 2002

Page, S., *The Difference: How the Power of Diversity Creates Better Groups, Forms, Schools and Societies*, Princeton University Press, 2007

Pandhi, N. and J. Saultz, 'Patients' perceptions of interpersonal continuity of care', *Journal of the American Board of Family Medicine*, 19 (2006), pp. 390–396

Park, L. E., J. Crocker and K. D. Mickelson, 'Attachment styles and contingencies of self-worth', *PSPB*, 30 (2004), pp. 1243–1254

Park, W. W., 'A comprehensive empirical investigation of the relationships among variables of the groupthink model', *Journal of Organisational Behavior*, 21 (2000), pp. 873–887

Penn, M., *Microtrends: Surprising Tales of the Way We Live Today*, London: Penguin, 2007

Pfeffer, J. and R. I. Sutton, 'Knowing what to do is not enough: turning knowledge into action'. *California Management Review*, 42:1 (1999), pp. 83–108

   The Knowing–Doing Gap: How Smart Companies Turn Knowledge into Action, Cambridge, MA: Harvard Business School Press, 1999

Pierce, J. L., D. G. Gardner, L. L. Cummings and R. B. Dunham, 'Organisation-based self-esteem: construct definition, measurement, and validation', *Academy of Management Journal*, 32 (1989), pp. 622–648

Pierce, J. L., D. G. Gardner, R. B. Dunham and L. L. Cummings, 'Moderation by organisation-based self-esteem of role condition-employee response relationships', *Academy of Management Journal*, 36 (1993), pp. 271–288

Plaut, S. M., 'Boundary violations in professional–client relationships: overview and guidelines for prevention,' *Sexual and Marital Therapy*, 12 (1997) pp. 77–94

Pontin, J., 'Authenticity in the age of its technological reproducibility: do social technologies make us less sincere?', *Technology Review*, August 19, 2008, www.technologyreview.com/view/410686/authenticity-in-the-age-of-its-technological-reproducibility

Porter, M., 'Clusters and the new economics of competition', *Harvard Business Review*, 76 (1998), pp. 77–90

Powell, G. N. and S. Foley, 'Romantic relationships in organisational settings: something to talk about', in G. N. Powell (ed.), *Handbook of Gender and Work*, Thousand Oaks, CA: Sage, 1999

Putnam, R., 'Bowling alone: America's declining social capital', *Journal of Democracy*, 6 (1995), pp. 65–78

   Bowling Alone: The Collapse and Revival of American Community, New York: Simon & Schuster, 2000

   'E pluribus unum: diversity and community in the twenty-first century', *Scandinavian Political Studies*, 30 (2007), pp. 137–174

Qiu, T., W. Qualls, J. D. Bohlmann and D. E. Rupp, 'The effect of interactional fairness on the performance of cross-functional product development teams: a multilevel mediated model', *Journal of Product Innovation Management*, 26 (2009), pp. 173–87

Rappaport, A., 'The economics of short-term performance obsession', *Financial Analysts Journal*, 61 (2005), pp. 65–79

Ray, C. A., 'Corporate culture: the last frontier of control?', *Journal of Management Studies*, 23 (1986), pp. 287–297

Reicher, S., A. Haslam and N. Hopkins, 'Social identity and the dynamics of leadership: leaders and followers as collaborative agents in the transformation of social reality', *Leadership Quarterly*, 16 (2005), pp. 547–568

Rink, F. and N. Ellemers, 'Diversity as a basis for shared organisational identity: the norm congruity principle', *British Journal of Management*, 18 (2007), pp. S17–S27

Rogers, C., *On Becoming a Person*, Boston, MA: Houghton Mifflin, 1961

Rosenberg, M., *Nonviolent Communication: A Language of Life*, Encinitas, CA: PuddleDancer Press, 2003

Roth, G. and A. Kleiner, *Car Launch*, New York: Oxford University Press, 2000

Rousseau, D., 'Psychological and implied contracts in organisations', *Employee Responsibilities and Rights Journal*, 2 (1989), pp. 121–139

Rushworth, J. and M. Schluter, *Transforming Capitalism from Within*, Cambridge: Relational Research, 2011

Ryff, C. D. and C. L. M. Keyes, 'The structure of psychological well-being revisited', *Journal of Personality and Social Psychology*, 69 (1995), pp. 719–727

Ryff, C., B. Singer, E. Wing and G. Love, 'Elective affinities and uninvited agonies', in C. Ryff and B. Singer (eds.), *Emotion, Social Relationships and Health*, Oxford University Press, 2001

Salovey, P., and J. D. Mayer, 'Emotional intelligence', *Imagination, Cognition, and Personality*, 9 (1990), pp. 185–211

Salz, A., 'The Salz Review: An Independent Review of Barclays' Business Practices', April 2013, available at http://online.wsj.com/public/resources/documents/SalzReview04032013.pdf

Schaubroeck, J., D. R. May and F. W. Brown, 'Procedural justice explanations and employee reactions to economic hardship: a field experiment', *Journal of Applied Psychology*, 79 (1994), pp. 455–460

Schein, E. H., *Organizational Psychology*, Englewood Cliffs, NJ: Prentice Hall, 1980

Schluter, M. and D. Lee, *The R Factor*, London: Hodder & Stoughton, 1993
    The Relational Manager: Transform Your Workplace and Your Life, Oxford: Lion Hudson, 2009

Schutz, W., *FIRO: A Three Dimensional Theory of Interpersonal Behavior*, New York: Holt, Rinehart & Winston, 1958
    The Human Element: Productivity, Self-Esteem and the Bottom Line, San Francisco, CA: Jossey-Bass, 1994

Seabright, P., *The Company of Strangers: A Natural History of Economic Life*, Princeton University Press, 2004

Senge, P., O. Scharmer, J. Jaworski and B. S. Flowers, *Presence*, London: Nicholas Brealey, 2005

SHARE, Share homepage, www.share.org

Shephard, G., *Shephard's Watch: Illusions of Power in British Politics*, London: Politico's Publishing, 2000

Sherif, M., J. White, C. W. Sherif, W. R. Hood and O.J. Harvey, *Intergroup Conflict and Cooperation: The Robbers' Cave Experiment*, Norman, OH: University of Oklahoma Institute of Intergroup Relations, 1961

Shinn, S., '21st century engineer', *BizEd* (January–February 2005), pp. 18–23

Siegel, E., *The Frances Sanders Lesson and Two Related Works*, New York: Definition Press, 1974

Simon, B. and S. Sturmer, 'Respect for group members: intragroup determinants of collective identification and group-serving behavior', *Personality and Social Psychology Bulletin*, 29 (2003), pp. 183–193

Simon, H., 'Bounded rationality and organizational learning', *Organization Science*, 2 (1991) pp. 125–134

Simons, D. J. and C. F. Chabris, 'Gorillas in our midst: sustained inattentional blindness for dynamic events', *Perception*, 28 (1999), pp. 1059–1074

Skarlicki, D. P. and R. Folger, 'Retaliation in the workplace: the roles of distributive, procedural and interactional justice', *Journal of Applied Psychology*, 82 (1997), pp. 434–443

Spencer, L. and R. Pahl, *Rethinking Friendship: Hidden Solidarities Today*, Princeton University Press, 2006

Spretnak, C., *Relational Reality*, Topsham, ME: Green Horizon Books, 2011

Stewart, T. A., *Intellectual Capital: The New Wealth of Organisations*, New York: Doubleday, 1997

Stone, L., *The Family, Sex and Marriage in England, 1500–1800*, London: Weidenfeld & Nicolson, 1977

'Attention: the real aphrodisiac', Speech at the Emerging Technology Conference, San Diego, CA, December 2006

Straw, J. 'I felt uneasy talking to someone I couldn't see', *Guardian*, 6 October 2006

Sutton, R. I., 'Are you a jerk at work?', *Greater Good: The Science of a Meaningful Life*, December 1, 2007, http://greatergood.berkeley.edu/article/item/are_you_jerk_work

The No Asshole Rule: Building a Civilized Workplace and Surviving One That Isn't, London: Sphere, 2007

Tarnow, E., 'Towards the zero accident goal: assisting the First Officer monitor and challenge Captain errors', *Journal of Aviation/Aerospace Education and Research*, 10 (2000), pp. 29–38

Taylor, F. W., *Principles of Scientific Management*, New York: Harper & Brothers, 1911

Teach First, Teach First homepage, www.teachfirst.org.uk/TFHome/

Telegraph, '"Swarms of locusts" man in German coalition', 14 October 2005, www.telegraph .co.uk/finance/2923841/Swarms-of-locusts-man-in-German-coalition.html

'"Target culture" that led to Mid Staffs still exists in NHS, claims top surgeon', 25 January 2013, www.telegraph.co.uk/health/healthnews/9824256/Target-culture-that-led-to-Mid-Staffs-still-exists-in-NHS-claims-top-surgeon.html, accessed 31 May 2015

Thatcher, M., 'The lady's not for turning', Speech to Conservative Party conference, 10 October 1980

The Times, 'Bobby Robson's sadness over Newcastle's implosion', 20 October 2008

Thomson, K., *Emotional Capital: Maximising the Intangible Assets at the Heart of Brand and Business Success*, Oxford: Capstone Publishing, 1998

Thorne, S. E., M. Kuo, E. A. Armstrong, G. McPherson, S. R. Harris and T. G. Hislop, 'Being known: patients' perspectives of the dynamics of human connection in cancer care', *Psycho-Oncology*, 14 (2005), pp. 887–898

TNS, TNS Loneliness Omnibus Survey for Age UK, April 2014

Todorov, A., A. N. Mandisodza, A. Goren and C. C. Hall, 'Inferences of competence from faces predict election outcomes', *Science*, 308 (2005), pp. 1623–1626

Tornow, W. W. and M. London (eds.), *Maximizing the Value of 360-Degree Feedback*, San Francisco, CA: Jossey-Bass, 1998

Turner, M. E. and A. R. Pratkanis, 'Mitigating groupthink by stimulating constructive conflict', in C. de Dreu and E. van de Vliert (eds.), *Using Conflict in Organisations* (London: Sage, 1997), pp. 53–71

Turner, Y. and I. Hadas-Halpern, 'The effects of including a patient's photograph to the radiographic examination', Radiological Society of North America 2008 Scientific Assembly and Annual Meeting, Chicago IL, February 18–20, 2008, abstract available at http://archive.rsna.org/2008/6008880.html

Twenge, J. M., *Generation Me: Why Today's Young Americans Are More Confident, Assertive, Entitled – And More Miserable Than Ever Before* (New York: Free Press, 2006)

Tyler, T. R. and E. A. Lind, 'A relational model of authority in groups', *Advances in Experimental Social Psychology*, 25 (1992), pp. 115–191

Waterman, R., *The Frontiers of Excellence: Learning from Companies That Put People First*, Boston, MA: Nicholas Brealey Publishing, 1994

Weber, M., *The Theory of Social and Economic Organization*, Glencoe, IL: Free Press, 1924

Wheatley, M. J., *Leadership and the New Science: Discovering Order in a Chaotic World*, 3rd edition, San Francisco, CA: Berrett-Koehler Publishers, 2006
    'Relationships: the basic building blocks of life', 2006, www.margaretwheatley.com/articles/relationships.html

Whitman, W. 'Song of Myself', *Leaves of Grass*, New York: Penguin, 1986

Wiesenfeld, B. M., J. Brockner, and V. Thibauh, 'Procedural fairness, managers' self-esteem, and managerial behaviors following a layoff', *Organisational Behavior and Human Decision Processes*, 83 (2000), pp. 1–32

Willcocks, L., *The London Insurance Market: Modernisation or Muddle*, London: Knowledge Capital Partners, 2004

Willis, J. and A. Todorov, 'First impressions: making up your mind after a 100-ms exposure to a face', *Psychological Science*, 17 (2006), pp. 592–598

Wolf, R., 'Respect and international relations: state motives, social mechanisms and hypotheses', Paper presented at the 49th Annual Convention of the International Studies Association, San Francisco, CA, March 26–29, 2008

Zimbardo, P., *The Lucifer Effect: How Good People Turn Evil*, London: Rider & Co., 2007

Zohar, D., *Spiritual Capital: Wealth We Can Live by*, San Francisco, CA: Berrett-Koehler Publishers, 2004

INDEX

"We wouldn't have missed it for the world"

THE WOMEN'S LAND ARMY IN BEDFORDSHIRE 1939 – 1950

Stuart Antrobus

Book Castle PUBLISHING

First published October 2008
by
Book Castle Publishing
2a Sycamore Business Park
Copt Hewick
North Yorkshire HG4 5DF

ISBN 978 1 903747 93 3

Typeset and designed by Caroline and Roger Hillier
The Old Chapel Graphic Design
www.theoldchapellivinghoe.com

Printed in Great Britain by TJ International, Padstow, Cornwall

Cataloguing-in-Publication Data

Antrobus, Stuart
    We wouldn't have missed it for the world: the Women's Land Army
in Bedfordshire, 1939–1950/Stuart Antrobus.

ISBN 978 1 903747 93 3
1.   Bedfordshire, Women's Land Army. I. Title.
940.53161'094256 – dc 22

Front cover: Harris's farm, Bletsoe, May 1942. Harvest group of land
girls from the Women's Land Army hostel at Milton Ernest. Back row
l–r: Gwen Varna, ?, Mary Pakes; front row l–r: Josephine Copp, Barbara
Stanton. *Source: M Smith*

Back cover: Great Barford land girls at Mr JH Brown's Willoughby Farm:
Nancy Karn on tractor and Ruth Bennett on cart. *Source: BLARS BT1081/2*

To the memory of my parents

Samuel and Hilda Antrobus

and to all Bedfordshire Land Girls

Bedfordshire land girls in St Paul's Square, Bedford, celebrate VE Day, 8 May 1945, marking the end of the Second World War in Europe. Grace Bramhall is on the extreme right. *Source: Antrobus archive. Courtesy of Beds Times*

Stuart Antrobus *Photo by Nicola Avery*

Stuart Antrobus was born and brought up in Cheshire and has degrees in history and librarianship from the Open University and the University of Loughborough. After teacher training in Nottingham, he taught for 15 years at Long Eaton School, Derbyshire, before moving on to a career in local government arts administration in Bedfordshire. He was the Manager of Leighton Buzzard Theatre and Arts Centre for 12 years. He has since taught social history in adult education in Bedfordshire with the Workers Educational Association (WEA) and Bedford Retirement Education Centre.

His decision to do detailed research into the Women's Land Army in Bedfordshire arose out of courses he taught on "Life on the Home Front in Bedfordshire during the Second World War". He has done historical research for Bedfordshire County Council on Bromham Watermill and Stevington Windmill, as well as on rights of way. He wrote the summaries for over 300 oral history interviews conducted as part of the "Changing Landscapes, Changing Lives" research project in mid-Bedfordshire, funded by the Heritage Lottery Fund. He has written a number of local history articles for Bedfordshire and national magazines.

Reviews of the author's previous award-winning internet publication *Bedfordshire Women's Land Army Internet Archive* through Bedfordshire Libraries' site http://tinyurl.com/2nq2up

"...a significant addition to our knowledge of the Women's Land Army and a valuable addition to the history of World War II in Bedfordshire"
   Dr Vernon Williams, Professor of History, Abilene Christian University, Texas

"...well structured, easily navigable"
   (judges for the Alan Ball Local History Awards 2007, the Library Services Trust)

"...very impressed with the extensive research and in particular its presentation on the web"
   Dr Margaret Bullock, formerly of the University of Leeds

"...a brilliant resource"
   Mary Gryspeerdt, Somerset Rural Life Museum, author of Back to the Land

"I am most impressed..."
   Nick Hill, Director, Eden Camp Museum, Yorkshire

"...a thorough and easy-to-use resource"
   Stephen Walton, Archivist, Imperial War Museum

"...easy to navigate and the language accessible, with many relevant and interesting photographs"
   Lynda Burrows, author of The Women's Land Army in East Anglia, 1939–1950

"...most impressed by the amount and depth of material...a thorough study"
   Melissa Hardie, Hypatia Trust, editor of Digging for Memories – The Women's Land Army in Cornwall

"It sets an example that could be taken up to develop a nationwide resource"
   Jane Howells, Editor, Local History News

Design for the Women's Land Army Veterans Badge presented by the British Government to former land girls in 2008 to recognise their wartime services. Garter King of Arms. *Source: DEFRA*

I am delighted to have been asked to contribute a preamble to this account of the Women's Land Army in Bedfordshire.

The Women's Land Army (better known as the Land Girls) worked to feed the nation during the war years as men went to fight. Between 1939 and its disbandment in 1950 more than 203,000 women served on the farms and market gardens of England and Wales. At its peak there were 80,000 women working on the land, and a further 4,000 women joined the Women's Timber Corps and worked in the forests supplying timber for the war effort.

These women made a vital contribution to the country during the dark days of the war. The work was long and arduous. Supplying the nation with food was no easy task, but they proved themselves more than equal to it, and the farmers, who were initially sceptical, eventually became their most ardent supporters.

When the war ended the Land Girls didn't get any formal recognition because they were a civilian organisation. Since then there has been a long and sustained campaign to achieve that recognition, and the decision by the Government in 2007 to acknowledge the contribution of the Women's Land Army and Timber Corps led to an enthusiastic response. The Women's Land Army badges will commemorate their service to the country and formally acknowledge the debt that we all owe them.

This book tells some of the stories of these remarkable women. It provides an important reminder of a period in our history when so many women contributed so much, and in doing so it should inspire and encourage us all.

Hilary Benn MP
Secretary of State for the Environment, Food & Rural Affairs
May 2008

Abbreviations

ATS	Auxiliary Territorial Service
BBC WWII PW	British Broadcasting Corporation Internet site (WWII People's War web pages)
BBC (WAC)	British Broadcasting Corporation (Written Archives Centre)
Beds Times	*Bedfordshire Times* and *Standard*
BLARS	Bedfordshire and Luton Archives and Records Service
BWAEC	Bedfordshire War Agricultural Executive Committee
CEMA	Council for the Encouragement of Music and the Arts
CLCL	'Changing Landscapes, Changing Lives' oral history project
CWAEC	County War Agricultural Executive Committee
DEFRA	Department for Environment, Food and Rural Affairs
ENSA	Entertainment National Services Association
GI	Colloquial term for an American serviceman
HER	Historic Environment Record, Bedfordshire County Council
HMSO	His/Her Majesty's Stationery Office
HQ	Headquarters
IWM	Imperial War Museum
Land girl	Colloquial term for member of the Women's Land Army
MAF	Ministry of Agriculture and Fisheries
MERL	Museum of English Rural Life, University of Reading
MoLNS	Ministry of Labour and National Service
POWs	Prisoners of war
TLG	*The Land Girl* (magazine)
TNA	The National Archives
TSO	The Stationery Office
WAAF	Women's Auxiliary Air Force
'War Ag'	Colloquial term for War Agricultural Executive Committee (WAEC)
WLA	Women's Land Army
WRNS	Women's Royal Naval Service
WSRO	West Sussex Record Office
YWCA	Young Women's Christian Association

CONTENTS

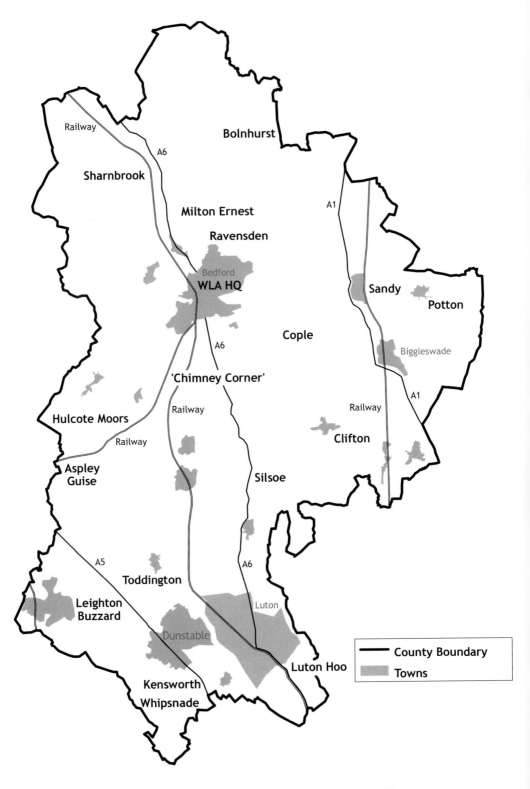

Women's Land Army hostel locations in Bedfordshire 1942–1950 *Map produced by Chris Wilson*

FOREWORD

It was not until 2005 that a memorial was erected in Whitehall to the seven million women who played their part in the Second World War – more than a year after animals had received their recognition with a statue in Hyde Park.

Women's contribution to the war, particularly on the Home Front, has always tended to be overlooked and undervalued, and none more so that the women and girls of the Women's Land Army who played such a vital role in keeping Britain fed throughout nearly six long years of war.

> 'Back to the land, we must all lend a hand
> To the farms and the fields we must go
> There's a job to done
> Though we can't fire a gun
> We can still do our bit with a hoe',

ran the official song of the WLA - who were usually referred to as Land Girls - and that's only part of what they did. There was ploughing, rat catching, milking cows, picking fruit, digging vegetables, sawing logs, hedging, ditching, helping with the harvest, collecting eggs – any job you can think of around the farm in all weathers, for a minimum wage of 28 shillings a week, and often not enough food to eat, and living in fairly primitive accommodation with farmers who were sceptical that 'a slip of a girl' would be any use to replace their regular farm hands who had gone off to fight or work in munitions factories.

Nearly 70 years after the outbreak of the Second World War, those who are still alive who worked on the land in the service of their country, are getting old. But they still have a fascinating story to tell. Of the work that they did, the hardships they endured, the responsibilities they carried – and the fun that they had. It is through books like Stuart Antrobus's marvellously detailed evocation of the life of the Land Girls in one part of Britain, Bedfordshire, with its farms and market gardens, that we, who were not there, but have reason to be grateful, can capture those days to build a picture of what it was like, a picture that fits into the great canvas of the Second World War, and how that war impacted on the lives of everyone in Britain in varied and different ways that still leave a legacy today.

It has taken far too many years for the Land Girls – and the 'Lumber Jills' or 'Polecats' of the Timber Corps – to get the recognition they deserve. Stuart Antrobus's book is one way of ensuring that that will happen, as well as telling a rich and absorbing story of going 'back to the land'.

Juliet Gardiner author of *Wartime: Britain 1939-45* (Headline, 2004)

Women's
Land Army

Women's
Timber Corps

The Government wishes to express to
you its profound gratitude for your
unsparing efforts as a loyal and devoted
member of the Women's Land Army/
Women's Timber Corps at a time when our country
depended upon you for its survival.

July
2008

Rt Hon Gordon Brown MP
Prime Minister

July 2008 Veterans Certificate, awarded to those who claimed their WLA Veterans Badge. *Source: DEFRA*

PREFACE

Life on the 'home front' in England during the Second World War has long been an interest of mine and area of research. In recent years I have led adult education courses on the topic throughout Bedfordshire. Out of this, and meeting a number of former wartime 'land girls', came my desire to find out what happened with regard to the Women's Land Army (WLA) in Bedfordshire – a subject which had not previously been researched in any depth.

Following initial research on the Women's Land Army nationally, I gave an illustrated talk on the WLA at Bedford Central Library on 27 January 2003 and managed to attract over 20 former 'land girls', as well as an interested general audience. One thing led to another and I found myself engaged on a self-imposed research project which occupied me, part-time, for some five years and led, finally, to the writing of this book.

It was not an easy subject to research, in that there was no official archive of Bedfordshire WLA organisational papers to sit down with in the county record office in Bedford (BLARS). I decided to approach it in two ways. I would interview as many former land girls (the colloquial name for members of the WLA) as I could who had served at some time in the 1940s in Bedfordshire. I would, at the same time, seek out whatever documents I could, nationally and locally, which would both reveal the organisation's history and its impact on the county.

One approach fed into the other. Not only did individual women I spoke to talk of their own particular experiences in the Land Army, either during the Second World War or afterwards, but they also provided me with primary sources – photographs, official letters and documents – which they had retained, and which had not found their way into archives. In addition, through the matters they raised in discussion, my research was pointed in new directions, offering clues and potential subject matter which added depth to the enquiry.

Since these former land girls were now in their late seventies and early eighties, it was clear that a high priority was to speak to as many as possible, in as much depth as they would agree to, so as to make the most of this vital personal primary source. In addition, I decided to make audio recordings of a number of interviews with representative women who had served both with independent farmers and in hostel gangs employed by Bedfordshire War Agricultural Executive Committee (Bedfordshire 'War Ag'). These oral histories would provide a permanent record for future historians to consult, long after these women were gone. (I had been disappointed to find nothing on Bedfordshire WLA experiences in the Imperial War Museum and this had spurred me to do something about it.) In addition, where I had not tape recorded interviews, I made notes of conversations and reminiscence sessions. Finally, I collected whatever written memoirs I could find from individuals or already published in village histories or local Bedfordshire magazines.

The resultant history is one very much written from the perspective of the working members of this unique women's organisation and, to some extent, the organisation's official view of how it worked. Ideally, had this history been written a few decades earlier, it would have benefited from the views of the farmers and market gardeners who employed these volunteer women workers, of the paid staff of the WLA county office and its volunteer Advisory Council members, of members and officers of the 'War Ag', and of a range of rural occupants who, as adults, came across this new group of young women and would have experienced the effect they had on village life. Sadly, few of those people just mentioned have put their thoughts down on paper in publicly-available sources.[1]

I have written elsewhere about my research methods[2] but, briefly, they involved collecting information from individuals through completed questionnaires plus, where possible, one-to-one interviews with former land girls. These then led on to a series of group reminiscence sessions held with women who had some shared experience in common, i.e. a particular hostel or that of being private farm employees. In turn, this led to an emphasis on collecting as many photographs as possible, with background information and names, which, together with donated or copied documents, formed an archive of Bedfordshire WLA material. This complemented the material already in BLARS and led to further areas of research.

One key enquiry was that of naming and locating all the various hostels which had been set up during and after the war to accommodate those land girls employed by the 'War Ag' as mobile gang workers. Local newspaper research plus a thorough review of the organisation's own magazine, *The Land Girl*, then enabled me to draw up a chronology. Following this, the relationship between the county WLA headquarters and the 'War Ag', plus the added dimension of YWCA involvements in providing a welfare role in hostels, needed to be explored through Ministry of Agriculture and Fisheries' papers in The National Archive at Kew and through articles in agricultural journals in the library of the Museum of English Rural Life, the Imperial War Museum and the British Library.

In order to complete a thorough exploration of the size of the land girl impact in Bedfordshire, I set about, with a team of keen volunteer researchers, poring over the card index to the service files of the WLA held by the Imperial War Museum in Duxford (covering approximately 200,000 young women in England and Wales). Although not totally comprehensive, this source, together with further names culled from newspapers and magazines, enabled the compilation of the Roll Call list at the end of this book. For the first time, a fairly definitive, county listing of former land girls who served in Bedfordshire has been recovered from authoritative sources. This will enable historians of the WLA, as well as family historians, to find out not only names but, through an associated internet site[3], further information on, plus photos of, a large number of these individual women who served their country but gained little subsequent recognition for their national service.

More analysis remains to be done on such topics as the background – where enrolled, former occupation, age on entry and length of service – of these young women, when time allows. This will be made public through articles in historical journals.

In the Personal Experiences chapters of this book women's own testimonies are given, most of them for the first time. The appendices at the end of the book enable the reader to put these personal stories in the context of the organisation's chronology, a typical farming year and the employment figures. End notes give sources for key information and expand, where necessary, with more information for the interested researcher. Sources and archive contact details are given for those who wish to do their own research.

It has been a fascinating research project, made all the more interesting through contact with so many former land girls who, despite remembering some of the hardships they suffered, almost always ended the conversation with such phrases as "they were the best years of my life" or "I wouldn't have missed it for the world".

For a healthy, happy job

Join the
WOMEN'S
LAND
ARMY

Seductive recruitment posters tempted young women, mostly in their late teens, into signing up as paid volunteers in the Women's Land Army from 1939 onwards. They were to take the place of men from farms and in market gardens who joined the armed forces. From 1942 this civilian labour force was expanded even more, following the conscription of young women between the ages of 19 and 30. *Image courtesy of the Imperial War Museum, London IWM PST 6078 Artist: Clive Uptton*

CHAPTER 1

The Women's Land Army National Organisation

INTRODUCTION

Over 11 years, from 1939 to 1950, some 203,000[4] paid volunteer members of the Women's Land Army (WLA) in England and Wales – 'land girls' as they were known – served as civilian workers on the farms and market gardens of England and Wales as a form of national service. Their labour proved to be vital in helping to produce food needed to feed the nation during the Second World War and the period of post-war austerity which followed. There was also a large WLA organisation in Scotland run by the Department of Agriculture for Scotland.[5]

FORMATION

The Women's Land Army administrative structure was organised as an agency of the Ministry of Agriculture, in secret, from April 1938 onwards, but young women were able to sign up for prospective membership early in 1939[6] in readiness for a possible outbreak of war. It was officially formed on 1 June 1939, three months before Britain's declaration of war with Germany. Its purpose was to provide a mobile labour force of young women to replace the men who would increasingly be called into the armed forces from agriculture and horticulture during the Second World War, which began for Britain on 3 September 1939. The WLA continued after the war ended, in 1945, and was finally disbanded on 30 November 1950.

The Women's Timber Corps was a separate part of the WLA, formed in April 1942 and disbanded on 31 August 1946. Its roughly 6,000 'Lumber Jills' worked in forests and timber mills.[7]

LADY DENMAN

The Women's Land Army was created and directed by Gertrude, Lady Denman. During the First World War she had been the Honorary Assistant Director of the first Women's Land Army[8] responsible for recruitment in the Southern Counties.

LADY DENMAN

Lady Gertude Denman, as a young woman during the First World War, had been the Honorary Assistant Director of the first Women's Land Army, 1917–1919. As war approached a second time in 1938, the Minister of Agriculture asked her to make preparations for a new Women's Land Army. She set up a national headquarters – in her country house at Balcombe Place, Haywards Heath, Sussex – and a county-based organisation, run by a mixture of volunteer women and paid officials. She relied heavily in each county on the leading members of the Women's Institutes, since she was also the Chairman of the National Federation of Women's Institutes. *Source: Antrobus archive, 1946 Bedfordshire WLA souvenir programme*

She had also chaired the National Federation of Women's Institutes since 1917, and had an unparalleled network of contacts throughout the country. This, and her outstanding leadership qualities, enabled her to quickly forge an effective national organisation based on county committees of volunteers and a core of paid officers and administrative staff. She provided her own large country house, Balcombe Place, near Haywards Heath in West Sussex, as the Headquarters for the WLA. The all-female staff moved there from London, on 29 August 1939. Lady Denman and her Assistant Director, Inez Jenkins, had 14 officers (seven of the senior members were regional officers) and 35 clerks and typists.[9]

CIVILIAN WORKERS

Despite the misleading term 'Army', the WLA was a civilian organisation, an agency of the Ministry of Agriculture. Its 'volunteers' were not to be those already employed in agriculture. They were to be new labour – females who were prepared to become additional full-time workers for the agricultural industry for the duration of the war. They were employed directly by farmers, from

September 1939 onwards, and billeted locally. Then, particularly from 1942, some were employed by county 'War Ags' (War Agricultural Executive Committees), which housed them in hostels and transported them daily to those farms which needed labour locally, according to seasonal needs. The land girls were not subject to military discipline, even after they joined under conscription, from 1942 onwards, but were recruited and provided with a distinctive uniform by WLA county headquarters. This gave them a sense of esprit de corps and marked them off clearly as essential war workers.

'THE LAND GIRL' MAGAZINE

Lady Denman established a monthly magazine for members of the WLA, published mid-monthly, initially as an unofficial periodical, then later funded by the Ministry of Agriculture. It was edited by Margaret Pyke who was based at the Balcombe Place WLA headquarters at Haywards Heath, Sussex. It cost 3d (1p) per copy, or 3 shillings (15p) a year (post free), and had to be subscribed to, although land girls were encouraged to pass it on to a larger number of readers in the organisation. The idea was to enable isolated land girls to keep in touch with

No. 4, Volume 5   JULY, 1944   Price 3d.

The Land Girl magazine was published monthly, priced 3d (1p) from April 1940 to March 1947. It was the way that the WLA's national HQ tried to keep in touch with land girls, but not everyone subscribed and only a minority got to see it. *Source: Antrobus archive. Courtesy of J. Caeiriog-Jones*

the organisation and for them to know what was going on nationally in the WLA. It contained Land Army news, articles, employment figures, photographs and drawings and letters from land girls. County organisations had an opportunity each month to say what had been going on in their area in the previous weeks.

It ran from April 1940 to March 1947 and eventually had a circulation of 21,000. Later, following a short break in 1947, due to a paper shortage, its successor periodical, *Land Army News*, was published from June 1947 to November 1950, when the organisation came to an end.

NUMBERS AND PAY

Some 17,000 volunteers had come forward at the outbreak of war and 1,000 were sent immediately into service. By December 1939, 4,500 had been found work but by April 1940 only 6,000 of the enrolled 11,000–12,000 recruits were in agricultural employment. Their pay, initially, was 28 shillings a week, ten shillings a week less, on average, than male farm workers.[10] It was not until late 1942 that there was a sudden rapid growth in numbers, following the introduction of conscription for young women. By September 1942 membership had reached 52,000.[11] By 30 September 1943 the WLA had an active membership of over 80,000 land girls.[12]

WOMEN DOING 'MEN'S WORK'

These young women workers, many of them from towns and cities and initially unused to both agriculture and country life, had to take on all areas of farming and horticulture, despite only limited training. They proved themselves more than capable in what had previously been 'men's work', whether in milking, animal husbandry, field work, pest control, tractor driving or all manner of hard physical work, throughout the country. Increasingly during the war farmers were also assisted, in many areas, by Italian prisoners of war, and, later, by German POWs, who both helped swell the agricultural labour force.

WAR SERVICE AND BEYOND

Land girls signed a pledge to commit themselves to the Land Army for the duration of the war but could leave if they married or were given permission to transfer to other war work. By the end of the war in 1945, numbers had dropped to 54,000 and many left to get married or return to their pre-war work. There was further recruitment and there were still 25,679 in February 1947.[13] Prior to disbandonment, on 30 November 1950, membership was down to 6,800.[14]

CHAPTER 2

The Women's Land Army Organisation in Bedfordshire

COUNTY COMMITTEE

Lady Denman, at the request of the Ministry of Agriculture in 1938, devised a national structure for a proposed Women's Land Army in the event of war, based on county committees, each chaired by a woman of her choice. These were often women she knew through her work as Chairman of the National Federation of Women's Institutes. For Bedfordshire, she chose Mrs Nora Whitchurch (who chaired the Bedfordshire Federation of Women's Institutes) as Chairman and Miss Marjorie Farrar was Honorary Organising Secretary (who worked part-time, unpaid, except for a small honorarium). Members of the committee were all unpaid. The county committee was comprised, as Lady Denman pointed out, "of women whose members are chosen for their knowledge of country life and local conditions".[15] The committee was an advisory body and the County Secretary, a salaried appointment by WLA headquarters (from 1941), was the only executive officer.

FIRST OFFICE

The WLA County Headquarters office was established in June 1939 at 2 St Paul's Square, Bedford, in the area of Shire Hall (now the Magistrate's Court, but then the headquarters of Bedfordshire County Council).

FUNCTIONS OF THE COUNTY ORGANISATION

The WLA HQ in Bedford was responsible for recruiting, providing uniforms, providing training and arranging suitable placements for volunteer land girls.[16] This was either with farmers who needed extra labour or with the county 'War Ag' (or WAEC). In the latter case the county WLA was responsible for housing and feeding them in hostels as well as for the welfare of these 'gang girls', who were directly employed by the 'War Ag' and supplied to local farmers according to seasonal needs. In Bedfordshire, the county WLA not only managed the hostels but appointed YWCA wardens to look after the welfare of these land girls.

Those young women who were employed and paid directly by the farmers were subject to standard conditions of service set out by the Women's Land Army, which had been negotiated nationally. Work had to be full-time and year-round. It was the responsibility of the county HQ to ensure that both the farmer and the land girl kept their side of the arrangement and both were reasonably happy.

Above the county set up was the WLA Regional Officer responsible for two-way communications between a number of county offices and the national office with regard to carrying out national WLA policy. They would come for visits of about two days on a regular basis.

CHANGES AT THE TOP IN BEDFORDSHIRE

From spring 1941 Mrs Lois Heydeman became the first paid County Secretary, replacing the post of Honorary Organising Secretary. She was appointed by the national headquarters at Balcombe Place, Haywards Heath, Sussex, and responsible to the Headquarters organisation for the welfare of every Land Army volunteer in the county.[17] In August 1941 Mrs 'J.B.' (Erica) Graham took over from Mrs Nora Whitchurch as County Chairman.[18]

NEW OFFICE

The office moved to 42 Harpur Street (where Eagle Court is now) in September 1942, where they shared a building with the Ministry of Food, on the opposite corner from Telephone House.[19] Hundreds of land girls were to visit there over the next seven years, as the organisation grew in numbers during the war years, then fell in the post-war years up to office closure in 1949. On entering, they passed through the green door under the WLA's sheaf of corn insignia.[20] The county headquarters was staffed by women administrators (with just one man, in charge of finance).

Gloria Crawley née Godfrey was a young woman straight from school when she joined the office staff in 1943 and worked for a year, filing and helping recruits with uniforms. When any land girl left the organisation, her uniform would be sold off, second-hand, to other land girls who were short of particular items and were not prepared to wait for their own worn clothes to be replaced. Gloria was from London and travelled back home each weekend. She remembers that the atmosphere could get rather bitchy at times, with so many women working together. She would be sent with messages between various members of staff to "tell Miss so-and-so" something, when they were not getting on so well.[21]

All the main offices were on the First Floor, with only Major Corbett, Finance Officer, and his assistant, Miss Myfanwy Jones, on the Second Floor. The office was open 9am–5pm Monday to Saturday, except 9am–1pm on Wednesdays (market day).

Name *D. S. Abraham*

No. *3H168*

You are now a member of the Women's Land Army.

You are pledged to hold yourself available for service on the land for the period of the war.

You have promised to abide by the conditions of training and employment of the Women's Land Army; its good name is in your hands.

You have made the home fields your battlefield. Your country relies on your loyalty and welcomes your help.

Signed *C. Denham*

Honorary Director

Signed *E Graham* Chairman Committee

Date *5th August 1941*

I realise the national importance of the work which I have undertaken and I will serve well and faithfully.

Signed *D. S. Abraham*

The pledge card was Lady Denman's way of getting her civilian land girls, who were not subject to military discipline, to commit themselves to doing their national service for the duration of the war. Her phrase "the fields are your battlefield" emphasised the importance of the work they were doing. If the country could not feed its people, then it could not win the war. *Source: D Stamford*

COUNTY SECRETARY

The County Secretary was responsible to the national WLA headquarters for filling the land girl requirements of the 'War Ag' and independent farmers, either by local recruiting or by 'importing' from counties with a surplus. She interviewed applicants with one other – usually the woman Chairman of the County Advisory Committee (or other committee member) – and arranged training for recruits.

She supervised county office organisation, especially finance, and supervised the county organisers. At least once or twice a week she would meet up with the County Chairman to discuss any difficulties.[22]

Externally, the County Secretary maintained contact with the county 'War Ag' and served on their Labour Sub-Committee and Hostel Sub-Committee. It was her job to ensure that hostels were inspected and to negotiate, when and where necessary, with the Ministry of Works, who either erected and furnished the hostel hutments or adapted and furnished the requisitioned houses which were converted into hostels.[23] Her salary was £250 per annum, plus a mileage allowance for necessary car journeys.[24]

NEW COUNTY SECRETARY

In March 1943 Mrs Heydeman was forced to resign through ill health and her Assistant Secretary, Mrs Ida Eugster, took over as Secretary, the post she held until the Bedfordshire office finally closed in November 1949 (a year before the WLA was disbanded).

OFFICE STAFF

The WLA county office included a number of sections under the County Secretary and Assistant County Secretary: employment, hostels, uniforms and welfare, and finance. In addition, a number of organisers (in the case of Bedfordshire, two) were responsible for different parts of the county.[25] Office staff did not wear uniform. When relevant members of staff went out to meet farmers or officials they wore WLA armbands to identify themselves.

The two members of staff whom most land girls in Bedfordshire were to get to know were Mrs Violet Sharman (the Uniform Officer) and Mrs Ada Truman (Records and Welfare Office). 'Shar' and 'Tru' were often seen, almost as a double act, at hostel socials and parties and threw themselves wholeheartedly into parades, sports days and their role as chaperones at early aerodrome dances put on by American forces.

Office staff and their roles changed over the years, but in 1946, the responsibilities were as follows: County Secretary, Mrs I. Eugster; Assistant Secretary, Miss Myfanwy Jones; County Organisers, Miss R. Digby and Mrs J. Nelson. The various section

Bedfordshire Women's Land Army Headquarters staff, Bedford, 1946. Left to right:
Back row: Mrs A. Truman, Miss B. Fuller, Major G. Corbett, Mrs V. Sharman.
Sitting: Mrs R. Digby, Mrs I. Eugster, Mrs 'J.B.' (Erica) Graham (Chairman, Bedfordshire WLA), Miss M. Jones, Mrs J. Nelson. *Source: BLARS (Graham archive). Courtesy of Jewell-Harrison Studios, Bedford*

officers were: Mrs V. Sharman, Uniform Officer; Mrs Truman, Records and Welfare Officer; Miss B. Fuller, Employment Officer and Major G. Corbett, Finance Officer, the only man in the Bedfordshire WLA HQ organisation.

In 1946 the (unpaid) Bedfordshire WLA County Advisory Committee was: Mrs 'J.B.' (Erica) Graham (Chairman), Mrs E. Horrel, Mrs J.G. Mills, Mrs G.H. Robinson, Mrs J. King, Mrs K.O. Andrews, Miss P. Read, Mrs Courage and Mrs N. Martin. Ex-officio member was Mrs Fowle, Regional Officer.[26]

COUNTY ORGANISERS

There were two mobile officers, each taking responsibility for the north or the south of the county respectively. It was their job to implement practical arrangements for land girls, whether employed by independent farmers or county 'War Ag'.

They inspected farms when a farmer first applied for WLA labour, to see if the place was suitable. They inspected every hostel at regular intervals. It was their job to report back to county office on farms, hostels and land girls and to investigate any complaints received. They would transport land girls from the nearest railway station to their appointed farms or hostels and keep in touch with them, as a 'welfare' link with the county office. They liaised continually with both farmers and 'War Ag' staff.[27]

COUNTY WLA OFFICE CLOSES

The Bedfordshire WLA county office closed its doors for good on 20 November 1949 and the administration for the remaining 300 land girls in the county was transferred to a joint Bedfordshire, Buckinghamshire and Northamptonshire office in High Wycombe. The *Bedfordshire Times* published an article entitled "Land Girls Rose to a Great Occasion". In it, the reporter writes of a peak period for the Bedfordshire WLA in mid 1940 [sic. This should be 'mid-1940s'] when, it is claimed "1,200 girls were working in this County". This figure is not borne out by the official figures published by the national WLA organisation in *The Land Girl*. The peak figure for Bedfordshire, on 29 September 1944, was 1,057.[28]

RECRUITMENT

Mrs Dallas, who had been in the Women's Land Army in Bedfordshire in the First World War, was instrumental in recruiting the first full-time volunteers in the first half of 1939 before war was declared and the organisation officially set up. 85 volunteers were working on farms in Bedfordshire at the outbreak of war.[29]

Initially, pre-war volunteers, in the spring and summer of 1939, who registered their interest in joining the WLA in the event of war, could express a preference

Nola Bagley, from Brightlingsea, Essex, was sent to serve as a land girl in Bedfordshire in 1943. She worked for Bedfordshire War Agricultural Executive Committee (the 'War Ag') and was based at Milton Ernest hostel in the north of the county. Like most recruits, she had her photograph taken in her new uniform. *Source: N Wallace*

The Women's Land Army had to compete for female labour with the three armed forces, nursing and essential war work in factories. This recruiting parade was one of a number of ways in which the WLA locally would try to keep in the public's eye and appeal to potential young women recruits. St Paul's Church, Bedford can be seen in the background. They are turning from St Paul's Square round to the Embankment on 1 June 1940. *Source: BLARS (Beds Times collection), Z50/13/312*

to be either 'mobile', meaning they were prepared to be sent anywhere in the country, or 'local', which meant they wished to be employed in their own county. They might even indicate that they could do only part-time work. Following the setting up of the official organisation and the clarification of conditions of service, including the requirement that farmers had to employ WLA members throughout the year and that recruits had to work full-time and be prepared to be mobile, rather than just work locally, this number was reduced to just 24 full-time volunteers registered by the end of December 1939. Some Bedfordshire volunteers were sent to other counties, because there was, as yet, no demand for them from Bedfordshire farmers.

Girls were interviewed at the county HQ, and, subject to a satisfactory medical note from their doctor (paid for by the Ministry of Agriculture), were enrolled on a list of potential land girls awaiting a placement. To indicate their registration in the WLA, they were issued with WLA enamel badges, carrying the emblem of the sheaf of corn (or fir tree, if they joined the Timber Corps). In addition, they were entitled to wear the optional WLA tie, which they had to pay for.

During the first two and a half years of the war, all land girls were true paid 'volunteers'. In the early years of the war, the majority of recruits were from the county and stayed in the county, provided farmers needed them at the time of recruitment. Otherwise they were sent to other counties where farm workers were needed. The introduction of female conscription, following the Conscription Act of November 1941, brought about an enormous increase in the numbers of women opting for the WLA as opposed to joining the services or other war work. They continued to be referred to as 'volunteers', but, nevertheless, had been conscripted in most cases, except where they joined voluntarily just before their call-up date to try and avoid unpleasant war work in munitions factories or military service.

PAY AND ACCOMMODATION

Half the pay – 14 shillings (70p) of the 28 shillings (£1.40) a week wage (in 1939–1940) – was deducted for bed and board at the private billets. The billet might be the farmhouse where the girl worked or the cottage of a farm worker or neighbour. If volunteers were not happy with the farm to which they had been allocated, they had to contact headquarters in Bedford, and request a move to another farm.

By December 1943, the working week in Bedfordshire had been shortened to 48

The three Bennett sisters, Hannah, Mary and Ruth, from Bedford, were all in the WLA. At least four other Bedfordshire families also provided three of their daughters as land girls: the Lowe, Wallis, Day and Pike families. Numerous other sisters enlisted but did not necessarily serve together. The Pearson twins were identical and served on the Priestley Farm at Flitwick in mid-Bedfordshire. The Virgin sisters were at Hulcote Moors hostel. Some farmers could not resist greeting the gangs from Hulcote with the query: "Which ones are the Virgins?" *Source: H Croot*

hours all the year round (it had previously been a 50-hour week in the summer) and the pay had risen to one shilling (5p) per hour – 48 shillings before stoppages – for those over 18 years old. Overtime pay, after two months' work, was 1s/3d (7½p) per hour on weekdays; and 1s/5d (8p) per hour on Sunday or Saturday afternoons (or other half-days). After paying for billets, land girls were to receive a minimum net wage of 22s/6d (£1.12½p) per week.[30]

Post-war, there were a number of improvements in pay and conditions in an attempt to both retain and recruit land girls. Land girls who had served as wartime volunteers for three years or more who were working elsewhere in the country would now be eligible for transfer to their own county.[31] In January 1947, two weeks paid holiday (previously one week) was announced for land girls nationally.[32] New age rates were announced in April 1949, ranging from 55 shillings (£2.75p) for under 18s to 71 shillings (£3.55p) for 21 year olds and over for a 47-hour week.[33] Women who stayed on the land after the disbandment of the WLA in November 1950 were paid 76 shillings (£3.80p).[34]

WELFARE VISITS

Local and District WLA representatives, all local unpaid volunteers, were allocated to the various parts of the county to keep an eye on the welfare of land girls and provide them with help and support, if they had problems. In February 1943 there were 36 local representatives in Bedfordshire, at a time when there were 517 land girls working in the county.[35] How effective this proved to be is open to question. Most of those interviewed by the author, as part of his research, could not remember any such visits.

EARLY ATTITUDES TO LAND GIRLS

Regarding the slow take-up of volunteers in the early period, farmers were not the only ones who were sceptical whether these young women, almost all of them from urban backgrounds, might be 'up to it'.

"To be quite honest, I rather wondered how 'Miss Modern' would tackle the hard work which anything to do with farming means," said Mrs Dallas (a land girl in the First World War), who had helped recruit them, "but I need not have had any doubts, for the Land Girl of today has already shown that she is just as anxious to do her bit as the Land Girl of yesterday."[36]

INDUCTION TRAINING

The original intention was that each volunteer would be given an initial training of at least four weeks, to give them a basic idea of what farming, whether milking, general farming (livestock or arable), or horticulture, was about. It was also

Land girls work on a haystack as schoolboys, with their gas masks in cases over their shoulders, look on. Great Barford, 13 May 1941. *Source: BLARS (Beds Times collection) BT1081/1*

designed to harden their muscles for the physical work they would be doing. Agricultural institutes such as the one at Moulton, Northamptonshire, were used as training centres for newly-recruited land girls. Later, training farms within Bedfordshire – the first at Luton Hoo, then at Toddington Park, and, later, Ravensden Farm – were established (see hostel details on p.240).

But it was not found possible to provide this for all land girls. Many, probably most, in Bedfordshire, had to learn on the job. Later, some were given training to drive a tractor or lorry or specialist training of another kind by the 'War Ag'.

HOLIDAY AND TRAVEL ENTITLEMENT

Holiday entitlement for land girls was the worst of all the female options for national service during the war. Munitions workers were entitled to two weeks' paid leave, those in the armed forces to four weeks' paid leave but land girls to only one week. Even then, given the nature of the seasonal work, this was to be taken at a time to suit the farmer. A railway warrant was issued to land girls after six months' work, provided that they worked at least 50 miles from home. This meant, in most cases, that members who worked a long way from their childhood home returned only twice a year, once for a week-long holiday and then for a few days over Christmas. Those who lived just over 50 miles away but were able to get home more frequently, using cheaper travel by bus or coach (or hitching free lifts), might use their travel warrants to visit a more far-flung part of the country for a holiday, since land girls could apply for a return train fare to anywhere in England and Wales.

One Bedfordshire land girl, for example, used this opportunity to travel free to Carlisle and then pay the difference to go on to the home in Scotland of one of her friends.

DISMISSALS

There were three main reasons for dismissal from the WLA: unsuitable conduct, repeated dismissal from employment, or refusal to resign although invited to do so. Unsuitable conduct covered a wide range of behaviour including failing to obey orders or to comply with WLA regulations. A significant number were dismissed for continual failure to return on time after leave.[37]

A WVS lady encourages a young woman to apply to join the Women's Land Army at an office in Leagreave, August 1941. Once an application was received, a potential recruit was formally interviewed at the county's WLA Headquarters in Bedford. *Source: Luton Central Library. Courtesy of Luton News*

BEDFORD WOMEN'S LAND ARMY CLUB

A Saturday afternoon club for girls who worked for independent farmers in the north of the county was set up in Bedford on 22 November 1941. Mrs Miriam Godber of Willington had raised £42 to set up the club funds. It was held from 1pm to 6pm at Bedford Girls' Club, above Braggins shop – the entrance being in Harpur Street, near the corner with Silver Street. The facilities included a games room, reading room, rest room, tea-room, kitchen and dancing hall. The walls were decorated with murals of Bedford scenes, painted by students from the town's women's teacher training college. Provided land girls could get transport into Bedford after their morning work on Saturday, the club enabled them to meet other land girls, many of whom worked on quite isolated farms, and were billeted in small villages or hamlets with little in the way of a social life. In addition, the land girls were allowed to bring along boyfriends for an hour or two.

BEDFORDSHIRE LAND ARMY NEWSLETTERS

As well as the national WLA monthly magazine, *The Land Girl*, each county would send out typewritten newsletters. Bedfordshire issued its own news sheets,

This photo of 1941 shows how long wartime queues outside shops could be, because of rationing. The Bedford Land Girls Club was held upstairs, above Braggins' store in Silver Street, on Saturday afternoons. The entrance was in Harpur Street (far right) round the corner. *Source: BLARS (Beds Times collection) BT 1085/4*

bringing isolated land girls up-to-date with the latest developments in the county. The May 1942 newsletter, for example, contained announcements about a new hostel, the second one in Bedfordshire, which had opened in Leighton Buzzard, gum boots (wellingtons) being in short supply and about active fund-raising for the Land Girls Spitfire Fund.

Recreational pool being played by land girls at the Bedford Women's Land Army Club, one Saturday afternoon in November 1941. *Source: Antrobus archive, 1946 Bedfordshire WLA souvenir programme*

The Bedfordshire newsletter transcribed below, of July 1942, included items on changes in HQ personnel, land girls' participation in a Luton parade, how they, at last, had been given permission to use canteens previously limited to the armed forces, and how WLA badges were no longer available because of metal shortages. It also announced the impending move of the WLA county office from 2 St Paul's Square to Harpur Street.

The News Sheet this month contains a very sad piece of information for all Volunteers in Bedfordshire. Mrs Dallas, the universally popular Hon. Uniform Officer, has had to give up her work for the Women's Land Army owing to pressure of household duties, and although we hope she will come to the Office whenever she can spare us a moment, it is very sad to feel she is obliged to relinquish the reins. A great many of our new Volunteers are not aware of the fact that Mrs Dallas, together with Miss Farrar, was responsible for all the WLA work before and at the outbreak of the War, nor that she herself was a Land Army volunteer during the last War.[38] Those who do know, however, and the present Office staff, will feel very sorry that her daily attendance at work has ceased.

Mrs Sharman has been initiated into the uniform work by Mrs Dallas, and has also taken on all the extra bookwork necessitated by the surrender of coupons by Volunteers which the Board of Trade have been obliged to enforce on the WLA at last. You will doubtless appreciate the fact that they have been very lucky not to have had to give up coupons until now, and we are very proud of the fact that nearly all our coupons have been sent in most promptly. Those few girls who have not yet sent them, should do so immediately.

Twenty-eight land girls took part in the United Day Parade in Luton on Sunday, the 14th June; they looked very smart and marched well.

By permission of the Army Welfare Officer for Bedfordshire, all WLA members in uniform are now allowed to attend Voluntary Concerts and Parties in addition to Canteens, and it is expected that Sunday Concerts at the Bedford Corn Exchange and elsewhere will be very popular. We are most grateful that this has been made possible.

The Office will shortly be moved to Harpur Street, opposite Telephone House, but we don't know the exact date yet.

No more WLA Badges are being made as the metal cannot be spared for those, so girls who already have them should treasure them and see that the pin is in good order.

Source: Antrobus archive

'GOOD SERVICE' BADGES: ARMLETS AND HALF-DIAMONDS

One way in which the County WLA organisation both kept in touch with land girls and praised and encouraged them was by having periodic ceremonies where members were awarded a further six-month red half diamond to add to their green WLA armlet, bearing the red piping and crown, indicating the patronage of Queen Elizabeth. Cumulatively these diamonds and half-diamonds indicated how long they had served in the WLA and could be worn on the left arm of their dressier (non-working) uniform for smart occasions. Often these award ceremonies were the occasion of a rally or party at one of the WLA clubs.

From September 1943 onwards, those land girls who qualified for their eighth

This two-year armband has two more half-diamond chevrons sewn on to it, thus indicating that the land girl had served at least three years in the Women's Land Army. Also shown is a Forewoman's badge, which was awarded when a land girl had completed a Forewoman's course organised by the 'War Ag'. A Forewoman was responsible for making sure that the right numbers of land girls were allocated and transported to the local farms each day, the work was done to the satisfaction of the farmers and timesheets completed. *Source: H. Hicks*

Half-diamond material badges in felt being presented by Mrs 'J.B.' (Erica) Graham to county land girls in November 1941. These were awarded for each six-months' service and sewn on to their green WLA armbands, indicating their length of service. *Source: BLARS (Beds Times collection) BT1245*

half-diamonds, having completed four years of satisfactory full-time service in the WLA, excluding any period spent in training, were entitled to a special armlet. It was scarlet, with the letters 'WLA' and four full diamonds embroidered on it in green.[39]

Six-year arm bands, first issued in autumn 1945, to those who had served throughout the full war-time period of WLA service, were yellow with green features.

Post-war, those few who had managed to achieve ten years of service were entitled to a special ten-year armlet.

BEDFORDSHIRE WLA AND ITS RELATIONSHIP WITH BEDFORDSHIRE 'WAR AG'

Nationally, from 1942 onwards, when hostel gangs of land girls were established, approximately one third of land girls were employed directly by county 'War Ags'.

In Bedfordshire, by 1944, about half of all county land girls were employed by Bedfordshire 'War Ag' and based in hostels (about 500 out of the total 1,000 women employed at the peak in 1943–44).[40] This required a close working relationship between the two organisations in the county. The WLA's Employment Officer liaised with the 'War Ag's' Labour Officer to ensure that requirements for labour were met and problems resolved. The position on the 'War Ag's' committees of the county's WLA Secretary ensured that the usage of land girl labour was fully utilised, once the prejudices of farmers had been overcome.

FARMERS CHANGE THEIR MIND

The organisation, it is claimed, had "revolutionized many farmers' ideas of women working on the land".[41] Certainly a study of newspaper articles, in that early 1939–1940 period, indicates a clear scepticism among the county's farmers that young, untrained women would be able to cope with the physical demands of work on the land. Over the border in Buckinghamshire, the Chairman of the National Farmers' Union Executive went so far as to give his opinion that "One man is equal to five very willing, unskilled girls".[42] This sort of prejudice undoubtedly led to the very low take-up of land girl recruits in the county and the reluctance of farmers to take them on until the early land girl recruits proved themselves and word got round that they were quite good workers. The same reluctance could be heard from a market gardener who suspected that these young women would find work growing onions too hard: "I don't think the land girls would stand the crawling".[43]

But a few weeks later the newspaper's agricultural correspondent is countering the argument: "Who was it who said that the land girls would be unable to cope with the unpleasant jobs to be found on any farm? Had the critic seen two girls picking Brussels sprouts on a farm at Thurleigh throughout the recent severe weather he would have revised his opinion. These girls are still busy among the sprouts and are making light of work which is not considered to be easy even for experienced hands."[44]

DIFFICULTIES AND DISPUTES

It would be wrong to assume that all was sweetness and light for land girls and their organisers and employers. There were difficulties on all sides. The practice of driving land girls out from their hostels to surrounding farms in open-topped lorries, in all weathers, led to a serious case of disruption at the Whipsnade hostel. Prisoners of war were always transported in covered wagons and the land girls did not see why they had to get wet and cold before or after a day's work. The land girls there downed tools and travelled up to the county office in Bedford to protest. There were so many of them that they were asked to go round to the 'War Ag' offices in St Paul's Square where they made their complaints known. The outcome of the dispute was that the hostel at Whipsnade was closed down and the land girls dispersed to other hostels in the south of the county, at Kensworth and Leighton Buzzard.[45]

A dispute at Leighton Buzzard hostel, where the same complaints were made by the land girls, resulted in a different outcome. They decided to refuse to go out in open lorries any more, but kept working by cultivating the garden around their hostel. Irate officials came down to the hostel to threaten them with dire consequences but the land girls stood firm and a covered lorry was provided.[46]

Some land girls got into trouble for refusing to carry out instructions or for failing to return to their place of work on time after having taken leave. Their employers, whether private farmers or the county 'War Ag', were faced with the same dilemma that the young women were civilian workers and the kind of sanctions and punishments available to the armed forces were not applicable to land girls. Despite doing essential war work they were not subject to military discipline. The ultimate sanction was to dismiss them, which defeated the whole point of the exercise in providing labour for the farms, and in some cases was what these particular land girls wanted.

Mr J.B. Graham, Secretary to Bedfordshire 'War Ag' (and husband of Bedfordshire WLA's county committee chairman, Erica Graham), wrote to the Ministry of Agriculture in September 1943, asking them to consider "the question of tightening up discipline in the Land Army's Hostels" which his committee believed was badly needed. His committee felt that the WLA should be given powers to "call in the aid of the police to apprehend an absentee and to take her back to her Hostel".[47] Nothing came of his protests.

ILLNESSES AND INJURY

There are no statistics for the number and type of illnesses and accidents suffered by land girls in Bedfordshire. The only evidence is that of the land girls themselves in their memoirs and occasional county WLA newsletters or County News items in *The Land Girl* magazine. Taking just one six-month period, January to June 1943, the national magazine (in County News items on Bedfordshire) refers, in February, to M. Green (WLA 102825) progressing favourably after sustaining severe injury[48] and that J. Smart (WLA95537) who had a serious accident would not lose the sight of one eye.[49] The experiences of those land girls who mentioned illnesses in Chapters 8 and 9 ranged from illnesses caught from contact with animals to injuries sustained mainly as a result of working with machinery or lifting heavy weights.

Land girls and local British and American servicemen enjoying themselves at a Hallowe'en party at Milton Ernest hostel. Ann Brodrick and Mary Codrington are in the centre. *Source: A Haynes*

FAMILY SPIRIT OF LAND GIRLS

The *Bedfordshire Times and Standard*, 18 November 1949, article spoke of how the "personal touch with each land girl" had been the keynote of the work carried out by the county's administrative staff. "At social functions big and small – and they have been many – a family spirit has prevailed." May festivities, various gymkhana and Farm Sunday open-air services, street processions, concert party shows, hostel birthday and Christmas parties, 'harvest homes' and inter-hostel sports events are given as examples of the active social life enjoyed by land girls. Particularly noted are the 'innumerable open invitations extended by local American aerodromes' which undoubtedly brought excitement and, sometimes, romance to Bedfordshire land girls, courtesy of their GI hosts (see the numerous memoir extracts in later chapters on both private farm and hostel land girls).

ROYAL SUPPORT

Queen Elizabeth showed her support for the WLA by becoming its Patron in July 1941.[50] Royal visits to the Bedfordshire WLA included that of the Duchess of Gloucester to Cople Hostel in March 1944 and the Duchess of Kent to open the Handicraft Exhibition at the Corn Exchange, Bedford, in July 1944. The most important post-war visit was by Princess Elizabeth in February 1946. (See Chapter 7 on royal visits.) Grace Cross, a Luton girl who had previously been a typist at Vauxhall Motors and joined the WLA in 1942, was chosen to represent Bedfordshire WLA in the national Victory Parade in London in June 1946, before the King and Queen.

PRIDE IN COMMITMENT

Even in the worst snow-bound winter of 1946–47, there were only two days when land girl drivers were not able to get their colleagues out to their work, in most parts of the county. Pride was also shown in that Bedfordshire land girls, at a time when some other counties' land girls went on strike in 1945 over the Government's treatment of them in terms of post-war benefits, kept on working "loyally, putting the needs of the country before their personal feelings".[51]

Two Bedfordshire land girls had received national recognition through the awards of British Empire Medals for service to the WLA – Elizabeth Day and Georgina Gray.

Phyllis Chiplin presents a book to Inez Jenkins, Chief Administrative Officer of the post-war WLA, watched by Mrs 'J.B.' (Erica) Graham, WLA county Chairman, 31 July 1947, Bedford. *Source: Antrobus archive (Courtesy of Beds Times)*

THE CLOSING DOWN OF BEDFORDSHIRE'S WLA ADMINISTRATION

The major event before the closing of the Bedford office was the day-long, large-scale 'harvest home' (held early in August 1949) when about 400 Bedfordshire land girls gathered at Hasells Hall, the WLA Sandy hostel, for inter-hostel sports, entertainment, dancing and fireworks. Presentations were made to the County Secretary and County Office staff.[52]

11 Bedfordshire land girls represented their county in the final disbandment parade at Buckingham Palace, London, on Saturday 21 October 1950 before Queen Elizabeth. They were Jean Bates, Mabel E. Bracey, Mary K. Goodwin, Audrey Winifred Hammond, Audrey Muriel Elizabeth Hislop, Constance Eyalyne Hopkins, Lillian Judge, Marion Ellen Morley, Anne Parker, Jean Elizabeth Scotchford and Ethel Stanton.[53]

A small number of Bedfordshire land girls, including Liz Day, served for ten years and at least one of the Bedfordshire land girls, Joan Garratt, served for the full 11 years in the WLA, enrolling on 23 March 1939 and leaving on the last day of the WLA, 30 November 1950.

Inter-hostel rivalry at Sharnbrook House sports day, July 1945. The last large WLA social event of this kind in Bedfordshire, for around 400 land girls, was held at Hasells Hall on 6 August 1949. *Source: BLARS (Beds Times collection) BT 2141*

Queen Elizabeth inspects land girls at the WLA disbandment parade at Buckingham Palace, 30 October 1950. Mabel Bracey, one of 11 representing Bedfordshire, is second from the right, front row. *Source: Museum of English Rural Life, University of Reading (Ref. P FW PH2/R72/1)*

The final event in the organisational life of the WLA in Bedfordshire was the Farewell Party (an estimated 30 were around the table) at Shire Hall, Bedford on 18 November 1950. Mrs Eugster, who had been first the Assistant County Secretary, then County Secretary for nine years, cut the cake. Mrs 'J.B.' (Erica) Graham reflected that the first tea party of the county organisation had been held in the same committee room 11 years before. Miss Amy Curtis, Chief Administrative Officer of the WLA, attended together with Mrs Martin, one of the original County Committee members. It was reported that 80% of the final Bedfordshire land girls were planning to stay on in agriculture after the official disbandment of the WLA on 30 November 1950.[54]

TO EVERY LIVESTOCK FARMER:

the Minister of Agriculture, Mr. R. S. Hudson, appeals for self-sufficiency on farms

Your land *must* feed your stock. You know only too well how difficult it was to carry stock through last winter. Supplies of imported feeding stuffs were short : they will be much smaller still next winter. For your own and your country's sake, do all you can to make yourself independent of imported supplies.

Grow more fodder crops. Make the utmost of your grassland. Make grass silage to replace imported cake. Dress every acre of your arable and grassland for greater yields.

Have *you* thought of all the possible ways of growing more feeding stuffs on your own farm ? Your County War Agricultural Executive Committee are distributing a leaflet called "Winter Feed." If you have not already had a copy, please get one. Act on the valuable advice it gives.

R. S. Hudson

MINISTER OF AGRICULTURE.

Issued by
THE MINISTRY OF AGRICULTURE & FISHERIES, London, S.W.I

From 15 January 1940, the government took control of livestock. Animals for slaughter had to be sold to the state at a guaranteed price. In this advertisement livestock farmers are being encouraged to grow the necessary crops to feed their own livestock, to minimise the need for animal feed to be imported. *Source: Bedford Central Library, Ampthill News 20 May 1941*

CHAPTER 3

Wartime Farming and the County War Agricultural Executive Committees

FARMING IN ENGLAND AND WALES AT THE BEGINNING OF THE SECOND WORLD WAR

Farming in most parts of the country had reached a low ebb by 1939. In terms of food production, over 60% of our food came from abroad. Never had the grazing acreage been so high and the ploughed-up acreage so low. Arable acreage was about 9 million; whereas 16 million acres were under grass and a further 5½ million was 'rough grazing' (once reasonable pasture).[55]

The Government, once the threat of war became clear, decided that there needed to be a central agricultural plan but with de-centralized execution. From May 1939 onwards, Britain's farmers had been offered £2 per acre in grant-aid to encourage the ploughing up of grassland, plus a basic slag subsidy to add lime to the soil. This led to 350,000 acres of ploughed land being added before the war started in the so-called 'Battle for Wheat'. From the commencement of war, a yearly quota of two million acres of additional ploughed land was set for 1940 (and exceeded by 100,000 acres); the same for 1941.[56]

The priorities for farming were set by reference to the fact that food output from each acre of land needed to be as great as possible: one acre of permanent grass (for animal fodder) fed one or two people; one acre sown with wheat fed 20 people; and one acre sown with potatoes fed 40 people. Potatoes and wheat were also heavy goods to transport from abroad on merchant shipping and the more that could be produced at home, the more shipping tonnage that was made available for other vital imports.

There were 48 million people to feed on our island and only about one million directly employed in the production of food, and most of those part-time, seasonal workers.[57] Increasingly, those men who worked on farms would need to be called up into the armed forces (50,000 skilled farm workers were absorbed

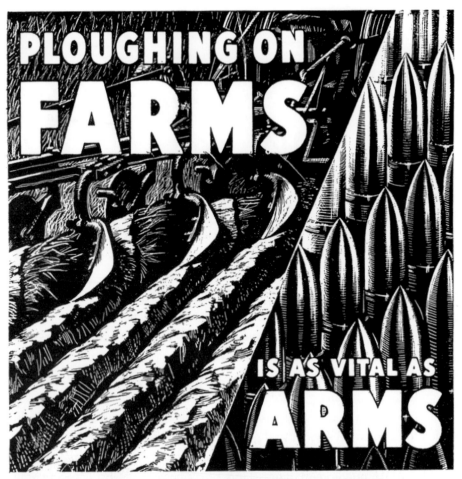

A government advertisement in *The Farmer and Stock-breeder* on 26 March 1940 urges farmers to plough: "The more we can grow, the more we can spend on munitions. Grow your own feeding stuffs." *Source: Antrobus archive*

by the armed forces in the first two years), so farmers were to be faced not only with enormous challenges in terms of increased food production targets but also a shortage of experienced labour to enable them to achieve those targets. From 1942 all male farm workers over 18 were 'called up', removing a further 100,000 men from the land. Machinery would enable the farmer to overcome some of his problems but Britain had been slower than America, Canada, Australia and the Soviet Union in embracing mechanisation. This was the background against which both the County War Agricultural Committees and the Women's Land Army were to operate during the Second World War.

COUNTY WAR AGRICULTURAL EXECUTIVE COMMITTEES (C.W.A.E.C.S) NATIONALLY

War Agricultural Committees were formed immediately on the outbreak of war on 3 September 1939. Their members had been selected before the war and were appointed directly by the Minister of Agriculture and Fisheries. They were leading farmers and nurserymen, with a good knowledge of local conditions, who had volunteered, unpaid, to help in the campaign to get full production from the land in their particular county.

These Executive Committees, numbering eight to 12 members, predominantly farmers, were given delegated powers by the Minister under the wartime Defence Regulations. There was usually at least one landowner, one representative from the farm workers and one woman representing the Women's Land Army. They formed Sub-Committees to cover different aspects of work, and District Committees to ensure that there was at least one Committee member in touch with every farmer, on up to say 50 or 60 farms, in his area of 5,000 acres. Later, some District Committees embraced a representative from every parish. The role was to tell farmers what was required of them, such as the growing of wheat, potatoes, sugar beet or other priority crops, and to help the farmers to get what

Ben (left) and Bill Barnett, harvesting, post-war, at Park Farm, Keysoe. During the war, Ben, who had a small-holding and was therefore in a reserved occupation, also worked on a number of farms for the 'War Ag' and was in the Home Guard. Bill served in the Royal Air Force during the war. Eventually he returned to farming. Ben married a land girl, Vera Jobling. *Source: V Barnett*

they needed in the way of machinery, fertilisers and so on to achieve the targets which were set them. They administered, locally, various grant and subsidy schemes, the rationing of feedstuffs and fertilisers and the provision of goods and services on credit.[58]

The writer Laurie Lee, working for the Ministry of Information, summed this up in *Land at War, the official story of British farming 1939–1944* with the following simple example:

> From Whitehall to every farm in the country the CWAECs formed a visible human chain which grew stronger with each year of the war. Here, roughly, is the way it worked. The Government might say to the Minister of Agriculture: 'We need so much home-grown food next year.' The Minister assured himself that the labour, tractors, equipment, and so on, would be forthcoming, and said to the Chairman of a County Committee: 'We've got to plough two million acres next year. The quota for your county is 40,000.'
>
> The Chairman said to his District Committee Chairman: 'You've been scheduled for 5,000 acres.'
>
> The Committee-man said to his Parish Representative: 'You've got to find 800 acres, then.'
>
> And the Parish Representative, who knew every yard of the valley, went to the farmer at the end of the lane.
>
> 'Bob,' he said, 'how about that 17-acre field – for wheat?'
>
> And Farmer Bob said, 'Aye'.[59]

The Sub-Committees covered the following concerns: Cultivations, Labour, Machinery and Land Drainage, Technical Development, Feeding Stuffs, Insects and Pests, Horticulture, Financial and General Purposes, Goods and Services and War Damage.[60]

The Committees employed paid officers such as the Executive Officer and assistants in each county and District Officers to keep the show running smoothly in every locality. Technical Officers were also employed to advise farmers about such matters as the lime requirements of their soils, the making of silage, the treatments of soil pests, the care of machinery and the improvement of livestock.

Farmers could get expert advice free, which contributed enormously to increase the output that farmers achieved.

Committees had their own Pest Destruction staff and where rats or rabbits had got too numerous, a team of trained land girls were employed to clear up the trouble. This became increasingly important as more and more corn was grown as one of the wartime priorities. An estimated one million tons of food annually was lost to pest damage, at a cost of £50 million.[61] Powers were given

Vera Roberts and Ellen Green, working to exterminate rats for Bedfordshire 'War Ag'. Vermin on farms accounted for millions of tons of food lost, pre-war. Now war was being waged on them with a vengeance. Rabbits, rats, mice, foxes, rooks, wood pigeons and moles were key targets. *Source: Antrobus archive, 1946 Bedfordshire WLA souvenir programme*

to CWAECs through Orders under the Defence Regulations to require farmers and landowners to destroy pests and, if not, for the CWAECs to do it themselves. Rabbits, rooks, rats and wood pigeons were among the worst offenders. Rats, for example, will eat one hundredweight of food each per year.

Rodent control had to be a continuing process, rather than merely a matter of seasonal campaigns in autumn and early winter, if extermination over large areas was to be achieved. Infestation orders also imposed duties on local authorities for urban areas. Poison baits, trapping, ferreting, shotguns and the use of the poison gas, Cymag, were the chief methods used by farmers, land girls and CWAEC pest officers to exterminate the pests.[62]

Threshing was another matter which the County Committees had to tackle. With so much corn being grown, steps had to be taken to organise threshing facilities in each county to ensure that farmers who did not have their own threshing machines got their corn threshed in a reasonable time. Each contractor had a definite zone of operation and was responsible for all the farms in a group of parishes, in such a way that cross journeys were avoided and each threshing team was kept fully employed.

In addition to the supervision of work done by private farmers, the County Committees, known colloquially as 'War Ags', farmed areas of land themselves, particularly those farms and areas of derelict land which no individual was willing to tackle properly. The clearing of derelict land and the drainage of wet lands were two of those difficult jobs on which many land girls were employed, particularly from 1942 onwards, when conscription brought in increased numbers of young women members of the Women's Land Army. Many of these were employed directly by the 'War Ags' and housed, as mobile labour gangs, in hostels located around each county. In addition, summer work camps set up by the 'War Ags' accommodated thousands of men and women, industrial and clerical workers from Britain's towns and cities, who volunteered to do paid work during their summer holidays, to help bring in the harvest. Even schoolchildren, over the age of 14, did their bit in the school holidays.

Nationally, there were 14 Liaison Officers appointed by the Ministry of Agriculture to act as a link between the Committees, via a grouping of counties, and the Ministry in Whitehall, London. Control of cropping was vital if farmers were to produce what the Ministry of Food required. Many farmers, used to being independent and making their own decisions on what to farm, did not take kindly to being told what to do. For some, it meant a complete revolution regarding what they farmed. While the cattle population was maintained during the war, there were large reductions in other livestock: sheep numbers fell by 30%, pigs by 58% and fowls by 46%.[63] In some Midland counties there was not a plough or a man who knew how to plough before the war, since livestock and grass were their specialities. Others did not take kindly to having to grow potatoes.

The idea of having County 'War Ags' was to make the task of mediating central dictates from national government more palatable by using well-respected local farmers to convey the war needs to farmers who knew them. Even so, when particular farmers failed to co-operate with this more democratic system, orders were served on them requiring them to plough up their grassland, or to grow given acreages of various crops, to clean out their ditches and drains, or apply adequate quantities of fertilisers. In the worst cases, recalcitrant or incompetent farmers – after first attempting to encourage and help them with advice and expertise – could be removed from their farms, by the dictate of the Minister of Agriculture, and their land farmed by someone else who would use the land to better advantage.[64]

"In 1939 fewer than one in six farmers owned a tractor and the vast majority of these were located in the south and east."[65] To aid the farmers, 'War Ags' set about introducing more and more machinery to facilitate the mass production of food now required by the war. Home production of tractors was greatly increased and machinery of all sorts brought over from America, thanks to the Lend-Lease scheme, and from Canada, through Mutual Aid.[66] Tractors increased 50% between 1942 and 1944.

Peggy 'Shirley' Richardson, a land girl from Potton WLA hostel, with a working horse. There were 30 working horses for every tractor in Britain in 1939. Rapid mechanisation was the only way that the greatly increased food production targets would be met. Tractors increased 50% between 1942 and 1944. *Source: T Cass*

They were distributed amongst the farmers, the dealers, and the machinery depots of the County Committees. Some of this machinery was quite novel for Britain – the caterpillar-tracked tractors and the first combine harvesters, which both cut and immediately threshed and bagged the corn in one mobile process. They cleared 36 feet in a single sweep, compared with the five-foot cut of the old horse-drawn binder. Training courses for both farmers and workers were needed, and for the

Night-time ploughing was sometimes the only way to meet the wartime targets for acres to be ploughed. Ministry of Agriculture advertisement in *The Farmers Weekly*, 5 March 1940.
Source: Courtesy of Farmers Weekly

mechanics who were to keep them going. Other machines were recognisable but much larger and more powerful than their predecessors.

Night ploughing was introduced where it was the only way that the work could be completed on time. Shifts of workers operated as drivers so that tractors barely stopped for a minute, even when their drivers were having a break. One tractor did the work of many horses and men. Some plough-tractors were able to draw up to five furrows at a time and more speedily than previously. But horses, where they had been retained, continued to do their bit, and did not need the carefully rationed fuel required by engines.

WARTIME AGRICULTURAL ACHIEVEMENTS

Food production achievements in Britain by the end of the Second World War were outstanding. "By 1944 there had, compared with pre-war production, been a 90% increase in wheat, 87% increase in potatoes, 65% increase in vegetables and 10% increase in sugar beet."[67] Overall, arable land increased by 63% between 1939 and 1944, from 8.9 million acres to 14.5 million acres.[68]

State agricultural planning undoubtedly played a major role in this achievement, together with the 'War Ags', the farmers (some 300,000, when wives are included) and their labour force, implementing this state strategy. The labour force included the land girls (a peak of over 80,000 in late 1943),[69] the POWs (20,000 in June 1943, rising to over 58,000 in June 1945[70]) and over 59,000 conscientious objectors.[71] In addition, casual, seasonal workers – men, women and schoolchildren, including those who joined 'harvest camps' – played a vital part in harvesting crops such as potatoes and corn. Equally, the mechanization of farming, more use of fertilizers, the making of silage, more scientific input and greater pest control played their part.

Threshing at Duloe, in the north of the county, outside St Neots, c. 1944. A caterpillar tractor is powering the threshing machine, but the traditional working horse is still being used to cart bags of grain away. *Source: F Hawkins*

MINISTER OF AGRICULTURE'S VISIT

Mr R.S. Hudson, the Minister of Agriculture, visits Bedfordshire and discusses progress with 'War Ag' committee members and officials in 1943. *Source: Bedford Central Library. Courtesy of Beds Times (1 October 1943 p7)*

CHAPTER 4

Bedfordshire War Agricultural Executive Committee

BEGINNINGS

Mr H.J. Humphreys, of Eversholt, was appointed the unpaid Chairman of the Bedfordshire War Agricultural Executive Committee (BWAEC) and Mr E.W. Russell was the salaried Executive Officer. The county headquarters' office was set up in Phoenix Chambers, St Paul's Square, Bedford and the first meeting of the Bedfordshire 'War Ag' was on Tuesday 5 September 1939. Its first instruction was to convert 10,000 acres of grass land into arable land. Amazingly, Bedfordshire farmers were able to have ploughed up 17,452 new acres, ready for the harvest of 1940.[72]

BEDFORDSHIRE – AGRICULTURAL POTENTIAL

Bedfordshire was still a predominantly rural, agricultural county with 250,000 of its 300,000 acres being farmed (approximately 50% grass and 50% arable). Two thirds of its subsoil was clay and one third (about equally divided) river gravel, greensand and chalk. It was noted for its market gardening. This was mainly on the gravel and greensand but sometimes on the better class of boulder clay in the east of the county. Crops of wheat, beans and clover were particularly successful.

PROBLEMS

Bedfordshire WAEC faced a number of problems: how to increase the farmed acreage on the clays, given the impeded drainage, and the low phosphate status of its soils. Farmers on the heavy soils relied less on farmyard manure and more on lime. Once the 'War Ags' got going, they offered a half-cost subsidy for ditching and mole draining. Track-laying caterpillar tractors were brought into use to enable cultivation on those heavy soils, previously avoided by farmers.

MACHINERY

Another challenge was how to rapidly increase the mechanisation of farms, through loaning, or assisting, farmers to buy tractors and specialist equipment to speed up all farming tasks and reduce the need for labour. The Government channelled equipment from North America – thanks to Canadian support and the Lend-Lease programme with the United States of America – through the Ministry of Agriculture to farmers locally via the 'War Ags'. Bedfordshire WAEC set up depots both providing and maintaining tractors and other equipment as required by independent farmers and its own farm managers at 'War Ag' farms.

Threshing equipment, and later the new combine harvesters, were provided by the 'War Ag' and offered through specialist contractors to tour each district of the county in as rational a way as possible, so as to minimise travel and costs. Increasingly, teams of hostel-based land girls were the labour force for these mobile harvesting and threshing gangs.

The 'War Ag' tractor repair depot, Newnham Street, Bedford. Iris Manning, Daphne Favell and Barbara Sowerby were among the land girl drivers who transported tractors and other machinery to the 'War Ag' farms which needed them around the county. *Source: I Cornell*

ARABLE FERTILITY

The average rainfall in Bedfordshire was 24 inches per year (falling occasionally to below 20 inches) and there were frequent periods of long drought. Nevertheless, clay soils could produce excellent swards and wild clover grew freely. One system adopted was the laying down of old arable land, thus enabling exhausted arable fields to be rested and accumulate fertility. Grass fields were broken up and cropped.

RECLAMATION

Bedfordshire 'War Ag' set about reclaiming areas of previously uncultivated land in the county, especially clay bushy land. Underdeveloped building land in a derelict state was taken over. Sandy and sandy loam land, badly infested with rabbits, was brought under control and into use. Five hundred acres of derelict clay land used only for rough grazing was cultivated. Waterlogged and semi-waterlogged land was drained, progressively. Bedfordshire 'War Ag' requested that the Internal Drainage Boards (set up by the Great Ouse Catchment Board) recondition the main watercourses and loaned them 11 excavator machines to assist.

Caterpillar tractors were vital when large-scale clearance of trees and bushes was needed to reclaim land to bring it into arable production. The Lend-Lease programme enabled large numbers of tractors and other essential farm machinery to be imported from North America, which enabled farmers to greatly increase productivity on the land. *Source: Antrobus archive, 1946 Bedfordshire WLA souvenir programme*

Common land growing gorse, bracken and such like was farmed for the first time in recent years. All together, the 'War Ag' took in hand 5,000 acres of otherwise unproductive land in the county.

CROPPING

Cereals and potatoes were the main crops of the war, but also vital were the vegetables and fruit produced in the market gardens and orchards of the north east of the county, where market gardens were well-established. New crops such as flax appeared in Bedfordshire, vital for the production of war materials such as canvas tents, camouflage, aircraft fabric and parachute-harnesses.

ALLOTMENTS

In the south of the county, Luton Corporation's Parks and Gardens Committee purchased farming equipment to recondition undeveloped land for the establishment of Borough allotments. Dunstable had a similar project. Those who already had allotments in the county cultivated them with increased vigour. Even the people in the towns were 'digging for victory' and helping to produce some of their own food.

LAND GIRL LABOUR ACCOMMODATION

Bedfordshire 'War Ag' also worked in conjunction with the Women's Land Army headquarters in Bedford to both help co-ordinate the flow of labour to the county's private farms and directly employ about half of the county's land girls (about 500 of the maximum number of 1,000 by 1943–44). These it housed in a mixture of requisitioned country houses or in a number of purpose-built hutments for 40 land girls, all strategically placed around the county, so that the young women were within about three miles of their usual work. This enabled mobile gangs of young women to go out each morning in small groups to work on whichever local farms needed their labour, for as long as they needed that labour, and to be returned each evening to their hostel in their own lorries. The land girls were employed directly by the 'War Ag', who paid them, and the farmers paid the 'War Ag' for their labour on a daily basis. Mr Whatling was in charge of Land Army labour, for the 'War Ag', and Mr Ted Foulkes, its Transport Officer, based at Turner's Yard, Goldington, Bedford. The Land Army appointed and paid Young Women's Christian Association (YWCA) Wardens and Assistant Wardens to look after the welfare of the land girls in each hostel.

PART-TIME WOMEN LABOURERS

In addition to these full-time agricultural workers, the Bedfordshire Land Corps (sometimes referred to as the Women's Emergency Labour Corps) were civilians who were either housewives or in employment elsewhere who offered to work, part-time, on local farms, and were organised by Bedfordshire 'War Ag', which provided the transport to get them to and from the farms. Housewives were shipped out every weekday afternoon to farmers who had requested extra help with seasonal jobs such as riddling potatoes or hoeing beet, and so on. Others, such as young women who worked in shops or offices, turned up outside the Corn Exchange in Bedford at 6.30pm in the evening and were transported in open-topped lorries to farms where they worked for three hours at a time. These auxiliary workers were vital, if farmers were to achieve the increasing targets set them each year of the war.[73]

BEDFORDSHIRE
WAR AGRICULTURAL EXECUTIVE COMMITTEE

WOMEN'S LAND ARMY

LABOUR IS NOW AVAILABLE from the following Hostels:

Milton Ernest	Silsoe
Bolnhurst	Hulcote
Ravensden	Toddington
Cople	Kensworth
Potton	Leighton Buzzard
Houghton Conquest	Whipsnade

Applications for labour from these Hostels should be made to the Labour Officer, Phœnix Chambers, High Street, Bedford. Tel. 3201 ex. 111.

E. W. RUSSELL
Executive Officer

Phœnix Chambers,
High Street, Bedford.
22nd September, 1943.

By September 1943, Bedfordshire 'War Ag' was employing hundreds of land girls directly, and sub-contracting them on a daily basis to local farms. The 'gang girls' were accommodated in 12 hostels, dotted around the county, some of them requisitioned country houses and others purpose-built huts. Further hostels were established in later years at Sharnbrook, Aspley Guise, Clifton and Sandy. Luton Hoo was a training farm with its own hostel which held some trainees for four week induction courses as well as its own directly-employed permanent land girls. *Source: Bedford Central Library. Courtesy of Beds Times [See Appendices for WLA Hostels table]*

WOMEN GIVE SPARE-TIME HELP ON THE LAND

A party of members of the Women's Emergency Land Corp, outside the Corn Exchange, Bedford, about to leave by lorry for an evening's work on the farms. *Source: H Croot. Courtesy of Beds Times (24 July 1942 p3)*

FARM CAMPS

Bedfordshire 'War Ag' set up three Farming Camps – at Blunham, Sharnbrook and Ampthill Park. Paid volunteers from towns and cities spent all or part of their annual summer holiday at these agricultural camps, enticed by the slogan 'Lend a hand on the land' and as an alternative to the holidays by the sea which were no longer possible with barbed wire surrounding many of the pre-war holiday resorts. Some were accommodated in bell tents, others in better equipped huts. Many got very sunburnt, especially the miners from South Wales who were used to working underground.

PRISONER OF WAR LABOUR

The further addition of foreign labourers by the use of prisoners of war – first Italian prisoners, then German prisoners – and of refugee and displaced persons from Europe boosted the agricultural labour force yet more. Finally, the contribution of teenage schoolchildren – boys and girls – gave seasonal boosts to the numbers employed on farms, during the school holidays. When labour shortages became desperate, soldiers would also be called upon, if they could be spared from their normal duties, and American GIs stationed in the northern airfields of Bedfordshire would sometime volunteer to lend a hand of their own volition.

INCREASING PRODUCTIVITY

Each year of the war, increasing targets were set for 'War Ags' and farmers to achieve. In 1943, Bedfordshire was set the challenge of cropping an additional 15,000 acres. Wheat and barley were in great demand for bread production, as the Government strove to avoid bread rationing. Only by maximising the use of machinery, fertilisers and labour was it possible. Issuing fertiliser permits was one of the many responsibilities of the 'War Ag'. The elimination of waste and the maximising of efficient ways of working were constantly brought home to farmers through propaganda notices and the issue of one and a half million 'Growmore' leaflets.

ACHIEVEMENTS

As in the country as a whole and thanks to the 'War Ag' committee, the land girls and all those who had done their bit to get in the harvests, Bedfordshire farmers achieved increases in food output which were miraculous.[74] Nationally, some six and a half million new acres were ploughed up between 1939 and 1944. Harvests of wheat, barley and potatoes increased by over 100%; milking cows increased by 300,000; other cattle by 400,000.

This was at the expense of fewer sheep, pigs and poultry but enabled the country to completely reverse its reliance on foreign food. In terms of calories, the net output had been quadrupled by 1943–44. By the end of the war, food imports had been reduced from 22 million to 11 million tons and Britain was producing well over 60% of its food. This was despite losing nearly 100,000 skilled male farm workers, who went off to fight, and thanks to the 117,000 women who replaced them.[75]

Hundreds of land girl recruits travelled from the mill towns of Yorkshire and Lancashire, as well as from other counties and London, to work in Bedfordshire during the Second World War. The greatest influx was in 1942 and 1943 when the conscription of women resulted in thousands being directed to work for county 'War Ags' to become the mobile labour 'gang girls' in agriculture. Young women who did not have family responsibilities had to opt for either the three women's auxiliary armed forces, nursing, war work in factories or chose to work on the land. *Photograph courtesy of the Imperial War Museum, London. D8855*

CHAPTER 5

Recruitment, Training and Proficiency Tests

RECRUITMENT

The minimum age for the Women's Land Army recruitment was 17 years,[76] a year younger than for the armed forces (and some managed to get in when only 16), and the maximum was normally 40 (although few were actually recruited above 30). Most young women were in their late teens when they joined and in their early to mid-twenties when they left. Most of them were born in the 1920s. A few were older on joining and therefore born earlier in the twentieth century. Some were born in the 1930s and served in the post-war years. What the WLA was looking for were physically fit young women, who had no dependants (and therefore, usually, were unmarried), who were mature enough to leave home and be willing to be sent anywhere in the country. Active recruitment ended in 1949 and the last members joined in March 1950 but the Land Army was not finally disbanded until 30 November 1950 . By this time, some 203,000 had served in the WLA in England and Wales.[77]

Publicity was the key to recruitment but was not easy, given the competing demands for female labour from other industries and the armed forces. Attractive posters and propaganda leaflets were the main means of appeal and methods of communication included marches through towns, stands at agricultural shows, and newspaper and cinema advertisements. The WLA had not only to appeal to potential recruits but also to publicise its work to farmers so that the availability of land girls would become known to potential employers in agriculture and horticulture.

They came from a wide range of jobs. Most were from ordinary, working class backgrounds, having previously worked in shops, offices, factories or in domestic service. Some came from more privileged families or were students but were in the minority. Some came from country backgrounds and therefore had some idea of what they were letting themselves in for but most were from towns and cities and were more susceptible to the rather rosy image of farm work portrayed in the recruitment posters offering 'A healthy, happy job'. The sun apparently always shone, you looked very smart and pretty and there was no indication of aching bones, calloused hands or the smell of cow muck.

A sample of personnel index cards for WLA recruits who ended up serving in Bedfordshire covers an enormous range of occupations: wages clerk, food packer, waitress (at a Lyon's corner house), woollen weaver, 'mother's help', dressmaker, canteen worker, machinist, hairdresser, factory 'hand', cashier, 'domestic', box maker, shop assistant, packer, typist, chemical worker, newspaper reporter, textile worker, boot and shoes 'hand', stenographer, seamless hosiery linker, philosophy student.[78]

Among the more unusual occupations undertaken by girls from Bedfordshire were 'feather mounter' for a Luton hat firm and a crayon sharpener at the Cosmic Crayon Company in Bedford.

This enamelled brass badge was given to successful applicants after their WLA interview. The royal crown indicates the patronage of Queen Elizabeth, who was always very supportive of the organisation. The badge could either be worn as a cap badge with the felt hat for formal occasions, or pinned on the green sweater, indicating membership of the WLA. (Members of the Timber Corps had a similar badge, with a fir tree in the centre, instead of the sheaf of corn of the standard WLA badge. They wore it on their beret.) *Source: Antrobus archive*

Potential recruits were normally interviewed at the relevant WLA county headquarters. In the case of Bedfordshire this was, from 1939 to June 1942, at 2 St Paul's Square, Bedford; then, from June 1942 until it closed in November 1949, at 43 Harpur Street. There were two on each interviewing panel – the full-time, salaried County Secretary and an unpaid, part-time member of the WLA County Committee, often the woman 'Chairman'. Questions might include "Are you frightened by cows?", "Have you a bicycle?" (since means of transport in the countryside were limited) and "Have you had any experience of farming or dealing with animals?"[79]

The interview was also an opportunity for the panel members to actually meet the young women and assess whether they appeared to have a strong and healthy physique and general temperamental suitability. A medical certificate had to be provided by each successful candidate's doctor, with the fee paid by the Ministry of Agriculture.[80] In addition, two character references were asked for. Finally, a check had to be made with the local labour exchange to ensure that candidates were not already in 'reserved occupations' (deemed essential to the conduct of the war). On average, only one in four applicants was successful.[81]

Pre-war volunteers, in the first six months or so of 1939, were enrolled – some 10,000 nationally – by being

"Now, Miss Fforbes-Wattson, have you had any experience of agricultural work?"

This wartime Punch cartoon illustrates the predominantly urban nature of the intake of young women into the wartime agricultural labour force, often with no previous experience of either farms or market gardens, nor of life in the country. Most young women who joined the WLA were from working-class backgrounds but some came from the middle classes. Their arrival in country areas was something of a culture shock for both residents and incomers alike. *Source: Punch magazine, 18 June 1941. Reproduced by permission of Punch Ltd, www.punch.co.uk*

asked to sign an undertaking to hold themselves available to work for three years on the land in the event of war. They received a WLA brooch badge as a sign of membership. Once the war started, recruits to the WLA were asked to pledge themselves for the duration of the war.[82] Once accepted, the recruit's name was listed on a county register and efforts made to find a farmer willing to employ her. This could take weeks or months and in some cases there was no demand for labour from the county's farmers for unskilled labourers and these young women had to be transferred to other counties where there was a demand. Until 1942 and the beginnings of conscription for women, volunteer recruits were issued with a

WLA membership card reminding them of their obligations and requiring them to sign a pledge to work for the duration of the war.

Co-ordinating supply and demand was a persistent problem for the WLA and matching recruitment to actual seasonal needs was very difficult, to say nothing of the initial reluctance of farmers to take on untried female labour. In addition, the varying needs of the changing war situation between 1939 and 1945 made it extremely difficult for the WLA. Enrolled strength reached a peak of almost 77,000 when, in September 1943, WLA recruitment was suspended[83], so that more female labour could be directed into aircraft production. At this time recruitment was so successful that about 1,000 young women a week were being attracted into WLA membership[84] and farmers were saying that 100,000 land girls were needed. A ceiling figure of 80,000 members was set for the WLA.

TRAINING FARMS IN BEDFORDSHIRE

The original idea was that girls would attend, when thought necessary, a four-week induction course at a nearby agricultural institute before joining a private farm. During initial training board and lodging was provided free, plus travel expenses, plus ten shillings pocket money. Silsoe Agricultural Institute did not exist then, so some early Bedfordshire recruits were sent to the Northamptonshire Institute of Agriculture at Moulton. The aim was to give them some idea of farm work and to toughen them up for hard physical labour.

Later specific farms in Bedfordshire were named as training farms where short training courses could take place. However, once large numbers of recruits began arriving in each county, particularly after conscription from 1942 onwards, it became impossible to offer this training to all and many land girls ended up training on the job at the farms to which they were allocated.

LUTON HOO

Luton Hoo Home Farm was the first designated training farm, offering training in both milking and dairy work and also, because it served a large country house, horticulture, from 7 July 1941.[85] It was announced as being the 'newly-opened training farm' in the August 1941 edition of *The Land Girl* magazine. Prior to the war it had been a residential training centre for Royal Horticulture Society students. Bedfordshire, being a county with a well-developed market garden sector, needed land girls with horticultural skills and aptitudes.

Accommodation at Luton Hoo was in the large brick-built house known as The Bothy, where, previously, unmarried young men undertaking gardening apprenticeships had been housed. The large walled garden offered opportunities for a range of specialist work in the glasshouses growing tomatoes and a wide range of fruit, some of them rather exotic.

The whole estate at Luton Hoo, around the large mansion, home of the Wernher family, was the wartime base for the army's Eastern Command, responsible for the defence of that part of England in the event of invasion by German forces. As a result it housed a wide range of personnel and a NAAFI which offered cigarettes, chocolates and other scarce commodities not generally available to the civilian population. The

Carting hay on the Luton Hoo estate. The first few weeks and months as land girls were a painful introduction to physical work, as their bodies had to be hardened up. Peggy Richardson (left) and Barbara Newell are working on the ground, passing up the hay to Phyllis with pitchforks. *Source: T Cass & I Davison. Courtesy of Luton News*

resident land girls benefitted from this and from the social life that the presence of so many men in uniform provided. Officers were billeted in and around the mansion.

Luton Hoo became the first specially approved WLA training farm in Bedfordshire in July 1941. Prior to that, those who were sent for initial training other than on the farm of their first employer had to go to agricultural institutes in other counties, such as the one at Moulton in Northamptonshire. Here, new recruits are working in the walled garden, harvesting onions with the Head Gardener, Alfred Daffurn. Those showing the most aptitude for horticulture would have been sent to market gardens in the county. A few were kept on as permanent land girl employees working on the estate's Home Farm. *Source: T Cass & I Davison. Courtesy of Luton News*

The farm bailiff was certainly impressed by at least one of the new land girl recruits, Phyllis Chiplin, who had undertaken milking training: she had "sat down and milked a cow right out at her first attempt. As she had never done any farm work in her life, this was a pretty good effort".[86] She later went on to become a leading Forewoman in the south of the county at the Whipsnade hostel. She led the Farm Sunday Parade of land girls at Wardown Park in June 1943.

Today the only hard evidence at Luton Hoo is a

Phyllis Chiplin, Forewoman, leading the contingent from Whipsnade WLA hostel at a Wardown Park parade, Luton, June 1943. *Source: M Cutler*

Toddington Park hostel, opened in 1942, housed both a permanent gang of 'War Ag' land girls and also small groups of trainees for a four-week induction course, after it became the second approved training farm in the county. Here they are pictured with their YWCA Warden and Assistant Warden, who looked after their welfare at the hostel on behalf of Bedfordshire WLA and the land girls' 'War Ag' employer. *Source: Antrobus archive. Courtesy of B Nicholls*

carved name on a wooden shelf of the potting shed recording the presence of 'Joy Collard. WLA. 1941–45'. She had obviously impressed the head gardener there, Alfred Daffurn, and had been kept on as a permanent land girl working for the Home Farm in the octagonal walled garden, growing fruit and vegetables.

TODDINGTON PARK

Although the hostel at Toddington Manor had been opened in November 1942 to house a permanent gang of land girls employed by the county 'War Ag', its role appears to have broadened by August 1944, when Toddington Park is described as "the latest training centre".[87] Irene Hulatt described the manor house inside as "stark and cold, bedrooms with eight bunk beds to a room, very stark lounge and dining room, huge kitchen and a warden who might have been trained in Colditz...," but admitted that, "Plain but good food was served."[88]

The hostel received a special WLA commendation in August 1944 for its 'excellent potato harvest'.

RAVENSDEN FARM

The county's third training centre was at Ravensden Farm, a mixed farm just north of Bedford, which offered initial training for land girls from May 1944 until December 1949. Ravensden House accommodated groups of between 16 and 30 female recruits, which were divided into two and given two weeks of milking (hand and milking machine) and dairy farming experience, and two weeks of arable farming experience in the fields of surrounding farms from Sharnbrook, Riseley, Melchbourne and Thurleigh to Poddington and Tempsford aerodromes. The farm was managed by Jack Stewart for the 'War Ag' and there were three land girl trainers. The three trainers and the Warden each had their own rooms in the hostel, and the trainee land girls shared bedrooms in the large farmhouse.

Margaret Perry (extreme right), an experienced land girl, trained young recruits in arable farming at Ravensden hostel, which was the third approved training farm, in the north of Bedfordshire. Training took place there from May 1944 to December 1949. It also housed a small permanent gang of 'War Ag' land girls who worked on local farms as required. *Source: M Chessum*

PLACEMENT ON FARMS

During the first two and a half years of the war, WLA recruits were placed on private farms and employed directly by those individual farmers, subject to nationally agreed minimum conditions regarding pay and hours worked. Then, following the introduction of conscription for women, and greatly increased numbers recruited by the WLA, 'War Ags' decided to directly employ large numbers of these new land girls and to house them around their counties in either requisitioned houses or in purpose-built hutment accommodation in gangs of up to 40 young women. This extra provision of accommodation was vital if large numbers of new workers were to be introduced into country areas, where previous waves of evacuees, refugees and billeted soldiers had already taken up existing housing.

Some women continued to be taken on by private farmers who needed permanent, all-year-round, workers. Nationally, about two thirds of land girls were employed on private farms. They undertook the whole range of work on the land, including milking, tractor driving, care of valuable stock, and market gardening. These young women had little or no chance of promotion or publicity from their work and were sometimes very isolated, with little contact with other land girls.

Eventually one third of land girls, nationally, were hostel or gang girls employed by 'War Ags' and sub-contracted to local farmers, as required. However, in Bedfordshire, the balance between those employed directly by private farmers and those employed by the 'War Ag' was 50/50[89]. This creation of a directly-employed mobile force, employed by the county 'War Ags' and housed in new hostels, was an innovative response to the rural housing shortage. This satisfied both the need for flexible seasonal work on farms, and the need for mobile gangs to provide workers for threshing contractors and other essential 'War Ag' drainage and reclamation projects.[90] These hostel gang workers also had the chance of some promotion as some were able to take on the responsibility, and a little extra pay, of gang leader, driver, forewoman, or even senior forewoman in a few situations.

FURTHER TRAINING

Whether new land girls had received four weeks of initial training or had been thrust directly on to farms and market gardens to learn 'on the job', there were further opportunities for most land girls to receive special training. Most common was the opportunity for those who wished to be taught to drive, with the aim of providing more farm workers who could use both tractors and the increasing range of new machinery which 'War Ags' were introducing to farms, in order to increase productivity.

Drivers were also important for the hostel gangs, in order to have their own

Rita Woodward demonstrating her driving skills on a Clophill farm, 25 March 1941. The fact that she is wearing her distinctive Land Army hat tells us that this was a publicity photo opportunity for the press. When land girls wore something on their head, when working, it was usually a headscarf. The uniform felt hats were kept for formal or smart occasions. *Source: BLARS (Beds Times collection) BT1049/2*

land girl transport enabling groups to travel out each day and be dropped off at various farms to do a day's work and then collected in the evening. These land girl drivers were paid a small addition to their pay. Some of them were given the title 'driver ganger' with some extra responsibility for making sure that the required labour was provided to each local farm, according to farmers' requests, and that the set work was achieved.

COUNTY OF BEDFORDSHIRE
WAR AGRICULTURAL EXECUTIVE COMMITTEE

This is to Certify that

Mary Beatrice Pates

has qualified as Forewoman in the services of
the above Committee

GRADE

Signed : *E. Russell*

Executive Officer.

Robert Dart

Date JANUARY 1944

Labour Officer.

Forewomen took on the responsibility of ensuring that 'War Ag' land girls from the hostels were allocated in the right numbers to individual farms, that the required work was done and that time sheets were completed. Farmers paid the 'War Ag' for the work done. The land girls were paid weekly by their employer, the 'War Ag'. Before appointment as a Forewoman the selected land girl attended a short course. *Source: M Smith*

FOREWOMAN TRAINING

Then, in 1944, the 'War Ag' decided to create Forewomen who were to take on the responsibility (previously that of Wardens) of ensuring that the relevant time sheets were completed and signed each day by farmers, confirming which land girls had been employed and for how many hours. Before these women were appointed, they were given short Forewomen training courses at county training farms and issued certificates. These Forewomen were also paid more for their responsibilities, some of which had previously been taken by the hostel Wardens. However, these Forewomen were not responsible for land girls when not working and they were not in authority over other land girls in any way comparable to petty officers in the armed forces. Land girls remained, always, civilian workers, not subject to any military discipline but contracted to work either for the 'War Ag' or for private farmers, many having pledged to work for the duration of the war, unless transferred to other war work or other circumstances (such as marriage) meant that they were no longer regarded as mobile.

PROFICIENCY TESTS AND CERTIFICATES

The first of the proficiency tests were held in July 1944. They were both practical and oral and conducted by working farmers, under the following categories:

Milking and dairy work, General farm work, Poultry, Tractor driving, Outside garden and glasshouse work, Fruit work, and Pest destruction.[91] Local newspapers frequently published the results of local tests and the level of certificate awarded.

The aim was to encourage land girls to stay on in agriculture after the war. These certificates would, like today's National Vocational Qualifications (NVQs), provide workers with evidence of their actual skills as assessed 'on the

A plastic WLA Proficiency badge indicated that the wearer had successfully completed at least one 'War Ag' proficiency test in a practical skill, from dairy work to tractor driving, from poultry husbandry to pest destruction. These tests were conducted by farmers, on the job. *Source: P Doyle*

job'. Not only was a certificate issued, which could be taken as evidence when seeking post-war work on farms and gardens, but also a bakelite 'Proficiency' badge to be worn on the successful land girl's uniform.

From July 1944 onwards, land girls could take proficiency tests in a wide range of land work skills. The aim was to encourage experienced land girls to stay on in agriculture or horticulture after the war. These vocational qualifications would enable them to demonstrate their skills and abilities to future farm employers. *Source: E. Day*

WOMEN'S LAND ARMY PROFICIENCY CERTIFICATE.

THIS IS TO CERTIFY THAT

Miss E. M. B. Day W.L.A. No. *86558*

HAS BEEN AWARDED A PROFICIENCY BADGE

IN *Outdoor Garden & Glasshouse Work*

AND HAS GAINED DISTINCTION.

Date *July 1947.* Signed *Ina Jenkins*

on behalf of the Women's Land Army.

CORRESPONDENCE COURSES

A minority of the land girls were sufficiently keen and interested to take on, on their own initiative, the study of agriculture through correspondence courses, while working full time as a land girl. The course outlined in Sackville-West's book *The Women's Land Army*[92] covers nine topics: the plant, the soil, grassland, tillage, arable crops, the animal, dairy farming, calf-rearing and the farm horse.

POST-WAR FULL-TIME AGRICULTURAL COURSES

One of the few benefits extracted from the government after the considerable outcry when the WLA was excluded from the scheme for post-war benefits, was the provision of a small number of grants to enable land girls to do full-time study at an agricultural institute. Two a year were granted to successful applicants in Bedfordshire. Among those who benefited were Margaret Perry, Georgina Gray and Elizabeth Day.

MINISTRY OF AGRICULTURE AND FISHERIES
WOMEN'S LAND ARMY

Bedfordshire *County Secretary*

Address 9, S.ᵗ Paul's Square,
Bedford.
18 . 6 . 42

Dear Miss Trott

NOTIFICATION OF TRAINING

A four weeks' training in general farm work starting on Monday, the 6ᵗʰ July, 1942 has been arranged for you, as a member of the Women's Land Army, with the Luton Hoo Estate at Luton Hoo, Beds.

During training you will be billeted at The Garden's Bothy, Luton Hoo Estate, Luton Hoo. You should be at the Bridge ~~The nearest station is~~ Street 'bus Depôt, Luton at 11.30 a.m. ~~on~~ ~~the 6ᵗʰ~~ ~~You should arrive on~~ when the Estate Van will ~~Please notify~~ meet you. Please travel in ~~of the time of~~ ~~your arrival as soon as~~ ~~possible.~~ uniform.

[P.T.O.]

Part of a letter inviting Zeita Trott to four weeks of general farming training at Luton Hoo Estate, a specially-approved training centre for land girl recruits in July 1942. At that time the Bedfordshire WLA county office was in St Paul's Square, Bedford. *Source: Z Holes*

CHAPTER 6

Bedfordshire Hostels

LAND GIRL GANG LABOUR ACCOMMODATION NATIONALLY

Nationally, the WLA, by January 1944, had 696 hostels accommodating some 23,000 land girls and employing 2,300 staff. Of these hostels, the WLA, through its county offices, directly ran 475 of them, the YWCA ran 146 and the County 'War Ags' ran 75. They accommodated approximately one third of land girls, whereas two thirds were billeted privately.[93]

Although hostel accommodation was fairly spartan, certainly by our standards in the 21st century, it provided a higher standard of amenity and comfort than the Ministry of Health considered necessary for other classes of war worker.[94] The hostels were either in requisitioned buildings or purpose-built hutments.

The policy was that hutment hostels were only to be erected when it was found impossible to requisition and adapt existing buildings.[95] This was because

New recruits at Luton railway station, en route to their hutment hostel in Hockliffe Road, Leighton Buzzard, May 1942. *Source: M Perkins. Courtesy of Luton News*

it was cheaper to adapt requisitioned buildings. The cost of building a hutment hostel was about £110 to £160 for each worker accommodated, whereas the cost of adapting existing premises was only £15 to £30 per worker.[96] Hostels were only to be established when it had been ascertained that billets were not available, because of the costs of labour and building materials and the cost of labour running hostels.[97] They should, ideally, be no further than three miles from the regular places of work.[98] This explains the wide distribution throughout Bedfordshire (see map showing hostel locations).

ACCOMMODATION SUBSIDY

County WLA committees were authorised to pay the difference between what each land girl contributed towards her bed and board and the actual cost. The difference was 20 shillings per week, per girl, on average. It was important, therefore, to try to ensure that each hostel was as fully occupied as possible, to keep the subsidy low, and it was difficult, economically, to operate a hostel for fewer than 20 workers.[99] In 1943 Bedfordshire hostels accommodated 113 girls at the beginning of the year, but the expected total by the end of the year was 442.[100]

REQUISITIONED COUNTRY HOUSES USED AS HOSTELS

In Bedfordshire a total of 12 country houses or farms were requisitioned and five purpose-built hostels erected to provide accommodation for land girls employed by Bedfordshire 'War Ag' (See table listing Bedfordshire hostels, on p.240). Luton Hoo Estate was taken over for a variety of military purposes at the beginning of the war. The Bothy (previously accommodation for young male gardeners in pre-war horticultural training) now housed land girls and the Home Farm was established as the first training farm for WLA recruits. Here they could learn to milk and do general farming on the Home Farm and were also introduced to fruit and vegetable growing in the large walled garden.

The first house requisitioned as a hostel in the south of the county, was Kensworth House, a large Victorian house for up to 50 land girls, outside Dunstable, in November 1942. It had previously housed the family of a wealthy Luton brewer and hat-maker. Around the same time, the requisitioned Toddington Manor was established not only as a hostel for a permanent gang of young women but also as a training farm for new recruits on a four-week initial course before being sent on to private farms.

Then, in January 1943, The Hollies, a small Georgian town house in Potton High Street was opened for up to 20 girls employed in the north-east of the county. In the centre of the county, Wrest Park Lodge, behind the church in the village of

Cople House accommodated up to 97 land girls employed by Bedfordshire 'War Ag'. They were taken out each day in lorries and deposited at local farms and market gardens as sub-contracted labour. Mrs Eugster (the fair-haired woman wearing a tie in the centre of the front row) was the County Secretary of Bedfordshire WLA. *Source: A Vyse*

Silsoe, was taken over as a hostel for about 30 girls and opened around June 1943. This was part of the Wrest Park estate.

In July 1943 Holcotmoors Farm (to give it its historic name) was opened as the Hulcote Moors farmhouse hostel for up to 18 'War Ag' land girls who were employed on neighbouring farms. This had been requisitioned from Sir Frederick Richmond of Westoning.

The largest land girl hostel established in a requisitioned country house was that at Cople House, east of Bedford, accommodating up to 97 in a three-storey building which had previously housed the Bedford banking family, the Barnards. This hostel was opened around September 1943 and was not closed until September 1950.

Sharnbrook House, the Georgian mansion situated on the High Street of the

The hutment hostels were very basic accommodation, built where there were no suitable large houses which could be requisitioned. The photograph shows off-duty land girls relaxing in front of the central entrance hall. This hostel, at Milton Ernest in the north of the county, was built to a standard Ministry of Works design to house 40 young women. *Source: D Filby*

village of Sharnbrook, was the furthest north of the requisitioned country house hostels for land girls. It was not listed when Bedfordshire 'War Ag' advertised the availability of labour from their hostels in September 1943 but was active by 1944 when, in June, the land girls were busy raising money by putting on a show in the village hall, in aid of the 'Salute the Soldier' week. It continued in use until around December 1949.

Further houses were brought into use after the end of the war. The Holt, the former manor house on the Square at Aspley Guise, opened in November 1946 as a land girl hostel. The following year, around June 1947, Clifton House, next to the Church in the village of Clifton, provided further accommodation for post-war land girls employed in the north-east of the county.

Finally, Hasells Hall, outside Sandy, which during the war had housed RAF pilots from the nearby Tempsford Aerodrome, now housed land girls from May

1948 (some of them from Aspley Guise when it closed around December 1948). It remained a hostel for some 18 months until closure in December 1949, as numbers still employed in Bedfordshire declined.

Most of the country house hostels in Bedfordshire had closed by the end of 1949, when the county WLA office closed, with only Cople and Silsoe holding on until the autumn of 1950 and the end of the organisation nationally.

Milton Ernest hostel, north of Bedford, was the first purpose-built hutment hostel for 'War Ag' land girls in Bedfordshire, opened on 16 February 1942, as the impact of female conscription brought a large increase in 'volunteers' to the Land Army. Leighton Buzzard followed soon afterwards, in the south, with a hutment hostel on Hockliffe Road, just outside the town, on 4 June 1942. Then came Bolnhurst hostel, also north of the county, opened on 19 October 1942. Each of these hostels housed 40 land girls and, like the country house hostels, were under the care of YWCA Wardens.

Whipsnade hostel, on the edge of the zoo, was opened on 15 February 1943 for 16 land girls under Derry Seymour, the Warden, with Daisy Beard as its first Forewoman. Some time after the D-Day landings of 1944, following a dispute with WLA management about having to travel in open lorries in freezing weather to local farms, and a token strike, the hostel was closed and some of the occupants transferred to Leighton Buzzard or Kensworth hostels.

'Chimney Corner' hostel, just south of Bedford (variously, and confusingly, described as Elstow hostel or Houghton Conquest hostel, but colloquially associated with the nearby pub name), was opened in July 1943. It was the largest of the hutment hostels, accommodating

'Vicky' Richards outside her dormitory hut at 'Chimney Corner' hostel, Houghton Conquest. Note the trays holding vegetable seedlings on the ground. Each hostel was encouraged to be partly self-sufficient in vegetables. *Source: V Cooper*

The dining room at Milton Ernest hostel, May 1942. After the evening meal, this became their recreation room, hence the dartboard on the wall. Despite a hard day's work in the fields, some of the land girls were keen to jitterbug (a lively jive dance) to a Glen Miller recording on their gramophone player. *Source: B Nichols. Courtesy of Beds Times*

up to 94 land girls (about the same size as Cople House hostel). It occupied a site (now an industrial estate) which held a munitions factory (some of it underneath the hostel!). It finally closed in 1950.

Most hutment hostels (the large hutment hostel at Chimney Corner was an exception) were of standard Ministry of Works design, with three wings (only two of them of brick), joined by a common entrance hall to form a T-shaped arrangement of dining cum recreation room (with kitchen plus warden's rooms beyond), a long dormitory hut (built of wood and asbestos sheets) and an ablutions wing for all washing (with boiler house attached to provide hot water). (See plan of typical hutment hostel opposite)

After the hot evening meal, the main socialising took place in the dining/recreation room. The dormitory hut had a concrete floor and no carpeting. There were bunk beds for 40 young women, on each side of the length of the dormitory, with a separate room at the end for the Forewoman. In some hutment hostels, as at Bolnhurst, there was no electricity, only oil lamps hanging from the ceiling for lighting. The space between the bunks was divided into cubicles for four girls, with two single wardrobes for their few personal clothes, and a small dressing table which acted as a boundary for their space. They also had box lockers under the bunk beds for their other personal belongings.

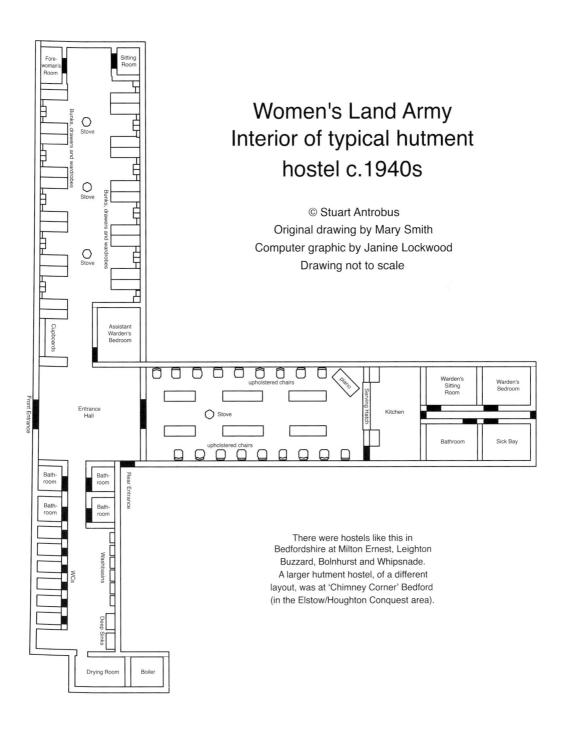

Women's Land Army Interior of typical hutment hostel c.1940s

© Stuart Antrobus
Original drawing by Mary Smith
Computer graphic by Janine Lockwood
Drawing not to scale

There were hostels like this in Bedfordshire at Milton Ernest, Leighton Buzzard, Bolnhurst and Whipsnade. A larger hutment hostel, of a different layout, was at 'Chimney Corner' Bedford (in the Elstow/Houghton Conquest area).

HOSTEL STAFF

Hostel staff varied, according to the size of the hostel. In general terms, the medium size hostels, accommodating around 20–30 young women, had two full-time resident members of staff: a Warden and Assistant Warden/Cook, with two part-time (non-resident) domestic staff. Larger hostels, with around 40 or more women, had, in addition, an Assistant Cook, who may or may not have been resident. Smaller hostels for around a dozen or so land girls consisted of a Cook/Housekeeper and one domestic.[101]

In Bedfordshire the majority of hutment hostels were for 40 girls and therefore had the maximum number of staff, with both resident Warden and Assistant Warden. A local handyman was employed to stoke the boiler to provide hot water

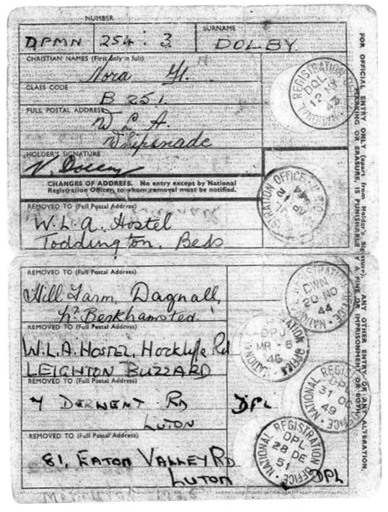

This national identity card shows how some land girls were moved from hostel to hostel and also to 'War Ag' farms as required during the war. *Source: A Norton*

for the ablutions block, where personal clothes were washed by individual land girls. Uniform working clothes were collected weekly for washing by a commercial laundry.

RECREATIONAL FACILITIES

The facilities and equipment for hostels were fairly standard and designed to allow for communal life. The dining room also had, as well as tables and chairs for eating, some comfortable easy chairs and recreational equipment such as radios, a piano, gramophone player and a dartboard. With the furniture rearranged, there was room for dancing.

DORMITORIES

When not using the dining/ recreation room, the dormitory was the other focal point of the land girls' evenings where they spent their spare time. A couple of coke stoves in the centre provided the only heating and the land girls sat around them, talking and smoking cigarettes (many girls smoked at that time to help them relax) while they compared their day's work on the various farms where they had been working.

Spartan bunk beds at Milton Ernest WLA hutment hostel. 40 land girls were accommodated in a single dormitory. *Source: B Nichols*

WELFARE

It was understandable that WLA officials preferred to find billets for land girls whenever possible, for reasons of cost. However, from the point of view of most land girls, hostels were preferable and more suitable. They ensured that a hot communal meal was guaranteed each evening (and the rationing benefits of a catering licence), and provided both the mutual support of other land girls and the social welfare safeguard of a resident Warden. This compared with the situation for many in private billets, usually in farm workers' cottages, where the wife would normally provide the hot meal for her husband at midday and would not, therefore, be necessarily willing to provide a hot meal just for the land girl in the evening. Land girls had to carry food with them, usually sandwiches, for their midday meal. It had also to be acknowledged that it was not possible, using volunteer WLA District Representatives and occasional visits, to ensure that a basic standard of care was provided for each land girl, especially in isolated locations.

BILLETS VERSUS HOSTELS

From the farmers' point of view, the provision of mobile gangs of workers accommodated locally, which could be varied in numbers to suit the job and hired from the 'War Ag' on a daily basis, was a far more preferable option than necessarily employing land girls all the year round, as was the case with land girls directly employed by independent farmers. It also solved the billeting problem which became difficult as the war progressed, with all available rooms in rural locations taken up with evacuees, servicemen or civilians employed as directed labour in the county.

YWCA INPUT

Whether the hostels were managed directly by the WLA or by the county 'War Ag', they turned, in Bedfordshire as in many counties, to the Young Women's Christian Association (YWCA) to provide Wardens with the responsibility for ensuring that the land girls in their charge were healthy and happy. At the same time the aim was to give them educational and recreational facilities.[10]

Some hostels had more leisure facilities than others. The post-war hostel at Aspley Guise offered table tennis.
Source: F Jones

Carefully posed photograph of studious land girls in the recreation room at The Holt, the old manor house on the Square, which became Aspley Guise WLA hostel in 1946. *Source: F Jones*

Potton hostel was one of the smallest hostels, occupying a town house accommodating about 20 young women. Here a small group of land girls celebrate their success in an inter-hostel competition in 1943. *Source: J Abbott*

Land girls taking part in Bedford's 'Wings for Victory' fund-raising parade, June 1943. *Source: BLARS (Beds Times collection) Z1002/1/18*

CHAPTER 7

Royal Visits, Parades and Major Events

Unlike the armed forces, the Women's Land Army, being a civilian labour force, was less often seen in parades during the war than the women serving in the armed forces – in the ATS, WRNS and WAAF. Nevertheless, they were called upon to do their bit in the main wartime fundraising parades, on Farm Sundays and on other special occasions.

RECRUITMENT PARADES

There was a Women's Land Army Rally in Bedford on Saturday 1 June 1940 in order to recruit new members, with parades down the High Street, both in the morning and in the afternoon. It consisted of land girls on both a farm wagon, drawn by a working horse, and a tractor. Afterwards there was a reception at the Swan Hotel for private farm land girls, when ten land girls were presented with six-months' 'good service' badges for their armbands.[103]

FUNDRAISING PARADES

Miss Read, the WLA's Luton Representative, arranged for a Land Army contingent from South Bedfordshire to take part in a Luton parade on 2 August 1942 before Admiral Sir Lionel Halsey.[104] 16 land girls presented a pageant at the Granada Cinema, as part of a Ministry of Information stage presentation on war work called 'Together to Victory' on Sunday 19 July 1942 which attracted a large crowd.[105]

'Wings for Victory Week' parade in Bedford, June 1943, was to raise money for more planes to be built for the RAF, went from De Parys Avenue, down Bedford's High Street to the Embankment and, finally, Russell Park. It included 100 land girls and a display of agricultural machinery. A mobile tableaux included a large bomb and anti-aircraft gun mounted on a lorry to lead the contingent, carrying a large notice saying, "These are Hitler's weapons" and followed by an arrow pointing to the land girls, saying "These are ours".[106]

Each July there were National Farm Sunday parades in Bedford, Luton and individual villages, of all who were part of the farming industry – farmers, farm workers, land girls, volunteers of the part-time Bedfordshire Land Corps, and others involved in food production – to record the role that they played in helping win the war by increasing food production and preventing starvation in this country. Tableaux involving land girls driving tractors and exhibiting farm machinery, livestock and produce were key elements of these parades.

BEDFORDSHIRE LAND GIRLS REPRESENT THEIR COUNTY IN LONDON

There were occasional opportunities when land girls from the county were able to represent their colleagues at national get-togethers in London, such as the party for the WLA held at Buckingham Palace by HM The Queen in July 1943, when Daisy Beard and Pat Johnstone attended.[107] Grace Cross represented Bedfordshire WLA in the Victory Parade in London on 8 June 1946.

ROYAL VISITS TO BEDFORDSHIRE INVOLVING LAND GIRLS DURING THE WAR

150 land girls provided the guard of honour, lining both sides of the drive, when the Duchess of Gloucester visited the WLA hostel at Cople on Wednesday 9 February 1944.[108] Flags of the British Empire, the United States and the USSR were flying above the entrance to the three-storey country house which was the accommodation for up to 94 land girls. Bunting adorned the house and Italian prisoners of war had been brought in to lay fresh gravel on the drive.

Apart from the usual county dignitaries, Mr H.J. Humpheys, Chairman of Bedfordshire War Agricultural Executive Committee and Mrs Ida Eugster, the WLA County Secretary attended. Mrs Erica Graham, Chairman of the Bedfordshire Women's Land Army Committee, was Her Royal Highness's guide.

The Duchess was reported to have had an "apt phrase and a cheery word" for all she met.

Mrs J. Dallas was one of those of the Advisory Committee who were presented. She had served in the Women's Land Army in the First World War, in charge of an agricultural training centre in Yorkshire and had helped set up the newly-formed WLA in Bedfordshire in 1939. Her husband, Mr W.W. Dallas, was

Occasional royal visits helped keep up morale and show the land girls that their work on the land was valued. The Duchess of Gloucester visited Cople hostel on 9 February 1944. *Source: Bedford Central Library. Courtesy of Beds Times*

Technical Officer to Bedfordshire WAEC. One of the land girls presented to the Duchess was Joyce Robbins, of Bedford, who had previously worked on the Duchess's Barnwell Estate.

Liz Day was chosen to present the Duchess, on leaving, with a basket of Bedfordshire rushes made by the land girls and containing eggs and apples surrounded by snowdrops, daffodils and anemones. This was chosen rather than a bouquet, to save the Lady in Waiting, Miss Sandford, having to carry the flowers around all day. Liz, the Forewoman, made a brief speech, at the top of her voice, so that all the land girls attending could hear.

The Duchess left, to rousing cheers, having said that she was "supremely happy" with all she had seen. As soon as the Duchess left, the land girls changed from their dress uniform into their dungarees and went out in their transport to the local fields to work.

The Duchess of Kent inspected uniformed war workers and opened the Services Handicraft Exhibition at the Town Hall, Bedford, 19 June 1944, and local land girls contributed. *The Land Girl* magazine reported:

> Some beautiful work was exhibited around our land girl maypole…Special mention must be made of Miss (Diana) Keable's fire screen, and an original set in leather (hat, bag and shoes) made by Miss (Joyce) Robbins which was specially commended by HRH.[109]

Earlier, in May, the Duchess had inspected war workers in Luton and ten land girls were included.[110]

Elsewhere in the county, in 1944 Princess Marina visited Luton Hoo training farm and Queen Elizabeth visited Biggleswade, in August 1944. Some land girls formed a guard of honour to line the route when HM the Queen visited the Biggleswade area to inspect the county's Home Guard under the command of her brother, Colonel the Honourable Michael Bowes Lyon.[111]

PRINCESS ELIZABETH'S VISIT TO BEDFORD, THURSDAY, 14 FEBRUARY 1946

The greatest event in the life of Bedfordshire Women's Land Army took place in Bedford on Thursday 14 February 1946. It was described in *The Land Girl* magazine as "the grandest ever undertaken by any county in Land Army history".

The Victory celebrations took place over three days but opened in the afternoon of Valentine's Day with a march past of some 600 Bedfordshire land girls. The 19-year-old Princess Elizabeth, in her first major public duty alone, took the salute, from a reviewing platform on St Paul's Square, accompanied by Lieutenant-Colonel Part, Lord-Lieutenant of Bedfordshire and Mrs Erica Graham,

The 19-year-old Princess Elizabeth, on her first official engagement alone, with Colonel Part on a day-long visit to Bedford on 14 February 1946. The highlight was a victory parade of 600 land girls from all over the county. Later, the Princess presented long-service armbands to 65 Bedfordshire land girls and made a speech reminding everyone how important their work on the land was in the difficult days of post-war austerity. *Source: Antrobus archive. Courtesy of Beds Times*

Chairman of Bedfordshire WLA Committee.

Land girls from both private farms and hostels marched down the High Street, led by the Bedford and Hertfordshire Regiment. There was an accompanying procession of agricultural vehicles, mainly drawn by tractors but a few by working horses.

The land girls who were driving the tractors managed an 'eyes right' at the appropriate moment, when passing the saluting base. But a newsreel camera captured the slightly embarrassing moment when, turning from the High Street

Princess Elizabeth, on the dais at St Paul's Square, Bedford, views the impressive parade of Bedfordshire land girls, watched by thousands of local men, women and children. They were led by an RAF band and followed by a tableau of tractor-led agricultural machinery. *Source: Antrobus archive. Courtesy of Beds Times*

into the rather congested road leading past Shire Hall towards the final cattle market end of the procession, traffic temporarily stopped, causing one tractor to run into the back of the trailer in front just after passing Princess Elizabeth.[112]

Apart from that, and a "grubby four-year-old who had to be evicted from the Special Visitors' Enclosure", the carefully-planned day went well. After the march past, brought to a conclusion by the office staff, attention changed to the Corn Exchange.

Here a land girl guard of honour lined the way to the entrance as the Princess entered to open a three-day exhibition, hand out long-service badges and give a short speech. Identical twin land girls, Betty and Jean Pearson, presented Her

Long-service armbands being presented by Princess Elizabeth (later, Queen Elizabeth II) in the Corn Exchange, Bedford, where she opened a three-day exhibition on agriculture, 14 February 1946. The basket of produce was presented by twin land girls Betty and Jean Pearson. *Source: Antrobus archive. Courtesy of Beds Times*

Royal Highness with a basket of farm produce, decorated with spring flowers and a huge bow in Land Army colours, and Anne Bridge presented her with a souvenir booklet, bound in vellum.

Lucinda Croft, who had served for six years in Bedfordshire, led the 65 land girls who were presented to HRH, most of them receiving four- or five-year armlets, in recognition of their wartime service in the Women's Land Army in the county. Mrs Eugster read out each girl's record, many including several years in one job, either milking or doing general farm work.

Princess Elizabeth then spoke to the invited audience of 900, including the 660 land girls: "You have all played your part in a great achievement. You have given unstinted and cheerful effort in conditions, sometimes unpleasant and always arduous..." and about what lay ahead "...peace with scarcity...the country still

Programme of Events

THURSDAY   14th FEBRUARY

3.0 p.m. Grand Parade of the Bedfordshire W.L.A.
Moving Tableaux and Demonstration
March Past from de Pary's Avenue.
Salute to be taken on St. Paul's Square by **H.R.H. Princess Elizabeth.**
3.15 p.m. H.R.H. Princess Elizabeth opens Exhibition of Agricultural
Work and Handicrafts by members of Bedfordshire W.L.A. and
distributes awards for long service.
W.L.A. Chorus will sing, conducted by Mr. Leslie Woodgate.
Mr. Colson, at the Organ.
Ceremony will be broadcast in St. Paul's Square.
5.0 p.m. H.R.H. Princess Elizabeth leaves.
Exhibition open to Public till 6.30.
Music by the 101st Convalescent Depot Dance Band.
Tickets for Tombola, etc.
8.0 p.m. Concert by W.L.A. Admission to W.L.A. only.
Prizes to Handicraft Competition Winners will be awarded.

FRIDAY   15th FEBRUARY

11 a.m. Exhibition opens.
Morning Coffee. Music by Orchestra under the direction of Louis de Jong
Ministry of Information Films. Showing continuously.
Afternoon Teas.
Prizes in Tombola drawn at 6.15 p.m.
6.30 p.m. Exhibition closes.
8.0 p.m. GRAND CONCERT by Bedfordshire W.L.A. and Guest
Artistes. Special performance by Miss E. Douglas Reid (by arrange-
ment with The Arts Council of Great Britain.)

SATURDAY   16th FEBRUARY

11.0 a.m. Exhibition opens.
Morning Coffee. Music by Orchestra under the direction of Louis de Jong.
Fun Fair—continuously. Teas, etc.
Prizes for Tombola, etc., drawn at 6.15 p.m.
8.0 p.m. GRAND DANCE.

**All proceeds from this Exhibition will be donated to the
Women's Land Army Benevolent Fund**

Bedfordshire WLA Programme of Events, 14–16 February 1946, Corn Exchange, Bedford
Source: Antrobus archive, 1946 Bedfordshire WLA souvenir srogramme (centre page)

Programme

The Artistes will be introduced by

MR. TREVOR HOWARD

(Appearing by kind permission of Individual Pictures, Ltd)
The Well-known Stage and Screen Star

"OH PEACEFUL ENGLAND" (*German*)
"JERUSALEM" (*Parry*)
Sung by Cople Hostel Chorus

"CHIMNEY CORNER"
A sketch by Leighton Buzzard Hostel

TAP DANCING AND SONGS
By Miss I. Randall

P. T. DISPLAY
by Elstow Hostel
(trained by Sgt. Inst. Jackson, A.P.G.T. 101 Convalescent Depot)

RECITATION
by Miss C. Woolven

GIPSY SONGS
by Sharnbrook House Hostel

MISS ELSPETH DOUGLAS-REID
DISEUSE

TEN MINUTE INTERVAL

Miss **ELSPETH DOUGLAS-REID**
appears by kind permission of
THE ARTS COUNCIL OF GREAT BRITAIN

"CRINOLINE LADY"
by Hulcote Moors Hostel

TAP DANCING
by Miss B. Nettleship

NURSERY RHYME QUADRILLES
by the Misses E. B. and Z. Woods and Miss S. Brown

"MOTHER RILEY'S AIR RAID SHELTER"
by Kensworth House Hostel

NEGRO SPIRITUALS
by Bobihurst Hostel

EURYTHMICS AND TABLEAU
by Leighton Buzzard Hostel

PIANO DUETS
by Miss J. Davenport and Miss B. Walton

MISS ELSPETH DOUGLAS-REID
DISEUSE

"I VOW TO THEE MY COUNTRY" (*Gustav Holst*)

"SONG OF LIBERTY" (*Elgar*)
Sung by Cople Hostel Chorus

MR. TREVOR HOWARD WILL CLOSE THE CONCERT

Cople Hostel Chorus was trained by Mr. J. Robinson and conducted by
Mr. Leslie Woodgate of the BBC

Leighton Buzzard Hostel was coached by Miss Robinson

A wide-ranging amateur concert was put on by Bedfordshire land girls to raise money for the Women's Land Army Benevolent Fund, 15 February 1946, Corn Exchange, Bedford. *Source: Antrobus archive, Corn Exchange, Bedford, concert programme 15 February 1946*

needs you, all of you and more besides to play your part in bringing us through the hard times we must expect before prosperity again returns." Only someone accidentally sitting back on to the keyboard of the hall's organ, causing a brief 'rude' noise – much to the young Princess's amusement – interrupted the vote of thanks by Mrs Erica Graham.

The Princess then toured the agricultural exhibition entitled 'How Victory Was Won on the Home Front', which was all around the hall, while the Women's Land Army Chorus, from Cople hostel, sang a selection of songs, trained by Mr J. Robinson and conducted by Leslie Woodgate of the BBC. The exhibition up in the gallery – Luton's contribution – included a section called 'Old Farming Days in Bedfordshire', which included old farming implements from Luton Museum. The father of land girl, Liz Day, a farmer from Odell, had to be called in beforehand to identify some of the, by now, obsolete items. The final section was a display of straw plaiting and objects of Bedfordshire folklore.

After the Princess left the public were allowed to enter and view the exhibition. In the evening there was a dress rehearsal concert – for land girls only – of the WLA concert for the public which was presented on Friday evening, 15 February.[113]

Some of the first Bedfordshire land girls at work with male farm workers on a farm in Lower Dean, 13 October 1939. Pamela Edgeworth was working as a secretary and Matilda Shaw was a philosophy student at St Hugh's College, Oxford before the outbreak of war and their decision to volunteer to join the WLA. In the early years of the war, male farm workers were able to remain on the farms, as their work entitled them to the status of a 'reserved occupation' or gave them six months' deferment, but they began to be called up into military service, leaving the farm owners or managers reliant on land girls, those men too old to be conscripted and conscientious objectors. *Source: BLARS (Beds Times collection) BT738/1*

CHAPTER 8

Personal Experiences: Life for Land Girls on Private Farms

LOCAL OR 'MOBILE': THE EARLY YEARS

From June 1939 until January 1942, almost all Women's Land Army volunteers worked directly for private farmers. These first volunteers to the Land Army were given the option of indicating their preference of either serving locally, meaning in their own county – sometimes even within daily travelling distance of their own home – or of being 'mobile', which meant being available to be sent anywhere in the country, where they were most required. If there was no demand for their labour in their own county, they had to decide whether they were prepared to be sent elsewhere in the country or withdraw from the organisation. Some young women took the opportunity to 'escape' from home and gain some independence by moving to another part of the country. This was in a time when most young women were expected to stay at home until they got married.

EXPANSION FOLLOWING THE INTRODUCTION OF CONSCRIPTION FOR WOMEN

From 1942 onwards, following the introduction of conscription, this option was removed completely. Conscripts, although still referred to as 'volunteers', since they had opted for the Land Army as opposed to national service in the armed forces, nurses or in war work in the factories, had to go where they were sent in the country. They could, after a number of years' service far from home, request to be transferred nearer to their home county, particularly if there were 'compassionate' circumstances such as a sick or elderly parent to care for.

Following the National Service Act of 18 December 1941 (calling up unmarried women between 20 and 30 years into auxiliary military service or vital industrial work; extending to 19 years of age in 1942) and the consequent increase in the number of young women coming forward to work on the land, the County War Agricultural Executive Committees (CWAECs or 'War Ags') began directly employing some land girls themselves. They accommodated them in hostels around each county. From February 1942 onwards, when the first 'War Ag'-employed hostel girls arrived and were set up at Milton Ernest (the first Bedfordshire hostel), the new land girls gangs provided a mobile labour force for Bedfordshire farmers. They were paid weekly by the 'War Ags' and sub-contracted to the farmers who were charged on a daily basis. Privately-employed land girls were still recruited and continued as before.

Privately-employed land girls formed roughly two thirds of the WLA nationally, over the whole period of the Land Army, from June 1939 to November 1950. The other one third were employed by county 'War Ags' and accommodated in hostels. But the proportions of private and hostel land girls varied from county to county. In Bedfordshire, at its peak, about half of land girls were in hostels and about half permanently on private farms. When Bedfordshire WLA achieved its peak employment of just over 1,000 young women in late 1943/early 1944, about 500 were private land girls and 500 'War Ag'-employed hostel girls.[114]

Life for private land girls was, then, the norm until 1942 and even after that year, the majority of those in the WLA, nationally, worked on, and lived on or around, private farms or market gardens. Each land girl was employed according to nationally-agreed conditions, established at the beginning of the war between the Women's Land Army and the farmers' representatives, through the Ministry of Agriculture and Fisheries. But whereas hostel land girls had a similar life style irrespective of which hostel they were in, life for private land girls varied considerably, dependent on the particular farm and farmer and the type of work they undertook.

Some land girls found themselves as the only young woman working on an isolated private farm. Because of this lack of company, and a lack of welfare support, life for private land girls could be more stressful. They also might have felt less sense of being in a national organisation, despite their uniform and title, than those who lived together in hostels. Certainly, having other land girls on the farm raised the chances of them being able to settle in and find some sort of social life locally, which would help overcome home-sickness and isolation.

LAND GIRL BILLETS

On leaving home, almost always for the first time, the young Land Army volunteer, usually aged around 17 or 18, was often exposed to rather trying circumstances at her farm or nearby billet. She might not only be home-sick but experiencing a totally different way of life in the countryside from that which she might have experienced in a town or city. She might not necessarily be welcomed, especially by the farmer's wife who might feel that the presence of a young woman was a threat. Almost everything she had to do was new to her and she had to pick up a lot in a short time.

Others were lucky and found friendly and supportive billets and farmers where they became one of the family.

The following accounts have been summarised by the author from interviews, questionnaires and brief memoirs from a range of former Bedfordshire land girls (their maiden name is given, except where not known) who, at some stage in their WLA service, experienced life as a land girl working directly for an independent farmer. (The first date given in brackets is that of the enrolment of the land girl into the WLA. The actual date when their service started might have been somewhat later and is given on an individual's Release Certificate. The final date is when they officially left the service.)

Betty Fuller (WLA 20580: 15 September 1939 – 30 July 1945)
Betty was one of these first volunteers to join the WLA when the war broke out in 1939. She began with four weeks of training doing milking on a farm in Kent. She first served in Hertfordshire, then transferred to Bedfordshire in November 1940 and worked at Northern Farm in Harrold, in the north of Bedfordshire. Here she did not only milking but also general farming and even specialist tasks such as thatching ricks. She transferred to Hertfordshire in March 1941 before returning to Bedfordshire in February 1942. She was to serve in the WLA throughout the entire duration of the war, finally leaving in July 1945.[115]

Betty Fuller (right) and another land girl thatching a rick at Northern Farm, Harrold. *Source: B Fuller*

Elizabeth 'Liz' Day (WLA 36558: 9 November 1940 – 30 November 1950)

Liz was the eldest of a family of seven children (two boys and five girls). At the beginning of the war she had joined the ATS, having been a part-time member of the Women's Legion of Motor Transport, a territorial organisation which trained in the evenings.

She was already 27 when she left the ATS and started her long Land Army career in Bedfordshire at Isaac Godber's nurseries at Willington (site of the present Garden Centre) where she stayed for over three years. (Isaac's son, Joseph, also worked there and later, after entering politics in the post-war years, became the Minister of Agriculture in Edward Heath's government.) There were three older men at Willington who were responsible for the glasshouses, and three land girls who assisted in picking tomatoes as well as other market garden work. Liz lived with Mrs Martha Spabbins in Station Road, Willington.

Her sisters, Helen and Jane also joined the WLA. Helen, who was 22 on entry and had been a kennel maid, joined at about the same time as Liz but later left and became a driver for the 'War Ag'. Jane, the youngest of the sisters, was 17 when she joined in June 1942 and left in October 1948. She worked on Godber's farm at Willington, with Albert, the horseman. They had a shire horse called Tommy and a Suffolk Punch called Pam. Tractors were beginning to come into use, and Liz was already an experienced driver.

Unusually, Liz and her sisters were from a farming background (Dungee Farm, Odell) and Liz had previously worked at Garner's dairy farm in Kempston. Technically, she should probably not have been accepted into the Land Army, since she had already been working full time in agriculture and the whole point of the WLA was to bring a new labour force into the countryside, but, of course, she was to be immensely helpful to the organisation because of her experience and know-how.

While at Godber's nursery she gained experience of steam sterilization of the greenhouse soil each winter, necessary to reduce the chances of disease and pests. A so-called portable steam engine, which did not move under its own steam but was pulled to each site, was brought in. It used Welsh steam coal and produced steam which was piped to the soil through a device placed six inches under the soil, one area at a time. It was her job to fire the steam engine up and then clear the clinker from it afterwards. She earned an extra one shilling a week 'dirt money'.

Liz worked in the outdoor gang most of the time at the nursery but in the summer tomato season, she would take an over-laden 2½-ton Commer lorry at least once a week to deliver 12-pound boxes of tomatoes to the wholesale markets in Coventry. Sometimes she had to find alternative routes, following bomb damage in the Midlands.

Liz Day trying out a Trusty Tractor and plough for market gardens, with Mr Caseby, the County Horticultural Officer, in the grounds behind Leighton Buzzard WLA hostel.
Source: E Day

She could appreciate more than most, just how difficult it must have been for those young women from towns and cities who found themselves doing hard physical work in the open air. She recollected, "I was used to the work and used to the weather. Those poor girls who had been hairdressers and allsorts, coming from the north…I remember collecting these girls from Cople (Hostel) for potato picking and I did feel sorry for them, bending down, and the weather too…I think they did well, very well." She was transferred to the large WLA hostel at Cople and given a room of her own there.

In terms of social life, "You made your own…Those of us at Willington or Great Barford used to meet at The Anchor [a Great Barford pub] on Friday night." There were May festivities and gymkhanas were "very popular". Because of her previous experience with horses, Liz could be seen annually in Russell Park, Bedford, on Farm Sunday, driving horses from Godber's nursery .

(See 'Life for Hostel Land Girls' for more about Liz Day.)[116]

Dorothy Hurren (WLA 12734: Spring 1939 – September 1944)

Dorothy signed up for the WLA in Bedfordshire as a volunteer in the spring of 1939, even before its official start in June 1939 and served in the county for almost the whole of the war, leaving in September 1944 in order to get married. She was sent for initial training to the Midlands Agricultural College at Sutton Bonington, near Loughborough, for four weeks. Some others were sent to the Moulton Agricultural Institute in Northamptonshire, since, at that time, there was no agricultural institute in Bedfordshire (Silsoe Institute was set up post war).

Dorothy was then sent to work at Home Farm, Southill Park (the Whitbread estate) and, later, to Chawston Manor, which was an accredited poultry farm, and poultry became her specialism. She worked here with her future husband, George Keightley, the chief poultry man, who was 20 years older than her. She left the WLA in 1944, when she married him, and they lived happily together for 48 years. He died in 1992, aged 93.[117]

Dorothy Hurren was in charge of the poultry at Chawston Manor Farm, but clearly had other interests as well. *Source: D Keightley*

Ann Brodrick (WLA 77088: 4 May 1942 – 14 September 1946)

Ann was living in Luton when the war started. Her father was in the armed forces and was responsible for the burning oil smoke screen arrangements there, designed to minimise the chances of aircraft attack on the vital industrial factories in the area, including Vauxhall's. She joined as soon as she got to know about the Women's Land Army. She was sent for training to a large farm in Hockcliffe. They were threshing and her job was to pitch sheaves up to the thresher. Safety measures were few and far between at that time and she had a near-miss accident, feeding the machine, which could have lost her her life or her limbs. She was saved by her pitch fork.

Ann had digs in a tiny cottage where her bed was made up in the hall, with her head against the front door. It was cold and she had been given very little in the way of food. It was so bad that she complained to the WLA county headquarters

The national press tended to either glamorize or make fun of land girls through cartoons in the early years when they were a novelty in the countryside. Ann Brodrick appeared in the wartime national press, in this glamorous Sunday Mirror photograph. *Source: A Haynes*

and moved to 'digs' in Chantry Lane, Kempston.

Her first job was milking, which is not what she had been trained to do. "We were just cheap labour actually," she recalled. "There were four land girls there. We skimmed the cream off the milk and scrumped apples." She had a grey pony and a trap to deliver milk into Bedford. Later, she moved to the first 'War Ag' land girls' hostel in huts at Milton Ernest, which she much preferred, because of the social life. But in 1945 she asked to move to Freddie Rawlins' farm at Biddenham.

She had worked there as a hostel girl and was treated as one of the family. She had her own Allis Chalmers tractor. She could drive lorry-loads of potatoes into Bedford and fetch the vet. She was 'dogsbody' but loved it. She got well fed there, as opposed to having very limited hostel food. Marjorie Rawlings gave Ann's food coupon book to Ann's mother, who was living on her own, by this time, in Luton.

Ann met her husband-to-be, 'Tich', on the Rawlins' farm. At the time of the VE Day, she was given time off to attend the victory celebrations in London. She slept on the railway station that night, before returning to Bedford.

Looking back on her years as a land girl, Ann remembered that some of the farmers were a surly lot. "They were not nasty to you; they just reacted to you as though you were not there." Some, like the ones on her final farm, were delightful but some were not so good. "I think they could have given us something to eat and drink at harvest time." Cold tea in bottles was often the only refreshment some of the land girls had.

Of the men on the farms during the war, there was the odd man who was Foreman, often an older man too old to fight. "They were usually OK working with the land girls."[118]

Iris Manning (WLA 130241: 14 July 1943 – 18 July 1950)

Iris was another land girl who was able to travel from home in Goldington to her place at Twinwoods Farm, Clapham. After leaving school, aged 15, she had worked in the office of Igranic engineering works in Bedford but when she was 18 was told that she would have to work in the factory on day and night shifts for the war effort. She decided instead to join the Women's Land Army, since her friend Jean Hartop was already in. Told at the interview that the WLA was very short of milking and dairy workers, she agreed to be sent for training at Toddington Park hostel, learning hand milking, in June 1943. She remembered that she was so nervous that she was shaking and the bucket she was milking into rattled. As a result, the cow kicked the bucket over and loads of cats suddenly appeared from nowhere and drank the spilled milk. They had clearly been waiting for such a thing to happen.

Posted to Twinwoods Farm, she was able to cycle there each morning, to be there at 6.30am for milking. Mr Sid Quenby, the farmer, said that he could tell the time by her, she was so punctual. The farm was immediately adjacent to the Twinwoods Airfield, from which Glenn Miller flew to his death. When she had finished milking she went to where she was needed on the farm. There were two other land girls at the farm, one from Clapham and one from Elstow.

On one occasion, she accidentally drove a tractor on to the runway at Twinwoods, as a Mosquito fighter plane was about to land. She was called before a senior officer to be told off.

Iris stayed there for just over two years. Deciding that she needed a change from a private farm, she went to Hulcote Moors hostel, near Cranfield in September 1945, for four months, and began work for the 'War Ag'. She soon afterwards got a job as a driver working from the 'War Ag's tractor depot in Goldington, delivering equipment to farms around the county, as required. She got to meet numerous land girls, as she visited farms where they were working.

She remembered that, on one occasion, she had been sent as a relief milker at a farm in Turvey where a land girl had been taken ill. Going to bed in the private billet, that first night, she found that there were fleas in the bed and so slept on the floor for the rest of the week. She was glad that for most of her time in the Land Army she was able to live at home. In her time off, she attended the Sunday evening concerts for the members of the Forces in the Corn Exchange in Bedford.

She stayed on in the Land Army until 1950, the final year – seven years' service, in all. Even after the end of the WLA, she stayed on to work for the 'War Ag' in their office at Phoenix Chambers, Bedford, until their agricultural machinery depot closed on 28 December 1951. Looking back, she commented, "I'm glad I did it. It taught me a lot."

Whereas Iris worked a lot with tractors, which played a vital part in helping farmers achieve increasingly high targets for food production, others worked with horses.[119]

Mary Bennett (WLA 69419: 30 March 1942 – 17 May 1947)

Mary was one of a family of nine children, six girls and three boys. Her father moved them to Bedford in 1932, when he was asked, as a civil engineer, to build a new brick factory for Bedford Brick Company in Kempston Hardwick. Locally it became know as Bennett's brickyard, although he had no money in it and it later became known as Coronation Brickworks and belonged to London Brick Company.

When the war came, three of the girls, Ruth, Mary and Hannah, all joined the

Mary Bennett (left), with fellow land girl, leading the prize milking cow, Genny IX, in a Bedford fund-raising parade, 'Wings for Victory Week', June 1943. *Source: M Spilling*

Land Army. Ruth joined first, and delivered milk in the Biggleswade area. Mary joined second and worked on Harold Brown's farm in Great Barford. Hannah joined last, to a farm in Pavenham.

Mary was 20 when she joined the WLA, after being a cashier at Liptons in Bedford. Mary's first billet in Great Barford was Mill House, at the top of the hill in the village of Great Barford, with Freddie Southill and his wife. Another land girl stayed there. Then they moved to stay with Mr and Mrs Marblin at Addingtons Road. Mary remembered that one land girl from East Finchley was removed from the Land Army because her father did not like what she was getting up to (which was not specified).

She worked a lot with working horses, as well as driving a tractor. There were three working horses on the farm: Phoenix, Gypsy and Festus. Phoenix had a tendency to rear up. The clanking of the lever on the rake started her off. Mary had to talk quietly to her to calm her down.

On one occasion, when she first started there, Mary was sent to collect Gypsy from a field. She sat on the horse, with no saddle and wearing wellingtons. Some male farm workers hit the horse and he headed off down a hill to the road. Mary did not know how to ride but just managed to stay on. That was her first and only time on the back of a horse. There were two men working the horses, which was a 'reserved' occupation, at the time she joined, which meant that the men could not be conscripted into the armed forces.

She was the only permanent land girl there, although other land girls came for large jobs such as stooking and threshing. Stooking was collecting up the sheaves of corn dispensed by the reaping machine. Three or four sheaves were stacked together, leaning on each other at the top to stand up and get dried out in the wind. Later they would be collected with a trailer and a rick made to store them in the farmyard for subsequent threshing.

"They warned me not to milk, because weekends would never be my own," but that was what she was taken on for. After early morning milking she went into the dairy, cooling the milk, while the cows went out into the fields. After breakfast, when it got light, Mary would go out into the fields, hoeing or thinning out seedlings. She would plough with a Ford tractor and pass the time singing songs such as 'One fine day' from the opera 'Madame Butterfly', as she worked. Sometimes working overtime was inevitable and then the land girls would earn extra but the gentleman farmer would not like it.

Socially the land girls in the Great Barford area tended to meet in the pub by the river. An American journalist was there once, writing down what they had been doing. Mary also visited the pub in Wilden and there were dances there. She was invited to dances at Thurleigh airfield but she had a fiancé so she stayed in and played 'ping-pong'. She did pick up one bad habit then: smoking. First it was Juilienne roll-your-own cigarettes that the boys used. Then she moved on to Woodbine cigarettes, and eventually to Player's Senior Service.

Twice, Mary paraded the prize milking cow, Genny IX – on a Farm Sunday parade and on the D-Day Parade in Bedford. All was well on the latter occasion until, parading down the High Street outside E.P. Roses's [now Debenhams] store, the cow decided to relieve itself. The crowd lining the street there was very amused but it did not go down so well with the platoon of American soldiers following behind, which had to march through the resultant mess.

While there she lost her engagement ring, when the horse pulled suddenly while harrowing and Mary never found it. Her fiancé was to be killed in Germany on the day after war officially ended. Later, a friend of hers took Mary to a hotel in Cornwall to help her recover.

After three years at Great Barford, Mary moved to Moorings Farm in the Kempston area, which grew potatoes and peas. She requested this move so as to be nearer to her dentists, who had proposed a course of treatment to cure a disease of the gum which had afflicted her. It also enabled her to live at home in Tavistock Street, Bedford, with her parents.

Mary never remembered seeing a copy of *The Land Girl* magazine and, after leaving the Land Army, did not get to hear about the various reunions, both local and national which happened after the organisation disbanded in 1950. This tended to happen more to the land girls who served on private farms, as opposed to those who worked for the 'War Ags' who served in hostels and, because of the sociable experience of living together, tended to keep in touch more after the war.

She finally left the Land Army in 1947, after five years service, having really liked being a land girl. She felt that most people appreciated what the land girls were doing for the war effort. She overheard people saying, "They do a grand job".[120]

Hannah Bennett (WLA 89769: 14 July 1942 – 17 May 1949)

Hannah, Mary's sister, decided to volunteer for the Land Army when she was 17 (nearly 18) years old, before she was due to be conscripted into National Service. Before this she had worked as a sales assistant in Woolworth's shop in Bedford. She did her initial training, during harvest time, on Harold Brown's farm at Great Barford where her sister, Mary, was. Ruth, their elder sister, also in the Land Army, was working on milk deliveries in the Biggleswade area.

The Bennett girls were one of at least five families in Bedfordshire from which three sisters had become land girls – the others were the Day family ('Liz', Helen and Jane), the Lowe family (Jean, Vera and Dorothy), the Pike family (Barbara, Elizabeth and Ivy), and the Wallis family (Helen, Freda and Elsie).

Hannah was sent to Mr Hensman's farm, in Felmersham. She had her meals with the farmer and his wife but slept in the servant's quarters. There was no electricity in the house or running water. Water had to be pumped into a tank in the roof from a well outside. A copper (a large metal bowl for containing water, heated by a fire below, within a brick fireplace) was used to produce hot water for the weekly washday. Oil lamps were used throughout the house for lighting and there was a jug and bowl in the bedroom for personal washing.

Food, however, was good. After she had finished milking each morning, commencing at six o'clock, she was given a breakfast of fried egg and bacon, with fried bread. Such a breakfast was not the norm for most land girls.

Mrs Hensman, who was the farmer's second wife and had previously been the

Ploughing in the Colmworth area *Source: Museum of English Rural Life, The University of Reading*

governess there, was kind to her, but insisted that she couldn't be called Hannah, as the workers would drop the aitch, so she had to be called 'Anne'.

Hannah had five cows to milk each day, by hand, but the farm's horseman relieved her from milking on every other Sunday, to enable her to have every other weekend off. Seven-day-a-week milking was the downside for those land girls who had taken up milking, particularly on small farms where there was less chance of relief milkers helping out. When she wasn't milking she helped out with general farming and took responsibility for the poultry. She also looked after two pigs.

There were three, then four working horses on the farm and Hannah had a near-accident, one day, when a horse nearly backed the hay cart she was on into the river and she could not swim. She found it hard, as did many land girls, particularly the smaller young women, to put the heavy harness on to the farm horses, particularly when the horse didn't want to co-operate. Several times she had to take three horses, at once, to Odell to be shod by the blacksmith. She sat on one horse and led the others.

At threshing time at the Felmersham farm, hostel land girls came to assist. Otherwise, for some private land girls, there was little contact with their fellow land girls who worked for the 'War Ag's mobile gangs.

Having a social life for land girls on private farms, particularly those which were more isolated, could be very difficult. But Hannah got friendly with a girl in the village and a farmer's daughter and the three of them went to the village 'hop' (dance) in Sharnbrook. She also remembered Mrs Sharman and Mrs Truman, from the WLA county office in Bedford, accompanying land girls, as chaperones, when they first attended dances at Little Staughton air base. She did meet some American servicemen, stationed at Sharnbrook, but preferred to play rounders on the village green with local boys. One night, however, she was stopped by a local policeman because her bicycle lamp was too bright (under the 'blackout' regulations) and she was actually fined.

Her friend's father was Head Gardener at Sir Richard Wells's place in Oakley and she had nectarines and other rare food treats when visiting the farm.

Sometimes she attended dances in Bedford and remembered borrowing her two sisters' Land Army coats to get her two friends in cheap to the Corn Exchange (those in uniform got in for half price). Underneath they had their dresses on. RAF Shortstown also held ballroom dances and there were buses every ten minutes from Bedford. She went out occasionally with British soldiers and sailors.

After two years at Felmersham, Hannah wanted to return home, so she moved to a Kempston farm where she looked after poultry and her mother allowed her to live at home, on condition that she helped with the housework.

The farmer she worked for was a bit devious and 'one for the girls'. This was not an unusual circumstance for some land girls and undoubtedly some male workers still working on the farms were susceptible to working in close proximity to female workers. At other farms, although there was no actual reason for concern, some farmers' wives were none too welcoming to these young women entering their world, particularly if the girls were attractive. This could make life difficult for land girls.

Hannah was also worried that her farmer employer was breaking wartime rules about feeding corn to hens which put her in a moral dilemma, since she had been brought up in a very religious household. He said that, if caught, she should take the blame since she'd get off lightly and he would pay her. She also disliked the fact that she had to wring the necks of any chicks which were poorly. Italian prisoners of war who were brought in to kill and pluck the hens were none too careful to check that they were actually dead. The stress she suffered as a result of this situation caused her to lose weight and become ill. She left there after 18 months.

She moved to College Farm, Oakley, where she was called 'Miss Bennett' and went out with Graham Oakley, one of the farmer's sons. She did horticultural work there and loved it. They grew strawberries, asparagus, peas, turnips, cabbages, cauliflowers and Brussels sprouts. Men did piece work there. There was an ex-RAF officer working there, who had been invalided out of the forces and was learning the business.

Hannah remembered that boys used to collect moorhens' eggs, using a punt along the river at Felmersham and Mrs Bishop cooking a big pan full of them.[121]

Barbara Harley (WLA 63979: 2 February 1942 – 30 January 1945)

"Farmers had little laughs at the expense of the Land Army girls raw from the towns. When I started learning to plough I was told to keep my eyes fixed on something in the far distance which would enable me to keep a straight line. When I had finished I found that I had a very crooked furrow indeed. I had been keeping my gaze fixed on a grazing cow as it had moved round the field.

"I started my Land Army service at Milton Ernest Hall and we used to go off to the fields every day singing our song:

"We, a band of jolly land girls, Oh how happy are we, Rising early every morning, To dig our way to victory. With a smile upon our faces, With a song we ride along, Out into the open spaces, To the farms where we belong."[122]

Stella Shelton (WLA 66026: 30 March 1942 – 18 December 1945)

Stella was a Clapham girl who, after school, joined H.H. Bennett, the school uniform manufacturers at Castle Lane, Bedford, where the museum is now. She was 19 when she joined the Women's Land Army, in March 1942, after a land girl had visited the factory in uniform. She had never been on a farm before and was terrified of cows, which was one of the questions often asked at WLA interviews. But, as she pointed out to the author, "You're full of verve at 19, aren't you?"

After the interview at the Harpur Street WLA office, she was sent for four weeks' training in milking on a working farm outside Luton, where there were five workers and the farmer. She was frightened to death when she first sat on her stool, stuck between two cows, but she got to like it. It was warm and she got a rhythm going. But her wrists really hurt for those first few weeks.

The cows were got in for milking at 6am each day and she finished at 5.30pm at night, seven days a week. She got one and a half days off a month. She remembered being paid £1/10s (£1.50p) per week and her 'keep' (the element of her pay deducted in advance for her food and accommodation costs). To get home on Saturday afternoons, she had to pay for her rail fare from Chilton Green (between Luton and Harpenden). There was a mile's walk to the station from the farm and she would usually get the bus from Bedford railway station to Clapham. Sometimes she brought her bike on the train, or left it in the Waiting Room at Chilton Station, for the ride back to the farm.

She was placed, after training at the Home Farm, at Hambros House, the estate of the London banking family, Hambros, in East Hyde. They were all right as employers but you had to "know your place", socially. She was billeted with Old Tom, the farmer, and his wife and children. Sometimes she walked with them into Harpenden to watch "the pictures" at the cinema there.

She was well fed, since the farmer's wife was a good cook but she had to wash up for the family after tea every night and 'do' her own room. She was allowed only one bath per week but she shared with another land girl so was able to have two a week. They had to do their own washing and ironing. The nearest pub where they could meet locals was the 'Leathern Bottle' near the park gates.

The other land girls there, from Bromham, had been there when she arrived and Stella thought they might have resented her arrival. There were 12 milking cows and, in addition, they had to clean out the pigs, teach the calves to drink and cut hay. There were three working horses on the farm, but no tractor. In addition to the cowman there were two male labourers.

After 16 months she got homesick – she had never been away from home before – and her mother was deaf and missed her daughter. She asked to be transferred to Mr Tinsley's farm, Church Farm, in Clapham, known for its horses, and was thus able to live at home.

She learned to drive a tractor there to do arable work such as ploughing and loved it. One of the tractors had metal cogs on the wheels and the other had big rubber tyres. Both were manufactured by Cases. There was also a small crawler tractor – an Alice Chalmers.

Flax pulling was one of the tasks on the farm, for which Tinsley's had a contract. Flax was used to produce parachute straps. The flax was pulled by machinery, using rubber belts.

Stella did a wide range of work there: milking, pig feeding and mixing 'swill' (Luton Council used to sell cooked waste, in moulds, for pig food), ploughing, operating the water cart, muck cart (she "always had warm feet doing that"), harvesting corn, hay making, harvesting sugar beet, threshing, pulling mangels, seed sowing and spreading artificial manure.

Stella Shelton with Sailor, the horse, having just cleared a field of kale in Clapham, 1945. *Source: S Forster Courtesy of Beds Times*

She learned a lot and was always busy. Other land girls working locally were Anne Fox, also at Church Farm, and Rose Richards, Barbara Probert and Anne Bridge at Park Farm. They lived very much in their own little world. They didn't get invited to dances in the area, never saw *The Land Girl* magazine and did not really mix with land girls from other farms. The only time Stella visited the WLA county office, in Harpur Street, Bedford, was to get items of new uniform.

There were two Italian prisoners of war (POWs) who lived at Park Farm, and 12 German POWs were driven over from their camp in Bolnhurst to work at Church Farm. She would not talk to them at first, since her brother was a prisoner of war in Germany, but she gradually got used to them and they were quite helpful.

One of the Italians, Leonardo, had been a young bank clerk in Naples. He was very polite. Another Italian man would flatter her with "Bella! Bella!". She did not take any notice of him. One of the 15-year-old English youths would teach the Italian men, keen to learn English, dreadful things to say in English to the housewives at their billets.

Stella found haymaking and harvesting very hard work. She got blisters. It was certainly a down-to-earth job as a land girl, in all senses of the term. But achieving a good milking yield was rewarding. She sang to her cows to encourage them to relax and let their milk down.

She liked the land girl uniform but was never asked to take part in any parade and so never wore the hat. The working uniform was practical dungarees.

Like most land girls, Stella was able to remember numerous incidents which occurred which now seem amusing but were not at the time. She had to look after pigs, which she found fascinating. There was an area of their pen which was partitioned off as the 'toilet' area but on one occasion, when feeding them, the pigs knocked her over and she fell in pig muck and had to be hosed down by another girl. She did not come up smelling of roses.

On another occasion, the land girls rose early, in the dark, as usual but when they entered the barn they fell over soldiers who had arrived overnight and taken refuge there. After that, the girls and the yard, were put 'out of bounds' to the soldiers.

It was not unusual, on some farms, for the remaining male workers to ask the land girls to do some of the jobs which they did not fancy doing, sometimes just to test them out or for 'a laugh'. Stella recalled that one of the sows had got out and had her baby pigs in a wood. She and another land girl were given a basket with a handle on either side and told to fetch the piglets home. The assumption was that the mother pig would follow her piglets but the girls were warned "don't make them squeal or she'll have you".

Stella and the other land girl found the sow, put the piglets gingerly in the basket and the mother followed. The young women were very relieved.

If you worked on the land during the war you were allocated an extra cheese allowance through the rationing system because of the hard physical work undertaken. Stella commented that she had cheese so much that her mother suggested that "...the mice'll be following you soon".

After the end of the war, Stella left the WLA in December 1945. "I thoroughly enjoyed it...very hard work but (was) very happy."

In later years, when married with young children, she would take them as a family, as seasonal labour, to go potato picking and broad bean picking.[123]

Mrs W. Farr (maiden name and WLA record not known)
"How I remember my Land Army days, happy, hard-working, full of laughter. I was such a green horn that I used to think cornstacks were put in the fields to make the countryside look pretty. I had a rude awakening when I had to thresh them and chaff and dust got into eye, nose and throat.

"One farmer sent me to feed the pigs. I had never seen such huge pigs. I wobbled unsteadily over to the sty, a bucket of meal in each hand and opened the gate. Whoops! A huge boar charged me, knocking me flat and covering me from head to foot in meal. And my clothes didn't exactly smell of sweet violets either. I got a lot of leg pulling for weeks afterwards.

"But we all seemed to thrive on it. We were rosy cheeked, healthy and had loads of fun. I wouldn't have missed it for the world."[124]

Zeita Trott (WLA 84908: 6 July 1942 – 20 April 1945)
Zeita, although born in Harpenden, Hertfordshire, was living in Luton when, on Christmas Day, 1939, her mother died. Although only 14 years old she ended up acting as 'Mum' to her family. She was small and found it terribly hard, physical work. She wanted to 'escape' and her paternal grandmother suggested joining the Land Army. She joined immediately she passed her 17th birthday, after an interview at the WLA's county office in Harpur Street, Bedford. She was quite happy with her uniform but she felt that it did not do a lot for shorter girls, in terms of appearance.

She was sent to Luton Hoo training farm for four weeks' training, where she stayed in the house called 'The Bothy', two to a room. They got up at 4.30am, learned milking, morning and evening, each day and did field work, hoeing and working in the greenhouses for the rest of the time. She had never been near a cow before but quite liked hand milking.

Her first posting was on a private farm, Brook Farm, Wymington. Mr Smith's farm was a mixed one, embracing both livestock and arable farming. She had a go

Zeita Trott showing off her smart new uniform, together with her waspish waist (the belt was not part of the uniform and was clearly needed to hold up the ill-fitting breeches). This was the outfit for leisure time or any smart occasions. Land girls, when working, never wore their hats or their WLA ties. They usually wore dungarees (or overall coats if they were milking) and wellingtons or boots. Many wore headscarves to protect their hair. *Source: Z Holes*

at most farm work there, except milking, the very thing she had trained in. She learned to work with horses, ploughing and disc harrowing. On one occasion, she was asked by the farmer to take a large shire horse, Punch, to be shod in Kettering. For some reason she walked all the way there but rode the horse on the way back home. Unfortunately, the horse was frightened by a vehicle on the way home and galloped the whole way, with Zeita clinging to his neck and mane. Her bottom was very sore by the time they got back to the farm.

There was one other land girl on the farm, Eileen Anderson, also from Luton. After working there for 15 months they both applied to move to the new hostel at Bolnhurst. Life was much more fun there, where they had "a good laugh".

A number of girls who had started on private farms asked to be moved to hostels, when they found out about the more sociable life there, but there were also instances where those who started off in hostels opted to move to a private farm, usually when a farmer had been particularly impressed with their abilities while working temporarily, in a gang, on his farm and wanted them to work for him exclusively.[125]

Mrs K.A. Scott (maiden name and WLA record not known)

"Unlike many other girls who ended up miles away from home, I, a Bedford girl, was given a job on a large (rural) estate at Kempston. There was just me and two men, both over 65.

"My first job was to feed chickens which were in a wire run in the middle of a field of cows. I was terrified of cows, but I thought they wouldn't notice me if I hurried. As I opened the gate they started running towards me. I dropped the buckets and ran to the chicken house where I locked myself in for over an hour, nearly overcome with fumes and the smell until one of the men came to look for me.

"After that the cows seemed to have it in for me. I was getting some manure from a small paddock, my back to some young bullocks, when one butted me from behind and I went head first into the dung heap.

"Another time I was biking home for lunch when the cows were being taken in for milking. Behind them were some troops from Grange Camp. Not wanting them to see a Land Army girl frightened of cows I rode through them when a tail flicked out and hit me in the face, knocking me off the bike. There I sat, my bike on top of me, a dirty face and the troops laughing.

"One day a gamekeeper asked whether I could kill and pluck a cockerel. I agreed, but it was a disaster. Thinking it was dead, I started to pluck it. I had just taken feathers off one side when it jumped off my lap and started to run and squawk around the room. Poor thing, it looked so funny, half-naked. It was the first and last chicken I tried to kill."[126]

Betty Gray (WLA 59345: 20 December 1941 – 18 August 1948)

After 14 months at Milton Ernest hostel (see Chapter 8), Betty transferred to a private farm at Caddington. She was there for two and a half years and the farmer taught her a lot, but when her father found out that the married farmer was having an affair with one of his land girls and she was expecting his baby, he insisted that Betty should leave such a place.

She moved to Inions Farm, Caddington, and was able to live at home and cycle to work each day, at 6.15am, for a 7am start. The farm was owned by the Powdrill family but managed by a Mr Massey. She preferred private farm work and enjoyed the responsibility. She learned to drive tractors and also worked with horses and did hand milking. There was another land girl working there.

Betty was a fit girl, through farming, and used to walk miles and miles in her spare time, with a girl friend. She lost the weight that used to make her self-conscious.

One job she did not like doing was cleaning out the calves' pen after they had

Betty Gray and
Clare Fletcher,
harvesting corn
at Manor Farm,
Caddington.
Source: B Nicholls

been in there all winter. The smell was vile. It was layer upon layer of dung. They had to cut it up and load it on to a cart to tip it out at the other end for manuring the fields. She also dealt with sheep and the farmer liked her helping with lambing because of her small hands.

Plucking and drawing poultry at Christmas time made their fingers sore and they got covered in fleas from the poultry. She had to have a bath at home after each session, so that she felt clean again. Despite that Betty concluded, "I really enjoyed it."

She was able to take part in the 1946 WLA parade in Bedford and all her life kept her WLA Proficiency test badge for General Farming. She was not, like all other wartime land girls, allowed to keep her dress uniform but she managed to keep a few smocks she had bought second-hand from the county office, which she used as a housewife about the house.[127]

Mrs Enid Peet (maiden name and WLA record not known)

"The blizzards of 1941 were sudden and fierce and many sheep died in snow drifts. As we recovered them and took them to the shed it was decided that we should at least get the wool off them.

"Farmhands (male) gathered round with many a wink and a nod to watch us girls coping with it, but we got our revenge. After lunch we took matchboxes and put the sheep ticks in them. With the boxes half open, we slipped them into the bulging pockets of the farm labourers.

"Discomfort, at first vague, showed on their faces as the ticks bit, followed by bewilderment and rage as we doubled up with laughter. We won the day and the respect of the men."[128]

Margaret Perry (WLA 111613: 22 March 1943 – 18 January 1949)

Margaret was brought up in Luton and was 15 when the war started. She liked outdoor work and would have liked to have done the three-year horticulture course at Luton Hoo when she was 16 but the course was fee-paying and her mother was a widow and could not afford it.

Instead, when she was 19 she was 'called up', under the Conscription Act, to do war work and she joined the Land Army. Ironically, she was sent to Luton Hoo to do four weeks' training: two weeks on dairy farming and two weeks arable work.

Her first post was in an isolated hamlet in the north-east of Bedfordshire, at Eyeworth. She lived in a small cottage with an old lady who was very good to her but conditions were very primitive. As at most country dwellings at that time, there was only an outdoor lavatory, a tin bath in the wash house for the weekly bath and water could only be heated in a copper by a coal fire.

She worked on a large farm of 1,200 acres, which was really three farms in one. W.J. Kendall had farmed there since the First World War. There were four land girls on the farm altogether, mostly from Bedfordshire but with one, Sheila Rennie, from Yorkshire.

The farm was mainly arable, so their work included a lot of hoeing to keep down the weeds. They worked with horses and, increasingly, with tractors. In the second year she was there a Massey-Harris tractor, fairly new to the county, was introduced and was driven by the man who later became her husband.

Margaret eventually got tired of living in an isolated place and transferred into dairying at a farm in Toddington owned by a syndicate of businessmen. There were 40 Ayrshire cows to milk, using Alfa-Lovell machinery. There was another land girl working there and they lived at the farmhouse but there was also a man who was a conscientious objector. He turned out not to be a happy man to be with and it was not an easy experience for her. It was winter: cold, snowy and dark. She stayed only two months.

She got a job tractor-driving at Dunton, near Eyeworth and working for the brother of the farmer she worked for first. She was reluctant to go back to the area but ended up with a very nice billet near Biggleswade for the summer. There were two other farm girls on the farm.

She enjoyed the greater degree of independence she had as a young woman away from home. She remembered cycling into London by herself, getting a lift for

opposite: Margaret Perry, from Luton, had wanted to do the three-year horticulture course at Luton Hoo but her mother was a widow and could not afford the fees. After joining the WLA Margaret went on to become a trainer at Ravensden and also took a correspondence course because she wanted to know more about farming. She subsequently completed a full-time agricultural course at the Northamptonshire Institute of Agriculture at Moulton, post-war. *Source: M Chessum*

part of the way on a lorry, and staying with aunts in Westminster and Wimbledon. She brought the bike back by train.

Her 21st birthday was around VE Day and she went into Luton to celebrate the end of the war in Europe.

Whilst in the Land Army, Margaret studied agriculture through a correspondence course, because she wanted to understand more about farming. 'The Farmer's Year' was her textbook. Later, after the war, when she decided to stay in the Land Army, two places on a full-time agricultural course were offered for Bedfordshire land girls, with the fees paid for by the government, and she got one of them. This was at the Northamptonshire Institute of Agriculture at Moulton, where most of the students were male and aged 18 or 19. The land girls were older and the only women. There were four ex-servicemen on their course.

She enjoyed the course, which was from September 1945 to 1946. with three terms which covered the seasons. They studied full time at the Institute and were billeted at the WLA hostel at Wilbury Castle in Wellingborough. They went to Moulton each morning for lectures and in the afternoon did practical work or went on visits. Tuberculosis testing (TT) legislation, to reduce tuberculosis (TB) in milking cattle, was being introduced at the time to develop TB-free dairy herds.

There was no obligation regarding the work she did after the course but she took a driving course with Bedfordshire 'War Ag' in Bedford and was offered a billet at Silsoe WLA hostel, where as well as the mobile gangs of land girls, some girls were employed directly by private farms but used the hostel as their billet.

In 1947, Margaret took up a position for the 'War Ag' as one of their trainers at the post-war training centre at Ravensden Farm, which Jack Stewart managed on behalf of the 'War Ag'. There were two other resident trainers, Betty Davies and Maureen Daley, each of whom had their own rooms. The hostel's Warden was Miss Bremner, who had previously been Warden at the county's first hostel at Milton Ernest.

Each month 16 new recruits arrived for induction into farming. Maureen Daley taught milking and Betty Davies assisted Margaret in teaching arable skills. She had eight girls at a time for field work and the groups changed with milking every fortnight. It was one of the most satisfying jobs that Margaret had, coming across a new lot of land girls every fortnight. In addition to the training work, she took the girls into Bedford on Thursdays evenings for recreation, as well as after lunch on Saturday. Mostly she was able to go home to Luton at the weekends, except when she was the relief milker, doing hand milking.

Ravensden land girls, as part of their training in field work, travelled out to a wide range of farms at Sharnbrook, Riseley, Melchbourne, Thurleigh, and Podington and Tempsford aerodromes.

There were some German prisoners of war working locally in the fields and they were a bit of a problem from her point of view. They, not surprisingly, "eyed the girls rather" and some girls were very willing. There was one particular girl who would not keep away. She would disappear at times. "What they got up to at the farm was none of my business," commented Margaret. Having said that, the Germans were recognised as hard workers, whereas most people felt that the Italian prisoners of war, though friendly, "weren't workers". Margaret had come across them earlier in her private farm days.

The nice thing about the confusingly-named Land 'Army', she remembered, was the fact that they were just civilian employees together, with no hierarchy of officers and other ranks and no military discipline. "We were free in the evenings" and there were some very intelligent girls to socialise with. "I didn't feel I was in the war – it was just my life. We didn't feel we were doing that much. We were doing a job. Towards the end, we were just waiting for our life to start. Things were going to be so much better after the war."[129]

Anne Fox (WLA record not known)

Anne was one of a number of Bedford High School girls who went on to serve in the WLA. She worked on Tinsley's Church Farm, Clapham. In this brief memoir, she remembers one occasion, while out 'bush-burning' when things went wrong in a field opposite the 'Angler's Rest' public house:

"We had been previously reprimanded for having our fires too far away from the hedge, thereby burning more grass than was necessary. We built our fire well under the hedge. It took us some time to get the fire going, but, alas, just as it blazed a gust of wind blew the flames into the hedge, singeing it badly, as we thought.

"Suddenly we realised that the flames had not only singed the foliage, but had also gained quite a hold on some dead wood in the trunks of the blackthorn. For a minute we panicked, then, simultaneously we began dragging away the branches we had pulled up preparatory to burning. With these safely out of the way, we began to throw earth on the fire to stop it spreading, but this was hopeless. I suggested water, so Jean ran down to the cottage at the bottom of the field and borrowed a bucket. In her haste she forgot to fill it on the way up. When she arrived panting, I grabbed the bucket and fled down the hill with it to the trough, filled it and ran back, and threw the water over the hedge, which was now burning well. After this I spent a hectic quarter of an hour fetching water. Of course the journey with the bucket was uphill. How I wished I had gone running more often at school, when requested to run up the hill before breakfast...I managed to get the fire in the hedge out, and to keep our fire going without further mishap. Proof of this adventure still remains to be seen in the hedge."[130]

Margaretta Clark (Initial service with Scottish WLA 1941 – December 1944. Joined WLA in England WLA 152612: 29 December 1944 – 18 March 1946, then 15 January 1948 – 17 June 1949)

Margaretta was born and brought up in Scotland. She was too young to join the armed forces when, aged 17, she joined the WLA in Scotland in 1941. She was trained at Craibstone College, near Aberdeen. They were taught how to saddle and work with Clydesdale horses and to drive tractors – in circles to start with. Arable work included growing potatoes. Animal livestock training embraced poultry work, including killing and dressing birds, and attending to pigs, sheep and cattle.

Her first posting on being transferred to the WLA in England was in the Leeds area, in Yorkshire and then Margaretta, with a friend, was transferred to Bedfordshire, to train land girls in hand milking – not always an easy job since she was a 'foreigner' and, aged 20, often younger than those she was training. She also acted as relief milker on a number of farms in north Bedfordshire before leaving on 18 March 1946, having married a farmer, Claude Eden from Carlton. She was later re-instated on 15 January 1948 and finally left the WLA on 17 June 1949.[131]

Kathleen Green (WLA 96987: 31 August 1942 – 29 October 1945)

Kathleen had worked in Marks and Spencer's store in Bedford before she joined the WLA in 1942 and was sent to Luton Hoo to train. She had always loved animals and chose to train to milk cows. Her father had owned a market garden before the war, so the long working days, seven days a week, came as no surprise to her. Most girls, especially those from towns and cities, found it a shock.

She worked for several farms and estates over the three years she spent in the Land Army, ending her service with a large farm at Ridgmont, owned by a 'gentleman farmer' who spent his day striding around his farm with his dogs.

She had to leave in 1944, on compassionate grounds, when her mother became seriously ill.[132]

Kathleen Green, previously an assistant at Bedford's Marks and Spencer shop, found herself milking cows for three years in the WLA. *Source: K Francis*

Mrs G.D.J. Jones (maiden name and WLA record not known)

"In the summer evenings during my Land Army days I helped with hay making and harvest. During my first summer I helped make the stack with the foreman, and when we had about three-quarters made, it slowly began to slip to the ground. It took many years for the foreman to live that down – he was constantly asked what he was doing on the stack for it to be so badly made."[133]

Rose Richards (WLA 148331: 1 July 1944 – 31 May 1946)

Rose had been brought up at Clapham Park, where her father was the butler to John Howard and her mother was cook. They lived at the South Lodge. Her first war service was at W.H. Allen's, the engineering factory in Bedford, where she helped make pumps for what later became clear were D-day landing vehicles. She became ill in the enclosed atmosphere of the factory and her doctor said she needed an open-air job. She applied to the WLA and impressed them at her interview because she could already drive, having previously driven on deliveries for a shop. She started as a land girl, milking for Mr Tinsley who had 30 milking cows at Park Farm, Clapham. She learned on the job and was able to stay at home. After milking and the subsequent dairy work she delivered the milk locally in a van. In the afternoon she washed the empty bottles and filled them for the next day.

There were two other land girls in the dairy at the farm, Mary McKenna and Doris Smart. Joyce Tinsley, one of Mr Tinsley's daughters and not a WLA girl, also worked in the dairy. Because there was a lot of water used in the dairy, they all wore wellingtons rather than boots. The other two land girls lived in private billets and did not get much to eat. Rose's mother used to invite them some evenings to join the family and eat jacket potatoes filled with minced bacon rinds. After the war both girls married local boys.

It was hard work in the Land Army, with long hours, often out in bad weather. Rose remembered that when the snow was bad, some winters, they had to get the tractor and trailer out to deliver milk, because it was impossible with the van.

When there was less milk to bottle than usual, she would do more field work.

They worked with prisoners of war, both Italians and, at other times, with Germans, who were based at Podington POW Camp. The Germans always had an armed British guard with them, whereas the Italians had more freedom. Mr Tinsley had some Italian POWs living in a caravan on his farm, which some villagers did not agree with. Rose remembered that some mornings, when the van would not start, the Italians would give a push to get it going.

In the summer, deliveries had to be even earlier so as to allow for harvest field work, often "until you dropped", late at night. The work also involved working on stacks. Rose was frightened of heights and the men had to use a ladder to get her down when it was finished.

Rose was able to meet other land girls when she attended dances at the Corn Exchange in Bedford. They heard Glen Miller's band playing but did not realise how famous he would become. The American and Canadian air force men also invited land girls to their dances at Twinwoods.

Rose's two years in the WLA ended with demobilisation at the end of May in 1946. She was able to take part, driving one of Tinsley's horse-drawn carts, in the February parade down Bedford's High Street before Princess Elizabeth.[134]

Catherine Bezant (WLA 74324: 27 April 1942 – 17 January 1947)

Catherine was aged 19 when, in 1942, she decided to join the WLA. She went to an office in Luton to be interviewed and was sent for training to Luton Hoo, where she learned milking. Her first post was at Wood End Farm at Marston Moreteyne. She went to St John's Station, Bedford, and caught the train to Millbrook. The farmer sent his daughter to pick her up. She was billeted up the road from the farm, at another farmhouse, Little Park Farm.

She did milking, looked after pigs – there were several sows and a boar – and collected eggs from the free-range hens who used to lay all over the place. The farmer had bought some goats but they were a bit of a disaster because they had fleas. There were three working horses and a pony, Polly, whom she looked after.

There were two other land girls on the farm, Albert the cowman, Frank, and two older men, Caleb and Mr K. They used to look after the land girls. They had been farm workers all their lives and were very good at their jobs.

There were about 30 milking cows and Catherine had to use an old 'sit up and beg' bicycle to go down the road each morning to collect them for milking. Each cow knew just where to go in the milking shed and if another one got in the way would bump it out of the way. They were very intelligent animals and the land girls knew them all individually. When the time came to round them up and take them to market, Catherine did not like it, because she had made friends of them.

The farmer was also a butcher and had a shop in the village. Every so often he killed a pig and they would have black puddings, made with the blood. He would also give the land girls sausages to take home. Caleb also kept a pig of his own and the farmer killed and butchered it at the farm.

The first land girls Catherine worked with left to get married. The next girl, Edie, worked there for a few years and also left to get married. Land girls, once married, were no longer regarded as being 'mobile' – capable of being sent anywhere in the country – and so were granted a 'willing release' from the WLA. Catherine stayed on the farm and worked seven days a week looking after the animals.

They started milking at six o'clock each morning and then returned home for breakfast. After that, there were various jobs to do, depending on the season. In the spring they spent most of their time in the fields, hoeing and weeding crops. They grew mangle-wurzels for cattle feed, and corn. Hay making was very hard work. The two old men did not think that the land girls should do this sort of work but they got used to the young women and got on well.

Occasionally, the land girls would walk over the fields, in summertime, up to Cranfield to go the cinema there, accompanied by a man to look after them. Usually in the evenings they were too tired to do anything but one or twice they cycled to the village hall when something was going on. Every other weekend, Catherine would travel home to Dunstable, on Saturday afternoon, and return by Sunday evening.

After a while working at Wood End she wanted to be nearer home so got a transfer to Barton to a beautiful farmhouse surrounded by a moat. There was a small airfield belonging to Luton Flying Club near the farm. The farmer had to have permission to send the cows to graze there. Catherine ended up spending hours preventing the cows from grazing on the middle of the airfield, since planes used it occasionally to land there. The job turned out not to be her idea of farming and she returned to Marston Moreteyne until Christmas 1946 when she left and returned home and to post-war life.[135]

Evelyn Archer (WLA 130232: 14 July 1943 – 28 Sept 1945)

Evelyn, from 1939, was working as a cashier in Green's, a Bedford shop later taken over by British Home Stores. As she approached the age of 21, she was anxious to avoid being 'directed' in to war work, with no choice of her own, and so decided to join the WLA. She went to the head office in Harpur Street, Bedford. She was hoping to be able to serve in Bedfordshire, even though a friend of hers had joined and been sent down to Kent. Evelyn was quite a shy person and was worried about leaving home.

She was accepted and was sent to the Hulcote Moors hostel, at Hulcote Moors Farm, while she waited for a place on a training farm course. They were taken out each day in a van to weed vegetables which were grown around the aerodrome at nearby Cranfield. There were some fun times when the air force pilots had a party and, the next day, the remaining 'goodies' were distributed to the land girls with a great big can of tea.

They also got invited to a dance at the airfield. None of the land girls had any fancy clothes to wear so they went in uniform. "We had got heavy shoes and we clumped across the floor and tried to dance with these...it was like an army trying to march. It was ridiculous."

Evelyn's training was at Mr Brown's farm in Great Barford, where she was taught to milk and helped with the harvest. Her billet was in a cottage where she had to share a double bed with another land girl. That was against the rules but she was too naïve to say anything.

While there, there was an incident when three land girls had to move a lot of calves from one side of the farm through a gate to the other side. They ended up with the calves running all over the place. The farmer's eldest son, who farmed Hill Farm, said, "I've never seen anything like it in my life."

[This kind of happening was not untypical and arose often out of the lack of proper training or demonstrations by farmers, allowing for the fact that often these young women knew nothing about animals, farms, farming or even country ways.]

Her first post after a month at Great Barford was at Beadlow Manor, outside Clophill. Captain Archer had numerous milking cows there and a milk round. Evelyn's billet there was with the wife of an RAF officer who had a tiny baby. She hated being alone so took a land girl in. Evelyn was given strict instructions not to wake the woman or the baby in the morning, so she had to creep about. She eventually asked for a move. Even then, it turned out that she had been there the longest of any land girl.

Next she was sent to Willington, and stayed until September 1945. In the better weather, she cycled and lived at home. In the winter months, she stayed with a kind woman in the village. She had a large bedroom but it was so cold, she could not get warm. But at least her landlady used to get up to make breakfast for her and pack her lunch, and a meal was always ready for her each evening.

At the Willington farm Evelyn got used to working with shire horses. She used to lead a pair of horses for the old man to plough. She was allowed to work on her own when haymaking. On one occasion she nearly knocked a shed down, backing a horse. On another, she was in the fields, driving a trailer from one heap of vegetables to the other, moving on when a fellow worker banged on the side of her tractor. Looking in her rear-view mirror, she wondered what the male worker was doing. He had been "spending a penny" and Evelyn, by moving the trailer, had removed his privacy.

The lack of privacy and of toilet facilities were a constant problem, also, for these young women – most of them used to working in buildings with toilet facilities: "when you're out in the fields, you had the hedge and nothing else". Working with men complicated the matter. WLA headquarters issued a memorandum directing land girls who were working with Italian prisoners of war to 'spend a penny' together, rather than alone.

In the winter there was the dreaded job of picking Brussels sprouts, going between two rows, pulling one plant up in each and banging them together, before throwing them in a pile. Workers wore a sack tied on their front to protect them from the mud.

Potato picking was another backbreaking job. Machinery dug up the potatoes and spun them out to be collected in sacks by hand and then a moving belt discharged damaged or misshapen ones. At a time when numerous labourers were required, gangs of land girls from Cople hostel would be delivered by lorry. Evelyn remembered that most of them were from Yorkshire and "a real laugh". When one girl came without her lunch, all the others gave her one of their sandwiches and a drink of their tea. Later they had four Italian prisoners of war to assist. One of them could drive the tractor. They were based at a camp in the Cople area.

"They were like young boys, really," she remembered. "There was no harm in them at all. One of them brought his exercise book every day and was trying to learn English. Over lunch we used to help him with the words. The other one was much more serious. We called him Henry. The Italian POWs would ask us to shop in Bedford for them, for things like combs and stuff for the hair…"

Later, Evelyn moved from the Danish Camp area to the farmer's new farm, Shrubbery Farm, Wilden.[136]

Dora Carlyle (WLA 65927: 21 February 1942 – 29 December 1945)
Dora was a cinema usherette at the Granada Theatre in Bedford before she joined the WLA. She volunteered because she did not want to be called up and put in the factories doing war work. After three months working on a mushroom farm in Ampthill and a longer period at Milton Ernest hostel, working for the 'War Ag' on a variety of farms, Dora transferred to work on a dairy farm because she loved working with animals. She worked on the farm attached to the Three Counties Hospital in Arlesey, where she lived in the nurses' home. She would rise at 4.30am to get dressed ready for milking

"I worked really hard. I used to have to get 60 cows up from the field to be milked with nothing other than a small hooded lamp, because we were not allowed lights due to the blackouts. I had to be out at 5am, get the cows ready, milk them by hand, not machine, then used to go for breakfast at 9am, after which I used to get two horses and plough the fields…I also used to pasteurise the milk and do threshing in the fields. Then I would bike eight miles home at weekends (on Saturday afternoons) from Arlesey to Foster Hill Road in Bedford to visit my family."

She met her husband, John, when he was stationed with the RAF at Henlow. She left the WLA after the war and they married in 1946. They were still together, she 84 and he 91 years of age, as she reminisced. "Sometimes I wonder how I did it all really, but I do not think hard work ever hurt anybody."[137]

Dora Carlyle in pristine white milking coat with one of her herd of Jersey cows on the estate farm at Three Counties Hospital, Arlesey. *Source: D Pontin*

Barbara Filbey (WLA 90465: 20 July 1942 – June 1945)

Barbara grew up in Bedford and worked for a high-class dressmaker, Gladys Clayton, after leaving Harpur Central School. When called up in 1943, aged almost 20, although offered a choice of going in the WAAF (Women's Auxiliary Air Force) or the WRENS (Women's Royal Naval Service), she opted to join the Land Army because she did not want to go away from home. She had a boyfriend who did not want her to leave the area. After a month's training at Luton Hoo she was sent to a private farm, Vicarage Farm, Kempston West End. This allowed her to stay at home and cycle to work each day. It was a 2,000-acre farm, both arable farming and milking cows. Freddie Ray was the farmer. She found it hard work. After morning milking, they used to have to go out in the fields and feed the 'dry cattle' – the ones that were not being milked. She worked with an elderly man who had a wooden leg – he had lost his leg in a threshing accident. They took hay out on a flat trolley and a large cart horse.

There were six land girls at the farm and the foreman said he did not want any of the men swearing in front of the girls. There was a tractor driver, three men who worked in the fields and one who looked after the horses. But by the time they had finished in the WLA, some of these girls were swearing worse than the men.

Her favourite job was muck spreading, since it kept your feet warm. They wore wellingtons and used to put hay in them to make them warm inside. The most interesting job, she felt, was feeding calves, which involved putting your hand in the milk and teaching them to feed with your fingers.

Apart from milking, Barbara and the other land girls learned as they went along. It was heavy going in the winter, harvesting sugar beet. The most miserable job, she found, was threshing. A steam engine drove the threshing machine, belching black smoke. The wind always seemed to blow in their direction.

She got quite good at building a stack, as the straw came from the threshing machine. It was quite an art, knowing how to start and how to build it and what to do with the middle.

The land girls were expected to do as much work as the men. There were not many jobs that the men helped them with.

Later she moved to Church Farm in Clapham, where there were more cows, because they had a milk round and they also delivered to Biddenham Dairies. Barbara used to take a horse and trap with the milk churns. They also had a little pony for that. On the way back from the dairies, they would call at the cake shop and get something to eat at lunchtime.

Once, when the foreman's daughter, Dianne, aged ten, was in the trap, the girl was given the reins, as Barbara delivered, but as Barbara got back on the trap, the pony bolted and flew down through Kempston. There were empty churns jumping up and down and two or three people shouting after it. There was nothing Barbara could do. Dianne was crying her eyes out. Somebody in a bread van saw the predicament, followed them and once the pony got to the farm lane, pulled in front of them. The pony stumbled and skinned both his knees.

On another occasion with another land girl with her in the trap, driving down Prebend Street, Bedford, one day with empty churns, two American servicemen were walking past and one called out, "Stop that buggy!"

The job that Barbara did not like was taking the bull to the cows for mating. She was "a bit on the prim side" and did not think it was a job for women. But being a land girl meant doing "men's work". They had to load 2½-hundredweight sacks of wheat, which in later decades would not be allowed because of health and safety legislation.

Whatever Barbara earned, she went halves with her mother. Money was very tight. She earned 48 shillings a week; a shilling an hour. A pair of stockings cost 1s/11d (about 10p). She used to make all her own clothes, and other people's as well, using her mother's old treadle sewing machine. When she was 17, her mother gave her £4 as a deposit on a new electric sewing machine and Barbara paid 1s/6d (7½p) a week to pay the hire purchase off.

She left the Land Army after she married and had a child.[138]

Barbara Cox (WLA 127173: June 1943 – May 1947)

Barbara joined the WLA in June 1943 and was able to work from home, which was Rook Tree Farm in Hulcote, near Cranfield. She worked at Hulcote Moors Farm, an arable and dairy farm, which was also a hostel for land girls employed by the 'War Ag'. Her father worked there at the farm. Prior to that she had travelled daily into Kempston to work for Cryselco, making electric light bulbs.

She learned to milk at Hulcote and started at 6am each day. There were 30-odd cows, all with their own names; some were Friesians and some Guernseys. Milk was collected in ten-gallon churns each morning at 8am and sent to London. Milking began again at 2.30 in the afternoon.

Unlike the other land girls who went out each day to different local farms, as required, Barbara stayed at the Hulcote farm all day and when not milking, worked in the fields. There were three tractors and three horses to work the farm. She never drove tractors but she did lead the horses, with someone behind guiding the hoe. "When they chain harrowed, a man walked behind with the reins to steer the horses. Root crops were mangel-wurzel, swede, potatoes, Brussels and cabbage to help the ration out."

She also took the horses to be shod in Woburn Sands, by a Mr Payne. In order to get on the back of the working horse, Barbara would lead it to a five-bar gate and climb up to get on its back. They were fairly gentle horses. Only one, called Snapper, had to have a muzzle.

The tractors were old Fordsons which were started on petrol and then run on paraffin. The tractor-driven ploughs only worked two furrows. But it was better than the single-furrow ploughs the horses had drawn.

Entertainment in the area was mainly going to the cinema in Cranfield and to dances at the RAF base at Cranfield aerodrome.

One night there was a dramatic incident, locally. A British plane, trying to get back after a night-time bombing raid in Germany, crashed into one of the stacks and there was a terrible fire. All six crew were killed.

German bombers dropped small bombs in the area one night and took a hedge out, and one bomb got lodged in a tree in the woods at Hulcote.

Barbara's dad was a special (part-time) constable and she was a voluntary, part-time Fire Guard, on certain nights.

"The people who worked on farms could get meat pies on a Wednesday from a Mrs Sturgess who lived at Water Hall. In the harvest time we would be working up until ten o'clock and later as we had double summertime."

Barbara left the Land Army in May 1947.[139]

Yvonne Frood (WLA 15996: 14 May 1943 – 30 March 1945)
Yvonne was a Yorkshire girl and after school had entered domestic service in Henlow. Her father had said to her, "Join the Land Army and put some roses in your cheeks." She joined, aged 18 in May 1943 and started with four weeks' training at Luton Hoo. She was placed at Park Farm, on the Shuttleworth Estate at Old Warden. At first she was lodged with the Foreman, Mr Fowler, but then was billeted at the Cowman's Cottage, with Mr and Mrs Bayliss, and their daughter Nancy, who was only two years younger than Yvonne.

Her job was hand milking with a pedigree herd of Jersey cows and she loved it there. She was able to take charge of the herd. There were three land girls from Cople Hostel who also worked there regularly. They would attend dances in Northill.

She left in March 1945 when she married Len Truin, a market garden worker.[140]

Dorothy Crowsley (WLA 77089: 11 May 1942 – 30 May 1945)
Dorothy was a Bedford girl who worked for Meltis on leaving school. She joined the WLA in June 1940 and her first job was rearing chickens in 'battery houses' at Lower Gravenhurst. In the summertime you could finish as late as 10pm. A friend

of hers from Meltis, Grace Sanderson, also joined then. They shared a bed in a small cottage and would lie awake half the night talking.

Later they moved to Biggleswade, where they worked in market gardening. They helped cultivate tomatoes and cucumbers in the summer and lettuces in the winter in large greenhouses owned by Mr Ives next to the cemetery. The labour force also included two old men and Italian prisoners of war, who were clever at making baskets in their spare time, which they would then sell for presents or swap for soap. Land girls from local hostels joined them when more labour was needed.

Dorothy's sister, Gladys Crowsley, joined the WLA at the same time and worked for Mr Godber at Willington.[141]

Sheila Stephens (WLA 192296: 3 March 1948 – 13 August 1949)

Sheila joined in March 1948 for the final few years of the post-war Land Army. She trained at Ravensden training farm and was then placed at Bolnhurst, working for the 'War Ag' (see Life for Hostel Land Girls). She later went to work at Manor Farm, Thurleigh, and worked privately for the farmer there for the rest of the time, although staying at the hostel as a billet. She met her husband-to-be on the farm, and remembered being embarrassed when going to have her engagement ring fitted. Her fingers were blistered because land girls were given no gloves to protect their hands.

Sheila learned to handle working horses – Belle was a shire horse and Blossom was a smaller Suffolk Punch. Every time the girls went to put their collars on, the horses would lift their heads to avoid it. Belle had a mind of her own and would only do what she felt like doing. If the gate was open, she would dash back to the stable.

There was always something to do on the farm. There were 65 Ayrshire cows to machine milk, plus pig and hens to looks after. The cows were fed only home-grown food – oats, wheat, barley, beans, curly kale and the Lucerne hay crop. Only protein additives were bought in. Six land girls worked there, with the men. One of the wartime German prisoners of war had stayed on and was a hard worker. The farmer's wife, Sheila's future mother-in-law, was a great baker and would come out into the fields with Scottish pancakes or scones for the land girls.

On Saturdays, after working in the morning, they rushed back to take their curlers out of their hair – they wore headscarves – and took the lorry into Bedford to meet their boyfriends. They would often go to the cinema – the Granada or Empire. Then lorries met them at night, in the middle of the town, to go back to the hostel. They met other land girls in the lorry park. Some weekends, Sheila

Many land girls worked in glasshouses, raising tomatoes and a range of vegetables. Horses were still being used on this market garden. 15 February 1943. *Source: T Kirkby*

would catch the Birch bus home, to stock up with food.

On Sundays, a lorry would come to take those land girls who wished to attend to St Peter's Church, Bedford – the land girls' church. They always wore their uniform hats bent a bit to make them individual.

Sheila was able to enjoy the companionship of a friend, Hazel, at the hostel, but after 17 months, Sheila had to leave. Her mother became seriously ill and Sheila was granted compassionate discharge. Her friend stayed on until the end, in November 1950, then also married a local farmer. They both lived on farms thereafter. In retirement, both friends ended up living in the same village, Turvey.[142]

Betty and Jean Pearson (WLA 12560 and WLA 120561: March 1943 – February 1946)

Betty and Jean, identical twins, were brought up in Birtley, County Durham. When they left Birtley railway station in March 1943 to travel to Bedford and join Bedfordshire WLA, all the family and friends turned out to wave them goodbye. At Bedford station they, together with other young women from Yorkshire and the North-East, were met by an army

The twins, Betty and Jean Pearson, from Birtley, County Durham, who served in the WLA working at Priestley Farm, near Flitwick. When Princess Elizabeth presented long-service awards to Bedfordshire land girls in the Corn Exchange, Bedford, 14 February, 1946, it was the Pearson twins who presented her with a basket of farm produce. *Source: B & J Pearson*

truck and the first thing they saw were lots of cycles being ridden by school boys in blazers and straw bengers [hats]. It reminded them of 'Tom Brown's Schooldays'.

They were placed at the Silsoe land girl hostel, which was Wrest Park Lodge. After two months, working for the 'War Ag' and travelling out each day to different farms and learning on the job, they were transferred to Walter Cole's farm near Flitwick, called Priestley Farm. They continued working there for three years, although they were billeted with 'War Ag' land girls at Silsoe.

Betty and Jean were very happy at Priestley Farm. The farmer and the farm hands were all very kind although they found the work very hard. The winter months were extremely trying. When they were picking Brussels sprouts in the snow, soaking wet, with hands red and cold, a few tears were shed and they felt sorry for themselves. But they were soon, as they put it, "knocked into shape". Mary Roberts (then Mary Cole), looking back to that time, noted "The hoeing and back-breaking jobs must have seemed endless to them, but they never complained".[143]

When extra labour was required, prisoners of war were brought in each day to work on the farm. Italian POWs wore brown tunics with yellow circular patches on their backs. Germans POWs were always accompanied by an armed British soldier. They were never allowed to work together. Three Germans worked quite regularly at Priestley Farm and were quiet hard-working men. One of them had come from a farming family in Germany. During school holidays, local schoolchildren would add to the labour in the fields, doing such jobs as 'singling' (or thinning out) sugar beet, and picking potatoes.

Working with horses was not without incident. Betty remembered, "We had to go bean-threshing at Woburn Abbey and I had the job of taking the horse and cart to fill it with bean stalks and then take it into the yard to put in the bullocks' troughs – but what I forgot to do was to allow for the hubs on the cart to go through the gates, and they caught the gate and as I went through the gate came away, and the horse took fright and so did the young bullocks and there was a right how-do-you-do – the farmer was far from pleased."

During the summer months, Jean and Betty's parents came down to Bedfordshire on holiday. Mary, the farmer's daughter, remembered, "They would come to the farm and sit on a grassy bank at the end of the field where Jean and Betty were working, waiting to share their lunch break with them."

The twins' moment of glory came in February 1946, the year after the war had ended and just before they left the WLA. They were chosen to present a basket of farm produce to Princess Elizabeth (our present Queen) at the Corn Exchange, Bedford, before a ceremony to present long-service badges to Bedfordshire land girls. Everyone was proud of them.

When they departed from the farm, Walter Cole, their employer for those three years, 1943–46, gave them a five pound Bond and a letter expressing his gratitude for their services: "I am very sorry you are leaving, but can quite understand your anxiety to be nearer home. The work I know has at times been very trying, although I never heard you complaining. I hope that you will be very happy in the future, but whatever happens, you can feel assured that you did what you could and did it very well during the war."

The young women had found peace in those days at Priestley Farm. "They were the best days of our lives." They had enjoyed the companionship of the other land girls. "It was a great privilege to serve in the Land Army, and one we would not have missed."[144]

MILKING COWS AND LOOKING AFTER FARM ANIMALS

Betty Harding (WLA 163843: 1 February 1946 – 18 August 1948)

When the Second World War started in 1939, Betty's eldest brother went off to war because he was a territorial soldier and her second brother went into the navy. Betty worked in a chemist's shop in Queen's Park, Bedford, after leaving school in Kempston. The war was over before Betty was 17, in December 1945 and able to join the Land Army. One of her aunts had a dairy farm and this had given Betty the idea that she would love to be a farmer's wife.

Betty started in 1946. After four weeks' training at Ravensden training farm, learning milking, she became a stock girl, looking after farm animals seven days a week and milking six days a week. One of the German prisoners of war milked for her on her one day off during the week. The farm was Church Farm, Dunton, near Biggleswade. There was one other land girl there who did the tractor driving. The farmer had three cottages, one for the horse keeper, one for another worker and one for his old aunt. Betty lodged with the old aunt.

Betty remembered the first time she tried to milk a cow on the training farm. "It's very difficult, you know. It looks easy but it jolly well isn't. You see this great big animal stuck in front of you. It looks so much bigger than when they're in the field. And you had a little stool and you had to sit on it and they said, 'Push your head into their groin and just give a pull (on their teats)'. Well, you can pull and pull and nothing comes, because the cow knows exactly that you are afraid, and withdraws its milk."

Betty was almost in tears the first time. She had a male teacher who said, "You're too nervous. You've got to try and relax". "He said that some people got on all right if they sang so I thought, 'I'll give it a try,' so I started to hum to myself, you see, and I think that relaxing, by trying to sing...I always sang (from then onwards) when I milked. They used to say, 'Hark at Betty, singing'. It was just because I was nervous. They were often love songs which everyone knew the words to, such as 'I'm in the mood for love'."

She learned the importance of cleaning. "That's very important. You always have to wash their udders before you start. You always had to wear a protective hat on your head, because you have to press your head tight in the cow's groin. It can't bring its foot up. Some cows love to kick the bucket. You get to know that. The ones that do it. There was lots of different knacks. And some of them you had to be quite frightened of, when they had really big horns and you'd got to put the chains around their head. Quite frightening, really, but you got used to it."

Mucking out was a daily chore, when the cows were out of the sheds, clearing the cow muck and piling it on the midden, scrubbing the floor and swilling down with water. In the summer the cows were out in the fields; in the winter, they had an enclosed paddock at the farm. After each winter, the paddock had to be cleaned out, when the men had nothing else to do. The cow muck and straw floor of the paddock got really high and had to be cut out. It was very labour intensive work.

At Church Farm, Betty had cows and pigs and young bullocks. "That was my domain. All the fields and all the rest, he had other people for. He'd got the tractor driver and the horse keeper. He'd got four horses. Every morning at six o'clock I had to milk. Four cows, I had to milk. Then there was the calves growing up, the different sizes…When they were a certain age, you took them off their mother.

"There was a technique where you had the milk in the bucket. You put your hand in and stuck your two fingers up, so that the calves started sucking them and thinking it was the teats. And you took your hand away and that's how you taught it to drink from the bucket." This was to enable the cow to be milked so that the farmer's wife could make butter from it.

"The job I hated was feeding the pigs. He always kept about 20. When you opened the door, they charged. In those days, you always fed them slops in a bucket. Left-over whey mixed with meal and stuff. Thick sloppy stuff. You always ended up with half down your trousers. It always had a sour smell. You couldn't wear those trousers any more then because it dried on all horrible and stiff. I used to creep to the gate, so I didn't think they'd know I was coming. But by the time you'd got the gate open, they were there. Horrible things, pigs.

"Meal was more or less made on the farm. In those days, they didn't have any combines; the corn use to be in stooks and you used to have to make a corn stack. This machine came and threshed all that stuff. There was always this stuff that wasn't sold. That was used for the (pigs)…The same with cows. They had meal and mangel-worzels, like a big turnip. They were chopped up for the cows. There was none of this business about nuts and pellets…

"I always had two hundred hens. They were in the field. Four hen houses on wheels, where they laid their eggs. The henhouses were moved, every now and then, so that that piece of ground didn't die completely. They roamed in the fields and went into the henhouses to lay their eggs. That is what is free range. A free range hen roams where it likes and then you have a lovely egg. The farmer's daughter – she was about 32 and because I was only 17 I thought she was ever so old – they were hers, the hens.

"She was so fussy with them. If one looked sick, she wrung its neck, straight away; she didn't want any disease. So one day she said to me, 'Betty, I think I'd better show you how to kill a hen.' Well, I was very squeamish. She brought it into the yard. She just got it and broke its neck. She gave me one and I pulled and pulled this small thing. All the blood started running down its neck; by that time I'd 'pulled' its head off and just dropped it and screamed. She said, 'Oh, you're not going to be any good.' That was the end of the hens.

"But I had all the dirty work, cleaning the hen houses out...She used to shut them up at night. I had to clean two dog kennels outside. I always got the mucky jobs. I loved it. They were the happiest years of my life. I really must say. I was my own boss. Nobody told me what to do. I just got on with my work and loved animals.

"Then, after 18 months, I suddenly began to get funny things – the cows had cattle ringworm. I was always one to hang round them...and I had one on my arm and one on my leg. Then I had another skin disease. I got really run down. So they – the Land Army – sent me off to Torquay for a holiday for two weeks. A beautiful place there...a Rest Home for land girls...It was once a private home...There was a beach there and we could go swimming. It was the first real holiday that I'd ever had in my life...I'd never been away for two whole weeks. You didn't have to do anything. You were looked after. Just a warden...I made friends with the other girls from all over the place...We had summer dresses on and shorts. It may have been August because my Grandma died in July and that was all to do with it. The stress. Me feeling low. Anyway, when I came back from there, I decided to go into a Women's Land Army hostel."[145]

(See Chapter 9 for Betty's hostel experiences.)

LUTON HOO

Kathleen Burgoyne (WLA 107321: 15 February 1943 – 18 March 1946)
Kathleen, a Luton girl, worked in a florist's shop after leaving school. When old enough to do National Service, but not wanting to work in a munitions factory, she opted for the Land Army.

On joining the WLA, Kathleen was sent to nearby Luton Hoo for training. There she caught the eye of the Head Gardener, Mr Alfred Daffurn, who asked her to stay on as a permanent land girl working for the Luton Hoo estate. She grew all manner of fruit and vegetables – tomatoes, all the green vegetables, soft fruit such as strawberries and raspberries, plums – as well as working in egg production. These were sold at the Farm shop to ATS girls who were just some of the various military personnel based in Luton Hoo park, which became the headquarters of Eastern Command during the war.

There were a dozen or so land girls employed permanently at Home Farm. Bernard Woods was the man in charge of the greenhouse, where Kathleen loved

Luton Hoo land girls in front of the conservatory in the walled garden. *Source: Luton Hoo Walled Garden Restoration Project/K Davies*

working. She remembered training fruit trees and bushes to grow along wires in the espalier manner.

One way in which they could earn extra money, was to get up early and clean out and light the fires in the coke stoves which heated the numerous glasshouses in the walled garden there.

At Christmas time there would be parties in the stable's coach house. And a dance in the ballroom of the mansion, hosted by Sir Harold and Lady Zia Wernher.[146]

Joy Collard (WLA 46343: 13 June 1941 – 30 November 1950)

Joy also worked full-time at Luton Hoo in the walled garden, after her initial period of training which began on 7 July 1941. She has left behind her carved name and the 'WLA' initials, with the years '1941–45', etched on the front of a shelf in the potting shed.[147]

Dorothy Hayward (WLA 12933: 9 October 1939 – 30 August 1944)

Dorothy wrote to *The Land Girl* magazine in February 1942 about her work in tomato growing at a large (unnamed) nursery in Bedfordshire:

> Dear Editor,
>
> I was interested in Doreen Sandberg's letter about tomato growing. My friend and I have both done this work at a very large nursery garden. Eight acres of glass! Our greenhouses were 187 feet long and held roughly 2,500 plants in each; there were 52 tomato houses and four for cucumbers. I honestly think it is one of the most interesting of all the various hand jobs; there are so many things one can learn.
>
> Here are a few tips for tomato growers:
>
> 1. Get a couple of khaki hankies, even if it means giving up a coupon or two. I found that one's hankies look really repulsive after wiping one's nose a couple of times. The green tomato stain comes off your face on to your hanky, and all your other clothes too, and it *will not* boil out! The stain doesn't show on the khaki.
>
> 2. *Don't*, whatever you do, wear silk underclothes for coolness; it's the biggest mistake you can make. Wear a light interlock vest and panties, shirt and dungarees, and always have a pullover or coat to put on when you go out into the open, even in the summer, for a few minutes.
>
> 3. Wear a shady hat, until the plants are big enough to offer some shade, and wear a beret or scarf round your head to keep your hair from being pulled about when turning above the wires or your hair will be green too.
>
> 4. Keep all cuts wrapped up, with self-adhesive bandage; there's a lot of germs in the wet-manured soil of a greenhouse, not to mention the fungus that sometimes attacks the plants. I always carried iodine, scissors and bandage with me to work.
>
> 5. Until one is used to the atmosphere inside the houses, try carrying a smelling bottle of frozen or liquid Eau de Cologne, as plants use up all the oxygen, and one finds it an awful job to keep awake sometimes, not to mentions headaches.
>
> 6. Wrap up well in the winter. Greenhouses are very, very cold when the furnaces are out while digging, flooding, manuring, etc., is in progress.
>
> Yours sincerely,
>
> D. Hayward, WLA 12,933.[148]

MARKET GARDENING

Many land girls worked in market gardens, in orchards and in glasshouses.

above: Greenhouse workers. The north-east area of Bedfordshire was most active in market gardening. *Source: T Kirkby*

left: Sylvia Burns was one of many who worked in the 1,000-acre Coxes Orange Pippin apple orchard at Cockayne Hatley. *Source: Antrobus archive, 1946 Bedfordshire WLA souvenir programme, p13*

Herb farm land girls, Leighton Buzzard. Stella Limon is on the far right. *Source: S Goldsmith*

Land girls working in the market garden at Woburn Abbey. *Source: C M Stokes. Courtesy of The Luton News*

CHAPTER 9

Personal Experiences: Life for Hostel Land Girls

The following accounts have been summarised by the author from interviews and from brief memoirs from a range of former Bedfordshire land girls who, at some stage in their WLA service, experienced life in one of the county's hostels for mobile gangs. (Dates in brackets are taken from their service record: the first date was when they were enrolled; the last when they were entered on the resigned or demobbed list. Actual service dates were in between and were given on their Release Certificate.)

BOLNHURST HOSTEL

The first five memoirs are from women who were at Bolnhurst hutment hostel, north of Bedford:

Joyce Irving (WLA90468: 27 April 1943 – 21 September 1946)

Joyce was born and bred in Bedford and lived there all her life. Called up to do National Service, she chose the Land Army instead of munitions. She was aged 20 when she was interviewed by Mrs Eugster, the County Secretary, and another woman at the county offices. Asked what experience she had of farming, she pointed out that her uncle had a farm and she liked animals.

Her uniform arrived a few days before she was due to begin and she was advised to put neats-foot oil on her shoes and boots to soften them in preparation. She started on an October Monday in 1942, taking her bicycle to Harpur Street, where the new recruits were collected by lorry and taken to the new hutment hostel at Bolnhurst. She knew two of the other girls, one of them from her school. After a drink of tea on arrival, Mrs Eugster and a 'War Ag' lady talked to them about the work they would be doing and arrangements in the hostel.

The hostel was run for the WLA by a YWCA (Young Women's Christian

Association) Warden called Miss E. McGinn, who turned out to be a very nice lady. There were 40 of them staying at the hostel.

They started straight away with eight of them following the 'War Ag' lady (in her car) on bicycles for three miles to Walker's farm in Keysoe. There they were set to pulling mangel-wurzels. They had had no initial training and were to learn everything 'on the job'. This was not unusual for many of the hostel land girls.[149]

Zeita Trott (WLA 84908: 22 June 1942 – 20 April 1945)

Zeita's first posting, after four weeks' training at Luton Hoo, was at Brook Farm, Wymington, with Eileen Anderson. Although they had a nice room in the farmhouse, they both decided it would be more fun if they moved to the new hostel at Bolnhurst. They were part of the first intake. There were 37 new land girls there and three 'old hands'. She met Joyce Irving there. As expected it was 'a good laugh'.

The hostel girls were taken out each morning to local farms, in small gangs, as required. They worked quite regularly at Walker's farm at Keysoe. They learned to drive tractors – Fordson, Massey, Ferguson, even the new caterpillar tractors. In winter they did a lot of hedging and ditching, when, if they were not careful, icy water would come over the tops of their gumboots (wellingtons).

Once they got settled into the hard physical work of the farms and the spartan conditions of the hostel huts, they began to develop a social life. There were dances at the surrounding north Bedfordshire airfields, which were taken over by the 8th American Army Air Force. She had three or four American boyfriends, over a period of years, and one, Jo Yoho from Ohio, corresponded with Zeita for a number of years after the war.

The presence of negro Americans (as black Americans were called then) was a new phenomenon in rural England at that time. Zeita remembered one day when she was hitching a lift on the A6, in order to catch a train in Bedford for Luton. An American GI lorry stopped to pick her up. She ended up between two very black guys, with about 40 other black soldiers in the back. They were very polite but it was a shock to see so many black men for the first time.

Her father used to have a quiet laugh at times, when she took some of her boyfriends home. She also took some of her fellow land girls home, who lived too far from home to be able to visit their own families at the weekends.

There were also concerts arranged by British soldiers, such as at the Pioneer Corps Camp at Colmworth, but these camps were not as attractive as the American bases, where there was no rationing and the American troops got paid three times as much as their British allies.

Zeita remembered being let into the Bolnhurst hostel through a window, having

Land girls with American GIs outside a Colmworth pub. (Left to right, front) Joe Yoho, Olive Turner, Zeita Trott, Doreen Kempster. 'Joho', as he was known, was Zeita's boyfriend at the time.
Source: Z Hole

arrived back after the 10pm curfew. One or two girls she knew got pregnant and she expressed surprise that there were not more. "We didn't know much about contraception in those days. Let's just say that a lot of us were lucky."

The young women tried to keep up appearances but make-up was limited and the living and working conditions they experienced made it difficult. They used to pierce each other's ears, using hot darning needles and a cork behind the ears.

Bathing, with just five inches of water allowed in the bath during the war, was not easy. The hot water was also limited to around six bath-fulls and once it ran out for the day, there was only cold to make do with. In the end, some of the land girls put modesty to one side and went in the baths in twos, or even threes, which made the water come higher and also allowed them to have more frequent baths than they would otherwise be allocated. There were no showers, just three baths, and five wash-hand basins which the 40 young women rushed to occupy each evening when arriving back at the hostel in their lorries.

Rats and mice were everywhere on the farms. Canvas gaiters were often worn around the lower legs. These protected the ankles from pitch forks and also stopped rats from running up their legs. Hay stacks used to 'heave' with mice and rats.

Zeita loved tractor driving. But she also learned the thatching of roofs at Milton Ernest. She once started a roof with Doreen Kempster but they hadn't finished by Friday evening so they worked all through the night – there was moonlight – so that they could go away for the weekend. When they got back on the Sunday, someone had set fire to it and it had been completely destroyed.

She also cared for livestock, remembering looking after six calves which had ringworm and were threatened with being put down. She managed to nurse them back to health.

She was lucky that her home was in Luton and she could get home at the weekends. Most land girls were from out of the county and too far away from their home to visit on a regular basis. Life in Luton was more affected by the war than in the rural areas of mid and north Bedfordshire. One of her relatives had evacuees. Her sister worked at Commer Cars factory which was hit by an enemy bomb, but she had escaped injury. There were Saturday dances in Luton, which she enjoyed.

At Bolnhurst hostel, they were very isolated. They had no newspapers and, most of the time, did not know what was going on in the war. "Perhaps it was a good thing," she reflected.

She was engaged, at one time, to a boy in the army and got lots of letters from him. But he lost his life in Tripoli. She later got engaged to a man in the navy and he was killed in action. This was the nature of life for many young women at that time – short-lived but intense relationships, which could end abruptly when the young man was killed or moved on to another theatre of war. "It was a sad time, wasn't it, if you think about it."

Zeita finally married a man in the Royal Air Force. Her father had married again, and started a second family. Zeita was at the christening of one of the babies at the Black Swan (the 'Dirty Duck') in Luton when she met her husband-to-be, a wireless operator and rear gunner. They had a nice wedding in Luton, despite the effects of the war, with five bridesmaids and a reception, at the end of 1945.

Zeita did not escape unharmed by her time working on the land. Lifting a very heavy bag of corn, she got a twisted gut and had to be sent to Kensworth hostel in the south of the county, for a month's convalescence. Many land girls sustained injuries through the hard physical work that they had to do, and some of them were injuries which they suffered from throughout their lives.[150]

Vera Jobling (WLA 135018: 11 August 1943 – 18 October 1947)
Vera was born in Thornaby on Tees in Yorkshire and it was whilst working in Stockton on Tees that she first saw some of her previous workmates in Land Army uniform. She decided to join and was sent by train to Bedford, where she was collected, with others, by a lorry. Vera Tate, later to become her best friend, and another new land girl called Lara had also travelled down together on the same train but Vera had not noticed them and was all on her own during the long journey.

Her first hostel was a large country house at Cople, where Mrs Stone, "a dominant woman", was the Warden. "She kept everybody in order. You daren't step out of line." There were over 90 land girls there, from Doncaster, London, Bedfordshire,

Newcastle and elsewhere. They were the first intake, in 1943. The house in Cople, formerly occupied by the Barnard family, owners of Barnard's Bank in Bedford, was a three-storey building that you could not see from the road.

Vera Jobling. *Source: V Barnett*

Her first job was at Godber's market garden at Willington. They grew tomatoes and chrysanthemums (they were allowed to work only 10% of the time on these, in order to sustain the seeds for post-war horticulture). Food was poor, with just horrible cheese sandwiches for their packed lunch. After only a few months, Vera developed appendicitis and after three weeks in Bedford hospital, she was sent home on sick leave for a month.

Later, at Cople hostel, Vera and her friend 'Sandy' (Kathleen) were wrongly blamed for coming back late to the hostel and climbing in through a window and got moved on to other, separate hostels. It was then, after about a year at Cople, where Vera drove a five-ton lorry, that Vera moved to Bolnhurst, where she was very happy for the next three years.

Life in the hutment hostel, after a country house, was extremely rough. There were only oil lamps for light, little in the way of carpeting and a poorly insulated wooden dormitory, with only a few coke stoves for heating. But the physical hardship of life in the huts was made up for by the camaraderie of the land girls there. Numerous life-long friendships were made and a great deal of fun enjoyed. Later she worked regularly at Turnpike Farm, Bolnhurst, which was run for the 'War Ag' by Mr Chandler, and that was where she first met Ben, her husband-to-be.

But life was not all fun. She had an accident to her foot, while ditching, which required a doctor to come out to the hostel to stitch it. On other occasions, when feeling unwell, land girls from Bolnhurst had to cycle to Kimbolton to see a doctor. Vera managed to avoid any further accidents but it was due to luck since there was no training in safety on the farms and many worked with dangerous machinery.

Working in the open air took some getting used to. In the summer they often got sunburnt but could not resist rolling up their dungaree trousers. Vera even remembers one occasion when she took off her blouse. "A bit brazen. Being in a crowd made us do what we did."

'Ponds' cream was the mainstay of women during the war in terms of skin care. She remembered that their mainstays were 'Outdoor Girl' lipstick and 'Californian Poppy' perfume. She went with others to RAF dances at Little Staughton, where a Lancaster Squadron was based, and to American bases at Thurleigh and Chelveston.

Land girl and farmer working in harmony: one of the newly-developed combine harvesters on the move at Kendall's farm in Eyeworth. *Source: BLARS (S Cooney) 2956/97*

The GIs called one of their halls 'Spamerina' (after the popular tinned processed meat, 'Spam'). There were endless supplies of doughnuts and cigarettes. The men there were gentlemen, she recalled, and she went out with one or two. But they could get up to mischief. She remembered, "You daren't hang your undies out at night. The Americans would come and take them. You looked in their huts and they were there, hanging up."

Food was quite good at the hostel to start with. They had a spotless cook, assisted by her daughter, Kathleen. But when those two left, the food got terrible. There were even protests over the semolina puddings.

Although she had not had any training before starting as a land girl, she did have training in lorry driving, given by the 'War Ag'. She was given lessons in Ginn's Yard, in Bedford, two hours a day for four weeks. Five out of six of the land girls undergoing driver training passed the driving test.

After the end of the war she married but worked part-time doing seasonal farm work and as a relief driver for Park Farm, Keysoe. This and Rutter's Farm were owned by the farmer, William Hartop, who employed Ben, her husband.[151]

Bolnhurst hostel 'War Ag' vehicle and driver, Jean Hartley. *Source: V Barnett*

Hedging and ditching. *Source: Antrobus archive. Courtesy of Beds Times*

Ethel Sweenie (WLA 123840: 3 June 1943 – 28 February 1946)

Ethel, originally from East Kilbride, Lanarkshire, had moved down to England with her family in 1942. While living with her aunt in Barnes, she got friendly with some girls in the Land Army and decided to join although, at 16, she was below the 17 years minimum age.

Young women at the age of 17 were less worldly-wise and more sexually ignorant in the 1940s than those in the 21st century. When her mother said to her, before leaving home to join the Land Army, "Don't ever bring trouble back to this house" (presumably referring to getting pregnant), Ethel had no idea what she meant. She was more interested in the arrival of her new uniform. She would dress up in it at 10 or 11 o'clock at night and walk up and down the road in it.

She was driving three-ton lorries by the age of 17. She remembered her driving test, in the Queen's Park area of Bedford, and having to reverse through five-bar gate entrances. After starting at Potters Bar, she was sent to Bedfordshire, to the Bolnhurst hostel but found the first few weeks, in autumn 1943, difficult, since all the other girls had been together for a good period, but she made a good friend, Peggy Deag, of Bedford.

The hostel girls had to get up at 6.30am each morning but Ethel, as a driver, had to get up earlier to fill up the vehicle's radiator with water (it was drained overnight in those days, since there was no anti-freeze).

Ethel felt that the wonderful atmosphere at the Bolnhurst hostel was as a result of most of the girls being so far from home that they had to develop their own social life. When she visited other hostels from time to time, to do driving, she noticed the difference in the degree of friendliness and sociability. She noticed that there were little groups of friends but no collective togetherness. The 'Bolnhurst beauties', as they called themselves, enjoyed excellent camaraderie. "You could have a laugh and a joke in the dining room and everybody joined in."

Everything was shared by the land girls. They were all short of money. By the middle of the war, their pay was one shilling an hour (for a 48-hour week) and 24 shillings were retained by the 'War Ag' for hostel accommodation and food. Her family returned to Scotland from the South East when 'doodle bugs' (German V1 rockets) started falling. Travel home from Bletchley to Scotland by train would take 14 hours during the war, when goods trains and military movements took priority. She was allowed only two free rail vouchers per year.

Land girls had to be in the hostel by 10pm at night, and lights out at 10.30pm. Like most hostels, they did have a wireless, but it frequently ran out of power, when the accumulator ran down and someone had to take the acid battery to be recharged at a local garage. At Bolnhurst, they did not even know that 'Victory in Europe' had been announced until the flares at Thurleigh aerodrome went up. It

Ethel Sweenie (second left) with American servicemen and other land girls at a wartime picnic.
Source: E Wildey

was Ethel who drove the Bolnhurst girls into Bedford for the VE-Day celebrations that night. "Everybody was happy."

The American air force men were very good to them. One American used to visit the hostel to write letters to his wife, asking the girls to add things. The Americans collected them three times a week and served them at their base with lots of decent food, and also brought them fresh fruit at the hostel. They were appalled at the spartan conditions at the hostel. "They thought we were in a 'borstal' because of our hard work and conditions." Ethel, when she first started in the Land Army was housed in a large house in Potters Bar on the main Barnet Road. There was the blue room, the yellow room, et cetera, and conditions were comfortable. Then she was transferred to the huts at Bolnhurst, housing 40 girls in bunk beds in one dormitory hut, with five horrible oil lamps for light and two little coke stoves for heat.

Ethel remembered an outbreak of veruccas, the foot condition, in the hostel. A chiropodist came out to the hostel because quite a few girls had them. Apparently, it came from their feet coming into contact with a sandy soil they had been working on. At other times, girls suffered from conditions brought on by their farm work. While threshing, for example, barley husks could get stuck in the back of their eyes. Ethel had to go to hospital to have a husk removed.

Not all the farmers they worked for, in their 'War Ag' gangs, were sympathetic employers. One farmer in Potton was "not a kind person. He used to spy on us with a pair of binoculars to see if we took any breaks in working." Working conditions were not ideal. There were no toilets, when working out in the fields. There was not even a glass of water. The land girls were given a flask to take out in the fields, but if one got broken, they would not get another one for a year. If their clasp broke on their lunch box, ants would get in to their food.

At Putnoe Farm they were treated totally differently. The farmer's mother let them work indoors when it rained. The land girls also worked with prisoners of war, first the Italians and then with German POWs (never the two together). The Italians had a reputation for laziness but friendliness; the Germans for being conscientious but not necessarily friendly. Needless to say, there were exceptions to disprove the stereotypes. However, Ethel recalled that the Italians they worked with would cheat by moving the sticks which the farmer had laid in order to show the area of potatoes each group had to pick.

The complaint that most land girls made was that often the prisoners of war were better treated than they were. When it rained, prisoners of war were brought inside to work and, usually, land girls would have to continue to work in the rain all day. Prisoners were often better fed, as well. "They were well fed compared with us." There were frequent land girl complaints about stale bread and awful potatoes.

Diets were not just limited by rationing and local food supplies. Cooking was limited by the facilities at Bolnhurst, with just one double–burner stove in the kitchen and one other small stove for the cook and assistant to work with.

Despite the hardships, the shared experience of hostel life made it easier for most land girls to cope with their life than was the case for some isolated land girls on private farms, where the same degree of company and support was absent. Hostel gangs would often spend the day singing together while they travelled to their farms, while they worked in the fields, and when they spent the evening together at their hostel. Usually it was the songs of the day. Often it was popular songs with newly-minted lyrics thought up by the land girls, often about themselves, such as "The Land Army – do or die!": "Don't turn away a Land Army Girl...She may be needed by and by. Every girl in the Land Army, She will do or die." They worked hard and played well.

At the very end of the war, on VJ Day, Ethel recollected, she had gone to 'The Wheatsheaf' pub in Colmworth, which was full of RAF men from Little Staughton, whereas Vera and Ruby had gone up to London for the celebrations.

Ethel left the Land Army after the February 1946 parade in Bedford. Her father had been demobbed and she missed home but after a few weeks she wished she had never left. She never again experienced the social life and togetherness that she enjoyed at Bolnhurst.[152]

These boisterous young women were not necessarily welcome when they visited the local villages. They were young. Many of them smoked. When they came across villagers in the village store, they might come across as knowing everything. They were mainly town and city folk. They stood out from country people because of their use of make-up or their ways. Villagers might resent their noise and laughter. Village girls frequently resented them taking their boys away from them at local dances. They threw caution to the winds, at times. They were in their late teens or early twenties. Their behaviour might have resembled that of students, away from home for the first time.

Sheila Stephens (WLA 192296: 3 March 1948 – 13 August 1949)

Sheila was born in Enfield, Middlesex, and was at school during the Second World War until the age of 16. With shorthand and typing skills she went in for clerical and secretarial work. After two years she decided that she would join the WLA in the last years of its existence, after a friend decided to join and persuaded her. When she went to the Oxford Street, London, recruiting office to join up, her father was amazed: "You've never even held a spade in the garden. You'd better come out and do some digging with me." In addition, she had a fear of animals, even cats and dogs, let alone cows and horses.

Her employer, a doctor, where she worked as the secretary, was disgusted that she would give up a comfortable, office job for work as a farm labourer. He would not speak to her for the two weeks before she left. But Sheila decided that she needed some adventure in her life.

She had already booked a holiday and asked, when signing up, if she would still be able to take it. The woman in the WLA office said, extremely misleadingly, "My dear, you'll find life in the Land Army will be one long holiday." Far from it, reflected Sheila, in retrospect.

She was transferred to Bedfordshire on 19 March 1948. When she caught the bus, with her luggage, to travel to the railway station, the conductor saw her uniform and said, "Hello, love. How long you been in?" Sheila burst into tears and said it was her first day. 11 girls met up at Kings Cross railway station, London. At Bedford Station they were met and taken to Ravensden House training hostel. A 12th girl, Josie Millwood, arrived late the next day and ended up being Sheila's lifelong friend.

Because she was petrified by animals she asked to do arable work but the first job she was given was to clean out a bull's shed, with the bull in it. She was 18 years old. The trainer tossed a mangel in the corner to distract the bull, while they hastily cleaned out the shed. Another job calling for speed was collecting bales of straw from a paddock where there was a nasty ram which delighted in chasing them.

'Milking girls' did milking training but Sheila was allocated to arable training and found herself hedging and ditching in awful weather, and muck spreading. When threshing an old stack of beans, they ended up so black they looked like chimney sweeps. She wrote to her parents but did not dare tell them what it was like. But the girls, mainly from the north of England, were very friendly. Only two were from London.

After this initial training, she moved to Bolnhurst hostel, also in the north of the county, working for the 'War Ag'. This hutment hostel had 40 bunk beds, which were awfully hard but had patchwork quilts, made and donated by Canadian ladies during the war. Sheila's first impression was of the porch area, full of "horrible muddy boots". They did not have any wellingtons, only hard soldiers' boots to start with. Her ankles were red raw, being a town girl and used to shoes rather than boots.

Every morning, during breakfast, the Forewoman came in and called out names, saying which lorry they had to get – 1, 2 or 3 (the van). The land girls were dropped off at various farms locally, and the farmer told them what they had to do for the day, until 5pm. She remembered at one farm sitting on the back of a cutting machine, cutting kale full of frost, where the land girls got showered with ice.

The girls sang songs in the back of the lorries, going to and from work. They would sometimes try to catch up the baker's van, on its round, to buy up what he could provide. They were always hungry. Sheila remembers the time that a farmer's wife took pity on them and took some hot Scottish pancakes to them in the field. The lady later became Sheila's mother-in-law, when she married the farmer's son.

At the end of the day the lorries would then reverse their route and collect the young women. Back at the hostel, there was a rush to get into the ablution block, to the right of the entrance, and be first in to the three baths. They were so desperate they ended up sharing with another, as they got so dirty and sweaty that they needed to have a bath every day. Then there were their clothes to wash in a number of large sinks in the washroom. Hostel life in the evenings was mainly

opposite: Sheila Hope née Stephens in 2003, still able to fit into her short land girl greatcoat, well over fifty years after her post-war service in the WLA. *Photo: S Antrobus*

sitting around the stoves, mending socks and chatting.

There were two cooks at the hostel, Molly and Bridie, from the locality, and a resident Warden. Food at the hostel was awful. All Sheila could remember was endless damson jam and she has never eaten any since her days in the Land Army. If you were late getting up in the morning, there was very little to make sandwiches with for the packed lunch, often just beetroot. If you were lucky, there was some cake.

On Sundays, a lorry would travel around the hostels picking up any girls wishing to attend St Peter's Church in Bedford, which she remembers as 'the Land Army church'. She wrote home to her parents every weekend, with a full diary of events from the week. (Unfortunately, she lost these letters, later in life, when moving house.) One weekend, Sheila's parents came to visit her at the hostel, which was apparently an 'unheard of' happening.

Eventually, Sheila went to work in private employment at Manor Farm, Thurleigh (See Chapter 8: Life for Land Girls on Private Farms).[153]

MILTON ERNEST HOSTEL

A significant number of women who met up and served at Milton Ernest hostel have also stayed in the Bedford area since the war. Between these and other accounts we can begin to get a rounded picture of life for the hostel land girls:

Doreen 'Dawn' Skeggs (WLA 138044: 21 September 1943 – 31 March 1950)
Dawn was born and brought up in London, where her father worked in Smithfield meat market. She was 12 when the war started and she and her brother were evacuated to Finningham, Suffolk, but after a few months, her mother took them home.

They experienced the 'Blitz' (heavy German 'blitzkrieg' bombing of civilians in London, in 1940). They used a brick shelter in the back garden, opposite the outside lavatory, during the air raids, but Father preferred to sleep under the home's kitchen table. They lived in terrifying times – they would stand at the front door watching the 'dog fights' in the sky between German planes and 'our Spitfires' [English planes]. They lived near to Woolwich Docks, one of the key targets for bombing and remembered an incident, one Saturday, when the area was lit up by flames and a lot of her school friends were killed. "It wasn't a pretty sight."

Dawn left school at 14 and late in 1940 their Mother took them to live on a relative's farm near St Albans. Dawn got a job in the tea bar at British Home Stores there. Father came to see them at the weekends. Uniformed servicemen would come in to the store, and she would see badly-scarred RAF officers, whose planes had been brought down in flames.

Early in 1942, Dawn transferred to a British Home Stores in London. She would have like to have joined the WRENS but being too young for the armed forces, falsified her birth certificate – altering 'seven' to 'six' (1926 instead of 1927) as her date of birth – and joined the Women's Land Army, actually aged 16½ . Her mother did not know. She was very good at arithmetic and the WLA would have liked her to join the Timber Corps, measuring trees for felling, but she wanted to work with animals and became a land girl. She was sent her land girl uniform in advance and went dancing at Covent Garden (the theatre now known as the Royal Opera House was converted into a ballroom during the war) and felt like a "top dog".

'Dawn' Skeggs driving land girls out to surrounding farms from Milton Ernest hostel. *Source: D Filby*

She met another young woman called Peggy Davis at Marylebone station in London and they travelled together to Bedford to join the hutment hostel at Milton Ernest. There were land girls there from all over the North Country – Yorkshire, Lancashire, Manchester, and Blackpool. "It was such a change. About five London girls, some Luton girls, about 30 girls from the north. They were a laugh." The mixed social classes and their varying accents caused amusement: "Now you didn't swear at me, did you? Why don't you speak English?"

Most of the young women had to learn on the job with no previous initial training. Some had never ever seen a farm let alone knew what went on in one. Dawn remembered that one such girl, Alice Forrest, straight from Manchester was sent to one of Dawn's farms where the farmer, with no explanation, directed her to go into the cowshed to "go round and wash all the cows ready for milking". He left her to get on with it but was furious when, later, he called in to hear her saying to a cow, "Hold yourself still while I wash yer face!"

Dawn soon learned to drive. A Wing Commander Vernon took her for her test, after training on a fire tender. She became one of the land girls who drove the others out to work on local farms each day in a 'War Ag' lorry, staying to work with the last gang and then driving them back, reversing the route, at the end of the day. She was paid ten shillings (50p) a week extra for this. They drove up to 30 minutes travelling time from the hostel, as far as Cockayne Hatley, Wymington or Radwell. Two, three or more girls were dropped at each farm, according to the requests of the farmers. The land girls were paid by the 'War Ag', which billed the farmers according to the weekly time sheets completed by each land girl and signed by the hostel Forewoman and the farmer.

They also found themselves working with prisoners of war, both Italian and German, on different occasions. Dawn was clear about the differences between them, in her experience. The Germans were "real gentlemen". She worked with one, Hans, who ploughed with a shire horse, with her leading the horse. He had a daughter the same age as Dawn and was very kind to her. The Germans were based at Colesden in a POW camp on the hill.

The Italians were, according to Dawn, different. When land girls needed to relieve themselves (no toilets in the fields), they had to go behind the low hedges surrounding fields. Four or five girls had to go together to keep "guard" so that some Italians POWs did not take advantage of them. She remembered that some "Romeos" amongst them wore hairnets and sang 'O Sole Mio'.

Ethel Eaton (left) and Edith Catchlove, a Forewoman. Ethel was the County Ploughing Champion and won many awards competing against men in Bedfordshire and the adjoining counties. *Source: Antrobus archive, 1946 Bedfordshire WLA souvenir programme*

Some of the work the land girls did was particularly unpleasant such as spraying crops with insecticides. At Cockayne Hatley they sprayed apples on the large Co-operative Wholesale Society orchards. The apples were later picked, graded in warehouses and stored in insulated rooms where they were gassed, to help preserve them. They then had to be washed and kept out 24 hours before they could be eaten.

A Swiss man, about five feet tall, who was the Manager, rode on a horse to inspect their work. Dawn, as a driver/ganger, negotiated with his foreman. When they were once asked to spread dried human manure on some ground, she negotiated rubber gloves and extra pay and refused to work when it was windy.

On one occasion, cow muck was four or five feet deep in a yard, after the cattle had been kept in over winter. It had to be cut in slices first, then forked on to a cart for spreading on the fields. After doing that job, they would sit on the surrounding wall, eating their sandwiches.

Farmer's wives would sometimes bring out jugs of fresh tea as opposed to the usual tea from flasks. Food at the hostel was very limited. Cornflakes and a piece of toast for breakfast. There were endless slices of "rubbery cheese" for sandwiches, which not only didn't suit Dawn but gave her migraine. So all she had to eat, often, was bread and jam and margarine. When it was hot, she used to take just bread and margarine and rub it on her arms to get a tan. There was a hot meal in the evening. She remembers a rather unusual dessert that they were given: prunes with Yorkshire pudding.

If the land girls were near a village, while working on different farms, they would sometime visit a pub during their half-hour midday break and there would be tasty sandwiches there. "They were nectar! Meat off farms, I suppose. A beef sandwich with half a shandy was heaven after cheese." Thanks to the hard work she kept her lovely slim figure.

The land girls would do every job a man would do, some of them very physically demanding. They built straw and hay stacks. They harvested in the traditional way – reaping, stooking, carting, threshing – as opposed to using the latest American 'combine harvester' machines which began to appear on farms, provided by the 'War Ag' depots. Dawn's least favourite job was hoeing: "Most boring job in the world. Up and down. Hated it!" It was a big change for Dawn, working in the countryside as opposed to a big city.

There were still some men on the farms, as well as the owners or tenant farmers themselves: men too old or boys too young to be in the armed forces, those with disabilities such as flat feet, conscientious objectors, and those engaged in other essential war work but who also worked part-time on the farms.

Milton Ernest hostel was very close to Thurleigh aerodrome, as was Charlie Measure's farm, where they often worked. The hostel was one of the landmarks used by pilots to see where they were. The land girls could see the American 'Flying Fortress' bomber planes 'limping home' after their daylight bombing raids over Germany. Quite a few crashed on landing. The land girls would meet the American servicemen in the local pubs, such as 'The Falcon', Bletsoe, 'The Queens Head' and 'The Swan' at Milton Ernest, which Glen Miller would sometimes visit and Dawn remembered seeing one day. (She once had a date with Johnny Desmo, Glen Miller's singer.) The GI servicemen would toast "the boys who didn't get back". They then got drunk. "They were only kids themselves," Dawn remembered.

British servicemen sometimes characterised the American troops as "over-paid, over-sexed and over here" but Dawn remembered them as "Great lads! If you were decent, and they knew you were decent, they didn't try anything on. Some land girls married Americans. After a day's work on the land, you were so tired you only wanted to go to bed – not with them." When she came across an "awkward situation" as a young woman, she used to think, "What would me Mum say? My Mum would kill me."

Not only did the Milton Ernest land girls attend dances at the nearby airfields, they also invited servicemen back to their hostel for the occasional dances. British soldiers came from their billets in Clapham or the barracks at Kempston. The land girls decorated their dining room hut with bales and sheaves of wheat borrowed from a local farm. A local three-piece band of local young men played for them "for a couple of quid" (£2).

Over time, the hard work and the responsibilities of being the post-war Forewoman at the hostel began to tell on her and a doctor recommended a complete break. She was sent for two weeks to the WLA Rest House at a cliff-top hotel in Torquay, in 1948. Not only did she have a valuable rest, she was able to see Olympic sailing in Torbay and meet some of the international sailors.

Some girls took to the life as land girls better than others. Some girls left to get married or to move to another district.

After the war, Dawn continued in the Land Army and took proficiency certificates in farming skills. She was able to use some of those skills on the smallholding she and her husband had, after the WLA ended in 1950. She had been in the Land Army for six and a half years. Despite the hard work, Dawn concluded, "It was a wonderful life...I wish I had those days over again."[154]

'Dawn' Skeggs, in her leisure time, knitting a 'fair isle' sweater for her brother. *Source: D Filby*

Nola Bagley (WLA 126906: 22 June 1943 – 29 December 1945)

Nola joined the WLA with another Brightlingsea, Essex girl, Jean White, and both were sent to a market garden farm at Margaretting, near Chelmsford. Their first job was to hoe, then pick out shoots from tomatoes. Tomato plants stain the hands terribly yellow which is hard to get off and their hands were soon blistered. They had so many varied jobs there that they ached somewhere different every day. They found themselves dabbing Sloan's liniment on them every night and must have reeked of the stuff. Sometimes they felt they were going to die with the pain and discomfort.

Then they were transferred to Bedfordshire to work for the 'War Ag', accommodated in a hutment hostel in Milton Ernest. This was a new way of life for them. 40 young women in their late teens lived together and worked somewhere different every few days, moving on to other farms when the previous job was done. Mostly it was hoeing. Some of the rows were so long they could not see the end of them. They also found themselves pulling mangels and sugar beet, and riddling potatoes with a machine which sorted the good from the bad and the small ones. Harvesting corn involved stooking the sheaves, then, when they were dry, loading them on carts and stacking them. By this time their blisters had burst and healed and turned to hard skin so that they did not hurt any more.

On Thursday nights they had a late night pass from the hostel warden to allow them an evening out in Bedford. They used one of their own trucks for transport. One night when it was very foggy, they found themselves driving up a roadside bank and nearly turning over. Luckily for them, they got it back on the road, although Nola found herself on the driver's, Barbara Watson's, lap at one point. For the rest of the way, two girls walked in front to help guide the lorry.

On another occasion, when they had gone out to a dance and knew they would be back late, they arranged to have one of the windows of the dormitory block left unlocked for them. But when they got back and climbed in through the window, Nola put her foot in a fire water bucket and water went all over the floor. They found themselves running around like mad things, thinking that any minute the Deputy Warden, Miss Stewart, would be after them. Fortunately, nobody came and they eventually dried the floor off and went to bed.

One hot day, Nola decided to leave off her socks and heavy working shoes and set off to work in her sandals. She soon discovered what a big mistake this was. The stubble of the harvest field scratched the skin round her ankles and daisy weed poisoned the raw places which were exposed. She had sore, blistered feet for weeks, which were very painful. She had learned the hard way that one had to cover up, however pleasant the weather.

Towards the end of her time in the WLA, she was working in a threshing gang with three other land girls and two male farm workers. They travelled round with their Northern's threshing machine to the farms which needed them. Each day they changed places around the machine so that one person did not get all the hard or dirty work all the time. They cleared the chaff and cavings from the base of the machine; they pitched sheaves to the man feeding the drum and, at times, were allowed to feed the drum. They really enjoyed the work as a team.

Threshing wheat was the best job. Threshing barley was horrible since it was full of spiky bits which penetrated their clothes if they had not got their drill coat on. Oats were also good to thresh but beans were filthy. They had to cover their hair but still the black dust penetrated their hair, eyes, nose and mouth and they got filthy. They were lucky to have baths and plenty of hot water at the hostel at the end of their day.[155]

Irene Cook (WLA 142624: 20 March 1944 – 14 September 1946)

Irene was unusual in being one of the minority of land girls who, whilst initially working for one independent farmer, was billeted with the 'War Ag' girls in a hostel. When she joined the WLA, aged 17½ years, she was sent to Moulton Agricultural College in Northamptonshire for six weeks' training. She was then placed on a private farm, milking for Mrs Lucas in Shillington. The downside of milking was that you were not entitled to regular weekends off.

Then she was moved to Mr Measure's farm in Thurleigh. Because he could not offer any billet, she was placed at Milton Ernest hostel, where she was known as 'Cookie'. She travelled to work each day on her bicycle. The farm was close to the American air force base at Thurleigh. She naturally attended dances there, with scores of other young women from north Bedfordshire. Their visits to the dances were very carefully controlled. They were collected in 'liberty wagons' (often colloquially known as 'passion wagons'), driven to the base and 'unloaded' directly into the hangar where the dance was taking place. At the end of the dance, their names were called out individually and they walked straight from the dance hall into the truck which had been reversed close to the entrance.

Irene got herself a very nice American boyfriend called Edward, from Pittsburgh, and they used to meet at the guard hut to the aerodrome. He gave her oranges and soap – items which were impossible to get for Britons but which were unrationed to Americans on their bases. Naturally he would get invited to the hostel and he would take doughnuts for the land girls. But he would never visit her at home.

At one time, Irene got ringworm from working with cows and had to be treated at a hospital in London. She was moved to another post.

Although she never worked with the hostel gangs, she maintained her friendship with Milton Ernest 'girls' all her life.[156]

Ann Brodrick (WLA 77088: 4 May 1942 – 14 September 1946)

Ann experienced life both as a hostel land girl and on a private farm. She remembered Milton Ernest hostel as being spartan, particularly the wooden-bottomed bunks, with only thin mattresses, but she never remembered not sleeping. She loved the hard physical work. "Absolutely loved it." She loved being out in the country and the fresh air. "I was desperate to marry a farmer because I wanted to carry on farming."

Some of the work was dreadfully boring, such as hoeing, but it was gang work, so there was the company of other land girls. Threshing took up a lot of time and was awful. She always seemed to be put at the dirty end where the chaff was. There were no masks to wear in those days; all they could do was tie headscarves around their heads. After a day out working, they all tried to get into the limited baths first – there were no showers. Not only was there no heating in the ablution block in winter, there were concrete floors.

Ann Brodrick worked both directly for private farmers and also for the 'War Ag' as a hostel girl before finally settling for life working on a farm where she was treated as one of the family.
Source: A. Haynes

There were two lorries – a Bedford truck and a dilapidated Ford truck and a Hillman van kept at the hostel. The two drivers fought to drive the Bedford vehicle. In the end they took it in turns. 'War Ag' mechanics maintained them. Ann became one of the two main drivers and so took out the hostel girls in one of the hostel lorries, each day, depositing a number at each farm on a particular route and staying and working with the last group. At the end of the day, she collected them all, in reverse order, and returned them to the hostel for their evening meal. They did not travel very far – as far as Melchbourne, Thurleigh or Riseley, usually.

She loved driving. "How many girls of 17 in those days would be taught to drive?" she reflected. It was a great opportunity in the Land Army, which needed its own drivers. She had learned to drive in a 20 foot lorry and remembered the challenge of hill starts.

Gangs were busy with harvesting in the summer and threshing in the winter, with other field work in between, as the season required. Ann also picked up girls in the evening who were doing overtime at harvest time. She would end up with a load of girls and their American GI boyfriends from local airfields in the back, just coming for the ride. They were good fun and attachments were formed, however briefly. The land girls saw the American planes heading off to bomb Germany each day on daylight raids. On their return the pilots would drop different-coloured flares to indicate to ground crew that they had injured or dead on board. The land girls got to know what these meant.

Americans also picked up land girls in their own military vehicles, to take them to dances on their bases. They provided the land girls' main entertainment. She remembered attending a concert at Thurleigh airfield given by Glenn Miller and his band, without realising the significance at the time. There were also dances in Bedford at the Corn Exchange. At other times, the Milton Ernest land girls socialised at 'The Swan', locally, or in her favourite pub, 'The Falcon', where years later former land girls were to hold yearly reunions. During the war, she recollected, rural public houses were suddenly inundated with women in breeches, drinking shandy, who would sit there with a half-pint, all night. "We didn't have any money."

They made their own entertainment at the hostel – "little shindigs". They had a wireless there and Ann loved jitterbugging to American dance band music. They would have their own dances and parties, sometimes with local troops – British and American attending. Mrs Ada Truman and Mrs Violet Sharman ("she was a darling"), from the county head office would visit and be good fun. They were known everywhere by land girls as 'Shar' and 'Tru'. Once they had an ENSA concert party entertaining them at the hostel and, as a fat woman sang, Ann disgraced herself by collapsing in a fit of giggles.

Ann was a very good-looking and slim young woman (she never weighed more than seven stones) and was chosen for a glamour photo with a lamb, the sort that made the Land Army seem a very attractive proposition but presented a totally false impression of the reality of work on farms. A professional photographer took the shot at Cave's farm, Ravensden and the resulting photograph appeared in the national press, in the Sunday Mirror. Just how different was the reality was illustrated by Ann's recollection that one of her boyfriends said to her, on a date, "Ann, your ears are filthy". She had been harvesting and was covered in dust. She insisted on returning to the hostel and washing again.

The daily routine of the hostel was to be out by 7.30am, after breakfast, but as a driver, she had to get up between 6am and 6.30am, so as to check the vehicle for oil and water before starting it up. Ann remembered the food there as "bloody awful" – the same cheese sandwiches every day for a packed lunch, carried out in individual tin boxes, with flasks of tea or cold tea in bottles. Some farmers, and farmers' wives were excellent and supplemented what little food the land girls were given, but others did not. "I think they could have given us something to eat and drink at harvest times." Some of the farmers were a surly lot. She remembered that John Saunder's mother at Clapham gave them rice pudding which was much appreciated.

Sometimes they worked the land around the American airfields and had to go through security checks, because there were bomb dumps there in concrete bays. The Melchbourne estate was a bomb dump and Milton Ernest was the centre of 'hush-hush' work.

Normally they would finish at 5.30pm but during harvest time, when there was double-summer time, it was traditional for tea to be given by the farmers to the workers and they stayed on until 10pm, since it was still light enough to be able to see to bring in the harvest. Horse-drawn carts were still being used, with side extensions to hold the sheaves or corn which were piled high. Straw ricks were then built. They started on the outsides and then bunged the sheaves in the middle, this way and that, so that they stayed up.

Winter found the land girls hedging and ditching. There were older men, who were too old to fight in the war, working on the farms. They were "OK" working with the land girls.

Occasionally, country house owners would "try it on" and ask for land girls to do vegetable work, such as picking asparagus, only to find that they were called upon to sweep leaves and pick daffodils. On such an occasion, Ann asked the butler for a phone, reported the situation and the land girls were removed.

As well as driving a truck, Ann learned to drive a tractor in an intensive course. Following this, she was summoned to a farm in the Dunstable area, but found no tractor in sight. She had been called under false pretences and was expected to peck (cut) thistles all week. Again she found a phone, reported the farmer and was removed the next day. Many land girls with less confidence no doubt suffered such abuses.

Because her home was in Luton, Ann was able to go home at the weekends. Out of her 40 shillings pay, then, she had just 24 shillings, after deductions for the hostel. Her brother, Tony, had "drawn the short straw" and been sent down the mines as a Bevan boy and hated it. Her father was out in Trincomalee, Ceylon (now Sri Lanka) with the Admiralty. Mother coped, as many women left on their own had to cope, during the war.[157]

opposite: Milton Ernest hostel's two lorries were kept in a makeshift straw garage which gave them sufficient shelter in the winter to enable them to start in the morning. When she was not working, it certainly helped if a land girl had her own bicycle to get into the nearest village or even further afield. *Source: D Clark*

Joyce 'Joy' Senior (WLA 144469: 16 May 1944 – 19 March 1946)

Joy was brought up in Batley in West Yorkshire and was a weaver before joining the Land Army. Until then she had always worn wooden clogs on her feet at work because the wool had to be kept damp or it would have broken. In order to escape this very hard work, which was a 'reserved' occupation – making essential uniforms for the air force and army blankets – she pestered her father to sign her application form to enable her to join the Women's Land Army.

She was called up to go to Bedford. No one in the family knew where Bedford was and got a map out on the kitchen table. They started looking in Scotland first. When her uniform arrived it was too big. It was not a good start. She had to use all her ration coupons (and some of her mother's) in order to get fixed up with underclothes and nightdresses for living in a hostel.

On the day she travelled down from Yorkshire, there were 20 other land girls on the train. They were met at the Midland railway station at Bedford and taken to Ravensden House farm for a month's training. She came out 'top of the class' in the courses. She was placed at Milton Ernest hostel, north of Bedford.

She learned to drive a 'War Ag' lorry, with Jack Stewart from Bolnhurst, over four weeks, and took her test, driving down the High Street in Bedford in an Army lorry. The army captain who was testing her arranged a date with her that night at the Granada cinema. She passed!

The first time she took a lorry out, delivering land girls to Oakley and Turvey, she was going up a hill in Oakley when the engine stalled, with 40 girls in the back. They were singing the song, 'She wore a yellow ribbon' at the time. She nearly had a heart attack but managed to double-declutch and got it started again without them knowing. On another occasion, Joy did not quite judge the entrance to the hostel right, on entering with a lorry. She knocked down one of the posts and paid a Mr Marshall to put it back up and keep quiet about it. Later, when caterpillar tractors arrived from the USA, Joy had to demonstrate them to farmers in Rushden.

When the land girls first started their work on the local farms, "Some girls were so tired at the end of each day that they just lay on their beds and we used to wrap them up with a blanket." Joy's job was to get up early, at about five o'clock in the morning, to light the fires in the hostel stoves, then get the van ready. She got an extra five shillings (25p) for doing that.

The hostel's YWCA warden at Milton Ernest at that time – a very large woman – was Mrs Lancaster, who was religious and strict but also very kind. Sometimes, when land girls could not get back in time from Bedford at the weekend, they would stay in the YWCA hotel next to the Granada cinema there, at a charge of one shilling (5p) for bed and breakfast. Mrs Lancaster phoned to check that they actually were there. The Assistant Warden at Milton Ernest was Miss Stewart, who was Jack Stewart's sister. The hostel's cook was called Rhoda. Joy's outstanding memories of the food there were of jam and bread and slab cake. (When at home, her mother would cook rice in batter, to taste like fish, and used paraffin oil to make pastry.) In a Greek restaurant in Bedford, she remembered, whale meat was on the menu at the height of food rationing and she quite enjoyed it.

The nearby American bases were very generous to the land girls, giving them their legs of turkey, since the GIs preferred turkey breasts. Joy soon got herself an American boyfriend, an instructor at Melchbourne, but he developed kidney problems and returned home to the USA where he died. Each Sunday she attended the American Army church, a tin hut at Melchbourne where she remembered the troops attending in full uniform, with rifles, ready to go to France. After the death of her American boyfriend, she was naturally upset and would not go to local dances. A farmer, Mr Mitchell in Wymington, invited her to his nephew's 21st birthday party and she was cajoled by her mates into going and bet ten shillings that she could not get a date there. She did, with a Lancaster bomber flight engineer who had just returned from a POW camp.

Because her home was so far away, like many land girls, she only visited her parents twice a year, when she was allowed free railway passes. But her two brothers, aged 18 and 11, once visited her, staying in the village, at the home of Mrs Purvey, their hostel cleaner.

Joy occupied herself, once, with a spot of sewing, making a bra and pants from an old nightie for a 'Mend and Make Do' exhibition at the Corn Exchange in Bedford. "Could never have worn them," she said. On another occasion, in her spare time, she was roped in to provide another person for the hostel choir. They were to give a concert in Northampton together with 12 girls from each of the other Bedfordshire hostels in a competition against Northamptonshire land girls. The problem was that Joy could not sing, so she had to mime and learn all the words of the songs – 'Rose of England', a Russian song and an American song.

Her only other performance experience was in the Christmas play at the hostel. Mrs Lancaster played Mary in the Nativity play in a nearby village, with a doll as Jesus in the cradle. "She looked as though she was warming her hands on the fire!" Two big girls from Birmingham were the angels and one had a candle. When Joy walked on, the angels were meant to follow. The audience heard, "Wait a minute; the bloody candle's gone out!"

There was one true-life dramatic moment during the war when she was on a stack working with German prisoners of war, in the Sharnbrook area. The older ones just wanted to show photographs of their families but one young German attacked her with a pitchfork, possibly trying to get the keys to the lorry from her.

Mrs Lancaster was Warden at Milton Ernest hostel from 1944 onwards. She had an Assistant Warden to help her and they were responsible for the welfare of the 40 land girls at the hutment hostel. YWCA wardens were appointed to each of the 16 hostels set up to house 'War Ag'-employed land girls. Luton Hoo training farm, at its own [17th] hostel, The Bothy, had a housekeeper responsible for the land girls, both trainees and permanent staff employed on the estate. *Source: D Filby*

Fortunately, another land girl, Mary McGuire, threw him off the stack. He had to be taken to hospital because of his injuries.

On an earlier occasion, when training as a driver with Jack Stewart of the 'War Ag' she had collected German prisoners of war from Tilbury Docks, to take them to their camp. There was always a British soldier with a rifle to guard them, but, according to Joy, with no bullets. She never worked with Italian POWs.

Working with animals on farms sometimes led to land girls contracting their diseases. Joy got ringworm from a cow. The hostel doctor was in Sharnbrook. He gave Joy some of the new M & B (penicillin) tablets but she proved to be allergic to them and "blew up with it". She was sent to a military hospital at Elton Hall for eight weeks to recover.

Joy left the WLA after the 14 February 1946 parade in Bedford. "It was the making of us," she said, reflecting on her land girl days. "I'd never (otherwise) have got away from home."

When she got married, the vicar could not resist saying, "Let Joy be unconfined". She had two children within 18 months.[158]

Mary Pakes (WLA 58931: 16 February 1942 – 16 February 1946)
Mary was born in Luton. When she joined WLA on 16 February 1942 she was working in one of the two large music shops in the town, S. Farmer and Co. The owner had gained two deferrals to her being called up for national service, because it took a long time to train staff in that particular trade and he did not want to lose her, but she wanted to 'do her bit' for the war effort. She was already a part-time member of the Civil Defence and the Red Cross and worked many hours in hospitals. Mother did not want her to be in the armed forces, because she was an only child. So she joined the WLA.

She did not know where she would be sent and was pleased when it turned out to be Milton Ernest in Bedfordshire. This would mean that she would be able to return home at the weekends. Most girls who had been called up were town girls. She felt sorry for the girls from Yorkshire who did not have travel passes home, except for two return rail tickets to anywhere in England, intended for their week's leave and Christmas. Mary did not waste her entitlement to two free rail passes per year: she went with friends, to stay at their homes in Scotland and had a free rail return to Carlisle. The following year she went for a holiday in Cornwall.

She was to be offered no formal training. When the new recruits were met by an open-topped lorry at Bedford railway station, it was bitterly cold and had been snowing. 'War Ag' men were cutting trees down at the time, so her first job was cutting off branches. It was hard work. She and 39 others were the first land girl intake to the Milton Ernest hostel. After work each day they were so tired, they used to sit round the old coke stove and "nodded off".

Then they made an effort and developed a social life. Bedford offered cinemas and dances and concerts. There were first aid courses and a land girl choir to join [the BBC Music Department was in residence in Bedford at that time]. She later took the choir in a lorry to Northampton to give a concert where she played the piano. Jean Tomkins and she both played the piano at the hostel. There were hostel sing-songs and local forces were invited. They occasionally visited Sharnbrook hostel, a large country house, not far away, for a few parties and even had inter-hostel sports competitions towards the end.

The hostel was comprised of specially-built huts. Miss Felicity Taylor of the YWCA was the first warden. "She was lovely, with her corgis and puppies." Eventually she had to give up because the concrete floors upset her legs. After her were various wardens, including Miss Lowe and a Mrs Lancaster (who later moved to America to live with her sister).

Land girls came and went over the years. One Yorkshire girl left early and said she wasn't coming back – she was homesick and an only child. But Mary wrote to her and persuaded her to return and she stayed. It was a caring environment. Mary had never experienced anything like that – communal living with girls from a wide variety of backgrounds, from London, Essex and Yorkshire. Whenever they later had a reunion and met up, "We're so natural with each other, like sisters. Still!"

Contact with the village was limited; there was little time except for visiting the local pub, 'The Queen's Head' in Milton Ernest. and sometimes to 'The Falcon' at Bletsoe. "By the time you'd walked down for a drink, it was time to walk back." They had to be back by ten o'clock at night.

Their uniform had been sent in advance. There was a shortage of greatcoats, so Mary had to provide her own trench coat. She got an overcoat eventually. She had both wellington boots and ordinary leather boots as well. "We were glad of them." Brown brogue shoes for 'walking out'. Dungarees and overall jackets were provided for work.

Not many girls did milking from the hostel. Instead, they went out in gangs to do seasonal work on the local farms. In the summer, especially, there were very long days, harvesting the corn. Threshing was the main occupation through the winter. "You can almost hear the drum going, even today!" Also in the winter – mangels, chopping tops off, going through the awful apparently 'hot' ache of freezing hands – then it was all right. Mary worked a bit with horses, carting then riding them back when the carts were empty.

She was also taught to drive. Until then she had stayed on one farm for a number of weeks. Once she was a driver, she took girls out to various farms and stayed with them during the day on the last 'drop'; then collected them all in the evening.

Like most land girls, she had her share of accidents. She was with two horses, one day, ploughing around a potato clamp (a mound of potatoes covered with soil to protect them from frost) when the machinery got caught up and she was dragged along under the plough. She had to be treated at Bedford Hospital for a chipped cartilage and take a long rest. It was damaged for the rest of her life and has recurred occasionally. No more tennis for Mary. On another occasion, after suffering a second bout of influenza she was granted a two weeks' break at the WLA rest-break house in Torquay. It was very nice weather and she arrived the day before the D-Day landing.

Mary Pakes was the first Forewoman to be appointed at Milton Ernest hostel. *Source: M Smith*

Mary was made Forewoman at the hostel. She had to do a four-week Forewoman's training course, based at Ravensden, and received her certificate in January 1944. The potential forewomen were taken round to see the various jobs done by land girls, including hedging and ditching demonstrations. There was even a trip to a sugar beet factory in Peterborough so they knew what happened to the produce they dug up.

She enjoyed being a Forewoman. She had her own room at the end of the dormitory. They all got on very well together. The only time they got into trouble was at Mr Rawlins' farm at Biddenham. It was very hot and they had been hoeing all day. One girl said, "I can't do any more!" She flopped down, threw away her hoe and they all did the same. They had only been down for a few minutes when the farmer came along, saw them and reported them. But he was very nice afterwards.

Farmers on the whole were very good but did not treat the land girls all that well at the beginning. They did not think they would be up to the job. "We had to prove that we were as good, or nearly as good, as men and that spurred you on!"

Mary remembered that the girls would sit out under the hedges in all weathers to eat their midday sandwiches. Later on, farmers' wives or managers' wives would invite them in and sometimes give them a 'sweet' (a dessert) that they, the farmer's family, were having.

They worked with Italian prisoners of war, for a short spell on a Podington farm. "They did not move very fast but they weren't a problem."

Some hostel land girls, like Betty Gray and Kitty Hollock, moved on to work for private farmers on a permanent contract. Mary still kept in touch with them. Mr Cave, a farmer from Ravensden, asked Mary to work permanently for him but she was enjoying herself too much at Milton Ernest and thought it would be too lonely, and so declined.

Mary felt that most land girls led a better life at the hostels. There was the camaraderie. Private farm billets were usually with farm labourers and their wives and you could never be sure of a welcome. Also, those private farm land girls had to make their own way into Bedford or their nearest town at the weekend whereas hostel girls had their own lorries and drivers.

Mary returned home to Luton on Saturday afternoons [all land girls worked till noon Saturday – a 5½-day week]. The return journey was on Sunday afternoon. She walked from the railway station down Midland Road to the Castle Lane lorry park where a hostel vehicle would collect those who had visited home. On one occasion her mother came over to see Mary but did not recognize her – she was so dirty after a day in the fields.

While at home, she would visit her boyfriend's home in Harpenden. He was a POW in Japan. She had met Eric before the war. There were no letters for a long, long time. Just a few lines to let his people know he was alive.

Before the Americans arrived, Milton Ernest land girls were allowed to play tennis, in the summer, and table-tennis, in the winter, at Milton Ernest Hall. That all stopped when Americans arrived and it became the centre for secret operations. Milton Ernest hostel girls were soon visiting the nearby American air bases for dances, chaperoned, initially, by staff from County Office or the warden from their hostel, but just for the first few times. The Americans were very generous with the land girls. There were trainer planes – 'Chugging Charlies' which operated over the fields where the land girls worked and American pilots used to drop written messages to land girls in the field, for a laugh. Some girls married GIs and Mary always kept in kept in touch with them.

The highlight of her Land Army career was on her last day, 14 February 1946, when she led the four-year armband contingent (rather than her own Milton Ernest contingent, of which she was Forewoman) marching down the High Street, Bedford, past the Princess, leading the entire parade. Land girls, being civilians, weren't included in post-war military parades. She had had to train in how to march, military style, at Kempston Barracks, then march through Radwell, shouting orders. Later that afternoon she was presented with an armband by Princess Elizabeth (the present Queen) in the Corn Exchange.

Eric, her fiancé, was one of the last POWs to return in 1945. The British

Mary Pakes led the 'four-year' contingent at the head of the WLA parade, Bedford, 14 February 1946, seen here passing St Paul's Square. *Source: Antrobus archive. Courtesy of Beds Times*

government arranged for them to return home via Manilla and across the USA, so that there was time to feed them up. They married in 1947 (the same year as Queen Elizabeth II – they had a letter from the Queen and Prince Philip, commemorating their Golden Wedding Anniversary on 8 April 1997, signed 'Elizabeth and Philip').

Eric's people had a farm where they bred Clumber spaniels. Mary and he lived there with them for the first years of their married life. After leaving the Land Army she was hoping to be a secretary to a farmer, using her Land Army experience and her previously-learned shorthand and typing skills. However, Arthur Davies, who knew her from her time in Farmer's music shop, asked her to be his secretary. He was both a seed merchant, covering Luton and Hitchin markets, and was the Musical Director/Conductor of the famous Luton Girls Choir, so the job was very varied.

Looking back on her Land Army experience, Mary concluded, "I wouldn't have missed it for the world. Although there was a war on."[159]

Betty Gray (WLA 59345: 20 December 1941 – 18 August 1948)

Betty, from Luton, was 17 when the war started and her father expected her to join him at Kent's factory, making meters, but she did not fancy factory work. Since a child she had spent summer holidays with her aunt in the countryside near Harlington and had always had a lot to do with animals and gardening. She decided to join the Land Army. She was sent to the Milton Ernest hostel, together with her school friend, Jean Tomkins. They were not given any initial training but were set to, as their first job, sorting rotting potatoes in a field, looking for good ones. She went on to do jobs such as hedging.

Her main friend at Milton Ernest was Elsie Howard from Dagenham. She used to take her home to Luton at the weekend because Elsie did not get to go home much. Later in life, Betty was to make Elsie's wedding dress for her.

Working clothes were washed by a local laundry for the land girls but they had to wash their own clothes. Betty took hers home to Mum – one lot one week, another the other week.

She liked all the work as a land girl but was something of a shy girl and did not relish the forced companionship of hostel life. Americans invited them to dances at nearby airfields but Betty did not go and when the land girls held dances at Milton Ernest hostel, Betty chose to work in the kitchen and serve the tea. "I wasn't one to mix very much. I was very shy. I was a bit on the plump side and, I'm afraid, at one place I worked at somebody used to make fun of me and it got to me. I decided to move to work on a private farm nearer to home." (see Chapter 8)

Betty was one of those land girls who had an accident while farming which left her with a life-long disability. She tore one of her ankles badly and had to have it strapped up for six months. Gradually, throughout her life, it got weaker and eventually, for over 30 years, she had to wear a calliper.

Despite having left the hostel at Milton Ernest and moved into private farming, she kept in touch with Mary Pakes, Jean Tomkins and Terry Goodwin throughout her life.[160]

Kathleen Hopkins (WLA 127178: 26 July 1943 – 30 March 1946)

Kathleen was raised in Luton and left school at 14, just before the war started. She worked in millinery and then in a grocery shop. From the age of 16, in 1941, she also did Civil Defence work, three nights a week, at the Old Police Station. A friend of hers joined the WLA and persuaded Kathleen to join when she was 18. She was placed at Milton Ernest hostel and remembered Miss Lowe, the Warden – "a very gentle person" – showing her round. Miss Stewart, Assistant Warden, had a room at the end of their dormitory and "laid the law down" throughout Kathleen's period there. Furniture was minimal, with a slim-line wardrobe shared by two girls, one chair and a little mat by the side of the bunk. There were just two army blankets to keep them warm in bed. Rhoda, a girl from the village used to wake them up in the morning with a school bell. "Come on, you girls. It's time you were up."

There was no initial training before joining the hostel. Kathleen's first job was mucking out a pig sty, then muck spreading. "You had to be careful you didn't get it down your wellies." She discovered that it was hard work on the land. In bad weather, they would sometimes be given indoor work such as plucking poultry in sheds, which she found horrible.

The hostel girls travelled out to farms in Stagsden, Felmersham, Turvey and all round the north-west of the county, two, three or four girls being dropped off at each farm to do various jobs. When she was on threshing gangs, she hated the dust. With only four baths for 40 girls, "You had to grab a bath as soon as you could." Some shared a bath as a way of getting a wash earlier and raising the level above the five inches of water they were allowed during the war.

Food was very limited at the hostel. One morning they each had one sausage in the middle of a large dinner plate. "Why on earth couldn't they put it on a smaller plate..." she commented. They each had a tin sandwich box with a handle to take out into the fields. There was no paper in which to wrap the sandwiches. Four pieces of bread were cut in half. 'Filling' for sandwiches was cheese or spam or jam, now and again but not very often. "If you were lucky and worked on a good farm, the farmer's wife used to come out with a can

'Lunch' sketch of land girl eating sandwiches and reading, drawn by fellow Bedfordshire land girl, Evelyn Shambley, for the 1946 Bedfordshire WLA Calendar. This also featured a post-war poem by Rose Perritt from Cople hostel. [See appendices for the poem.] *Source: Antrobus archive. Courtesy of E Wildey*

of tea and perhaps a few little cakes," especially at Dollimore's farm at Turvey.

Farmers were not too bad; some were better than others. They used to use sacks to cover themselves in rainy weather. The only other men left on farms were men too old to join the fighting forces. Italian prisoners of war sometimes joined them on threshing gangs.

At the hostel there were sing-songs and walks round the village in the evening. Social life usually revolved around the 'Queen's Head' public house in the village, where she would have a glass of cider. She would cycle there on Saturday afternoons. The only thing that worried the girls was when the next dance was coming up. There were village dances in Clapham, where they might meet some American servicemen. The GIs would also visit the hostel to see girls they were 'chatting up'. Kathleen was never interested in being a 'GI bride' but the Preator sisters at the hostel, Sylvia and Myra, both married Americans eventually.[161]

In Bedford, they would attend dances at the Corn Exchange on Thursdays when they had a late night pass, and Kathleen went out a few times with the pianist from the 'Embassy Band'. On Sundays at the Corn Exchange there were concerts for the armed forces and the land girls also attended. Kathleen attended concerts by Glen Miller and his Orchestra. Then there were sailors from Henlow Fleet Air Arm camp, soldiers from Kempston barracks and airmen from Cardington camp. Some land girls used to have autograph books and collect men's autographs. Kathleen still has some.

They were allowed a late-night pass (for after the usual 10pm curfew). If they missed the last truck back to the hostel, they would have to walk five miles back, in the 'blackout', unless they could hitch a lift. They then had to be let in through the dormitory window by a friend, preferably without the Assistant Warden hearing them. If they were caught, they might be banned for a few weeks from further late passes.

Kathleen took part in the great WLA parade in Bedford on 14 February 1946, as part of the Milton Ernest contingent. Mary Pakes, their Forewoman, had trained them in marching ready for the event. The RAF band led them as they marched down the High Street, past Princess Elizabeth. Later, the Corn Exchange was jam-packed with land girls for presentations and a tea.

Kathleen was demobbed a month later and got herself a job in Luton. She met her husband at the George Hotel there, while dancing. They married in 1949 and had 48 years together.

Looking back on her WLA experience, she reflected that it was "A great time. I'd do it all again. Hard work but I really enjoyed it. Enjoyed meeting people. We were so concerned with one another. It was like one big happy family...we keep in touch."[162]

Joan Wilding (WLA 17219: 24 June 1946 – 29 October 1948)

Joan was one of those teenagers who were seduced into joining the WLA by the government's advertising posters showing a young lady enjoying the sunshine and delights of the beautiful English countryside. She also persuaded her best friend, Celia Holt who lived next door, to join up with her. They had attended the same school in Manchester and did everything together. They were transferred from Lancashire to Bedfordshire and placed in employment by the 'War Ag' at Milton Ernest hostel.

One of her abiding memories was of the food, or lack of it. "We were always hungry. Breakfast and the evening meal were provided at the hostel and we were given a packed lunch for our mid-day meal. This was usually two slices of bread and 'marg', sometimes with meat but very often without any filling, a thin slice of cake and sometimes an apple. We looked forward to working on a farm where we were working with vegetables when we could augment our meal with raw carrots, turnip or swedes. We really appreciated the chance to harvest peas and particularly apples when we worked in the Cockayne Hatley orchards."

On one of the farms where they worked there were two very large Shire horses. One of them, Beryl, a lovely silver grey, became very attached to Joan. She was 'her' horse and as soon as Joan was dropped off the Bedford lorry at the gate the horse would gallop across the field to meet her for petting and cuddling. Joan rode her often and worked with her, ploughing and doing other work around the farm. On other farms Joan would drive the Massey Harris tractors but it was never as enjoyable as working with Beryl.

In the fields of that particular farm they came across a dilapidated house occupied by an old man who seemed to live the life of a hermit. It was extremely untidy and dirty inside but the land girls would be invited in to get warm. But even though they often had a raging thirst, they declined the opportunity to make a brew, once they caught sight of his stained pots and cups He had no bed, just one old chair in which he slept. When the land girls finally left, he gave Joan a bible with a lovely brass clasp, probably the most precious possession he had.

Another example of kindness was when an old farm hand with whom Joan had worked slipped a note in her hand as she left. He had put two 'threepenny bits' (value 2½p) in it for 'two cups of coffee' in Sandy on the way back to the billet. Joan still has the note and the two 'three-penny bits', which she saved. The note was signed 'A token of thanks for driving horse. I am yours. Sincerely, Beryl.'

The land girls regularly worked with prisoners of war, both Italians and Germans. Fraternisation was not officially allowed during the war but Celia, Joan's friend, became romantically attached to one of the German POWs in this post-war period, spending as much time with him as she could. (See Celia Holt's memoir, below.)

They also worked with prisoners from Bedford jail at times. One of them, a rather handsome lad, left a note for Joan after his last visit, promising to come back and marry her. Joan felt that was really something to look forward to – engagement and marriage to an ex-conman!

Working during the very severe winter of 1946–47 was horrendous but they had to continue. They sometimes worked knee deep in snow, which filled their wellingtons. Chillblains and frost-bite were commonplace. They had to pick Brussels sprouts with their bare hands because gloves were useless for that job, in those conditions.

After a day's work in the fields, their Bedford lorry would arrive to take them back to their Milton Ernest hostel. There was always a fight to be first on in order to get the seats next to the tailgate, at the back. The first off would be the first to the ablutions block and the hot water in the limited number of baths. It was not uncommon for two or even three girls to share a bath in order to thaw out. It was so cold in the winter that sometimes girls would even miss the evening meal in order to stay in the bath to keep warm.

But when the weather got warmer and they were in a happier mood, the girls would sing in the back of the lorry on their way to and from the hostel, even when they travelled through Bedford. Perhaps the singing was too loud, too bold or too bawdy on some occasions as they were banned, in the end, due to complaints by some of the more respectable inhabitants of the town.

The weekly entertainment which Joan looked forward to was the Saturday night dance at the Corn Exchange in Bedford where the attraction lay in the RAF boys stationed at Cardington. Romance was difficult and almost non-existent, if only because the land girls had to ensure that did not miss their lorry taking them back to Milton Ernest. If they did miss it, the late night bus only went as far in Milton Ernest as the 'Swan' public house. From there they were faced with a terrifyingly long walk down pitch black country lanes to the hostel. "You only missed it once," Joan remembered. "Never again!"

The hostel girls were from a broad cross section of society and from varying regions but "the ones who gave us the best time were undoubtedly the 'Scousers' [from Liverpool], of which there were four or five. They really kept us going and made life a little more pleasant."[163]

LAND GIRLS MARRY AMERICAN SERVICEMEN

With thousands of young American servicemen in north Bedfordshire from 1942 through to 1945, it was not surprising that there were frequent romances and relationships between land girls (as well as other young women in the county) and attractive GIs. Most romances were short-lived or casual but for some, these romances led to engagement and even marriage. From just one station alone, Thurleigh airfield – 'Station 111' – there were 141 marriages between American men and English women.[164]

Myra Preater (WLA 144338: 15 May 1944 – 18 April 1946) from Milton Ernest hostel married an American and left for America as Mrs Trulock, a GI bride. Her sister
Sylvia Preater (WLA 152508: 18 December 1944 – 18 April 1946) also fell in love with an American, Gerry Wiley, a B 17 pilot from Texas and they got engaged. But she couldn't bear to leave England. He returned home to the United States and they corresponded but the relationship petered out. Then, almost 30 years later, after

Eileen Tomlins, a Sharnbrook hostel land girl, marries Andrew Pollack, an American serviceman from Pennsylvania. After Eileen moved there to join her husband she was not able to return to England until her mother died in 1962. *Source: A Faulkner*

both had been married then divorced, they ended up meeting, falling in love again and marrying. They lived in Texas for ten years then moved to England to spend their last days together, happily married, in the Cotswolds.[165]

Peggy 'Shirley' Richardson (WLA 51548: 21 August 1941 – 16 April 1945), from Bedford, joined the WLA aged 16, in the autumn of 1941, having lied about her age. She trained at Luton Hoo, then worked for the 'War Ag', based at the Potton hostel. She loved ploughing with horses, which she said were big but gentle. She was only five feet, one and half inches tall, but was proud throughout her life of the muscles in her forearms, which she said she gained from hand milking and from loading hay and threshing. She went by the name of 'Shirley' because there were a couple more named 'Peggy' in her hostel and she loved the child film star Shirley Temple.

Rinaldo Di Paul was an American of Italian background from Philadelphia and over here with the American 8th Army Air Force, based at Little Staughton. On furloughs he went with other GIs into Potton to go to the dances there and met Peggy. He took her to see the large planes he worked on as a mechanic. He was quite a comedian and won over Peggy. They married on 10 February 1945 at St Joseph's Roman Catholic Church, Bedford. She resigned from the WLA on 4 April 1945 as she was pregnant with her son Parris. She remembered having to put her arms out in front of her to protect her stomach whilst attending the VE-Day celebrations in Bedford at the end of the war in Europe. Her son was born at what is now De Parys Hotel, Bedford, on 27 November 1945.

Rinaldo was obliged to leave for the USA in February 1946, leaving Peggy and her son behind but, as a war bride, she was able to sail on the liner Queen Mary for New York on 17 April 1946 so as to join him in Philadelphia (one of 3,000 war brides). They lived the rest of their life together in America.[166]

Peggy Davis (WLA 132638: 28 July 1943 – 31 August 1945)
Peggy came from Luton and joined the WLA in August 1943. She was placed at Milton Ernest hostel as a 'War Ag' land girl. She worked for two years at Manor Farm, adjacent to Thurleigh airfield. It was in Milton Ernest's village pub, 'The Swan', that 'this pretty, bronzed and healthy young lady melted Joe's heart'. 'Joe' (as everyone called him) was in fact Walter Albertson, a member of the ground crew who helped keep the American B-29 bomber planes airborne on their relentless daytime raids on wartime Germany. He had come over to England in the Queen Elizabeth liner with 17,300 other troops and had arrived at Thurleigh on 6 September 1942.

Peggy and Joe fell in love and were married at Christ Church, Luton, on 14 July

1945, two weeks before Joe was posted back to America, since the war was now over. Peggy had to wait for eight months before she was able to join him in New York on 1 March 1946. Joe left the forces after the war but was called up as a Reservist to take part in the war in Korea. He finally left the armed services in September 1967 and on 9 October of that year, they returned to England where they were to spend the rest of their life together, first living in Bedfordshire and finally near Ely.[167]

Peggy Davis marries 'Joe' Albertson, 14 July 1945 in Luton.
Source: P Albertson

RELATIONSHIPS WITH POWS

Less frequently there were relationships between English land girls and either Italian or German prisoners of war. Fraternisation, as it was called, was not just frowned on but would provoke hostile reactions during the war from most British people, for obvious reasons. The WLA HQ warned land girls in 'Headquarter's Notes' in March 1943 of the dangers of being 'over-friendly' when working, for instance, with Italian prisoners of war : "...there is a world of difference between courteous behaviour and foolish overfriendliness...friendship will only lead to embarrassment and unhappiness".[168]

LAND GIRL MARRIES GERMAN POW

Celia Holt (WLA 172162: 24 June 1946 – 18 October 1948)
Celia joined the WLA in the summer of 1946, with Joan Wilding, and both were transferred from Lancashire to Milton Ernest hostel. They found themselves working for long periods in the apple orchards of Cockayne Hatley, pruning then harvesting apples from thousands of trees. It was here that Celia first met Harry Müller, a German POW. The summer was hot and the land girls rubbed Vaseline

Celia Holt *Source: C Müller*

on themselves, thinking it would give them a good tan. The only colouring they got was from the dirt and dust which stuck to them. Then the German POWs, who had been potato picking in a nearby field, appeared and began good-natured banter to the effect of "Do you call that work?"

Harry was 19 and Celia 17 and over the next few weeks Celia and he got to see each other, while working, and got very friendly. Post-war, German POWs were allowed to travel within five miles of their camp and Celia and Harry decided to meet up privately in the Tempsford area, well away from prying eyes. No one knew about their meetings. But after a few weeks, Harry brought the news that the POWs were going to be moved away. A few other land girls had become friendly with German POWs and the news of imminent separation was shocking.

Fortunately for them, the move was cancelled but eventually the time came for the POWs to be repatriated to Germany. Harry got permission to stay for a while and work on the estate of Sir Malcolm Stewart at Hatley and was billeted with his foreman, John Norman and his wife Barbara. Celia and Harry got engaged and when Celia discovered she was pregnant they married and she left the WLA.

The marriage ceremony took place in Manchester and, because Harry was a German ex-POW, the church was packed out with people curious to "see a German". Celia was determined to join Harry in Germany and start a new life together but, at first, only Harry was allowed to enter occupied Germany. It was heartbreaking for Celia but Harry began the long process of gaining authority for Celia to join him.

It was on 29 January 1949 that Celia left England for Frankfurt in Germany. She did not know how she had plucked up the courage to go through with it. The journey was two days' long and difficult and she was treated as a displaced person. She was only 19 years old, pregnant and found herself in a strange country where she did not speak the language and was regarded as one of the enemy. At first, it was very lonely, with Harry out at work all day, but then she got herself an office job with Americans there, when Harry's father offered to look after their son, Johnny. Gradually she picked up the German language. Later they had a daughter. Harry died in 1985 and Celia remained in Germany, as a widow, and had four grandchildren. She kept in touch with Joan Wilding over the years and they visited each other.[169]

The following accounts tell of the experiences of young women in other Bedfordshire hostels, at Cople, Aspley Guise, Clifton, Toddington, Silsoe, Whipsnade, Kensworth, Leighton Buzzard, 'Chimney Corner' near Houghton Conquest, Ravensden, and Hulcote Moors:

COPLE HOUSE HOSTEL

M.A. 'Jacqueline' Hindle (WLA 180818: 18 April 1947 – 6 August 1949)

In 1945 Jacqueline saw a Women's Land Army poster as she was walking on her way to work in a factory, down Blackburn Road in Accrington, Lancashire, and decided she would join, there and then. She visited the local Labour Exchange to get information and applied.

After a medical examination in Preston, she was told she was too short (she was only five feet tall) and was only just 17, when 17½ was the approved minimum age for entry to the WLA. She argued her case to her interviewer: "Nelson was only small and look what he did" and she was signed up. Only then did she tell her father and her grandmother, whom she knew would not approve (her mother had died when Jackie was three years old and she had been brought up by her grandmother). It was near the end of the war and, with her two brothers in the army, she felt a bit lonely at home. She also wanted to 'do her bit' for the country while she could.

Her WLA uniform arrived in a kit bag one Saturday afternoon and she was informed she was to start in two weeks' time. She tried on her uniform and showed her pals who immediately wanted to join, themselves, but their mothers would not let them.

Her father had given way, reluctantly, and when he saw her off at Accrington railway station, he gave her a large white £5 note, in case she got into trouble and needed to come home. She joined the train with about 20 others from Liverpool, Morecambe and other parts of Lancashire and ended up at the hostel at Cople, outside Bedford, on the road to Sandy. "It was idyllic, coming from Lancashire – you know, all soot and grime – then going down there, with its lovely thatched cottages."

It was her first time away from home and sleeping in a strange bed. She was shy and undressed under her blankets because she had never had to share a bedroom before. She had been learning to play the ukulele, which her father had bought her, but the hostel Warden made her go outside and sit in a field, well away, when she wanted to play it. Out of the ten girls in her room, four were called Mary (her first name) so she adopted her confirmation name, which she preferred, of Jacqueline. Despite that, because she was the only one from 'the North' they nicknamed her 'Enoch' because of her Lancashire accent. Enoch was the name of a comedian who was well-known at that time through a radio show 'Over the Garden Wall'.

Jacqueline started by trying to milk cows but after two weeks was placed on a market garden near Sandy. Here she helped grow tobacco in the greenhouses, as well as the salad crops – tomatoes and cucumbers. There were fields full of lettuces, which she had to hoe manually. When a motorised cultivator was introduced she had a go but accidentally cut up a field full of lettuces and was banned from doing it again, by the farmer.

Gangs of girls were sent out to work on local farms and market gardens in the Cople and Moggerhanger area, cutting cabbage, picking sprouts in the winter, pulling onions and picking potatoes. Some of the work was back-breaking, especially at threshing time.

German prisoners of war worked with the land girls and, later, some of the local girls, including land girls, married them, especially when, after the war,

Cople House land girls picking peas. *Source: F Wallis*

Land girls harvesting onions, with Mr Cook, in a field between Moggerhanger and Sandy. *Source: B Hills*

some of the German young men wanted to stay in Britain. One of the German POWs she worked with was Hans, who helped her when working with horses. He later married Daisy May, a land girl from Birmingham.

Jacqueline, being short, had to stand on a box even to put the workhorses' halters on and get them ready in the reins, to handle them. There were two big shire horses, which she used for ploughing.

Jacqueline got to like hostel life, with plenty going on after work and even occasional coach trips to Southend. She remembers that they always listened to the comedy programme, ITMA (It's That Man Again, starring Tommy Handley) on Sunday afternoons and other BBC radio programmes.

In their spare time, some evenings, they walked to 'The Five Bells' public house, where they met 'RAF boys' (pilots and ground crew) from RAF Henlow and RAF Cardington and drank lemonade, since the younger ones were not allowed to drink alcohol. It was there that she met her husband-to-be, Arthur, whom she married after she left the Land Army in 1950. They rented Potton House in nearby Potton.

Reflecting on her days in the WLA she concluded, "It was an idyllic time for me, because I lived in a lovely place, with lovely friends and people. You couldn't want for anything more."[170]

Elizabeth 'Liz' Day (WLA 36558: 9 November 1940 – 30 November 1950)

The coming together of girls from both north and south in the country led to some social difficulties at hostels. Liz noted that girls from the north did not care for the girls from the south at first but when they got used to each other it was all right. "They (those from the North) were some of the best…(but) they said we spoke 'too posh', like the BBC…" She noticed how well the northern urban girls got on together in hostels and reflected that it was probably their experience of working in mills and factories. They much preferred the gang work life of the hostel land girls rather than the often lonely and isolated life and work of those working on independent farms.

Liz was 27 on joining and had had considerable earlier farming experience.[171] She was given specific responsibilities whilst being billeted at Cople House hostel, where she had her own room. Before that, there was a short course at the training farm at Ravensden. She remembers that, as part of it, they went on a visit to see a sugar beet factory in Peterborough. Later, one of her more unusual jobs was taking any land girls who had 'nits' (head lice) into Bedford for treatment. She remembered one such trip to the cleansing station in the bad winter of 1947.

She recollected that, at one time, she was responsible for a gang of schoolgirls from Bedford High School who were allowed to work for a few weeks in the fields during term time, helping to harvest tomatoes from a seven acre site. Miss Westaway, the Headmistress, was not going to let them work near to men where they might hear bad language and she would sometimes come out in her car to keep an eye on them. Quite a lot of local women also did seasonal work on local farms and market gardens at harvest time.

Another of Liz's responsibilities for the 'War Ag' was to go round to every hostel in the county and encourage land girls to grow their own vegetables. At the requisitioned country houses at Cople, Ravensden, Kensworth and Silsoe their gardeners were able to stay on. "It was very good where a house was taken over and a gardener left – he knew what to do. But it was a job to make him realize it was tons of cabbages you wanted, not a nice bed of asparagus." 'Chimney Corner' hutment hostel did not have any garden but the hostel at Milton Ernest and Leighton Buzzard did. She remembered Leighton Buzzard as having "a lovely bit of ground there", producing excellent onions. She worked a lot with Mr Randall, the 'War Ag' Horticultural Officer.

The problem was that at the hutment hostels you could not get the labour to do voluntary gardening. Land girls who had spent hours labouring in the fields were not inclined to spend even more time in the evenings and at weekends tending to a hostel garden, despite the need to be as self-sufficient in food as possible. Sometimes, if a girl was not very well, the doctor would say, "Give her some light

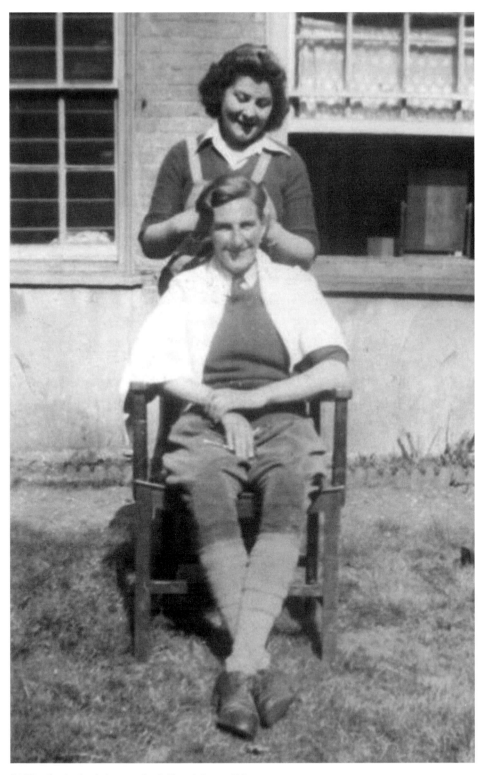

'Liz' Day having her hair cut at Cople Hostel. *Source: E Day*

A small garden in front of Milton Ernest hostel, post-war. The huts have been renovated with a 'lick of paint'.
Source: D Filby

jobs in the garden".

Liz made the most of her time in Bedford during the war, when the BBC Music Department was resident in the town. "I used to cycle in to symphony concerts and hoped that 'Jerry' [German] planes didn't come over." She remembered the conductors – Sir Adrian Boult and Dr (later, Sir) Malcolm Sargent. Speaking of the latter, "I remember his conducting 'The Wasps' [by Vaughan Williams]. He looked so nice – he was a dapper man – a very thin waist – I remember looking at him and thinking of wasps."

The highlight of Liz's personal time in the WLA was when, at Cople Hostel, there was a visit by the Duchess of Gloucester to inspect the land girls. She did not know until the day, but she had been chosen to present of a basket of tomatoes, eggs and a huge bunch of snowdrops and aconites, picked from the hostel garden. Her fellow land girls said, "For goodness sake speak up. We can never hear what anybody says." And during her interview with the author, although it was recollecting a time some 60 years before, she raised her voice and enunciated perfectly her speech, "Your Royal Highness…"

In the Bedford parade of 1946, Liz drove a tractor down the High Street, past Princess Elizabeth. Later, the princess opened an exhibition of agricultural works and handicrafts. Luton Museum had loaned some ancient items of agricultural implements and Liz's father had to be called upon to identify some of these rare items, for labelling.

Rather than being demobilised, as the majority of Bedfordshire land girls were after the February 1946 parade, Liz decided to stay on in the WLA, post-war. She transferred to horticulture, where the work was somewhat lighter than general farm work, since she was quite a small person. She worked briefly with gangs doing experimental work with Unilever at Colworth but then she ended as a 'groundsman' at the women's physical education teacher training college in Bedford. She learned the specialist skills from Will Rogers, the groundsman at the High School, Bedford. She liked playing hockey and cricket, herself, and at the interview for the job said, "I'm only used to grass as cattle fodder but I do know what I like to play on." (She was to stay on at the college for 30 years. A well-travelled representative from Fisons, who knew all the leading groundsmen, once pointed out to her that she was the only woman head 'groundsman' in the country.)

In 1947 Liz took four WLA proficiency tests and gained three distinctions (93% in General Farm Work; 96% in Outdoor Garden and Glasshouse Work; 100% in Market Garden and Fieldwork). The only reason she did not gain a distinction in Milking and Dairy Work was that she had not done any milking for years and the cow "wouldn't let it [the milk] down".

Because of her interest in agriculture she had already done a correspondence course on 'Elements of Agriculture' in 1944, conducted by the College of Estate Management. At the end of the war, she was one of the fortunate ones who got a grant to do a full-time course in horticulture for which she got paid both her wages and her fees (this and the donation of £150,000 to the WLA Benevolent Fund were the only token gestures made by the government following Lady Denman's – Honorary Director of WLA – resignation in 1945 over the failure to offer post-war gratuities to land girls). Her course was from 9 October 1947 to 27 August 1948 at the Kent Horticultural Institute at Swanley.

It was while she was there that she heard that she had been awarded the British Empire Medal for services to the WLA. The letter notifying her was in an envelope marked 'Prime Minister' and informed her that she was not to say anything to anyone for three weeks. The letter was signed 'George Rex' [King George VI]. "I was tickled pink getting a letter from 'George'." Once the news was out, she

By this personal message I wish to express to you

Elizabeth Mary Blair Day

my appreciation of your loyal and devoted service
as a member of the Women's Land Army from
9th November, 1940 *to* 30th November, 1950
Your unsparing efforts at a time when the victory
of our cause depended on the utmost use of the
resources of our land have earned for you the
country's gratitude.

Elizabeth R

Liz Day received a copy of Queen Elizabeth's congratulatory certificate after ten years' service with the WLA in Bedfordshire. Only 31 members nationally were decorated for distinguished service. Liz Day and Georgina Gray were the only two Bedfordshire land girls to be awarded medals for their outstanding service to the WLA service. Each was awarded the British Empire Medal. Not until 2008 did every surviving member of the WLA have the opportunity to receive a WLA Veteran's Badge. *Source: Antrobus archive*

was ribbed by all her fellow students at Swanley who came up with their own rude abbreviations as alternatives to BEM. They wrote 'NBG' on her dormitory door, standing for "No Bloody Good" (but only in jest). Her brother wanted to know what that made them (the family).

Liz never wore her decoration for any special occasion, yet she was only one of two land girls who were honoured in this way in the county in the 1940s. The other recipient of the BEM in Bedfordshire was Georgina Gray in January 1947. When Liz left the WLA in November 1950 she had served for ten years, although she was never awarded the special ten year armband. She did receive a congratulatory certificate from Queen Elizabeth, who was royal patron of the WLA and felt that land girls had not been treated well by the government after their wartime service.

Her Land Army socks, Liz said, lasted her for a long while afterwards.[172]

ASPLEY GUISE HOSTEL

Frances 'Frankie' Guttridge (WLA 161896 27 October 1945 – 18 September 1947)

Frankie was evacuated during the war from Lewisham, London, to Hastings, then to Wales, and finally to Daventry, Northamptonshire. She loved life in the countryside and so joined the post-war Land Army, aged 18, after a brief spell as a clerk at Lewisham Town Hall.

After working on private farms at Potton and a brief spell at the 'Chimney Corner' hostel, when she learned to drive, she was posted to The Holt, a former manor house in the centre of Aspley Guise, which became a new WLA hostel for the post-war period, 1946 –48.

She eventually became a Forewoman there and shared a bedroom with Dora, a driver who took out the mobile gang to surrounding farms each day. Among other places, including market gardens, she worked at Salford Water Mill with Fred Bass, who managed it. She remembered farmers delivering sacks of corn with horse and cart. They sometimes worked in the fields with prisoners of war. The Italians were friendly but Frankie found that some of the Germans were sullen and rude.

The 'Anchor' pub, across the square from the hostel, was very convenient for the hostel land girls. There was a cinema in Bletchley and there were also socials and dances in the Aspley Parish Hall. Local girls accused the land girls of 'stealing' their boys. At the weekends and on Thursday evenings they travelled to Cranfield, Cardington or Bedford for dances. Land girls were not officially allowed to give lifts to men in their 'War Ag' trucks but they got round it by giving their boyfriends headscarves to wear when being given lifts to a dance, so that they looked like girls in the back. Joan Taylor attended a fancy dress dance in Bedford as 'The Ghost of Aspley Guise'.[173]

Some Saturday afternoons, Frankie would hitch a lift home to London, along the A5 (Watling Street) because she could not afford the train fare.

Boyfriends were only allowed inside the hostel for invited parties. Normally they had to wait outside for their girlfriends. A large Cedar tree by the front drive of the house enabled the land girls to take turns to kiss their boyfriends goodnight before the 10pm deadline for being in the hostel.

During the freezing winter of 1946–47, the land girls at Aspley Guise were unable to get out to their local farms because of snow drifts. To occupy them and girls at other hostels, the 'War Ag' provided them with paint and held an inter-hostel contest to see who could spruce up their accommodation the best. Aspley Guise came second among the requisitioned houses in the 'Brighter Hostels' competition.

Frances left the Land Army in order to marry a local hairdresser, Bill Jones, who was also an excellent accordion player with a local dance band. After marriage, she worked for a further year for Frank Summerford at Mill Lane Farm, Salford, She remembered him as a man with huge hands who could carry 20 hen's eggs at a time.[174]

Sylvia Bunnett (WLA 180033: 12 March 1947 – 16 July 1948)
Sylvia, known to her friends as 'Bunnie', was another London girl, from Edmonton. She managed to join the WLA six months before the minimum 17 years on entry, but the organisation kept her on at the Toddington training farm until she was 17. She joined with her elder sister, Gladys, who was later discharged because of a heart condition. Sylvia was placed at The Holt, Aspley Guise and became a friend of Frankie Guttridge.

There were many pranks and japes played by the hostel girls. Rosa McEver, an Irish girl, was not a member of the WLA but worked as one of the kitchen staff at the hostel. She indulged in frightening the girls with stories of a 'ghost' and several girls had woken up in the night and sensed some sort of presence in their room. In order to find out who or what was causing it, they set up a bucket of water over the door to their room. Sure enough, the 'ghost' – who was Rosa – was soaked and her trick revealed.[175]

Sylvia later married local man, Jim Cox.[176]

Josephine 'Josie' Walton (WLA 154146: 1 March 1945 – 18 November 1948)
Josie started as a land girl, milking cows, at Home Farm, Westoning, where she had been brought up. She loved the work – calling the cows up, milking, mucking them out and taking the cows to pasture. "It meant taking them across the High Street and up Sampshill at just about the time my compatriots were waiting sleepy-eyed to catch the bus to their dreary office jobs. By this time I had done two hours' work, and after a pleasant cycle ride behind the plopping cows and a swift ride back with my feet off the pedals I would be ready for a good breakfast. Of course, it wasn't always fine and sunny but those times don't come so readily to mind."[177] Later, she became the resident milker at Ravensden training farm. The downside of milking was the seven day week, milking cows twice a day.

After VJ Day (Victory over Japan), Josie moved to Hayfield Farm, where she gained a proficiency badge for calf rearing, and then on to Ravensden Training Farm and Hostel where she became the Resident Milker under the Manager, Jack.

When her parents moved to Ampthill in 1947, Josie took the opportunity to move to the Aspley Guise hostel, which involved just a five and a half day week

The Holt, Aspley Guise, a post-war WLA hostel (now Moore Place Hotel)
Source: Antrobus archive

and a variety of field work. She still gained a badge for calf rearing, when she worked at Hayfield Farm, Aspley Guise.

Not surprisingly, with a mix of young women forced to live together in the close proximity of the hostel dormitories, there were tensions from time to time and not everyone got on with their neighbours. One of the land girls had adopted the habit of smoking Turkish cigarettes which were sometime the only cigarettes available thanks to war-time rationing and the smell was quite offensive to those not smoking. Josie decided to resort to verse in order to make the point and left the following poem on the offender's bed:

Oh Lucy, dear
Why must it be
You make our lives a misery
By smoking Turkish
Early morn
You bring us headaches
With the dawn.

Lucy got the message.

Josie took part in the WLA exhibition of handicrafts at the Corn Exchange, 14–16 February 1946, which was opened by Princess Elizabeth when she came to review the 600-strong parade of Bedfordshire land girls (see Chapter 7 on royal visits).

When the hostel at Aspley Guise closed in the slow post-war rundown of the WLA in the autumn of 1948, she was one of those briefly transferred to the last of Bedfordshire hostels to be opened, at Hasells Hall, Sandy.[178]

She married a local man and became Josie Rowe.[179]

CLIFTON HOSTEL

Betty Harding (WLA 163843: 1 February 1946 – 18 August 1948)

After having worked on private farms, milking, Betty decided she would like to try life at a WLA hostel, working for the 'War Ag'. "I was a bit fed up having to work weekends. When you're young, you feel you'd like to be going different places and I was always working Saturdays and Sundays.

"So I asked for a transfer and they sent me to Clifton Hostel, near Shefford…it was a very big house, turned into a hostel. And I was sent out then with the other girls in the lorry every day, to different farms. That was another experience really. Because I'd never lived with others…I was quite a shy person…I never could bring myself to undress in front of everyone else. I used to go to the bathroom and put my pyjamas on and have a wash. But when I'd been there a little while I got used to the other girls stripping off and I used to think, well it's stupid me hiding in a bathroom, you know, and I got a bit hardened to things.

"The room I went in I had to share with five other girls, lots of bunk beds. It's quite an eye-opener when you sleep with five other girls. Some of the swearing that went on – my Father was very strict about swearing; he wouldn't have any swear words. These young girls from London, they swore like troopers. But they had hearts of gold, really.

"They were all from London. I didn't realise, in those days, how different they were from us. For one thing, the food. I'd been brought up to eat very good, humble food. Potatoes and gravy and vegetables and meat. If they put it in front of the Londoners, they wouldn't eat it. All they wanted was to go down to the fish and chip shop and buy fish and chips. They ate rubbish, even in those days. They really did. We did shepherd's pie which was nicely cooked, or steak and kidney pie and they'd push it on one side. Off they'd go and cycle to the village and buy food.

"And they were rough, as well, They sometimes, when it came to bedtime, and they'd been out for the evening, they just used to jump into bed in their knickers and, poor as we were, my Mum had always taught us to get undressed, wash and get our pyjamas on. They didn't bother about all that. The first thing they did in the morning was sit up and put their make-up on. It was quite an eye-opener, really.

"The biggest eye-opener was when one of the girls came and sat on my bunk bed one day and she was absolutely lousy (infested with lice). I thought, 'My God, she's 'crawling'.' I went and told another girl, who used to work with children. I thought, well I don't know what they look like, really. She came and looked and said, 'You are' and told the Warden. And then we all had to go, marching in and have our hair washed with this stinking stuff and a turban round it for 24 hours. I said, 'My goodness, I've reached 17 and it's the first time I've had lice in me hair.'"

Every day or week they were sent to different farms, doing field work. "The first job I went to was pulling beetroot. That was horrible because you had to pull the tops off. Your hands were so sore by the end of the day, where you screwed. You tried gloves but you could not screw tops off properly so you had to take your gloves off. We had red hands and were so sore.

"One of the nicest jobs – there was an apple orchard at Cockayne Hatley [near Wrestlingworth]. I should say there was a million trees there, belonging to the Co-op [Co-operative Wholesale Society]. We had to prune them. None of us girls knew a thing about pruning. We were told, 'Each tree's got to be no taller than six foot.' The foreman did sort of come round but, I mean, if one of these apple trees had an apple on them...we did hack them about...all the pieces that fell off them fell into the middle of the rows and one girl took them all to the end, and the forelady ['forewoman'] built a big fire.

"It was in October and November and it was lovely to have this big fire and have a warm and, at dinner time, we toasted all our sandwiches on the fire and we used an Oxo [meat extract] cube, which were a penny (less than ½p) in those days, and put it in a flask and take that to drink. We'd all sit round the fire. It was a very nice time.

"It was very hard work. Land work is not easy because you're bending all day.

Margaret Scaife and Margaret Coulin, working in the Co-operative Wholesale Society apple orchard at Cockayne Hatley, pause briefly for the local press photographer in May 1948. *Source: Bedford Central Library. Courtesy of Beds Times*

You can imagine, your back kills you at the end of the day. But we all used to sing on the way home from the fields to the hostel. It was a big old truck with canvas sides.

"We had two trucks and sometimes you'd drop off at that farm and then another dozen at that one or just two at that farm. The driver used to drop them and she had to work at the last place.

"If it was pouring with rain up to dinner time, you could be 'rained off', you see. This particular day we were rained off. The truck was going into Bedford so the driver said, 'Anybody want to go into Bedford?' so, of course, we all said yes, quickly changed into our clothes and went into Bedford."

German boyfriend

"There used to be seats at Bedford bus station and we got talking to these two German prisoners of war. One thing led to another and I started going out with him [Heinz Schwarz]. It was October…His camp was at Tempsford. We were taken into Bedford every Wednesday evening and every Saturday dinner time and had to catch the ten o'clock truck back home.

"After Christmas he got his papers to say he was gong to be repatriated and sent back to Germany and so he said he'd like me to come back with him. We wrote to the Home Office and they said that the only way I could go back with him was if we got married. Really it was all stupid. I'd got no more intentions of getting married than flying to the moon. But I was in love and I'd got to go with him – I couldn't bear him to go away. So we made arrangements to get married. From Tempsford he went to Clapham, because Clapham was the camp where they [POWs] were sent before they were sent home.

"When the Warden at Clifton Hostel heard, she wasn't having a German anything to do with her hostel, so I got married in February [1948]. Mother was also the same; she said her husband had been wounded in the war, her boys had all fought in the war – she wasn't going to have anything to do with any German. She gave me an ultimatum that if I married him, I needn't come home any more. And then I got turned out of the hostel. So Heinz was sent back to Germany. It was a very sad time for me, really.

"At the Easter, I was quite upset because I hadn't got a mother any more, and I got Interflora to send her a nice bouquet and then she wrote back and said that she'd like to see me whenever I wanted to come. Eventually I did get to visit my mother but she said not to go when my brother was there because he'd been in the Forces with the Chindits in Burma and had had a hard time. So I used to see her when I knew my brother wasn't in. I didn't speak to my own brothers and sisters right until my mother died. I'm a bit sad about that."

Toddington Park

"But then the Land Army found me another hostel that took me in, at Toddington. I stayed there until the July when I got the papers to go to Germany. The Warden was an Irish lady. She told me she could tell me a good few atrocities that the English had done against the Irish. She said, 'Don't take any notice. There's good and bad in the whole world.' She was a very lovely lady, she really was. She said, 'You've got to treat people as you find them.'

"The room I was given was the old studio where the artist

Land girls from the Toddington Park hostel put on a promotional display to recruit casual workers to help bring in the harvest on the local estate farm. One of the girls dresses as Britannia to evoke patriotic sentiment and the banner refers to the work that the land girls did, with 'Providence' or nature, to grow the crops which helped feed the nation. *Source: Antrobus archive, 1946 Bedfordshire WLA souvenir programme*

painted…a lovely room…the whole of one side was window, and we had four single beds in – no bunks or anything. It had its own bathroom. When I walked in and said who I was, one of the girls said, 'Good God, we expected some old fogey when we heard 'Mrs Schwarz' was coming' and I was just a young girl. I got on very well with the other girls I shared with. I kept in touch with them for quite a long time. But only the one girl I kept in touch with until she died two years ago; she went to live in Tasmania. And a few years back, Heinz and I went to stay with her. She married a German prisoner of war, like I did. That's why I kept in touch with her. She emigrated."

In July 1948, Betty moved to Pforzheim, to join Heinz. They lived with his mother, who was very good to her, because there was no accommodation anywhere in the area. The town had been fire bombed by RAF planes on 23 February 1945, when over 17,000 people were burnt to death and 83% of the town's buildings destroyed. Betty could not speak German and was very homesick. Eventually they moved back to Bedfordshire.[180]

SILSOE HOSTEL

Betty and Jean Pearson (WLA 120560 and 120561: 17 May 1943 – 28 February 1946)
The Pearson twins, from the North East, were placed at the Silsoe land girl hostel, which was Wrest Park Lodge, a small manor house behind the church, just outside the Wrest Park estate. In the early days there was a definite problem between those from the North and those from the South and they could not 'get on'. It reached a peak when, on one occasion during a meal, a row broke out and the pudding plates were thrown around the dining-room. Eventually things settled down and they all became friends.

They had to get up at 6am and make their sandwiches, which usually consisted of grated cheese, for lunch. The sandwiches were packed in tin luncheon boxes to keep out the rats and mice in the fields. During the first two months, when they learned on the job, they were allocated to various local farms doing threshing, hoeing and planting. Eventually they got settled on Walter Cole's farm near Flitwick, called Priestley Farm. They continued working there for three years, although they remained billeted with 'War Ag' land girls at Silsoe.

The Pearson twins enjoyed life at the hostel, where the Warden looked after them. They got up to the usual pranks young people indulge in when housed together: making apple-pie beds or putting holly in the sheets. The land girls also convinced themselves that they had their own ghost, "which frightened the living daylights out of us". There were reports of a lady and a boy ghost visiting one girl's bedroom and walking between the beds, door handles turning on bedroom doors and the sound of chairs being moved in the dining room through the night.

The hostel girls developed their own social life. They were often invited to an American camp for a night out, with wonderful dance bands playing and "lots of lovely cakes which we didn't have". A British soldier called George, from a nearby camp, used to come over to the hostel and play the piano for the girls to dance to. When any of the land girls got married, they would go to the garden shop in the town and borrow hoes and forks and form a guard of honour outside the church.

The twins were also involved in the life of the village, which had two pubs and a church. They were asked if they would like to teach at the Sunday School. They had difficulty understanding the Bedfordians' dialect and the children could not understand their north-east accents, at first. The Pearson twins would go to a lovely thatched cottage, where "two dear, elderly ladies gave us instructions for the Sunday School lessons". After a while the young women gave it up because they used to stay at the weekends with some relatives in Bedford.[181]

SOUTH BEDFORDSHIRE HOSTELS

Mary Hickey (WLA 107329 15 February 1943– 19 July 1947)
Mary served in the south of the county, at various times being based in the WLA hostels at Whipsnade and Leighton Buzzard. Here she tells of her experience in her own words:

"My father was working near London helping to clear landmines. When the situation began to get worse, we decided to move to Luton. I had an older brother and a younger brother and sister. As I approached my 18th birthday, my father told me to make up my mind as to what I was going to do, otherwise he said, 'You'll be put into war work, and that won't be easy.' I thought that, as I'm not the sort of person to take lots of orders, the best thing to do would be to find somewhere that was more relaxed.

"I knew nothing about the country. The nearest we had to a cow was the churn in the dairy next door where we bought our milk. My

Mary Hickey worked for the 'War Ag', variously, at Whipsnade, Kensworth and Leighton Buzzard hostels.
Source: M Cutler

family worked in the rag trade, we were townies!

"Anyway, away I went to the town hall to join the Land Army. Once home, I decided to tell my family over tea. 'By the way, I've joined the Land Army today!' They laughed. My father thought it was hysterical, 'With shoes like that!'

"The first place I was billeted was Whipsnade. We slept in a hut that was used, pre-war, by the waitresses that used to work at the Zoo. They had stoves in the middle of the room with pipes going up into the roof; very primitive but warm. For going out, we were given breeches, green woolly jumpers, woollen socks, hats and a great coat. For working we wore jumpers, dungarees, shirts and coat.

"The war effort had taken over the land that was attached to the Zoo; most of the wild animals had gone and it was now used for growing food. The parrots were left and they soon learned to swear because the girls came from all walks of life. Many of them would say b***** off when someone came to the door! We enjoyed it although the job was very hard, especially working on the threshing machine. It was hell. I met Barbara on my first day. She was a giggler, although that stopped when mice came through the door and then the giggles turned to tears.

"That happened on our first day. We didn't like it very much.

"We then moved to Leighton Buzzard where we did general farm work, Brussels sprouts and potato picking, hay making, et cetera. The nicest place that we stayed in was Kensworth, a lovely house, altered to create more bedrooms and bathrooms. We enjoyed it there; it had a library with huge windows and a legend of the headless huntsman who used to ride by at night. Of course, we loved all that. There was lots of fun attached to it.

"Sometimes we would be let out in the evening but 'lights out' was at ten o'clock. We would wait outside the hostel, get a lift to Bedford Corn Exchange on the back of someone's motorbike and go 'living it up' with the Yanks [American servicemen]. Coming home, a friend would let us into the hostel but that stopped when someone told the warden what was going on. When we found out who it was (what we thought was a dear old lady), we decided that we would dress up as ghosts. We put white sheets over our heads and knocked on her door making ohhhhhhhhhhhh noises. Well, the poor old dear left about a week later, so that worked! But we worked hard and played hard.

"We were up at about 6.30am and then given a packed lunch in a tin box before being dropped off at one of the farms. Some farmers were not very nice; they didn't want us girls there. We could appreciate that because they had lost good experienced farm-hands and in place they were given a couple of giggling females. They were at a loss because, as willing as we were, we didn't know much about farm work and none of us really wanted to either.

"I learned to smoke as a land girl. This happened because one day we were given a cow shed to clean out. It was filthy, with lots of manure and the smell was terrible. One of the chaps in the shed told us that we would have to roll it up to get it out. So we rolled the manure up, just like a carpet! The smell got worse as we did this. He said, 'What you need is a fag.' I told him that we didn't smoke, he said, 'You soon will!' He got out a little tin box and rolled cigarettes for us. It was marvellous! We couldn't smell anything else after that!

"There was one particular farm where we dreaded going. We drew lots to see who would be sent. When our names were called we'd say, 'Oh no, please not me!' One particular time, three of us were sent there, chewing gum and smoking cigarettes that we'd got from the Americans. We were cocky too because we knew how to use the pitchfork. As we stood there the farmer came out, a gangling man, who stared at us. 'Girls!' he said, tut-tutting away. We started to giggle. 'Get your hands out of your pockets and put those fags out!' His wife, though, was lovely. She used to feed us big slabs of bread pudding and give us hot drinks.

"One farmer came from Somerset and had brought with him his own recipe for cider. When we went hay-making he would give us bottles of cider to drink, 'Coming up, sunshine!' he would call. There were many good, funny sides to our work. On leaving one farm, the farmer told me that he would miss me. 'You're the only woman I know that can handle a pitchfork.' This was quite a compliment!

"On another occasion I was sent to a farm with lots of pigs. Well, I love pigs, especially piglets. The farmer had told me that he had a little job for me working with the piglets. When I got there, the farmer told me to hold the piglets by their back legs. He then castrated them!

"Spending a penny wasn't much fun when working in the fields either. We sometimes had to walk a long way to find somewhere that was out of sight of the men who were also working on the farm! Once we climbed into a field with a bull in it. My friend Barbara and I crept along, hoping it wouldn't see us!

"Mrs Clementine Churchill (the wartime Prime Minister's wife) visited us for the day at Leighton Buzzard hostel. She chatted to us, asking us if we liked our jobs. Of course, we said yes! She was a very charming person. I must have enjoyed the work because after I had been doing the job for three years, I signed up for another year. It was a very free life.

"During my time in the Land Army I learned a lot of things; how to notice wild strawberries growing by the side of a lane that no-one else would see, or birds nesting.

"The Queen, when she was Princess Elizabeth, presented me with my four years' service green arm band, with WLA written across it. We had gang leaders; I was a gang leader eventually. There were new girls joining up all the time. They thought they would have a good time!"[182]

Stella Limon (WLA 69083: 25 March 1942– 30 May 1945)

Stella was a Luton girl and on leaving school worked as a clerk for an insurance company. Once the war started her plan was to join the Wrens, once she was 18 but, in the meantime, once she was 17 she thought she would follow the example of some of her female colleagues and join the WLA. The idea was to transfer to the forces once she was 18.

She was sent to Leighton Buzzard hutment hostel, to be employed by Bedfordshire 'War Ag'. As were most hutment hostels, it was a T-shaped assembly of three huts – dormitory, ablutions block and dining room/kitchen, joined by a small entrance hall – designed to accommodate 40 young women. To the rear was a half-acre garden, where they grew their own vegetables.

Stella Limon was based at the Leighton Buzzard hutment hostel in Hockliffe Road.
Source: S Goldsmith

The irony was that it had originally been accommodation for Italian prisoners of war but they complained that it was too cold in there and, because of the Geneva Conventions, they were transferred to elsewhere. Clearly, land girls were deemed to be capable of putting up with the conditions. Stella remembered that in winter the fire buckets kept by the coke stoves would be frozen solid each morning. In the summer, they would be sometimes kept awake at night by the sound of earwigs dropping on to the floor.

Those first few weeks in the new uniform were uncomfortable. The corduroy breeches were stiff and made a noise as they moved. Both their heavy shoes and the working boots were agony to wear. Blisters developed on their feet and weals where the tops of the boots rubbed their ankles. But once they were broken in, they were effective and comfortable.

Well-brought-up young women like Stella were shocked to hear the bad language of those recruits from the East End of London, whose language was extremely "colourful". Stella wondered what she had let herself in for.

They travelled out each day to local farms and immediately found themselves potato picking, with a sack tied round their waist, collecting potatoes which had been unearthed by a machine. These had to be loaded on to a trailer and later into one-hundredweight bags or stored under straw and earth-mound clamps. Their muscles protested during that first week.

Later in the year they found themselves hedging and ditching, learning such skills as using a bill hook and then a large scythe. Looking back, Stella wondered how she ended her land girl career with her hands and feet intact.

One issue that continued to upset the girls was that when they were transported early in the morning out to farms in the area, even though it was often raining or in freezing winter weather, they were in the back of open lorries. They were either soaked or so cold by the time they arrived that they were in no state to start work. They put in a request for a canvas top to be put on the lorry but, in spite of promises, nothing happened.

Finally, the land girls had had enough and refused to go to work until they got cover on their lorry. Instead they worked in their hostel garden, hoeing and weeding the Brussels sprouts. It wasn't long before a member of the county staff from the WLA headquarters office in Bedford arrived to threaten them with various regulations, if they didn't do what they were told. The land girls held firm and had been sensible enough to keep working, albeit not where they were supposed to be. Their action worked and the next day a lorry came with a cover on it.

Stella remembered the summers as being hot and sunny. Double summer time was introduced to give farmers more daylight hours in which to gather the corn harvest. The land girls, and all other farm workers, started at seven in the morning and worked until late in the evening.

One barley harvest somewhere between Whipsnade and Studham was particularly memorable. A large field had been ploughed for the first time in living memory and barley sown. The crop had grown to an enormous size, well above the land girls' heads. Their job was to go round the fields three times with their scythes, to make enough room for the tractor and harvester to operate. The barley heads cut into their skin and, to make matters worse, they disturbed a wasps' nest and the wasps attacked them.

On another occasion, working near to Chalton, there was a firing range just over the hill. They heard the crack of rifles and every so often a whine overhead and something landing in a sheaf of corn. They never thought anything about it until they were joined one day by local airmen, who had volunteered to help with the harvest. The first time the men heard the whine they flattened themselves on the ground. The land girls just stood open-mouthed until they were dragged down as well. The RAF men explained the damage a ricochet bullet could do to you. Soon after that the Air Force had the firing range shut down until the harvest field had been cleared.[183]

KENSWORTH

Eileen Fuller (WLA 90463: 20 July 1942 – 19 October 1946)

Eileen, a Dunstable girl, was called up for a month's training at Luton Hoo before being sent to the newly-opened Kensworth House WLA hostel, a delightful country house which had once belonged to a Luton brewer. She was pleased that she was able to get home at the weekends. Her brother was missing in Singapore and her mother had taken the news very badly.

As at all hostels, the hostel gangs of mobile land girls did seasonal work on local farms, as required: threshing, picking potatoes or Brussels sprouts. "One of the worst jobs was picking 'Brussels' on cold frosty mornings – as soon as you picked them the frost would melt on your fingers. It was a hard life but very healthy. The food was nice and we had a good cook."

It was a very cold winter when she joined and after about six months Eileen developed paralysis in her face through driving in open lorries out to the local farms each day. She was then given work in the gardens surrounding the house, helping to grow vegetables to help feed the land girls living there.

When the house opened as a hostel there were about 20 young women; all except two local girls were from London. There ended up being forty land girls there. "It was a lot of fun, living with a lot of girls and I remained friends with one girl in particular. We sometimes had parties (like little dances); the local boys and soldiers were invited along."

Eileen was discharged in 1946 when she had to leave to nurse her mother, who was ill at the time.[184]

'CHIMNEY CORNER', HOUGHTON CONQUEST

Mrs P.E. Guyver (Maiden name and WLA record not known)

Mrs Guyver looked back to her days as a 'War Ag' land girl at 'Chimney Corner' hostel near Elstow and Houghton Conquest:

"I think back to those days of hard work – no fun cutting cabbages with ice on them, your legs covered with sacking to keep out the cold. The harvesting, the threshing machine – I always had the job of cutting the band of the sheaves and feeding the drum – coming home filthy dirty with the odd barley ear that had managed to penetrate your clothes or down your back. Still, the one blessing was that those harvesting got the first chance of a bath!

"How did we all survive? Well we did and I think the friendship of the girls in your dormitory made up for the less good times. There was always talking and telling stories over the potato riddling machine and a good sing-song on the way to and from the farms."[185]

Eileen Wortham (WLA 154032: 26 February 1945 – 8 November 1947)

Eileen joined the WLA, aged 18, in 1945. She had been evacuated to Northampton from London as a child of 12 but at the age of 16 she returned to London and had to take on war work in a factory. "I hated being shut indoors all day and really missed the country life I had come to know and so volunteered for the Land Army."

She was initially sent to Toddington WLA hostel for four weeks' training. Each morning they would climb into the back of a lorry and be dropped off at their place of work for the day. "I was mostly sent to Bennett's Pear Tree Farm, Elstow, where I worked on the threshing machine. I also spent time at the Cockayne Hatley orchards, Mark Young's farm at Cople and also at another farm, Hammer Hill, Haynes, where I recall having to muck out the bull shed. The farmer would move the bull into an adjacent shed with just a thin partition between us. The bull would constantly be banging and head butting against the partition while we worked. I also recall that particular farmer had a rather risqué sense of humour and was often chastised by his wife for making us young girls blush with his jokes."

Eileen recalled that the hostel was comprised of three blocks of dormitories, each divided into two sections with six sets of bunks accommodating 12 girls. There were two 'ablution rooms' with two sinks and six toilets each. "We had to walk through one dorm to reach the other. Girls from separate 'dorms' did not really tend to mix a great deal. Friendships were mostly formed with those you shared with."

They were out very early each morning in all weathers performing manual and often dirty work and so, on return to the 'dorms' at the end of the day, there was always a rush for the baths. There were no laundry facilities and they had to wash clothes every day in the sinks and hang them out on makeshift lines between the dorms to dry.

The food was not very good, generally. There was a large urn providing ready-sweetened tea which tasted awful and stewed. Those who preferred unsweetened tea got their own large teapot and made their own tea, fresh.

"After our evening meal we would often go to St John's café in Bedford for steak pie and chips. We were given a packed lunch to take with us each day, mostly cheese or corned beef sandwiches with not much filling. Some farmers' wives would kindly give us meals or refreshments."

They did not see much of their hostel Warden, except when they had to go to her to ask for an iron to press their clothes. She did not regularly visit the dorms, according to Eileen.

Eileen left the Land Army in November 1947 and a year later married a local lad from Elstow, whose father owned the threshing tackle she had worked on at Bennett's Farm in the village. They remained in Elstow for the rest of their lives.[186]

Irene Wright (WLA 145672: 10 June 1944 – 28 April 1945)

"I came to Bedford in 1943 aged 17 when I joined the Women's Land Army. I was sent to Toddington Manor for my training and from day one it was hard work doing all the jobs that men would normally have done. There was nothing glamorous about being a land girl – we would be up at six and working by seven a.m. in winter in the pitch dark. Chilblains and blisters were part and parcel of daily life.

"It was a hard time. We had to work in the fields with farm labourers who were then more or less pensioners because all the young men had gone to war and we had to do everything on the land that a man could do. We had to plough, we had to build the peat pits for the carrots and the potatoes, we had to milk the cows, drive the tractors – everything. It was exhausting but I loved every minute of it.[187]

"It was drawing to the end of 1943 and the end of my training in the Women's Land Army. The coming weekend was to be a weekend back into civilization. It was cold and I was tired, my feet were recovering from blisters after breaking in my issue hobnail boots, my face and nose quite pink, my nails broken, my hands rough, and my blonde page boy bob looking like a haystack but I was quite proud of my little duck egg muscles that had formed on my upper arms.

"Eight of us piled into a WLA truck, which took us from Toddington Manor and dropped us at the Toc H in Bedford. After booking in we had some idea between us of painting the town red. We decided that we would go dancing at the Dujon Ballroom we had discovered in the High Street. We decided to wear our Land Army uniforms – not exactly glamorous and yet certainly had sex appeal for the boys, and we felt safer in it too.

"I scrubbed up quite well, even my hair recovered its shine and except for my bra strap breaking and one of the girls kindly pinning it back with a safety pin (no sewing equipment!) we were set to go.

"No sooner in the Dujon than a half drunk 'Yank' [American serviceman] grabbed me onto the dance floor, causing me embarrassment by telling me, 'You're the gal I've been waiting for all my life' and he wasn't going to take no for an answer. Suddenly this handsome sailor in Fleet Air Arm uniform tapped the

A 'War Ag'
mobile gang
of land girls
threshing
from the
stack at
Lodge Farm,
Toddington.
*Source: The
Museum of
English Rural
Life, The
University of
Reading*

Yank on the shoulder, saying, 'My girl, mate', and the American politely released
me.

"There we were, Ken and I dancing and arguing when suddenly the pin on my
bra came undone and the end of Ken's thumb had a spot blood on it and I made
a dash for the 'ladies'...We were together all evening, apart from the 'excuse me's.
He walked me back to the Toc H and we said our goodnights and there were stars
in my eyes and a happy twinkle in Ken's.

"The next day he took me punting on the river and we walked and enjoyed a
milkshake in a milk bar.[188]

"I then moved to 'Chimney Corner' [which is now an industrial site]. We used
to be got up very early in the morning and the lorries used to pick us up and take
us to wherever we had to go to start work...

"The first harvest we were sent to Whipsnade Zoo, much of which had been
ploughed up to feed the animals still living there. We were harvesting oats. The
horse pulled the machinery which cut the oats and turned out stooks which we
set up, eight stooks together leaning into each other, to dry. It was very hard,
dusty work. The oats scratched our arms until they bled...

"The field we were in belonged to the camels but a temporary fence was
in place to stop the camels damaging the crops. One of these camels was very
pregnant and making a huge noise. We all decided to make the noise back to
it. All of a sudden, these furious camels decided that enough was enough and
charged through the fence. No one had ever told us how fast a camel could run.
There were stooks, land girls and camels everywhere. We headed for the nearest

ditch, which we had been advised to do if a swarm of bees attacked us. This was a swarm of camels!

"Eventually a very red-faced elderly zoo keeper had the camels under control, saying 'Who was the bloody ring leader of that little fiasco? Don't you know you could have caused my baby to abort?' While saying this he had his arms round the pregnant camel which was slobbering all over him and none of us could keep a straight face. Finally he pointed to me and my mate and said, 'Right, you gels, tomorrow morning, can muck out the elephants'.

"Eventually I went to work on a private farm and I finished my Land Army days there.

"Without the Women's Land Army food would not have been produced in the quantities that it was produced and yet at the end of the war we were never recognised or given any honours for our steadfastness to duty to our country."[189] *Irene and Ken married in January 1945 and were together for over 60 years.*

RAVENSDEN

Eleanor 'Biddy' Deighton (WLA 148770: 9 August 1944 – 28 February 1946)

Eleanor 'Biddy' Deighton *Source: E Cust*

Biddy Deighton was a Yorkshire girl who enrolled in 1944 and was transferred to Bedfordshire. She was to be employed by a private farmer but was first sent to Ravensden House WLA training centre in the north of the county and has recorded a few recollections. "At the time it sounded a million miles away from home. I joined at York with my friend Muriel and we travelled together to Ravensden Hostel. We were put in different sections and were put into rooms with bunk beds in. In my room were eight girls and we were referred to as 'milking girls'. We were given a cow each morning and late afternoon to milk by hand (can't have been easy on the cows). During the day we learnt about dairy farming.

"At the end of the month we were given written tests. I remember I got B+, which I thought was good when I realised how frightened I was of cows before going there." When she left Ravensden Biddy was the only one out of the eight 'milking girls' who went on to a dairy farm, She was eventually placed on Home Farm, Cranfield. There she did machine milking and, in between milking, tractor driving and general farm work. She later transferred to Essex.[190]

HULCOTE MOORS

Betty Hurst (WLA 132640: 28 July 1943 – 29 July 1944)

Betty had previously worked in munitions for a year at Elstow, packing mortar bombs which she did not like. Her brother had gone into the navy, her sister into the air force and Betty became a land girl. She joined the hostel at Hulcote Moors, which was an old farmhouse, outside Cranfield. The 20 girls there were from all over the country. She was able to cycle home each weekend.

They used to get up at half past six each morning. The warden's husband, Mr Whatling, who worked for the 'War Ag', used to play a recording of 'Moonlight Becomes You' in order to wake them. After breakfast they set off in a lorry to the fields for half past seven. They would be dropped off in small gangs at somebody's farm and work there all day. They did outside manual work – no milking.

The first day she worked she was building a haystack. She was terrified of heights but she had to go up the ladder and sheaves were passed up to her. She was terrified and wondered how she was going to get down.

She learned on the job without any initial training. She learned to drive a tractor with Geoff Ping.

The closeness of the hostel to the wartime aerodrome at Cranfield led to some incidents with airmen. One Lancaster bomber plane came down in the next field to them, one night. Two English pilots died in the crash but three other crewmen managed to get to the hostel at three o'clock in the morning. One was a French-Canadian, another Australian and the third a New Zealander. The land girls kept in touch with the airmen after that happened. Parties were held at the hostel and airmen would come over. One of the airmen's wives was a superb cook and made the most delicious meals and cakes. No one asked her where the ingredients came from!

Betty's father was too old to go into the army and kept his job at the brick works at Marston. Just part of the brickworks were kept going but the bricks were just piled up because there was little building going on during the war.

Betty enjoyed her time in the Land Army: "It was wonderful. I absolutely loved it."[191]

Cicely Redman (WLA 154971: 24 March 1945 – 19 April 1947)

When she left school, Cicely worked as a dressmaker machinist for Gladys Claytons in Harpur Street, Bedford. She cycled there and back from Wootton each day. Following a wartime experience when she thought her house had been hit by a 'doodlebug' bomb, she began fainting whenever she heard a plane go over, and her doctor recommended she leave the job in the town and work outside. She decided to join the WLA and got accepted.

The irony was that she got posted to Hulcote Moors hostel and her first job was hoeing at Cranfield Aerodrome, surrounded by aeroplanes. She then went on, like all hostel girls, to do all kinds of field work at local farms. She never did milking although she did feed calves and she delivered on a milk round. She was given just a one-hour lesson in driving one lunchtime and set off on her own in the van on her first milk round. She did not even know where the reverse gear was, but she managed. Milk was in two-gallon cans and milk was ladled out, using a pint or a half-pint measure, into customers' jugs at each house. There were no bottles or plastic cartons. The money for the milk was collected once a week by going round with a leather bag.

After the morning milk round, Cecily would then join other land girls in field work, harvesting or threshing. They were out in all weathers. Sometimes they worked with Italian prisoners of war; sometimes with German POWs.

She then worked for a number of private farms, the first one in Salford. She was able to live at home and travel each day to the farm. Her second farm at Box End, Kempston, was a poultry farm. She looked after the poultry. She did not kill them but she did pluck and dress hundreds of them after they had been killed.

She ended up working for Biddenham Dairies, taking milk into Bedford. She had quite a large van and the run she most dreaded was one down a slope to a farm, where there was only about three inches clearance each side of her wing mirrors. She used to hate that but she had to do it every day. She also did some bookwork in the farmer's office.

When Princess Elizabeth came to inspect the WLA on 14 February 1946, she saw some of the dresses that Cicely had made ready for the land girls' concert on 15 February. Cicely used a lot of butter-white muslin, which was used to filter milk in the dairy, and made a dress out of it, with purple ribbons to decorate it. It made a lovely off-the-shoulder dress, thanks to her dressmaking skills.[192]

Audrey 'Peggy' Clark (WLA 126425: 19 June 1943 – 18 March 1946)

Having left school during the war, Peggy, a Cardington girl, worked for a printing firm in Bedford, which was a reserved occupation not requiring her to do any other war work. But she promised her cousin, Edna, that she would go with her to do whatever war work she signed up for. This turned out to be working for the WLA. Peggy knew that this would be hard work – her father had told her – but she did not want to let Edna down, they were such good friends.

It turned out to be very hard, physical work but she enjoyed the companionship of the other land girls so much. They were sent to work for the 'War Ag' at Hulcote Moors hostel, which was a farmhouse accommodating 18 young women.

Hulcote Moors hostel girls supposedly welcoming American servicemen to the area. *Source: A P Tedder*

The social life they enjoyed helped to compensate for the hard work they did. There were dances at nearby RAF Cranfield and dances at the American airfields further north, at Thurleigh. The American servicemen came to collect the land girls in a truck. Once there, on the airfield, they had wonderful food, completely free of the rationing the British girls were used to. Peggy also attended the dances in Bedford at the Corn Exchange, including one where Glenn Miller's band played.

The Hulcote hostel girls worked over a wide area of mid-Bedfordshire, including Ampthill, Marston and Maulden. They were usually told the night before where they would be working the next day. They set off with their packed lunch in a metal box. But one day a pig on the farm where she was working somehow managed to open it and ate her lunch. Fortunately, the farmer's wife came to her rescue and gave her something to eat.

There were twin sisters, Joyce and Hilda Virgin, staying at the Hulcote hostel and if a farmer phoned up the hostel, the Warden, Mrs Whatling, would say I'll send Peggy and the two Virgins. Naturally, when the lorry arrived at the farm with a load of land girls, the farmer would ask, "Which two are the Virgins?"

Being a local girl, Peggy was able to go home on Saturday afternoons for the weekend. She cycled to Cardington and back. Her brother was in the army so there was only her mother and father at home.

Wartime military activity occasionally affected them. One night an Allied plane came down in their orchard and the land girls had to spend the night in the farmhouse cellar, in case it exploded. On another occasion, a plane came down locally and a pilot with a German-sounding accent knocked on the hostel door, but he turned out to be Polish and therefore an Allied pilot.

The bathroom in the farmhouse was a long room with wash hand basins all along the walls and a bath in the same room, so that there was no privacy; some would be bathing while others washed at the sinks. Restrictions on the amount of water you used – just five inches of hot water in a bath – led to the bath at the hostel being used by two girls at a time, sitting back to back. Soap was difficult to get and sometimes they resorted to buying men's shaving soap.

Social life included occasional visits to the 'Swan' at Cranfield. They would walk there across the fields in their wellingtons, carrying their shoes to change into once they got to the surface roadway, leaving their wellingtons by the gate.

One outstanding event in their social life was the time that 20-year-old Peggy was voted the first land girl May Queen by her fellow land girls at Hulcote Moors. The crowning event was held at the farmhouse. Her mother and father provided the bouquets of flowers for her and her attendants and her guard of honour was fellow land girls with hoes, rakes and forks. Then she took part, in her May Queen costume, in a fund-raising parade in Bedford, from De Parys Avenue down the High Street to the Embankment and Russell Park. A newsreel film crew came along and filmed it and locals were able to see it at the cinema.

Towards the end of the war, she met her husband-to-be at RAF Cranfield.[193]

Peggy Clark is voted Britain's first WLA May Queen by her fellow land girls at Hulcote Moors hostel, Cranfield, 6 May 1944. *Source: A P Tedder*

Zoe Odell (WLA 123681: 3 June 1943 – 29 February 1944)

When Zoe joined the WLA, under conscription, she thought she would be sent far away, somewhere like Wales. But she was sent to Hulcote Moors, near Cranfield. She had joined the WLA against the wishes of her father who said, "If you join the Land Army, you don't come in this house". When her uniform arrived she had to take it to her aunt's house, a few doors away and when she left to begin her service, her father told her, "Don't come home". She had to stay at the hostel and did not go home for quite a while. Her father thought she was joining the WLA just to 'get off' with farmers. Her mother dared not say anything.

The first farm that Zoe was sent to work at was Charlie Howe's farm in Lower Shelton, Marston. She had never been on a farm before. He said to her, "Do you know anything about ploughing?" When she said, "No" he got out his old tractor and showed her how to plough a furrow and set her off.

As it happened, it was exactly opposite her parents' house, so, at dinner time, she popped over to see her mum, who was delighted. "Oh, it's so nice to see you. Will you come and have a bit of dinner?" When her father came home from work that afternoon, mother told him about Zoe's work. "I'd better go over and see what she's doing." When he saw the good job Zoe had made of the ploughing, he relented. "You're making a good job of that. You can come back home at the weekend."

Work as a hostel land girl was hard. They were out in all weathers. They had hobnail boots rather than wellingtons and they were heavy. They were given an oil-skin jacket and a 'sou'wester' hat.

Food was rationed with set amounts to live on each week. For their packed meal there was bread, a small amount of margarine and a little bit of cheese. When their ration was used up there was nothing else. One day when they were working at Barnes' farm in Marston, the farmer was told that they were eating just bread, with no filling and he rang up the WLA county headquarters in Bedford to complain. "We've got land girls and they've hardly got anything to eat. My wife's having to bring them in and give them some dinner." He said that he had never know anyone being "packed up" like that in all his life. "You can't work on that."

This stirred things up at headquarters and an investigation was set up. It turned out that the Warden had been keeping back some of the land girls' rations for her own family. She was sacked and someone else took over. The food got better and they had ham sometimes.

Most of the work they did was field work, hoeing all day, then harvesting and threshing, seasonally. Later Zoe went to work at Davies' farm locally, and eventually married the farmer. She then worked with her husband, getting up at 5.30 in the morning, sharing the hand milking and doing a milk delivery round. She loved the life.[194]

Stacking straw at Sharpenhoe, as it comes from the threshing machine. *Source: Luton Central Library. Courtesy of Luton News*

CHAPTER TEN

Summary and Conclusions

The development of the Women's Land Army in Bedfordshire in the 1940s, to a large extent, mirrored developments in other counties in England and Wales, between 1939 and 1950. The start was very slow, despite enthusiastic recruitment figures, with farmers extremely reluctant to take on inexperienced female workers, when they had been used to, and still had some, experienced male workers. It is not yet possible to put figures to the numbers of young women who enrolled in Bedfordshire but had to be transferred to other counties in order to be placed on farms. Certainly there appears a considerable discrepancy between the larger numbers enrolled and the smaller numbers employed in the county.[195]

Once the conscription of women, after the Conscription Act of November 1941, began to have effect from 1942 onwards, much larger numbers of members were both enrolled in, and transferred from elsewhere in England to, Bedfordshire. Parallel with this increase in the numbers of young women volunteering for work on the land, as opposed to joining the three armed services, becoming nurses or undertaking essential war work in factories, was the decision that the county 'War Ags' would directly employ large numbers of land girls and accommodate them around each county, in either requisitioned houses or in purpose-built hutment hostels.

Nationally in England and Wales the proportion of these 'hostel' land girls was one third, as opposed to two thirds employed directly by private farmers. In Bedfordshire the proportion was fifty-fifty, with approximately 500 young women employed by Bedfordshire WAEC and 500 employed by private farmers, over the peak period of 1943–44 (when, nationally, the 'ceiling' figure was 80,000 land girls in England and Wales).

Including the training farms (two out of three of which also housed permanent mobile gangs) there were 16 hostels located strategically around Bedfordshire to accommodate the mobile labour gangs of land girls employed by Bedfordshire 'War Ag'. A 17th hostel at Luton Hoo accommodated trainee land girls (as well as those permanently employed by the estate). These hostels included 12 houses accommodating from 16 to 97 land girls in each. Nine of these were requisitioned during the war: Cople House, Hulcote Moors Farm, Kensworth House, The Bothy at Luton Hoo, The Hollies in Potton, Sharnbrook House, Toddington Manor, Ravensden House and Wrest Park Lodge at Silsoe. After the war a further three houses, The Holt at Aspley Guise, Clifton House and Hasells Hall, near Sandy, were established as hostels. The other five hostels were purpose-built Board of Trade hutments, ranging from ones accommodating up to 40 land girls, as at Bolnhurst, Leighton Buzzard, Milton Ernest and Whipsnade, and the exceptionally large hutment hostel at 'Chimney Corner', just south of Bedford in the Houghton Conquest/Elstow area, accommodating up to 94. (See appendices for table giving more details of these hostels.)

The peak number of land girls in Bedfordshire at any one time – just over 1,000 in the 1943–44 period – compared with just under 2,000 each in Northamptonshire and Buckinghamshire, 1,300 in Cambridgeshire and over 2,300 in Hertfordshire, but Bedfordshire was the smallest of these counties.[196]

In the early years of the presence of the WLA in Bedfordshire, there were voices, particularly amongst the farming and market garden community, who raised doubts about to what extent, if at all, land girls would be able to provide the type of labour skills needed by the agricultural and horticultural industries. There was a clear prejudice in favour of male labour and against female labour for most activities requiring physical strength and even those who did take on land girls had anxieties as to how effective they would prove to be. Those who were the pioneer land girls had a lot to prove to their employers about their abilities to cope with the demands of the job. The proven success of many of those land girls in the first two or three years led to more farmers taking on their own land girls, as prejudices were broken down.

The real impetus to the acceptance of land girl labour by reluctant farmers was the withdrawal of the Reserved Occupation status of male farm workers from 1943, when all men over 18 were required to join the armed forces. This left farmers dependent on women workers (the majority of them signed-up 'land girls'), conscientious objectors, men too old or not fit enough to be in the armed forces and prisoners of war, first Italians and then Germans. Other part-time and seasonal workers included schoolchildren and 'holiday farm' paid volunteers.

By the 12 May 1944, *The Bedfordshire Times* is paying tribute to "the Women's Land Army who have come from all corners of England and from every walk of life to do a tough job and have come out with flying colours".[197]

The success of the WLA in Bedfordshire, as in other counties, depended on the relationship between the WLA as represented by its county headquarters staff and its individual members (the land girls) with the other elements of the wartime farming community. These were the individual private farmers who employed land girls on their farms, the 'War Ag' (the largest single employer of female labour) as represented by its Labour Officer at Phoenix Chambers, Bedford, and the YWCA who provided Wardens and Assistant Wardens for the hostels to look after the welfare of the land girls. In the end, it was down to individual relationships between the professional officers of each of these organisations or elements. There were inevitable tensions but ways were found to work together.

Analysis remains to be done on the length of stay of individual land girls at private farms or in hostels and the reasons given – occasionally revealed by the service record cards – as to why they left. Fairly frequent reasons for being dismissed, or being given an 'unwilling release', included refusal to obey instructions,

American visitor, Mr MacFarlane, a guest of farmer Joseph Godber of Willington, who had six land girls working there, praised the Land Army, speaking at the Land Army Club in Bedford. "You can take it from me that the Land Army is doing a good job of work – the best of all the women's services, I think – with less hullabaloo and less publicity than all the others." Mrs Erica Graham is on the right. *Source: BLARS (Graham archive) X464. Courtesy of Beds Times (31 July 1942)*

failure to return after leave, insubordination, or being pregnant but not married. Getting married was one of the acceptable reasons for being given a 'willing release', since married women were not regarded as any longer being 'mobile'. Other reasons for a 'willing release' by the organisation were 'compassionate grounds' including having parents or other family members to care for.

The 'War Ag', possibly because they had such draconian powers over farmers in their area during the war, felt particularly frustrated that they could not exercise more control over their employee land girls. They protested to the Ministry of Agriculture that land girls should be subject to military discipline and that they should be able to instruct the police to bring workers back, when they refused. They found it hard to accept, perhaps because of the misleading title of Land 'Army' and the uniform, that these young women were civilian workers.[198]

The experience of land girls throughout their period in the Women's Land Army varied considerably, according to individual situations and circumstances. There were considerable differences between those employed directly by private farmers on their farms and those employed by the 'War Ag'. The latter formed daily mobile gangs of workers – of varying size – who travelled out each day from their hostel. The key aspect of the hostels was the shared communal experience of hostel life, with its own social activities and welfare support.

The quality of life as a private farm land girl depended on a host of factors – whether one was the only land girl on the farm or market garden, whether one was billeted on the farm or in a cottage in the area and, most importantly the relationship between land girl and farmer, fellow farm workers and also the farmer's wife or billet landlady.

Where more than one land girl worked on the farm or market garden, then at least there was not complete isolation of the land girl and the chance of friendship and support when times got difficult. Isolation and loneliness could be very hard for the young WLA woman. More so, perhaps, for the majority who had been used to urban life and its many services and conveniences, compared with the restrictions and deprivations of life in relatively remote rural areas. Most of the recruits were also in their late teenage years, some as young as 17 (or less, if they cheated) and were away from home for the first time. Communication with home was limited to writing letters, since few had access to telephones in their homes.

Another way in which the experience of land girls differed, irrespective of whether they worked on private farms or were from hostels, was caused by their distance from the parental home. Some land girls were able to stay in their home county of Bedfordshire; a few were even able to live at home and cycle each day to their farm. Others, including some from London, were able to go home at the weekend, on Saturday afternoon, and return on Sunday evening. This led to a

Land girls put on a concert (thought to be at Hasells Hall hostel, Sandy, post-war). *Source: L Freestone*

divergence of social experience and the degree to which individuals were able to maintain contact with home and local friends.

Those living hundreds of miles from home were usually able to return only twice a year – once for their one week's paid leave (at a time to suit the farmer) and once for a few days at Christmas. A free travel pass was issued after each six months' satisfactory work and could be to anywhere in England or Wales.

On the other hand, those who lived in hostels developed their own social life at weekends which those who were able to regularly visit home missed out on. There were clearly benefits for each group. The lone land girls on the private farms might suffer more from these restrictions, unless they were able to make friends locally and integrate themselves into village life.

Theoretically, mechanisms for welfare such as the District Representatives appointed to keep an eye on local land girls and give support, as required, were in place. The reality, according to those I have interviewed who served in

Milton Ernest hostel girls having a break from summer work in the fields at Rawlins' Farm, Biddenham, 1945. *Source: N Wallace*

Bedfordshire, was that such support and concern was less obvious on the ground, where it was up to the land girls to stick up for themselves, often, in disputes with farmers or those with whom they were billeted. When things got bad enough, land girls had to contact the WLA HQ in Bedford to report problems and seek solutions. Often this would involve transfer to another farm or billet.

Personal development and education of the land girls also varied enormously during the wartime period. Some land girls took the opportunities to learn new skills whenever possible on the farms. These included the opportunity to learn to drive tractors and operate machinery or become specialised milking or dairy workers, for example. Later, they were able to take proficiency tests and gain certificates so as to be able to demonstrate the skills that they had acquired during their years in the Land Army. This not only gave satisfaction but also opened up future career prospects for those who envisaged a post-war future working in agriculture or horticulture. A few took a correspondence course which enabled them to use their academic abilities, which had been frustrated by the intervention of war, when otherwise they might have gone on to further or higher education. Post-war, a limited number of full-time course bursaries enabled a few former land girls to study at agricultural institutes and go into careers in charge of farms or as agricultural secretaries.

For the vast majority, their period of national service on the land was a relatively brief rural interlude in a life which would be spent mostly in urban areas and activities. At least they had learned what life was like in the countryside and on farms or in market gardens, what went on there, how important it was for the country as a whole, and gained an appreciation of values other than those of town and city dwellers. Some, not surprisingly, married farmers or farm workers and would spend the rest of their lives in their adopted environment. Biologists, no doubt, might comment on the enrichment of the rural gene pool which arose from this mass immigration of women from elsewhere in the country.

Wherever one lived and whatever one's age during the war, it was an intense period of change, uncertainty and dislocation. As young people – most land girls were in their late teens or early twenties – this period of enforced labour on the land, thrown together with people they would otherwise not have met, was, for many, the equivalent to going away to college for a few years (or, perhaps more apposite, the enforced national service that many post war young men experienced). It was a chance to leave home and become independent but within an organisation which gave structure to their lives and the opportunity to develop as a person away from their previous social background.

Some thrived as a result; others found it hard to cope with. Most appeared to have come out of it, feeling that they had at least 'done their bit' for their country during a time of war and hardship, even those who served post-war when austerity and food rationing continued.

Whatever the hardships they suffered individually, almost all those I interviewed ended their conversations in the same way, by saying that they were "the best years of my life" and "I wouldn't have missed it for the world".

On being discharged from the WLA every member was issued with a Release Certificate showing their period of service. This one was issued to Joyce Irving in September 1946. *Source: J Ingle*

NOTES

PREFACE

1 BLARS (Graham archive) is an exception. Occasional references occur in the letters of Erica Graham, Chairman of the Bedfordshire WLA, which give a few insights into the organisation, from the perspective of this leading, committed part-time Council member.

2 See my article in Local History Magazine (January/February 2007, No 111), pp 12–16

3 See Bedfordshire Libraries' Virtual Library local history web pages:
www.galaxy.bedfordshire.gov.uk/webingres/bedfordshire/vlib/0.wla/wla_home.htm

CHAPTER 1

4 Speech by the Earl of Huntingdon in London to 130 (out of a national total of 230) land girls and WLA staff who had completed ten years of service in the WLA. LAN, March 1950 (Vol 3, No 10) p3.

5 Peak figure of Scottish WLA of 7,976 in November 1943 (including 1,744 employed by Scottish 'War Ags'). Total overall figure for Scottish WLA membership unknown. There was also a small WLA mobile group on the Isle of Man and another on five islands of the Isles of Scilly. Recruitment to the organisation in Northern Ireland was very low, partly because compulsory National Service was never introduced there. In addition, in England and Wales, there was a WLA Auxiliary Force of women, recruited by the WLA each spring and summer, able to offer a short period of full-time work between four weeks and six months, which was intended to help cover the need for an enlarged labour force at harvest time and other seasonal bursts of activity ('Information for Women's Land Army Representatives', February 1943 p12; Antrobus archive: MAF HMSO Return label No.5).

6 A handbook on 'National Service' was published on 25 January 1939 and delivered to every household in the country. In it Sir John Anderson MP, Lord Privy Seal, outlined the many ways in which men and women might 'fit themselves for National Service'. Women were invited to enrol ready for the eventuality of war for, amongst other options, 'a mobile force consisting of women who are ready to undertake all kinds of farm work in any part of the country' (p24).

7 4339 by December 1943 in England and Wales were employed by the Home Timber Production Department of the Ministry of Supply. Sackville-West (1944) p95. For more on the work of the Timber Corps see Home Timber Production Department, Ministry of Supply (1944/1997): Meet the Members. Approximately 2,000 further women worked for the Timber Corps in Scotland.

8 1917–19, employing some 23,000 women. Huxley (1961), p159

9 Twinch (1990), p67

10 But by December 1943 they earned one shilling (5p) an hour; 48s (£2.40p) per 48-hour week. WSRO 5926 Denman papers, File 7

11 Murray (1955) p159

12 75,900 land girls is given (presumably for the previous month) in TLG. Oct 1943 (Vol 4, No 7) p16. Murray is inconsistent when he writes of membership being 'still 3,000 below the 'ceiling' of 85,000' by the end of June 1944; Murray (1955) p210, then of a peak of 87,000 having been reached in August 1943, Murray (1955) p180, and also referring to the 'ceiling' strength having been reduced to 80,000 in July 1943, Murray (1955) p209 (but failing to give his primary source for all these figures). Certainly, at a time when farmers were calling for there to be 100,000 land girls, the government implemented a freeze on recruitment between August 1943 and 3 January 1944, Twinch (1990) p121–2. Thereafter, 80,000 was the ceiling on total WLA membership.

13 TLG, March 1947 (Vol 7, No 12) p16

14 Short (2007) p105

CHAPTER 2

15 BBC (WAC) Script: 6 August 1943, Women's Land Army birthday broadcast to Australia, para 4
16 TNA MAF 59/29 Introduction, para 3
17 TLG May 1941 (Vol 2, No 2) p11
18 BLARS Graham archive, letter from Lady Denman to Mrs Graham, 5 June 1941
19 Antrobus archive: Bedfordshire WLA newsletter, July 1942; TLG, October 1942 9 (Vol 3, No 7) p13
20 *Bedfordshire Times* 18 November 1949, p5
21 Antrobus archive. Notes on interview with Gloria Crawley, 14 January 2006
22 BLARS (Graham archive). Letter from Lady Denman to Mrs 'J.B.' Graham, 5 June 1941.
23 TNA MAF 59/29 Appendix B, para 2
24 Tillet (1988) p6
25 TNA MAF 59/29 Appendix A and Appendix B, para 2
26 BLARS Z290/8/8 (1946 souvenir programme, pp6 and 8)
27 TNA MAF 59/29 Appendix B, para 4
28 TLG, October 1944 (Vol 4, No 7) p16
29 *Bedfordshire Times* 18 November 1949, 'County offices close...', p5
30 WSRO 5926 Denman papers, File 7
31 TLG January 1945 (Vol 5, No 10) p9
32 TLG January 1947 (Vol 7, No 10) p1
33 LAN April 1949 (Vol 2, No 10) p3
34 LAN October 1950 (Vol 4, No 5) p1
35 WSRO 5926 Denman Papers File 5. Statistics for London Conference 12 February 1943
36 TLG, January 1941 (Vol 1, No 10) p6
37 The author hopes to carry out an analysis of service records of land girls serving in Bedfordshire, relating to former occupations, county of origin, age on entry, length of service and reasons for leaving. These will subsequently be published on his Bedfordshire Women's Land Army web pages and in local history magazines.
38 First World War, 1914–1918
39 WSRO 5926 Denman papers, File 6
40 1946 Bedfordshire WLA souvenir programme, p6
41 *Bedfordshire Times* 18 November 1949, p5
42 *Bedfordshire Times* 17 November 1939, p3
43 *Bedfordshire Times* 12 January 1940, p5
44 *Bedfordshire Times* 9 February 1940, p5
45 Article on Beds WLA at Kensworth by Irene Millest in *War and the Three Villages* (1995); Gwendoline Morgan née Morris http://www.bbc.co.uk/ww2peopleswar/stories/89/A5505789.shtml
46 Stella Goldsmith née Limon 'Bedfordshire Land Girl Memoir'; http:/tinyurl.com/2nq2up
47 BLARS WW2/AC2/17 Letter from J.B. Graham to the Ministry of Agriculture and Fisheries, 30 September 1943
48 TLG February 1943 (Vol 3, No 11) p12
49 TLG June 1943 (Vol 4, No 3) p13
50 TLG, July 1941 (Vol 2, No 4) p8
51 *Bedfordshire Times* 18 November 1949, p5
52 *Bedfordshire Times* 18 November 1949, p5
53 *Bedfordshire Times* 27 October 1950, p6
54 *Bedfordshire Times* 24 November 1950, p6

CHAPTER 3

55 Easterbrook (c. 1940s), Hammond (1954); HMSO (1951)
56 Short (2007) p25
57 Ministry of Information (1945/2001) p32
58 Anthony Hurd 'War Agricultural Committees – Why and How?' in *The Land Girl* February 1944, pp2–3
59 Ministry of Information (1945) p12
60 Easterbrook (1940s) p9
61 Short, pp56–7; Sackville-West quotes an estimated 2½m tons, but does not give her source.
62 About a thousand trained land girl pest controllers were said, by Sackville-West (p54), to 'tour the farms with great gusto'.
63 DEFRA website 'Agriculture during World War Two' (Accessed: 20 May 2007)
64 Short (2006) pp158–178
65 Short (2006) p16
66 Short (2006) pp95–96
67 HMSO. 'How Britain was fed in wartime: food control, 1939–45' (1946) p5
68 DEFRA website, 'Agriculture during World War Two' (Accessed: 20 May 2007)
69 DEFRA website, 'Agriculture during World War Two'; Hammond, 'Food and Agriculture', p78
70 Hammond, 'Food and Agriculture' p79
71 Short (2007) p13

CHAPTER 4

72 *Farmers Weekly* 31 May 1940, p17 quoted in Short (2007) p25
73 Antrobus archive: 24 May 2005. Correspondence with Helen Laurance née Young, who worked as an organiser for Bedfordshire 'War Ag' both with the Emergency Land Corps and in encouraging land girls to grow vegetables in the ground around their hostels. Her husband was a District Agricultural Officer with Bedfordshire 'War Ag'; BBC WWII PW Article ID: A3757683
74 *Agricultural Statistics* 1939–1944 (1947); 1945 (1948) HMSO
75 Short (2007) Chapters 2 & 3, pp16–54

CHAPTER 5

76 Initially the minimum entrance age had been 18 years and many counties tended to look for a minimum of 17½ years, but reasonable maturity was what was the deciding factor. Those employed in the WLA Forestry Section had to be over 21 years old, which became the age minimum when the Women's Timber Corps began enlistment in 1942.
77 *Land Army News* March 1950 (Vol 3, No 8) p3
78 Antrobus archive. Transcriptions of WLA service records relating to young women who served in Bedfordshire 1939–50.
79 Antrobus archive. Feedback from interviews by Stuart Antrobus with former Bedfordshire WLA land girls.
80 Sackville-West (1944) p17
81 MAF 59/5. Letter from Mrs I. Jenkins to Miss Stopford, MoLNS, 20 December 1941
82 MAF 59/15. 10 June 1939 Circular from Inez Jenkins
83 MAF 59/5 MoLNS minute, 17 September 1943
84 MAF 59/5 WLA Circular 146, 16 March 1943
85 Luton Hoo Estate Archive 0001/15: Letter, 14 June 1941 from Lois Heydeman, Beds WLA HQ, to Captain Burrett, Estate Manager, confirming Specially Approved Farm Training status.

86 *The Land Girl* Aug 1941 (Vol 2, No 5) p11
87 *The Land Girl* Aug 1944 (Vol 5, No 5) p12
88 Antrobus archive. Personal memoir by Irene Hulatt née Wright
89 1946 Bedfordshire WLA souvenir programme, p6
90 Hammond 'Food and Agriculture' p78
91 Sackville-West (1944) p99
92 Sackville-West (1944) p100

CHAPTER 6

93 Short (2007) p114
94 TNA MAF 47/153. Letter from Minister of Health to Ministry of Works, 8 June 1943
95 TNA MAF 47/143. Letter 2 January 1943
96 MAF 47/143. Para 12, p15, 19 May 1943
97 TNA MAF 47/143. Memo to executive offices of County 'War Ags' in England and Wales, 19 May 1943
98 TNA MAF 47/143. 19 May 1943 Para 12 on Hostels
99 WSRO 5926 Denman papers: WLA Leaflet No. 6 Employment of Regular Force Volunteers, Section 7. Accommodation, p7
100 WSRO 5926 Denman papers: WLA Leaflet No. 6 Employment of Regular Force Volunteers, Section 7. Accommodation, p7; TNA MAF 47/143 Existing hostel beds and likely additional beds for 1943
101 WSRO 5926 Denman papers. Procedure for establishing and running hostels for members of the WLA, October 1941. Section F
102 Twinch (1990) p72
103 *Bedfordshire Times* 31 May 1940 p7

CHAPTER 7

104 *The Land Girl* August 1942 (Vol 3, No 5) p12
105 *Bedfordshire Times* 24 July 1942 p5
106 *The Land Girl* July 1943 (Vol 4, No 4) p10 (letter from Mrs J. Eugster, Beds WLA County Secretary)
107 *The Land Girl* August 1943 (Vol 5, No 5) p13
108 *The Land Girl* March 1944 (Vol 4, No 11) p9; *Bedfordshire Times* 11 February 1944 p6
109 *The Land Girl* August 1944 (Vol 5, No 5) p12
110 *The Land Girl* June 1944 (Vol 4, No 3) p13
111 *Bedfordshire Times* 28 July 1944
112 IWM Film and Video Archive, newsreel footage WPN 256
113 *Bedfordshire Times* 15 Feb 1946, p7; *The Times* 15 February 1946, p7; *Bedford Record* 19 February 1946, p1; *The Land Girl* March 1946 (Vol 6, No 12) p12

CHAPTER 8

114 1946 Bedfordshire WLA souvenir programme, p6
115 Antrobus archive: completed questionnaire by Betty Fuller & IWM service record
116 Stuart Antrobus interview with Elizabeth Day, No. 5, IWM Sound Archive 24643
117 Antrobus archive. Brief unpublished memoir & captions to photographs by Dorothy Keightley née Hurren, 2003
118 Stuart Antrobus interview with Ann Haynes née Brodrick, No. 11, IWM Sound Archive 24649
119 Stuart Antrobus interview with Iris Cornell née Manning, No. 2, IWM Sound Archive 24640

120 Stuart Antrobus interview with Mary Spilling née Bennett, No. 3, IWM Sound Archive 24641

121 Stuart Antrobus interview with Hannah Croot née Bennett, No. 6, IWM Sound Archive 24644; Carmela Semeraro interview with Hannah Croot née Bennett, CLCL 206

122 Barbara Hartwell née Harley, *Bedfordshire on Sunday* 24 April 1977, p5, col7

123 Stuart Antrobus interview with Stella Forster née Shelton, No. 4, IWM Sound Archive 24642

124 *Bedfordshire on Sunday* 24 April 1977, p5, cols 1–2. Maiden name not given

125 Stuart Antrobus interview with Zeita Holes née Trott, No. 8, IWM Sound Archive 24646

126 *Bedfordshire on Sunday* 24 April 1977, p5, cols 2–3. Maiden name not given

127 Stuart Antrobus interview with Betty Nichols née Gray, No. 18, IWM Sound Archive 24665

128 *Bedfordshire on Sunday* 24 April 1977, p5, col 4. Maiden name not given

129 Stuart Antrobus interview with Margaret Chessum née Perry, No. 1, IWM Sound Archive 24539

130 K.M. Westaway *Old Girls in New Times*, Bedford: F.R. Hockliffe Ltd., 1945 pp66–67 (Illustration facing p57). Card missing from WLA service records at Imperial War Museum (therefore service dates not known).

131 Handwritten memoir by Margaretta Eden née Clark and correspondence with her husband, Claude Eden, 18 February 2006 (Antrobus Archive)

132 Antrobus archive: brief memoir by Kathleen Francis née Green, 2003

133 *Bedfordshire on Sunday* 24 April 1997, p5, col 4. Maiden name not given

134 Stuart Antrobus interview with Rose Hakewill née Richards, No. 12, IWM Sound Archive 24650

135 Memoir by Catherine Henman née Bezant; Yates (2006) pp69–72

136 Carmela Semeraro interview with Evelyn Huckvale née Archer, CLCL 125

137 *Bedfordshire Times* 14 February 2008 p20; Stuart Antrobus interview with Dora Pontin née Carlyle, 29 March 2008

138 Carmela Semeraro interview with Barbara Filbey née Probert, CLCL 045

139 Carmela Semeraro interview with Barbara Tovey née Cox, CLCL 122

140 Antrobus archive, notes from author's meeting with Yvonne Truin née Frood, 1 November 2005

141 Antrobus archive, unpublished hand-written memoir by Dorothy Yates née Crowsley

142 Stuart Antrobus interview with Sheila Hope née Stephens, No. 9, IWM 24647

143 Roberts (1991) p95

144 Roberts (1991); Antrobus Archive, personal memoir article by Betty and Jean Pearson from their local church magazine, 'The Torch', February 1998

145 Carmela Semeraro interview with Betty Schwarz née Harding, CLCL 154

146 Antrobus Archive, notes on conversation with Kathleen Davies née Burgoyne, 21 November 2006

147 Courtesy of the Luton Hoo Walled Garden Project research team, Luton Hoo Estate

148 Letter in TLG, February 1942, (Vol 2, No 11) p11

149 Stuart Antrobus interview with Joyce Ingle née Irving, No. 7, IWM 24645; Colin Burbage interview (13 mins) with Joyce Ingle and three other former Bedfordshire land girls – Peggy, Joan and Mary (surnames not given), on his CD 'On the Home Front: Memories of Wartime Life 'Somewhere' in England', originally recorded in 1989 [CB sound, 12 Glamis Walk, Bedford, MK41 8LG]

150 Stuart Antrobus interview with Zeita Holes née Trott, No. 8, IWM 24646

151 Stuart Antrobus interview with Vera Barnett née Jobling, No. 15, IWM 24653

152 Stuart Antrobus interview with Ethel Wildey née Sweenie, No. 16, IWM 24663

153 Stuart Antrobus interview with Sheila Hope née Stevens, No. 9, IWM 24647

154 Stuart Antrobus interview with 'Dawn' Filby née Skeggs, No. 10, IWM 24648

155 Antrobus archive, brief unpublished handwritten memoir by Nola Wallace née Bagley, 2007

156 Dr Vernon Williams interview with Irene Saunders née Cook, 24 April 2006; Jenny Ford interview

with Irene Saunders née Cook, BEDFM:2001/146, courtesy of Bedford Museum

157 Stuart Antrobus interview with Elizabeth Ann Haynes née Brodrick, No. 11, IWM 24649

158 Stuart Antrobus interview with Joyce 'Joy' Case née Senior, No. 13, IWM 24651

159 Stuart Antrobus interview with Mary Smith née Pakes; Antrobus archive, brief typed memoir

160 Stuart Antrobus interview with Mary Nichols née Gray, No. 18, IWM 24665

161 Sylvia Preater's story of engagement to an American pilot at the end of the war but subsequent separation and eventual marriage nearly thirty years later, is told in Joanna Lumley's book *Forces Sweethearts*, Bloomsbury, 1993, published in association with the Imperial War Museum, p 189.

162 Stuart Antrobus interview with Kathleen Cox née Hopkins, No. 17, IWM 24664

163 Antrobus archive, brief unpublished memoir by Joan Wellings née Wilding, February 2008

164 For more about life at Thurleigh airfield during the Second World War, see the video documentary *Thurleigh Memories*, by Dr Vernon Williams, Director, East Anglia Air War Project, Abilene Christian University, Texas, USA. DVD ISBN 0-9708927-8-0

165 J Lumley *Forces Sweethearts: Wartime Romance from the First World War to the Gulf* (1993) Bloomsbury p 189

166 Antrobus archive. Biographical information and photograph from Peggy DiPaul's daughter, Theresa Cass, 2007

167 I am indebted to Peggy Albertson, and to Ralph Franklin, British representative of the 306 Bombardment Group and founder-curator of Thurleigh Airfield Museum, for biographical information on both 'Joe' and Peggy, and the quotation from his eulogy at Joe's funeral in 2006. See also the video documentary *Thurleigh Memories* (see above) which includes brief extracts from oral history interviews with Peggy and Joe Albertson.

168 *The Land Girl* March 1943 (Vol 3, No 12) p 7

169 Antrobus archive: brief handwritten memoir by Celia Müller née Holt, 2008

170 Summarised, with her approval, from the transcription of a tape-recorded interview by Nora Myles with 'Jacqueline' Hunt née Hindle recorded on 19 April 2007 as part of a BA in History and Sociology course at the University of Central Lancashire.

171 See p 82–3 of Chapter 8 on *Life for Land Girls on Private Farms*

172 Stuart Antrobus interview with Elizabeth 'Liz' Day, No. 5, IWM 24643

173 Letter from Joan Ison née Taylor to Stuart Antrobus, 1 June 2005

174 Ted Enever *Cockney Kid and Countrymen*, The Book Castle, 2001, p 100; Stuart Antrobus interview with Frances Jones née Guttridge in 2005 and 2008

175 Ted Enever *Cockney Kid and Countrymen*, The Book Castle, Dunstable, 2001, pp 101–102

176 Antrobus archive notes on an interview with Sylvia Cox née Bunnett, Frances Jones née Guttridge & Josephine Rowe née Walton, 2005

177 Josephine M Rowe née Walton, article on 'Westoning' in *Bedfordshire Magazine*, Vol 24, Winter 1993, p 114

178 Josephine M Rowe née Walton, article on 'Woburn' in *Bedfordshire Magazine*, Vol 24, Spring 1994, p 168

179 Interview by Stuart Antrobus with Josephine Rowe née Walton, 2005

180 Carmela Semeraro interview with Betty Schwarz née Harding, CLCL 154

181 Antrobus Archive, personal memoir article by Betty and Jean Pearson from their local church magazine, 'The Torch', February 1998

182 Antrobus archive, notes on meeting with Mary Cutler; BBC *People's War* archive ID A5484152 (1 September 2005); Yates (2006) pp 74–76

183 Antrobus archive. For her full written memoir, covering her experience at Leighton Buzzard and Cople hostels, visit the following Bedfordshire Libraries' Internet web pages: http://tinyurl.

com/2nq2np and follow the links from the Bedfordshire Women's Land Army contents page to 'Bedfordshire Land Girl Memoir'.

184 Yates (2006) pp72–73

185 Antrobus archive. Undated local newspaper cutting. Maiden name unknown

186 Antrobus archive. Brief written memoir by Eileen Wagstaff née Wortham

187 Irene Wright née Hulatt *Snapshots from Bedford Guild House* (2004) p17. Courtesy of Biograph

188 Antrobus archive. This extract first appeared as part of a longer article entitled 'Stars in My Eyes' in *The Fisherman*, the parish magazine of St. Andrew's Church, Bedford, February 2005.

189 Antrobus archive. Handwritten memoir extracts provided by the author, Irene Hulatt née Wright

190 Antrobus archive. Brief written memoir in letter of 31 October 2006

191 Carmela Semeraro interview with Betty Fitton née Hurst, CLCL 044; Antrobus archive, brief handwritten memoir, July 2005

192 Carmela Semeraro interview with Cicely McKeegan née Redman, CLCL 171

193 Carmela Semeraro interview with Peggy Tedder née Clark, CLCL 194

194 Carmela Semeraro interview with Zoe Sinfield née Odell, CLCL 049

CHAPTER 10

195 See appendices for table and graph showing actual employment figures for Bedfordshire WLA. Research into the service cards for those members who were enrolled in Bedford reveals individuals who were subsequently transferred to other counties, presumably because at the time of enrolment there were no further land girls needed in Bedfordshire. Occasional county newsletters also refer to these transfers but further statistical analysis of almost 3,500 cards needs to be done to reveal what proportion transferred to other counties soon after enrolment in Bedfordshire.

196 Antrobus archive. Figures derived from monthly county returns in *The Land Girl* magazine

197 *Bedfordshire Times* 12 May 1944 p4

198 Post-war, the Ministry of Agriculture was admitting that it had been unfortunate that the term 'Army' had been used to name the body of paid volunteer civilian workers who undertook service on the land for the duration of the war. That and the issue of a distinctive uniform had led the recruits to consider themselves on a par with those women in the armed services, despite not being subject to military discipline and not (except for those in the Timber Corps) employed by the state.

LIST OF ILLUSTRATIONS

BEDFORDSHIRE WOMEN'S LAND ARMY TIMELINE 1939–1950
including national developments which affected Bedfordshire land girls

1 9 3 9

EARLY 1939
- First Bedfordshire 'land girl' volunteers signed up before the outbreak of war by Mrs J. Dallas (First World War WLA volunteer) and Miss G.M. Farrar, and asked to wait to be notified of a farmer who needed their labour in Bedfordshire. (61 volunteers had to be transferred to other counties during the autumn, because of a lack of demand from Bedfordshire farmers for land girl labour.)
- Nationally agreed 28 shillings (£1.40p) weekly pay (10 shillings less than the average farm wage at that time) for a 50-hour week (48 in winter). Half that (70p) to pay for food and accommodation.
- Bedfordshire WLA headquarters office opened, 2 St Paul's Square, Bedford, following official establishment of Women's Land Army (WLA), 1 June 1939.
- National WLA headquarters set up at Balcombe Place, Haywards Heath, West Sussex on 29 August 1939.
- First 'Chairman' of the County Committee: Mrs Nora Whitchurch, of Great Barford House, Bedford; Honorary Organising Secretary: Miss Marjorie Farrar of Chicheley Hall.

SEPTEMBER 1939
- Sunday 3 September: declaration of war between Britain and Germany.
- Mr H.J. Humphreys, of Eversholt, appointed unpaid Chairman of the Bedfordshire War Agricultural Executive Committee (BWAEC or 'War Ag') by the Minister of Agriculture, Sir Reginald Dorman-Smith (February 1939 – May 1940).
- Mr E.W. Russell is appointed the salaried Executive Officer. 'War Ag' headquarters office: Phoenix Chambers, St Paul's Square, Bedford.
- Tuesday 5 September: First meeting of the Bedfordshire 'War Ag'.

NOVEMBER 1939
- 'All is not well with the land girls. Many of them left good jobs to undergo training and now find that farmers are unwilling to engage them. In Bedfordshire there is considerable scepticism about their worth...Perhaps the land girls will come into their own later on, but there is no doubt that the scheme has been bungled and that some of the girls are bitter about it. For reasons of patriotism many have given up careers only to find that their services are not wanted.'
  Beds Times 17 Nov 1939 p3

DECEMBER 1939
- Enrolled volunteers employed in Bedfordshire by end of December 1939: 24
  The Women's Land Army (1944) p95

1 9 4 0

JANUARY 1940
- 'Too Hard for Land Girls?': Talking about growing onions, Mr Mark Young, Junior, Sandy market gardener, said "I don't think the land girls would stand for the crawling".
  Beds Times 12 Jan 1940 p5

FEBRUARY 1940
- 'Hardy Land Girls': 'Who was it that said that land girls would be unable to cope with the unpleasant jobs to be found on any farm? Had the critic seen two girls picking Brussels sprouts on a farm at Thurleigh throughout the recent severe weather he would

have revised his opinion. These girls are still busy among the sprouts and are making light of work which is not considered to be easy even for experienced hands.'
Beds Times 9 February 1940 p5

APRIL 1940
• Calling up of farm workers aged 20 years upwards who have not received six months postponement through being in 'reserved occupations'.

MAY 1940
• 'Appeal for Land Girls at Bedford': 'Appeals for recruits to the Women's Land Army... were made to a public meeting in the Corn Exchange, Bedford on Thursday afternoon ...Lady Lucas Tooth, chief speaker, said that the war of 1940 was a women's war in a sense which could not have been imagined in 1914. Today women were not only replacing men – they were running essential services at home (in this country). Miss N. Bowers, for the Women's Land Army, said that recruits were needed for farm work and members of the WVS (Women's Voluntary Service) could help best by using their personal influence on suitable young women.'
Beds Times 3 May 1940 p7

• I June 1940 : rally of the Women's Land Army held in Bedford when intending recruits could obtain full particulars of enrolment and conditions. Saturday recruiting stall in Market Square. Recruiting parades held from 11am to 12.30pm and 2.30 to 4.30pm, consisting of land girls on a horse-driven farm wagon and a tractor.
Beds Times 31 May 1940 p7

JULY 1940
• 50 volunteers employed in Bedfordshire, so far.
The Land Girl July 1940 (Vol 1, No 4)

SEPTEMBER 1940
• Mrs J. Dallas reports that 60 copies of *The Land Girl* magazine had been sold in Bedfordshire (56 land girls actually employed to that date).
The Land Girl Sep (Vol 1, No 6) p 10

NOVEMBER 1940
• Mrs J. Dallas reports that there are 65 subscribers to *The Land Girl* magazine in Bedfordshire (as against 74 enrolled members, some 66 of them working in the county).

• Miss G.M. Farrar, County Secretary, donated a first copy to every volunteer at that time in training or employment in Bedfordshire.
The Land Girl Nov 1940 (Vol 1, No 8) p 10

• WLA 'A Few Facts About What It Is Doing': 'At the end of October there were seventy-six members of the Women's Land Army in Bedfordshire, though this by no means represents all those who have been enrolled since the war, as there have been many transfers to other counties. Of these seventy-six working in this County, forty are employed in dairy work, one does a motor milk round, five are on poultry farms, two in food production in private gardens, two as timber measurers under the Forestry Commission, and there are also a number of tractor drivers and general farm workers. Two Land Army members have recently been married. There have been eighteen farmers and market gardeners who have been good enough to give preliminary training, many of whom have kept the trainee in regular employment. The general opinion in this County is that the Land Army is proving its worth.'
Beds Times 29 November 1940 p4

DECEMBER 1940
• 55 land girls employed in Bedfordshire.
Official WLA figures listed in *Sackville-West* (1944) p95

1 9 4 1

JANUARY 1941
- 'Please Come Back'. An appeal from WLA national headquarters to volunteers who had trained and begun with the WLA but left during the first 18 months.
  The Land Girl January 1941 (Vol 1, No 10) p8

MARCH 1941
- National appeal in *The Land Girl* magazine for members to recruit other new volunteers.
- New WLA minimum wage from 1 March 1941: 32 shillings (£1.60p) (for up to 48 hours a week) for land girl billetted off the farm; 16 shillings (80p) for land girl billeted on the farm (plus free board and lodging), plus overtime pay.
  The Land Girl March 1941 (Vol 1, No 12) p8

APRIL 1941
- 19 Bedfordshire land girls completed one year's service; 21 have completed six months' service; 40 volunteers transferred to other counties (which explains low 'employed' figures for Bedfordshire WLA).
- Several recruits have been trained at Northamptonshire Agricultural Institute, Moulton.
- 74 subscribers to *The Land Girl* magazine.
  The Land Girl April 1941 (Vol 2, No 1) p11

MAY 1941
- Bedfordshire WLA Tea Party on St George's Day in Bedford arranged by Mrs J.A. (Nora) Whitchurch and Honorary Organising Secretary, Miss G.M. Farrar. Over 50 land girls present. Mr H.J. Humphreys, Chairman of Bedfordshire 'War Ag' presented half-diamond armband chevrons to 12 land girls who had completed 18 months' service; two girls received their second half-diamond; and two, their first half-diamond (a half-diamond chevron represented six months' service). It was announced that Miss Farrar was leaving the county. 'Her cheerful manner and understanding ways will long be remembered.' Miss Bower, HQ Organiser from WLA national headquarters, spoke encouragingly to the girls and a warm welcome was given to Miss Lois Heydeman, the new salaried County Secretary.
  The Land Girl May 1941 (Vol 2, No 2) p11

JULY 1941
- HM Queen Elizabeth agreed to become Patron of the WLA.
  The Land Girl July 1941 (Vol 2, No 4) p8

AUGUST 1941
- Six Bedfordshire land girls attend the newly-approved training farm at Luton Hoo. The work of Miss Phyllis Chiplin (WLA 47099) particularly praised. 102 Bedfordshire subscribers to *The Land Girl*.
  The Land Girl August 1941 (Vol 2, No 5) p1

SEPTEMBER 1941
- 'In the Event of Invasion', land girls encouraged to stick to their jobs and carry on but advice given on how to disable tractors if in real danger of capture by the enemy.
  The Land Girl Sept 1941 (Vol 2, No 6) p1

OCTOBER 1941
- Miss Brazier, Bedfordshire land girl, won second prize in a national *The Land Girl* magazine photographic competition.
  The Land Girl Oct 1941 (No 7, Vol 2) p5 (see *The Land Girl* Nov 1941 (Vol 2, No 8) p11 for the photo)

NOVEMBER 1941
- Mrs 'J.B.' (Erica) Graham (Chairman, Bedfordshire WLA County Committee) opened the WLA Club (at the Girls' Club premises on Harpur Street, Bedford) on 22 November 1941 and presented Good Service badges: 14 for two years; two for 18 months, two for one year, 21 for six months. Mrs Godber had raised £42 through a dance and from friends to launch the club.
  The Land Girl Dec 1941 (Vol 2, No 9) p13
- Bedford Land Girls Club opens every Saturday afternoon 1pm–6pm for land girl

'recreation and social intercourse'. Facilities: games room, reading room, rest room, tea room, and kitchen plus dancing hall.

- Announcement that Bedfordshire 'War Ag' had handed over four hostels to the WLA. Mrs Graham said she was confident the girls would find them ideal homes.
  Beds Times 28 Nov 1941 p8 (See February 1942 for first opening of these hostels)

DECEMBER 1941
- Land girls who have already volunteered will be regarded as engaged in vital war work in relation to the new National Service Act, and will not therefore be 'called up' to other work.
  The Land Girl Dec 1941 (Vol 2, No 9) p5
- New issue of overcoats very much appreciated.
  The Land Girl Dec 1941 (Vol 2, No 9) p13
- Minimum wages raised from 29 December 1941: 38 shillings for 48-hour week (or 18 shillings with free bed and board).
  The Land Girl Jan 1942 (Vol 2, No 10) p5
- 140 land girls employed in Bedfordshire.
  Sackville-West (1944) p95

1 9 4 2

JANUARY 1942
- Dorothy Hayward (WLA 12933) wrote to *The Land Girl* magazine about her work in tomato growing in a very large nursery in Bedfordshire (eight acres of glass, 187 feet long; 52 tomato houses with 2,500 plants in each, plus four glasshouses for cucumbers). (Nursery's name not given).
  The Land Girl Feb 1942 (Vol 2, No 11) p11

FEBRUARY 1942
- 16 Feb 1942: Milton Ernest hutment hostel opened under the YWCA Warden Miss Felicia Taylor. "Despite severe weather everyone has stuck to the new work manfully."
  The Land Girl April 1942 (Vol 3, No 1) p11

MARCH 1942
- 'Farmers should give as long notice as possible of their labour requirements and they should be prepared to train their own women if this is at all practicable'. Letter sent to the National Farmers Union from the national WLA HQ. Currently, no trained volunteers were unemployed.
  Beds Times 20 March 1942 p4

APRIL 1942
- Women's Timber Corps (a branch of the WLA) is formed. Its members became known as 'lumber jills'. They wore the same uniform as other land girls except for a special green beret and a Timber Corps badge with a fir-tree emblem. They were employed by the Home Timber Production Department of the Ministry of Supply.
- Miss Clemence Dane, in a BBC radio broadcast, 20 April 1942, makes the first reference to the WLA as the 'Cinderella service', in the sense of being taken for granted and its importance overlooked.

MAY 1942
- 'Hard Work and Good health'. Article and photographs, taken in canteen and dormitory, of land girls at the new Milton Ernest hostel. 40 'healthy and weather-tanned' girls from Bedfordshire and London had a visit from Miss E.W. Moore from the YWCA headquarters. Daily routine outlined.
  Beds Times 29 May 1942 p6

JUNE 1942
- 4 June 1942: Leighton Buzzard hutment hostel for 40 opened (second YWCA hostel in county for land girls). Warden: Miss Whipp.

- Bedfordshire had 180 *The Land Girl* magazine subscribers.
  The Land Girl June 1942 (Vol 3, No 2) p 13
- Sunday 14 June: 28 land girls took part in the United Nations Day parade in Luton.
  Bedfordshire WLA news sheet July 1942

JULY
1942
- As part of a 'War Work Campaign', 16 land girls presented a pageant at the Granada Cinema in Bedford, Sunday 19 July 1942.
  The Land Girl Aug 1942 (Vol 3, No 5) p 12
- Bedford Women's Emergency Land Corp formed of women who volunteer to work, part-time, for a minimum of 48 hours on the land. Recruits drawn from housewives, shop assistants and women in other occupations who work all day long but are willing to spare one or more evenings or half-days off to do spare-time work on farms. Collected by lorries from the Corn Exchange at 6pm by the 'War Ag' and returned after work.
- American visitor, Mr MacFarlane, a guest of farmer Joseph Godber of Willington, who has six land girls working there, praised the Land Army, speaking at the Land Army Club in Bedford. "You can take it from me that the Land Army is doing a good job of work – the best of all the women's services, I think – with less hullabaloo and less publicity than all the others."
  Beds Times 31 July 1942 p 6

AUGUST
1942
- Bedfordshire WLA has contributed £40.3s.0d (£40.15p) to the Land Army 'Spitfire Fund' (£5,691. 5s. 10d raised nationally, which enabled the RAF to buy the first Typhoon fighter plane, called *The Land Girl* and featuring the WLA badge).
- Miss Read, Luton, arranged for a group of land girls from South Bedfordshire to march in the Luton parade, 2 August 1942, before Admiral Sir Lionel Halsey.
  The Land Girl Aug 1942 (Vol 3, No 5) p 12

SEPTEMBER
1942
- Land girls in uniform (previously excluded) to be admitted to canteens run by the Council for Voluntary Work in Bedfordshire.
  The Land Girl Sep 1942 (Vol 3, No 6) p 7
- Mrs Erica Graham, County WLA Chairman, of Lodge Farm, Toddington, organised a Harvest Home outing for land girls, with tea at Whipsnade Zoo, Saturday 26 September 1942.

OCTOBER
1942
- Bedfordshire WLA HQ has moved to 43 Harpur Street, Bedford (Telephone 2937), almost opposite the new Telephone Exchange, and next to the Potato Board Office.
  The Land Girl Oct 1942 (Vol 3, No 7) p 12

NOVEMBER
1942
- Minister of Agriculture, Mr R.S. Hudson (May 1940 – August 1945), visited the county on Saturday 14 November 1942 and praised the farmers for their increase in arable land acreage. He inspected land drainage schemes.
  Beds Times 20 Nov 1942 p 4
- Two new Land Army hostels opened at Bolnhurst in the north (hutment for 40) and Kensworth House in the south (requisitioned house for approximately 40), plus a new training hostel for four week courses at Toddington Park in mid-Bedfordshire.
- Ministry of Information films had been shown at the two hostels so far. 'War Ag' officers held a 'Brains Trust' evening at Leighton Buzzard and Milton Ernest hostels (Bolnhurst hostel to be next).
  The Land Girl Dec 1942 (Vol 3, No 9) p 12

DECEMBER
1942
- 'War on Farm Pests': Article on how good crops are ruined by rats and on the 'War Ag's active policy of extermination of rats, sparrows, squirrels and other vermin, plus

mice and voles in market gardening.
Beds Times 25 December 1942 p4

• 'Women's Land Army Party' arranged by Bedford WLA Club for 250 Bedfordshire land girls, Saturday 19 December 1942, at the Dujon Café, Bedford, plus inauguration of the nation-wide Women's Land Army Benevolent Fund. Cheque for £23 donated by Bedfordshire land girls. Entertainment provided by recently-formed Milton Ernest hostel choir and three local airmen, under leadership of Miss Prowse of the BBC, based in Bedford. Mrs Miriam Godber's 'Welfare Fund' provided for party.
Beds Times 25 Dec 1942 p7

• 492 land girls employed in Bedfordshire.
The Women's Land Army (1944) p95

1 9 4 3

JANUARY 1943
• 'The Women's Land Army are hoping to double the numbers of workers during the year, and they are extending their scheme of hostels, but they would like to place more girls with individual farmers. [It is also proposed] ...to organize gangs of business and professional men and women who will be available during the weekends...'
Beds Times 1 Jan 1943 p4

• 'Restoring Fertility to Derelict Acres'. Food is now produced at Whipsnade Zoo where only animals once roamed.

• Italian POWs engaged in drainage work in Elstow.
Beds Times 22 Jan 1943 p4

• 506 land girls employed in Bedfordshire.
The Land Girl Jan 1943 (Vol 3, No 10) p16

• Hostel opened in Potton at The Hollies, King Street, a small town house accommodating 20 land girls including nine from Lincolnshire. The first YWCA Warden was Mrs Stone.
The Land Girl Feb 1943 (Vol 3, No 11) p12

FEBRUARY 1943
• The Women's Land Army employed 53,500 land girls at this time nationally.
The Land Girl Feb 1943 (Vol 3, No 11) p12

• 'Land Girls Beat Men at Ploughing': Monday 1st February, 1943 at Woburn Park. Friendly ploughing match between WLA and male farm workers. Girls won first, second and third places: Ethel Eaton, Rhona Carter and Edith Catchlove.
Beds Times 5 February 1943 p3

• Reclaiming land at Wilstead. Land girls used tractors between Wilstead and Houghton Conquest, pulling up bushes, to add 30 acres of high-cropping land.
Beds Times 12 Feb 1943 p4

• 520 land girls employed in Bedfordshire.
The Land Girl Feb 1943 (Vol 3, No 11) p16

• 15 February 1943: Whipsnade hutment hostel opened, near to The Green, Whipsnade for 16 volunteers (formerly housing weekend waitresses at nearby zoo).
The Land Girl April 1943 (Vol 4, No 1) p12 'County News'

MARCH 1943
• Demonstrations by land girls: farmers impressed at New Buildings Farm, Husborne Crawley, 3 March 1943. Organised by 'War Ag' to show 'those farmers who are rather sceptical about work that can be undertaken by members of the Women's Land Army'.

- Miss Daisy Beard, a former kennel assistant, was the first forewoman to be engaged in Bedfordshire WLA.

  Beds Times 26 Feb 1943 p4 and *Beds Times* 5 March 1943 p7

- 541 land girls employed in Bedfordshire.

  The Land Girl March 1943 (Vol 3, No 12) p16

APRIL 1943

- 'ENSA concerts are now being held regularly at all the hostels and all volunteers living near enough to attend are welcome to do so.'

- Uniform Department: 'Please do not wear half uniform and half mufti [civilian clothes] and strings to the hats. Land Girls are not cowboys.'

  The Land Girl April 1943 (Vol 4, No 1) p12

- 567 land girls employed in Bedfordshire.

  The Land Girl April 1943 (Vol 4, No 1) p16

MAY 1943

- 'Use Horses More': advertisement encouraging farmers to save fuel because of shortages.

  Beds Times 21 May 1943 p6

- 614 land girls employed in Bedfordshire.

  The Land Girl May 1943 (Vol 4, No 2) p16

JUNE 1943

- Mrs Lois Heydeman compelled through ill health to leave Bedfordshire WLA HQ office staff; replaced by Mrs Ida Eugster.

- Silsoe hostel (requisitioned Wrest Park Lodge House) opened last week. Warden: Mrs Stone (formerly of Potton hostel); Assistant Warden: Miss Sanderson. Elstow ['Chimney Corner'] and Hulcote Moors hostels to open soon.

  The Land Girl June 1943 (Vol 4, No 3) p13

- 'Wings for Victory Week' 12–19 June in Bedford (target £500,000). 16 land girls marched down High Street and 18 tractors and trailers in parade, Saturday 19 June 1943.

- "We secured a large bomb and anti-aircraft gun mounted on a lorry to lead our contingent carrying a large notice saying 'These are Hitler's weapons' and followed by an arrow pointing to our Land girls saying 'These are ours'."

  The Land Girl July 1943 (Vol 4, No 4) p10

- 663 land girls employed in Bedfordshire.

  The Land Girl June 1943 (Vol 4, No 3) p16

JULY 1943

- 4 July 1943: National Farm Sunday processions in Bedford, Luton and individual villages.

- 771 land girls employed in Bedfordshire.

  The Land Girl July 1943 (Vol 4, No 4) p16

AUGUST 1943

- Recruitment to Women's Land Army is closed by a decision of the War Cabinet (because of need for more workers in the aircraft production industry).

- Daisy Beard and Pat Johnstone (Bedfordshire land girls) represented the county at a WLA fourth birthday party at Buckingham Palace given by HM the Queen. Pat Johnstone also broadcast to America via the BBC.

- Two new hostels opened recently [July 1943]: Houghton Conquest [a hutment hostel for up to 94 land girls, near 'Chimney Corner'. Warden, Miss Lamb] and Hulcote Moors Farm [a small hostel for 16 near Cranfield. Warden, Mrs Whatling].

  The Land Girl Aug 1943 (Vol 4, No 5) p13

- Advertisement entitled 'John Bull's Daughters' included a drawing of a land girl harvesting and a poem 'Diana drives the tractor'.

  Beds Times 13 Aug 1943 p10

- BBC WLA broadcast (29 August, 1.15pm, Home Service) referred to the uniform rationing clothing coupon arrangements, WLA correspondence courses in agriculture and horticulture and the introduction of WLA Proficiency Tests.
  Beds Times 13 Aug 1943 p9
- 792 land girls employed in Bedfordshire.
  The Land Girl Aug 1943 (Vol 4, No5) p 16

SEPTEMBER 1943
- 180 land girls arrived immediately before the ban on further recruitment. Cople House hostel opened (accommodating up to 97 girls).
  The Land Girl Oct 1943 (Vol 4, No 7) p 13
- 'WLA Labour Is Now Available' public notice to farmers, issued by Bedfordshire 'War Ag', 22 September 1943, referring to 12 hostels: Milton Ernest, Bolnhurst, Ravensden, Cople, Potton, Houghton Conquest, Silsoe, Hulcote Moors, Toddington, Kensworth, Leighton Buzzard, Whipsnade.
  Beds Times 24 Sept 1943 p6 (Advertisement)
- 904 land girls employed in Bedfordshire.
  The Land Girl Sep 1943 (Vol 4, No 6) p 16

OCTOBER 1943
- Minister of Agriculture visits Bedfordshire.
  Beds Times 1 October 1943 p7
- Exceptionally dry season. Early and heavy harvest.
- Gymkhana held at Elstow, 11 September, arranged by Mrs Graham and the County staff. Excellent weather attracted large crowds. Side-shows manned by land girls and three hostels organised their own stalls.
- Cups given by Mrs Graham, Mrs Mills, Alan Wood and R. Dent. The Lord Lieutenant, Colonel Part attended. A dance was held in the evening. Cheque for £150 to be sent to the WLA Benevolent Fund.
  The Land Girl Oct 1943 (Vol 4, No 7) p 13
- Mrs Martin of Box End House, Kempston, held her first informal Land Girls Club meeting for girls in the Kempston and Stagsden area.
- 965 land girls employed in Bedfordshire.
  The Land Girl Oct 1943 (Vol 4, No 7) p 16

NOVEMBER 1943
- 'Bedfordshire Not Short of Milkers...There are a number of Land Girls in dairy work waiting to be placed with milk producers.'
  Beds Times 5 November 1943 p4
- 997 land girls employed in Bedfordshire.
  The Land Girl Nov 1943 (Vol 4, No 8) p 16

DECEMBER 1943
- 40 more girls from the North and 40 girls from Essex welcomed to Bedfordshire over the last two months.
- New temporary hostel opened in Luton.
- Threshing in full swing.
- 12 girls (who started as land girls in autumn 1939) qualified for their four-year armlet.
- Agricultural correspondence courses in full swing.
- The first Proficiency Tests will be held early in the New Year (1944).
- 1006 land girls employed in Bedfordshire.
  The Land Girl Dec 1943 (Vol 4, No 9) p 16

1 9 4 4

JANUARY 1944

- Recruitment nationally to the WLA was re-opened on 3 January 1944 for milking and other responsible jobs.

  The Land Girl Jan 1944 (Vol 4, No 10) p 10

- 990 land girls employed in Bedfordshire.

  The Land Girl Jan 1944 (Vol 4, No 10) p 16

FEBRUARY 1944

- 'The Chairman and County staff would like to thank all the volunteers who entertained them so liberally at Christmas parties. Lectures on health and beauty have been given at all hostels managed by the WLA and we were lucky in having Mrs Godfrey Phillips, the National Association for Health Education, as our lecturer. These talks were so popular that we hope to arrange a weekend session at our WLA club for all privately employed volunteers who were not able to go to the hostels.'

  The Land Girl Feb 1944 (Vol 4, No 11) p 13

- The Duchess of Gloucester visits Cople hostel, Wednesday 9 February 1944. 150 land girls provided a guard of honour.

  Beds Times 11 February 1944 p7 (photo p6) and *The Land Girl* March 1944 (Vol 4, No 12) p9

- 973 land girls employed in Bedfordshire.

  The Land Girl Feb 1944 (Vol 4, No 11) p 16

MARCH 1944

- Bedfordshire land girls have contributed an average of 12s/6d (62½p) each to the WLA Benevolent Fund to date.

  WLA Benevolent Fund Bulletin No 3, May 1944

- 974 land girls employed in Bedfordshire.

  The Land Girl March 1944 (Vol 4, No 12) p 16

APRIL 1944

- 26 clothing coupons were given up by every land girl at the beginning of the rationing period to allow for uniform during the year.

  Beds Times 21 April 1944 p4

- 967 land girls employed in Bedfordshire.

  The Land Girl April 1944 (Vol 4, No 1) p 16

MAY 1944

- Training hostel opened at Ravensden House Farm, north of Bedford.

  Beds Times 20 October 1944 p4

- Peggy Clark, elected by fellow land girls at Hulcote Moors hostel as Britain's first Land Army May Queen is crowned at a coronation at Cranfield 6 May.

- Ethel Eaton wins a ploughing competition at Eaton Socon.

  Beds Times 20 October 1944 p8

- WLA procession from De Parys Avenue to Russell Park, Bedford, Sunday 14 May 1944: '...a tribute to the Women's Land Army who have come from all corners of England and from every walk of life to do a tough job and have come out with flying colours'.

  Beds Times 12 May 1944 p4

- 992 land girls employed in Bedfordshire.

  The Land Girl May 1944 (Vol 4, No 2) p 16

JUNE 1944

- Services Handicraft Exhibition held in Bedford, opened 19 June by the Duchess of Kent. 'Some beautiful work was exhibited around our land girl maypole. Special mention must be made of Miss Keable's (3796) fire screen, and an original set in leather (hat, bag and shoes) made by Miss Robbins (42994) which was specially commended by HRH (Her Royal Highness).'

  The Land Girl Aug 1944 (Vol 5, No 5) p 12

- Rest houses for land girls set up at Torquay and Llandudno, funded by the British War Relief Society of USA, where a few land girls from Bedfordshire were able to enjoy a break after years of hard labour in the WLA.

  The Land Girl June 1944 (Vol 5, No 3) p9

- 'Land Girls Put On a Show'. WLA concert of 'mirth and melody' in aid of the 'Salute the Soldier Week' and Red Cross POW Fund, in Sharnbrook village hall.

  Beds Times 16 June 1944 p1

- 999 land girls employed in Bedfordshire.

  The Land Girl June 1944 (Vol 5, No 3) p16

JULY 1944
- First complete series of Proficiency Tests had been completed.
- 987 land girls employed in Bedfordshire.

  The Land Girl July 1944 (Vol 5, No 4) p16

AUGUST 1944
- Some land girls formed a guard of honour to line the route when HM The Queen visited the Biggleswade area.

  The Land Girl Aug 1944 (Vol 5, No 5) p1

- 1006 land girls employed in Bedfordshire.

  The Land Girl Aug 1944 (Vol 5, No 5) p16

SEPTEMBER 1944
- Bedfordshire's Gymkhana in aid of the WLA Benevolent Fund was held in Bedford. 'The Land Army rose spendidly to the occasion and a very merry time was had by all. A display of 'Haute Ecole' riding by Mr Gloster and his famous horse 'Mavourneed' was much appreciated.'

  The Land Girl Sep 1944 (Vol 5, No 6) p11

- Four-year armlet party held at the WLA Club in Bedford, with Mrs Dallas as the hostess. Mr Lawrence of Bedfordshire 'War Ag' gave a talk on Young Farmers Clubs. American comfort parcels were distributed to each volunteer. 13 out of 37 were unable to attend owing to pressure of harvest.

  The Land Girl Oct 1944 (Vol 5, No 7) p13

- 1042 land girls employed in Bedfordshire.

  The Land Girl Oct 1944 (Vol 5, No 6) p16

OCTOBER 1944
- Ravensden House WLA training centre syllabus outlined. 'These girls are carefully selected and it is hoped that they will not be confused with daily 'gang-labour'.'

  Beds Times 20 Oct 1944 p4

- Musical afternoon at WLA Club in Harpur Street, Bedford, with musical accompaniment by Mrs Rogers, Warden at Ravensden.

- 'Miss Cornelius, our new organiser in the south of the county has replaced Miss Ellison who now takes over in the north.'

- 1057 land girls employed in Bedfordshire.

  The Land Girl Oct 1944 (Vol 5, No 7) p16

NOVEMBER 1944
- 1053 land girls employed in Bedfordshire.

  The Land Girl Nov 1944 (Vol 5, No 8) p16

DECEMBER 1944
- 17s/3d (86p) raised on average per Bedfordshire land girl for the WLA Benevolent Fund to date.

  WLA Benevolent Fund Bulletin No. 4 Dec 1944 p2

- Hulcote Moors set a new county record by passing the £100 mark for money raised for the WLA Benevolent Fund.

- Two excellent CEMA (Council for the Encouragement of Music and the Arts) concerts have been arranged at Cople and Elstow hostels.

  The Land Girl Dec 1944 (Vol 5, No 9) p12

• Shire Hall Christmas Party for privately employed land girls from across the county.
  The Land Girl Feb 1945 (Vol 5, No 11) p 12
• 1044 land girls employed in Bedfordshire.
  The Land Girl Dec 1944 (Vol 5, No 9) p 16

1 9 4 5

JANUARY 1945
• 'Special consideration will be given in future to volunteers with three or more years' service in the Land Army, who are working away from home but who want to transfer to their home counties.'
  The Land Girl Jan 1945 (Vol 5, No 10) p 9
• Wounded military personnel from the local convalescence home were entertained by hostels in the north of the county (Bolnhurst, Milton Ernest, Sharnbrook and Hulcote Moors).
  The Land Girl Feb 1945 (Vol 5, No 11) p 12
• 1033 land girls employed in Bedfordshire.
  The Land Girl Jan 1945 (Vol 5, No 10) p 16

FEBRUARY 1945
• Four more CEMA concerts at hostels.
• Miss Digby, new Organiser for Bedfordshire, and Mrs Grand, Hostel and Welfare Officer, are welcomed at the Bedford WLA HQ.
• Lady Denman, Honorary Director of the WLA, announced, on 17 February 1945, her resignation after nearly six years' service with the national organisation she created. This was in protest against the Government's announcement that land girls would not be getting the post-war gratuities and other benefits which others such as those in the Forces and Civil Defence would. Her resignation was designed to draw public attention to what she saw as an injustice and to attempt to bring about a change of heart by the Government.
• Miss Squire, YWCA, attended Milton Ernest hostel's third birthday party.
  The Land Girl April 1945 (Vol 6, No 1) p 13
• 1008 land girls employed in Bedfordshire.
  The Land Girl Feb 1945 (Vol 5, No 11) p 16

MARCH 1945
• Lady Denman requested that WLA county staff stay in their posts to continue the smooth running of the Land Army.
  The Land Girl March 1945 (Vol 5, No 12) p 2
• 19 March: nine land girls completed proficiency tests in milking and dairy work, two gaining Distinction certificates.
  The Land Girl April 1945 (Vol 6, No 1) p 13
• Land reclamation at Bolnhurst. Use of steam-powered tractor with a winch to pull the roots out. Use of prisoners of war.
  Beds Times 16 March 1945 p 4
• 966 land girls employed in Bedfordshire.
  The Land Girl March 1945 (Vol 5, No 12) p 16

APRIL 1945
• Congratulations to Hulcote Moors for achieving 'best working hours' and to Leighton Buzzard for 'best garden'.
  The Land Girl April 1945 (Vol 6, No 1) p 11
• No WLA girls on strike in Bedfordshire, despite land girls from Buckinghamshire WLA

at their Linslade hostel striking last week over the question of post-war gratuities.
Beds Times 20 April 1945 p4

- 992 land girls employed in Bedfordshire.
  The Land Girl April 1945 (Vol 6, No 1) p16

MAY
1945
- 8 May: VE Day – end of war in Europe.
- 60,600 land girls still employed nationally at the end of the war, 28 April 1945.
  The Land Girl May 1945 (Vol 6, No 2) p16
- Photo of land girls with a decorated milk trolley (to celebrate end of war) delivering milk to householders.
  Beds Times 11 May 1945 p3
- Land girls encouraged to look out for the potato pest, the Colorado beetle, and report and send specimens to the Ministry of Agriculture.
  Colour leaflet inserted in *The Land Girl* May 1945 (Vol 6, No 2) p3
- Government announced proposals for the post-war treatment of the Women's Land Army. No concession on gratuities or clothing grants. Instead, promises of post-war training facilities and a grant to the WLA Benevolent Fund of £170,000.
- Mrs F.C. (Inez) Jenkins becomes Chief Administrative Officer of the WLA (no new Honorary Director in place of Lady Denman).
- 26 May 1945: second WLA May Queen crowned at Hulcote Moors hostel.
  The Land Girl June 1945 (Vol 6, No 3) p13 and *Beds Times* 1 June 1944 p3
- 966 land girls employed in Bedfordshire.
  The Land Girl May 1945 (Vol 6, No 3) p16

JUNE
1945
- Three land girls (all in WLA since 1939) represented the organisation at the Victory Thanksgiving Service at St Paul's Church, Bedford: Diana Keable, Peggy Burton and Betty Fuller.
- Edith Catchlove (four and a half years service) led a contingent of 30 land girls in the Luton Victory Parade on Thanksgiving Sunday.
- A senior Resettlement Advice Officer, Ministry of Labour, had been touring hostels, giving talks on careers after the war.
- Miss Williams, Regional Officer resigned. Bedfordshire HQ, welcomed Mrs Nelson as Eastern Area Organiser, to replace Miss Ellison. Mrs Place, Assistant Secretary, had resigned through ill health.
  The Land Girl June 1945 (Vol 6, No 3) p13
- 961 land girls employed in Bedfordshire.
  The Land Girl June 1945 (Vol 6, No 3) p16

JULY
1945
- Minister of Agriculture informed WLA county secretaries that the organisation will be needed 'at least until the harvest of 1948'.
  The Land Girl July 1945 (Vol 6, No 4) p1
- 'Grand Garden Party and Dance', Sharnbrook (WLA and WAEC) for hostel land girls.
- 939 land girls employed in Bedfordshire.
  The Land Girl July 1945 (Vol 6, No 4) p16

AUGUST
1945
- 15 August: VJ Day (Victory in Japan). Two-day celebrations for the final end of the Second World War, following the surrender of Japan.
- Elstow and Silsoe hostels celebrated second birthdays recently.
- Miss M.M. Jones promoted to Assistant Secretary at Bedford HQ; Miss Young appointed third WLA Organiser.
- Two dances organised at Corn Exchange, Bedford, in aid of WLA Benevolent Society.

- Two tennis matches recently between Bedfordshire 'War Ag' and WLA land girls and staff: 'War Ag' won by narrow margin.
- 907 land girls employed in Bedfordshire.

  The Land Girl August 1945 (Vol 6, No 5) p 16

SEPTEMBER 1945
- Ministry of Agriculture regretted it was not possible to grant an early release from WLA, despite end of war, since it was vital for the harvest to be secured.

  The Land Girl Sep 1945 (Vol 6, No 6) p 1

NOVEMBER 1945
- Government announced a system of releases for members of WLA who joined for 'duration of the war'.

  The Land Girl Nov 1945 (Vol 6, No 8) p 1

DECEMBER 1945
- 14 Bedfordshire land girls among those from around the country who were present and two (Joan Garratt and Mildred Hull) were presented with armlets for six years or more service, at the Mansion House, London (800 volunteers in England and Wales plus 80 officials and office staff worked since autumn 1939).

  The Land Girl Dec 1945 (Vol 6, No 9) p 1 and *The Land Girl* Feb 1946 (Vol 6, No 11) p 13

1 9 4 6

JANUARY 1946
- Bedfordshire Women's Land Army recently took over management of YWCA hostels and 'farewell' parties were held.

  The Land Girl Feb 1946 (Vol 6, No 11) p 13

- Miss Bower, from the WLA national headquarters, attended a conference of district representatives at the Bedfordshire WLA Chairman's house, outside Bedford.

  The Land Girl Feb 1946 (Vol 6, No 11) p 13

- 'Awards to Land Girls' A party for 200 land girls was held at Shire Hall on 25 January 1946. Mrs Dorothy Fowle, Eastern Regional Officer, presented 'good service' half-diamond badges to 14 members and yellow armbands (for six years' service) to two others.

  Beds Times 25 Jan 1946 p 6

FEBRUARY 1946
- Princess Elizabeth's visit to Bedford. 600 Bedfordshire land girls marched past the 19-year-old future Queen at St Paul's Square, before a tea and presentation in the Corn Exchange. This event, on Valentine's Day, was only part of three days of celebration, 14–16 February 1946 that marked the high spot of the Women's Land Army in Bedfordshire. 65 land girls received long service (four or six years) armlets, including Lucinda Croft, who had missed the Mansion House presentation through injury. A three-day exhibition was entitled: 'How Victory Was Won on the Home Front'.

  Beds Times 15 Feb 1946 p 7 and *The Land Girl* March 1946 (Vol 6, No 12) p 12 and *The Times* 15 Feb 1946 p 7

MARCH 1946
- WLA nationally needed 30,000 new members, as many wartime volunteers are demobilised.

  The Land Girl March 1946 (Vol 6, No 12) p 1

- Bedfordshire land girl numbers down to about 600.

  Beds Times 31 May 1946 p 4

MAY 1946
- 60 new land girls recruited to Bedfordshire since 1 April 1946. Mrs Eugster said that although demobilisation had reduced the Bedfordshire WLA strength to 600, membership was now at about 800.

- The new intakes were trained at Toddington Park and at Ravensden (milking training).
  Beds Times 31 May 1946 p4
- Land girls (including some from Bedfordshire WLA) attended a course at Northamptonshire Institute of Agriculture.
  The Land Girl May 1946 (Vol 7, No 2) p5

JUNE 1946

- County's Weekend of Thanksgiving and Celebration. Ten land girls attended.
  Beds Times 7 June 1946 p3
- Recruiting by Bedfordshire WLA showed 'steady' results and a special 'broadcasting' van was to appear at all outdoor county functions over the next three months.
- G. Goss chosen to represent Bedfordshire WLA at the London Victory Parade on 8 June 1946.
  The Land Girl June 1946 (Vol 7, No 3) p13
- Talks on 'food waste' by Ministry of Food officials at several hostels.
- 12 'original' hostel members receive scarlet (four-year) armbands from the County Secretary.
- Leighton Buzzard hostel celebrated its fourth birthday recently.
- Wrest Park Lodge hostel, Silsoe, celebrated its third birthday party on Empire Day.
- Bedford HQ sorry to lose Mrs Nelson, County Organiser, who was to be replaced by Miss Fuller (who previously served as Employment Section Officer). Miss Collier takes over as Employment Section Officer.
  The Land Girl June 1946 (Vol 7, No 3) p13
- More Land Girls Wanted: 120 land girls were present at the Royal County Theatre, Bedford, when an interval appeal during 'Lorna Doone' was launched for a relief milking scheme. There was a guarantee of two years work then further training.
  Beds Times 21 June 1946 p4

JULY 1946

- At the Bedford HQ, Miss N.G. Burke was welcomed as the replacement for Miss Stringer as County Organiser in the south. Miss K.M. Chage, Hostel Section Officer, was leaving this month.
- Proficiency tests in milking and dairying are held at Thurleigh and Ravensden.
- Prize-winning stock from Mr Godfrey's farm, Clophill, shown by P. Yirrell and H.H. Wallis, land girls, at the agricultural show at Wrest Park this month, where the WLA had a recruiting display.
  The Land Girl July 1946 (Vol 7, No 4) p13
- 'Replacing POW Labour: Important Work for the Bedfordshire WLA.' As a result of the recent recruiting drive the WLA had a large pool of surplus labour. The Bedfordshire force had risen from a 'rock-bottom of 530' to 760. Mrs Eugster said that "Farmers were not finding (German) POW labour as good as it had been".
- Billeting of the land girls a chief problem – two new hostels needed in Bedfordshire (Aspley Guise hostel opened around November 1946; Clifton hostel did not open until around June 1947).
- Two former Bedfordshire land girls, Mrs Malcolm McMullen (formerly at Sharnbrook hostel) and Mrs Joseph Burby (formerly at a farm in Riseley), both GI brides, reported as having met up in America.
  Beds Times 12 July 1946 p4
- Milking and Dairy Work proficiency test held at Blackburn Hall, Thurleigh, on 25 July 1946.
  Beds Times 2 Aug 1946 p4

AUGUST
1946
- 'Milking Without Tears: Land Girls Get Their Proficiency Badges.' Girls who passed their hand milking certificate gained a weekly increase of 2s/6d (12½p).
  Beds Times 2 Aug 1946 p4
- 'How Bedfordshire Depends on German Prisoners of War': Were POWs to be withdrawn from the county, the Bedfordshire population would be reduced by 4,100 men. Restlessness and 'go-slow' policy by POWs (2,400 POWs employed on Bedfordshire farms and market gardens). Farmers forced to bribe them to work and then, in addition, feed them.
  Beds Times 9 Aug 1946 p7
- 'WLA Hostels Nearly Full' and it is hoped to open others. Miss N. Davis (Assistant Secretary, Bedfordshire WLA) reported that recruiting is satisfactory, with some recent volunteers from the north country.
  Beds Times 30 Aug 1946 p6
- 'Timber!': the Women's Timber Corp (a branch of the WLA which was formed in April 1942) is disbanded, 31 August 1946. (There was no significant presence of 'lumber jills' in Bedfordshire.)
  The Land Girl Sep 1947 (Vol 7, No 6) p1

SEPTEMBER
1946
- Proficiency tests in general farm work are held this month.
  The Land Girl July 1946 (Vol 7, No 4) p13
- 693 land girls employed in Bedfordshire.
  The Land Girl Sep 1946 (Vol 7, No 6) p16

OCTOBER
1946
- 18 October 1946: successful fancy dress dance for WLA at the Corn Exchange, Bedford. Over 250 land girls attended.
  The Land Girl Dec 1946 (Vol 7, No 9) p13
- 680 land girls employed in Bedfordshire.
  The Land Girl Oct 1946 (Vol 7, No 7) p16

NOVEMBER
1946
- 681 land girls employed in Bedfordshire.
  The Land Girl Nov 1946 (Vol 7, No 8) p16
- Hostel opened at Aspley Guise at The Holt, former manor house.

DECEMBER
1946
- Lectures on hygiene had been given in all hostels and a successful concert tour by artists from the Arts Council of Great Britain.
- 14 December: Christmas party for privately employed land girls at Shire Hall.
  The Land Girl Dec 1946 (Vol 7, No 9) p13
- 661 land girls employed in Bedfordshire.
  The Land Girl Dec 1946 (Vol 7, No 9) p16

1 9 4 7

JANUARY
1947
- Two weeks paid holiday per year announced for land girls nationally.
  The Land Girl Jan 1947 (Vol 7, No 10) p1
- New Year's Honours: Miss G.M. Gray (WLA 58933, Bedfordshire) awarded the British Empire Medal (BEM) and now undergoing a Government training course at Moulton College.
- New Year's Day: Land Army girls attended the pantomime in Bedford – topical WLA references won much applause.
- 24 January 1947: Grand Party Dance at Corn Exchange, Bedford. Advertisement for

dancing partners brought a good response from as far afield as Twickenham.
The Land Girl Feb 1947 (Vol 7, No 11) p13

- 672 land girls employed in Bedfordshire.
The Land Girl Feb 1947 (Vol 7, No 11) p16

FEBRUARY 1947
- 'One More Furrow': Minister of Agriculture recently sent a letter to every land girl encouraging them to continue in the Women's Land Army.
The Land Girl Feb 1947 (Vol 7, No 11) p1

- All ex-members of WLA who completed at least two years' service and received a willing release by VJ Day (15 August 1945) entitled to receive a certificate signed by the Queen.
The Land Girl Feb 1947 (Vol 7, No 11) p6

- Miss Medley-Costin, the new Regional Officer, paid a visit to Bedfordshire.
The Land Girl Feb 1947 (Vol 7, No 11) p13

- 663 land girls employed in Bedfordshire.
The Land Girl Feb 1947 (Vol 7, No 11) p16

MARCH 1947
- Final edition of *The Land Girl* magazine, after seven years. A smaller newsletter, *Land Army News*, would replace it after a delay caused by the fuel crisis.

- 619 land girls employed in Bedfordshire.
The Land Girl March 1947 (Vol 7, No 12) p16
(No further county employment figures for Bedfordshire and other counties published, following the end of *The Land Girl*; local newspapers the only occasional source of figures.)

APRIL 1947
- Bedfordshire and Hertfordshire Regiment invited 400 land girls to a grand concert.
Land Army News June 1947 (Vol 1, No 1) p3

JUNE 1947
- First edition of *Land Army News* published (Vol 1, No 1). Free to WLA members in private employment. Hostel members to share copies. Only four pages but larger (just over A4) format. No photographs or drawings.

- 'Brighter hostels' competition in Bedfordshire: first prize – Cople House; second prize – Aspley Guise; Hutments: first prize – Milton Ernest (oldest hostel); second prize – Leighton Buzzard.

- New hostel at Clifton House to be opened shortly.

- Pauline Collier (ex-land girl) appointed the new Employment Officer at the County Office.
Land Army News June 1947 (Vol 1, No 1) p3

JULY 1947
- A warm welcome was given to Inez Jenkins, WLA Chief Administrative Officer, when she toured Bedfordshire on 31 July 1947. She saw girls in training, at work and taking proficiency tests.

- She presented long service badges and proficiency tests certificates at a large gathering at Kempston Barracks. Cople Hostel provided special entertainment during the evening.

- 100 new recruits welcomed to Bedfordshire from Derbyshire, Lancashire and London/Middlesex.
Land Army News Aug 1947 (Vol 1, No 3) p3

AUGUST 1947
- Proposed increase in minimum wage for agricultural workers, including a maximum board and lodging deduction to be fixed for land girls billeted by their employers (no longer any county by county variation).

- Land girls invited to let their local representatives know what form of recreation or education they would like provided for hostels, clubs or local groups this winter.

- The Women's Employment Federation suggested future careers for land girls.
  Land Army News Aug 1947 (Vol 1, No 3) p1
- Congratulations to Miss E.M.B. Day (WLA 36558 Bedfordshire) on gaining three distinctions in recent proficiency tests. 'Liz' Day gained 100% for field work, 96% for outdoor garden work and 93% for general farm work.
  Land Army News Aug 1947 (Vol 1, No 3) p 2

SEPTEMBER 1947
- A number of Bedfordshire land girls were attending courses at agricultural colleges.
- WLA Gymkhana held at Stevington to help raise money for the WLA County Welfare Fund.
  Land Army News Oct 1947 (Vol 1, No 5)

OCTOBER 1947
- Land girl B. Simner attended the Milking and Dairy Show at Olympia, London, to represent Bedfordshire Young Farmers Club, 31 October. She tied for first place in the Poultry Judging Competition.
  Land Army News Dec 1947 (Vol 1, No 7)

NOVEMBER 1947
- A number of Bedfordshire WLA members passed their tractor driving proficiency tests this month.
- A Fancy Dress Dance was held in Bedford with great success – 50% in fancy dress. Mayor of Bedford, J.A.Canvin, and WLA County Chairman, Mrs 'J.B.' Graham judged the competition.
  Land Army News Dec 1947 (Vol 1, No 7)

DECEMBER 1947
- 'Party at the Palace' given by Princess Elizabeth and the Duke of Edinburgh, 16 December. WLA had presented the newly married couple with a breakfast table of inlaid mahogany and clock (chosen by the princess).
- 689 land girls employed in Bedfordshire.
  Land Army News Jan 1948 (Vol 1, No 8) p1

1 9 4 8

JANUARY 1948
- 16 January, three Bedfordshire land girls – Lucinda Croft, Joan Garrett and Irene Skevington – joined with 426 other eight-year land girls (out of 773) at a party given in their honour by the National Farmers Union in Caxton Hall, London. Miss B. Fuller (County Organiser) and Mrs Robinson (Committee Member) also attended.
- 26 January, announcement by Minister of Agriculture that the WLA would go on for a further two or three years.
- 250 land girls attended 'Cinderella' pantomime at the Royal County Theatre, Bedford.
- Bolnhurst hostel entertained 44 children from local Dr Barnardo's Howard Home, Bedford, to tea, with a present for each child. Father Christmas (resembling an RAF Sergeant) arrived with two bags full of presents. Mrs Sutton, Assistant Warden, on duty. Mrs Truman, WLA Welfare Officer, led community singing and the children sang carols.
  [More details in *Beds Times* 9 Jan 1948 p5 Col 4]
- Recent recruits to Bedfordshire WLA from Huntingdonshire, Lancashire, Yorkshire, Lincolnshire, London and Middlesex.
- Visits by land girls to county factories: Vauxhall Motors, Cryselco and Meltis.
  Land Army News Feb 1948 (Vol 1, No 9) p3

FEBRUARY 1948
- Sixth anniversary of Milton Ernest hostel celebrated with Dawn Skeggs (four and a half years veteran) cutting the cake with the County Secretary.
  Land Army News April 1948 (Vol 1, No 11) p3

MARCH 1948
- 14 March: Beginning of national and local recruitment campaign for WLA. Urgent need to fill 1,500 vacancies, nationally, in 'War Ag' gangs.

APRIL 1948
- Toddington and Kensworth hostels were taking glove-making classes with visiting instructress from Bedford Education Authority.
- Death of Ethel Eaton, outstanding tractor driver and winner of the County Ploughing Competition at Eaton Socon, 1943, announced.
- County WLA head office shortly to lose Miss P. Collier, Employment Officer.
- New hostel to open shortly near Sandy, at Hasells Hall. Working party of land girls were currently getting the kitchen garden ready. They hoped to be settled in a few weeks' time.
  Land Army News April 1948 (Vol 1, No 11) p1

MAY 1948
- 'Pastures new. Vacancies. Bedfordshire. Wanted for pigs and poultry farm, girl with technical knowledge, able to instruct students. Cottage billets. Wages above minimum.'
  Land Army News May 1948 (Vol 1, No 12) p1
- 'Smiling Girls in Apple Blossom Time'. Margaret Scaife and Margaret Coulin shown in photo engaged in pruning over one million apple trees in Co-operative Wholesale Society's orchard in Cockayne Hatley.
- 'Hasells Hall at Sandy is now being put into shape by the Ministry of Works for use as a hostel.'
  Beds Times 7 May 1948 p6

JUNE 1948
- Land Army county committees disappeared, together with District Representatives (both unpaid elements of the WLA organisation) but there would still be a WLA County Organiser. A Welfare Committee was to be set up in each county.
  Land Army News Feb 1948 (Vol 1, No 9) p1
- Land girls shown 'Combatting the Colorado Beetle Menace'. Land girls from Houghton Conquest ('Chimney Corner' hostel) have been trained to inspect crops locally.
  Beds Times 4 June 1948 p6
- Mrs Inez Jenkins (who had helped Lady Denman in 1938 set up the WLA nationally, as Assistant Director) resigned as Chief Administrative Officer: 'now needed in her own home'. Her role was taken by Miss Amy Curtis (ex Women's Royal Naval Service Superintendent, Portsmouth Command, then Ministry of Labour).
- Only quarterly visits to employers by the County Organiser (previously monthly visits).
- Proficiency test awards listed for Bedfordshire.
- Recent hostel dances were held at Leighton Buzzard, Toddington and Kensworth in aid of the local welfare fund. Generous collections at Cople House. Many hostels were saving for Sunday motor coach trips. Aspley Guise hostel took part in a Music Festival organised by Bedford Rural School of Music, 22 May.
  Land Army News June 1948 (Vol 2, No1) p3

JULY 1948
- Berets now to be the official headgear for land girls, in place of the original felt hat.
- Congratulations to Elizabeth Day of Bedford, eight-year veteran, on the award of the British Empire Medal (BEM) for services to the WLA.
  Land Army News July 1948 (Vol 2, No 2) p1
  'Her humour and keenness for her work typifies the spirit of the Land Army at its best.'
  Land Army News Aug 1948 (Vol 2, No 3) p4 'County News'

AUGUST
1948
- WLA stand at County Agricultural Show, Cardington Road ground, Bedford: 'an interesting and unique 'stand' built of straw and decorated with large bunches of vegetables'.
- Miss Fuller, Warden, given farewell party at The Holt, Aspley Guise hostel. The land girls' gift was an electric clock and a butter dish.
  Land Army News Aug 1948 (Vol 2, No 3) p4 'County News'
- 'Land Girls Travel Time. Dissatisfaction at Hostel'. Previous special additional payments in Bedfordshire for land girls while travelling from hostel to work and back was withdrawn now that pay had been increased to 68 shillings (£3.40p) per week. Now only paid if travel times exceeded 30 minutes each way. Land girls who drove lorries now to be paid extra ten shillings (50p) per week, and not the previous 12s/6d (62½p).
  Land Army News Aug 1948 (Vol 2, No 3) p6
- Miss Betty Pentelow from Bromham (land girl from December 1941), passed with distinction as one of 80 land girls taking the nine-month course at the Northamptonshire Agricultural Institute, Moulton, and won prize for best student. She wanted to be a farm secretary. Elizabeth Day and Jean Prole also passed.

SEPTEMBER
1948
- 'Some of our readers may have heard that hostels in their own counties are closing and wonder if the Land Army is no longer needed; this is certainly not the case, it is needed but in a different way. If a smaller number is to be employed on field work, there will be plenty of opportunities in other branches: milkers are desperately wanted now.'
  Land Army News Sep 1948 (Vol 2, No 4) p1

1 9 4 9

MARCH
1949
- Miss Curtis, Chief Administrative Officer from WLA HQ, visited Bedfordshire WLA, 24 March.
  Land Army News April 1949 (Vol 2, No 11) p3

APRIL
1949
- New wage rates ranging from 55 shillings (£2.75p) per week for under 18s to 71 shillings (£3.55p) for 21 and over for a 47-hour week (from 51 shillings to 66 shillings for 44 hours). Additional pay for overtime.
- Bolnhurst hostel closed, end of April.
- Hostels in county now benefitting from the Hostels Welfare Fund for new curtains, cushions and lampshades, wireless sets, gramophones and pick-ups, sewing machines and hair dryers, etc.
- Milking and Dairy Work proficiency test results.
  Land Army News April 1949 (Vol 2, No 11) p3

MAY
1949
- Seventh anniversary hostel party at Leighton Buzzard.
  Land Army News June (Vol 3, No 1) p4

JUNE
1949
- Tenth anniversary of establishment of Women's Land Army.
- Miss P. Gilbert, a County Organiser, leaves, succeeded by Miss I. Walker.
- Clifton hostel second anniversary party held.
- Dressmaking classes are held for privately employed land girls.
  Land Army News June 1949 (Vol 3, No 1) p4

AUGUST
1949
- 'Land girls hold own Harvest Home'. Photo and article on large gathering of 400 Bedfordshire land girls at Hasells Hall, Sandy, for a nine-hour revelry on Saturday 6 August. Inter-hostel sports events in afternoon on the grass terrace of the country

house. Tea, presentations then a concert and dance followed by fireworks.
Beds Times 12 Aug 1949 p4

- WLA recruiting advert slide shown during film programme at Picturedrome Cinema, Bedford, and Savoy Cinema, Luton.
- Messrs Bacchus Ltd, Bedford, and Blundells Ltd, Luton, each lent a window for WLA recruitment drive displays.
Land Army News Aug 1949 (Vol 3, No 3) p4

SEPTEMBER 1949
- 'If Land Girls wonder why their own county no longer has a Land Army office but has to share one, the reason is that now the Land Army is smaller it is wasteful to have as many offices as before. A lot of attention is also given to the cost of running hostels and in counties where there are a good many vacant beds some hostels are being closed.'
Land Army News Sep 1949 (Vol 3, No 4) p1

OCTOBER 1949
- Minister of Agriculture announced, in a statement to the House of Commons (31 October 1949) that the WLA was to be disbanded in November 1950: "Now that there are more regular workers in agriculture there is not the same need to go on recruiting extra labour from the towns and, therefore, the Land Army's purpose has been achieved and the organisation can go into honourable retirement."
- Recruitment for work with the County War Agricultural Committees had been stopped (within the limit set by demand, girls would be accepted up to 31 March 1950, for employment with individual farmers).
Land Army News Nov 1949 (Vol 3, No 6) p1

NOVEMBER 1949
- 'Land Girls who rose to a great occasion' County office in Bedford closes. From 20 November, until 30 November 1950, the land girls of Bedfordshire (as of Northamptonshire) would come under the regional administration of the Buckinghamshire County Secretary at its office in High Wycombe.
- Approx 300 land girls now employed in Bedfordshire and steadily decreasing.
Beds Times 18 Nov 1949 p5

DECEMBER 1949
- 'Hostels have been closing : Toddington, Ravensden, Sharnbrook, Clifton, Hasells [Sandy].'
Land Army News Jan 1950 (Vol 3, No 8) p4

1 9 5 0

FEBRUARY 1950
- 25 February : supper party given at Someries House, Regents Walk, London (Ministry of Agriculture luncheon club) by the County Welfare Committees, nationwide, for 130 Land Girls and staff who had completed ten years service (230 invited). Speech by the Earl of Huntingdon. He spoke of the total number of land girls who had served in the Land Army as being 203,000 (compared with 23,000 in the First World War).
- Ten-year service badges (made in metal) 'made to last forever – something to be worn with pride'.
- WLA Benevolent Fund total, raised by members and friends, £184,000.
Land Army News March 1950 (Vol 3, No 8) p3

APRIL 1950
- Closing of 'St Elmo' WLA Rest Break House in Torquay (Llandudno closed 'some time ago').
Land Army News April 1950 (Vol 3, No 11) p1

MAY
1950
- Mrs Winston Churchill at YWCA hostel, Clapham Road, Bedford. Photo included a land girl, Miss Phyllis Raynor, in working uniform.
  Beds Times 26 May 1950 p10

JUNE
1950
- Before 30 November 1950 all land girls remaining in agriculture would be provided with a booklet giving them useful information about wages, insurance, income tax and other matters.
  Land Army News June 1950 (Vol 4, No 1) p1

JULY
1950
- 'Each land girl who remains at work on the land (after November 1950) will be allowed to keep her complete outfit of uniform free of charge ...
  'Those who are in possession of a WLA bicycle on loan or hire will be allowed to buy their machines for a very modest sum ...
  'Land Girls who are now in Agricultural Executive Committee employment and who intend to stay in agricultural work will in general continue to live in their hostels which, though no longer managed by the WLA, will be run on much the same lines.'
  Land Army News July 1950 (Vol 4, No 5) p1
- Miss Ramage, County Secretary had to resign due to ill health. Mrs J. Hirst appointed to succeed. Miss Walker left the Land Army. County Organisers now: Miss Fuller, North Bedfordshire; Miss Kennedy, South Bedfordshire.
  Land Army News July 1950 (Vol 4, No 5) p4
- 'Chimney Corner', Houghton Conquest hostel closed.
  Antrobus archive, questionnaire re WLA: Vivyan 'Vicky' Cooper née Richards

SEPTEMBER
1950
- Hostels closed at Leighton Buzzard and Cople.
  Land Army News Sep 1950 (Vol 4, No 4) p4

OCTOBER
1950
- Increased agricultural wages for women: 76 shillings (£3.80p) for a 47-hour week.
  Land Army News Oct 1950 (Vol 4, No 5) p1
- 'Pool Labour: Farmers to Run Own Scheme'. Decision of Bedfordshire and Huntingdonshire Agricultural Executive Committees to close down their hostels and end all pool labour. At beginning of 1951, Farmers Union branches to look into the possibility of setting up their own co-op scheme.
  Beds Times 6 Oct 1950
- 'Bedfordshire Girls in Land Army Farewell'. Report on the farewell parade at Buckingham Palace (prior to November disbandment). 500 land girls inspected and presented with long-service badges. Bedfordshire representatives listed.
  Beds Times 27 Oct 1950 p6

NOVEMBER
1950
- Final edition of *Land Army News*, including text of Queen's farewell speech at final WLA parade, Buckingham Palace, Saturday 21 October 1950. Message from the Minister of Agriculture. Article on the history of the WLA over 11 years of national service.
  Land Army News Nov 1950 (Vol 4, No 6) pp1-2
- 'Happy End to Women's Land Army'. Farewell party at Shire Hall, Bedford, on Saturday 18 November (WLA officially ended 30 November 1950). 80% of remaining Bedfordshire land girls were staying on the farms. Mrs Erica Graham recalled that Bedfordshire WLA's first tea party had been in the same committee room – they had come full circle. Miss Amy Curtis, Chief Administrative Officer of the WLA, attended. Miss Phyllis Chiplin presented her with a book on Bedfordshire. Miss I. Eugster, County Secretary for nine years, cut the cake. Officers and Mrs Martin, original committee member, listed as attending.
  Beds Times 24 Nov 1950 p6

BEDFORDSHIRE WAR AGRICULTURAL EXECUTIVE COMMITTEE AND DISTRICT COMMITTEES
(Personnel at 5 December 1940)

EXECUTIVE COMMITTEE
Mr H.J. Humphreys, Berrystead, Eversholt (Chairman)
Mr N.B. Foster, Northbridge, The Avenue, Ampthill
Mr B. Hartop, Gable House, Ickleford, Hitchin
Mr E.H. Horrell, Knotting
Mr C.H. Inskip, Clifton Bury, Shefford
Mr H.E. White, 13 Hardwick Road, Bedford
Mrs N. Whitchurch, Great Barford House, Bedford *

DISTRICT COMMITTEES
Ampthill
Mr N.B. Foster, Northbridge, The Avenue, Ampthill (Chairman)
Mr H. Hobbs, Birchmoor Farm, Woburn
Mr H. Davies, West End House, Haynes
Mr R.P. Burton, Great Farm, Maulden
Mr W. Brittain, Wood Farm, Flitwick

Bedford
Mr E.H. Horrell, Knotting (Chairman)
Mr W.T. Elgey, Church Farm, Podington
Mr C. Spencer-Thomas, Honeydon, Bedford
Mr F. Bath, Roxton Manor, Bedford
Mr H.J. Cook, Felmersham, Bedford
Mr F.J. Potter, 30 Cardington Road, Bedford
Mr C.H. Gardner, Kitchen End, Silsoe

Biggleswade
Mr C.H. Inskip, Clifton Bury, Shefford (Chairman)
Mr A. Cope, Beeston, Sandy
Mr J. Billington, 202 Hitchin Road, Stotfold
Mr E.M. Street, Langford, Biggleswade
Mr R.G. Kendall, Dunton, Biggleswade
Mr T.H. Ream, Portobello Farm, Sutton

Luton
Mr B. Hartop, Gable House, Ickleford, Hitchin (Chairman)
Mr R.O. Andrews, Chalton Cross, Luton
Mr F.J. Manning, Streatley, Luton
Mr E. Gray, Eaton Bray, Dunstable
Mr N.S. Barber, Green End Farm, Kensworth

* Chairwoman, Bedfordshire County Committee, Women's Land Army
Source: BLARS WW2/AC 2/5 (pp1–2 359)

BEDFORDSHIRE WOMEN'S LAND ARMY HOSTELS 1942–1950

17 hostels were set up by Bedfordshire WLA and the County War Agricultural Executive Committee (Bedfordshire 'War Ag' or CWAEC) from 1942 onwards to accommodate mobile groups of land girls. They were run by the Women's Land Army who appointed Young Women's Christian Association (YWCA) Wardens and other staff. These hostels for 'gang girls' ranged in size and type from ones for just 16 land girls, and the early Ministry of Works hutments for 40 young women, to a large requisitioned country house for up to 95. Three of these hostels were training farms/centres, which housed recruits attending four-week induction courses, as well as full-time workers.

Ordance Survey map reference	Location of hostel hutments or name of house or farm	Opened	Closed	Accommodation maximum housed
SP94233590	ASPLEY GUISE The Holt	November 1946	December? 1948	House 40?
TL08675841	BOLNHURST	19 October 1942	April 1949	Hutment 40
TL03974332	'CHIMNEY CORNER' (Houghton Conquest/ Elstow area)	July 1943	July 1950	Hutment 94
TL16603915	CLIFTON Clifton House	c. June 1947	by December 1949	House 40?
TL10474811	COPLE Cople House	c. September 1943	by September 1950	House 97
SP94084035	HULCOTE MOORS Farm	c. July 1943	March 1947?	Farmhouse 18
TL04331855	KENSWORTH Kensworth House	c. November 1942	c. October 1949	House 40+
SP93432543	LEIGHTON BUZZARD	4 June 1942	by September 1950	Hutment 40
TL10191789	LUTON HOO Estate The Bothy training centre only	7 July 1941	March 1946	Gardener's Bothy (house)
TL01385648	MILTON ERNEST	16 February 1942	31 March 1950	Hutment 40
TL22424930	POTTON The Hollies	c. January 1943	August? 1948	House 20+
TL06025534	RAVENSDEN Ravensden House plus training centre	May 1944	by December 1949	Farmhouse 30
TL18925000	SANDY Hasells Hall	May 1948	by December 1949	House ?
SP99485972	SHARNBROOK Sharnbrook House	c. early 1944?	c. December 1949	House 25?
TL08343556	SILSOE Wrest Park Lodge	June 1943	September? 1950	House 32
TL00312985	TODDINGTON Toddington Park plus training centre	November 1942	by December 1949	House 24?
TL00991775	WHIPSNADE	15 February 1943	1944?	Hutment 16

© Stuart Antrobus 2008

THE FARMING YEAR

The following is not a definitive list of all farms' activities in the 1940s but looks back to the experience on one Bedfordshire farm and is made up using typical extracts from a diary kept by identical twin land girls, Joan and Betty Pearson. They came from the North East of England and spent three happy years working at the Priestley Farm, near Flitwick, Bedfordshire.

The author is grateful for the kind permission of Joan and Betty Pearson and of Mary Roberts, the author of the book 'Farm of My Childhood' in which this first appeared.

JANUARY

We went out topping. In other words we had to take the tops out of Brussels sprouts. It would be freezing cold. You had to flick the snow off to find the tops.

Putting cabbage stalks in the furrows to be ploughed in for fertilizer.

If wet outside, sorting onions in the loft where they had been stored until required.

Cleaning mangolds. Cleaning beetroot.

Putting up potatoes from the potato pit. Potatoes were stored under straw and covered with soil in the autumn ready for use. Someone shovelled potatoes into a machine; someone else turned the handle and the potatoes came up a conveyor belt for sorting.

FEBRUARY

Digging leeks if ground was not too hard. Weeding parsley.

Dung flinging from the heaps already on the field. Turning dung from one side of a narrow yard to the other. A job we did not like doing, as we smelt dreadful. The girls would not sit next to us going back in the truck because we smelt so awful.

Harrowing with horses, after a field had been ploughed. This was done to break up the soil.

MARCH

Weeding parsley. Cleaning beet. Pulling rhubarb. Preparing ground for sowing onion seeds. The onion bed was prepared by pulling a large roller over the ground. Sowing fertilizer ready for setting potatoes. Planting cabbage plants – a back-breaking job. Planet hoeing peas. A planet hoe was an implement with long handles attached to a wheel fixed between two blades. This was pushed along the rows to cut out the weeds.

APRIL

Hoeing cabbage. Pulling rhubarb. Digging up parsnips. Still leek digging. Sowing fertilizer ready for potatoes.

MAY

Singling out beetroot. Setting Brussels sprouts. Cutting cabbage and parsley.

JUNE

Picking peas. Crawling along rows of beet, thinning them out. Setting leeks.

JULY

Stooking corn. Weeding onions and parsley. Threshing oats.

AUGUST

Setting kale plants. Pitching corn. Stooking corn. Pulling onions.

SEPTEMBER

Spreading shoddy (pressed waste fibre sent from London by rail) over the fields, ready to be ploughed in. Pulling onions. Picking beans. Cutting lettuce. Bunching parsley.

OCTOBER

Topping sprouts. Digging sugar beet (chopping off the tops with a sharp curved knife, with one hand behind your back in case you chopped off a hand by mistake!). Cutting cabbages. Gleaning potatoes (picking up, into a basket, all potatoes left on the ground by the potato digger).

NOVEMBER

Flinging dung over the field ready to be ploughed in. Picking tops off Brussels sprouts.

DECEMBER

Picking sprouts. Plucking fowls.

Other jobs during the year included stone picking (cleaning a piece of land of stones, ready to be ploughed). These stones would be carried to the headland (the edge of the field), from where they would be used to fill in the deep ruts in the cart tracks of the farm.

Undated illustration of a land girl and her working horse returning to the farm after a day's work. *Artist unknown. Source: Antrobus archive, 1946 Bedfordshire WLA souvenir programme (back cover)*

BEDFORDSHIRE WOMEN'S LAND ARMY EMPLOYMENT FIGURES
1939–1950

Year	Month	Figure	Source
1939	end December	24	Vita Sackville-West (VSW) *The Women's Land Army* (1944) p95
1940	February	27	*Bedfordshire Times* 9 Feb 1940 p5
1940	July	50	*The Land Girl* magazine Volume 1 (4) (see County Returns)
1940	August	51	*The Land Girl* magazine Volume 1 (5)
1940	September	56	*The Land Girl* magazine Volume 1 (6)
1940	October	63	*The Land Girl* magazine Volume (7)
1940	end October	76	*Bedfordshire Times* 29 Nov 1940 p4
1940	November	61	*The Land Girl* magazine Volume 1 (8)
1940	December	55	*The Land Girl* magazine Volume 1 (9) and VSW p95
1941	January	57	*The Land Girl* magazine Volume (10)
1941	February	—	—
1941	March	50	*The Land Girl* magazine Volume 1 (12)
1941	April	57	*The Land Girl* magazine Volume 2 (1)
1941	May	64	*The Land Girl* magazine Volume 2 (2)
1941	June	70	*The Land Girl* magazine Volume 2 (3)
1941	July	86	*The Land Girl* magazine Volume 2 (4)
1941	August	97	*The Land Girl* magazine Volume 2 (5)
1941	September	107	*The Land Girl* magazine Volume 2 (6)
1941	October	115	*The Land Girl* magazine Volume 2 (7)
1941	November	121	*The Land Girl* magazine Volume 2 (8)
1941	December	140	*The Land Girl* magazine Volume 2 (9) and VSW p95
1942	January	151	*The Land Girl* magazine Volume 2 (10)
1942	February	158	*The Land Girl* magazine Volume 2 (11)
1942	March	201	*The Land Girl* magazine Volume 2 (12)
1942	April	228	*The Land Girl* magazine Volume 3 (1)
1942	May	244	*The Land Girl* magazine Volume 3 (2)
1942	June	311	*The Land Girl* magazine Volume 3 (3)
1942	July	345	*The Land Girl* magazine Volume 3 (4)
1942	August	364	*The Land Girl* magazine Volume 3 (5)
1942	September	392	*The Land Girl* magazine Volume 3 (6)
1942	October	407	*The Land Girl* magazine Volume 3 (7)
1942	November	448	*The Land Girl* magazine Volume 3 (8)
1942	December	492	*The Land Girl* magazine Volume 3 (9) and VSW p95
1943	January	506	*The Land Girl* magazine Volume 3 (10)
1943	February	520	*The Land Girl* magazine Volume 3 (11)
1943	March	541	*The Land Girl* magazine Volume 3 (12)
1943	April	567	*The Land Girl* magazine Volume 4 (1)
1943	May	614	*The Land Girl* magazine Volume 4 (2)
1943	June	663	*The Land Girl* magazine Volume 4 (3)
1943	July	771	*The Land Girl* magazine Volume 4 (4)
1943	August	792	*The Land Girl* magazine Volume 4 (5)
1943	September	904	*The Land Girl* magazine Volume 4 (6)

1943	October	965	*The Land Girl* magazine Volume 4 (7)
1943	November	997	*The Land Girl* magazine Volume 4 (8)
1943	December	1006	*The Land Girl* magazine Volume 4 (9)
1943	end December	990	VSW p95
1944	January	990	*The Land Girl* magazine Volume 4 (10)
1944	February	973	*The Land Girl* magazine Volume 4 (11)
1944	March	974	*The Land Girl* magazine Volume 4 (12)
1944	April	967	*The Land Girl* magazine Volume 5 (1)
1944	May	992	*The Land Girl* magazine Volume 5 (2)
1944	June	999	*The Land Girl* magazine Volume 5 (3)
1944	July	987	*The Land Girl* magazine Volume 5 (4)
1944	August	1006	*The Land Girl* magazine Volume 5 (5)
1944	September	1042	*The Land Girl* magazine Volume 5 (6)
1944	October	1057	*The Land Girl* magazine Volume 5 (7)
1944	November	1053	*The Land Girl* magazine Volume 5 (8)
1944	December	1044	*The Land Girl* magazine Volume 5 (9) and VSW p95
1945	January	1033	*The Land Girl* magazine Volume 5 (10)
1945	February	1008	*The Land Girl* magazine Volume 5 (11)
1945	March	966	*The Land Girl* magazine Volume 5 (12)
1945	April	992	*The Land Girl* magazine Volume 6 (1)
1945	May	966	*The Land Girl* magazine Volume 6 (2)
1945	June	961	*The Land Girl* magazine Volume 6 (3)
1945	July	939	*The Land Girl* magazine Volume 6 (4)
1945	August	907	*The Land Girl* magazine Volume 6 (5)
1945	September	875	*The Land Girl* magazine Volume 6 (6)
1945	October	845	*The Land Girl* magazine Volume 6 (7)
1945	November	827	*The Land Girl* magazine Volume 6 (8)
1945	December	822	*The Land Girl* magazine Volume 6 (9)
1946	January	799	*The Land Girl* magazine Volume 6 (10)
1946	February	698	*The Land Girl* magazine Volume 6 (11)
1946	March	654	*The Land Girl* magazine Volume 6 (12)
1946	April	599	*The Land Girl* magazine Volume 7 (1)
1946	May	567	*The Land Girl* magazine Volume 7 (2)
1946	June	594	*The Land Girl* magazine Volume 7 (3)
1946	July	628	*The Land Girl* magazine Volume 7 (4)
1946	August	628	*The Land Girl* magazine Volume 7 (5)
1946	September	693	*The Land Girl* magazine Volume 7 (6)
1946	October	680	*The Land Girl* magazine Volume 7 (7)
1946	November	681	*The Land Girl* magazine Volume 7 (8)
1946	December	661	*The Land Girl* magazine Volume 7 (9)
1947	January	672	*The Land Girl* magazine Volume 7 (10)
1947	February	663	*The Land Girl* magazine Volume 7 (11)
1947	March	619	*The Land Girl* magazine Volume 7 (12) (final issue)
1948	January	689	*Land Army News* Jan 1948 p3
1949	November	300*	*Bedfordshire Times* 18 Nov 1949 p5
1950	November	?	*Bedfordshire Times* 24 Nov 1950 p6

*approximate

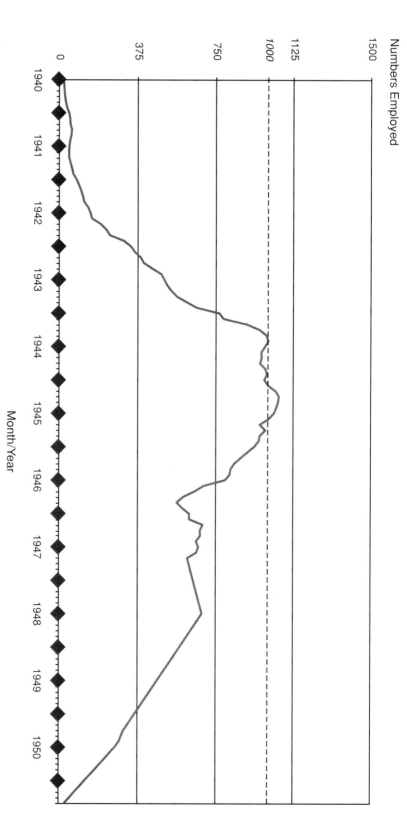

Notes

1 The figures in the previous table and on the graph above are for employment in Bedfordshire. Many more young women were enrolled in Bedfordshire but transferred to other counties to work, because there were not vacancies on Bedfordshire farms, at the time of their enrolment. WLA service file index cards held by the Imperial War Museum, Duxford (microfilm copies at the National Archives, Kew) indicate which females were enrolled in Bedfordshire but transferred for service in other counties of England and Wales.

2 Once *The Land Girl* magazine ceased to be published, post-war (last edition in March 1947), there was no regular publishing of land girl enrolment figures. Very occasional figures can be derived from copies of the *Bedfordshire Times* and *Land Army News*.

WOMEN'S LAND ARMY UNIFORM ISSUE

First issue on joining	Supplementary issue (after one month's service)	Replacements (one year from date of first issue if worn out)
1 pair breeches	1 pair breeches	1 oilskin
1 pullover	3 pairs stockings	1 pair breeches
3 pairs stockings	1 pair gumboots or	2 pairs dungarees and
2 overall coats	1 pair boots (according to	1 overall coat or
3 shirts	nature of employment)	2 overall coats and
2 pairs dungarees		1 pair dungarees
1 hat		1 hat
1 oilskin		2 shirts
1 pair shoes		6 pairs stockings
1 pair leather boots		1 pair shoes or boots or 1 pair
with leggings		gumboots and 1 pair leather
1 armlet (when available)		boots with leggings
1 badge (when available)		
1 great coat (with shoulder		
tabs)		

Source: WSRO 5926 (File 2)

WOMEN'S LAND ARMY BENEVOLENT FUND

The Fund was formed on 30 July 1942 and registered as a war charity. Lady Denman was its Chairman and Her Majesty the Queen was Patron. During the war the Benevolent Fund relied mainly on fundraising by land girls. As Lady Denman explained in the 1946 Bedfordshire WLA Souvenir Programme, 'The Women's Land Army Benevolent Fund has seldom made a public appeal for money during the course of the war. Call it pride, or an inferiority complex prompted by the thought that there might be causes more deserving than their own. Today, however, the Fund *is* a most deserving cause. Land girls have no gratuity to help them settle to civilian life again. In cases of need the Benevolent Fund is trying to fill this deficiency.'

At that time the Fund was helping more than a hundred members each week with grants towards the expenses of illness and convalescence (before the National Health Service had been established), towards the expenses of training for civilian jobs and towards re-settlement. The Fund also had a Homecraft Training Centre near Bury St Edmunds, where members who were about to be married and were setting up homes could receive a month's training in domestic skills.

right: WLA Benevolent Fund advertisement, inserted in copies of *The Women's Land Army* by Vita Sackville-West, c. 1945. *Source: Antrobus archive*

THE WOMEN'S LAND ARMY
BENEVOLENT   FUND
★
PATRON: HER MAJESTY THE QUEEN

Lonely Battle

Although serious accidents are rare, hardly a day passes without some Land Girl getting hurt.   That is why the Land Army Benevolent Fund has been set up.

Land Girls, of course, come under National Health and Unemployment and Workmen's Compensation. But, in a hard world, that does not cover everything. Many of them are working hundreds of miles away from home and friends, and the great advantage of the Benevolent Fund is that help can be given personally and privately.

These girls are playing a vital part in the Battle of the Land.   For some of them it is a lonely battle. But they are fighting it proudly, and we can make it less lonely by showing that we are ready to help them if they have bad luck.

After the war, many Land Girls will want training to enable them to earn their living in a peaceful world.   In so far as the Benevolent Fund has money available, it will help to give this training.

Please send Donations to:—

THE   WOMEN'S   LAND   ARMY
BENEVOLENT   FUND,
6 CHESHAM STREET,
LONDON, S.W.I.
★

The Women's Land Army

A world of chaos, a world at war,
Destruction as never seen before,
A world of heartbreak, world of fear,
And misery so hard to bear.
Armies wrong, and Armies right,
Marching forth to kill and fight,
And screaming death rained from the sky
And lo, the toll of death was high.

An Army came, but not to kill,
Only hungry mouths to fill,
An Army clad in brown and green,
About the countryside was seen,
Around the farmyards, on the roads,
With horses, carrying heavy loads,
A women's army, firm of hand,
Had come to conquer on the Land.

In lonely ones, or gangs together,
In the strange fantastic English weather,
That never a moment may be lost,
In tearing winds and biting frost,
They tended livestock, planted seed,
Tilled, manured, conquered weed,
Picked potatoes, cabbage, beet,
So that England still could eat.

Now a world at peace, a world still mad,
A world all blasted, weary, sad,
A lot more hungry mouths to fill,
The green Army is needed still,
Little reward will come their way,
But beauty in their hearts will stay,
That comes to those that understand,
The love of a horse, the love of the land.

Rose Perritt
WLA 134339
served in Bedfordshire,
working for the 'War Ag'
based at Cople hostel

ROLL CALL OF BEDFORDSHIRE LAND GIRLS

The following list is of the maiden names of women who were members of the Women's Land Army and who served in Bedfordshire for at least six weeks between 1939 and 1950. Most served for several years. It has been compiled by Stuart Antrobus (with the assistance of a team of volunteers) from the WLA service records held by the Imperial War Museum, plus other documentary sources including Bedfordshire newspapers and copies of *The Land Girl* magazine and *Land Army News*.

Some of the first names of land girls appear to have been misspelled but have been accurately transcribed from the original records. The surnames recorded are maiden names, except where (Mrs) has been added after the surname to indicate that the person was married on enrolment in the WLA, in which case their married name is given. In those few cases where two or more women have identical first and surnames, then their unique WLA numbers have been added to clarify which individuals are recorded.

For a current updated version of the list below, see the 'Roll Call' web pages on the Internet at: http://tinyurl.com/2nq2up

Irene May	Abbott	Doreen Mary	Allison	Irene	Arding
Jean	Abbott	Sarah Ann	Allott	Annie Collin	Arkless
Daphne Sylvia	Abraham	Martha	Allport	Edith Margaret	Armitage
June Eileen	Abraham	Patricia Elsie	Allsobrook	Renee	Armitage
Lilian Margaret	Abrams	Eileen Lucy	Allsworth	Doris Evelyn	Armstrong
Josie Wilson	Abthorpe	Vera Moreen	Allwood	Lilian Mary	Armstrong
Patricia Rosemary	Acton	Temperance	Alston	Margery	Armstrong
Joan	Adams	Margaret Mary	Altobelli	Joyce Muriel	Arnold
Lena Joan	Adams	Lily	Ambler	Ivy	Arrowsmith
Mary Jean	Adams	Margaret S	Ambler	Anne	Arthur
Winifred Linden	Adams	Eileen	Anderson	Mary Elizabeth	Ashby
Cynthia Louise	Adamson	Ellen Margaret	Andrew	May	Ashcroft
Eileen	Adamson	Lucy Catherine	Andrew	Lily Mabel	Ashdown
Elizabeth	Adamson	Edith Gladys	Andrews	Violet May	Ashford
Jean	Adamson	Iris Evelyn	Andrews	Muriel Constance	Ashman
Barbara Elizabeth	Adby	Sylvia Mary	Andrews	Sylvia	Ashpole
Peggy Rita	Adlem	Winifred Mary	Angell	Eleanor Rose	Askew
Sylvia Mary	Ager	Mary	Ansal	Mary Geraldine	Askham
Delys	Aistrop	Barbara	Ansell	Muriel	Askin
Kathleen Mary	Albone (Mrs)	Betty	Anstee	Iris	Asser
Joan Betsy	Alcock	Hazel	Anstee	Sheila	Astle (Mrs)
Violet Edith	Aldridge	Stella	Anstey	Amy Jessica	Astling
Sarah Ellen	Alexander	Beryl	Appleby	Elsie	Atkins
Olga	Allan	Betty Olive	Appleby	Lily	Atkins
Elsie Muriel	Allen	Edna W	Appleby	Mary	Atkins
Hilda Rose	Allen	Mary Vera	Appleby	Alicia May	Atkinson
Joan	Allen	Dorothy	Appleton	Doreen	Atkinson
Joan Mary	Allen	Irene	Appleton	Evelyn Marjorie	Atkinson
Joan Phyllis	Allen	Patricia	Appleton	Marjorie	Atkinson
Marjorie Rose	Allen	Margaret	Appleyard	Helen	Attenborough
Mary	Allen	Evelyn Florence	Archer	Joyce	Attwell
Vera Eileen	Allen	Lilian	Archer	Barbara Sheila	Attwood
Kathleen	Allingham	Muriel	Archer	Nina Kathleen	Aubrey
Annie	Allinson	Queenie Amina	Archer	Joyce Lydia	Austin

Pamela	Avis	Violet Lilian	Barker	Calma Olive Myrtle	Beeson
Jean Nora	Baber	Agnes Mary	Barlow	Olive	Beever
Olive	Backhouse	Elizabeth Ann	Barnard	Doris Evelyn	Beevers
Ellen	Bacon	Kathleen Mary	Barnes	Marie Stella	Begg (Mrs)
Jean	Bacon	Olive Marie	Barnes	Janet Ivy	Behmber
Margaret	Bacon	Laura	Barnes-	Vera Margaret	Beischer
Nola Jean	Bagley		Barrington	Winifred Elizabeth	Beischer
Rosetta	Bagley	Frances Ann	Barnet	Bernice Doreen	Bell
Edith	Bagnall	Elizabeth	Barnett	Daphne	Bell
Dorothy	Bagshawe	Frances Lucy	Barnett	Eileen Winifred	Bell
Pamela Blanche	Bailey	Ivy L	Barnett	Ivy Peggy	Bell
Agnes Mary	Bainbridge	Lilian M	Barr	Joyce Annie	Bell
Mary Ann	Bainbridge	Doreen	Barrat	Margaretta	Bell
Florence	Bairstow	Elvina Florence	Barrett	Nancy Barbara	Bell
Angela	Baker	Frances	Barrett	Nora Elizabeth	Bell
Betty Sheila	Baker	May	Barrett	Pamela Gladys	Bell
Evelyn May	Baker	Muriel Winifred	Barrett	Winifred Annie	Bell
Jeannette Louisa	Baker	Rosina Beatrice	Barrett	Rosa Guilia	
Jessie Edith	Baker	Winifred Mary	Barrett	Caterina	Bellini
June Audrey	Baker	Ada Rose	Barron	Elsie Florence	Benford
Kate Mary	Baker	Patricia	Barrs	Alma	Bennett
Megan Barbara		Joyce	Barstow	Dorothy	Bennett
Alice	Baker	Gladys Winifred	Barter	Florence Alfreda	Bennett
Patricia	Baker	Rose	Bartlett	Hannah	Bennett
Patricia Helen	Baker	Catherine Stella	Barton	Jeane Ethel	Bennett
Rosina Florence	Baker	Lilian Beatrice	Barwell	Kitty	Bennett
Norah	Balding	Maud Roma	Barwick	Mary	Bennett
Brenda Jessie	Baldry	Betty	Basill	Norah	Bennett
Dorothy Stella	Baldwin	Catherine Doris	Bass	Ruth	Bennett
Kathleen	Baldwin	Daisy	Bass (Mrs)	Patricia	Benney
Doreen	Ball	Joan	Bassett	Eileen	Benson
Dorothy	Ball	Dorothy Jean	Batchelor	Mary Elizabeth	Benson
Maisie	Ball	Audrey May	Bates	Doreen Vivienne	Bentley
Grace Violet	Ball	Jean	Bates	Winifred	Bentley
	(WLA 102185)	Stella Eileen	Bates	Annie	Benton
Grace Violet	Ball	Yvonne	Bath	Pauline Fiona Ruby	Beresford
	(WLA 170792)	Florence Lilian	Batt	Rebecca	Berger
Irene	Ballard	Frances Lydia	Batt	Marie	Berlemont
Patricia Clarice	Baller	Gwendoline	Battersby	Joan Eileen	Berry
Vera	Bamford	Dora	Battrick	Margaret Isobel	Betts
Margaret Jean	Bandy	Muriel	Battye	Marie Louise	Betts
Audrey Elizabeth	Banes	Irene May	Baxter	Margaret Long	Bevan
Clara	Barber	Phyllis Mary	Baxter	Mary	Beveridge
Edna Doreen	Barber	Alma	Bayley	Catherine Hilda	Bezant
Eileen Josephine	Barber	Ethel	Bayliss	Patricia Violet	Biddis
Jeanne	Barber	Mavis	Beacham	Violet Daisy Harriet	Biddlecombe
Mary Margaret		Daisy Irene	Beard	Elsie	Biggs
Kathleen	Barber	Mabel	Beard	Beatrice Georgina	Billham
Phyllis Ellen	Barber	Ruth	Bearman	Winifred Evelyn	Billings
Alice Ivy	Barclay		(Mrs)	Dorothy Rebecca	
Hazel	Barclay	Frances	Beck	Deacon	Billington
Daphne Myra	Barker	Constance Mona	Beckett	Mary	Billington
Mamie	Barker	Rosina	Bedford	Edith Ellen	Bilsborough

Stella	Binns	Josephine Marie	Bowkett	Gladys	Brown (Mrs) (WLA132662)
Marjorie	Birch	Jean	Bowler		
Betty	Bird	Hilda Grace	Bowles	Gladys	Brown (WLA142629)
Eileen Joyce	Bird	Beryl Joan	Bowley		
Elizabeth	Bird	Joan Olive	Box	Joan	Brown (WLA142623)
Marie Joan	Bird	Mabel	Bracey		
Margaret Minnie	Bird	Marjorie	Bracey	Joan	Brown (WLA155352)
Doreen Marjorie	Birdsall	Rona	Bradford		
Joyce Florence	Bishenden	Joyce Edna	Bradley	Joyce	Brown
Gwendoline Ellen	Bishop	Lily Emily	Bradley	Kathleen	Brown
Joyce Magdalene	Bishop	Pat	Bradley	Margaret	Brown
Frances	Blackburn	Doreen June	Bradstock	Mary	Brown
Joyce	Blackwell	Daphne Patricia		Muriel Elsie	Brown
Elizabeth		Catherine	Brady	Nellie	Brown
Rutherford	Blaikie	Regina	Brady	Olga	Brown
Phyllis Winifred	Blain	Catherine	Braine	Olive	Brown
Dora May	Blake (Mrs)	Grace	Bramall	Rhoda	Brown
Catherine	Bland	Joan	Bramhall	Ruth Elizabeth	Brown
Doris	Bland	Daphne Iris May	Branch	Sheila Marion	Brown
Joyce	Bland	Martha	Brandwood	Mary	Browne
Bessie	Blankley	Florence	Brasier	Dorothy Alexandra	Bruce
G	Blay	Elizabeth Alice	Braybrook	Olive Edna	Brumwell
Gladys	Blenkinsopp	Eileen	Breach	Elsie May	Bryan
Gwendoline	Bliss	Eileen Beatrice	Brewer	Ivy	Bryant
Patricia Mary	Bloom	Anne Katherine		Jasmine Pearl	Bryant
Mavis	Bloomer	Mary	Bridge	Margaret Gladys	
Nellie	Blower	Joy	Bridge	Mavis	Bryant
Doris	Blunt	Hilda Mabel	Bright	Madeline Jean	Buck
Freda Annie	Blunt	Margaret Mary	Brindley	Jean	Buckenham
Margaret	Blyth	Mary Audrey	Britten	Grace Vera Frances	Buckeridge
Jennie	Boak	Patricia	Britton	Audrey Gertude	Buckingham
Bertha	Boal	Muriel	Broad	Irene Mary	Buckingham
Edna May	Boden	Linda Jessie	Broadberry	Joy Ellen Patricia	Buckland
Rachel Daphne	Bodington	Elsie May	Brockett	Edna	Buckle
Lucie	Bolton	Elizabeth Ann	Brodrick	Hilda Patricia	Buckley
Joyce Evelyn	Bond	Joan	Brogden	Mary	Buckley
Mabel	Bone	Elizabeth	Bromham	Matilda Elizabeth	
Doreen	Bonnett	Esther Cathrine	Bromley	Mary	Buckley
Irene Dorothy	Boon	Kathleen	Brook	Grace VF	Buckridge
Irene Dorothy	Boone	Honor Sylvia	Brooks	Margaret EH	Buery
Agnes	Booth	Joyce Barbara	Brooks	Elizabeth	Bullen
Margaret Christine	Booth	K	Brooks	Irene Maud	Bullen
Margaret Catherine	Borshell	Josephine	Brookshaw	Margaret	Bullen
Joy	Borthwick	Edith Mary	Broughton	Sheila Margaret	Buller
Joan Iris	Bosley	Kitty Marguerite	Broughton	Bertha	Bullock
Ann	Bottomley	Barbara Edith	Brown	Bertha Grace	Bullock (Mrs)
Doreen	Bottomley	Dorothy May	Brown	Florence Annie	Bullock
Ethel	Bottomley	Eileen Phyllis	Brown	Kathleen Mary	Bullock
Audrey Sheila	Bottoms	Emily	Brown	Marjorie	Bullock (Mrs)
Barbara Priscilla	Bouch	Emily Elizabeth	Brown	Margaret	Bundock
Margaret Enid	Bourlet	Ethel Anne	Brown	Muriel Ellen	Bundy
Rose Emily	Bowers	Florence Marie	Brown	Doris Mabel	Bundy
Agnes	Bowes			Edith Mary	Bunker

Jean	Bunker	Margaret	Care	Ann	Cheshnutt
Sylvia Joan	Bunnett	Clara Mollie	Carlyle	Freda Lilian	Chessum
Gladys Irene	Bunnett (WLA 111713)	Dora H	Carlyle	Marjorie Grace	Chesters
		Dorothy Maud	Carlyle	Nina May	Childerley
Gladys Irene	Bunnett (WLA 180032)	Constance	Carney	Sylvia Audrey	Childs
		Stella Joyce	Carpenter	Doris May	China (Mrs)
Doreen Frances	Burchell	Jean	Carr	Phyllis	Chiplin
Valerie Anne	Burden	Joan	Carr	Joan Olive	Chisholm
Doreen Joan	Burgess	Kathleen Avis	Carr	Elsie	Christy
Iris Georgina Lilian	Burgess	Flora Ella	Carroll	Aileen Ivy	Church
Joan Betty	Burgess	Kathleen Jean	Carroll	Jean Margaret	Church
Margaret Ellen	Burgess (Mrs)	Louie	Carroll	Margaret Betty	Church
Marjorie	Burgess (WLA 190104)	Freda May	Carter	Marjorie	Church
		Frieda Emmeline	Carter	Sylvia May	Church
Marjorie	Burgess (WLA 62715)	Jean	Carter	June	Clacher
		Rona Kathleen	Carter	Eva Doreen	Clamp
Pamela	Burgess-Allen	Alice	Cartwright	Alice Mary	Clark
Gladys	Burgoyne	Frances Annie	Cartwright	Audrey Peggy	Clark
Kathleen	Burgoyne	Gladys Ruth	Carty	Barbara Kathleen	Clark
Josephine	Burke	Marjorie	Cashmore	Betty Alma Edith	Clark
Kathleen	Burke	Madge	Castle (Mrs)	Betty Winnifred	Clark
Jean	Burnage	Yvonne June	Castleman	Dora Ellen	Clark
Gwynneth	Burns	Edith Clematis	Catchlove	Edna May	Clark
Margaret Nancy	Burns	Margaret	Catley	Eileen Maude	Clark
Sylvia Mary	Burns	Elizabeth	Catterall	Ivy	Clark (Mrs)
Pauline	Burr	Laura	Cattrick	Joy Marian Anna	Clark
Freda Daisy	Burrell	Gladys	Caulfield	Kathleen Ivy	Clark
Phyllis Alice	Burrett	Hilda Frances	Causby	Mabel	Clark
Madge	Burrows	Stella	Caves	Mabel Doreen	Clark
Patricia Mary	Burtenshaw	Vera Eileen	Caves	Madeline Dora Dorcas	Clark
Constance Joyce	Burton	Irene Maria	Cawood		
Iris Mary	Burton	Evelyn Doreen	Cearns	Margaretta Helen	Clark
Jeanette	Burton	Doreen Florence	Chaffe	Marion	Clark
Peggy	Burton	Constance Gertrude	Chalkley	Rose	Clark
Sylvia Jean	Burton	Nicole Irene	Challier	Brenda Louise	Clarke
Ethel	Busby	Mavis	Chalton	Mary Evelyn	Clarke
Edith	Bushell	Irene Alice	Chamberlain (Mrs)	Olive	Clarke
Joyce	Bussey			Betty	Clarkson
Emily Buiness	Butchart	Dorothy Jessica	Chance	Dora Lilian	Clarkson
Barbara Alice Clare	Butler	Sylvia	Chance	Pamela	Clayson
Doreen Joyce	Bygrave	Brenda Florence	Chandler	Mary	Clayton
Olive Mabel		Elizabeth D	Chandler	Jean	Clegg
Dorothy	Bygraves	Freda Elizabeth	Chandler	Florence Joan	Clements
Annie Edith	Caddick	Joan Mary	Chandler	Matilda Winifred	Cleverly
Eileen Winifred	Cain	Kitty	Chandler	Sylvia Ethel	Clewley
Olive May	Cakebread	Margaret Ruth	Chandler	Joan	Clifton
Ursula	Callus	Jean Birgitte	Chapman	Hilda Evelyn Alice	Clinker
Elizabeth	Cameron	Alice	Chappell	Joan	Cloran
Marguerite	Cameron	Daphne Lilian	Chappell	Magdalene	Coady
Gladys Elizabeth	Campbell	Charlotte	Chard	Phyllis May	Coates
Cora	Camps	Muriel	Cheetham	Violet	Coates
Betty Evelyn	Campsie	Marion Edith	Cherry	Joan	Cobb
Muriel	Caplin	Barbara Julia	Chesham	Denise Miriam	Cobden

Cynthia	Cobley (Mrs)	Mavis Joan	Cooper	Alice	Crawford
Joyce Rosetta	Cocker	Monica Audrey	Cooper	Ethel Ruth Ina	Crawley
Elizabeth Prole	Cocking	Violet Joyce	Cooper	Isabel Elsie	Crawley
Gwendoline Elsie	Cockings	Lillian Cynthia	Coote	Joan Phyllis	Crew (Mrs)
Matilda Mary Eliza	Codrington	Muriel	Coote	Joyce Hatfield	Cribb
Hannah	Coe	Olive	Copley	Amy	Crick
Florence Ida	Coggins	Joyce Mary	Copp	Rose Ellen	Cridge
Muriel Evelyn	Colbourne	Peggy Beryl	Coppard	Joan	Crisell
Florence Alice	Colbridge	Dorothy Joyce	Copping	Betty Irene	Crisp
Betty	Cole	Joan	Corby	Elisabeth Gifford	Crockett
Edith Barbara	Cole	Betty	Corker	Iris	Croft
Elizabeth	Cole	Pat	Corner	Kathleen May	Croft
Hilda Jean	Cole	Phyllis	Corner	Lucinda Maud	Croft
Trixie Maud	Cole	Mary Beryl	Cornes	Doreen	Crosby
Thelma	Coleman	Doreen Joyce	Cornish	Grace Lilian	Cross
Joy Monica	Collard	Mavis	Cornwell	June Diana	Cross
Elsie	Collier	Lilian	Corp	Sylvia Hermione	Cross
Pauline Hobson	Collier	Irene	Corwood	Margaret	Crotty
Gwendoline Joan	Collins	Mary Amelia	Cosgrove	Gladys Mabel	Crow
Helen Philomena	Collins	Ethel May	Cotterill	Dorothy Frances	Crowsley
Patricia Iris	Collins	June Daphne	Cotton	Gladys Joan	Crowsley
Yvonne Betty	Collins	Doris Joan	Couchman	Nancy	Crowther
Bettina	Collis	Margaret Edna	Coultrip	Vera	Crowther
Gladys Beatrice	Collis	Norah Bridget	Courtney	Stella Frances	Crump
Sylvia Carmel	Collis	Pearl Primrose	Coutts	Phyllis	Crutchley
Catherine	Colton	Anne	Cowley	Marian	Cufter
Patricia Joan	Colville-Smith	Audrey May	Cowley	Barbara Francis	Cumberland
Winifred Noel	Colyer	Edith	Cowley	Constance Eileen	Cumner
Annie Alice Mary	Colyer	Lavinia	Cowling	Patricia Margaret	Cunniffe
Noreen Dorothy	Colyer	Barbara Phyllis	Cox	Catherine	Cunningham
Nora Elizabeth	Condell	Dorothy Vera	Cox	Elizabeth Betty	Cunningham
Margaret	Conlin	Eileen Elsie	Cox	Joan Mary Beatrice	Cunningham
Sally	Conlon	Gertrude Eleanor	Cox	Sheila Ann	Cunningham
Catherine	Connor	Ivy Anne	Cox	Marjorie	Currant
Iris Rosalie Elsie	Conway	Jean Patricia	Cox	Gwyneth Joan	Curren
Audrey	Cook	Joan Eveline	Cox	Diana Nona	Curry
Dorothy	Cook	Maureen Elizabeth	Cox	Doris Emily	Curtis
Dorothy Evelyn	Cook	Muriel Joan	Cox	Jean	Curtis
Irene Florence May	Cook	Olive Joan Eileen	Cox	Nellie	Curtis
Joan Margaret	Cook	Rita	Cox	Phyllis	Curtis
Mary Doreen	Cook	Vera	Cox	Iris Daphne	Cutts (Mrs)
Peggy Isabel	Cook	June	Crabbe	Edna May	Daffin
Joyce Marjorie	Cooke (Mrs)	Barbara May	Cracknell	Phyllis	Daglish
Marjorie	Cooke	Joan Evelyn	Cracknell	Evelyn Laura	Daisley
Irene	Coolbear	Rita Florence	Craft	Joyce	Daisy
Ruby Grace	Coombs	Eileen May	Cramhorn	Maureen	Daley
Marjorie Grace	Coop	Dorothy Gladys	Crampton	Alice Winifred	Daly
Daphne Mary	Coop (Mrs)	Kate	Cranage	Mavis Irene	Damon
Audrey Jill	Cooper	Phyllis	Cranbrook	Mary	Danahar
Ida	Cooper		(Mrs)	Edith	Daniel (Mrs)
Jeanne Barbara	Cooper	Beatrice Mary	Crane	Mabel Edith	Darts
Jessie Agnes	Cooper	Betty	Crane	Jean	Davenport
Joyce Mary	Cooper	Queenie	Crannage	Gwyneth	Davey

Joan Mabel	Davey	Sheila	Dean	Yvonne G	Doreè
June Florence	Davey	Sheila Doreen	Dean	Joan Helen	Dorey
June Rosina	Davidson	Deborah Mary	Deane	Barbara	Doughty
Pamela Ann	Davidson-Pratt	Josephine Sylvia	Deane	May Florence	Dovey
		Minnie Barbara	Dear	Clarice	Dowd
Dora	Davies	Kathleen	Deegan	Doris May	Dowie
Elizabeth Myfanwy	Davies	Edith Eleanor	Deighton	Ivy Georgina	Downer
Gwyneth May	Davies	Mary Nessa	Deighton	Alice	Downes
Jennet Amelia	Davies	Lily Francis	Dell	Audrey Anne	Downie
Kathleen	Davies	Gladys Catherine	Delvenne	Vera Kate	Downing
Kathleen Joan	Davies	Joan Mary	Denison	Margaret Ada	
Marion	Davies	Hilda	Dennell	Priscilla	Downs
Marjorie Joyce	Davies	June Pamela	Dennis	Maureen Florence	Downs
Muriel	Davies	Averil Anstice	Dent	Sybil Eileen	Downs
Winifred	Davies	Beatrice	Dent	Alice Ann	Dowsett
Ada	Davis	Dorothy Patricia	Denton	Beryl	Draper
Doreen Evelyn	Davis	Elizabeth Grace	Denton (Mrs)	Audrey Maureen	Driver
Hazel	Davis (Mrs)	Joyce Mary	Denton	Dorothy	Dronsfield
Joan Lilian	Davis	Rose May	Denton	Margaret	Druce
Lily	Davis	Caroline	Deswarte	Betty Margaret	Drury
Marion Annie	Davis	Patricia	Devereaux	Dorothy	Dryden
Olive May	Davis	Patricia Florence	Devlin	Eileen Brenda	Duce
Peggy Iris	Davis	Doris Amelia	Dew	Sheila	Duerden
Doran	Davison	Peggy Margaret		Anne	Duffy
Joan Frances	Davison	Joan	Dexter	Betty Christine	Duggan
Jean Dorothy	Dawes	Ivy Winifred	Dibben	Kathleen	Dumpleton
Dorothy Mabel	Dawick	Hannah	Dible	Mary	Dumpleton
Alice Maude	Dawkins	Annie	Dickens	Joan Marie	Dunn
Amy Anita	Dawson	Prudence	Dickens	Lilian	Durber
Dorothy	Dawson	Evelyn Lucy	Dickins	Irene Mary	Durkin
Gladys Hilda	Dawson	Irene Mary	Dickins	Olive Marion	Durston
Barbara Hilda	Day	Florence Maude	Dicks	Audrey Mary	Dutton
Barbara Joyce	Day	Rhoda	Diemer	Elizabeth Betty	Dutton
Elizabeth Mary Blair	Day	Cecilia Eileen	Dines	Irene Joyce	Dye
Ethel May	Day	Tryphena	Dingle	Violet Grace	Dymock
Gladys May	Day	Olwen	Dinsdale	Rose Lilian	Earl
Helen Diana	Day	Harriet	Ditchburn	Josephine Mary	Earlam
Jane Constance	Day	Jennie	Dixon	Edna	Earnshaw
Mary	Day	Mary Isabella	Dixon	Sheila	East
Rose Ann	Day	Nellie	Dixon	Joyce Edyth	Eatherley
Ruby	Day	Dorothy Maud	Dobson	Ethel Lorna	Eaton
Ruth Emily	Day	Elsie	Dockerty	Mary Edith	Eaves
Sylvia Mary	Day	Isabella	Dodd	Pamela	Edgeworth
Sylvia	Daynes	Muriel Joyce	Dodd	Teresa	Edmond
Mary Jean	Dazley	Margaret Florence	Dodson	Agila Mary	Edwards
Joan Kathleen	Deag	Ivy	Doherty	Annie Ellen	Edwards
Margaret	Deag	Anne Campbell	Doig	Delma	Edwards
Rose	Deakin	Nora Florence	Dolby	Doris	Edwards
Audrey	Dean	Olive M	Dolezal	Dorothy	Edwards
Josephine	Dean	Ailsa A	Donald	Gwendoline Faye	Edwards
Mary	Dean	Sheila Irene	Donald	José Freda	Edwards
Patricia Ellen	Dean	Mary	Donohue	Joyce	Edwards
		Patricia	Donovan	Nellie	Ehrlich

Marjorie Alice	Elborough	Annie	Evers	Daisy Veronica	Flannery
Kathleen	Eldon	Mary	Evers	Beryl	Flaxmer
Doreen	Elford	Joan	Evershed	Beryl Margaret	Fleckney
Daphne Gladys	Elliff	Anastasia Mary	Ewart	Dorothy	Fleming
Zoë Christine	Ellingham	Edith Nora	Ewles	Lucy Ann	Fleming
Jocelyn	Elliot	Dorothy Betty	Facer (Mrs)	Nellie	Fleming
Eileen	Elliott	Eileen Joan	Fahey	Clara	Fletcher
Eileen Patricia	Elliott	Heather Margaret	Fair	Eileen Florence	Fletcher
Vera Cynthia	Elliott	Margaret	Fairclough	Joan	Fletcher
Celia Alvey	Ellis	Mima	Fairley	Ruby Valentine	Fletcher
Christine	Ellis	Constance Creamer	Fall	Rosina Alice	Flewers
Constance Margerate	Ellis	Pauline Frances	Fardoe	Eva Hilda	Flexon
Doreen Evelyn	Ellis	Betty	Farmer	Betty May	Flitton
Ethel	Ellis	Grace	Farmer	Dorothy Julia	Flitton
Eunice	Ellis	Doreen May	Farquhar	Patricia Killick	Flood
Florence	Ellis	Doris Elizabeth	Farrah	Constance E	Flower
Joy	Ellis	Jean	Farrar	Mary Elizabeth	Foames
Muriel	Ellis	Joyce	Farren	Beryl	Foers
Olive	Ellis	Diana Goodman	Farrow	Lily	Fogg
Peggy	Ellis	Elsie	Farrow	Clarice Evelyn	Fohrwesser/ Foster
Violet May	Ellis	Louise	Farrow		
Marion	Ellison	Edna Mary	Faulkner	Jeanette	Foley
Hilda Maud	Elms	Daphne Alexandra	Favell	Violet Vera	Folley
Elsie May	Elson	Mary	Favell	Dulcie Madeline	Fontaine
Sadie May	Elwell	Audrey Joyce	Faver	Joyce	Fontana
Joan	Emerton	Joan Evelyn	Feasey	Hilda May	Foote
Josephine Wade	Emery	Mona	Feather	Barbara Lilian	Ford
Moira	Emery	Joan Mary	Felce	Edna May	Ford
Audrey Olive	Emmens	Betty Joan	Feltham	Johanna Maria	Ford
Edna	Emmett	Maureen Lilian	Fenner	Lydia	Ford
Rosina Helen	Emmett	Betty Beryl	Fensham	Alice	Forrest
Marjorie Ellen	Emmons	Florence	Fensome	Peggy	Forrest
Margaret	Engstrom	Freda May	Fensome	Mary	Foster
Joan Dorothy	Euinton	Elsie	Fenwick	Clarice Evelyn	Foster (previously Fohrwesser)
Hilary Gwendolen	Evan-Jones	Hilary	Fenwick		
Barbara Winifred	Evans	Annette Stewart	Ferry		
Dorothy	Evans	Gladys Patricia	Figgins	Bertha Dorothy	Fox
Dulcie Lillie	Evans	Barbara Maud	Filbey	Dorothy Florence	Fox
Florence Eileen	Evans	Dorothy	Filby	Dorothy May	Fox
Frances Alice	Evans	Agnes	Finch	Kathleen Una	Fox
Grace Doris	Evans	Edith Mary Celia	Finch	Marjorie Anne	Fox
Jean	Evans	Elizabeth Joan	Findley	Mary	Fox
Joan	Evans	Elsie	Firth	Mary Ellen	Fox
Lily	Evans	Hilda	Firth	Maude	Fox
Margaret Louise	Evans	Jean	Firth	Olive Mary	Fox
Margaret Olwen	Evans	Betty Lily Edna	Fish	Dorothy	France
Margaret Primrose	Evans	Audrey	Fisher	Jean Grace	Francis
Ruby Emmeline	Evans	Betty Rugeley	Fisher	Violet	Frankland
Marguerite Elizabeth	Everett	Jessie Evelyn	Fisher	Joyce	Frappell
Joyce	Everidge	Margaret Joyce Beverley	Fisher	Rosemary	Fraser-Harris
Lilian Dora	Everitt	Mary Margaret	Fisher	Annie Isobel	Freckleton
		Eileen	Fishwick	Irene	Freedman
				Mary Jean	Freeman

Violet Amy	Freeman	Jean Josephine		Doris May	Gosling
Celia	French	Lilian	Gibson (Mrs)	G	Goss
Kathleen Florence	French	Patricia Joan	Giggle	Phyllis Louisa	Gough
Mary	Froggatt	Kathleen May	Gilbert	Mabel	Goulding
Iola Yvonne	Frood	Sylvia Sarah	Gilder	Lilian Victoria	Gower
Betty	Frost	Ellen Barbara	Giles	Diana F	Grandage
Doreen Charlotte	Frost	Irene Margaret	Gill	Esmé	Granville
Eva Elsie	Frost	Maureen	Gill	Jean Margaret	Gration
Mabel Alice	Frost	Margaret Grace	Gillard	Joan	Graves
Marjorie Florence	Fry	Dorothy Isobel	Gillgrass	Sheila	Gravestock
Mary	Fullen	Bonnylin Alice	Gillies (Mrs)	Betty	Gray
Betty Mary	Fuller	Patricia Rhoda	Gillies	Doris	Gray
Eileen Mary	Fuller	Doreen Brenda	Gilligan	Edna Annie	Gray
Vera Francis	Furlong	Patricia Lilian	Girling	Elizabeth Jane	Gray
Beryl Gertrude	Gabbert	Marion Eileen		Georgina Mary	Gray
Marjorie	Gable	Betty	Gittins	Ivy Berther	Gray
Doris Edith	Gadsby	Barbara Nancy	Gladden	Julia	Gray
Betty Edna	Gage	Peggy	Gladstone	Marjorie Agnes	Gray
Molly	Gage	Elizabeth Joyce	Gleave	Vera	Gray
Phyllis May	Gage	Joan Irenée Edith	Glennie	Winifred	Gray
Annie	Gallagher	Rona	Glinn	Winifred Elizabeth	Gray
Eileen	Gallant	Miriam	Godber (Mrs)	Elizabeth Anne	Greaves
R	Gammon	Ellen May	Godfrey	Rosamund Irene	Greaves
Marian	Gant	Rosina	Godfrey	Audrey Mary	Green
Audrey May	Gardner	June	Godwin	Barbara	Green
Iris	Gardner	Edna May	Goetz	Betty Violet Rose	Green
Isabel	Gardner	Iris Dorothy	Gold	Daisy Kathleen	Green
Patricia Elizabeth	Garner	Marjorie Stella	Golder	Denise Evelyn	Green
Joan Mary	Garratt	Vera Daphne	Goldsmith	Elsie	Green
Annie	Garside	Pauline	Goldstein	Ella Verdun	Green
Evelyn Fanny	Garton		(Mrs)	Frances Ivy	Green
Sheila Daisy	Garvey	Margaret	Goldsworthy	Iris	Green
Elsie Florence	Gastrell	Rosalind Mary	Goodall	Kathleen	Green (Mrs)
Jean	Gates	Violet Maud	Goodall	Kathleen May	Green
Alice Marguerite		Josephine Elizabeth	Goode		(WLA96987)
Joan	Gaunt	Emily E	Goodlet	Margaret Olive	Green
Joan Charlotte	Gaunt	Celia	Goodmaker	Patricia Margaret	Green
June Olive	Gay	Betty Marie Rita	Goodman	Shirley Alice	Green
Joan Betty	Gazeley	Joyce Awdrey	Goodman	Sylvia	Green
Joan Ettie	Gearey	Rose Ord	Goodricke	Sheila	Greenan
Catherine	Gee	Ivy Georgena	Goodson	Joan Sara Maud	Greener
Eileen	Gegg	Barbara Mary	Goodwin	Mary Teresa	Greenland
Valerie Iris	Gegg	Josephine	Goodwin	Annie	Greenwood
Joyce	Gelder	Mary Kathleen	Goodwin	Daisy	Greenwood
Margaret Anne	Gellatly	Mary Veronica	Goodwin	Eileen Norah	Greenwood
Florence	Genders	Pamela Violet	Goodwin	Mavis	Greenwood
Kathleen May	George	Teresa Margaret	Goodwin	Vera	Greenwood
Joan Kathleen	Gerrard	Celia	Goodyear	Elizabeth Natalie	Greg
Zena Rose	Gething	Mary Helena	Goodyear	Agnes	Gregory
Dorothy	Gibbons	Molly Annie	Goodyear	Irene	Gregory
Margaret Ethel	Gibbs	Marjorie	Gordon	Mildred	Gregory
Nora Elizabeth	Gibbs	Joan	Gore	Phyllis	Gregory
		Elizabeth	Gorvett	Rose Ann	Gregory

First name	Surname	First name	Surname	First name	Surname
Christine Mary	Gregson	Joan Winifred	Hammond	Dorothy Veronica	Hart
Josephine	Grenier	Mary Constance	Hammond	Joyce Sylvia	Hart
Edna Maud	Grevett	Margaret Alice	Hampton	Olive Agnes	Hart
Kathleen Mary	Grey	Kathleen	Hancock	Ruby Doreen	Hart
Lilian Constance	Griffin	Doris	Hand	Winifred Edith	Hart
Rose Marie	Griffin	Grace	Hand	Jean	Hartley
Violetta Ivy	Griffin	Kathleen	Hanna	Joan	Hartley
Beryl Mary	Griffiths	Constance Elizabeth	Hansen	Jean Edith	Hartop
Gladys	Griffiths	Gladys Marjorie	Hanson	Lilian Maud	Hartwell (Mrs)
Iris Elsie	Griffiths	Joan	Hanson	Mary Louise	Harvey
Lily	Griffiths	Joan	Harbidge	Florence Mary	Harwood
Myra	Griffiths	Marion	Hardacre	Betty	Harwood
Rachel	Griffiths	Bette Noeleen	Harding	Dorothy	Haslam
Doris Evelyn	Grindell	Mary	Harding	Joan	Haste
Lilian	Gripton	Kathleen Irene	Harding	Joan	Haswell
Sylvia Laura	Gross	Violet	Harding	Audrey Lilian	Havard
Frieda May	Grove	Mildred Elsie	Hardy	Joan Violet	Haw
Winifred Mary Elizabeth	Grundon	Edith	Hargreaves	Hazel Dorothy	Hawkins
Constance	Gudgeon	Barbara	Harker	Doreen	Haworth
Elsie May	Guest	Joan Doris	Harle	Hazel Lillian	Haworth
Frances Marie	Guttridge	Barbara Jane	Harley	Sylvia Joyce	Hawthorn
Iris	Haddock	Grace	Harling	Joyce Ellen	Hayden
Barbara	Hague	Margaret Helen	Harling	Mary	Hayden
Doris	Haigh	Peggy Beatrice	Harmsworth	Evelyn	Hayers
Edith Nellie	Haines	Alice	Harper	Lucy	Hayes
Irene Mary	Haines	Gwendoline	Harper	Sheila Mary	Hayes
Joan	Haines	Julia Sheila	Harps	Dorothy	Hayman
Joan	Hales	June Audrey	Harpur	Louise	Haynes
Mary	Haley	Lilian Amy	Harpur	Mary Francis	Haynes
Monica Olive	Haley	Irene Eileen May	Harries	Theresa	Hayter
Elma Doris	Halfpenny	Doris	Harris (WLA114938)	Dorothy Nora Mary	Haywood
Daphne Ida	Hall	Doris	Harris (WLA181199)	Georgina Elsie	Haywood
Doris May	Hall	Edna Josephine	Harris	Louise	Haywood
Dorothy	Hall	Ethel	Harris	Sarah	Hazeldine
Bertha	Hall	Ethel Emma	Harris	Margaret Geraldine	Hazelton
Edna	Hall	Gwendoline Joan	Harris	Sheila Mary	Hazelton
Ivy Irene	Hall	Joan Elizabeth	Harris	Patricia May	Hazlewood
Joyce	Hall	José	Harris	Joyce Eveline	Head
Margaret	Hall	Joyce Winifred	Harris	Sheila	Head
Sylvia Margaret	Hall	Olive	Harris (Mrs)	Freda	Heal
Matilda	Halling	Phyllis Elaine	Harris (Mrs)	Doreen	Heales
Dorothy May	Halliwell (Mrs)	Eliza Mary	Harrison	Gwendolyn May	Heath
Maureen Janet	Halls	Freda	Harrison	Joan	Heath
Rose	Hallworth	Gladys	Harrison	Joan Violet	Heath
Jane Elizabeth	Halsey	Jean	Harrison	Diana José	Heathcote
Frances	Hamilton	Joan Mary	Harrison	Joyce Evelyn	Hellis
Jacqueline Raymonde	Hamilton	Joyce Grant	Harrison	Betty Winifred	Hellyer
Audrey Winifred	Hammond	Lilian Dorothy	Harrison	Margaret Mary	Hellyer
Dorothy Primrose	Hammond	Margaret	Harrison	Nina Rosa	Helman
Edwina Florence	Hammond	Elsie	Harrold	June Mary	Helme
				Norma Maureen	Hemmett
				Marion Lillian	Hemming

Vilma Joy	Henbrey	Joan Mary	Hinton	Kathleen Florence	Hopkins
Catherine Ellen	Henderson	Mabel Joan	Hinton	Audrey	Hopkinson
Daphne June	Henderson	Norah Eleanor	Hiorns	Muriel	Hopper
Clara Mary	Henman	Doris Brenda		Elizabeth	Hopwood
Alwyn Margaret	Henry	Kathleen	Hird	Lily	Hornby
Barbara	Henshaw	Gertrude	Hirsch	Doris Emily	Horning
Jean Gladys	Herald	Minnie	Hirshorn	Marjorie Hilda	Horning
Constance Eileen	Herbert	Lilian May	Hirst	Joyce	Horridge
Gladys Irene	Herbert	Audrey Muriel		Audrey Isobel	Horsbrugh
Rosabel	Herkes	Elizabeth	Hislop	P	Horsbrugh
Joan Patricia	Herly	Edna	Hitchen	Hetty	Horsenail
Frances Peggy	Herniman	Elsie Gertrude	Hoather	Betty	Horsier
Edna	Herring	May Violet	Hoather	Betty	Horsler
Joyce Irene	Hewitson	Constance Edith	Hobbs	Olive Isobel	Horsler
Beatrice	Hewitt	Dorothy Eileen	Hobbs	Kathleen Constance	Horsley
Elizabeth Dora	Hewitt	Joan Beryl	Hobbs	Dorothy Gladys	Horsted
Annie	Heywood	Daphne Joan		Joan Patricia	Horswill
Florence Grace	Hibbard	Gwendoline	Hobkirk	Kathleen Rose	
Vera	Hibbert	Annie	Hobson	Georgina	Horton
Mary Ursula	Hickey	Gladys	Hobson	Irene May	Hoskins
Doreen Frances	Hickmott	Mariane	Hodges	Annabelle Lucy	Houghton
Amy Phyllis	Higgins	Joan	Hodgson	Dorothy	Houghton
Norah	Higgins	Nancy	Hodgson (Mrs)	Josephine Peggy	Houghton
Doris	Higginson	Joyce Lily	Hogan	Mary Elizabeth	
Maud Ethel	Higgs	Ailsa	Hogg	Nancy	Hounslow
Georgina May	Highfield	Esther	Hold (Mrs)	Frances	Houston
Doris	Hignett	Barbara	Holden	Doris May	How
Ada Margaret	Hill (Mrs)	Jean Rose	Holder	Joyce Katherine	How
Florence	Hill	Mary	Holdroyde	Amelia Doris	Howard
Ivy Lily	Hill	Kathleen Mary	Holdstock	Beatrice Nellie	Howard
Joyce	Hill	Audrey	Holland	Elsie Minnie	Howard
Joyce Alice	Hill	Emily Sally	Holland	Lillian	Howard
Joyce Vera	Hill	Mary Elizabeth	Holland	Margaret	Howard (Mrs)
Margaret Dorothea		Mildred Althea	Holliday (Mrs)	Frances Joan	Howarth
Lizzie	Hill	D	Hollingdale	Yvonne Lilian	Howdee
Marjorie	Hill	Laura Violet	Hollingdale	Ethel May	Howe
Gladys Joan	Hills	Joan Seymour	Hollis	Gladys Vera	Howe
Pamela Winifred	Hills	Margaret Ada	Hollis	Joyce Evelyn	Howe
Pansy Gertrude		Enid Mary	Holmes	Pamela Margaret	Howe
Clare	Hills	Jenny	Holmes	Thelma	Howe
Evelyn Mary	Hillyard	Dorothy	Holroyd	Margaret	Howe-Double
Vera	Hillyard	Vera	Holroyd	Hilda Maude	Howell
Avril Marjorie	Hilton	Celia	Holt	Gaynor	Howells
Gladys	Himsworth	Ellen	Holt	Elizabeth Mary	Howick
Mary Agnes	Hinchliffe	Freda	Holt	Phyllis	Howitt
Olive	Hinchliffe	Kathleen Beryl	Holt	Iris Doreen	Howlett
Ann Elizabeth	Hind	Nellie Annie	Holt	Gwendoline	Hoy
Audrey Joan	Hinde	Patricia Kathleen	Holt	Barbara	Hubbard
Isobel Mary	Hindle	Vera	Holt	Monica	Hubbard
Mary Alice	Hindle	Joy	Holton	Nancy Irene	Hubbard
Marjorie	Hinds	Pamela Kathryn	Homan	Edna Mary	Huckle
Audrey	Hines	CE	Hopkins	Gladys	Hudson
Hazel Rosemary	Hinton	Gladys	Hopkins (Mrs)	Joan Maisie	Hudson

Penelope Jane	Hudson	Ruth	Inman	Irene Alice	Johnson
Vera Isabella	Hudson	Lily Pearl	Inns	Joan	Johnson
Gladys Martha	Hughes	Joyce Doreen	Irons	Joyce Dorothy	Johnson
Margaret	Hughes	Joyce Edith	Irving	Margaret	Johnson
Mary Theresa	Hughes	Beryl Claire	Isaacs	May Dorothy	Johnson
Nora Edna	Huke	Daphne	Ives	Nora	Johnson
Jean Marion	Hulatt	Doreen Pearl	Ives	Pamela	Johnson
Joyce Maisie	Hulatt	Irene Margaret	Jacks	Vera Lily	Johnson
Joyce Margaret	Hulford	Christine	Jackson	Alice Barbara	Johnston
Edna Violet	Hull	Joan	Jackson	Monica	Johnston
Mildred	Hull	Joan Alys	Jackson	Frances Patricia	Johnstone
Rose Emily	Hull	Lillian	Jackson	Eva	Johnston-
Vera Florrie	Hull	Lilian Patricia	Jackson		Sparks
Ruth Lilian	Hulme	Mary Maureen	Jackson	Ann Lorraine	Jones
Elizabeth Muriel	Hulse	Rosalie	Jackson	Audrey	Jones
Dora Josephine	Hume	Miriam Fanny	Jakes	Brenda Mary	Jones
Elizabeth Elsie		Audrey	James	Diana	Jones
Norma	Humphrey	Margaret L	Jamieson	Doreen	Jones
Violet Susan	Humphrey	Ivy Elizabeth	Janaway	Doreen Elisabeth	Jones
Ada Maud	Humphreys	Alice	Jarvis	Edith	Jones
Maisie Jean	Humphreys	Daphne Mary	Jarvis	Eileen Mary	Jones
Betty	Humphries	Joan Doris	Jauncey	Gladys	Jones
Barbara Elizabeth	Hunt	Kathleen	Jay	Gwendoline	Jones
Edna Marion	Hunt	Winifred May	Jaynes	Gwendoline Jessie	Jones
Margaret	Hunt	Nora May	Jeakings	Hannah Isobel	Jones
Peggy	Hunt	Kathleen Dorothy	Jeanes	Hilda Beatrice	Jones
Jeannette	Hunter	Marion Kathleen	Jeans	Irene Mary	Jones
Audrey Mary	Hurdiss	Freda Rose	Jeeves	Ivy Louise	Jones
Florence	Hurdiss	Dorothy Margaret	Jefferies	Jean	Jones
Hetty	Hurley	Joyce Maud	Jeffreys	Joan	Jones
Jessie	Hurrell	Vera	Jeffs	Joyce	Jones
Doreen Grace	Hurren	Florence Elizabeth	Jelley	Lilian Julia	Jones
Doris Eva	Hurren	Vera Doris	Jellis	Margaret	Jones
Betty	Hurst	Dorothy Gertrude	Jenkins		(WLA135427)
Doreen	Hurst	Edna Viola	Jenkins	Margaret	Jones
Elsie	Hurton	Nora Madge	Jenkins		(WLA81011)
Rita	Hushion	Gwendoline Vera	Jennings	Mary Eluned	Jones
Winifred	Hutchinson	Mary Elizabeth		Monica Mary	Jones
Doris	Huxtable	Ann	Jepps	Noreen	Jones
Patricia	Hyatt	Helena May	Jessop	Norma Fay	Jones
Patricia Irene		Vera	Jobling	Pearl	Jones
Knowler	Hyde	Frances Ida	Johns	Peggy	Jones
Doreen JE	Hyder	Amy	Johnson	Joyce	Jordan
Bridget Mary	Hyland	Catherine		Betty Eileen	Jordon
Queen Mary	Hymns	Rosemary	Johnson	Betty Eva	Jordon
Joan	Ilderton	Edna Elizabeth	Johnson	Mabel	Jowett
Isabella	Illidge	Edna May	Johnson	Constance Agnes	Judd
Joan	Illingworth	Eileen Mary	Johnson	Dora May	Judd
Irene Pamela	Ilsley	Elizabeth	Johnson	Lilian	Judge
Gladys Elizabeth	Impey	Evelyn Hermione	Johnson	Betty May	Julyan
Florence Joan	Inckle	Gladys	Johnson	Rose Lilian	Juniper
Joyce Lillian	Ingram	Gladys Mabel	Johnson	Nancy	Karn
Kathleen Helen	Inker	Irene	Johnson	Katherine	Kassalitus

Rosaleen Albertina	Kattenhorn	Hilda Margaret	Kimber	Carinthia A	Lane
Sheila Elizabeth		Doreen Iris	King	Catherine	Lane
Mary	Kavanagh	Dorothy	King	Doris May	Lane
Doreen	Kay	Elizabeth Mildred	King	Edna	Lane
Vera	Kay	Ena	King		(WLA130239)
Violet	Kay	Jean Dorothy	King	Edna	Lane
Diana Phylis	Keable	Hilda Mabel	King		(WLA158270)
Edna May	Keen	Margaret Eileen	King	Iris	Lanfear
Hanna Theresa	Keen	Patricia Margaret	King	Brenda Edith Mary	Langdon
Mary	Keenan	Violet Joan	Kingham	Joan Olive	Langford
Margaret	Keene	Ethel Evelyn Violet	Kingsland	Violet Elizabeth	Langford
Gertrude	Keens	Yvette Pamela	Kingston-	Blanche Muriel	Langrish
Joyce Irene	Keeper		Jones	Eileen Mildred	Langton
Audrey Mavis	Keith	Gladys May	Kinnear	Mary	Langton
Eunice Esme	Kellow	Iris May	Kinnear	Dorothy	Lannon
Marguerite	Kelly	Doreen	Kinvig	Brenda Margaret	Large
Madeline	Kelsey	Constance Florence	Kirby	Mary	Large
Lily	Kemble	Elsie Joy	Kirby	Mary Veronica	
Gladys	Kemp	Ivy Joy	Kirby	Agnes	Larke
Doreen Mary	Kempster	Jean Ivy	Kirby	Eva Sarah	Larkin
Elsie	Kempster	Margaret Grace	Kirby	Joan	Larkin
Joyce Isobel	Kendall	Veronica	Kirwin	Phyllis	Laverick
Alice	Kendray	Helen Gertrude		Carrie	Law
Ada	Kendrick	Mary	Kitchener	Betty	Layfield
Mary Emma	Keneford	Joan Lesley	Kitson	Joan Gladys	Le Boutillier
Vera Rose	Kennard	Margaret Evelyn	Kneen	Winnie	Lea
Alice	Kenneally	Vanda Eileen	Kneen	Jean Elsie	Leader
Barbara	Kennedy	Betty Jane	Knight	Esther Lilian	Leather
Irene	Kennedy	Doris Margaret	Knight	Audrey Madge	Lee
Margaret	Kennedy	Jessie G	Knight	Betty Vera	Lee
Dora	Kenningley	Ruby Rose	Knight	Faith Betty	Lee
Edith Maude	Kenrick	Muriel	Knightson	Florence Brenda	Lee
Gladys Winifred	Kenswood	Eileen Mary	Knott	Jean Mary	Lee
Beryl Mary	Kent	Lois Patricia	Knowles	Lilian	Lee
Gertrude Jean	Kent	Dorothy Mary	Kolesnick	Margaret Veronica	Lee
Elsie Ethel	Kenward	Dorothy Louisa	Lacey	Minnie Violet	Lee
Gladys Winifred	Kenward	Jacqueline Marie		Nellie	Lee
Miriam Jean	Kerner	Claire	Laird	Vera Joyce	Lee
Christine	Kerridge	Edith Newton	Lake	Doreen	Leeson
Ivy Veronica	Kerry	Joan Vera	Lake	Hannah	Lefcovitch
May Florence	Kerry	Olive	Lake	Minnie	Lefcovitch
Margaret	Kershaw	Dorothy	Lamb	Cora	Leicester
Mary	Keyes	Eliza	Lamb	Eveleigh	Leigh
Eleanor Alice	Keyworth	Elsie Mary	Lambkin	Mary Ann	Leighton
Irene Stella Ann	Kibble	Rosina Patience		Jean Mary	Leith
Doris May	Kidd	Lilian	Lammas	Rita Kathleen	Leonard
Doreen	Kiddell	Iris Jenny	Lammert	Dorothy Frances	Lepine
Beatrice Toni	Kidson	Madaleine Maud	Lancashire	Lily	Levey
Patricia Margaret	Kilbey	Audrey Genevieve	Lancaster	M	Levey
Eileen	Kilbride	Elma Irene		Abigail	Levine
Joan Betty	Kiln	Winifred	Land	Hannah	Lewin
Rose Emily	Kilsby	Margaret	Land	Bessie	Lewis
Ruby	Kilsby	Sylvia Shirley	Landsman	Betty Joyce	Lewis

Betty Lucille	Lewis	Margaret	Lough	Gladys Violet	Mann
Doris	Lewis	Elizabeth Margaret		Iris Joan	Manning
Edna May	Lewis	Ethel	Lovell	Peggy May	Manning
Eileen Olga	Lewis	Joan Ada	Lovell	Eileen Ellen	Mansell
Elizabeth	Lewis	Kathleen Gertrude	Lovell	Sylvia May	Manser
Joan Evelyn	Lewis	Mary	Lovell	Irene	Mansfield
Winifred	Lewis	Mary June	Lovell	Florence Emma	Mantell
Pauline	Libby	Elizabeth Esther	Lovett	Audrey Doreen	Manwaring
Eileen Mary	Liddell	Dorothy Mabel	Lowe	Elizabeth Lydia	Manyweathers
Georgina	Light	Dorothy Maude	Lowe	May	Maples
Barbara Eileen	Lightfoot	Edith	Lowe	Edith Alice	Marchant
Norah Kathleen	Lilley	Jean	Lowe	Kathleen Valentine	Margan
Violet Rose	Lilley	Vera Mary	Lowe	Irene Violet	Markham
Mary E	Lillieo	Mary Elizabeth		Phyllis	Markham
Audrey	Limbert	Catherine	Lowndes	Winnie Irving	Markham
Stella Margaret	Limon	Jean Eleanor	Lucas	Olive Winifred	Marks
Audrey Jean	Lincoln	Lavinia	Lucas	Eva	Marriott
Joan	Lindley	Wendy Gillian	Luckey	Mary Elisa	Marsburg
Laurel	Lindley	Hazel Mary	Luddington	Lilian Jessie	Marsh
Lily Victoria	Lindop	Doris May	Ludlow	Mary	Marsh
Marjorie Winifred	Lindsay	Norah	Lumsden	Olwyn Jean	Marsh
Dorothy Cynthia	Linegar (Mrs)	Mary Eileen	Lunt	Phyllis May	Marsh (Mrs)
Cynthia Winifred	Linford	June	Luscombe	Rose Hilda	Marsh
Doreen	Linford	Edith Emily	Luxton	Amelia Beatrice	Marshall
Joy Dorothy	Linford	Beryl	Lye	Elizabeth Edith	Marshall
Dorothy	Ling	Iris May	Lynch	Gwendoline	Marshall
Dorothy Francis	Lingard	Moira E	Lynch	Katharine Mary	
Cicely Margaret	Link	Elizabeth Irene	Lyne	Crommelin	Marshall
Justine Emmeline		Joyce	Lynn	Lena Elsie	Marshall
Marguerite	Lipschutz	Lilian Ethel	Lyons	Margaret Rutt	Marshall
Ivy May	Lipscombe	Margaret	Lyons	Mary	Marshall
Margaret	Lister	Marjorie Sylvia	Lyons	Sheila	Marshall
Eileen Rose	Litchfield	Mary	Lyons	Margery Barbara	Martell
Maude Ethel	Litchfield	Thelma Eileen Rita	Mabbitt	Dorothy	Martin
Annie	Little	Joan	Mabbott	Ethel Joan Elaine	Martin
Lillian Ellan	Littlejohn	Kathleen	MacDonald	Hilda May	Martin
Diana	Littleton	Millicent	MacDonald	Hilda Rose	Martin
Joan	Littlewood	Olive Emily	MacDonald	Joyce	Martin
Doreen	Livingston	Joan	Mack	June	Martin
Sarah	Lobb	Veronica Grace	MacManus	Olive	Martindale
Doris	Lockhart	Ethel Elizabeth	Madeley	Doreen Phyllis	Maskell
Audrey	Lockwood	Winifred Ursula	Maher	Doris Mary	Maskell
Daphne Margaret	Lockwood	Susan	Mahoney	Annie	Mason
Joan	Loft	Lily	Mair	Barbara Helen	Mason
Evelyn Dorothy	Long	Clarice	Makinson	Faith	Mason
Joyce Margaret		Renée	Males	Grace Joyce	Mason
Maud	Long	Doris	Mallatratt	Irene	Mason
Jennie Martha	Longmate	Roma Marla	Mallone	Ivy	Mason
Ruby Florence	Lorch	Ellen Mary	Maloney	Paulette Barnes	Mason
Phyllis Mary	Lord	Betty Hayden	Malpas	Eve Maude	Massey
Violet Rose Jane		Joyce Mary	Malpass	Betty	Massingham
Angèle	Lorenz	Madge	Malsher	Thelma Grace	Mathers
Margaret Patricia	Lorn	Florence Elizabeth	Mann	Irene Lilian	Mathews

Lilian	Mathews	Mary Jane	McMinn	Peggy Kathleen	Mores
Stella Jean	Matson	Irene	McNally	Beryl May	Morgan
Kathleen May	Matthews	Freda	McPherson	Jean	Morgan
Ethel Margaret	Mattison	Aileen Doris	McSweeney	Joan Margaret	Morgan
Violet May	Mattox	Marie Kathleen	McSweeney	Winifred	Morgan
Ida	Maudsley	Evelyn May	Mead	Gladys	Morley
Muriel Joan	Maunder	Olive VR	Mead	Marion Ellen	Morley
Rose Marie	Maxwell	Winifred	Mead	Hilda Mary	Morrell
Olga	May	Margaret	Meaghan	Bessie	Morris
Rita Doreen	May	Beatrice Anne	Measures	Constance Lucy	Morris
Masie Elizabeth	Maycock	Dorothy	Meggitt	Dora	Morris
Margaret	Mayes	Olive Rose	Mehew	Evelyn Rebecca	Morris
Irene	Mayfield	Iris	Melia	Gwendoline	
Jean Ann	Mayfield	Catherine Margaret	Mellor	Hounslow	Morris
Annie	Mayhew	Winifred	Merrilees	Joan Rose	Morris
Barbara Joyce	Mayhew	Dorothy Mabel	Merrill	Marie	Morris
Phyllis	Mayling	Rita Mary	Merritt	Phyllis	Morten
Matilda Ann	McAllister	Margaret	Metcalf	Jill	Mortimer
Joan Alice	McAward	Joyce Edith	Middleditch	Kathleen June	Mortimer
Mavis Jean	McCabe	Olwen Jean	Middleton	Ada	Morton
Mollie	McCann	Cecilia	Milburn	Audrey	Morton
Hilda Evelyn	McCarron	Muriel Constance		Jean Isobel	Moseley
Isabelle	McCartney	Phyllis	Miles	Elizabeth Mary	Moss
Grace Elizabeth	McClaren	Agnes Crawford	Miller	Gabrielle	Moss
June	McClean	Frances Evelyn	Miller	Edna	Mostyn
Josephine	McCluskey	Jean	Miller	Sheila Dorothy	Mott
Ruby Phyllis	McCluskey	Renee	Miller	Ethel Maud	Mount
Bernadette Anne	McCormack	Audrey Irene	Mills	Enid Mary	Moxen
Margaret Mary	McCrorie	Edith Margaret	Mills	Kathleen Kenward	Moy
Doreen	McCulloch	Eileen	Mills	Georgena	Muckle
Joan	McDermott	Eileen Agnes	Mills	Aileen	Muckleston
	(Mrs)	Elsie	Mills	O	Muckleston
Joyce Lilian		Joan Kathleen Ada	Mills	Barbara Joan	Mudd
Kathleen	McDiarmaid	Kathleen Mary	Mills	Eileen Nora	Muffett
Ethel Gertude	McDonald	Molly	Mills	Violet Mary	Mulcahy
Katherine	McGovern	Joyce Patricia	Millward	Irene May	Mullins
Mary	McGovern	Hazel Muriel	Millwood	Jean Hannah	Mundy
Christina Catherine	McGregor	Agnes Beverley	Milne	Doreen	Munns
Maureen Agnes		Edna	Milton	Doris M	Munro
Kelly	McGuinness	Margaret	Milton	Christina Ann	Murdoch
Patricia Mary	McHale	Gladys Patience	Minns	Catherine Joyce	Murphy
Doris Jean	McIntyre	Beryl Jean	Mitchell	Grace Charlotte	Murphy
Annie Simpson	McKay	Dorothy Kathleen	Mitchell	Edna	Murray
Mary	McKenna	Elsie Irene	Mitchell	Ellen	Murray
Monica	McKenna	Kathleen May	Mitchell	Ivy Vivian	Murray
Edith Jeanett	McKibbin	Pamela	Mitchell	Jean Margaret	Murray
Grace Elizabeth	McLaren	Ellen Sheila	Mooney	Kathleen Rosalind	Murrell
Jessie Rose	McLaren	Louisa Florence	Moor	Mary	Musgrave
Jasmine Pearl	McLean	Edith Helen	Moore	Joan Flora	Musselwhite
June	McLean	Joan Constance	Moor-Radford	Eva Kate	Myers
Florence May	McLellan	Florence	Moran	June Adela	Myes
Bridget	McLoughlin	Margaret	Moran	June Marie	Napolitano
Nora	McManus	Patricia	Moran	Doris May	Nash

First name	Surname	First name	Surname	First name	Surname
Peggy	Nash	Patrica Irene	O'Brien	Violet D	Palfreyman
Lucilla Dasiy	Nason	Veronica	O'Brien	Dorothy Ethel	Palmer
Winifred Marjorie	Naughton	Winifred	O'Brien	Edna	Palmer
Florence	Neale	Dorothy Joan	O'Connell	Freda	Palmer
Gladys	Neale (Mrs)	Eileen	O'Connell	Heather Georgina	Palmer
Winifred May	Needham	Minnie Gladys Mary	O'Connor	Mildred Mabel	Palmer
Ivy Mary	Neenan	Nora	O'Connor	Muriel Evelyn	Panting
Kathleen Mary	Nelsey	Sheila	O'Connor	Thelma	Pape
Isabel Margaret	Nelson	Eileen Daisy	O'Dell	Dorothy	Papworth
Joyce Constance	Nelson	Phyllis	O'Dell	Amy R	Parcell
Betty	Nesbitt	Mary	O'Donoghue	Mavis Doreen	Parcell
Dorothy	Nesbitt	Edna	O'Hare	Joyce Isobel	Paris
Dorothy Muriel Barbara	Nettleship	Theresa	O'Keefe	Doreen Mabel	Parish
Wendy Patricia	Nettleton	Dorothy Lily	O'Keeffe	Gladys	Park
Harriet	Newbury	Lilian	O'Leary	Annie	Parker
Maisie Leonora	Newbury	Catherine	O'Loughnan	Bridget Mariota	Parker
Sybil Doreen	Newbury	Annie Kate	O'Neill	Doris	Parker
Frances	Newby	Mary Eileen	O'Neill	Elizabeth Sarah	Parker
Barbara	Newell	Norah Winifred	O'Riley	Lucy May	Parker (Mrs)
Doreen Mary	Newiss	Mary Margaret Teresa	O'Shea	Mary	Parker
Doris Lilian	Newman	Lorna	Oakes	Mary Gladys	Parker
Kathleen Ruth	Newman	Mavis Mary Betty	Odell	Winifred Grace	Parker
Peggy Eileen	Newman	Zoe Constance Freda	Odell	Mary	Parkinson
Audrey	Newson	Violet Kathrine Joan	Offen	Winifred	Parkinson
Amanda	Newton	Joan	Oldham	Joy Christine	Parmenter
Helen	Newton	Eileen	Olding	Margerie	Parnell
Jean Muriel	Newton	Joan Daphne	Oldreive	Joyce Lilian	Parrott
Joan	Nicholls	Lily	Oldroyd	Eira Joan	Parry
Muriel	Nichols	Alice Mary	Oliver	Joan	Parsons
Edith	Nicholson	Doris Margaret	Oliver	Kathleen Hilda	Parsons
Enid Audrey	Nicholson	Nancy Isabel	Oliver	Patricia Pearl	Parsons
Frances	Nicholson	Joan Florence	Orman	May	Partridge
Patricia Ann	Nipper	Ivy Daisy Amelia	Osborne	Doreen	Patterson
Hazel June	Nixon	Daisy	Otter	Hazel	Payling
Rachel Monica	Noah	Renee	Oughton	Clarice Audrey	Payne
Sheila Edna	Nobbs	Joyce Millicent	Owen	Dorothy Joan	Payne
Elsie	Noble	Margaret	Owen	Violet Anne	Peacock
Enid Lily	Noble	Margaret Dorothy	Owen	Amy	Pearce
Irene Adelaide	Noble	Iris Joan	Owens	Bessie Winifred	Pearce
Muriel Gladys	Noble	Marjorie Mary	Oxnard	Florence	Pearce
Winifred	Norledge	June	Pack	Ida Maud	Pearce
Mary Ann	Normington	Dorothy	Page	Kathleen	Pearce
Marjorie	Norris	Florence	Page	Margaret	Pearce
Betty Frances	Northwood	Kathleen Marie	Page	Beatrice May	Pearson
Betty	Norton	Miriam	Page	Betty	Pearson
Betty Irene	Norton	Moira	Page	Doris	Pearson
Doreen	Norton	Vera Ellen	Page	Dorothy	Pearson
Gladys	Nunn	Ruth Margaret	Paice	Elizabeth Jane	Pearson
Gwendoline Annie Mary	Nunn	Mary Beatrice	Pakes	Jean	Pearson
Irene Alice	Nutt			Joyce	Pearson
Patricia	O'Brien			Mildred	Pearson
				Winifred	Pearson
				Beryl Mildred	Peat

Catherine Gladys	Peat	Mabel Elsie	Pinnock (Mrs)	Margaret Florence	Pullen
Joan	Peat	Margaret	Pitcher	Barbara	Pumfrey
Kathleen Edith	Peat	Bernice Winifred	Pitt	Constance Audrey	Purcell (Mrs)
Iris Winifred	Peck	Bessie	Pitt	Edith May	Purkiss
Joyce Betty Olive	Peck	Patricia Mona	Pitts	Kathleen Violet	Purkiss
June Pamela	Peck	Phyllis Mary	Plater	May	Purvis
Kathleen Elizabeth	Peck	Peggy Joyce	Platt	Jean Winifred	Pye
Rosina Daisy	Peck	Annie	Plews	Irene Margaret	Pyrke
Betty	Pentelow	Edna May	Plows	June Mary	Quick
Pauline Dora Mary Edith	Percival	Grace Ellen	Plummer	Rosina Doris	Quick
Joan	Percy	Dorothy Lilly	Plumridge	Mary Alma	Quinn
Winifred Ethel	Percy	Doreen	Polhill	Maisie	Rabjohn
Joyce	Perrin	Iris Victorine	Pollock	Gladys	Race
Pauline	Perrin	Kathleen May	Ponting	Ruth Irene	Racher
Rose	Perritt	Dorothy Joan	Poole	Margaret	Radcliffe
Joyce Lilian	Perry	Sheila Jean	Pope	Lalage Muriel	Radwell
Margaret Jeanne	Perry	Gene Rosina	Porter	Dorothy May	Rainbow
Gwendolen Lillie	Perryman	Margaret Millicent	Porter	Joan Liffin	Ramsay
Kathleen N	Perryman	Mary	Porter	Phyllis	Ramsbottom
Myrtle Eileen	Perryman	Marie Ann	Porthouse		(Mrs)
Doris Maud	Pestell (Mrs)	Joan Mary	Postans	Mary	Ramsden
Beatrice	Peters	Hazel Josephine	Potten	Vera Mary	Ramsden
Daphne Lois	Peters	Elsie Rose	Poulton	Edith	Ramsey
Margaret Eileen	Peters	Rosemarie Joyce	Powell	Maria	Ramsey
Marion May	Peters	Joyce	Poxon	Marie Florence	Randall (Mrs)
Mary	Peters	Margaret Ada	Poyner	Iris Mary	Randell
Eileen Ruby	Peterson	Phyllis Constance	Pratt	Enid	Ranshaw
Eileen Mary	Pettifer	Myra Rosalind	Preater	Ada	Ratcliffe
Sylvia	Pettit	Sylvia Marie	Preater	Kathleen Doris	Raven
May	Phelan	Daphne Maud	Prentice	Marguerite	Rawes
Ivy	Philips	Mary Doreen	Prentice	Doreen	Rawlings
Dorothy Joan	Phillip	Audrey	Preston	Doris Joan	Rawlins
Doris Hilda	Phillips	Ellen	Preston	Violet Lily	Rawson
Dorothy May	Phillips	Jean	Preston	Jean	Ray
Kathleen Ann Rose	Phillips (Mrs)	Winifred Celia	Preston	Audrey	Raynor
Nesta Gwenllian	Phillips	Audrey Maisie	Price	Ada Jessie	Read
Catherine	Phillipson	Doris	Price	Margaret Alice	Read
Nellie	Phillipson	Nellie Kathleen	Price	Daphne May	Ream
Jean Burns	Philpott	Vilma Nadine	Price	Evelyn	Redknap
Agnes	Pickering	Eileen	Priestley	Cicely May	Redman
Eileen Constance Lilian Gladys	Picts	Olive Mildred	Prigmore	Gladys Daisy Jean	Redman
Sheila Doreen	Picts	Amy	Prince	Phyllis May	Redman
Amy	Pierce	Maggie Florence	Prince	Dorothy	Reed
Eileen Winifred	Piesse	Clara	Pritchard	Joyce	Reed
Iris	Piggott	Margaret Bertha	Pritchard	Mabel Kathleen	Reed
Barbara Jane	Pike	Joyce Irene	Pritchett	Phyllis Mary	Reed
Elizabeth May	Pike	Marjorie Beatrice	Proctor	Doris	Reekie
Ivy Maud	Pike	Bertha Jean	Prole	Nancy Elyned	Rees
Barbara Mary	Pilgrim	Joyce	Prudden	Joyce Hilda	Reeve
Mary	Pinder	Kathleen Mary	Prutton	Maud Mary	Reeves
Barbara Joyce	Pinnock	Beatrice Mary	Pugh	Violet	Reeves
		Joan Vyvyan	Pugh	Florence	Regan
		Betty	Pullen	Sylvia Thursa	Reid

Sheila Winifred	Rennie	Joyce Pamela	Robbins	Joyce Margaret	Rogers
Doris Eileen	Restall	Constance Audrey	Roberts	Letitia Esther	Rogers
Martha Veronica	Revell	Doris May	Roberts	Mabel Florence	Rogers
Betty	Reynolds	Gabrielle Theresa	Roberts	Mary	Rogers
Edna Bernice	Reynolds	Gladys Nellie	Roberts	Phyllis	Rogers
Joan	Reynolds	Gwenllian	Roberts	Rachel	Rogers
Margaret Joan	Reynolds	Inga Doris	Roberts	Rachel May	Rogers
Nellie Margaret	Reynolds	Joan	Roberts	Muriel	Rogerson
Queenie Gladys	Reynolds (Mrs)	Margaret Ellen	Roberts	Frances Mary	Rollaston
		Marie	Roberts	Irene May	Rolles
Joyce Doreen	Rhind	Mary Margaret		Florence	Rollett
Edna	Rhodes	Pamela	Roberts	Violet	Rosborough
Gladys Mary	Rhodes	Phyllis Grace	Roberts	Irene Gertrude	Rose
Adelaide Eleanor	Richards	Vera Davies	Roberts (Mrs)	Pamela Joan	Rose
Gladys	Richards	Daphne	Robertson	Doris Pearl	Rosen
Mary Elizabeth	Richards	Diana Nesta	Robertson	Phyllis	Rosenshine
Peggy Iris	Richards	Doreen Mary	Robins	Isabel Margaret	Ross
Rose Vickery	Richards	Gladys	Robins	Jean Marie	Ross
Sylvia	Richards	Margery Winifred	Robins	Alice Beryl	Round
Violet	Richards	Audrey	Robinson	Ina Elizabeth	Routledge
Vivyan Leila	Richards	Barbara Gertrude	Robinson	Elsie Edna	Rowe
Beatrice	Richardson	Beryl	Robinson	Maisie	Rowe
Beryl Ethel May	Richardson	Bessie Florence	Robinson	Edith May	Rowell
Doreen Pamela	Richardson	Dora Helen	Robinson	Florence Rose	Rowland
Dorothy	Richardson	Doreen May	Robinson	Joyce Mary	Rowlands
Gladys Dorothy	Richardson	Dorothy Helen	Robinson	Hilda Elizabeth	Rowlett
Isabel	Richardson	Edna Frances	Robinson	Margaret Mary	Rowley
Mabel	Richardson	Gladys Irene	Robinson	Myrtle Barbara	
Margaret Irene	Richardson	Hilda Edna	Robinson	Primrose	Rowley
Marjorie	Richardson	Jean	Robinson	Vera Joan	Rowley
Moyra	Richardson	Kathleen de Renzie	Robinson	Patricia Ellen	Royall
Peggy Kathleen	Richardson	Kathleen Fanny		Kathleen Annie	Ruck
Sheila Mary	Richardson	Mary	Robinson	Dorothy Maud	Rudd
Violet Florence	Richardson	Marian Annie	Robinson	Joan Louisa	Rudkin
Ethel M	Richer	Marjorie	Robinson	Ruby May	Ruffett
Doris Ellen	Riches	Mary	Robinson	Josephine	Runeckles
Joyce Edna	Riches	Pauline Maria	Robinson	Yvonne	Runeckles
Mary Lucy Dorcas	Riches	Winifred	Robinson	Betty	Rush
Edna	Richmond	Doris Edith	Robjohns	Jean Marie	Rushen
Dawn Freda Mary	Richold	Irene Florence	Robson	Joyce	Rushton
Eileen Joyce	Rick	Margaret	Robson	Patricia	Rushton
Gertude Ellen	Rick	Mary	Robson	Ella Maureen	Russell
Betty Isobel	Rickerby	Phyllis	Robson	Ivy Edith	Russell
Margaret	Rickers	Margaret Helen	Roche	Ivy Frances	Russell
Frances Huntley	Ricketts	Florence Margaret	Roddis	Mabel	Russell
Jean Renee	Riddell	Minnie	Roddy	Ruby Ethel	Rust
Joan Eva	Riddy	June Cynthia	Rodwell	Olive	Rutter
Mary	Riding	Kathleen Stephanie	Roe	Anne	Ryan
Sheila	Riding	Pauline Barbara	Roe	Kathleen Maud	Ryan
Margaret	Rigby	Charlotte A	Rogers	Margaret	Ryan
Claudette Pearl	Ring	Daphne Elizabeth	Rogers	Mary Theresa	Ryan
Jocelyn Theresa		Ellen Edna	Rogers	Una Patricia Lucy	Ryan
Maud	Roach	Florence Mary	Rogers	Joyce Amelia	Ryell

Mary	Ryland	Joyce Dorothy	Sears	Kathleen Frances	
Gillian	Sadler	Barbara	Seath	Mary	Single
Madge Beatrice	Saile	Betty Doreen	Seddon	Gladys May	Singleton
Joan	Salisbury	Marie Lowies	Sellence	Bessie	Sireling
Rita	Salisbury	Edith Emily	Semaine	Gladys Mildred	Skeen
Dorothy	Salt	Annie Mabel	Senior	Doreen 'Dawn'	Skeggs
Lorna	Salter	Elfreda	Senior	Helena Joan	Skelton
Alice May	Sambridge	Joyce	Senior	Joyce Marguerite	Skelton
Doreen Edna	Sampson	Violet	Setter	Frances Edith	Skevington
Muriel Edna	Sams	Dorothy May	Sewell	Irene Amy	Skevington
Joan Diana	Samuel	Evelyn	Shambley	Lena	Skevington
Brenda Christine	Sandall	Elsie	Shane	Mary	Skinner
Mabel Martha	Sanders	Grace Alice Eveline	Sharp (Mrs)	Olive Rose	Skinner
Mary Rose	Sanders	Joyce Margaret	Sharp	Ellen	Skipp
Grace	Sanderson	Elizabeth	Sharpe	Cecilia	Slater
Brenda	Sands	Lilian Annie	Sharpe	Doreen Winifred	Sletcher
Florence Joyce	Sands	Kathleen Mary	Sharrock	Lucy	Sloane
Jean	Sands	Irene Florence	Shattock	Patricia Mary	Small
Sheila Mary	Sarsby	Florence Mary	Shaw	Doris Elizabeth	Smart
Brenda Iris	Saunders	Gladys	Shaw	Florence Elizabeth	Smart (Mrs)
Connie	Saunders	Margaret Anne	Shaw	Margaret	Smart
Doreen Winifred	Saunders	Marjorie	Shaw	Audrey Annie	Smith
Eileen Lilian	Saunders	Mary Matilda	Shaw	Beryl Joyce Pamela	Smith
Gene Helena	Saunders	Rima	Shawmarsh	Betty Doreen	Smith
Hazel Mary	Saunders	Betty	Sheard	Constance Lillian	Smith
Trixie Doris	Saunders	Pearl Maureen	Sheehan	Daisy Ruth	Smith
Vera Mary	Saunders	Emily	Sheldon	Dorothy	Smith
Betty	Saunderson	Cecilia Monica	Shelton	Dorothy Kathleen	Smith
Edith Sarah	Saunderson	Stella Beatrice	Shelton	Dorothy Sheila	Smith
Eileen	Savage	Vera	Shelton	Eileen Jennifer	
Ivy Jean	Saville	Doris	Shepherd	Lucy	Smith
Margaret	Scaife	Hester	Shepherd	Elsie	Smith
Marie Teresa	Scanlon	Vera	Shepherd		(WLA 131083)
Phyllis Patience	Scarlett	Joan Pretoria	Sheppard	Elsie	Smith
Doris	Schofield	Marguerite Joan	Sheppard		(WLA 179397)
Eleanor	Schofield	Marjorie	Sheridan	Ena Mary	Smith
Eva	Schofield	Joyce Maraim	Sherlock	Ethel Jane	Smith
Winnie	Scholefield	Bella	Sherman	Evelyn Edith	Smith
Jean Elizabeth	Scotchford	Eileen	Sherriff	Evelyn May	Smith
Rosemary Minnie	Scotchford	Kathleen	Shipp	Freda	Smith
Jane Mary	Scott	Joan	Shirley	Gertrude	Smith
Jean	Scott	Gladys Mabel	Short	Gertrude May	Smith
Joan Gladys	Scott	Jeanette	Short	Gladys	Smith
Margaret	Scott	Winifred Helen	Shortland	Helen Margaret	Smith
Ruby Grace	Scott	Christine Sarah	Shouler	Hetty Lillian	Smith
Marjorie	Scrivener	Joan Alice	Shouler	Hilda	Smith
Patricia D	Scully	Myriam Alice	Silvester	Irene	Smith
Joan	Seagrave	Christina	Sim	Iris	Smith
Betty	Seamark	Ivy Lilian	Simmons	Ivy	Smith
Violet E	Sear	Beryl AJ	Simons	Jay Audrey	Smith
Dorothy Elizabeth	Searle	Una Muriel	Simons	Jean	Smith
Ethel	Searle	Joan Iris	Simpson`	Jean Pauline	Smith
Jean Dorothy	Searle	Dorothy Joan	Sing	Jean Rosemary	Smith

Joan	Smith
Joyce Mary	Smith
Margaret Ellen	Smith
Margaret Ruth	Smith
Margery Ena	Smith
Marjorie	Smith (WLA 122246)
Marjorie	Smith (WLA 174763)
Marjorie Edith	Smith
Mary	Smith
Mary Ann	Smith
Mary Doreen	Smith
Mary Helen	Smith
Maud	Smith
Muriel Petrie	Smith
Natalie Margery	Smith
Nellie Evelyn	Smith
Nellie Hallam	Smith
Nellie Mona	Smith
Olive Rosina	Smith
Pamela Mary	Smith
Patricia Elizabeth	Smith
Phyllis Christine	Smith
Phyllis Joan	Smith
Phyllis May	Smith
Rita	Smith
Rose Olive	Smith
Sylvia	Smith
Vera	Smith
Veronica	Smith
Irene	Smithies
Ethel	Smithson
Myra Hilda	Snape
Sarah Elizabeth	Snape
Louisa May	Snell
Phyllis May	Snell
Florence Alice	Snodden
Pauline Elizabeth	Snowdon
Iris Elsie May	Snowling
Victoria Madeleen	Snowling
Dorothy Emily	Snoxell
Madeleine	Somerset-Butler
Stella Augusta	Sonnenstein
Doreen Edna	Southern
Patricia Violet	Southey
Barbara	Sowery
Margaret Keith	Spark
Audrey Betty	Sparks
Alice Mary	Spedding
Mary Kathleen	Speight
Dorothy	Spence
Margaret Mary	Spencer (Mrs)
Mary Kathleen	Spencer
Sandra	Spens-Black
Louisa Martha	Spicer
Peggy Lilian	Spicer
Bessie Mary	Spiers
Constance Mary	Spratley
Sheila Margaret	Sproule
Nellie Mary	Squibb
Helena Elizabeth	Stacey
Olive	Stacey (Mrs)
Barbara Emily	Stafferton
Jacqueline Joan	Stafford
Betty	Stagg
Lilian Fern	Stanbrook
Lilian Mary	Standbrook
Irene May	Standing
Isabel	Stanford
Joan	Stanley
Barbara Joan	Stanton
Cynthia Elizabeth	Stanton
Ethel May	Stanton
Ethel	Stanyon
Irene May	Stapleton
Joyce Myrtle	Starkey
Peggy Mavis	Starkey
Mavis Audrey	Stearn
Doreen Avis Francis	Stedman
Florence Ada	Steel
Joan Thelma	Steel
Aranka	Steinberg
Olive Ruth	Stephens
Sheila Jean	Stephens
Annie	Stephenson
Doris	Stephenson
Elizabeth	Stephenson
Georgina	Stephenson
Lucy	Stephenson
Olive May	Stephenson
Shirley	Stephenson
Joan Doreen	Stern
Dorothy	Stevens
Stella May	Steward
Jean	Stewart
Joan Forbes	Stewart
Pickering Grace	Stewart
Doris May	Stock
Doreen	Stockdale
Cynthia Elizabeth	Stockley
Millicent Irene	Stocks
Winifred May	Stoddard (Mrs)
Doreen Mary	Stokes
Rita Olive Squires	Stokes
Elsie May	Stone
Marjorie Joy	Stone
Olive Jean	Stone
Emily	Stoner
Betty	Stones
Helen Mary	Stops
Alice Joyce	Stott
Hilda	Stradling
Eileen Louisa May	Strange
Kathleen	Strange
Olga Jean	Stratton
Thelma Doris May	Stratton
Joan Mary Ann	Street
Madge Elizabeth	Street
Pamela Hilda	Street
Hilda Winnie Maud	Streeton
Irene Elizabeth	Streets
Barbara Mary	Strike
Marjorie	Stringward
Ena Daisy	Strong
Irene	Stuart
Jenney Garrett	Stubbs
Kathleen Daisy	Stubbs
Phyllis Ethel	Studd
Eileen Ann	Studman
Alma Lilian Jane	Sturge
June Angela Edwina	Sturt
Barbara	Stutchbury
Joyce Rosemary	Sugars
Florence May	Sullivan
Edith	Summerbell
Daisy Rose	Summerlin
Barbara Eileen	Sumner
Beryl	Sumner
Joyce	Sumpter
Ruth Elizabeth	Surkitt
Eileen	Sushams
Joyce	Sutcliffe
Evelyn Violet	Sutters
Betty	Suttle
Edith Hettie	Sutton
Dorothy	Swain
Sylvia Ruth	Swales
Vera	Swales (WLA 94696)
Vera	Swales (WLA 166187)
Hilda	Swann
Phyllis Jean	Swanwick
Ethel Elizabeth	Sweenie

First Name	Surname	First Name	Surname	First Name	Surname
Eileen Mary	Sweet	Ann	Thomas	Bessie Florence	Tompsett
Hilda Lilian	Sweet	Betty Mar	Thomas	Agnes	Tones
Rosina Ellen	Swoish	Elsie	Thomas	Margaret Mary	Toohey
Bessie	Sykes	Hilda	Thomas	Dorothy	Topham
Elsie	Sykes	Mary Elizabeth	Thomas	Joyce Marie	Topliss
Bessie	Symon	Mavis Elizabeth	Thomas	Irene Alice	Toseland
Ivy Barbara Joan	Symons	Peggy	Thomas	Lillian May	Towers
Eileen Mary	Syratt	Sheila	Thomas	Joyce Evelyn	Towle
Margaret Townsend	Tack	Vera	Thomas	Joan Winifred	Townend
Annie	Tait	Marjorie Rose	Thomason	Margaret Doreen	Townsend
Dorothy	Talbot	Ellen	Thomasson	Patty	Townsend
Christine	Tangye	Evelyn May	Thomlinson	Phoebe Florence	Townsend
Mabel Alice	Tarbottan	Averil Irene May	Thompson	Barbara Ellen	Toyer
Ivy	Tarbotton	Barbara	Thompson	Winifred	Traskowskie
Gertrude	Tate	Edith	Thompson	Gladys	Travis
Vera	Tate	Elizabeth Edna	Thompson	Daphne Grace	Treadwell
Mary	Tattersall	Jean Mary	Thompson	Suzanne Evelyn	Trethowan
Kathleen Nellie	Tattman	Lillian Blanche	Thompson	Winifred Mary	Triggs
Maisie	Tavener	Linda Ellen	Thompson	Phyllis Janet Doreen	Trimingham
Alwyn	Taylor (WLA149029)	Margaret	Thompson	Jean Doreen	Tromans
Alwyn	Taylor (WLA153614)	Margaret Louise	Thompson	Zeita Helga	Trott
Betty	Taylor	Mildred	Thompson	Mary Elizabeth	Trowbridge
Betty Joan	Taylor	Muriel Evelyn	Thompson	M Christine	Truscott
Doris Joyce	Taylor	Vera Margaret	Thompson	Florence EM	Trusler
Dorothy May	Taylor	Winifred	Thompson	Doris May	Trussler
Edna	Taylor	June Isobel	Thomson	Mavis Doreen	Tuck
Eileen Rosemary	Taylor	Dora	Thorley	Eileen	Tucker
Elizabeth Joan	Taylor	Irene	Thorley	Dorothy Margaret	Tuffnell
Eva May	Taylor	Cissie Florence	Thornton	Audrey Millicent Patricia	Tugwood
Gwen	Taylor	Doreen	Thornton	Evelyn May	Tully
Irene Edith	Taylor	Gladys	Thurland	Phyllis Irene	Tunney
Isabella	Taylor	Doreen Phyllis	Tidman	Veronica	Tunstall
Joan Margaret	Taylor	Christina	Tierney	Irene Constance	Turnbull
Margaret	Taylor	Gwendolyn Lydia	Tiffin	Annie	Turner
Marjorie	Taylor	Dulcie Kate	Tilbrook	Dora	Turner
Mary	Taylor	Hilda Amy Patricia	Tilly	Joyce Clara	Turner
Moelfie Jean	Taylor	Margaret	Tiltman	Joyce Edna	Turner
Pamela Jean	Taylor	Beatrice Winifred	Timpson	Louise	Turner
Philippa Margaret Harrison	Taylor	Maureen	Tingle	Margaret	Turner
Vera Doreen	Taylor	Doris Margerie	Titcombe	Marjorie	Turner
Vera Mavis	Taylor	Elsie Jean	Titmuss	Olive Doreen	Turner
Winifred Pearl	Taylor	Pamela Nancy	Tizzard	Vera	Turner
Joyce Edna	Tearle	Francis	Tobin	Barbara	Twigg
Gladys Lillian	Tedder	Gladys May	Todd	Margaret	Twiname
Julia	Tempest	Mary	Todd	Dorothy Mabel	Tyers
Sheila	Terry	Marguerite Joan	Tofield	Florence Evelyne	Tysoe
Doreen Dorothy	Tester	Edna Margaret	Tomkins	Sheila Ann	Tysoe
Esmé	Thackray	Jean	Tomkins	Rosamond Mary	Tyson
Joyce	Thirkettle	Nancy Anne	Tomkinson	Betsy Vera	Tyzack
		Betty May	Tomlin	Doreen Nellie	Underwood
		Eileen	Tomlins	Violet Elizabeth	Underwood
		Sheila Mary	Tomlinson		
		Eileen Dorothy	Tompkins		

Phyllis Ethel	Unsworth	Freda	Wallis	Marie	Watkinson
Louisa Francis	Unwin	Helen Florence	Wallis	Sheila	Watkinson
Phyllis	Unwin	Ivy	Wallis	Kathleen Mary	Watkis
Bessie Irene	Upson	Margaret	Walsh	Barbara	Watson
Barbara Gladys	Upton	Patricia	Walsh	Eileen	Watson
Joyce Eleanor	Upton	Betty	Walters	Irene Rose	Watson
Mary Elizabeth	Usmar	Betty	Walton	Iris Lilian	Watson
Margarita	Valente	Harriett	Walton	Jessie Dorothy	Watson
Hilda May Helsby	Valiant	Josephine Mary	Walton	Joan	Watson
Gladys	Vandersteen	Lilian Maude	Walton	Lilian Mabel	Watson
Mary Ann	Vango	Sylvia Olive	Walton	Marion Rose	Watson
Olive	Varden	Brenda	Wanless	Marjorie Elaine	Watson
Marjorie	Varley	Iris Joan	Warboys	Patricia	Watson
Gwendoline Iris	Varna	Margaret	Warboys	Sheila	Watson
Margaret Joyce	Venn	Monica	Warboys	Margaret Edith	Watson-Baker
Gwendoline	Vernon	Lilian	Warburton	Ida	Watt
Nellie	Vernon	Audrey Hilda	Ward	Barbara Virginia	Watts
Sarah	Vernon	Barbara Ruth Enid	Ward	Delia Ann	Watts
Marjorie Rose	Verrell	Betty	Ward	Elizabeth Esther	Watts
Norah Beatrice	Viles	Constance Audrey	Ward	Margaret Mary	Watts
Eileen Florence	Vince	Dorothy Gladys	Ward	Mary Kathleen	Watts
Marion	Vince	Ellen Mary	Ward	Rose Elizabeth	Watts
Eileen Marjorie	Vine	Joan Alice	Ward	Yolande Marie	Way
Winifred Alice	Vinn	Joan Isabella	Ward	Betty	Wayman
Minnie Elizabeth	Vinnell	Joyce	Ward	Alice	Wears
Greta Joyce	Virgin	Margaret	Ward	Caroline Cordelia	Webb
Hilda Margelé	Virgin	Mary	Ward	Gwendoline	
Joan Mary	Waddington		(WLA154977)	Priscilla	Webb
Gertrude Mary	Wade	Mary	Ward	Joan	Webb
Eileen Joan	Wadman		(WLA165843)	June Margaret	Webb
Mary Josephine	Wafer	Philippa	Ward	Kathleen Hetty	Webb
Eva Emily	Wagstaff	Alma Joan	Wareham	Peggy Doreen	Webb
Joan	Wagstaffe	Marjorie	Wareham	Rose Elizabeth	Webb
Violet Doreen	Wainwright	Hilda Doris	Waring	Elizabeth	Webster
Betty Doreen	Waite	Marjorie Agnes	Warner		(WLA177614)
Vera	Waites	Mary	Warner	Elizabeth	Webster
Kathleen Emily	Walden	Nina Lucy	Warner		(WLA178957)
Marian	Wales	Alma Ida	Warren	Letitia Thyrza	Webster
Gwendoline Daisy	Walford	Betty	Warren	Matilda Harrison	
Dorothy	Walker	Dora Kathleen	Warren	Scott	Webster
Ellen	Walker	Helen	Warren	Vera	Webster
Helen Edith	Walker	Kathleen	Warren	Joan Catherine	Weedon
Hettie Elizabeth	Walker	Lilian Ethel	Warren	Rita Elizabeth	Weeks
Mary Ann	Walker	Margaret	Warren	Denise Edith	Welch
Patricia	Walker	Vera May	Warren	Phylis Mary	Welch
Peggy Doreen	Walker	Elizabeth Ada	Warwick	Laura	Welford
Gladys	Wallace	Violet May	Warwick	Jean Alma	Wells
Kathleen	Wallace	Audrey Gladys	Wass	Pearl	Wells
Betty	Waller	Margaret Vina	Wass	Phyllis Ruth	Wells
Eileen Makala	Waller	Lilian Mary	Wassell	Ruby Lilian	Wells
Lily	Walley	Gwendoline Mary	Waterman	Agnes	Welsby
Edith Lillian	Wallis	Brenda	Watkins	Lilian	Welsby
Elsie May	Wallis	Gladys	Watkins	Dorothy	Welsh

Jean Elizabeth	Welton	Sylvia Joyce	Whitworth	Marjorie Doris	Williamson		
Maisie Elizabeth	Welton	Kathleen	Whybird	Sylvia	Williamson		
Joyce DW	West	Gwendoline Ruth	Whybrow	Annie Eileen	Willis		
Mary Elizabeth	West	Marjorie	Whyment	Beatrice May	Willis		
Iris	Westall	Margaret	Whyte	Irene Victoria	Willis		
Sheila Mary	Westfield	Freda Phyllis	Wickens	Pauline Mary	Willis		
Eileen	Westmoreland	Patricia Jean	Wickham	Joan	Willmore		
Florence	Westnead	Nancy Olive	Wicks	Patricia Kathleen	Willoughby		
Sylvia Joan	Weston	Joyce Esther	Wilby	Jessie	Willshaw		
Barbara Joan	Westover	Agnes	Wilcock	Elsie Florence	Willson		
Eva	Whale	Mary	Wilcock (Mrs)	Gladys Ada	Wilshaw		
Florence Edith	Whalley		(WLA111700)	Alice Maud	Wilson		
Muriel Ellen	Wharam	Mary	Wilcock	Edna	Wilson		
Peggy	Wharton		(WLA171542)	Elizabeth	Wilson		
Doris Irene	Wheatley	Nora Ruby	Wilcox	Elizabeth Margaret	Wilson		
Irene	Wheatley	Clara	Wild	Elsie	Wilson		
Kathleen Louise	Whelan	Jacqueline Ruth	Wild	Elsie	Wilson (Mrs)		
Mabel Elizabeth	Whiffin	Edna Mary	Wilderspin	Ethel	Wilson		
Patricia May	Whiles	Catherine Emily	Wilding	Frances	Wilson		
Rera	Whitaker	Gladys Rose	Wilding	Frances Josephine	Wilson (Mrs)		
Lilian Evelyn	Whitbread	Joan	Wilding	Isabella	Wilson		
	(Mrs)	Shirley Virginia	Wilding	Jean Catherine	Wilson		
Audrey Marjorie	White	Audrey	Wildman	Joan Margaret	Wilson		
Bertha Kate	White	Alma Grace	Wiles	Joyce	Wilson		
Dorothy Margaret	White	Iris Edith	Wiles		(WLA122276)		
Edna	White	Mable Beatrice	Wiles	Joyce	Wilson		
Jean Mildred	White	Cicely Grace	Wilkinson		(WLA130248)		
Jessie	White	Eleanor Mary	Wilkinson	Joyce Louise	Wilson		
Joan Gwendolin	White	Freda Regina	Wilkinson	Margaret	Wilson		
June Emily	White	Madge	Wilkinson		(WLA145529)		
Nancy	White	Margaret	Wilkinson	Margaret	Wilson		
Patricia Jean	White	Margaret Emily	Wilkinson		(WLA197718)		
Phyllis	White	Mary Audrey	Wilkinson	Muriel	Wilson		
Veronica Kathleen	White	Pauline Brenda	Wilkinson	Norah	Wilson		
Barbara Eileen Joan	Whitehead	Queenie	Wilkinson	Olive Joan	Wilson		
Ivy	Whitehead	Sylvia	Wilkinson	Rose Ann	Wilson		
Zita Joan	Whitehead	Marjorie Louise	Wilks	Ruth	Wilson		
Diana Christobel	Whiteman	Annie Adeline	Williams	Sheila May	Wilson		
Gwendoline	Whiteman	Audrey Rosa	Williams	Sheila Robetta	Wilson		
	(Mrs)	Bertha	Williams	Rachel Russell	Windham		
Sylvia Audrey	Whitewood	Cecilia	Williams	Annie Patricia	Wineley		
Adelaide Alice	Whitfield	Dorothy M	Williams	Pamela	Wingfield		
Alice Margaret	Whitfield		(Mrs)	Kathleen	Winks		
Audrey	Whiting	Frances Mary	Williams	Bessie Evelyn	Winn		
Joyce Helena		Katherine	Williams	Betty IRM	Winrow		
Pauline	Whitney	Kathleen Mary	Williams	Dorothy Irene	Winstone		
Beryl Elsie	Whittaker	Marjorie	Williams	Kathleen	Winterbottom		
Agnes	Whittingham	Mary	Williams	Sybil	Winterburn		
Rosina	Whittingham	Muriel	Williams	Olga Louise	Wise		
Sheila Mary	Whittington	Olive Mary	Williams	Joan Elizabeth	Witham		
Winifred Joan	Whittington	Rose	Williams	Violet Hope	Withycombe		
Glenys Jean	Whitworth	Veronica Mary	Williams		(Mrs)		
Sylvia Eileen	Whitworth	Joan	Williamson	Zena Betty	Wombell		

Barbara Turner	Wood	Celia Margaret	Woolven	Pearl Alma	Wright
Chrissie	Wood	Violet Margaret	Woolven	Violet Emily	Wright
Constance Alice	Wood	Monica	Worboys	May	Wroe
Doris Ellen	Wood	Eileen Millicent	Worrall	Margaret	Wyatt-Parr
Edith	Wood	Helen Margaret	Worrall	Hilda I	Wyeth
Ethel Winifred	Wood	Ivy Christine	Worsley	Irene	Wylie
Hilda May	Wood	Eileen Dorothy	Wortham	Mary Ruth	Wynans
Joan	Wood	Barbara Jean	Wottrich	Gladys Winifred	Wynn
Lilian	Wood	Anne	Wray	Iris Beatrice	Yarnold
Dorothy	Woodcock	Doris Edith	Wray	Joan Eileen	Yates
Vera	Woodcock	Florence Hilda	Wray	Lilian May	Yates
Monica	Woodhall	Hazel	Wray	Marie	Yates
Gladys May	Woodhouse	Muriel Eve	Wray	Mary Jane	Yates
Gwendoline Vera	Woodhouse	Margaret	Wride	Margaret	Yearsley
Rosemary May	Woodhouse	Agnes	Wright	Christina Ellen	Yeoman
Doris Evelyn	Woodley	Audrey	Wright	Pamela Julie	Yirrell
Beatrice Mary	Woodlock	Barbara Kathleen	Wright	Sylvia	Yockney
Jean Rhoda	Woodman	Daphne	Wright	Eileen	York
Barbara May	Woods	Doreen Dolores	Wright	Mavis Kathleen	Youells
C	Woods	Florence Ellen	Wright	Agnes Lily	Young (Mrs)
Daphne Joan	Woods	Irene	Wright	Bertha	Young
Ena Rose	Woods	Irene	Wright (Mrs)	Evelyn	Young
M Zilpha	Woods	Ivy Doreen	Wright	Irene Lilian	Young
Mary Joyce	Woods	Joan Evelyn	Wright	Joan Winifred	Young (Mrs)
Eileen	Woodward	Lilian Joan	Wright	Joyce	Young
Evelyn Mary	Woodward	Marjorie Frances	Wright	Molly	Young
Muriel	Woodward	Marjorie Hilda	Wright	Phoebe	Young
Phyllis	Woodward	Olive	Wright	Sylvia G	Young
Jean Lilian	Woolcot	Patricia Marjory			
Mary	Woolhouse	Eleanor	Wright		

SOURCES AND BIBLIOGRAPHY

PRIMARY SOURCES

OFFICIAL WOMEN'S LAND ARMY PAPERS

Following the disbandment of the organisation at the end of November 1950, it appears that the Women's Land Army (WLA) papers from its national headquarters were not deposited in any official archives and that documents were destroyed. The exceptions to this were that the index cards to WLA service records were saved (see Imperial War Museum and National Archives) and Lady Denman's personal papers were held by her family (see West Sussex Record Office). The Women's Land Army was a branch of the Ministry of Agriculture, Fisheries and Food (MAF) and papers and correspondence between the WLA and the Ministry, and with other government departments regarding the WLA, can be viewed at The National Archives (TNA) under MAF Records. Papers from some WLA county headquarters can be found at the National Archives but not for Bedfordshire.

The original WLA index cards to the service records (incomplete) are kept at IWM, Duxford and can only be viewed by prior arrangement. There are 158 boxes of cards covering over 200,000 young women who served in England and Wales, in alphabetical order of maiden name (with duplicate cards made out under their new surname, when members married). These brief personnel details of individual members of the Women's Land Army (Second World War only) can most easily be viewed, on microfiche only, at The National Archives at Kew.

The main official record of the wartime work of the WLA (as far as 1944), still in print thanks to a reprint by the Imperial War Museum in an expanded version which includes 'Poems of the Land Army', is:

Sackville-West, V. *The Women's Land Army* (1944, reprinted 1993) The Ministry of Agriculture and Fisheries/IWM

Those interested in the work of the Timber Corps, should consult:

Timber Corps of Women's Land Army *Meet the Members, A Record of Timber Corps of Women's Land Army* (1944/reprinted 1997) Bristol: Bennet Brothers Ltd/IWM

The following major (but fairly rare) printed source of detailed information on the Women's Land Army organization and of practical information for land girls should also be consulted by those wishing to have a detailed understanding of the national organization. Reference copies of the manual can be consulted at the libraries of the Imperial War Museum, Museum of English Rural Life, The Women's Library and at the British Library (by those holding a reader's pass):

Shewell-Cooper, W.E. *Land Girl: A handbook for the Women's Land Army* (1941) The English Universities Press

DOCUMENTS RELATING TO THE WOMEN'S LAND ARMY IN BEDFORDSHIRE

The names of those young women who served at some point between 1939 and 1950 in Bedfordshire have been recovered by the author, with the help of a team of volunteers, from the service records and from other sources, including Bedfordshire newspapers. They are listed in the Roll Call on pages 249–271.

Although occasional references can be found to Bedfordshire in those WLA papers held in the national collections mentioned above, the bulk of documents shedding some light on the Bedfordshire WLA experience are held by Bedfordshire and Luton Record and Archive Service (BLARS) in Bedford. Some documents and photographs have been deposited by individuals; the rest are to be found in the papers of the Bedfordshire War Agricultural Executive Committee. BLARS and Bedford Central Library Heritage Library also hold transcriptions and summaries of a number of oral history recorded interviews by Carmela Semeraro with former Bedfordshire land girls (See BLARS and Bedford Central Library below).

Listed below are the key references to papers and visual material in the main archive collections relating to the WLA, Bedfordshire WLA and individual land girls, War Agricultural Executive Committees and the Ministry of Agriculture, Fisheries and Food.

306 BOMBARDMENT GROUP MUSEUM

A small museum open at weekends only during the tourist season (April to October) includes a permanent section on the Women's Land Army in Bedfordshire, especially uniforms and photographs.

BBC WEB SITE

See Archives for how to access WW2 People's War 'oral history' written memoirs by former Bedfordshire land girls.

WW2 People's War is an online archive of wartime memoirs contributed by members of the public and gathered by the BBC. The archive can be found at bbc.co.uk/ww2peopleswar.

There are several memoirs by former Bedfordshire land girls, giving insights into land girl life, especially that of 'War Ag'-employed hostel girls, including:

Mary Cutler née Hickey regarding life in the hostels at Whipsnade, Kensworth and Leighton Buzzard (Article ID A5484152).

Olwen Jean Russell née Middleton regarding life at Leighton Buzzard hostel (Article ID 4359738).

Eileen Fuller regarding life at Kensworth hostel (Article ID A3882602).

For the life of a land girl directly employed by a private farmer, see

Catherine Henman née Bezant (Article ID A7764528) and Mary Spilling née Bennett (Article ID A2674307).

BBC WRITTEN ARCHIVE CENTRE

BBC radio scripts (not audio recordings) from programmes relating to the WLA and its work, including a number of broadcasts by Lady Denman (Hon. Director of the WLA) and other officers from the national organization, are held here, covering 72 broadcasts from 2 June 1939 to 27 October 1950.

BEDFORD CENTRAL LIBRARY HERITAGE LIBRARY

Bound copies are held of the Marston Vale Oral History Project material (transcriptions of the interviews conducted by Carmela Semeraro and summaries of the interviews made by Stuart Antrobus). Copies of the original sound recordings are held in tape form by BLARS, as well as further copies of both transcriptions and summaries. The full title of the project was 'Changing Landscapes, Changing Lives'. The collections include nine interviews (all by Carmela Semeraro, except Interview 122 which was by Stuart Antrobus) with former members of the Women's Land Army who served in Bedfordshire in the 1940s:

Barbara Probert née Filbey	Interview 042 (Z 1205/042)
Betty Fitton née Hurst	Interview 044 (Z 1205/044)
Zoe Sinfield née Odell	Interview 049 (Z 1205/049)
Barbara Tovey née Cox	Interview 122 (Z 1205/122)
Evelyn Huckvale née Archer	Interview 125 (Z 1205/125)
Betty Schwarz née Harding	Interview 154 (Z 1205/154)
Cicely McKeegan née Redman	Interview 171 (Z 1205/171)

Peggy Tedder née Clark   Interview 194 (Z 1205/194)
Hannah Croot née Bennett   Interview 206 (Z 1205/206)
(Additionally, Interview 097 was with Jean Caeriog-Jones née Redman who was a Bedford girl who
served with the WLA in Buckinghamshire: Z 1205/97.)

Digitised versions of the above recorded interviews, together with other selected interviews
from the 'Changing Landscapes, Changing Lives' oral history project, may be available for listening
to in the Heritage Library, by arrangement with the Local Studies Librarian. (The original cassette
recordings are held at The Forest of Marston Vale, Forest Centre, Station Road, Marston Moretaine,
Bedfordshire, MK43 0PR. www.marstonvale.org)

The Heritage Library also contains hard copies of the following Bedfordshire newspapers
covering the period 1939–1950, which can be consulted every Tuesday and on other days (except
Sunday) by arrangement:
Bedford Record, Bedfordshire Times. These, together with the following local newspapers from
around the county, can also be consulted on microfilm (at any time during the opening hours of
Bedford Central Library):
Ampthill News, Biggleswade Chronicle, Dunstable Gazette, Leighton Buzzard Observer, Luton News.

BEDFORD MUSEUM

Oral history sound recordings and transcriptions, plus artefacts, including items of WLA uniform.
Interviews by Jenny Ford with former land girls who served in Bedfordshire:
BEDFM:2001/145 Mrs 'Dawn' Filby née Skeggs (Interview recorded 5 April 2001)
BEDFM:2001/146 Mrs Doris Oakley née Dew (Interview recorded 5 April 2001)

BEDFORDSHIRE COUNTY COUNCIL HISTORIC ENVIRONMENT RECORD (HER)

This key source of information on the county's archaeological sites and landscape features holds
the following:
Aerial photographs of WLA/'War Ag' land girl hutment hostels in 1940s:

Bolnhurst	RAF 10 Aug 1945: 106G/UK/635/3163 (H20)
'Chimney Corner'	RAF 7 June 1946: 106G/UK/1562/3209 (WA 19)
Leighton Buzzard	RAF 12 Dec 1946: CPE/UK/1897/4272 (QB5)
Milton Ernest	RAF 7 June 1946: 106G/UK/1562/3033 (Y 13)
Whipsnade	RAF 11 Oct 1945: 106G/UK/914/4022 (No ref.)

(At the time of writing, there were physical remains on the ground only of the Bolnhurst hostel.)
Photographs/drawings of buildings requisitioned as WLA/'War Ag' land girl hostels and/or
training farms:

HER 3676	Aspley Guise, The Holt
HER 6645	Clifton House
HER 4239	Cople House
HER 14368	Hulcote Moors Farm (Holcotmoors Farm on O.S. maps)
HER 5725	Kensworth House
HER 6889	Luton Hoo, The Bothy
HER 5872	Potton, The Hollies
HER 9544	Ravensden House Farm
HER 3454	Sandy, Hasells Hall
HER 1115	Sharnbrook House
HER 15664	Silsoe, Wrest Park Lodge
HER 5313	Toddington Manor

BEDFORDSHIRE LIBRARIES LOCAL HISTORY WEB PAGES http://tinyurl.com/2nq2up

An extensive range of material collected by the author during the research for this book is made available courtesy of the Virtual Library site. It includes descriptions by Stuart Antrobus of hostels and training farms, a comprehensive, illustrated WLA (national and local) timeline 1939–1950, and an extensive archive of photographic images.

A Roll Call of land girls who served in Bedfordshire leads on to 'More Information' regarding numerous individuals, including period photographs. (At the time of writing, some very short newsreel film footage of the 14 February 1946 WLA parade in Bedford can also be viewed on the Internet site, by permission of the Imperial War Museum.)

BEDFORDSHIRE AND LUTON RECORDS AND ARCHIVES SERVICE (BLARS)

Selected documents relating to the Women's Land Army and Bedfordshire War Agricultural Executive Committee:

War Agricultural Executive Committee papers

WW2 AC/1/1 Correspondence 1939–1940, including Ministry of Agriculture circular letters

WW2 AC/1/2 Correspondence 1940, including billeting and hostels for land girls, and agricultural machinery census of June 1939

WW2 AC/2/1 Letter books: September 1939–February 1940

WW2 AC/2/2 Letter books : February–April 1940

WW2 AC/2/3 Letter books: April–June 1940

WW2 AC/2/4 Letter books: June–September 1940

WW2 AC/2/5 Letter books: September 1940–January 1941, includes Direction Order on Duke of Bedford regarding grazing sheep and cows with deer in Woburn Park, and destruction of rats during threshing, and use of schoolboy labour

WW2 AC/2/9 Letter books: November 1941–February 1942

WW2 AC/2/10 Letter books: February–May 1942 re reluctance of owner to allow the house's use as a billet for the WLA

WW2 AC/2/11 Letter books: May–August 1942 re enforcement of Possession Order regarding Toddington Park House, required as accommodation for WLA

WW2 AC/2/12 Letter books: September–November 1942 re compensation for owner of Toddington Park Farm, requisitioned as accommodation for WLA

WW2 AC/2/14 Letter: 9 March 1943 – threat of cultivation order on Sir P. Malcolm Stewart re his land in Sandy; need for more WLA workers in the county

WW2 AC/2/15 Letter: 29 March 1943 re requisitioning Cople House for use as land girls hostel

WW2 AC/2/16 Letter: re concern at suspension of WLA recruiting 1943

WW2 AC/2/17 Letter: 30 Sept 1943 to Ministry of Agriculture re tightening up discipline of land girls in hostels, and Letter: 1 December 1943

AO/C1/31 Agricultural Officer (Land Agent) correspondence January 1935–June 1946

AO/C3/12 Agricultural Officer (Land Agent) correspondence January 1939–December 1943, includes WLA memorandum of 25 May 1939 to Chairman and Organising Secretaries of county WLA committees, and circular letter from the Ministry of Agriculture to local authorities in possession of farm institutes re short courses of instruction for inexperienced recruits

AO/C4/7 Agricultural Officer (Land Agent) correspondence April 1939–July 1941 re possible use of land at Whipsnade

X464/23–28 Women's Land Army 1939–50 leaflets

X464/25 List of 'War Ag' committee members 29 January 1946; list of wardens at Bedfordshire WLA hostels; *Bedfordshire Times* photo 2 August 1945 WLA Sports and Fete, Sharnbrook

X464/26 Photographs of Princess Elizabeth on visit to Bedford 14 February 1946

Z50/13/312 Photographs of WLA parade turning from St Paul's Square towards Embankment past Murkett's Garage 1 June 1940

Z50/100/68 Photographs of Women's Land Army at Sharnbrook House 1940–1945

Z50/142/796 Photographs of Land Army girls celebrating VE Day St Paul's Square, Bedford 8 May 1945

Z229/50 Sale of Cople Estate 20 September 1947

Z290/8/8 Programme for Women's Land Army exhibition and rally 14–16 February 1946, including photographs and a brief history of Women's Land Army in Bedfordshire during the war years 1939–1945

Z1002/2 Photographs in album showing Bedford 'Wings for Victory' fund-raising parade 12–19 June 1943, including land girls

Z1039/2/19 Photograph of Victory Parade, The Mall, London 8 June 1946, with land girls marching past inspection podium

Z1198/1/2 Women's Land Army Course (nine 'papers')

Z1198/2/1 Letter welcoming new 'volunteers', giving useful advice and uniform lists, not dated (c. 1940–46)

Z1198/2/5 Bedfordshire WLA County News sheet 16 April 1946

Z1198/3/1 Bundles of copies of *The Land Girl* magazine (1940s)

Z1205 'Changing Landscapes, Changing Lives' oral history interview transcripts and summaries of over 350 interviews with people who lived and worked in the Marston Vale area of mid-Bedfordshire during the twentieth century. (Sound recording copies held but not currently available to the public at BLARS; see Bedford Central Library.)

EAST ANGLIAN AIR WAR ARCHIVES, ABILINE, TEXAS, USA

The following seven videotape oral history interviews with former Bedfordshire land girls by Dr Vernon Williams (Professor of History, Abilene Christian University, Texas) were made on 29 April 2006, at Bedford Central Library, England, by arrangement with Stuart Antrobus:

Vera Barnett née Jobling; Joy Case née Senior, Doreen 'Dawn' Filby née Skeggs, Ann Haynes née Brodrick, Zeita Holes née Trott, Joyce Ingle née Irving, Irene 'Cookie' Saunders née Cook.

Dr Williams also conducted videotape oral history interviews with Joseph 'Joe' Albertson (former American serviceman) and his English wife (former Bedfordshire land girl) Peggy Albertson née Davis at Ely, England on 29 August 2003.

BRITISH LIBRARY

The three major contemporary source books – Sackville-West (1944), Shewell-Cooper (c. 1940) and Home Timber Production Department, Ministry of Supply (1944) – are held, together with almost 50 other books on the WLA, including numerous memoirs, yet none specifically relating to the Bedfordshire experience.

The following PhD thesis, which contains an extensive bibliography and extracts from primary sources, can be obtained, in microfilm form, from the British Library through the Inter-library loan system and consulted in your local library:

Bullock M.H. *The Women's Land Army 1939–1950: a study of policy and practice with particular reference to the Craven district* (2002) Leeds: University of Leeds (A hard copy of this thesis can also be consulted at the Brotherton Library, University of Leeds.)

IMPERIAL WAR MUSEUM, LONDON
Sound Archive

18 recorded audio interviews by Stuart Antrobus with a range of former Bedfordshire land girls can be heard at the IWM Sound Archive, by prior arrangement:

Vera Barnett née Jobling (Interview 15)	IWM ID 24653
Joyce Case née Senior (Interview 13)	IWM ID 24651
Margaret Chessum née Perry (Interview 1)	IWM ID 24539
Iris Cornell née Manning (Interview 2)	IWM ID 24640
Kathleen Cox née Hopkins (Interview 17)	IWM ID 24664
Hannah Croot née Bennett (Interview 6)	IWM ID 24644
Elizabeth Day (Interview 5)	IWM ID 24643
Doreen 'Dawn' Filby née Skeggs (Interview 10)	IWM ID 24648
Stella Forster née Shelton (Interview 4)	IWM ID 24642
Rose Hakewill née Richards (Interview 12)	IWM ID 24650
E. Ann Haynes née Brodrick (Interview 11)	IWM ID 24649
Zeita Holes née Trott (Interview 8)	IWM ID 24646
Sheila Hope née Stephens (Interview 9)	IWM ID 24647
Joyce Ingle née Irving (Interview 7)	IWM ID 24645
Betty Nichols née Gray (Interview 18)	IWM ID 24665
Mary Spilling née Bennett (Interview 3)	IWM ID 24641
Ethel Wildey née Sweenie (Interview 16)	IWM ID 24663

(Brief sound extracts from these interviews can be heard through the Bedfordshire Libraries' Virtual Library local history web pages by clicking on the 'More Information' section of the 'Roll Call' web pages, under their maiden names, for example: Ethel Sweenie re life at Bolnhurst hostel. (See http://tinyurl.com/2nq2up)

Film and Video Archive

Rare newsreel footage (only one minute long) showing Princess Elizabeth (later Queen Elizabeth II) inspecting 600 Bedfordshire land girls on 14 February 1946 in Bedford is held in the Film and Video Department of IWM and can be viewed by prior arrangement. (See also Bedfordshire Libraries, above)

Printed Book Collection

Has a range of printed books, journals, newspapers and pamphlets relating to the WLA, including copies of printed land girl memoirs. Also provides a Recommended Reading list on the WLA.

Photograph Archive

Includes copies of the Ministry of Information 'Battle of the Land' official collection of photographs showing the WLA at work in 1942, WLA training in 1940 and Timber Corps training in 1943.

Department of Documents

Private papers and memoirs of former land girls from around the country (but not, at the time of writing, from Bedfordshire).

Art Collection

Includes collections of WLA posters and of paintings by the war artist Evelyn Dunbar on the subject of land girls during the Second World War (as well as paintings by other artists of land girls during the First World War and Second World War).

LIDDELL HART ARCHIVE, KINGS COLLEGE, UNIVERSITY OF LONDON

Reference Code: GB99 KCLMA Denman. Title: Denman, Lady Gertrude Mary (1884–1954) 1939–45 material: 1½ boxes. These are photocopies of the original papers deposited by Lady Denman's family with the West Sussex Record Office, Chichester.

MUSEUM OF ENGLISH RURAL LIFE (MERL), UNIVERSITY OF READING

MERL's Library holds an excellent archive of photographs of the Women's Land Army, as well as a wide-ranging collection of agricultural journals for the period 1939–50, including articles and letters relating to the Women's Land Army and War Agricultural Executive Committees.

THE NATIONAL ARCHIVES

A select list of some of the Board of Agriculture papers on the Women's Land Army and wartime farming:

MAF 32 National Farm Survey: Individual Farm Records (1941–43 in England and Wales, including unique survival of the census returns for 4 June 1941 for each farm)

MAF 47/82 Policy on Provision of Hostels 1940–1944

MAF 47/96 Hostels for Agricultural Workers – Management and Welfare 1941–1944

MAF 47/143 Hostels and Billets for Agricultural Workers including the WLA 1943

MAF 59/4 Enrolment of volunteers 1938–1941

MAF 59/5 Enrolment of volunteers 1942–1943

MAF 59/6 Enrolment of volunteers 1944–1950

MAF 59/7 Organisation up to the outbreak of war 1939

MAF 59/8 Recruitment of auxiliary forces for seasonal work 1939–1942

MAF 59/9 Expenses of County Committees 1939–1942

MAF 59/10 Staff files 1939–1942, including list of duties of county secretaries

MAF 59/11 Staff files 1942–1943

MAF 59/12 Staff files 1947–1950

MAF 59/13 Trainees – instructions and general correspondence 1939–1940

MAF 59/14 Reports of conferences 1939–1942

MAF 59/15 Instructions to County Committees, circular letters and memoranda 1939–1944

MAF 59/16 Instructions issued to County Committees, circular letters and memoranda 1946–1949

MAF 59/17 Forms and leaflets used 1939–1950

MAF 59/18 Recruiting posters 1939–1949

MAF 59/19 Personal allowances and billeting 1939–1946

MAF 59/20 Wartime organization 1940–1945

MAF 59/21 *The Land Girl* volumes 1 and 2 1940–1942

MAF 59/22 *The Land Girl* volumes 3 and 4 1943–1944

MAF 59/23 Select Committee on National Expenditure 1940–1941

MAF 59/24 Headquarters organisation, 1940–1945

MAF 59/25 Conditions of employment 1943

MAF 59/26 Demobilisation arrangements 1944–1946

MAF 59/27 Post-war organization 1945–1950

MAF 59/28 Committee on the Employment of Women in Agriculture 1947–1950

MAF 59/141–163 Women's Land Army (photographs of activities) e.g. 59/162 Training photographs

MAF 68 Agricultural Returns (statistics from the annual census returns showing totals by parish and county)

MAF 73 National Farm Survey: maps (showing the boundaries of each agricultural holding in England and Wales)

MAF 80/3086 Joint WLA and WAEC Sub committee

MAF 421/1 Ministry of Food: Women's Land Army: Index cards (A–Z) to service records of the Second World War 1939–1948 (on 808 microfiche)

MAF 900/179 162–179 Specimens of Classes of Documents Destroyed (regarding the Women's Land Army) e.g. 900/179 Recruiting broadcasts 1947–1949

Ministry of Information – INF 2/143 Illustrative material concerning the Women's Land Army

WEST SUSSEX RECORD OFFICE (WSRO)

Lady Denman's papers relating to the Women's Land Army

WSRO Burrell Accession 5926

Files 1 and 2 Papers relating to the WLA headquarters

File 3 Papers relating to Lady Denman's address to the All-Party Agricultural Committee of the House of Commons (graph showing WLA employed members, September 1939–May 1943)

File 4 Leaflets, brochures and forms relating to the WLA

File 5 Papers relating to WLA rallies and conferences 1939–1945

File 6 Papers relating to WLA uniforms 1939–1945

File 7 Papers relating to WLA wages 1939–1945

File 8 Miscellaneous papers relating to the WLA (20th century)

THE WOMEN'S LIBRARY, LONDON METROPOLITAN UNIVERSITY (TWL)

This archive holds an entire run of *The Land Girl* magazine from Vol 1, No 1 April 1940 to Vol 7, No 12 March 1947 and its successor, *Land Army News*, from Vol 1, No 1 June 1947 to Vol 6, No 6 November 1950.

These periodicals give a unique insight into the development of the WLA nationally (including Scotland) and into county developments through the 'County News' section. Each monthly copy of *The Land Girl* also gives a list of figures of enrolled membership for each WLA county in England and Wales, over the period April 1940–March 1947.

A Bedfordshire Land Girls 60th Anniversary 'Get Together' was organised by Stuart Antrobus at Bedford Central Library on 14 February 2006. The author is seen with just a few of about 80 former Bedfordshire land girls who attended. HM the Queen send sent her good wishes for the event. On 14 February 1946, as Princess Elizabeth, she had inspected over 600 of them in Bedford at a grand Victory parade.

PRINTED AND SECONDARY SOURCES

BOOKS

All books were published in London, unless otherwise stated

Burton E. *What of the Women: A Study of Women in Wartime* (1941) Frederick Muller Ltd

Calder A. *The People's War (Britain, 1939–45)* (1969) Jonathan Cape

Douie V. *Daughters of Britain: An Account of the Work of British Women during the Second World War* (1950) Oxford: V Douie

Doyle P. and Evans P. *Home Front: British Wartime Memorabilia 1939–1950* (2007) Ramsbury, Marlborough: Crowood Press

Easterbrook L.F. *Achievement in British Farming* (c. 1940s) The Pilot Press

Foreman S. *Loaves and Fishes: An Illustrated History of the Ministry of Agriculture, Fisheries and Food, 1889–1989* (1989) HMSO

Gangulee N. *The Battle of the Land* (1943) Lindsay Drummond

Gardiner J. *Wartime: Britain 1939–1945* (2004) Headline Book Publishing

Hammond R.J. *Food (History of the Second World War; United Kingdom Civil Series, 3 volumes)* (1951–62) HMSO

Hammond R.J. *Food and Agriculture in Britain, 1939–45: Aspects of Wartime Control* (1954) Stanford, California: Stanford University Press

HMSO *National Service: The Handbook: A Guide to the Ways in Which the People of this Country May Give Service* (1939) HMSO

HMSO *The Statistical Digest of the War* (1951) HMSO

Home Timber Production Department, Ministry of Supply *Meet the Members, a Record of Timber Corps of Women's Land Army* (1944/1997) Bristol: Bennett Brothers Ltd (reprinted by Imperial War Museum)

Huxley G. *Lady Denman GBE, 1884–1954* (1961) Chatto and Windus

Ministry of Information *Land at War* (1945/2001) HMSO/reprinted by TSO

Montford F. *Heartbreak Farm: A farmer and his farm in wartime* (1997) Stroud: Sutton Publishing Ltd

Murray K.A.H. *Agriculture* (1955) HMSO

Powell B. and Westacott N. *The Women's Land Army, 1939–1950* (1997) Stroud: Sutton Publishing Ltd

Roberts M. *Farm of my Childhood* (1991) Dunstable: Book Castle

Rose S.O. *Which People's War? : National Identity and Citizenship in Wartime Britain* (2003) Oxford: Oxford University Press

Sackville-West V. *The Women's Land Army* (1944/1993) The Ministry of Agriculture and Fisheries/ reprinted by IWM

Shewell-Cooper W.E. *Land Girl, a Manual for Volunteers in the WLA* (c. 1940) English Universities Press

Short B. (and others) (eds) *The Front Line of Freedom: British Farming in the Second World War* (2006) British Agricultural History Society

Street A.G. *Hitler's Whistle* (1944) Eyre and Spottiswoode

Tillet I. *The Cinderella Army: The Women's Land Army in Norfolk* (1988) Dumfries: I. Tillet

Twinch C. *Women on the Land* (1990) Cambridge: Lutterworth Press

Tyrer N. *They Fought in the Fields* (1988) Sinclair Stevenson

Ward S. *War in the Countryside* (1988) Cameron Books

Winnifrith Sir J. *The Ministry of Agriculture, Fisheries and Food* (1962) George Allen and Unwin

ARTICLES IN JOURNALS AND CHAPTERS IN BOOKS

Antrobus S. 'Researching the history of the Women's Land Army' in *Local History Magazine* No. 111 (Jan/Feb), pp 12–16 (2007)

Brew B.G. 'Women's Land Army Training' in *Agriculture, Journal of the Ministry of Agriculture* 50, pp376–378 (1943)

Burrows L. 'The Women's Land Army in East Anglia, 1939–1950' in *Suffolk Review* 43, pp 1–31 (2004)

Clarke G. 'Life on the home front: The Women's Land Army' in *Auto/Biography* 9, pp81–88 (2001)

Clarke G. 'The Women's Land Army, 1938–50' in Short B. (and others) (eds) *The Front Line of Freedom: British Farming in the Second World War* (2006) British Agricultural History Society

Dallas J.W. & Russell E.W. 'Experiences in Land Reclamation: Bedfordshire' in *Journal of the Royal Agricultural Society of England* Vol 102 pp 109–114 (1941)

DEFRA 'Agriculture in World War Two' at www.defra.gov.uk/esg/work_htm/publications/cs/ farmstats_web/WWII (accessed 30/05/2007) (2007)

Denman G. 'The Women's Land Army' in W. Hutchinson (ed.) *Hutchinson's Pictorial History of the War. A Complete and Authentic Record in Text and Pictures* Vol 4 pp47–51 (1940)

Hurd A. 'War Agricultural Committees – Why and How?' in *The Land Girl* Vol 4, No 11 (Feb 1944) pp2–3 (1944)

Jenkins I. 'They Served on the Land: A Tribute to the Women's Land Army 1939–50' in *Agriculture. Journal of the Ministry of Agriculture* 57, pp403–407 (1950)

Storey N. 'Land Girls' in *Family Tree Magazine* (Nov 2006) pp8–11 (2006)

Twinch C. 'Lend a Hand on the Land' in *Bedfordshire Magazine* Vol 25, No 199 (Winter 1996) pp286–290 (1996)

Yates J. and King S. 'Women's Land Army' in *Dunstable and District at War from Eyewitness Accounts* pp69–76 (2006) Dunstable: The Book Castle

Harvesting in the brickfields of mid-Bedfordshire in the 1940s. The brickyard chimneys were a familiar background to many farms in the area, particularly where poor-quality land had been reclaimed for wartime productivity. *Source: J Bennett*

ACKNOWLEDGEMENTS

I would like to begin by thanking all my colleagues at Bedford Central Library for their help and encouragement.

Beyond that, my especial thanks go to Dr Margaret Bullock for reading the entire first draft of the book and giving helpful advice about its structure. To Dr Keith Agar for reading the chapters on wartime farming and the war agricultural committees and making suggestions. To Nicola Avery for proof-reading sections of the book, facilitating the scanning and use of the numerous photographs and giving immense support to the whole research project by creating the associated Internet site through Bedfordshire Libraries. To Ros Wong for continued support and encouragement, for proof-reading the entire book and for creating such a detailed index. To Sylvia Woods and Lynne Marshall for the final proof-read. Any remaining errors or omissions are my own.

I am immensely grateful to the following volunteers who gave up their time to assist me by researching the WLA service records at the Imperial War Museum, Duxford: Irene Davison, Richard and Lynne Marshall, Dave Moore, Mick Trundle and Sylvia Woods. Additionally I would like to thank Abbey Kemp for her research on the coverage of the WLA in Bedfordshire local newspapers in the 1940s. Their work enabled me to create the definitive list of young women who served as land girls in Bedfordshire (see Roll Call). I am also very grateful for the assistance of Penny Stanbridge, Irene Davison, Sylvia Woods, and Richard and Lynne Marshall when computer inputting the data. I am particularly grateful to those 18 women who agreed to be interviewed in depth by me about their experiences serving with the Bedfordshire Women's Land Army in the 1940s. Those tape-recorded interviews are now lodged with the Sound Archive of the Imperial War Museum (see the section on Sources for details): Vera Barnett (née Jobling), Joyce Case (née Senior), Margaret Chessum (née Perry), Iris Cornell (née Manning), Kathleen Cox (née Hopkins), Hannah Croot (née Bennett), Elizabeth Day, Doreen 'Dawn' Filby (née Skeggs), Stella Forster (née Shelton), Rose Hakewill (née Richard), Ann Haynes (née Brodrick), Zeita Holes (née Trott), Sheila Hope (née Stephens), Joyce Ingle (née Irving), Betty Nichols (née Gray), Mary Smith (née Pakes), Mary Spilling (née Bennett), and Ethel Wildey (née Sweenie).

In addition, I am most grateful to Carmela Semeraro for permission to use the sound recordings and transcriptions of the major oral history project in Mid-Bedfordshire, 'Changing Landscapes, Changing Lives', directed by her and for which I wrote the summaries. These include an interview by me with Barbara Tovey (née Cox) and further interviews with former land girls conducted by Carmela Semeraro: Hannah Croot (née Bennett), Betty Fitton (née Hurst), Evelyn Huckvale (née Archer), Cicely McKeegan (née Redman), Barbara Probert (née Filby), Zoe Sinfield (née Odell), Peggy Tedder (née Clark), Betty Schwarz (née Harding). (For more details see Sources.)

The following 180 women very kindly completed questionnaires for the author regarding their WLA service: Jean Abbott (née Herald), Hilda Abbott (née Howell), Peggy Albertson (née Davis), Mona Appleyard (née Feather), Patricia Bailey (née Benney), Margaret Ball (née Smart), Alice Barley (née Harper), Vera Barnett (née Jobling), Joyce Bennett (née Smith), Dorothy Bettles (née Copping), Lilian Bettles (née Standbrook), Rosemary Birch (née Denton), Daphne Bowes (née Barker), Peggy Briggs (née Herniman), Elizabeth Brockett (née Greaves), Dora Carrick (née Battrick), 'Joy' Case (née Senior), Olive Cattanach (née MacDonald), Hazel Chapman (née Payling), Margaret Chessum (née Perry), Vera Cobb (née Lowe), Joyce Colbeck (née Gelder), Ethel Collyer (née Richer), Joan Constable (née Hobbs), Vivyan Cooper (née Richards), Jacqueline Cooper (née Hamilton), Iris Cornell (née Manning), Josephine Costin (née Runeckles), Kathleen Cox (née Hopkins), Sylvia Cox (née Bunnett), Hannah Croot (née Bennett), Eleanor Cust (née Deighton), Mary Cutler (née Hickey), Helen Daniels (née Stops), Kathleen Davies (née Burgoyne), Gladys Dawson (née Park), Elizabeth

Day, Teresa Day (née Scanlon), Irene Day (née Thorley), Audrey Ellison (née Dutton), Marion Ellison, Daphne Everett (née Ives), Ena Farrington (née Woods), Lily Felce (née Bradley), Betty Fensham, Dawn Filby (née Skeggs), Hazel Filsell (née Millwood), Betty Fitton (née Hurst), Sheila Fleck (née Richardson), Freda Flegg (née Wallis), Stella Forster (née Shelton), Gladys Fowler (née Collis), Kathleen Francis (née Green), Joyce Franklin (née Hulatt), Celia French (née Slater), Betty Fuller, Eileen Fuller, Vera Gee (née Hull), Veronica Gilbert (née Tunstall), Doris Gilbert (née Farrah), Louisa Gill (née Unwin), Stella Goldsmith (née Limon), Sybil Greenslade (née Downs), Rachel Griffiths (née Rogers) Rose Hakewill (née Richards), Ellen Hallum (née Bacon), Joy Handscombe (née Holton), Jean Harpin (née Davenport), Joyce Harris (née Malpass), Gwendoline Harris (née Heath), Doreen Harvey (née Kempster), Elsie Hawkins (née Firth), Frieda Hawkins (née Carter), Vera Hawkins (née Tate), Ann Haynes (née Brodrick), Hilda Hicks (née Bright), Doreen Hoar (née Bradstock), Joan Hoar (née Gore), Zeita Holes (née Trott), Pauline Holmes (née Wilkinson), Sheila Hope (née Stephens), Eileen Hornsby (née Gegg), Olive Horsford (née Hart), Evelyn Huckvale (née Archer), Irene Hulatt (née Wright), Doris Hunt (née Smart), Doris Ingle (née Beevers), Joyce Ingle (née Irving), Joan Ison (née Taylor), Frances Jones (née Guttridge), Rita Keen (née Stokes), Dorothy Keightley (née Hurren), Iris King (née Patrick), Rona Kirkby (née Glinn), Gladys Kirtland (née Carty), Joan Knell (née Brown), Peggy Lancaster (née Wharton), Madge Larkins (née Wilkinson), Nora Lilly (née Dolby), Ruby Liscombe (née Coombs), Patricia Lovell (née Allsobrook), Muriel Ludlam (née Cox), Florence Maples (née Snodden), Constance Martin (née Wood), Elsie Martin (née Wilson), Teresa McGettigan (née Goodwin), Cicely McKeegan (née Redman), Mary Mechem (née Goodyear), Annie Moran (née Dickens), Audrey Morfoot (née Mills), Celia Müller (née Holt); Beryl Murphy (née Richardson), Betty Nicholls (née Gray), Doris Oakley (née Dew), Sylvia Odell (née Walton), Jean Parrish (née Tomkins), Maureen Parsons (née Daley), Barbara Payne (née Robinson), Jean Pearson, Betty Pearson, Joan Peck (née White), May Perkins (née Godfrey), Joan Petri (née Lovell), Elsie Phipps (née Elson), Myra Plester (née Griffiths), Dora Pontin (née Carlyle), Betty Potton (née Bird), Joan Potts (née Le Boutillier), Barbara Probert (née Filbey), Bessie Rabbitt (née Pitt), Christine Ramsay (née Shouler), Jane Ritchie (née Day), Edna Robinson (née Harris), Peggy Robinson (née Hunt), Josephine Rowe (née Walton), Irene Saunders (née Cook), Vera Saunders, Trixie Schreiner (née Saunders), Betty Schwarz (née Harding), Jean Sharp (née Scotchford), Olive Sharp (née Turner), Zoe Sinfield (née Odell), Margaret Smith (née Bird), Mary Smith (née Pakes), Dorothy Spendlove (née Batchelor), Mary Spilling (née Bennett), Eileen Stacey (née Elliott), Daphne Stamford (née Abraham), June Stapleton (née White), Margaret Stead (née Kennedy), Marion Steen (née Clark), Marguerite Stephens (née Everett), Mary Stokes (née Henman), Mabel Stratford (née Bracey), Marie Strong (née Berlemont), Audrey Sutton (née Hurdiss), Emily Swales (née Brown), Jean Tayles (née Lowe), Peggy Tedder (née Clark), Phyllis Tembey (née Coates), Elsie Thomas (née Wallis), Monica Thorne (née Cooper), Barbara Tovey (née Cox), Yvonne Truin (née Frood), Dorothy Vincent (née Walker), Ada Vyse (née Ratcliffe), Phyllis Wadsworth (née Laverick), Nola Wallace (née Bagley), Eileen Waller (née Litchfield), Audrey Watson (née Hislop), Joan Wellings (née Wilding), Mary Westrope (née Wilkinson), Ethel Wildey (née Sweenie), Sylvia Wiley (née Preater), Ena Willis (née Smith), Betty Wood (née Feltham), Joan Wright (née Corby), Dorothy Yates (née Crowsley).

In addition, the following people kindly provided information about their relatives or friends who were formerly land girls: Eric Abbott (re Jean Herald); Michael Barratt (re Myrtle Beeson and Rona Glinn); Stevie Bennett (re Joyce Smith); Hazel Brand (re Helen and Jane Day); Sue Brecknock (re Gladys Minns); June Brown (re Rachael Griffiths), Lynda Brown (re Winifred Daly); David Chapman (re Elizabeth Dutton); Nick Cooke (re Maud Litchfield); Irene Davison (re Barbara Newell); Raymond Ellison (re Ethel Busby); Rachel Etherington (re Dorothy Lamb); Melanie Horn (re Betty Feltham); Peter Jennings (re Dorothy Meggitt); Sue Jewsbury (re Jean Lee) Sheila Johnson (re Irene

Mullins); Tracey Johnson (re Lily Mair); Sally Myers (re Eva Myers); Nora Myles (re 'Jacqueline' Hindle); Ann-Marie Norton (re Nora Dolby); Christine Paice (re Ruth Paice); John Partridge (re Joan Wright); Jane Patten (re Margaret Fisher); Paul Quenby (re Jean Hartley); Frances Shah (re Elsie Elson); Gillian Sharp (re Olive Cakebread); Barry Sinfield (re Doris Lane), Norman Willis (re Kensworth hostel and its land girls).

I am indebted to the archivists, librarians, historians and other staff at the following institutions (with particular thanks to individuals named in brackets): BBC Written Archive Centre (Jeff Walden); Bedford Central Library, Reference and Local Studies (Nicola Avery and Barry Stephenson); Bedford Museum (Jenny Ford and Ann Hagen); Bedfordshire County Council, Heritage and Environment Section (Stephen Coleman); Bedfordshire and Luton Archives and Records Service (BLARS) (James Collett-White and Nigel Lutt); British Library, London; DEFRA (Dermot McInerney); East Anglian Film Archive (Amelia Hamer);Imperial War Museum, Duxford (Brenda Collins, Stephen Walton and Pamela Wright); Imperial War Museum, London; Liddell Hart Archives, Kings College, University of London; Luton Central Library (Mark Stubbs); Luton Hoo Walled Garden Project (Charlotte Phillips, Susan Mitchell and the late Martin Smith); Luton Museum (Dr Elizabeth Adey); Museum of English Rural Life, University of Reading (MERL); The National Archives, Kew; University of Southampton, School of Education (Dr Gill Clarke); West Sussex Record Office, Chichester; The Women's Library, Metropolitan University, London.

The following kindly gave permission for extracts and/or photographs to be quoted from their publications: Julie Eldridge (Bedford High School for Girls) for photo of and memoir by Anne Fox from 'Old Girls in New Times'; Ted Enever for material on Aspley Guise hostel land girls in 'Cockney Kid and Countrymen'; Jewell-Harrison Studios, Bedford; Jean Yates for memoirs by Mary Cutler (née Hickey), Eileen Fuller, and Catherine Henman (née Bezant) in 'Dunstable at War'; Mary Corbett of Biograph for Irene Hulatt's contribution to Snapshots from the Guild House; and the editors of Bedfordshire Times and The Luton News.

Others who have helped in various ways: Ruth Boreham, Colin Burbage, Lynda Burrows, David and Susan Butter, Jean Caeiriog-Jones (for the generous donation of copies of The Land Girl magazine), David Clark, Roger Day, Alan Edwards, Ralph Franklin, Frank and Mary Godber, Doreen Greenaway, Esther Gregory , Beryl Hyde, Nora Jackson, Helen Laurance, Harold Mennie, Irene Millest, Lesley Squire, Marion Turner, Dr Vernon Williams and his students at Abilene Christian University, Texas, USA, Chris Wilson and Pamela Wright.

I am grateful to the others, too numerous to mention by name, who assisted me in many ways during my research, particularly those former land girls who loaned or donated photographs from that period of their lives or put me in touch with other former land girls.

Finally, thanks to Paul Bowes and Sally Siddons of Book Castle Publishing, and Caroline and Roger Hillier of The Old Chapel Graphic Design, for helping me see this through to publication.

Every reasonable effort has been made to contact the copyright holders, but if there are any errors or omissions Book Castle Publishing will be pleased to insert the appropriate acknowledgement in any subsequent printing of this publication.

ARCHIVES

306 Bombardment Group Museum
Thurleigh Airfield Business Park, Thurleigh, Bedfordshire MK44 2YP
www.306bg.co.uk

BBC web site
('WW2 People's War' oral history archives of memories of former land girls: enter 'Bedfordshire'
AND 'ww2' AND 'land army' in search box)
www.bbc.co.uk/ww2peopleswar/categories/index.shtml

BBC Written Archives Centre
Peppard Road, Caversham Park, Reading RG4 8TZ
Tel. 0118 948 6281
www.bbc.co.uk/heritage/more/wac.shtml

Bedford Central Library (including Heritage Library)
Harpur Street, Bedford MK40 1PG
Tel. 01234 270102/350931
www.bedfordshire.gov.uk
click on Libraries>About Your Library>Bedford Central Library>Bedfordshire Heritage Library

Bedford Museum
Castle Lane, Bedford MK40 3XD
Tel. 01234 353323
www.bedfordmuseum.org

Bedfordshire and Luton Archives and Records Service
Riverside Building, County Hall, Cauldwell Street, Bedford MK42 9AP
Tel. 01234 228833 or 363222
www.bedscc.gov.uk/archive

Bedfordshire Libraries (Virtual Library web pages)
www.bedfordshire.gov.uk
click on Libraries > Local and Family History > Subjects> Second World War> Women's Land
Army> History of Bedfordshire Women's Land Army

British Library
96 Euston Road, London NW1 2DB
Tel. 020 7412 7332 (Visitor Information) Tel. 020 7412 7676 (Reader Information)
www.bl.uk/catalogues/listings.html (for catalogue of books and documents)

East Anglian Air War Project
ACU Box 28130, Abilene Christian University, Abilene, Texas 79699-8130, United States of America
www.acu.edu/anglia

Imperial War Museum
Lambeth Road, London SE1 6HZ
Tel. 020 7416 5320
www.iwm.org.uk click on Collections

Liddell Hart Archives
Kings College London, Strand, London WC2R 2LS
Tel. 020 7848 2015
www.kcl.ac.uk/iss/archives/visiting

Luton Museum
Wardown Park, Luton LU2 7HA
Tel. 01582 546722
www.luton.gov.uk/museums

Museum of English Rural Life
The University of Reading, Redlands Road, Reading RG1 5EX
Tel. 0118 378 8660
www.merl.org.uk

National Archives
Kew, Richmond, Surrey TW9 4DU
Tel. 020 8876 3444
www.nationalarchives.gov.uk/searchthearchives/catalogue.htm

West Sussex Record Office
3 Orchard Street, Chichester, West Sussex PO19 1DD
Tel. 01243 753602
www.westsussex.gov.uk click on Libraries and Archives>Record Office

The Women's Land Army Museum
Little Farthingloe Farm, Folkestone Road, Dover, Kent CT15 7AA
Tel. 01304 212 040

The Women's Library
London Metropolitan University, Old Castle Street, London E1 7NT
Tel. 020 7320 2222
www.thewomenslibrary.ac.uk

INDEX
COMPILED BY ROS WONG

Pages in **bold** indicate illustrations

LIST OF SUBSCRIBERS

Peggy Iris Albertson (née Davis)
Mona Appleyard (née Feather)
Barbara Ashworth (née Lightfoot)
Patricia (Paddy) Bailey (née Benney)
Rosemary Birch (née Denton)
Kathleen Booker (née Bracey)
David Bradley
Peggy Briggs (née Herniman)
Daphne Myra Bowes (née Barker)
Moira Brockbank
Elizabeth Anne Brockett (née Greaves)
Sylvia M Burns
Stan & Theresa Cass (née Di Paul)
Margaret Chessum (née Perry)
Marjorie Clark
Mary Patricia Clarke (née Walsh)
Joyce Colbeck (née Gelder)
Ethel Colyer (née Richer)
Nick Cooke
Jacqueline Cooper (née Hamilton)
Vicky Cooper (née Richards)
Iris Cornell (née Manning)
Josephine Costin (née Runeckles)
Kathleen Cox (née Hopkins)
Gladys Dawson (née Park)
Elizabeth Day
James Dyer
Audrey M Ellison (née Dutton)
Dianne Ellison
Fred Ellison
Marion Ellison
Raymond Ellison
Lewis & Vivienne Evans
Daphne Everett (née Ives)
Marion Field
Joyce Franklin (née Hulatt)
Betty Fuller
Eileen Fuller
Eddie Grabham
Sheila Green (née Minns)
Rachel Griffiths (née Rogers)
Rose Ann Gwinnett (née Day)
Joy Handscombe (née Holton)
Doreen Harvey (née Kempster)
Elsie Hawkins (née Firth)

Emma Hayfield (née Chapman)
Terry & Marion Hext
Ruth Margaret Hoggarth (née Paice)
Sheila Jean Hope (née Stephens)
Evelyn Huckvale (née Archer)
Gillian & Jacqueline Hurd
Hilary C Jones
Rita Keen (née Stokes)
Iris Doreen King (née Patrick)
Mary King (née Lovell)
Florence Marples (née Snodden)
Hazel Mayes (née Brace)
Teresa McGettigan (née Goodwin)
Margaret Minns
Irene May Mullins
Sally Myers
Joyce Osborne
Mrs Paine
Jane B Patten
Jean & Betty Pearson
May Perkins (née Godfrey)
Angela Pitkin
Myra Plester (née Griffiths)
Shela Porter
Jane Ritchie (née Day)
Josephine Rowe (née Walton)
Irene (Cookie) Saunders (née Cook)
Betty Schwarz (née Harding)
Jean Sharp (née Scotchford)
Olive Sharp (née Turner)
Margaret Minnie Smith (née Bird)
Mary Smith (née Pakes)
Eileen Stacey (née Elliott)
Mabel Stratford (née Bracey)
Marie V Strong (née Berlemont)
Emily Swales (née Brown)
Jean Tayles (née Lowe)
Phyllis May Tembey (née Coates)
Elsie Mary Thomas (née Wallis)
Mary Isabel Uggur (née Hindle)
Betty Wadsworth (née Laverick)
Nola Wallace (née Bagley)
Eileen Rose Waller (née Litchfield)
Mrs J Wood

THE WINDMILLS AND WATERMILLS OF BEDFORDSHIRE: PAST, PRESENT AND FUTURE

Hugh Howes

Over a hundred windmills and watermills in over 80 parishes once played a crucial role in Bedfordshire's rural industrial economy. Most of the mills which still existed before the Second World War have long since disappeared together with a whole way of life swept away by a modern industry.

Several do survive, although most are in a ruinous state. Stevington windmill and the watermills at Bromham and Stotfold, however, have not only survived but are open to the public and this book offers an invaluable guide in explaining their features to the modern visitor.

It also provides a history of milling in the County including some insights into the skills of those that worked at these mills. It then examines all the other surviving wind and watermills and some of the problems concerning restoration, conversion and after –use of this important part of the County's heritage.

Book Castle PUBLISHING

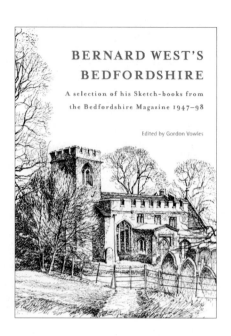

BERNARD WEST'S BEDFORDSHIRE
A selection of his Sketch-books from the Bedfordshire Magazine 1947–98

Edited by Gordon Vowles

For the entire fifty year life of the *Bedfordshire Magazine* from 1947, Bernard West's Sketch-book was a highly popular feature. Whether village or townscape or individual building or countryside, it was also accompanied by a knowledgeable, lively, often trenchant commentary. The combination fully exhibited his wide-ranging talents as architect, local historian, artist and conservationist.

This is a book which should have a wide appeal, but especially to those who have an interest in Bedfordshire's past and its continued preservation.

Book Castle PUBLISHING

JOURNEYS INTO BEDFORDSHIRE

Anthony Mackay

This book of ink drawings reveals an intriguing historic heritage and captures the spirit of England's rural heartland, ranging widely over cottages and stately homes, over bridges, churches and mills, over sandy woods, chalk downs and watery river valleys.

Every corner of Bedfordshire has been explored in the search for material, and, although the choice of subjects is essentially a personal one, the resulting collection represents a unique record of the environment today.

The notes and maps, which accompany the drawings, lend depth to the book, and will assist others on their own journeys around the county.

Anthony Mackay's pen-and-ink drawings are of outstanding quality. An architectural graduate, he is equally at home depicting landscapes and buildings. The medium he uses is better able to show both depth and detail than any photograph.

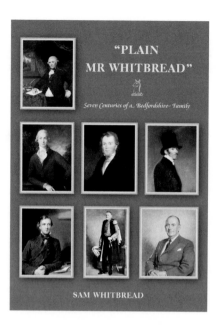

"PLAIN MR WHITBREAD"
Seven Centuries of a Bedfordshire Family

Sam Whitbread

The Whitbread family have been a part of Bedfordshire life since at least the 13th century (and probably earlier). From small beginnings as peasant farmers, through appointments as local officials to the founder of the Brewery, one of the most notable success stories of the Industrial Revolution, and his son, the radical Whig politician and follower of Fox, the Whitbreads have gradually made their presence felt, first locally and later nationally. Six Whitbreads sat in the House of Commons for a total of 128 years, while at the same time building roads, bridges and hospitals, improving cottages and the local churches, and serving as magistrates, High Sheriffs and Lord-Lieutenants of the County.

The book's title is taken from the fact that at least two members of the family were offered peerages but preferred to "remain plain Mr Whitbread".

The author originally conceived the book as a simplified family history for his children and grandchildren but it will also appeal to those interested in the local history of Bedfordshire.

The narrative ends with the death of the author's father in 1985, but the author has added a "postscript" outlining the first seventy years of his own life.

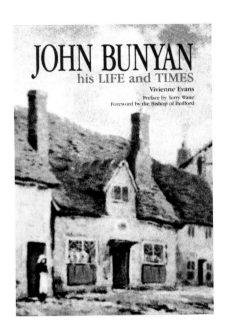

JOHN BUNYAN
His Life and Times

Vivienne Evans

Born to a humble family in the parish of Elstow near Bedford, John Bunyan (1628–1688) became one of the world's most widely read Christian writers – The Pilgrim's Progress eventually being translated into over two hundred languages.

This lively book traces the events of his life with its spiritual turmoil and long imprisonment, as well as discussing many of his writings. Clearly seeing Bunyan as a product of his time and place, it also explains the intriguing social, political and religious background of the turbulent seventeenth century.

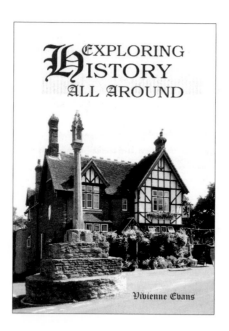

EXPLORING HISTORY ALL AROUND

Vivienne Evans

A handbook of local history, arranged as a series of routes to cover Bedfordshire and adjoining parts of Hertfordshire and Buckinghamshire. It is organised as two books in one. There are seven thematic sections full of fascinating historical detail and anecdotes for armchair reading. Also it is a perfect source of family days out as the book is organised as circular motoring/cycling explorations, highlighting attractions and landmarks. Also included is a background history to all the major towns in the area, plus dozens of villages, which will enhance your appreciation and understanding of the history that is all around you!

Book Castle PUBLISHING

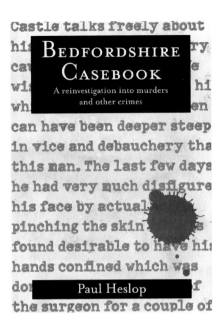

BEDFORDSHIRE CASEBOOK
A reinvestigation into murders and other crimes

Paul Heslop

This is a book about crime and punishment in Bedfordshire. It focuses mainly on the time when perpetrators were hanged for murder and lesser crimes, or sentenced to hard labour, or transported abroad for what today would be regarded as minor offences.

They range from the 17th century incarceration of John Bunyan, whose 'crime' was to preach outwith the established church; to rape and terror perpetrated by the man they called The Fox, on the South Bedfordshire borders in the 1980s. 'Domestic violence' features: the brutal murder of his wife by Joseph Castle in Luton in 1859, and the murder of 23-year-old Ruby Annie Keen at Leighton Buzzard by Leslie George Stone in 1937. We have the murder of Old Sally Marshall, at Little Staughton, in 1870; a Luton mugging that ended up as murder when William Worsley, convicted on the evidence of an accomplice, was hanged; and the A6 murder at Deadman's Hill, the infamous Hanratty case, still topical today.

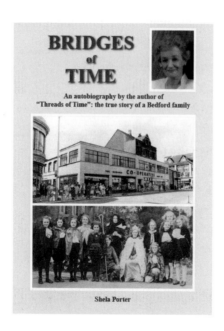

BRIDGES OF TIME

Shela Porter

The unfolding of a traumatic span of seventy years, this gripping autobiography tells the story of a woman's struggle, mostly in Bedford, to achieve happiness as she battles against fate and finally finds peace and contentment in her later years.

Ambitions to become a teacher are thwarted when she is taken out of school at fourteen. Marriage at twenty and the birth of three children in the first three years lead to a lonely life on a council estate as her marriage breaks down and her violent and immature husband leaves the family home.

Now widowed and lonely as her children leave home, Shela begins a questionable relationship with a man whom she eventually marries after his strictly Catholic wife dies. Two years in India follow and then several in Yorkshire as her unhappiness with an unfaithful and controlling husband results in a nervous breakdown and a return to Bedford with a pressing need to re-establish her life yet again.

In her early sixties, with all thoughts of romance firmly dismissed from her mind, she meets the caring and gentle man who becomes her new husband and who nurses her back to health while encouraging her to write regularly again.

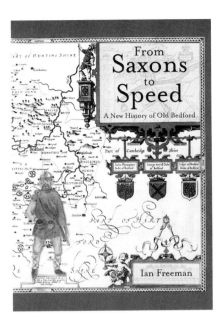

FROM SAXONS TO SPEED
A New History of Old Bedford

Ian Freeman

The early history of Bedford town has been treated in a somewhat perfunctory way by previous local historians. This is understandable because information from the "Dark Ages" is sparse whereas there is a plethora of information readily available from later centuries.

This book is an attempt to fill that gap, using what firm information there is, supplemented by intelligent speculation when necessary. As a result, a number of generally accepted "facts" are put into question, and, in some cases, shown to be wrong.

The book begins with the Saxon period through the times of King Offa and King Alfred when the settlement and basic structure of the town was being laid out. It goes on to the Norman and Platagenet periods and describes how those invaders and rulers left their mark on the town.

Finally, it looks at the town as depicted in John Speed's map of the town which he published in 1610. It describes those streets and buildings which have survived from that time and discusses some of the prominent people who have lived in the town from time to time.

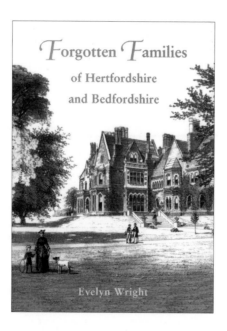

FORGOTTEN FAMILIES
of Hertfordshire and Bedfordshire

Evelyn Wright

This book tells the story of families once famous but whose fame is now mainly forgotten. They all lived in Hertfordshire and Bedfordshire in the 16th and 17th centuries, and include the Bechers of Renhold (of Becher's Brook fame), the Mordaunts of Turvey Abbey, Lady Cathcart of Tewin, the Bull family of Hertford, the Nodes family of Stevenage, the Docuras of Lilley and the Wicked Lady of Markyate Cell. All the families were related to each other, forming an intricate network over two counties: Hertfordshire and Bedfordshire. The author is one of their 20th century descendants. The book includes pedigrees showing the relationship between various families, and illustrations of many of the manor houses and mansions in which they lived.

Evelyn Wright was born in the village of Wingfield in Suffolk, and moved to Bedfordshire soon after her marriage in 1952. During a busy life bringing up five children, running a Nursery School and looking after elderly parents, she has always found time for writing. Evelyn is married to John Wright, a Chartered Surveyor, and they live in Aspley Heath in Bedfordshire.